THE NEW YORK ROAD RUNNERS CLUB
COMPLETE BOOK OF
RUNNING

RANDOM HOUSE
NEW YORK

THE NEW YORK ROAD RUNNERS CLUB
COMPLETE BOOK OF
RUNNING

RANDOM HOUSE
NEW YORK

 BY FRED LEBOW, GLORIA AVERBUCH, AND FRIENDS

The New York Road Runners Club Complete Book of Running
Copyright © 1992 by New York Road Runners Club

Grateful acknowledgment is made to the following for permission to reprint previously published material:

Susan Foster: Eighty black and white illustrations. Reprinted by permission of Susan Foster.

Hershey Foods Corporation: Pasta Salad Combination recipe. Copyright © 1991 by Hershey Foods Corporation. Reprinted by permission of Hershey Foods Corporation.

Human Kinetics Publishers: Excerpts from *Nancy Clark's Sports and Nutrition Guidebook* by Nancy Clark, Champaign, IL: Leisure Press, 1990. Copyright © 1990 by Nancy Clark. Reprinted by permission.

Lilac Bloomsday Association: Excerpts from *Bloomsday Training Guide* and several children's puzzles from Lilac Bloomsday Literature. Reprinted by permission.

New York Road Runners Club: Excerpts from *New York Running News.* Reprinted by permission of New York Road Runners Club.

The Quaker Oats Company: "Gatorade Heatwave Fluids: The Inside Story" and excerpts from "Beat the Heat Infocard." Reprinted by permission of The Quaker Oats Company.

Road Runners Club of America: Excerpts from *Children's Running: A Guide for Parents and Kids.* Copyright © 1989 by Road Runners Club of America. Reprinted by permission.

Running *magazine:* Excerpts from "Cliff Temple's Guide to Running," Parts 1–3. Reprinted by permission of *Running* magazine.

Runner's World *magazine:* Women's Races, Running Games, and 75 Great Races reprinted by permission of *Runner's World* magazine. Copyright © 1992, Rodale Press, Inc., all rights reserved.

Library of Congress Cataloging-in-Publication Data

The New York Road Runners Club complete book of running / by Fred Lebow, Gloria Averbuch, and friends.
    p. cm.
  Includes index.
  ISBN 0-679-40980-7
  1. Running. I. Lebow, Fred. II. Averbuch, Gloria, 1951- .
III. New York Road Runners Club. IV. Title: Complete book of running.
GV1061.N43 1992
796.42—dc20   92-16254

Manufactured in the United States of America

First Edition

New York Toronto London Sydney Auckland

In memory of my father, Bernard Averbuch, my strength and inspiration (1919–91). —G.A.

To my family: Michael, Simcha, Schlomo, Sara, Esther, and Morris.—F.L.

Throughout the book, frequent references are made to several of the NYRRC's ongoing programs and regular publications. They include:

- *Fitness Features*, a regular series of NYRRC promotional spots written and broadcast by Gloria Averbuch throughout the week on WABC Radio in New York. The book includes excerpts from these broadcasts, which have aired since 1982.
- *Fitness Forum*, also featured throughout the book, is a regular column of medical/training advice in *New York Running News,* the magazine of the NYRRC.
- All information in this book—including statistics and records—is the most current available as of July, 1992.

Photo Credits

- Photo of Stu Mittleman by Ken Levinson. Reprinted by permission.
- Photo of Carl Lewis by Kathryn Dudek. Reprinted by permission.
- Photo of the Chemical Corporate Challenge by Michael DeVito. Reprinted by permission.
- Photo of Tom Brokaw by Will Cofnuk. Reprinted by permission.
- Photo of Anne Marie Letko and Tom Fleming by Gloria Averbuch. Reprinted by permission.
- Photo of Norb Sander by Michael Tighe. Reprinted by permission.
- Photo of Eamonn Coghlan by Kathryn Dudek. Reprinted by permission.
- Photo of PattiSue Plumer by Victah Sailer/Agence Shot. Reprinted by permission.
- Photo of Kathrine Switzer and Nina Kuscsik. Reprinted by permission.
- Photo of Lynn Jennings by Victah Sailer/Agence Shot. Reprinted by permission.
- Photo of Juma Ikangaa by Victah Sailer/Agence Shot. Reprinted by permission.
- Photo of Grete Waitz by Victah Sailer/Agence Shot. Reprinted by permission.
- Photo of Shorter, Rodgers, and Lebow by Nancy Coplon. Reprinted by permission.
- Photo of marathon water cups by Nancy Coplon. Reprinted by permission.
- Photo of Linda Down by Nancy Coplon. Reprinted by permission.
- Photo of NYRRC Pee-Wee Division by Victah Sailer/Agence Shot. Reprinted by permission.

Foreword

Nearly 20 years after the running boom and the publication of thousands of books and articles on the sport, you might well ask: "What could possibly be left to say about runners and running?"

But runners require continuing motivation, new goals, and information about refined training techniques. They need to know about the cutting edge in sports nutrition and medical treatment, about aging and exercise, time management, the new array of cross training alternatives, and the latest resources—from health and equipment to race contacts. And yet they need to remember the basics, the sound principles that keep them running far, fast, and healthy.

To satisfy runners' ongoing needs, Fred Lebow has inspired the ultimate running book, a manual covering every aspect of the sport for all levels, from the beginner to the elite.

The New York Road Runners Club Complete Book of Running represents the greatest combination of expert advice and insights ever compiled in one volume. The material is derived from the very best minds and bodies in the sport. The book includes the words and writing of world-class athletes (many of whose careers were made by winning NYRRC events), as well as contributions from medical experts, sports psychologists, nutritionists, and running coaches. It even includes the thoughts of some average runners, whose words represent the experience of the club's nearly 30,000 members.

For most runners, catching up with the elite is—literally and figuratively—a rare opportunity. *The New York Road Runners Club Complete Book of Running* offers a unique insight into the pros and what they know. In these pages, they give their views on everything from training and racing to children's running and fitness, masters and women's running, and more.

The New York Road Runners Club (NYRRC) is the source of enormous expertise. It is from the NYRRC—with its years of experience in every aspect of the sport of running—that this book has been assembled. Virtually every NYRRC resource was used, from the ground-floor library to the sixth-floor office of *New York Running News*, the NYRRC magazine.

Surely the authority of the contributors and the depth of resources used to compile this book make it the most comprehensive, up-to-date, one-stop runner's manual available, a book that, like the NYRRC, brings together the elite and the average runner in a common arena. I hope that it meets your running reference needs, and that the words and advice in these pages offer continuous support, motivation, common sense, and guidance.

Gloria Averbuch
New York City, 1992

CONTENTS

Part 5—Nutrition

Part 6—Fitness and Safety

Part 7—Health and Medicine

Part 8—Aging and Exercise

Part 9—Children's Running and Fitness

Part 10—Women's Running

Part 11—Walking

Part 12—The Running Lifestyle

Part 13—Running Equipment

Resource List

About the Contributors

The New York Road Runners Club Complete Book of Running is based on original interviews, articles, vignettes, and adapted writings of the running world's best and brightest. The advice and insights conveyed in these pages are the words not of one author, but of a panel of contributors. Following is an alphabetically arranged list of these contributors; each entry in the list includes a brief biographical sketch. Grateful acknowledgment is made to all these contributors and to the publications that have granted permission to reprint articles and excerpts from previously published magazines and books.

Kim Alexis is a supermodel who has appeared on over 400 magazine covers. In addition, she hosts the television program *The Healthy Kids Show* on The Family Channel. Alexis is a mother of two young sons and a marathoner and triathlete.

Mark Allen is the three-time winner of the Ironman Triathlon in Hawaii and the eight-time winner of the Nice International Triathlon. He was also the winner of the NYRRC's first triathlon and has been among the top finishers in the Trevira Twosome.

Tzvi Barak, P.T., Ph.D., O.C.S., is a Manhattan physical therapist specializing in orthopedics. A runner, he has been a medical volunteer with the NYRRC since 1984.

Beryl Bender Birch has been NYRRC's wellness director since 1981. She has been one of the foremost specialists in the field of yoga for athletes and yoga therapy for 22 years and is the author of a book on those topics.

Gordon Bloch has represented the United States in World Cup competition and run 2:33:01 for the marathon. She is a four-time recipient of the NYRRC Runner of the Year award. A free-lance writer and editor in the health and fitness field, she also works as a running coach.

Tom Brokaw may be best known as the anchor of *NBC Nightly News with Tom Brokaw*, but in his "other life" he is an avid runner and a member of the NYRRC Leadership Council.

Amby Burfoot, who won the 1968 Boston Marathon, is the executive editor of *Runner's World* magazine. In his 30 years of running on the roads, he has covered more than 100,000 miles.

Nancy Clark, M.S., R.D., sports nutritionist and runner, is the author of *The Athlete's Kitchen* and *Nancy Clark's Sports Nutrition Guidebook*. She is the staff nutritionist for Boston's SportsMedicine Brookline, one of the largest athletic injury clinics in New England.

Eamonn Coghlan is the world indoor record holder in the mile (3:49.7), the 1983 World Champion in the 5000 meters, and a three-time Olympian for Ireland. A 10-year resident of New York, Coghlan has run many NYRRC races. He currently resides in Ireland and works for Execom Communications, an executive communication training company.

Nancy Coplon has been the photo editor of *New York Running News* since 1984. In addition, her photos have appeared in such publications as *Newsweek* and *Runner's World*.

Ted Corbitt, one of the founders of the New York Road Runners Club, at one time held the American record in the 50-mile, 100-mile, and 24-hour runs. In addition, he was an Olympian in the marathon at the 1952 Games in Helsinki. Corbitt currently works as a physical therapist in New York City.

Marcus Daniels is a Montclair, New Jersey, body work practitioner whose focus is deep tissue balancing. He treats runners of all levels, some of whom are quoted in this book.

Elliott Denman is a journalist and champion race walker. He is an Olympian who participated in the 1956 Games in race walking. He is also a member of the International Amateur Athletic Federation panel of race walking judges and serves as the New Jersey Athletics Congress race walking chairman.

Margaret Dessau, M.D., is a certified internist and member of the faculty of Columbia University Medical School in New York. She is also a contributor to *New York Running News* and an accomplished runner. At her peak, she won a 10K race in Tokyo in 36 minutes.

Joe Douglas is both a "founding father" and coach of the Santa Monica Track Club. He is a prominent supporter of the New York Games and of Fred Lebow's attempt to rekindle the sport of track and field in the United States. He expresses that support by bringing his best athletes to compete in the meet every year.

Tom Fleming, a 2:12:05 marathoner, is a two-time winner of the New York City Marathon and has held five American road bests at various distances. He is currently the coach of Nike Running Room, one of the nation's top teams, and is also the coach of several national class high school runners. Fleming, who has also served as a U.S. coach in international competition, works at the grassroots level of the sport as well, designing fitness programs for local recreation departments and businesses. Since 1978, he has owned and operated Tom Fleming's Running Room, a running equipment store in Bloomfield, New Jersey.

Susan Foster, a graphic designer and illustrator, is also a sub-three-hour marathoner and NYRRC Runner of the Year nominee in her age category.

Marilyn Frender is captain of the NYRRC sports massage team and a licensed massage therapist in New York. She coordinates the year-round efforts of the 75 to 100 volunteer massage therapists in major NYRRC events.

Peter Gambaccini is a writer for *Runner's World, The Village Voice, Diversion,* and *Sport,* and a features editor of *New York Running News.* He is also an accomplished runner, having won over 40 track and road races.

Thom Gilligan, a 2:20 marathoner, heads Marathon Tours, a travel agency specializing in trips to races around the world. He has been associated with the NYRRC for over a decade.

Bob Glover is director of educational programs for the NYRRC and head coach of the club's classes. Founder and coach of the elite women's team, Atalanta, he is also the author of best-selling books on running.

Cliff Held is head coach/director of Craftsbury Running Camp in Vermont—one of the most popular running camps in the country. He has been a coach in the NYRRC running classes, and currently coaches several teams that include runners of all levels. Held is also a competitive masters runner.

Don Imus, a pioneer of "shock radio," is the host of the *Imus in the Morning Program* on New York's WFAN radio. He is also a NYRRC member and part of the WFAN broadcast of the New York City Marathon.

Lynn Jennings is the six-time women's USA National Cross Country Champion, the all-time record for that number of titles. She is also the three-time World Cross Country Champion. Jennings holds the world best for the eight kilometers on the roads and is a two-time Olympian. She won the NYRRC Runner's World Midnight Run in 1991.

Don Kardong is a 1976 Olympic marathoner and senior writer for *Runner's World* magazine. He is also the president of the Association of Road Racing Athletes.

G. Thomas Kovacs, a certified sports chiropractor, is director of Sports Chiropractic Services in Manhattan. He is also a runner and triathlete who has served as an NYRRC medical volunteer and clinic panelist.

Nina Kuscsik is the winner of the first official women's Boston Marathon (1972), a two-time winner of the New York City Marathon, a former 50-mile American record holder, and chairman of various women's long-distance running committees. She is also on the board of directors of the NYRRC.

Carl Landegger is a prominent businessman and long-time member of the NYRRC board of directors. Landegger and the other three authors of "International Marathoning" in Chapter 41—**Renee Landegger, Michelle Jordan,** and **Janet Nelson**— have completed a total of 69 marathons around the world.

David E. Martin is professor of physiology in the Department of Cardiopulmonary Care Sciences at Georgia State University in Atlanta. He has had a life-long research interest in the physiology of athletic performance, particularly with runners and jumpers. Martin, who also heads several committees of The Athletics Congress, has been an adviser or coach to some of the nation's top distance runners for the past 15 years. He is looking forward to running his thirtieth marathon in the near future.

Stu Mittleman achieved an extraordinary string of ultramarathon successes in the 1980s. During that decade, he set American 100-mile, 1000-mile, and six-day records, the latter two of which still stand. He is the three-time national 100-mile champion and set a world record in the 1000-mile run in 1986. Mittleman is founder and director of The Fitness Evaluation Center in New York City.

Don Mogelefsky is the managing editor of *New York Running News* and a two-time New York City Marathoner.

Gary Muhrcke is the winner of the first New York City Marathon in 1970 and the winner of the first Empire State Building Run-Up in 1978.

He is the founder and owner of the Super Runners Shop chain of stores, located throughout the New York metropolitan area.

PattiSue Plumer is an Olympian and multi-time American national champion in the 3000 and 5000 meters. She is also the American record holder in the 5000 meters, with a time of 15:00. The winner of the 1990 Fifth Avenue Mile, Plumer works as an employment and labor law attorney in Palo Alto, California.

Mary-Giselle Rathgeber, M.S., R.D., a regular columnist for *New York Running News,* is on the staff of The Preventive and Sports Medicine Center in New York. She also serves as nutrition consultant to *Esquire Health & Fitness Magazine* and *The Image Workshop* on the Lifetime cable television network.

Bill Rodgers is one of history's most accomplished road runners. He is the four-time winner of both the New York City and Boston Marathons. An Olympian and winner of other numerous prestigious road races and awards, he is currently a top masters competitor.

Andres Rodriguez, M.D., is the president of the International Marathon Medical Directors Association (IMMDA), and the medical director of the NYRRC. Rodriguez and medical coordinator Yolanda Rodriguez set policy and supervise all club races. For the New York City Marathon, they oversee approximately 1500 medical personnel—the largest medical staff ever assembled for a sporting event.

Peter Roth is the treasurer of the NYRRC and is also on the board of directors. He is author of a book on running and travel, and was an executive producer of the running film *On the Edge.* As president of Kidselebration, he produces and sells children's products to the toy and gift markets.

Alberto Salazar changed the face of marathoning worldwide in the 1980s by winning three New York City Marathons: the first, in 1980, was then the fastest ever for a first-time marathoner, and the second was a then world record of 2:08:13. He simultaneously held the American record in the 5000 and 10,000 meters. He currently works for Nike as the international coordinator for athletics.

Norbert Sander, M.D., is the head of The Preventive and Sports Medicine Center in New York City. He is also the winner of the 1974 New York City Marathon, a contributor to *New York Running News,* and a NYRRC clinic participant.

Harold Selman, M.D., a psychiatrist, and **Maryellyn Duane, Ph.D.,** a psychologist, are co-captains of the New York City Marathon Psyching Team. They are also both marathon runners.

Mona Shangold, M.D., a NYRRC clinic speaker and club member for 15 years, has long been at the forefront of research and information regarding women and exercise. She is currently the head of The Sports Gynecology and Women's Life Cycle Center at Hahnemann University Hospital in Philadelphia. In addition, Shangold is the author of a number of books in her area of expertise.

George Sheehan, M.D., the renowned running philosopher, is a regular columnist for *Runner's World* magazine and, most recently, the author of *Personal Best*. He has also been a top runner in his age group for many years.

Frank Shorter is the 1972 Olympic gold medalist in the marathon and the 1976 Olympic marathon silver medalist. His gold medal performance has been credited as a major catalyst for the American running boom. Shorter is currently an accomplished masters runner and duathlete.

Francie Larrieu Smith can boast a running career with the greatest longevity and versatility of any American runner ever, man or woman. She has made five Olympic teams and two World Championship teams for distances from 800 meters to the marathon. She has held 17 American outdoor track records, which she set from age 16 to 38.

Doug Stern is an aquatics consultant and competitive athlete. His swim instruction is extensive and includes all ages from high schoolers to senior citizens, and people from various sports backgrounds. He is a contributing writer for several publications, and his deep water running classes are part of the NYRRC program.

Tracy Sundlun is coach of the New York-based team, Warren Street Social and Athletic Club, ten-time national TAC team champions at distances from 5 kilometers to the marathon. Among his athletes is Pat Petersen, seven-time NYRRC Runner of the Year. Sundlun also works closely with the NYRRC in his position as executive director of the Metropolitan Athletics Congress.

Kathrine Switzer is perhaps best known for being one of the first women to run the Boston Marathon. Switzer, the winner of the 1974 New York

City Marathon, was also head of the highly successful Avon women's running circuit. She currently broadcasts running events for ABC-TV.

Cliff Temple, a journalist and coach, has been the *Track & Field* correspondent of *The Sunday Times*, London, since 1969. He has covered six summer Olympic Games, and in the past 20 years, he has coached—among others—a number of British Olympians.

Grete Waitz is the nine-time winner of the New York City Marathon and the six-time winner of the Women's Mini Marathon. In those NYRRC events alone, she set a total of five world bests. Waitz is also an Olympic silver medalist and 1983 World Champion (both in the marathon), and the five-time winner of the World Cross Country Championships.

Dan Weiner, M.D., is a New York City plastic surgeon and avid runner. **Mickey Lawrence,** also an avid runner, heads Image Impact, Inc., a special events marketing company. Together they have developed and distribute Sports Proof, a skin care product designed for runners.

Joe Weisenfeld, D.P.M, has been a medical volunteer at NYRRC races since 1979. Weisenfeld currently serves as the chief of podiatry for the NYRRC Medical Committee and is the medical coordinator at the start of the New York City Marathon.

Priscilla Welch holds a range of masters world records, including the marathon (2:26:51). A native of Great Britain and an Olympian in the marathon, she resides in Boulder, Colorado. She won the 1987 New York City Marathon.

Bob Wynn has been working with the NYRRC since 1982. He is currently a coach with City-Sports-For-Kids. He is also an athletic associate at the Allen Stevenson School in Manhattan, where he teaches physical education to those in kindergarten through third grade.

Thanks also go to Paul Friedman, Hemant Patel, Cristopher Maloney, Raleigh Mayer, *Runner's World* magazine, Carol Connolly, Tom Allen, and Angela Miller for their various contributions.

About the New York Road Runners Club

The New York Road Runners Club (NYRRC), a nonprofit organization, was established in 1958 to develop the sport of running for competition and physical fitness. The club has grown from its initial membership of 42 to become the world's largest running club, with more than 29,000 members worldwide.

The NYRRC conducts more than 120 events a year, including races covering distances of less than 1 mile up to 100 miles. Many of these races are major international events, such as the New York City Marathon, the Fifth Avenue Mile, the Advil Women's Mini Marathon, the New York Games, and the Chemical Corporate Challenge series. In its New York offices the club features a comprehensive international library, an audiovisual center, and a runners' store. It also sponsors art and photography exhibits. Throughout the year, the club invites prominent athletes, coaches, and other running and fitness experts to lecture as part of the club's clinic and workshop series. To plan and implement these events, the club maintains an office of approximately 45 workers. A network of thousands of volunteers supplements the efforts of this core staff.

NYRRC Race Calendar

The NYRRC publishes an extensive road race calendar. It includes dates and telephone numbers for over 500 area races, plus a world marathon schedule and other information. The calendar, which is sent to all club members, can also be obtained by sending your request with an S.A.S.E. to the NYRRC. Following is a summary of the club's major events in 1992, listed by month:

January	Runner's World Midnight Run
February	Empire State Building Run-Up
	Sheraton New York Bagel Run
March	Brooklyn Half-Marathon (Gatorade Grand Prix Event #1.
	Advil New Runner/New Racer Clinic
April	NY Health and Racquet Club Backwards Mile

	Trevira Twosome
	Roosevelt Island Spring 10K
May	Chemical Corporate Challenge
	Alamo Alumni Run
	Advil Mini Marathon Tune-Up
	Carey Limousine Wall Street Rat Race
	Advil Mini Marathon (women only)
	The New York Games
June	Chemical Corporate Challenge
	Westchester Half-Marathon (Grand Prix Event #2)
July	Tavern on the Green Breakfast Run (members only)
August	K-Rock Reservoir Run
	New York City Triathlon
	Hispanic Half-Marathon (Grand Prix Event #3)
September	Roosevelt Island Fall 10K
	Fifth Avenue Mile
	Race for the Cure (women only)
	Staten Island Half-Marathon (Grand Prix Event #4)
October	Chemical Corporate Challenge Championships
	NYC Marathon Computer Run
November	New York City Marathon
	Annual Pete McArdle Memorial Cross Country Classic
	NYRRC Turkey Trot
December	Winter Series 10 Mile/10K (members only)

Other NYRRC events and programs include running classes, power yoga workout training, deep water running classes, race walking, the Achilles Track Club for disabled runners, and an extensive Junior Road Runner series.

The NYRRC running classes are nearly as old as the New York City Marathon. In the 1970s, coach Bob Glover came to me with the idea of starting the classes. He has headed them ever since. Approximately 25,000 people have graduated from the classes as of the end of 1991, and about 500 of these students run the marathon every year.

I first took the class in 1985, initially in an attempt to get my 10k time down from 47 to 44 minutes. I attended weekly on Tuesday nights; within a year, I took that significant chunk off my time.

The classes have been a remarkable success. For example, I met one woman in Central Park recently who after two years of classes, improved her 4:45 marathon time by almost one hour.

I find various aspects of the classes beneficial. Most of these benefits apply to any group running you do. First, classes teach runners to run right, teaching conscientious stretching, warmup, and cooldown routines. Classes also include other tips and racing information. Second, they offer invaluable shared experience. Learning alone can't possibly offer the range of insight and experience available in a class. Third, running with the class is safer on dark winter evenings. And, finally, classes are great motivators. It's hard to do speedwork alone, but it's a lot easier with the combination of group support and being committed to taking a class.

When I'm in a race, I can tell how I'm doing by locating my classmates. I know from experience whose pace is my pace. Because the classes are so well tailored, those within a group are evenly matched in ability. If I'm lagging behind my classmates, I know I'm not running well.

There's also the social side of the classes to consider. Classmates share their experiences not only in class but also socially, like over pizza afterward. Just ask former running class coach Cliff Held, who met and married one of his students.

—Fred Lebow

Leadership Council

In 1991 the NYRRC established the Leadership Council to ensure the optimal and enduring operation of the club. Members of the council are drawn from New York City's business and community leaders, many of whom are also avid runners. The current Leadership Council includes: Herman Badillo, former Bronx borough president; Elizabeth Barlow Rogers, Central Park administrator; Tom Brokaw, anchor of *NBC Nightly News*; Bill Chaney, chairman of Tiffany & Co.; Barbaralee Diamonstein Spielvogel, chair of The New York Landmarks Foundation; Timothy Healy, president of the New York Public Library; George Hirsch, publisher of *Runner's World*; Carl Landegger, chairman of Black, Clausen; Bill Perkins, district manager of the Board of Elections; Bill Rodgers; Howard Rubenstein, president of Howard Rubenstein Associates; Valerie Salembier, publisher of *Family Circle*; Percy Sutton, chief executive officer of Inner City Broadcasting; Grete Waitz; and Paula Zahn, co-anchor of *CBS This Morning*. A 14-member board of directors also assists when needed in guiding the club.

New York Running News

In 1958 noted marathoner Ted Corbitt put out the first edition of a running publication on a mimeographed sheet, and so became the first publisher of *New York Running News*, the nation's oldest running magazine. The quarterly publication, for years edited on the kitchen tables of a handful of club faithfuls, began with a print run of 600 copies. In 1972 Fred Lebow took over as publisher. The current circulation of the bimonthly magazine is 30,000, and the marathon issue is 75,000. A subscription to *New York Running News* is included with NYRRC membership.

Community Service

To protect and enhance Central Park and the city of New York, the NYRRC has developed several community service programs. After all, this 26,000 acres of parkland is an oasis for runners. The park is also the finish line of the New York City Marathon, an event that brings thousands of guests to New York.

The NYRRC is committed to building a stronger and safer New York. Various events of the past years, from economic recession to park safety, have presented particular challenges. Community service provides a vehicle for those who want to slow the growth of urban problems with positive programs of action.

The Safety Program. What began as a safety patrol of more than 400 volunteers has evolved into a full-scale program providing running pairing services, an educational series, a group running program, a daily patrol, and a safety gatehouse in Central Park.

Reservoir Maintenance. The NYRRC underwrites the salary of a full-time reservoir maintenance worker.

City-Sports-For-Kids. This year-round fun and fitness program for youths from 5 to 12 aims to promote physical fitness, develop self-esteem through sports, and build bridges among children of different socio-economic, religious, ethnic, and racial backgrounds.

Social Action

The NYRRC believes that running can and should be a vehicle for positive social action. To this end, the club has conducted the Homeless Shelter Running Program, the Rikers Island Prison Running Program, and the Urban Running Program for children. City-Sports-For-Kids is currently the fastest-growing social action program offered by the club.

The NYRRC welcomes inquiries from other running clubs and individuals who want to create social action or community service programs in their communities.

The Achilles Track Club

One of the most remarkable success stories of the NYRRC is the Achilles Track Club. Perhaps no aspect of the running movement better demonstrates the range of the sport's potential. The Achilles Track Club began in 1982 as an NYRRC program to introduce disabled people to the sport of running. It was conceived by Dick Traum, an NYRRC board member and amputee. Having himself run 10 marathons and one 100k race, Traum knew the possibilities of the sport for the disabled.

Traum had spent time in Canada, and participated in five Terry Fox 10k runs for cancer research. (Fox, an amputee suffering from cancer, inspired millions of people with his run across Canada. Although he eventually died of his illness, runs in his name have raised $90 million for cancer research.) Traum saw that disabled people of Toronto were more visible and more active than those in New York. After racing in

Canada, he was inspired to start the Achilles Track Club, named for the Greek hero Achilles, admired for his strength but renowned for his vulnerable heel.

Traum went to Fred Lebow and suggested soliciting interest for the club via the NYRRC's 1100 members who worked as medical and health care professionals. Fred, who was excited about the concept, was convinced it would catch on. "Even if you only get three people, it'll still be a success," he said. There were two responses. "It'll still be a success," Lebow told Traum again.

Traum initially established an eight-week course. Then, NYRRC coach Bob Glover got involved and suggested that the course be converted into a permanent program. The first course, which began on November 10, 1982, with two people, grew to six people by January. By 1991, the Achilles Track Club had mushroomed to over 3000 members from 35 chapters in the United States and approximately 70 chapters worldwide.

Achilles athletes, who run, walk, and use wheelchairs, represent an entire range of disabilities, from amputations, blindness, cerebral palsy, and paraplegia to epilepsy, diabetes, multiple sclerosis, traumatic brain injuries, cancer, heart disease, and arthritis.

The Achilles philosophy is to encourage members to participate in road races with the general running public as well as in events specifically designed for the physically challenged, for instance, the Paralympics. Approximately 500 Achilles members have completed a marathon, and a total of 115 participated in the 1991 New York City Marathon. Members have also competed in marathons in Beijing, Warsaw, Toronto, London, San Francisco, and Los Angeles.

Another Achilles philosophy is to improve the quality of life of its members. As of 1992, the club has conducted eye, leg, and wheelchair programs. As part of the eye program, Drs. Richard Koplin and John Seedor, both of the New York Eye and Ear Infirmary, perform surgery at no cost to Achilles members who can't afford the $25,000 price of surgery or to whom the surgery is otherwise unavailable. In addition to donating the doctors' services, the infirmary also donates the use of its facilities. Airlines provide free transportation for Achilles members, and the West Side YMCA in New York provides accommodations at modest rates.

The leg program provides artificial legs for amputee runners. The wheelchair program, still in its infancy, has provided five sports wheelchairs to the Beijing chapter of the club and has donated wheelchairs to athletes in Russia, Poland, and Colombia.

Who Are Some of the Runners of the Achilles Track Club? Linda Down, a New Yorker with cerebral palsy, gained worldwide fame in the 1982 New York City Marathon. After completing the race, an achievement documented by network television, she was invited to meet President Reagan at the White House. Down is a board member of the Achilles Track Club and helps other members by serving as a coach. She is also an inspirational speaker for the United Way. Down completed her first marathon in just over 11 hours. Since that time, she has done 10 marathons, with a best time of under 8 hours.

Fifty-plus-year-old Jere Munro, who has multiple sclerosis, founded the Achilles Track Club in Boston. In April, 1991, in cooperation with the Boston Athletic Association, he was responsible for setting up an Achilles division in the Boston Marathon. Among the 14 Achilles runners in that race were two visually impaired runners from Beijing. This marked the first time that disabled Chinese athletes, in any sport, left their country and competed in a mainstream event. On the day of the Boston Marathon, President Bush awarded Munro the Points of Light Foundation Award for his contribution.

Daniella Zahner was a world-class skier hoping to represent her native Switzerland in the Olympics when a car accident left her legs seriously injured. She now runs with crutches, and her time of 4:13 in the 1991 New York City Marathon established a world record in its category. That year, she was also named the Achilles Track Club outstanding female performer. Zahner is also a volunteer who escorts Achilles members in races.

Jeffrey Dutton, M.D., has small bowel syndrome. Twenty feet of his intestines were removed some years ago. Consequently, his total intake of liquid and solid food is ingested intravenously. While training for the New York City Marathon in 1984, Dutton concluded, "If I can run a marathon, I can get through medical school." He applied to medical school and in June 1991 completed his medical studies.

Disabled athletes don't just participate in races for fun and fitness. There are world- and national-class athletes in this category. Among them is Michael Keohane, a 1992 Olympic Trials marathon qualifier, 1990 Goodwill Games USA team member, and a past NYRRC Runner of the Year in his age group. Keohane was born with a congenital disability: he has no left forearm or hand. Nevertheless, he says, "I played any sport I could find," and he took up golf after meeting a one-armed golfer who taught him how to play. He played soccer for nine years and in high school began running. Keohane ran his first marathon at age 22, recording a time of 2:30. Three years later, he ran 2:16:20.

I not only support having disabled people participate in NYRRC events, but also hope eventually to have special events focusing on the disabled. As for elite wheelchair racers, they participate in the Boston and Los Angeles marathons, but in New York, we don't have an appropriate course. It's suitable for the everyday wheelchair athlete, but not for the superathlete. Boston doesn't really accept wheelchair athletes slower than three or four hours. We accept wheelchair athletes as slow as seven or even ten hours. I've been accused of discriminating against wheelchair athletes, but just as I discriminate against fast wheelchair athletes, Boston discriminates against slow athletes.

—Fred Lebow

NYRRC Membership

For more information about the NYRRC, simply include an S.A.S.E. with your query addressed to 9 East 89th Street, New York, NY 10128, or call (212) 860-4455 for information. The NYRRC is open Mondays through Fridays from 10 a.m. to 8 p.m., Saturdays, 10 a.m. to 5 p.m., and Sundays, 10 a.m. to 3 p.m. Membership is $25 per year and includes monthly race and premium mailings and a subscription to *New York Running News*. All proceeds from race fees and membership dues are used to support and develop the innovative programs and quality events produced throughout the year by the NYRRC.

Introduction

When Fred Lebow took up jogging in 1969, he found his niche—both personally and professionally. A European immigrant schooled only in religious studies, Fred is a former garment district executive whose only previous running experience was escaping from the Nazis. Yet this man has made footracing a social movement. With Fred's creativity, the marathon race became an international festival and the sport of running became the vehicle for scores of other athletic and social events. Fred took a simple sport and, with a stroke of daring and imagination, made it a global passion.

Fred's genius has been to marry the most unlikely partners: a marathon to the streets of New York City; a mile race to posh Fifth Avenue; runners to the stairs of the Empire State Building. In addition to his matchmaking, Fred has made a commitment to the development of the sport of running, from grassroots participation to the revival of track and field in the United States.

Behind Fred's public facade is a zealous and sometimes difficult person. He applies complete devotion to running and promotes comparable attention from his small staff of nonprofit wage earners. When Fred gets an idea, New York Road Runners Club staff tremble, but soon they are working double-time on the dream or scheme.

I've watched Fred operate for years now, and my observations support a theory about the roots of his greatness. Fred belongs to a group unique in history: Eastern European Jews who, as children—by wits and luck—escaped annihilation by the Nazis. Jerzy Kosinski, Roman Polanski, Bill Graham, and others like Fred were refugee children who grew up to be profoundly successful—and flamboyant. Crazy, perhaps; controversial, undoubtedly; and visionary, absolutely.

Fred was already a role model and motivator—an unlikely race director who, while wearing running shoes, brought his message of health and fitness all the way to the White House—when he was struck with cancer in March of 1990. No amount of running or fitness could have prevented this insidious, often fatal, disease. But Fred has made his victories in the race against cancer perhaps the most significant of his running career, and his story of exercising through the pain and trauma of disease is the most inspirational chapter of his remarkable life.

"Fred, This Run's for You" was the theme of the 1991 New York City Marathon fund-raising drive for cancer research. Each of the contributors to this book has participated in this spirit to create The NYRRC Complete Book of Running. *Fred, this book's for you!*

—Gloria Averbuch

My Life as a Runner with Cancer

Runners are attuned to their bodies. They sense even tiny physical changes, the kinds that affect performance and general well-being. It was my running that first alerted me to my own illness, and my running that rehabilitated me from its ravages.

Before I noticed any specific symptoms of disease, my running was definitely off. In January 1990, my usual 9- or 10-minute-per-mile training pace inexplicably slowed to 13 or 14 minutes per mile. I thought an old knee injury might be the reason, but I felt no knee pain. I had no other particular aches or fatigue—just an odd sense of weight bearing down on me. And I was disoriented. For example, Gloria Averbuch, my writing partner for years, was disturbed when, during our regular session to prepare my magazine column, I was literally unable to string a thought together. Then, at the annual NYRRC Awards Banquet on February 10, I took the dais, started to speak, but the words came out wrong. I even confused the names of two people I know quite well. Those near and dear to me had suspected I was in trouble. Now they were sure.

On Monday following the banquet, NYRRC staff and friends Brian Crawford and Sandy Sislowitz arranged for me to go to Dr. Norb Sander. Norb made an appointment for an MRI (magnetic resonance imaging) scan the next morning. I wasn't particularly concerned about my condition at this point. After all, I didn't feel bad. I had no headaches, no fatigue. Surely nothing could be seriously wrong.

But by the time the fourth doctor examined me during the morning of the MRI, I was making speech errors, my sight was blurred, and I grew weak and unable to maintain normal posture. To the doctors, something was clearly wrong with the left side of my brain— maybe an inflammation, maybe something worse. True to form, I initially resisted their instructions to check into the hospital for more comprehensive testing.

Nevertheless, I finally checked into Mount Sinai Hospital, where I met Dr. Seymour Gendelman. Rather than launch into a discussion of my MRI, he instead pulled out his NYRRC membership card and started to chat about running. He told me he had even run the New York City Marathon. He was the first of several of the dozen-odd doctors involved in my treatment who were NYRRC members. I was struck by this discovery. For all my talk about the ubiquitousness of running, I only half believed the sport was a significant part of our culture. When I met all those running doctors, I realized how truly mainstream the running movement has become. And I took personal comfort in having runners for doctors. Not only could they understand me better than nonrunners, but they also supported my need to keep exercising during even the bleakest days of my illness.

Dr. Gendelman soon turned his attention to the issue at hand. The MRI revealed at least three tumors, one of which was two inches in diameter, considered a huge mass. There was significant swelling, which was exerting tremendous pressure on my brain—hence the speech problems, weakness, slumping, etc. Cortisone was immediately prescribed to reduce the swelling. Then Gendelman told me that in order to determine if the tumor was malignant or not, a tissue sample would have to be extracted.

There are several types of tumors. One is lymphoma, preferable to malignant melanoma or glioblastoma. These latter are the most aggressive tumors known. "What's the worst-case scenario?" I asked Dr. Gendelman. "If the tumor were a melanoma or glioblastoma, you probably wouldn't have more than three to six months to live," he explained.

I was numb. "I don't know what he's talking about," I told myself. "I don't have any symptoms. I don't have headaches. I can still exercise. I'm a healthy person. I live clean and am basically unstressed. I can't be sick."

Gendelman continued to talk, saying a brain biopsy would have to be conducted, explaining how it would be performed. But I was only half listening, my mind hearing over and over the death sentence proclaimed a few moments before. The tumors could not be removed surgically for several reasons. First, they were extensive, making it difficult to guarantee successfully excising all of the mass. And, they were on the left side of the brain, where, as Gendelman says, "God, in His infinite wisdom, put most of our ability." Trying to remove the tumors could well have left me without speech and paralyzed on my right side.

I poured my fear into exercise. During my first stay in the hospital, my room was located near a circular rooftop. I figured there were probably about 67 loops to a mile running out there. I did that 67-lap run faithfully while I was in the hospital until snows came and the security guards made me stop for fear I'd slip and fall.

A brain biopsy is a major operation. I have a scar on my head where I was cut to remind me of that. (In fact, I have five scars on various parts of my body as mementos of all operations related to my cancer: two on my head, two on my neck, one on my knee.) Although I was laid up, I had to remain active physically. Anyone who exercises can understand— my mind needed it more than my body. I didn't run the day following the brain biopsy, but I got up and walked 12 steps. I felt pretty weak, so I went back to bed. But each day I walked a bit more—for 5 minutes, then 10 minutes. I walked in the hospital hallway. It wasn't a good hallway, but it would have to do. By my calculations, 70 lengths made a mile. I worked my way up to a half-hour walking in that hallway.

A biopsy of a tumor is not always conclusive. That's because the tissue is different throughout the mass. Sure enough, my first biopsy was inconclusive. The mass could be toxoplasmosis, an infection. It could be cancer. Thus I began the emotional roller coaster ride through hope and despair.

After I recovered from the biopsy, there were three more weeks of tests—CAT scans and more types of blood tests than I ever imagined existed. I was even tested for HIV because what I had was not unusual in AIDS patients. Four weeks after the biopsy, I was finally able to go home. I kept up my exercise, but suddenly one day felt a pain just below my right knee. Again, my running provided a crucial early warning.

A vascular surgeon examined me, testing my blood circulation and pressure. I had thrombophlebitis, a blood clot, very possibly related to my brain tumor. I couldn't be put on anticoagulants, the typical medication for phlebitis, because they might cause my tumors to bleed. Instead, I was immediately scheduled for surgery.

It was about this time that Republican Party Chairman Lee Atwater had been diagnosed with cancer, but he eventually died from a blood clot. A runner who regularly put in six miles a day, Atwater was only 40 years old when he died. Panic invaded me for the first time since my troubles began. I made a connection and felt an eerie identification with Lee Atwater.

A blood clot, if it travels to the heart, can kill instantly. Because I couldn't be treated with drugs, the surgeons instead fitted me with an umbrella filter. The filter was inserted through a tube and opened right above the vein to trap any part of the clot that might break off. To this day, I have my umbrella right below my abdomen working inside me.

After the procedure, I started walking again. It was mental therapy. I always walked in the morning, hoping the peace of mind the exercise gave would help carry me through the tense days in the hospital. As my condition grew more complicated, I kept up exercising to release the tension of my fears. And more, exercise became my personal statement of gratitude and defiance. Running had warned me of my illness (for which I'll always be thankful), and running, I felt, would help me fight the disease.

My physical fitness was critical. I used it to make sure I didn't stagnate. You can be sick in bed, unable to do almost anything, but you can still wiggle your fingers and toes. I found this out through experience. Over the months in and out of hospitals, I believed that if I let myself be ruled by disease, I could succumb to my own laziness. I fought that tendency with exercise.

After the surgery on the blood clot, the doctors decided to do a second brain biopsy. An elaborate steel head halter, a heavy contraption weighing about 20 pounds, was screwed onto my head. A series of three-dimensional photographs was taken to ensure that the doctors inserted a needle in exactly the right spot. During the biopsy, I had to remain awake. I had to indicate that movement and speech were not impaired by the procedure. My head remained in the helmet after the biopsy sample was retrieved. The surgeon himself took the sample to the hospital lab to be sure he'd extracted sufficient matter for testing. He was gone, it seemed, a lifetime before they unscrewed me from the implement of torture. The entire operation, which took only an hour and a half, seemed to last a century.

I'd been warned of the slim chance—3 to 5 percent—of not surviving the second biopsy procedure. "I'm probably going to end up in a wheelchair," I thought during the operation. "God is telling me something about my attitude against wheelchair racers in the New York City Marathon." Since I emerged from that surgery—my motor faculties intact—I've found my views rather softer on the topic of wheelchair-bound athletes!

I'd spent a total of eight weeks in the hospital by the time the second biopsy was complete. During those weeks, I was cheered by many visitors—from world-class athletes to sponsors, friends, and, of course, my family. Most visitors, however, didn't greet me in my bed. I was usually walking or actually running through the hospital. When Eamonn Coghlan came to visit, he joined me in one of my courses, an 11-lap-to-the-mile route. "You won the Millrose miles by running 11 laps," I reminded him. "Yes, this feels like 11 laps to the mile," he agreed with a smile.

Dr. Gendelman told me the result of the second biopsy: lymphoma. My prognosis was much better than it could have been with other types of tumors, and I would immediately begin a course of chemotherapy. Lymphoma, he explained, had a variable response to the treatment, some tumors rapidly shrinking, others growing. And because lymphoma is common in AIDS patients, I had yet another series of blood tests for HIV.

When Gendelman and all my guests had gone that day, I was alone with my thoughts. It all finally sunk in. I thought over the 58 years of my life. Anger and grief overcame me, and tears ran hot down my cheeks. A nurse came in. I quickly turned my head into the pillow. I didn't want her to see me crying.

When I woke the next morning, I was a renewed person. I felt wonderful, transformed. I was determined to get the better of my illness, and I have not succumbed to tears and despair since then. I got up and continued my walking regimen.

On the journey to save my life, I then started chemotherapy, a horrible odyssey of nausea, weakness, weight and hair loss. I felt like Methuselah in his nine hundredth year—yet I continued to proclaim myself the healthiest cancer patient on earth. And I continued to work—via telephone. Although I couldn't attend the weekly races in Central Park, I watched them from the window of my 10th-floor hospital room. I saw them all—from 4 miles to 20k. The runners must have been told where I was because many raised their arms to wave as they passed the hospital building.

The first day back in my own apartment, I decided to walk in Central Park. I was tired before I started. But I was spurred on by greetings from the doorman I used to pass on my daily runs during my pre-disease days. Every day I went walking, starting with one mile, and by the third day I walked 2¾ miles in one hour. After about three weeks of walking, I was able to insert short bursts of running, 10- to 15-yard jogs, into my walking routine. I never thought running could be so difficult! I was amazed how I could be jogging and every walker in the park could still pass me. But with each day I improved, inserting more and longer intervals of jogging. One minute of running became ten, and eventually, I worked my way up to past levels of training.

Then I began a 31-day cycle of radiation at Memorial Sloan-Kettering Cancer Center. Because the hospital is within blocks of my apartment, it was convenient to walk there for treatments. This was the only convenience, however. My insurance company refused to cover the expense of the treatment (although I'm delighted to thank Al Gordon in these pages for personally paying for my radiation therapy) and the treatment itself, like the chemotherapy, made me violently ill. With chemotherapy, I lost my hair. With radiation, I lost my trademark beard. Initially, I became bloated, then I lost weight. Eventually I was down to 124 pounds from my running weight of 144. I had no hair, and very little meat on my bones. But I had made great progress in my recovery. One day I managed an entire lower loop of the park running. It took me 30 minutes to cover the 1.7 miles.

By August, I had completed my chemotherapy and radiation treatments. I underwent another MRI to see if the treatments had worked. Dr. Lisa DeAngelis, with the guidance of Dr. Jerry Posner, the major world authority on malignant brain tumors, had been directing my treatments. Dr. DeAngelis smiled, "You're doing very well." I was officially in remission. The dosages of cortisone and phenobarbital were tapered off. My body was becoming my own again.

Why did I get this cancer? Probably no one will ever know. And although the cancer is in remission now, it could occur again any day. The truth is that the human body fails—sometimes from aging, sometimes from accidents, sometimes from illness and disease. Pills, operations, doctors' guidance, and the love of family and friends all aid recovery. But there is something more, something crucial to overcoming the failure of the body, and that is physical fitness.

When I look back over my experience with cancer, I am struck by how little other patients exercise. At Mount Sinai, younger, fitter patients than I didn't move a muscle. Only one other patient—a 2:48 marathoner—ever seemed to join me in activity. I realized that the NYRRC had developed fitness programs for youths, the homeless, and the incarcerated, but we had neglected the sick. In the midst of my treatment, Allan Steinfeld said the club had been approached to use the marathon in a fund-raiser for cancer research. "Forget it," I said. I'd never wanted to use the marathon for fund-raising of any kind. But the next day while I was at Sloan-Kettering for a radiation treatment, I saw two boys, probably 8 and 10 years old. Like me, they were bloated and hairless. These boys brought home to me the utter tragedy of cancer. And children, I've learned, have even less chance to survive the disease than adults. I returned to the club that day and told Allan to go ahead with the fund-raiser.

In 1990, over $1.2 million—matched by government funds—was raised in the Stop Cancer New York City Marathon drive. In 1991, additional funds were raised. The campaign continued in the 1992 Marathon. I'm delighted at the tremendous success of these fund-raising efforts, and I am gratified to be able to give something back for my own good fortune in fighting cancer.

When I became ill, I got the best doctors, treatment, and advice. And then I did more. I moved my hands, my legs. I made my blood pump. Other patients at Mount Sinai would ask me, "Why do you do this?" I'd respond, "The question isn't why I'm doing this, but why you aren't."

I know it's sometimes hard to get motivated to run even in the best of health and under the best conditions. Part of my desire to run is to stay in shape to race. Even after cancer therapy, I walked, then ran, with the goal of getting back into racing. However, I was no longer racing to break a 7-minute-per-mile pace. I'm delighted now to break 10 minutes per mile.

I've raced a lot since my illness. (By the time you read this, I hope to have run the 1992 New York City Marathon.) I was slow and I sometimes had to walk in the earlier races. Often I was so far back in the pack that I found myself among the disabled members of the Achilles Track Club. "Now you qualify for our team," laughed Dick Traum, the group's leader and my dear friend.

Exactly one year after I was diagnosed with cancer, I returned to the hospital to learn if the cancer was still in remission. I was very nervous before the tests, as were my friends and colleagues. On the day I got the results, my friends and staff were assembled in my office. "I'm okay," I said. Then I turned to Allan Steinfeld and said, "Let's go for a run." We did the two laps of the Central Park reservoir in 36 minutes—the fastest I had covered that course since getting sick. I felt wonderful—inside and out.

If it weren't for my friends, particularly those who originally forced me to go to Norb Sander to find out about my odd behavior, I doubt that I would be here today. My illness was hard on me, sure, but it was also hard on them, especially Allan Steinfeld, who carried my responsibilities at the NYRRC as well as his own during my illness and recovery. Allan has been my partner in creating the club's events. If I dream the impossible, Allan implements it. And Allan has served as my coach in my running comeback. Even now when I race I hear Allan's voice in my head, "Pick it up, you can do it!"

Things were going pretty well after my one-year checkup until six months later. I woke up with a swelling in my throat. I went to Sloan-Kettering, where I was told, "We have to operate." Here I go, back on the roller coaster, I thought. The lump was a carcinoma of the thyroid, but not the same kind of cancer I had in my brain. Compared to the brain cancer, this was nothing. The tumor was removed and has never recurred.

Since my illness, I have been taking my life back, slowly but confidently. My body has changed. I'm not as strong as I was before, but I can manage more and more each day. I'm thinner, but I've always been fairly "runner thin." But the real change is inside me, a change I understand best through my running. I'm glad to be alive and I live with that feeling every day. It's like being a beginner again, in love with the idea of my body moving along, content with the weather, the seasons, and the sound of each footfall.

Fred Lebow
New York City, 1992

Fred Lebow's Comeback Race Results

Race	Time	Pace per mile
Snowflake 4 Mile (Feb. 17, 1991)	40:37	10:09
Staten Island Half-Marathon (Sept. 22, 1991)	2:27:19	11:14
Turkey Classic 5 Mile (Nov. 23, 1991)	45:29	9:05
Winter Series 10K (Dec. 8, 1991)	59:18	9:33
Four-Mile Holiday Run (Dec. 22, 1991)	34:56	8:44
Season Opener 5 Mile (Jan. 5, 1992)	43:40	8:44
Rogaine 5K (March 1, 1992)	25:32	8:13*
Lisbon Half-Marathon (Mar. 8, 1992)	2:04:36	9:31

* Best time for the distance in two years.

Part 1: Training

1

For Beginners

All runners, at one time or another, are beginners. Although as a beginner you are not yet ready for major marathons or Olympic competitions, you can reap all the benefits of running more quickly and dramatically than seasoned runners. As a beginner you also bring a special freshness and excitement to the sport, a vitality that sometimes fades with experience.

Grete Waitz's Ten-Week Beginner's Program

What can you expect as a beginner? For starters, you will gain a new awareness of your body. Running will improve your stamina. It will help you control or reduce your weight (most beginners lose one half to one pound per week). And running provides a new relationship with nature; if you've never really felt the sun, wind, or rain on your face, you will now!

So how should you begin? Grete Waitz has outlined a ten-week program specifically for beginners.

Grete Waitz says her "running" program is actually a "jogging" program because you must jog before you can run. Both running and jogging are enjoyable and beneficial, but one precedes the other, and then

3

they are done in balance. In fact, every running program, no matter what level, includes some jogging. Before beginning the program, consider a few of Waitz's facts and tips from her book *World Class:*

Run at a conversational pace. While jogging you should be able to talk comfortably without being winded. Make a commitment to train with a friend. When motivation is low and excuses are easy to find, that commitment to meet your training partner will see you through.

We have a saying in Norwegian, "Hurry slowly." Getting fit is done by gradually and progressively increasing training. Beginners often feel my program is too slow; however, although the heart and lungs respond quickly to exercise, muscles and joints take much longer. That is why those who immediately run far and fast usually end up injured, burned out, or both. On the other hand, if the program is too strenuous, take your time, even longer than ten weeks, if necessary. Stay with a given session as long as you feel you must, and move ahead when you feel you are ready.

This program is designed to bring you from your armchair to running 3¼ miles (5 kilometers plus) continuously. It is based on running three days per week. You should space those days out to allow for sufficient recovery between efforts. If you are not using a track to gauge the distances, you can approximate them. With experience, you will begin to get a sense of how long it takes you to run each segment and to complete the workout. Then you will be able to use time as a basic indicator of distance. (However, the point is not to run for time, or to time yourself.)

Studies have shown that the ideal amount of exercise for optimum fitness is 20 to 30 minutes three times a week, done at a moderate level of intensity. This program will get you fit. You should realize that those who run more than this amount are doing so for reasons beyond fitness. (If this eventually becomes the case for you, you can explore more advanced programs in this book.)

Use the first four weeks to get a general education. Pay close attention to your body; learn to read its signals of fatigue and stress, or when you can push beyond them. It's like studying another language. It may seem foreign at first, but eventually you will learn to understand the meaning of various physical sensations.

After ten weeks, you may stay at the level you have reached, or you may want to increase, with the goal, for example, of running a race.

However, to maintain basic fitness, simply continue doing the schedule for week 9.

Before beginning this program, be sure you have a physical and consult your physician about your basic health and fitness.

Ten-Week Beginner's Program

Week 1
- Alternately jog/walk (eight of each) 100-yard segments, for a total of 1 mile.
- Same workout for all three days.

Week 2
- Alternately jog/walk (five of each) 200-yard segments, for a total of 1 1/4 miles.
- Same workout for all three days.

Week 3
- Alternately jog/walk, varying the segments between 200 and 400 yards, for a total of 1 1/2 miles.
- Same workout for all three days.

Week 4
- Alternately jog/walk, but walk only half the distance of each jog. Vary the segments between 1/4 and 1/2 mile, for a total of 1 3/4 miles.
- Same workout for all three days.

Week 5
- Day 1: 1/2-mile jog, 1/4-mile walk, 1/2-mile jog, 1/4-mile walk, 1/2-mile jog, for 2 miles total.
- Day 2: 3/4-mile jog, 1/2-mile walk, 3/4-mile jog, for 2 miles total.
- Day 3: 2-mile jog, no walk.

Week 6
- Day 1: 1/2-mile jog, 1/4-mile walk, 3/4-mile jog, 1/4-mile walk, 1/2-mile jog, for 2 1/4 miles total.
- Day 2: 1-mile jog, 1/4-mile walk, 1-mile jog, for 2 1/4 miles total.
- Day 3: 2 1/4-mile jog, no walk.

Week 7
- (Only jogging, no walking from this point on; however, you can vary the pace of the jog.)

- 2½-mile jog.
- Same workout all three days.

Week 8

- 2¾-mile jog.
- Same workout all three days.

Week 9

- 3-mile jog.
- Same workout all three days.

Week 10

- 3¼ miles total (5 kilometers plus).
- Congratulations! You're no longer a beginner.

Tom Fleming's Beginner's Guide to Running for Fun and Fitness

I've noticed that for some people the physiological motion of running is very easy. I've watched a very big man, 220 pounds, run very economically, with a very good gait. Usually these people are naturally athletic. They find running simple. There's no batting a ball; there's no fielding. All you need is yourself and a decent pair of shoes. I think that's why running is so appealing to most people. Obviously it must be easy if so many people attain an acceptable level of fitness and stay with the sport so long.

Is there any personality trait that makes someone a good runner? That's probably one of the hardest questions to answer. There are some people who have excelled who don't have the greatest talent, but they're bright enough and realistic about their goals. They know what they have to do to achieve those goals. And this is true for all levels.

Are the really good runners smarter? Not necessarily. I've known some who weren't. But then you've got to factor in an incredible God-given innate ability. There's something else that makes the great ones different. I think that, number one, they had a good mother and father; the genetics are right. Of course, they also have great desire. I can spend hours talking about the nature of desire, will, and guts.

What makes running an integral part of someone's life? That may be an unanswerable question. Some people have no idea why they wake up every morning and have to get in their run. But they'll tell you what the end result is: They feel better and they don't get the headaches they used to at their jobs. The average person is running for both fitness and stress relief.

After an initial time period, running does become easier. You can always remember that first week, those first few runs. What people enjoy, whether you're talking about an elite runner or a jogger, is that you do improve fairly quickly.

How long this takes varies from person to person. I've seen some rather overweight people, for example, who weren't athletic at all, who started running and within three months made big changes. I don't just mean in how they looked, but their entire attitude. They felt more confidence in themselves and more confident about exercising.

The point is to take it gradually, particularly for those people who want to lose weight. Many times I advise them to begin with a walking program, because running may be too difficult. But I'll promote the activity either way, because I know sooner or later they're going to want to start jogging or running.

Regardless of your reasons for wanting to begin a program of running, use some common sense:

1. Start at the doctor's office. A thorough checkup is recommended before undertaking an exercise program. It is useful to explain to your doctor the details of any exercise program you intend to do. A stress test is recommended if you are over age 40.

2. Keep a diary, a running/exercise log. You can track your progress by recording the times and distances you run, even how you feel, who you run with, and the weather. Be accurate about what you write, as this record can greatly instruct you in the future.

3. In terms of clothing, always put comfort before fashion. Wear loose clothing. Your feet will expand during a training run, so make sure you purchase shoes that are large enough. You should run in well-cushioned training shoes.

4. Never push it. Use the talk test to determine if your pace is appropriate: You should be able to converse comfortably while running. Run with the same style you use to walk, a relaxed effort with your own natural form and rhythm. Do not hesitate to alternate running and walking.

5. Know your body. Get in the habit of checking your pulse—in the morning before getting out of bed, during daily tasks, and dur-

ing running. This will give you a gauge of both your general health and your fitness level. (To determine your pulse, see Heart Rate Monitor Training, Chapter 4.)

6. Four feet are better than two. Train with a friend. It makes the running easier, and the commitment and motivation stronger.

7. Develop your own training routine. Any time of day and any place is fine, as long as you are consistent in exercising. If you prefer to vary your fitness routine, do other exercises or sports on nonrunning days.

8. Try to avoid aches and pains by practicing good exercise habits, such as an organized and thorough warmup and cooldown. Easy-paced running is an effective warmup. The cooldown is most essential, and should include a stretching routine for muscle flexibility.

9. To avoid injuries, heed the following: Don't run in worn-down shoes; avoid uneven surfaces; don't be impatient and run too far or too fast too soon. If you feel a suspicious pain, or if you feel ill, take off until the condition improves.

10. Set no limitations. While using common sense and being cautious is the best guarantee for long-term enjoyment and acquiring the benefits of running, don't underestimate your potential ability. There are times it feels great to go for it!

For the total newcomer to running, Cliff Temple offers six golden rules:

1. Run more slowly than you think you should.

2. Don't run as far as you think you should.

3. Run more often than you think you should.

4. Exchange experiences with other runners whenever practical (shared training runs are ideal).

5. Try to find a local running club that offers coaching that is specific to newcomers.

6. Read running magazines and books from cover to cover, and always keep issues handy in case an injury or training query turns out to be *your* problem or question next week.

Cliff Held Says Slow and Steady

The most important message I stress to beginners is to learn to love the sport. Like other endeavors, if running is not undertaken properly, it can be difficult and discouraging. It sometimes takes a while to learn to enjoy it. That doesn't necessarily happen overnight.

In order to start properly, the beginners in the NYRRC running classes combine running and walking. Most novices make the mistake of deciding right away to run one mile. That's this number, this distance, they have in their head. But they don't realize how far one mile really is. This kind of approach—taking on too much too soon—usually results in feeling pain, or becoming injured or discouraged.

The goal of the class is to get beginners eventually running 20 minutes without stopping, and to be introduced to the sport in a positive and enjoyable way.

Gordon Bloch's Convenience Approach

To me, the beauty of running is that you can do it anywhere. Other exercise seems so cumbersome in comparison: You have to go to a gym, or change into a bathing suit, or buy expensive equipment. Although each person has to find his or her own exercise formula, the simplicity of running gives it a great advantage.

Here are some tips for beginners:

1. Find a training partner.
2. If necessary, join a health club and run on an indoor track or treadmill.
3. Seek out local road races.
4. Join in on group runs, or set up groups of your own.
5. Take a fitness vacation, or attend a running camp.
6. If you're injured, try to adopt a "Zen-like" attitude. Keep in shape with cross training.

Francie Larrieu Smith's Advice from Experience

Be patient; don't expect too much too soon. I highly discourage young people from competing in road races. I think it's great to expose them to fun running, but it kills me to see a child running the marathon.

A lot of beginners don't realize that some pain is natural. Even the most seasoned runners experience pain. When I come back after a lay-off due to injury and I'm forced to start at the bottom, I, too, experience some aches and pains. It's important to know that it passes. Just make sure to go by the book, building slowly by adding only 10 percent a week.

I think you can know the signs of injury trouble with experience. Exercise helps you to get to know your body. I know when something is serious or not. I believe I've come to know my body so well that I can judge if and when it's time to see a doctor. This is not only the case with running injuries, it's true even with illnesses, like the flu.

I hope that people gain some sound training knowledge with this book. I meet people every day who still basically don't seem to know what to do. They read about someone's training in a running magazine and they copy it. One thing people need to realize is that there is no one program that works for everyone.

Another thing I tell runners is that no matter how inexperienced a runner you may be, there is nothing wrong with being intense. You don't know what you might discover. True, there are those who just don't have the genetics to be great. But then there are the "late bloomers." In running, as in any athletic event, there may be latent talents you never expected would blossom.

Do It Together

Exercise programs are followed better when working out with a spouse. In one study, nearly 50 percent of men who exercised alone quit their program after one year, while two-thirds of those exercising with their wives stuck with it.

—Fitness Features

Run with Rover

"Running with your dog is probably one of the safest things you can do for yourself, and it can be great for the animal as well," says Mimi Noonan, DVM, a veterinarian at the Animal Medical Center in Manhattan and NYRRC member, who runs daily with her two-year-old rottweiler, Keffer, along the East River. You are much less likely to be harassed or attacked when running with a canine, she says (even an animal not trained to attack assailants), although you and the dog should still never run alone in an area and at a time that you feel unsafe.

According to runner Jack Sanford, author of *Running with Your Dog*, and quoted in *Runner's World* magazine, if you intend to run with your dog, begin with ordinary obedience training, like the basic commands (sit, stop, come when called, etc.). Then begin walking with the dog over a set route several times a week. As this becomes easier and more controlled, substitute some jogging for walking.

The most important thing to remember when running with a dog, Noonan says, is that dogs are like people when it comes to getting in shape. "Just as you wouldn't enter a marathon without training, you can't take your pet on 10-mile runs without working up to them." Start by taking your dog on warmup or warmdown jogs. Increase the distance gradually. Most dogs should be able to run up to 30 to 40 minutes at your training pace after a few weeks.

If you wish, and the dog responds well, you can add longer runs—again, building gradually—of up to two or three hours. "I've known people whose dogs went with them on all their marathon training runs, with both of them loving it," says Noonan.

Several precautionary measures are in order, however, when running with a dog. First, she suggests that the animal be given a physical examination by a veterinarian, in case there are any underlying health problems that would make running hazardous. Once past that hurdle, another health and safety step is making sure the animal gets enough water (again, like people) before, during, and after your runs. In addition, Noonan says, heed signs of canine thirst—panting, salivating, slowing down, wanting to stop at puddles—even if you're not thirsty.

Another potential problem, especially in urban areas, is broken glass, rough pavement, and other things that can hurt a dog's paws. Watch for limping or favoring of one leg, suggests Noonan. "Most dogs will keep running through pain, even on three legs if they have to," says Noonan (remind you of any runners you know?), "so it's up to you to be alert."

Always keep your dog on a leash when running together. "People love the idea of letting their dog run free, but in most places it's just dangerous. Besides, worrying about your dog, other dogs, people, cars, bikes, roller skaters, etc., will distract you from your running."

Dogs shouldn't run until they are at least one year to 18 months old. Before then, canine bones are still developing, and the pounding of running can cause growth deformities. "It's the same reason doctors don't recommend that young children engage in distance-running programs," says Noonan, adding that her dog just started running at age 2.

In addition, certain types of dogs should never run. These include the brachycephalic breeds with flat faces and short noses, such as pugs, boxers, and Boston terriers. "They can't move enough air into their lungs when breathing heavily, especially in hot weather," Noonan explains.

Finally, some dogs simply don't take to running, and should not be forced to.

Fred Lebow's First Experiences

My most vivid memories of beginning to run are of how little anyone seemed to know about the sport and how little was available in the way of information and equipment. Not only did I have trouble getting any decent shoes, but when I went to a newsstand to try to find a running magazine, it was hopeless. "Running," I told the vendor, who looked quite puzzled. "You know—track and field." His eyes lit up in seeming recognition. Then he handed me *Road & Track*, a magazine about cars.

I started running one mile along the Central Park reservoir. In one of my first runs, I saw an old-time runner and we started talking. He was a regular racer who ran events at Van Cortlandt Park. He encouraged me to race too. "But I'm 38 years old," I told him. "Well, I'm old enough to be your father, and I'm doing it!" he replied.

When I started running, I had the idea I had to be very good to participate. I remember how embarrassed I was the first time I called to inquire about a race and had to tell the official I was 38 years old. One of my first races was a five-miler near Yankee Stadium. People who raced were fairly serious in those days. There were only 60 people, and I came in 59th, beating a 70-year-old. But I was pleased I was able to finish without walking.

These days, it's perfectly acceptable to do a five-hour marathon. People run 4:59 and they're ecstatic. When I ran my first marathon (4:09), I was depressed that I didn't break four hours. A majority of runners in New York don't break four hours. I think it's great that now time no longer determines or affects participation.

When I began running, I sought advice from a multitude of people—athletes and coaches. Running was so foreign to me, and to those around me. It seemed hard to get advice. The questions were very basic then, like: Why do this sport in the first place?

In 1970 I was talking with Gary Muhrcke and Norb Sander (two early winners of the New York City Marathon). Gary took me outside to show me how to run, how to lift my legs. Like many people at the time, I used to believe running wasn't natural, that you had to learn how to do it. I was surprised when Gary finally said, "It's nothing special. Just do it; it's a natural movement."

The great thing about this sport is that it's never too late to begin, and there's so much support to do so. Jack Rudin is 68 years old. He is one of our marathon sponsors, and has been involved with running and racing for years. His father was a marathoner. It's only recently that he's started walking (and perhaps eventually running) in our events. I see how he gloats over his achievements, how happy he is. It's great.

Introduction to Training Terms

A variety of training philosophies, advice, and programs are followed by beginners as well as advanced runners. Many programs are similar in principle, and many experts' views support each other. Yet different athletes stress different aspects of the sport—its benefits, techniques, and goals. Remember, no training program can account for the individual circumstances of each runner. As with any training program, the ones in this book can be adapted, if and how necessary.

The basic training techniques are defined below.

Fartlek

Fartlek, which means "speed play" in Swedish, was popularized as a form of training by Gosta Holmer, a Swedish Olympic coach for 33 years. In essence, it consists of bursts of speed in the middle of a long run—basically a less structured form of interval training. "Fartlek brings us back to the games of our childhood," according to Cliff Temple. "A child plays while sitting, walks some steps, runs to its mother, walks or runs back to the playground, makes a longer excursion to get a toy.... The swift but short runs dominate and develop the inner organs."

What appeals to so many runners about fartlek training is that it takes the pressure off of doing more structured, timed intervals on the track. In addition, it's a good alternative to a track workout in bad weather. Whereas you might cancel a track workout on a rainy, windy day when the desired times would be impossible to achieve, there is no reason to skip a fartlek workout. In fact, in this case, it's also good practice for racing under tough conditions.

While fartlek is an effective method of quality training, at the same time it also seems a natural extension of the recreational aspect of running, as the name "speed play" indicates.

Interval Training

While most elite runners begin their careers on the track, the majority of average runners have been introduced to the sport via the roads and road racing. A good number of these runners find the track foreign and intimidating. The track can be a rewarding new challenge and an important tool in training. What's more, for a true test of ability, nothing surpasses running the 400-meter oval.

According to Cliff Temple, whose ideas about interval training are given here, many runners have an aversion to running on the track. However, by using that simple 400-meter oval, you can improve your distance-running performances more effectively than with yet another road run. In addition, many still have the impression tracks are for the elite. That is simply not so.

How does track running help a runner? On a track, you most likely will run a series of relatively short repetitions over distances from 400 to 1000 meters. Due to the brevity of each effort compared to your normal 45 minutes of steady running on the road, each run can be at a considerably faster pace than you are used to.

On a steady road run, your pulse rate might remain around 120–140 beats per minute most of the way. But at the end of a single hard 600- or 1000-meter run you could push your pulse up to 180 or more. As your body adapts to the higher demands, it becomes still more physiologically efficient. And don't forget, these shorter intervals can be done on the road if a track is unavailable, and that same purpose will still be served.

At first, it is best to be conservative. You'll know you have been if you finish the session feeling you could have done a little more. If necessary, adjust the sample workouts outlined in the book to achieve that feeling. As you gain conditioning, you can increase, and eventually move ahead to the next level of program.

Cliff Temple's Golden Rules of the Track

1. Always run in a counterclockwise direction.
2. Never warm up on the inside two lanes. Use an outer lane or the grass infield.
3. If you have to cross the grass infield, make sure no one is throwing a javelin, discus, or hammer.
4. If, during a hard training run, someone is walking, standing, or running more slowly on the inside lane ahead of you, shout "Track!" which is the standard warning signal.

Interval Training Tips

1. Don't use the same interval session every time; allow yourself three or four variations of a session to check progress. (The programs and philosophies in this book allow for such variations.)
2. You don't necessarily need to use a track, but do employ permanent and easily identifiable landmarks.
3. Be strict with yourself in timing your recovery period.
4. If possible, get someone to time your runs and the recoveries.
5. Make sure you warm up properly before the beginning of each session.
6. Interval training has countless variations, which can be adjusted as you become fitter; you can increase the number of runs, amend the distance run, or reduce the amount of interval recovery.
7. Don't expect every single session to show an improvement in times. The fitter you get, the more difficult that becomes.
8. Make allowances for diverse weather conditions, e.g., run with the wind rather than against it where possible, but note the conditions in your training diary.

One caveat: If you're new to the track, take the opportunity to get used to running on turns. This can be quite stressful, particularly on the inside leg, which incurs a torque not experienced when running in a straight line. This is even more the case on indoor tracks, which are usually smaller and have more and tighter turns than outdoor tracks. It's no wonder that indoor tracks are the source of high injury risk. You might want to take a few weeks to adapt by running an increasing number of easy laps on the track before beginning hard efforts.

Balance is another way to avoid potential injury. You can lessen stress by alternating directions. Cliff Temple's golden rules point out that track etiquette and safety require running in the counterclockwise direction. However, if the track isn't crowded, or you're willing to run your workout in outside lanes, it's possible to change directions. Speaking at a clinic in Philadelphia in 1982, Olympic 1500-meter bronze medalist and New York City Marathon champion Rod Dixon related that he would run 20 quarters on the track during his building phase: alternating five in the clockwise direction, five in the counterclockwise direction.

This caveat applies even if you're not taking up speedwork. Many people run recreationally on the track or are tempted to find an indoor facility in inclement weather. Often personnel at these tracks will switch the running direction periodically throughout the day. If staff at your facility does not, request it, explaining why.

Hill Training

Like the Fleming program outlined in Chapter 3, Cliff Temple advocates the use of hill training. He recommends a one- to two-mile warmup jog, and stretching exercises for gluteal (buttocks) muscles, quadriceps, hamstrings, calves, and Achilles tendons. Afterward, a one- to two-mile jog is recommended for a cooldown. But he cautions against hill work if you have existing calf or Achilles injuries.

According to Temple, the muscle groups used to tackle the resistance provided by a hill are virtually the same as those used for sprinting, although their range of movement is different, so by running a series of uphill efforts it is possible to simultaneously improve strength and, indirectly, speed. Hill running should give the well-conditioned runner a good return for the time and effort invested in it.

To avoid running steep downhills and to allow for sufficient recovery from an uphill leg, Temple advocates running hills in a "D" shape. Athletes run hard 80 to 100 meters up the straight line of the D, then gently jog around the curved part in a gradual descent to the start of the next circuit. If the course is grass and free of hazards like stones and glass, Temple encourages athletes to run in bare feet to allow the fullest range of natural leg movement. If this type of "D" course is impractical, as a variation to running up a hill and jogging straight back down, two short, parallel roads that are connected at top and bottom can be run up and down in a square-shaped course.

While sprinting short hills is designed to develop dynamic, blazing speed, there are other methods and purposes for running hills. Training should reflect the nature of its use. Thus, you need not always run hill workouts that require you to charge up at full speed. Temple points out that for the distance runner, the hill must be looked on as something to be negotiated effectively and economically with as little disruption to the running rhythm as possible. In this case, don't view a hill as something that has to be climbed as quickly and vigorously as possible.

A good hill session for the distance runner includes a number of hills or a short loop with hills that can be run a number of times. As you approach each hill, concentrate on keeping the upper body relaxed and letting the legs do as much of the work as possible. As you reach the top of each hill, concentrate on running over the top until the gradient eases. Then pick up natural rhythm again. It is almost like trying to pretend the hill isn't there, Temple points out.

The Buddy System

What appeals to so many people about running is that you can do it alone, at any pace you like, and let your mind wander or problem-solve. There's no need to make and keep appointments, to chat when you don't feel like it, or to run slower or faster than you want to in order to accommodate someone else's pace. So it's easy to see why runners get hooked on the solitude.

On the other hand, there's nothing like the "support system" of a training buddy or group. This is true for a myriad of reasons, from safety and companionship to getting the encouragement to go the distance or get through a tough workout.

Then there's the balance that comes from socializing with a group. Says Francie Larrieu Smith, "I'm pretty intense during interval sessions, but I like the socializing with a group when we step off the track."

The support of a running partner or group is always useful, especially for speedwork. However, it isn't always easy to find a partner who trains at the same pace or is on the same rhythm on a given day. In addition, even among equally matched runners, some excel over shorter distance intervals, some over longer stretches.

So try this buddy system: Use each other for incentive by giving one runner a head start or varying the distance for each runner. For example, when planning to do 400-meter intervals, one runner could take a 200-meter head start; or, setting off together, one runner could finish with 200 meters, while the other continues on for 400 meters (or, in the case of fartlek, three light poles and six light poles). Both runners benefit from being pushed and from encouraging each other.

Gordon Bloch on Training Partners

When I first started running, what kept me going was a commitment to meet someone. I was a high school girl trying to stay in shape in the off-season from team sports. I met my running partner every day for months at exactly 6:30 a.m. We didn't miss a day, except for illness. If one of us overslept, the other would throw rocks at the bedroom window to wake up the tardy partner. After a few months of this, I was hooked on the running routine for good.

I now have two regular training partners. I think running partners or groups are so important. The most important reason is safety. Particularly as a woman, you are limited in what you can and should do alone. Running by yourself—even during the day—is just asking for trouble. In addition to the safety factor, we run together for companionship, and to remind each other how important a part of our lives this activity is.

Tom Fleming on Running with a Group

Group running encourages consistency. Throughout my entire career I've run with partners and groups. Currently, our group trains together several times a week. It's a weekend ritual.

Most people like to run with others. Just the act of meeting makes the workout more enjoyable. When it comes to the hard work, I think people do it better when they're together. They drive off each other's energy. Then they share a light moment. Even if the individual workouts are different, it's worth it just to start and finish together. Obviously the advantages are more psychological than physical, but nonetheless, it gets the job done.

Bob Glover on Running with a Group

Sometimes the social aspect of running is an important aspect of the workout. From coaching the NYRRC running classes and coaching a team, I've seen how much it helps to be in a class, or to be on a team. Particularly in the winter months, it's easy to quit or taper off. But when runners come out to the Tuesday night class, even if they're not full of energy, they usually do better than they thought they would. Even if a person swears he or she is totally unmotivated to run on a particular occasion, I say just come out and do stretching exercises with the class.

Tom Fleming's Training Program for 5K to the Marathon

Although running— and sports training in general—has made enormous advances since the early days of the running boom, the basic principles of training have not changed. "From the mile to the marathon, sound training principles are the same," says Tom Fleming.

The focus of Fleming's program is a strong mileage base. Fleming feels that although some may be able to run long-distance events on relatively low mileage, it is not advisable. According to Fleming, "What seems to be getting a lot of attention is how good you can be by doing the least amount of work. What I say is, let's look at how much better you can be by doing the proper amount of work."

To experience steady improvement in your running, and to enjoy a long, healthy running career, Fleming believes you have to put in a relatively substantial amount of mileage at some point in your training cycle. This is especially true with running a race, like a marathon or even a 10k. "If you are short on time or motivation, it is wiser to adjust your goals rather than to try to do more or longer racing with less training," he says.

In the late 1960s there were two important trends in distance running that gained wide popularity. One was called LSD (long, slow distance), the American equivalent of a system embraced most notably by New Zealand coach Arthur Lydiard. A joke began to circulate that if you ran long enough and slow enough, you'd become long and slow.

23

That's why the second trend was important, to balance the first. It was called interval training.

Although Fleming points out that he doesn't completely agree with everything in the Arthur Lydiard system, he feels the basis of that philosophy is absolutely sound. As a beginner, as well as at the beginning of a training cycle, you need to develop endurance and strength. There's only one way to do that, and Lydiard gave the same prescription to everyone, from half milers to marathoners—two or more months of base building, consisting of long, slow distance running.

If you're an average runner who, for example, does one marathon a year, Fleming believes you will get the best results from a solid, progressive training program characterized by relatively high mileage training. He contends you can then be successful, and have a healthy career, because you've built a strong base rather than taking risks by cutting corners with lower mileage. The most commonly asked question by the beginners who come into Fleming's running-shoe store is, "How do I get faster?" He says he always tells them, "Get stronger and you'll get faster." To do that, you've got to build a good mileage base.

If you're a serious runner, you may be asking, "What about speedwork?" Of course you need the fast running, acknowledges Fleming, "but you can't build a house without a foundation."

Fleming is even a believer in what is called "overdistance training." He defines it as spending a week or two at some point running relative maximal mileage—i.e., the most you can comfortably tolerate. This is not mandatory in his training program, but it is an option for the serious runner.

For example, for a 30-mile-a-week runner, this might mean slowly building (no more than 10 percent per week) to a couple of 50-mile weeks. This is not meant to be a permanent rise, just a brief period of heavier training. In building your base mileage, you build strength and conditioning. In testing your upper limits with overdistance training, you can gain both conditioning and confidence.

"World-class athletes are always trying to go right to the limit. That's what it takes to make it to the top," Fleming reflects. At some point in their training, distance runners may try overdistance training. Runners like Bill Rodgers have experimented with running as much as 50 percent more than their usual mileage for one to two weeks. "Eventually they go right to a ceiling, and bump into it, but they learn not to go over it," comments Fleming. One of the benefits of heavy training is that you quickly learn to read your own body.

In addition to the training benefits, many runners try overdistance training for the mental edge—to gain the confidence which comes from their ability to reach their limit. And this applies to everyone, not just the elite.

The Program

Tom Fleming's program is based on some of the most successful methods of distance running. In designing the system, Fleming incorporates elements popularized by running pioneers Arthur Lydiard and Bill Bowerman with other well-established training elements to create a multiphase program. The phases are not meant to be done simultaneously; while some can be done together, others absolutely should not (e.g., hill work and fartlek). Some need not be done at all. For example, a beginner could experience significant improvement simply by doing Phases One and Two. Imperative, however, is balance. Balancing mileage, intensity, and rest is essential to making this—and any training program—successful.

Bowerman's Hard/Easy Method

Hard/easy is generally recommended as the premise of all training programs. It simply means that for every hard effort, a sufficient rest period is required to recover and assimilate the benefits of training. This easy period varies in length, depending on the individual as well as the intensity of the effort. A runner might follow a hard effort one day with an easy run or a day off the next, or easy running for two or more days following.

Phase One: Lydiard's Endurance Mileage

This distance phase, which builds endurance, ultimately helps a runner to become more efficient—therefore faster—by developing aerobic capacity. As a result of a recent emphasis on shorter, faster mileage, Fleming feels this essential base training has been compromised. "Although this phase is generally accepted as being essential, very few do it thoroughly," he says.

Studies have shown that athletes need to slow down their distance runs (a claim also substantiated in Chapter 4, Heart Rate Monitor

Training). Therefore, Fleming emphasizes that the base phase should not consist of anaerobic running; Phase One should be run at conversation pace, generally for six to eight weeks.

Phase Two: Tempo Runs

A tempo run is done at a strong pace, approximately 20 seconds per mile slower than 10k race pace. This pace is held for about 15 to 25 minutes in the middle of a longer distance run (with the segments before and after used as warmup and cooldown periods). This type of running is done in the first third of the season, as a way of adapting to faster interval running.

Phase Three: Hill Repeats

Hill repeats should be done on a sufficient grade but not on a steep hill, a maximum of one-quarter mile in length from base to top. One- to one-and-a-half minutes per repeat is an adequate amount of stress. These efforts should be strong, but not done at full speed. After running uphill, a slow jog down minimizes jarring to the quadriceps and knee joints. In this phase, Fleming's athletes average eight hill repeats, one time per week, for six weeks. The hill phase begins at the end of the base distance phase. Fleming has found that initially runners are able do four repeats. They can generally add two more repeats per session.

Phase Four: Fartlek

Fartlek is basically interval training, but with less structure. While many runners are familiar with the term fartlek, some do it incorrectly. Fleming's top athletes run a total distance of nine miles, five at most of fartlek effort. However, computing with either time or distance is possible. As an example of time, the workout Fleming's athletes do consists of a total running time of one hour, with three minutes hard, two minutes easy for 30 minutes in the middle of the run. This is done one time a week for four to six weeks. This type of run is done in cycles throughout the year, except during the endurance phase, when it is not done at all.

Phase Five: Interval Training

Interval training usually starts at the beginning of the competitive season. Prescriptions here for distance runners are to do 800- to 3000-

meter repeats, once each week for six to eight weeks, depending on the length of the competitive season. The recovery phase for Fleming's athletes is based on time, but it is also common to use distance for recovery, e.g., jogging a 400-meter recovery lap around the track. Although intervals are customarily done on a track, there is no need to be restricted to one. Fleming's team also does intervals on measured distances in a park.

An advanced runner might do four times 800 meters at race pace, for example. However, it is recommended that a beginner might want to do the intervals slower than race pace. If a runner tolerates a workout well, Fleming shortens the rest period rather than speeding up the interval. "Psychologically, it seems to be easier on the athlete," he says.

In the beginning of the season runners concentrate on longer intervals, and during the actual racing phase, the intervals become shorter and faster. This aids "sharpness" by developing the speed and efficiency of leg turnover..

Training Tips

1. Training should be progressive and consistent.
2. All training programs should be individualized. Each runner can learn to identify a perfect blend of ingredients to develop his or her specific strengths. This is done through coaching and personal experience.
3. Each type of training has its own specific effect.
4. Each program should be tailored to the event for which the runner is training.
5. Carefully planned, realistic, short- and long-range goals guarantee successful results.
6. With an experienced eye, a coach or training partner who knows the athlete's individual running style and mechanics can help that person determine when to cut back, or when to push on. If running form begins to fall apart, it is often a sign the workout is falling apart as well.
7. Build on strengths; don't waste time trying to improve weaknesses. If a runner has great endurance but limited speed, Fleming believes it is more productive to develop the ability to maintain

a high level of aerobic running than to spend time and effort trying to develop a kick or sprint ability.

Tom Fleming's Training Pyramid

RACING

Sharpening
Phase
Shorter/Faster Intervals

Strength/Speed Phase
Tempo Runs, Hill Repeats, Fartlek, Longer Intervals

Endurance Phase
Distance Runs (easy runs, also done as cross-country runs, circuit runs)

Percentage of Yearly Training
Endurance Phase   35%
Strengths/Speed Phase   55%
Sharpening Phase/Racing   10%
Easy run—conversation pace.
Tempo run—hard, but in control.

Hills—should be approximately 200–400 meters long, not extremely steep.

Intervals—are given in minutes, so you may use a watch and do them on a training loop, or go to a track and convert them into specific distances.

Pickups—150–200 meters in length (or pick objects for distance, such as five light posts). The pace is quick, but not an all-out sprint. They are inserted during a distance run at will, and should not be so taxing as to require stopping for recovery. Shorter pickups of 50–100 meters should be done before hard workouts and races.

A First Time Marathoner's Story

In the spring of 1991, 31-year-old Angel Jimenez walked into Tom Fleming's running store. Jimenez was clearly an athlete of some kind, and turned out to be an Olympic-style Tae Kwon Do champion who ran about 25 miles a week for fitness. He told Fleming he wanted to run a race, and added, "I'm entering the New York City Marathon." The New York City Marathon was in November, less than six months away.

Fleming felt it was too soon for him to run the marathon. He tried to discourage him, but to no avail. Jimenez announced he wanted to start to do speedwork to prepare for racing. Fleming managed to quash that idea. He cautioned Jimenez against doing any interval running for at least four months, and put him on the high-mileage buildup outlined below. Fleming stressed that for a novice like Jimenez the object of the marathon is to complete it, not race it.

After building his base of training, Jimenez was invited by Fleming to run with his team once a week during their medium efforts. His ability to keep up with top-class athletes became his "speedwork" (a tempo run) and served to bolster his confidence. By September, Jimenez had participated in 5k and 10k races to feel the difference between racing and training.

Little did Fleming anticipate the emergence of Jimenez's talent. He responded very well to training. He lost 18 pounds from his already muscular body. He was well prepared for the marathon, and ran a smart race, going out slowly. He experienced the joy of passing people throughout the second half of the race, which he finished in 2:41:50.

To prevent the almost universal mistake of taking up training too quickly after the excitement of running a successful marathon, Fleming emphasized several weeks of easy running before Jimenez rebuilt his mileage base for the next goal.

Angel Jimenez's Training Chart

Week of	Days Running per Week	Total Miles (with races)
7/1/91	7	58 (5-mile race)
7/8	6	50
7/15	7	62
7/22	7	60
7/29	6	56
8/5	7	61 (5k race)
8/12	6	57
8/19	7	68
8/26	7	68
9/2	7	67 (5-mile race)
9/9	7	65
9/16	7 (first 20-miler)	70
9/23	7	70 (10k race)
9/30	6 (second 20-miler)	67
10/7	7 (third 20-miler)	78
10/14	7	54 (10k race)
10/21	7	55
10/28	7	31 + 26.2 mile NYC Marathon in 2:41:50

Training Charts

Advanced Beginner

The 26-week advanced beginner level training program is designed for the 50- to 55-minute 10k runner. At this level you've probably already run several races. This program will help you to gear your training toward improving your race times.

Fleming uses a 26-week time frame because, as he emphasizes, there are no shortcuts. If you want to experience steady improvement, you have to have both the patience and determination to stick to a plan. It is often the case that people are tempted to change suddenly because of what a friend is doing or because of a program they read about in a running publication.

Patience is particularly important as you may need to hold yourself back. Stick to the schedule, even if at times you feel so good you'd like to skip a phase or part of the program.

The first 12 weeks of all the programs is strictly devoted to building the base. On the advanced beginner level, base building continues right through to the 17th week. It is Fleming's view that runners at this level can improve tremendously simply by being consistent. No fancy workouts are needed in this stage.

During the 17th week, short pickups during the normal distance run are included once a week to help give you a sense of the faster pace you will encounter in a race. The pickups can be done for several light posts, with plenty of jogging and resumption of normal training pace in between each.

Racing every three to four weeks is probably plenty at this level, and mixing up the distances, i.e., 10k, 5k, five miles, four miles, etc., will help give you a variety of opportunities to test your new endurance.

Intermediate

The intermediate-level runner is someone in the 44- to 50-minute range for 10k. The intermediate level training program is basically the same as the beginner's program but the mileage is slightly higher. During the initial 12-week base building, training mileage slowly increases from 25 miles per week to 35 miles per week. Daily training amounts can be varied according to your personal habits and preferences. Fleming tends to make the Sunday run the long one for the week.

In the 13th week, moderate interval training begins. These intervals can be done on the track or on the roads or trails, wherever you normally do your workouts. The intervals should be done at approximately your current 10k race pace. It is not so important to determine exactly how fast you are going, as long as you've increased your pace substantially, but without straining in the effort. Recovery between intervals should consist of very easy jogging for at least the same amount of time as the hard effort. Perhaps a little more recovery will be needed in the beginning, until you become accustomed to such efforts. (Note: You should expect to feel a little sore or sluggish in the legs in the early going. Don't worry, this is the body's natural adaptation process to the increased training effort.)

26-Week Advanced Beginner Level 10K Training Program

for the 50 – 55-minute 10K runner

Wk	Monday	Tuesday	Wednesday	Thursday
1	2 miles easy	2 miles easy	3 miles easy	2 miles easy
2	2 miles easy	2 miles easy	3 miles easy	2 miles easy
3	2 miles easy	2 miles easy	4 miles easy	2 miles easy
4	2 miles easy	2 miles easy	4 miles easy	2 miles easy
5	2 miles easy	3 miles easy	4 miles easy	3 miles easy
6	2 miles easy	3 miles easy	4 miles easy	3 miles easy
7	2 miles easy	3 miles easy	4 miles easy	3 miles easy
8	2 miles easy	3 miles easy	4 miles easy	3 miles easy
9	3 miles easy	3 miles easy	4 miles easy	4 miles easy
10	3 miles easy	3 miles easy	4 miles easy	4 miles easy
11	4 miles easy	4 miles easy	4 miles easy	4 miles easy
12	4 miles easy	4 miles easy	4 miles easy	4 miles easy
13	4 miles easy	4 miles easy	4 miles easy	4 miles easy
14	4 miles easy	4 miles easy	4 miles easy	4 miles easy
15	4 miles easy	4 miles easy	4 miles easy	4 miles easy
16	4 miles easy	4 miles easy	4 miles easy	4 miles easy
17	4 miles easy	4 miles easy	4 miles w/4 pickups	4 miles easy
18	4 miles easy	4 miles easy	4 miles w/4 pickups	4 miles easy
19	4 miles easy	4 miles easy	4 miles w/5 pickups	4 miles easy
20	4 miles easy	4 miles easy	4 miles w/5 pickups	4 miles easy
21	4 miles easy	4 miles easy	4 miles w/6 pickups	4 miles easy
22	4 miles easy	4 miles easy	4 miles w/6 pickups	4 miles easy
23	4 miles easy	4 miles easy	4 miles w/6 pickups	4 miles easy
24	4 miles easy	4 miles easy	4 miles w/6 pickups	4 miles easy
25	4 miles easy	4 miles easy	4 miles w/6 pickups	4 miles easy
26	4 miles easy	4 miles easy	4 miles w/6 pickups	4 miles easy

Wk	Friday	Saturday	Sunday	Total for Week
1	Rest day	2 miles easy	4 miles easy	**15 miles**
2	Rest day	2 miles easy	4 miles easy	**15 miles**
3	Rest day	2 miles easy	5 miles easy	**17 miles**
4	Rest day	2 miles easy	5 miles easy	**17 miles**
5	Rest day	2 miles easy	5 miles easy	**19 miles**
6	Rest day	2 miles easy	5 miles easy	**19 miles**
7	Rest day	3 miles easy	6 miles easy	**21 miles**
8	3 miles easy	Rest day	**Race**	**21 miles**
9	Rest day	3 miles easy	6 miles easy	**23 miles**
10	Rest day	3 miles easy	6 miles easy	**23 miles**
11	Rest day	3 miles easy	6 miles easy	**25 miles**
12	3 miles easy	Rest day	**Race**	**25 miles**
13	Rest day	3 miles easy	6 miles easy	**25 miles**
14	Rest day	3 miles easy	6 miles easy	**25 miles**
15	Rest day	3 miles easy	6 miles easy	**25 miles**
16	2 miles easy	Rest day	**Race**	**25 miles**
17	Rest day	3 miles easy	6 miles easy	**25 miles**
18	Rest day	3 miles easy	6 miles easy	**25 miles**
19	Rest day	3 miles easy	6 miles easy	**25 miles**
20	2 miles easy	Rest day	**Race**	**25 miles**
21	Rest day	3 miles easy	6 miles easy	**25 miles**
22	Rest day	3 miles easy	6 miles easy	**25 miles**
23	Rest day	3 miles easy	6 miles easy	**25 miles**
24	2 miles easy	Rest day	**Race**	**25 miles**
25	Rest day	3 miles easy	6 miles easy	**25 miles**
26	2 miles easy	Rest day	**PEAK RACE**	**25 miles**

26-Week Intermediate Level 10K Training Program
for the 44 – 50-minute 10K runner

Wk	Monday	Tuesday	Wednesday	Thursday
Distance/Base Building Phase				
1	3 miles easy	4 miles easy	3 miles easy	4 miles easy
2	3 miles easy	4 miles easy	3 miles easy	4 miles easy
3	3 miles easy	4 miles easy	4 miles easy	4 miles easy
4	3 miles easy	4 miles easy	4 miles easy	4 miles easy
5	3 miles easy	5 miles easy	4 miles easy	4 miles easy
6	3 miles easy	5 miles easy	4 miles easy	5 miles easy
7	3 miles easy	5 miles easy	4 miles easy	5 miles easy
8	3 miles easy	5 miles easy	4 miles easy	5 miles easy
9	3 miles easy	4 miles easy	5 miles easy	4 miles easy
10	3 miles easy	5 miles easy	4 miles easy	5 miles easy
11	4 miles easy	5 miles easy	4 miles easy	5 miles easy
12	4 miles easy	5 miles easy	4 miles easy	5 miles easy
Intervals/Speed Introduction Phase				
13	3 miles easy	4 miles easy	5 miles, 6 x 1 min. @ 10K pace	4 miles easy
14	4 miles easy	4 miles easy	6 miles, 6 x 1 min. @ 10K pace	4 miles easy
15	4 miles easy	4 miles steady	6 miles, 4 x 1:30 mins. @ 10K pace	4 miles easy
16	4 miles easy	4 miles easy	6 miles, 4 x 1:30 mins. @ 10K pace	4 miles easy
17	4 miles easy	4 miles easy	6 miles, 3 x 2 mins. @ 10K pace	4 miles easy
18	4 miles easy	4 miles easy	6 miles, 3 x 2 mins. @ 10K pace	4 miles easy
19	4 miles easy	4 miles easy	6 miles, 2 x 3 mins. @ 10K pace	4 miles easy
20	4 miles easy	4 miles easy	6 miles, 2 x 3 mins. @ 10K pace	4 miles easy
21	4 miles easy	4 miles easy	6 miles, 3 x 2 mins. @ 10K pace	4 miles easy
22	4 miles easy	4 miles easy	6 miles, 4 x 1:30 mins. @ 10K pace	4 miles easy
23	4 miles easy	4 miles easy	6 miles, 6 x 1 min. @ 10K pace	4 miles easy
24	4 miles easy	4 miles easy	6 miles, 2 x 3 mins. @ 10K pace	4 miles easy
25	4 miles easy	4 miles easy	6 miles, 3 x 2 mins. @ 10K pace	4 miles easy
26	4 miles easy	4 miles easy	5 miles, 4 x 1 mins. @ 10K pace	4 miles easy

Wk	Friday	Saturday	Sunday	Total for Week
				Distance/Base Building Phase
1	3 miles easy	3 miles easy	5 miles easy	**25 miles**
2	3 miles easy	3 miles easy	6 miles easy	**26 miles**
3	3 miles easy	3 miles easy	6 miles easy	**27 miles**
4	4 miles easy	3 miles easy	6 miles easy	**28 miles**
5	4 miles easy	3 miles easy	6 miles easy	**29 miles**
6	4 miles easy	3 miles easy	6 miles easy	**30 miles**
7	4 miles easy	3 miles easy	7 miles easy	**31 miles**
8	4 miles easy	2 miles easy	**Race**	**30 miles**
9	5 miles easy	4 miles easy	7 miles easy	**32 miles**
10	5 miles easy	3 miles easy	8 miles easy	**33 miles**
11	5 miles easy	3 miles easy	8 miles easy	**34 miles**
12	4 miles easy	2 miles easy	**Race**	**32 miles**
				Intervals/Speed Introduction Phase
13	5 miles easy	4 miles easy	8 miles easy	**33 miles**
14	5 miles easy	4 miles easy	8 miles easy	**35 miles**
15	4 miles easy	3 miles easy	**Race**	**33 miles**
16	5 miles easy	4 miles easy	8 miles easy	**35 miles**
17	5 miles easy	4 miles easy	8 miles easy	**35 miles**
18	4 miles easy	3 miles easy	**Race**	**33 miles**
19	5 miles easy	4 miles easy	8 miles easy	**35 miles**
20	4 miles easy	3 miles easy	**Race**	**33 miles**
21	5 miles easy	4 miles easy	8 miles easy	**35 miles**
22	4 miles easy	3 miles easy	**Race**	**33 miles**
23	5 miles easy	4 miles easy	8 miles easy	**35 miles**
24	4 miles easy	3 miles easy	**Race**	**33 miles**
25	5 miles easy	4 miles easy	8 miles easy	**35 miles**
26	3 miles easy	2 miles easy	**PEAK RACE**	**30 miles**

26-Week Advanced Level 10K Training Program
for the 38 – 44-minute 10K runner

Wk	Monday	Tuesday	Wednesday	Thursday
Distance/Base Building Phase				
1	4 miles easy	6 miles easy	4 miles easy	6 miles easy
2	4 miles easy	7 miles easy	4 miles easy	7 miles easy
3	5 miles easy	7 miles easy	5 miles easy	7 miles easy
4	5 miles easy	8 miles easy	5 miles easy	8 miles easy
5	6 miles easy	8 miles easy	6 miles easy	8 miles easy
6	6 miles easy	8 miles easy	6 miles easy	8 miles easy
7	6 miles easy	8 miles easy	6 miles easy	8 miles w/2 mi. tempo run
8	6 miles easy	8 miles easy	6 miles easy	8 miles w/2 mi. tempo run
Hill Work Phase				
9	7 miles easy	6 miles easy	7 miles, 4 x uphill	7 miles easy
10	7 miles easy	6 miles easy	7 miles, 5 x uphill	7 miles easy
11	7 miles easy	6 miles easy	7 miles, 6 x uphill	7 miles easy
12	7 miles easy	6 miles easy	7 miles, 6 x uphill	7 miles easy
Long Interval/Strength Phase				
13	7 miles easy	6 miles steady	7 miles, 3 x 4 mins. @ 10K race pace	7 miles easy
14	7 miles easy	6 miles steady	7 miles, 4 x 3 mins. @ 10K race pace	7 miles easy
15	7 miles easy	6 miles steady	7 miles, 6 x 2 mins. @ 10K race pace	7 miles easy
16	7 miles easy	6 miles steady	7 miles, 8 x 1:30 mins. @ 10K race pace	7 miles easy
17	7 miles easy	6 miles easy	7 miles, 3 x 4 mins. @ 10K race pace	7 miles easy
18	7 miles easy	6 miles easy	7 miles, 4 x 3 mins. @ 10K race pace	7 miles easy
19	7 miles easy	6 miles easy	7 miles, 6 x 2 mins. @ 10K race pace	7 miles easy
20	7 miles easy	6 miles easy	7 miles, 8 x 1:30 mins. @ 10K race pace	6 miles easy
Faster Interval/Peaking Phase				
21	5 miles easy	5 miles easy	7 miles, 4 x 2 mins. @ 5K race pace	5 miles easy
22	5 miles easy	5 miles easy	7 miles, 6 x 1:30 mins. @ 5K race pace	5 miles easy
23	5 miles easy	5 miles easy	7 miles, 8 x 1 min. @ 5K race pace	5 miles easy
24	5 miles easy	5 miles easy	7 miles, 4 x 2 mins. @ 5K race pace	5 miles easy
25	5 miles easy	5 miles easy	7 miles, 6 x 1:30 mins. @ 5K race pace	5 miles easy
26	5 miles easy	5 miles easy	7 miles, 8 x 1 min. @ 5K race pace	5 miles easy

Wk	Friday	Saturday	Sunday	Total for Week
			Distance/Base Building Phase	
1	4 miles easy	4 miles easy	8 miles easy	**36 miles**
2	4 miles easy	4 miles easy	9 miles easy	**39 miles**
3	5 miles easy	4 miles easy	9 miles easy	**42 miles**
4	5 miles easy	4 miles easy	10 miles easy	**45 miles**
5	6 miles easy	4 miles easy	10 miles easy	**48 miles**
6	6 miles easy	6 miles easy	10 miles easy	**50 miles**
7	6 miles easy	6 miles easy	10 miles easy	**50 miles**
8	6 miles easy	6 miles easy	10 miles easy	**50 miles**
			Hill Work Phase	
9	7 miles easy	6 miles easy	Race	**50 miles**
10	7 miles easy	6 miles easy	10 miles easy	**50 miles**
11	7 miles easy	6 miles easy	10 miles easy	**50 miles**
12	7 miles easy	6 miles easy	Race	**50 miles**
			Long Interval/Strength Phase	
13	7 miles easy	6 miles easy	10 miles easy	**50 miles**
14	7 miles easy	6 miles easy	10 miles easy	**50 miles**
15	6 miles easy	4 miles easy	Race	**47 miles**
16	7 miles easy	6 miles easy	10 miles easy	**50 miles**
17	7 miles, 4 short pickups enroute	6 miles easy	10 miles easy	**50 miles**
18	6 miles easy	4 miles easy	Race	**47 miles**
19	7 miles, 5 short pickups enroute	6 miles easy	10 miles easy	**50 miles**
20	6 miles easy	3 miles easy	Race	**45 miles**
			Faster Interval/Peaking Phase	
21	7 miles, 6 short pickups enroute	5 miles easy	10 miles easy	**44 miles**
22	4 miles easy	3 miles easy	Race	**39 miles**
23	7 miles, 7 short pickups enroute	5 miles easy	10 miles easy	**44 miles**
24	4 miles easy	3 miles easy	Race	**39 miles**
25	7 miles, 8 short pickups enroute	5 miles easy	10 miles easy	**44 miles**
26	4 miles easy	3 miles easy	**PEAK RACE**	**39 miles**

26-Week Competitive Level 10K Training Program
for the 34 – 38-minute 10K runner

Wk	Monday	Tuesday	Wednesday	Thursday
Distance/Base Building Phase				
1	6 miles easy	6 miles easy	6 miles easy	6 miles easy
2	6 miles easy	7 miles easy	6 miles easy	7 miles easy
3	6 miles easy	7 miles easy	7 miles easy	7 miles easy
4	6 miles easy	7 miles easy	7 miles easy	7 miles w/tempo run
5	7 miles easy	7 miles easy	7 miles easy	7 miles w/tempo run
6	7 miles easy	8 miles easy	7 miles easy	8 miles w/tempo run
7	7 miles easy	8 miles easy	7 miles easy	8 miles w/tempo run
8	7 miles easy	8 miles easy	8 miles easy	8 miles w/tempo run
Hill Work Phase				
9	7 miles easy	8 miles easy	8 miles, 6 x uphill	8 miles easy
10	7 miles easy	8 miles easy	8 miles, 8 x uphill	8 miles easy
11	7 miles easy	8 miles easy	8 miles, 10 x uphill	8 miles easy
12	7 miles easy	8 miles easy	8 miles, 10 x uphill	8 miles easy
Long Interval/Strength Phase				
13	7 miles easy	8 miles easy	9 miles, 3 x 5 mins. @ 10K race pace	6 miles easy
14	7 miles easy	8 miles easy	9 miles, 5 x 3 mins. @ 10K race pace	6 miles easy
15	7 miles easy	8 miles easy	9 miles, 6 x 2:30 mins. @ 10K race pace	6 miles easy
16	7 miles easy	8 miles easy	9 miles, 10 x 1:30 mins. @ 10K race pace	6 miles easy
17	7 miles easy	8 miles easy	9 miles, 3 x 5 mins. @ 10K race pace	6 miles easy
18	7 miles easy	8 miles easy	9 miles, 5 x 3 mins. @ 10K race pace	6 miles easy
19	7 miles easy	8 miles easy	9 miles, 6 x 2:30 mins. @ 10K race pace	6 miles easy
20	7 miles easy	8 miles easy	9 miles, 10 x 1:30 mins. @ 10K race pace	6 miles easy
Faster Interval/Peaking Phase				
21	7 miles easy	8 miles easy	9 miles, 6 x 2 mins. @ 5K race pace	6 miles easy
22	7 miles easy	8 miles easy	9 miles, 8 x 1:30 mins. @ 5K race pace	6 miles easy
23	7 miles easy	6 miles easy	9 miles, 12 x 1 min. @ 5K race pace	6 miles easy
24	7 miles easy	8 miles easy	9 miles, 6 x 2 mins. @ 5K race pace	6 miles easy
25	7 miles easy	8 miles easy	8 miles, 8 x 1:30 mins. @ 5K race pace	6 miles easy
26	6 miles easy	6 miles easy	8 miles, 12 x 1 min. @ 5K race pace	6 miles easy

Wk	Friday	Saturday	Sunday	Total for Week
				Distance/Base Building Phase
1	6 miles easy	5 miles easy	10 miles easy	**45 miles**
2	6 miles easy	6 miles easy	10 miles easy	**48 miles**
3	7 miles easy	6 miles easy	10 miles easy	**50 miles**
4	7 miles easy	6 miles easy	12 miles easy	**52 miles**
5	7 miles easy	7 miles easy	12 miles easy	**54 miles**
6	7 miles easy	7 miles easy	12 miles easy	**56 miles**
7	7 miles easy	7 miles easy	14 miles easy	**58 miles**
8	8 miles easy	7 miles easy	14 miles easy	**60 miles**
				Hill Work Phase
9	8 miles easy	5 miles easy	**Race**	**54 miles**
10	8 miles easy	7 miles easy	14 miles easy	**60 miles**
11	8 miles easy	7 miles easy	14 miles easy	**60 miles**
12	8 miles easy	5 miles easy	**Race**	**54 miles**
				Long Interval/Strength Phase
13	9 miles easy	7 miles easy	14 miles easy	**60 miles**
14	9 miles easy	7 miles easy	14 miles easy	**60 miles**
15	7 miles easy	5 miles easy	**Race**	**52 miles**
16	9 miles easy	7 miles easy	14 miles easy	**60 miles**
17	9 miles, 6 to 8 short pickups enroute	7 miles easy	14 miles easy	**60 miles**
18	7 miles easy	5 miles easy	**Race**	**52 miles**
19	9 miles, 6 to 8 short pickups enroute	7 miles easy	14 miles easy	**60 miles**
20	7 miles easy	5 miles easy	**Race**	**52 miles**
				Faster Interval/Peaking Phase
21	9 miles, 6 to 8 short pickups enroute	7 miles easy	14 miles easy	**60 miles**
22	7 miles easy	5 miles easy	**Race**	**52 miles**
23	9 miles, 6 to 8 short pickups enroute	7 miles easy	12 miles easy	**58 miles**
24	6 miles easy	4 miles easy	**Race**	**50 miles**
25	7 miles, 6 to 8 short pickups enroute	7 miles easy	12 miles easy	**55 miles**
26	5 miles easy	4 miles easy	**PEAK RACE**	**45 miles**

26-Week Intermediate Level Marathon Training Program

for the 3:30 – 4:00 marathon runner

Wk	Monday	Tuesday	Wednesday	Thursday
Distance/Base Building Phase				
1	3 miles easy	4 miles easy	3 miles easy	4 miles easy
2	3 miles easy	4 miles easy	3 miles easy	4 miles easy
3	3 miles easy	4 miles easy	4 miles easy	4 miles easy
4	3 miles easy	4 miles easy	4 miles easy	4 miles easy
5	3 miles easy	5 miles easy	4 miles easy	4 miles easy
6	3 miles easy	5 miles easy	4 miles easy	5 miles easy
7	3 miles easy	5 miles easy	4 miles easy	5 miles easy
8	3 miles easy	5 miles easy	4 miles easy	5 miles easy
9	3 miles easy	4 miles easy	5 miles easy	4 miles easy
10	3 miles easy	5 miles easy	4 miles easy	5 miles easy
11	4 miles easy	5 miles easy	4 miles easy	5 miles easy
12	4 miles easy	5 miles easy	4 miles easy	5 miles easy
Intervals/Speed Introduction Phase				
13	3 miles easy	4 miles easy	5 miles, 6 x 1 min. @ 10K pace	4 miles easy
14	3 miles easy	4 miles easy	6 miles, 6 x 1 min. @ 10K pace	4 miles easy
15	3 miles easy	4 miles steady	6 miles, 4 x 1:30 mins. @ 10K pace	4 miles easy
16	3 miles easy	4 miles easy	6 miles, 4 x 1:30 mins. @ 10K pace	4 miles easy
17	3 miles easy	4 miles easy	6 miles, 3 x 2 mins. @ 10K pace	4 miles easy
18	4 miles easy	4 miles easy	6 miles, 3 x 2 mins. @ 10K pace	4 miles easy
19	3 miles easy	3 miles easy	4 miles easy	6 miles, 2 x 3 mins. @ 10K pace
20	3 miles easy	4 miles easy	6 miles, 2 x 3 mins. @ 10K pace	3 miles easy
21	3 miles easy	3 miles easy	6 miles, 3 x 2 mins. @ 10K pace	4 miles easy
22	3 miles easy	4 miles easy	6 miles, 4 x 1:30 mins. @ 10K pace	4 miles easy
23	3 miles easy	3 miles easy	3 miles easy	5 miles, 6 x 1 min. @ 10K pace
Tapering Phase				
24	3 miles easy	3 miles easy	5 miles, 2 x 3 mins. @ 10K pace	4 miles easy
25	2 miles easy	3 miles easy	5 miles, 3 x 2 mins. @ 10K pace	3 miles easy
26	3 miles easy	3 miles easy	5 miles, 4 x 1 mins. @ 10K pace	3 miles easy

Wk	Friday	Saturday	Sunday	Total for Week
				Distance/Base Building Phase
1	3 miles easy	3 miles easy	5 miles easy	**25 miles**
2	3 miles easy	3 miles easy	6 miles easy	**26 miles**
3	3 miles easy	3 miles easy	6 miles easy	**27 miles**
4	4 miles easy	3 miles easy	6 miles easy	**28 miles**
5	4 miles easy	3 miles easy	6 miles easy	**29 miles**
6	4 miles easy	3 miles easy	6 miles easy	**30 miles**
7	4 miles easy	3 miles easy	7 miles easy	**31 miles**
8	4 miles easy	2 miles easy	**Race**	**30 miles**
9	5 miles easy	4 miles easy	7 miles easy	**32 miles**
10	5 miles easy	3 miles easy	8 miles easy	**33 miles**
11	5 miles easy	3 miles easy	8 miles easy	**34 miles**
12	4 miles easy	2 miles easy	**Race**	**32 miles**
			Intervals/Speed Introduction Phase	
13	5 miles easy	3 miles easy	10 miles easy	**34 miles**
14	5 miles easy	3 miles easy	10 miles easy	**35 miles**
15	4 miles easy	3 miles easy	**Race**	**32 miles**
16	5 miles easy	3 miles easy	12 miles easy	**37 miles**
17	5 miles easy	3 miles easy	14 miles easy	**39 miles**
18	3 miles easy	2 miles easy	**15K or 10 mile race**	**36 miles**
19	4 miles easy	3 miles easy	16 miles easy	**39 miles**
20	4 miles easy	3 miles easy	18 miles easy	**41 miles**
21	4 miles easy	2 miles easy	20 miles easy	**42 miles**
22	3 miles easy	2 miles easy	**20K or half mar. race**	**37 miles**
23	4 miles easy	3 miles easy	17 miles easy	**38 miles**
				Tapering Phase
24	4 miles easy	3 miles easy	15 miles easy	**37 miles**
25	4 miles easy	2 miles easy	13 miles easy	**32 miles**
26	2 miles easy	Rest day	**THE MARATHON**	**42.2 miles**

26-Week Advanced Level Marathon Training Program

for the 3:00 – 3:30 marathon runner

Wk	Monday	Tuesday	Wednesday	Thursday
Distance/Base Building Phase				
1	4 miles easy	6 miles easy	4 miles easy	6 miles easy
2	4 miles easy	7 miles easy	4 miles easy	7 miles easy
3	5 miles easy	7 miles easy	5 miles easy	7 miles easy
4	5 miles easy	8 miles easy	5 miles easy	8 miles easy
5	6 miles easy	8 miles easy	6 miles easy	8 miles easy
6	6 miles easy	8 miles easy	6 miles easy	8 miles easy
7	6 miles easy	8 miles easy	6 miles easy	8 miles w/2 mi. tempo
8	6 miles easy	8 miles easy	6 miles easy	8 miles, w/3 mi. tempo
Hill Work Phase				
9	7 miles easy	6 miles easy	7 miles, 4 x uphill	7 miles easy
10	7 miles easy	6 miles easy	7 miles, 5 x uphill	7 miles easy
11	7 miles easy	6 miles easy	7 miles, 6 x uphill	7 miles easy
12	7 miles easy	6 miles easy	7 miles, 6 x uphill	7 miles easy
Long Interval/Strength Phase				
13	7 miles easy	6 miles easy	7 miles, 3 x 4 mins. @ 10K race pace	7 miles easy
14	7 miles easy	6 miles easy	7 miles, 4 x 3 mins. @ 10K race pace	7 miles easy
15	5 miles easy	6 miles easy	8 miles, 6 x 2 mins. @ 10K race pace	7 miles easy
16	5 miles easy	6 miles easy	8 miles, 8 x 1:30 mins. @ 10K race pace	7 miles easy
17	5 miles easy	6 miles easy	8 miles, 2 x 6 mins. @ 10K race pace	7 miles easy
18	5 miles easy	6 miles easy	8 miles, 3 x 4 mins. @ 10K race pace	7 miles easy
19	4 miles easy	6 miles easy	7 miles easy	8 miles, 4 x 3 mins. @ 10K race pace
20	4 miles easy	6 miles easy	8 miles, 6 x 2 mins. @ 10K race pace	6 miles easy
21	4 miles easy	6 miles easy	8 miles, 2 x 6 mins. @ 10K race pace	5 miles easy
22	5 miles easy	6 miles easy	8 miles, 3 x 4 mins. @ 10K race pace	7 miles easy
23	4 miles easy	6 miles easy	7 miles easy	8 miles, 6 x 2 mins. @ 10K race pace
24	3 miles easy	6 miles easy	8 miles, 2 x 4 mins. @ 10K race pace	5 miles easy
Tapering Phase				
25	3 miles easy	6 miles easy	8 miles, 3 x 3 mins. @ 10K race pace	5 miles easy
26	3 miles easy	6 miles, 6 x 1 min. @ 10K race pace	5 miles easy	4 miles easy

Wk	Friday	Saturday	Sunday	Total for Week
				Distance/Base Building Phase
1	4 miles easy	4 miles easy	8 miles easy	**36 miles**
2	4 miles easy	4 miles easy	9 miles easy	**39 miles**
3	5 miles easy	4 miles easy	9 miles easy	**42 miles**
4	5 miles easy	4 miles easy	10 miles easy	**45 miles**
5	6 miles easy	4 miles easy	10 miles easy	**48 miles**
6	6 miles easy	6 miles easy	10 miles easy	**50 miles**
7	6 miles easy	6 miles easy	10 miles easy	**50 miles**
8	6 miles easy	6 miles easy	10 miles easy	**50 miles**
				Hill Work Phase
9	7 miles easy	4 miles easy	**Race**	**50 miles**
10	7 miles easy	6 miles easy	10 miles easy	**50 miles**
11	7 miles easy	6 miles easy	10 miles easy	**50 miles**
12	7 miles easy	4 miles easy	**Race**	**48 miles**
				Long Interval/Strength Phase
13	7 miles easy	6 miles easy	10 miles easy	**50 miles**
14	7 miles easy	6 miles easy	10 miles easy	**50 miles**
15	8 miles easy	4 miles easy	13 miles easy	**51 miles**
16	8 miles easy	4 miles easy	15 miles easy	**53 miles**
17	8 miles, 4 short pickups enroute	4 miles easy	14 miles easy	**52 miles**
18	8 miles easy	4 miles easy	**15K or 10 mile race**	**53 miles**
19	7 miles easy	4 miles easy	16 miles easy	**52 miles**
20	8 miles, 5 short pickups enroute	4 miles easy	18 miles easy	**54 miles**
21	7 miles, 6 short pickups enroute	4 miles easy	20 miles easy	**54 miles**
22	5 miles easy	3 miles easy	**20K or half mar. race**	**51 miles**
23	7 miles easy	4 miles easy	17 miles easy	**53 miles**
24	6 miles, 6 short pickups enroute	4 miles easy	15 miles easy	**47 miles**
				Tapering Phase
25	6 miles, 6 short pickups enroute	4 miles easy	13 miles easy	**45 miles**
26	4 miles easy	3 miles easy	**THE MARATHON**	**51.2 miles**

26-Week Competitive Level Marathon Training Program
for the 2:40 – 3:00 marathon runner

Wk	Monday	Tuesday	Wednesday	Thursday
Distance/Base Building Phase				
1	6 miles easy	6 miles easy	6 miles easy	6 miles easy
2	6 miles easy	7 miles easy	6 miles easy	7 miles easy
3	6 miles easy	7 miles easy	7 miles easy	7 miles easy
4	6 miles easy	7 miles easy	7 miles easy	7 miles w/tempo run
5	7 miles easy	7 miles easy	7 miles easy	7 miles w/tempo run
6	7 miles easy	8 miles easy	7 miles easy	8 miles w/tempo run
7	7 miles easy	8 miles easy	7 miles easy	8 miles w/tempo run
8	7 miles easy	8 miles easy	8 miles easy	8 miles w/tempo run
Hill Work Phase				
9	7 miles easy	8 miles easy	8 miles, 6 x uphill	8 miles easy
10	7 miles easy	8 miles easy	8 miles, 8 x uphill	8 miles easy
11	7 miles easy	8 miles easy	8 miles, 10 x uphill	8 miles easy
12	7 miles easy	8 miles easy	8 miles, 10 x uphill	8 miles easy
Long Interval/Strength Phase				
13	6 miles easy	8 miles easy	9 miles, 3 x 5 mins. @ 10K race pace	6 miles easy
14	6 miles easy	8 miles easy	9 miles, 5 x 3 mins. @ 10K race pace	6 miles easy
15	6 miles easy	8 miles easy	9 miles, 6 x 2:30 mins. @ 10K race pace	6 miles easy
16	6 miles easy	8 miles easy	9 miles, 10 x 1:30 mins. @ 10K race pace	6 miles easy
17	6 miles easy	8 miles easy	9 miles, 3 x 5 mins. @ 10K race pace	6 miles easy
18	7 miles easy	8 miles easy	9 miles, 5 x 3 mins. @ 10K race pace	6 miles easy
19	6 miles easy	6 miles easy	8 miles easy	9 miles, 6 x 2:30 mins. @ 10K race pace
20	6 miles easy	8 miles easy	9 miles, 10 x 1:30 mins. @ 10K race pace	6 miles easy
21	6 miles easy	8 miles easy	9 miles, 3 x 6 mins. @ 10K race pace	6 miles easy
22	6 miles easy	8 miles easy	9 miles, 4 x 4:30 mins. @ 10K race pace	6 miles easy
23	6 miles easy	6 miles easy	8 miles easy	9 miles, 6 x 3 mins. @ 10K race pace
24	6 miles easy	8 miles easy	8 miles easy	8 miles, 6 x 2:30 mins. @ 10K race pace
Tapering Phase				
25	6 miles easy	8 miles easy	7 miles easy	8 miles, 6 x 2 mins. @ 10K race pace
26	6 miles easy	8 miles easy	6 miles, 6 x 1 min. @ 10K race pace	6 miles easy

Wk	Friday	Saturday	Sunday	Total for Week
				Distance/Base Building Phase
1	6 miles easy	5 miles easy	10 miles easy	**45 miles**
2	6 miles easy	6 miles easy	10 miles easy	**48 miles**
3	7 miles easy	6 miles easy	10 miles easy	**50 miles**
4	7 miles easy	6 miles easy	12 miles easy	**52 miles**
5	7 miles easy	7 miles easy	12 miles easy	**54 miles**
6	7 miles easy	7 miles easy	12 miles easy	**56 miles**
7	7 miles easy	7 miles easy	14 miles easy	**58 miles**
8	8 miles easy	7 miles easy	14 miles easy	**60 miles**
				Hill Work Phase
9	8 miles easy	5 miles easy	**Race**	**54 miles**
10	8 miles easy	7 miles easy	14 miles easy	**60 miles**
11	8 miles easy	7 miles easy	14 miles easy	**60 miles**
12	8 miles easy	5 miles easy	**Race**	**54 miles**
				Long Interval/Strength Phase
13	9 miles easy	6 miles easy	16 miles easy	**60 miles**
14	9 miles easy	6 miles easy	16 miles easy	**60 miles**
15	7 miles easy	5 miles easy	**Race**	**53 miles**
16	9 miles easy	6 miles easy	18 miles easy	**62 miles**
17	9 miles, 6 to 8 short pickups enroute	6 miles easy	18 miles easy	**62 miles**
18	7 miles easy	5 miles easy	**15K or 10 mile race**	**56 miles**
19	8 miles easy pickups enroute	6 miles easy	20 miles easy	**63 miles**
20	9 miles, 6 to 8 short pickups enroute	6 miles easy	20 miles easy	**64 miles**
21	9 miles, 6 to 8 short pickups enroute	6 miles easy	20 miles easy	**64 miles**
22	7 miles easy	5 miles easy	**20K or half mar. race**	**57 miles**
23	8 miles easy	6 miles easy	18 miles easy	**61 miles**
24	8 miles easy	6 miles easy	16 miles easy	**60 miles**
				Tapering Phase
25	8 miles easy	6 miles easy	14 miles easy	**57 miles**
26	4 miles easy	4 miles easy	**THE MARATHON**	**60.2 miles**

Advanced

The advanced-level runner is capable of running 10k in 38 to 44 minutes. It is at this level that Fleming believes you can benefit from the addition of some tempo running during the seventh and eighth weeks. Four weeks of hill work is introduced as a prelude to the faster work done during the Long Interval/Strength Phase. Note also that the mileage of the advanced level is slightly higher than that of the intermediate.

The strength intervals are done once a week at 10k race pace either on the road or track, whichever is the preference. To determine what distances to run on the track, simply estimate how much distance you cover, for example, during a three-minute interval. If you are a 42-minute 10k runner and thus averaging about seven minutes per mile, half-mile repeats would be done at about 3:30. Therefore, a workout of 4 × 3 minutes could be 4 × 800 meters (half-mile) in 3:30 with three to three-and-a-half minutes, rest between each. When done on the road, the rest should be the same amount of time or distance as the interval.

Also added to the schedule are short pickups done during on your normal Friday run, but only during weeks when there is no race.

The final Faster Interval/Peaking Phase is added during the last six weeks. During this phase, the mileage is cut slightly, which should help you feel a little more spring in your legs, and the intervals are done closer to 5k race pace.

Competitive

The competitive runner is one who is classified as a 34- to 38-minute 10k runner. The difference between this level program and the advanced program is, as for the others, more mileage. In the beginning, you do 45 miles per week and build to a maximum of 60 miles per week. During the initial eight-week Distance/Base Building Phase, you do tempo runs once per week from week four through week eight. The hill work and intervals are similar to the advanced level, except that the amount increases on the competitive level.

Marathon Training

It is Tom Fleming's belief that, first and foremost, you are all distance runners, so whether you are training for the 10k or the marathon, the initial 12 weeks are always the same. After about 12 weeks, you have built enough of a base to add some speedwork with the goal of running a 10k, or to increase the long run to become accustomed to the demands of a marathon. Therefore, you'll note that on each level the 10k and marathon programs are almost identical, except that for the marathon, an allowance is made for the Sunday run to become increasingly longer. In addition, longer races are suggested to accustom the body to the marathon race experience.

Heart Rate Monitor Training

On the beginner level, the guidelines for the proper amount of running and exercise are fairly clear. What's more difficult, but equally important, is to establish a safe, effective pace. As runners progress and become more serious, the questions become even more refined and specific. How do I train most efficiently? How much speedwork should I do—and how hard should it be done—and how much long-distance running will best maximize my potential? How can I get the most out of training without getting injured?

Overtraining is a common and understandable mistake. And it's a classic one. Who hasn't acted on that feeling that if a little is good, more must be better? With the excitement and enthusiasm that come from fitness and athletic achievement, it isn't always easy to tell when we're overdoing it. In fact, sometimes it seems almost impossible to avoid that trap.

Experienced runners know the rules of preventing overtraining and overracing, which is all well and good on paper. But runners are complex people—very often compulsive overachievers. Therefore, it will come as little surprise when Cliff Held estimates that almost all the athletes he has encountered run too hard, particularly their speedwork. "Their perception of training effort is not accurate. In fact, runners are notoriously inaccurate," says Held. It is no wonder, then, that he believes 95 percent of all injury results from overtraining.

49

For the beginning runner, the goal is also to prevent overtraining, so that he or she will not become "turned off" to the sport by injury or illness. For the more experienced runner, the issue is how to achieve a high level of fitness without crossing that fine line into the injury zone.

There has long been established a sound basis of scientific information on the proper amount and intensity of training. However, until fairly recently, it was very difficult to apply it accurately. That's because it was based on perceived effort. With the use of a heart rate monitor, there is no guessing. Guidelines are all in the numbers: precise and specific.

Exactly what is a heart rate monitor, and how does it work? There are various types of heart rate monitors, but the device Cliff Held uses fits like a belt right below the chest and is accompanied by a watch that picks up the heartbeat signals from the belt. Based on heart rate formulas, once your set of numbers is determined for various workouts, you merely program the device. It then emits a beep if your heart rate either rises above or falls below the desired zone.

When using a heart rate monitor, in addition to following the directions for operating and maintaining the device, you should be aware of another tip Cliff Held offers. Do not store the monitor in a plastic bag after training. The moisture from perspiration will adversely affect the device.

Science has determined a great deal of what we need to know about exercise and heart rate. We know that there are optimal training zones based on heart rate. Once maximum heart rate (MHR) has been determined, other heart rate information for training can be gleaned.

You can determine your MHR by using a simple formula (see p. 52) that gives a rough figure, or for greater accuracy, you can take a stress test on a treadmill. For those who are a bit more ambitious, or who do not want to spend money on a stress test, here is a self-test composed by Cliff Held. Find a long hill and run up it as hard as you can. When you truly feel you are giving it your absolute maximum effort and cannot run a step harder, check your heart rate. That should be a fairly accurate reading of your MHR.

At the other end of the heart rate scale is the resting heart rate (RHR). RHR, like MHR, is an indicator of health and fitness. Trained athletes tend to have low resting pulses, some in the 40s or even 30s in beats-per-minute. You should become familiar with your RHR so you know what the norm is when you are fit and healthy. Resting pulse rate should be measured before getting out of bed in the morning as often as possible—ideally every day. If you wake up and it's high—as high as 75 beats per minute in the case of a fit person—you'll know you're either sick (or on the verge or it) or have overtrained. When you are fatigued, ill, or injured and are forced to cut back training, tracking your MHR and RHR can help you stage a proper comeback.

Like any single method, using heart rate to gauge training is most effective with experience. But how do you best gain that experience? It is inefficient to stop mid-run to measure your pulse and compute your heart rate. That's when the ease and effectiveness of a heart rate monitor are most apparent.

Training Zone

Training zone refers to the range in which aerobic benefit is achieved. The high end of the training zone is MHR. The low end of the training zone is 60 percent of the MHR.

Cliff Held prescribes workouts based on percentages within the training zone (see below). Any time you exercise within the low limit to the MHR, you are acquiring cardiovascular benefit, says Held. Below that 60 percent, though you're burning calories, you are not attaining aerobic benefit.

According to Held, the heart rate monitor keeps a runner from training too hard, as well as from "sandbagging," or taking it too easy. In most cases, with a heart rate monitor, runners initially feel that they are doing just that—running too easily. They are surprised that the device directs the body to run slower than they are used to, yet they are still within the training zone. Use of the heart rate monitor assures proper pace and training benefits, as well as sufficient (and safe) recovery from strenuous efforts.

The heart rate monitor confirms that quality is more important than quantity. "I've seen runners do 90 miles a week, but a lot of those are 'junk miles'," says Held. "The monitor proves it's better to do 60 to 70 quality miles."

Held has had a 95 percent rate of improvement among those he has trained over the years using heart rate monitors. One of them is Susan Foster, a 37-minute 10k runner who had not broken three hours in the marathon for many years. Says Held, "In analyzing her training together, we found she was not getting the benefit of her mileage." She had some junk miles. After training with a heart rate monitor, in January 1992 in the New Orleans Marathon, run in snow and 17-mile-per-hour headwinds, she won the race, breaking three hours. Three other of Held's runners, who had trained with heart rate monitors, also ran personal best times and received awards in the same race. At least one other of those runners had a training program characterized by junk mileage.

Cliff Held's Heart Rate Formula

There are various formulas for measuring heart rate. A number of them add or subtract for a whole list of variables—from current health to different levels of fitness. Cliff Held acknowledges that while some of these formulas may be more accurate than the one he uses, most are more difficult to compute. Besides, the only way to determine exact maximum heart rate is to take a stress test. Otherwise, Held's formula has proved fairly accurate—and it is definitely simple.

Men—220 minus your age (add 10 if you are already fit, i.e., running or involved in another exercise program).
Women—226 minus your age (add 10 if fit).
Beginners, do not add 10.

Because these formulas were determined using the average population, if someone is physically fit, Cliff Held adds 10 points to the first number (i.e., 230, 236). In his experience, this 10-point addition has been fairly accurate.

Thus, a 40-year-old fit woman charts the following as a scale of her training zone, which is used to determine all workouts:

MHR is 196 beats per minute.
90%—176
80%—157
70%—137
60%—118

For a 40-year-old fit man, the numbers are:

> MHR is 190 beats per minute.
> 90%—171
> 80%—152
> 70%—133
> 60%—114

Training with a Heart Rate Monitor

Following are Cliff Held's various recommendations for heart rate monitor training.

Beginner

First, consult a physician before taking up running or any exercise program. If you are over age 30, and/or overweight, or if you have been sedentary for 10 years or more, get a checkup. Do not use a heart rate monitor as a substitute for a fitness test.

It takes a beginner at least six months to get completely acclimated to running. During this time, speed is not important. The point is gradually to increase mileage at a safe pace.

If you're just getting into the sport, *never run above 70 percent of your MHR*. Sixty to 70 percent is recommended. Maintain that level for at least three months. After that, you may continue to maintain basic training at that heart rate level, or add one to two workouts per week during which you intensify your effort to raise your heart rate five to ten beats.

You should stay at this level for at least six months before moving on to the intermediate phase. Otherwise, you can stay where you are and continue to maintain basic fitness.

Intermediate

Use of the heart rate monitor is not necessary for warmup or cooldown. Warmup and cooldown can be 1 to 1½ miles of easy jogging before and after the workout. But use the monitor for speedwork.

1. Most intervals should be done at 90 percent of maximum heart rate, but not higher. (Depending on the type of workout, intervals usually total 1½ to 2½ miles of hard running.)

2. For mile intervals and fartlek—which are longer intervals—80 to 85 percent of maximum heart rate.

The heart rate monitor is especially effective to gauge the length of recovery between efforts. Often the key isn't how hard you work out, but how long you recover. For example, if you run 880 yards, with a two-minute recovery, how do you really know if that is too much or too little rest? Recovery is achieved as soon as you drop to or below 120 beats per minute. Then you're ready to go again.

Also use the heart rate monitor for a long sustained effort, whether it is 6 or 18 miles. Your pace should be comfortable, conversational, 65 to 70 percent of MHR for advanced beginners, up to 80 percent for more experienced runners; for your regular run (not recovery from hard runs) 65 to 75 percent of MHR, and recovery run (done the day after a hard workout or race) 60 to 70 percent of MHR. (If the pace feels like you're walking, add a 10-beat increase.)

Results

Is the heart rate monitor successful? According to Held's experience with average runners, it is. Of the first group of 16 marathoners he had trained using the device, 15 of them ran personal bests. In addition, with heart rate monitor training he has noticed a significant decrease in the number of aches and pains among the runners with whom he works.

As a competitive masters runner himself, Held believes in the device because of personal experience and because he has seen other athletes he respects get good results with it. Elite athletes such as Ingrid Kristiansen and Rob de Castella use heart rate monitors, as do endurance athletes in other sports. Concludes Held, "Heart rate monitors are logical, and because I believe in a conservative approach to coaching, using one makes intellectual sense."

Cliff Held always uses a heart rate monitor for his hard workouts and quality runs. There are those who wear a heart rate monitor during races, as well. World record holder Ingrid Kristiansen is among them. But not Held. "It would take the fun and the spontaneity out of the race," he feels.

While the heart rate monitor certainly would seem to be the most logical training tool, Cliff Held warns that it is just a training device. You don't have to get locked into it. You don't have to use it every time you run. Using it is part of Held's serious side. Then there's his bottom line.

"For all but those who make a living at it, the first and foremost aspect of running is that it should be fun and enjoyable. I do a family run once a week with my wife, and it's considerably slower than my usual pace. On these days, the important thing is to talk and to have a good time. What good would it do me to wear a heart rate monitor?"

And of course, like all training methods, nothing is absolute. Held qualifies the belief in the total accuracy of the heart rate monitor. "No one factor always directly correlates to results. There are too many other variables, like weather and general health. And, as with any endeavor, there's the psychology of success, and just plain luck."

He also cautions, "The heart rate monitor is a training tool, not a training plan. How well you use the tool depends on how skilled the advice is you're getting, or how well you stick to a program." But in general, Held reasons, anything that is more training-specific betters one's chances of success.

The bottom line, says Held: "It's a device which is as good as any other. That means it's only as good as the people who use it."

If You're Measuring Your Pulse by Hand

While you're exercising, check your pulse at the wrist, not the neck. Recent studies have shown that applying pressure to the carotid artery in the neck can slow your heartbeat by 3 to 12 beats per minute, which can cause you to miscalculate the intensity of your workout.

* * *

Don't bother to check your pulse every time you exercise. Sometimes checking your pulse is not an imperative part of your workout. For one thing, particularly if you are doing it by hand, it can be very inefficient. Some people fail to find their pulse for 20 to 30 seconds after they've slowed down. In the meantime, the heart rate quickly comes down, making any kind of calculation inaccurate. According to an article in *Glamour* magazine, many teachers and trainers are using the rate of perceived exertion (RPE) instead. This rating system—based on a scale of 0 to 10—indicates how hard you *feel* you're exercising. One expert believes that RPE puts the focus back on the exerciser, encouraging her or him to tune into the body rather than rely on a theoretical figure.

That's not to say that target heart rate should be abolished altogether. Pulse rate is helpful in initially determining your own RPE for a certain activity. Pulse counting is also recommended for pregnant women or those with chronic health conditions such as diabetes (because small increases in pulse can have adverse effects), or when exercise conditions change: heat, humidity, and altitude can all affect heart rate.

—Fitness Features

Your Training Diary

Keeping a diary can be a valuable training aid. A diary provides you with both knowledge and perspective. It helps you to analyze your training and discover what works best for you. By analyzing your diary, successful cycles can be repeated and cycles that lead to breakdown, injury, or poor performance can be eliminated.

For every level of runner, the diary is an important tool. For the beginner, getting into the habit of keeping a diary reinforces the fitness lifestyle. For the intermediate runner, it is a motivation to improve further and to set new goals. And for the advanced, it is essential in tracking and evaluating intense, complicated training. "Because you invest so much in your sport, the diary is also important in its function as a coach, psychiatrist, and conscience. It gives you the opportunity to contemplate your training and to be counseled by it," according to Grete Waitz.

It is also important not to become a slave to the diary. A diary should be a motivator, not something that goads you to do more and more just to be able to write it down. It should be a record of sensible achievement, effective training regimes, and relevant feelings and reflections.

According to Tom Fleming, training can be recorded on anything—from a book designed as a running diary to a loose-leaf notebook or desk diary. Some runners use computers to record their training and racing. Whatever format you choose to record your running, it should include the following information:

1. Date and day of the week.
2. Distance or time run; the course or place running occurred.
3. Overall evaluation of the run: weather, type of effort (e.g., hard,

    moderate, easy), feelings, comments (e.g., felt sluggish on uphills), training partner or group.

4. Pulse—resting (taken in the morning while still in bed), training pulse, when and where relevant or of interest to you.

5. Weight, measured before run.

6. List of planned upcoming races.

7. Long- and short-term goals—Chart goals with a suggested time frame of up to one year. Significant goals should be written in the front of the book as a reminder. Never lose track of where you want to go, and how you want to improve.

While most serious and elite runners know the value of a diary, it can be an extremely useful tool for everyone. New York Road Runners Club member Mary Ellen Howe took up running with great enthusiasm, particularly after losing 25 pounds in less than one year. However, a new job and an arthritic condition in her knee recently caused her to run with more care.

To monitor her training, she keeps a diary, of which she says the following: "Staleness in my running is almost always due to overtraining, lack of sleep, or crossing multiple time zones during business travel. Recognizing the problem should be easy, but often is not unless I check the comments in my running log. When I see too many notations saying "felt slow, tired, or legs were dead," I know that it is time to cut my mileage 25 to 50 percent, catch up on sleep, and get a massage."

Tom Fleming says, "I'm a stickler. I've got 24 years worth of my own very detailed training diaries. My main reason for keeping a diary is to record all workouts and races. This enables me to look back over the work done, and evaluate if and how it has brought me toward my goals."

It is important to evaluate your running in this regard. Good results don't just happen by accident. They are the product of a consistent, progressive training program, one which can best be built and improved by analyzing past results.

Tom Fleming, as a coach, reads his athletes' diaries, but asks that they keep them mostly for their own benefit. "I ask them to write down—in their own handwriting—their goals. It's always great to see something like Anne Marie Letko's diary of 1991. Together we decided on a goal, which she wrote down: to make the World Championships team and to run 32:20 for 10,000 meters (nearly a minute faster than her previous best time). She improved her time to 32:26, made the World

Championships team, and she won the World University Games. We specifically set a time goal because I believe she needed something that she could grasp. Time is something all runners can understand. We all live by the clock."

One of the main uses of a training diary is to gain perspective. It is very difficult for any athlete, no matter what level, to assess the overall effectiveness of training while it is being done—despite years of experience. That's because so many factors—goals, aging, relative progress—are constantly changing.

Anne Marie Letko looks back over one year to get a good benchmark of her training progress. At that time, training seasons and cycles begin to repeat, so there is an aspect of completion. Thus she can use the diary as a source of comparison to new cycles. She sees what she did right, and when she was at her peak. And she sees what preceded trouble, like a down period in performance or the onset of an injury.

"Athletes forget," says Fleming. "They improve, and later when they are stuck on a plateau, they forget that improvement. With a diary, if they get stuck in a rut, proof of their better days is in black and white. In addition, it is important for an athlete to verbalize his or her aspirations."

But one of the most important factors for keeping a diary is a positive attitude. "If I'm feeling down in September, not doing well, I'll look back at May–a great month," says Letko. "Then I fully understand that you can't always be that up. I still had that great period of time on which to look back." With this perspective, she can be more patient, and wait for a peak cycle to come again, as it inevitably does.

"Can you talk yourself into a performance? Absolutely," says Fleming. "I've done it myself. 'Boston Marathon' reads the heading in large letters in my 1983 diary, which I wrote down months before the race as a source of inspiration. I weighed 170 pounds, 15 pounds overweight, as I stood on the starting line of that race. I had only done one or two good long runs. My diary entries reflect the fact that I absolutely talked myself through that race, and I managed to run in the low 2:14s. That has to be a record for the fastest fat man in the world! "

Anne Marie Letko also uses her diary to enhance her confidence. For example, she looks back at what she did during last year's cross-country season immediately preceding the upcoming cross-country season. "I look at the good workouts, and I see what results came from them. I feel better prepared for the upcoming season. Just seeing how I progressed knocks down a lot of psychological barriers."

However, while using the diary's past performances is a good learning tool, it is not a precise guide for the future. "I don't necessarily duplicate what I did the year before," says Letko. What Letko and Fleming do seek to do is duplicate the *pattern* of success, not necessarily the workouts and races themselves.

Confidence, inspiration, and patience are also the privilege of other runners who keep a diary. Says Letko, "A lot of average runners really get into keeping a diary. Maybe they don't need to study it every day, but it can keep them feeling up. If you're sitting inside in January and there's a blizzard, and maybe you're sick, you can get out the diary and look back at what you did in the spring. It can make you realize that a time like that will come again."

You don't always have to use a training diary as an educational tool. "Sometimes you like to look it over just for the heck of it," she says. Letko feels that it has an even deeper value than as a training guide. "Even if you don't write down all the details of your day—and I try not to do that in my training diaries for specific reasons—you can still look back at what you wrote and recall other things that were going on in your life." For Letko, looking at the places, and the people she was with, evokes an entire range of memories. "I can visualize how it might be when I'm 45, retired from competition. I'll look back at my diary when I was in my prime and be able to say, 'This is what I once did.'"

Anne Marie Letko's Diary

To illustrate Tom Fleming's point and show how athletes and their coaches use athletes' handwritten perceptions and expressions in their diaries, Anne Marie Letko has provided a sample reproduced here in facsimile.

WEEK #27—This week is unique, says Letko. Although it was a mid-season period, in which the emphasis was on strength work, she ran a race. "It was a fantastic week," says the athlete of the high-volume running and the successful race. But yes, it does go against sound training principles. This is not generally a period during which she would race. "It shows I broke the rules," says Letko. "We're all crazy. I bet if you analyzed the programs of other top runners, you would see they break the rules, too. But it gives them confidence. Here I had a high-mileage, high-quality week, and I ran a race. I felt good; I ran fast. The race didn't seem to affect me adversely. The fact I did it gives me a sense of invincibility."

YEAR TOTAL	TOTAL MILEAGE	1991
2243	FOR WEEK #27 93	**JULY**

Am – Ran 7³/4 mile loop {49:00}; felt OK; hot tub
Pm – DEL VAL TRACK; warm up about 3 miles + strides; ☐ 17
1000m → 69, 2:19, 2:53 jog 400; 8×400m w/200 jogs between
warm down after 400's   {69, 69, 69, 68, 69, 68, 68, 67} MONDAY **1**

Am – Ran about 8 miles very slow w/ Jim; humid; tight + sore
Pm – Ran Hampton loop (4.9 miles) {30:50} very rainy ☐ 13
lifted weights downstairs; sauna
                                TUESDAY **2**

Pm – Ran 4 miles very easy {26:45}
Ran 4× strides + jog to make 5 miles total ☐ 5
hot tub
                                WEDNESDAY **3**

Am – Ran 2 miles slow in early morning (at home)
9:30 → LONG ISLAND 5K → 1st: 15:40 [4:55,10:00,15:05] ☐ 15
course record; felt pretty comfortable, eased last
mile + picked up last 200m.
        Pm – Ran 5 miles easy   THURSDAY **4**

Am – Ran 10 miles at Gorge {6:30 pace}; feel good
from race
Pm – Ran Hampton loop easy; sauna ☐ 15
                                FRIDAY **5**

Am – 9.7 mile loop at Tom's {53:30}; very humid!
Pm – 5 miles on Del Val trails; 4×400 w/ 200 walk/jog ☐ 18
on track [66.5, 66.8, 65.5, 66.1] warm down
                                SATURDAY **6**

Am – Ran 10 miles easy at Gorge (about 6:45 pace)
sauna   very humid (☺)! ☐ 10
                                SUNDAY **7**

WEEK #34—This is a week that represents the tapering period. "I was at full speed capacity," says Letko. This is also a special week in her career as it precedes the 1991 World Championships in Tokyo. The workouts here provide her with special memories as well as confidence because they were done after traveling to a nice place, yet she succeeded in doing them in oppressive weather conditions. The week ends on August 25. Two days later, in the heats for the 10,000 meters, she ran her personal best time, 32:26.

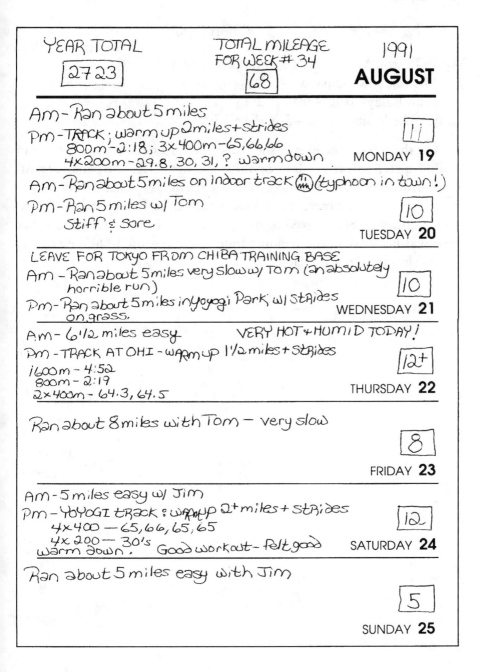

YEAR TOTAL
| 2723 |

TOTAL MILEAGE
FOR WEEK # 34
| 68 |

1991
AUGUST

Am - Ran about 5 miles
Pm - TRACK; warm up 2 miles + strides
    800m - 2:18; 3x400m - 65,66,66
    4x200m - 29.8, 30, 31, ? warm down
| 11 |
MONDAY **19**

Am - Ran about 5 miles on indoor track 🏃 (typhoon in town!)
Pm - Ran 5 miles w/ Tom
    Stiff & sore
| 10 |
TUESDAY **20**

LEAVE FOR TOKYO FROM CHIBA TRAINING BASE
Am - Ran about 5 miles very slow w/ Tom (an absolutely
    horrible run)
Pm - Ran about 5 miles in Yoyogi Park w/ strides
    on grass.
| 10 |
WEDNESDAY **21**

Am - 6½ miles easy   VERY HOT + HUMID TODAY!
Pm - TRACK AT OHI - warm up 1½ miles + strides
1600m - 4:52
  800m - 2:19
  2x400m - 64.3, 64.5
| 12+ |
THURSDAY **22**

Ran about 8 miles with Tom — very slow
| 8 |
FRIDAY **23**

Am - 5 miles easy w/ Jim
Pm - YOYOGI track; warm up 2+ miles + strides
    4x400 — 65, 66, 65, 65
    4x200 — 30's
warm down. Good workout - felt good
| 12 |
SATURDAY **24**

Ran about 5 miles easy with Jim
| 5 |
SUNDAY **25**

Actual Schedule/Events in April and May

April: Boston Milk Run 10K—1st place, 32:48
    Mt. Sac 10K—passed
    Penn Relays 10K—3rd in 32:43
May: Nike Women's 8K—5th place 25:48

On the next three events she listed, she passed. Instead, Letko ran a 3000-meter time trial, alone on the track, in 9:03.05—a personal best. Comments Fleming, "It was early in the season, so instead of undergoing the pressure of a race, and risking getting beat, I preferred to emphasize confidence. She proved to herself she could run fast." In fact, her time was better than the winning time at the Boston 3000-meter race, which she chose not to run.

RACING SCHEDULE
1991:

APRIL: early - time trial
    or 4/7 - Boston Milk Run 10K?
      ↓ more time trials
      4/20 - Mt. SAC 10K ⌈ Colette Murphy, Sammie
                         Gobowski, Patty Murray, Laura
    or ⌈ | Lemona, Maria Servin, Shelly
                        | Steily, Sylvia M., Maria T., etc.
      4/25 - Penn Relays 10K ⌊ are already confirmed
                      [Lynn Jennings &
                         Elaine Van Blunke]

MAY : early - _time trials_? (Freihofer's 5K if I
                               can't find any track?)

    5/12 - Nike Women's 8K
    5/18 - 3000m at Boston
    5/25 - 1500m at Boston   (Metrowest)
    or Ridgewood 5K (as a tune-up)

In June, Letko passed on the Boston and New York races. Instead, she ran a 1500-meter time trial, alone on the track, on 5/28. Her time of 4:18 was a personal best. Says Fleming, "When she did that by herself, without being pushed by anyone else, she gained the confidence to realize she can perform well in a race."

Letko's diary entry for June 13:
TAC/US CHAMPS/WORLD TRIALS 10,000m.
AM—ran 4 miles very light; hot tub
PM—race at 7:55 p.m. cooler & breezy. 3m warmup + strides. 32:50, 3rd place, Going to Tokyo! (with Lynn Jennings + Francie Larrieu Smith). Last 400m in 67 secs. I *can* sprint!

Racing Schedule 1991: This represents a unique feature of Tom Fleming's coaching. He believes in having Letko write down her tentative racing schedule, and her year-end goal (again, in her own handwriting). Writing down the goal solidifies it in her mind. Adds Fleming, "*I* don't write it, nor does she just say it. *She* puts it down in black and white. Then, I can hold it up to her in the end as proof." In February 1991, Anne Marie Letko's 10,000-meter best time was 33:05. Her goal sheet for a target race one half year later reads, 32:0? In that race, she ran 32:26. Not only is this a substantial improvement, but her prediction is extremely accurate.

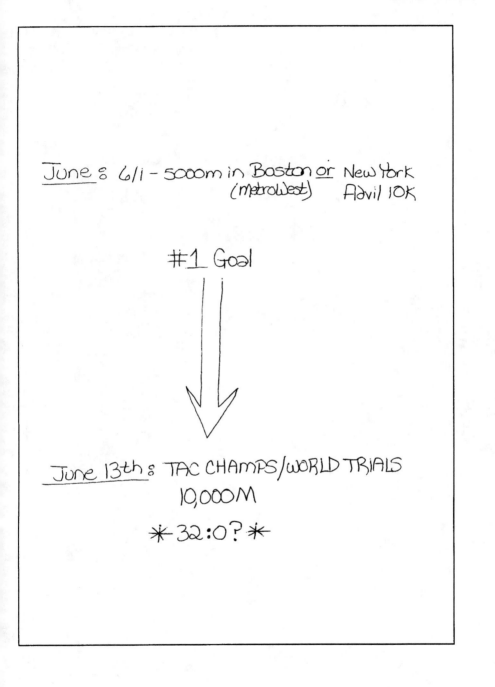

June : 6/1 - 5000m in Boston or New York
            (metroWest)   Advil 10K

#1 Goal

June 13th : TAC CHAMPS/WORLD TRIALS
              10,000M
            * 32:0? *

Coaching

6

A coach brings out the best in an athlete—physically and mentally. There's an art to the craft of coaching. As Stanford University coach Brooks Johnson once said, "Coaching is no different from what a choreographer does with a dance or what a playwright does with a play." A coach also serves as a supporter, a mentor, a friend, and a psychologist. According to Francie Larrieu Smith, "Having a coach has helped my longevity and the direction of my training and career. I get more from myself if someone like a coach is watching me during my workouts. I don't always do this–only for interval sessions. The hard-paced and other runs I do by myself. For every runner, whether jogger or world-class athlete, there are ups and downs. Those who are self-coached can become stagnant or bored. At least occasionally, it might be good for those people to seek out some coaching advice."

Do you need a coach? One of the beauties of the sport of running is that you can do without—and be a success. Take, for example, Joan Samuelson. "I train alone a lot of the time," she says, "and I am currently self-coached. I have never thrived in an atmosphere of a lot of runners. I have always chosen to live away from that. I have very few friends who run. My philosophy on running is, I don't dwell on it, I do it."

While coaching is not mandatory, would you benefit from having a coach, or from coaching advice? Based on the experience of most of the athletes in this book, and on observing the thousands of runners who have been guided by coaches in the NYRRC classes, the answer to that question is a resounding yes. Toshiko D'Elia puts it like this, "Everyone needs a good coach. That person is like an outside observer, an evaluator, anoth-

69

er set of eyes. Bob Glover has been coaching me since 1977. I would not have been running this long without my coach."

While having a coach may seem impractical for most runners on all but the advanced or elite level, that does not preclude seeking and acquiring coaching advice. There are many types of coaching situations. In addition to one-on-one private coaching, there are running classes, clubs, Y's, running camps, and other organizations through which informal coaching is available. Even more experienced runners can offer some valuable advice and insights, which can be considered a form of coaching.

In addition to the educational aspect of coaching, there are other benefits you can derive—from motivation to the camaraderie of sharing your experience. A coach can provide not only advice, but also perspective and support.

"As a coach, I try to keep people from taking their running too seriously," says Gordon Bloch, a NYRRC coach from 1984 to 1992. "New Yorkers in particular can be such an intense bunch. The typical student in the running class is a classic New Yorker: very successful in his or her work, used to putting out a hard effort and getting positive results. You tell people like this that improvement in running is a gradual process, but sometimes they don't get it. They throw themselves into it too intensely, getting injured or disillusioned, or they don't come back to the class. A more positive outcome is that they come back with a lower-key attitude and approach. The better they are, the worse it can be. Those with some athletic background who are in a higher level class get the most caught up. The surprising part is that women are usually more sensible than men. I find this in their approach to sports in general. I have no concrete evidence, but they seem more willing to listen to so-called voices of authority, or reason."

Grete Waitz cautions that a coach/athlete relationship should not be built on blind faith, but on communication—an exchange of ideas and information. She suggests that you work together with a coach to construct a training program, even if you are a beginner. You know yourself better than anyone—from your body to your time commitment and training goals. Fill your coach in and be sure to understand the training exercises and goals your coach suggests for you.

And remember, not all coaches will be right for you, nor will you be right for them. "I have a few requirements about who I will coach," says Tom Fleming. "I think a person has to stay with a program at least one year. That's the only way to know if it works. If I sense an athlete won't stick with a program, I won't work with him or her. There have been some people I suspect are in this category who have asked me to help them and I've turned them down."

"I've been running for over 20 years; I read all the books and articles, yet I need a coach. Why?" asks Fred Lebow. "I still have to be told, to be encouraged. Allan Steinfeld has a knack for that. If he's not training with me, I miss it. I just ran 45 minutes for five miles, but I bet if he were there, I could have broken 45.

"When I think of coaches who are most inspiring, I think of Fred Thompson, the outstanding mentor of the Atoms Track Club, based in Brooklyn," says Lebow. "Fred has made Olympians and shaped young lives."

Post-Workout Craftsbury Cooldown Routine

This routine, created by Cliff Held, takes 10 to 20 minutes total and should be done after every run. Unless otherwise indicated, hold the stretch for 30 to 45 seconds and repeat three or four times. "Progression" refers to the transition from one exercise to another. This routine is taken from the Craftsbury running camp.

Wall Pushup. Stand three feet from wall, feet apart and flat on ground, hands on wall, arms straight for support. Lean hips forward, and bend knees slightly. This exercise stretches the calf.

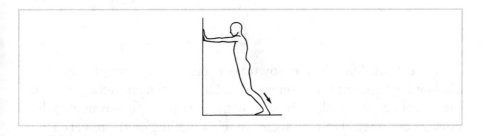

Progression: Bring one foot forward, with knee bent. Lift back foot's toe up. Lower your upper body to waist height. Stretches muscle under calf.

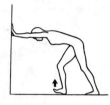

Progression: Feet together, rock back on heels, hands on wall, forming a jackknife with the body. Stretches hips, shoulders, and lower back.

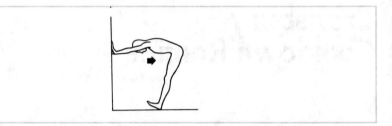

Back Scratch. Place palm of hand on bottom of opposite bent elbow; gently push the arm up until it touches the ear, and your hand reaches down, or "scratches," your back. Guide your hand down your back as far as comfortably possible by gently pushing on the elbow. Change hands and repeat. Stretches triceps and shoulders.

Hamstring Stretch. Lie down with one leg up straight up in the air, one leg bent with foot on ground. Lay towel over arch; gently pull the towel as you push against it with your foot (to the point where muscles contract). Hold 30 seconds; relax. Pulling on the towel encourages hamstring to increase range of motion and strength.

Progression: Turn foot outward so the toes point away from body to stretch outer hamstring fibers. Stretches and strengthens hamstrings and calves.

Trace the Alphabet. With the foot in the air, circle it in large tracings of A-B-C-D...Z. Develops ankle strength and flexibility.

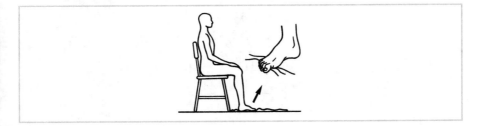

Foot Crunch. Lay the towel on ground. Grab the towel with the toes until the arch tires. Strengthens foot muscles, good for those who

suffer from plantar fasciitis.

Progression: Hook toes under a chair. Keep knees bent (situp position). Hold position until shin tires. Good for those who suffer from shinsplints.

Quadriceps Stretch. Kneel (do not sit) on knees; lean back with body erect, arms to the side. Hold 15 seconds. Come back to original kneeling position. Repeat three times.

Heel to Buttock. Stand on one foot. Lift the other foot (bend knee) with the opposite hand. Attempt to raise the heel of the lifted foot to buttocks. Keep the trunk upright. Hold 30 to 40 seconds. Repeat three or four times. Change legs and repeat. Also stretches the quadriceps.

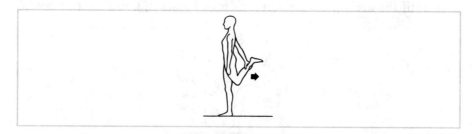

Hip/Lower Back Stretch. Get into a sitting position. Cross left leg over right bent leg. Hug the left knee to the chest. Twist the trunk of your body and look over your left shoulder. Change legs and repeat, looking over your right shoulder.

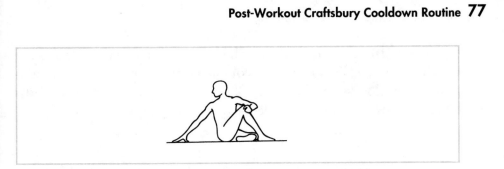

Iliotibial Band Stretch. Lie on your side with both legs bent in running position. Bring the bottom bent leg up toward your chest. Then bring the top bent leg up back toward buttocks in back. Hold for 30 seconds.

Progression: Lie on your back, knees bent. Hug your shins to your chest. Stretches hamstrings and lower back.

Progression: With your feet on the ground, raise your hips up in the air until the torso forms a flat plane. Hold 30 seconds, lower. Repeat ten times. Stretches quadriceps and lower back.

Groin Stretch. Seated, draw your feet together until the soles are nearly touching. (They can touch completely if you are flexible enough.) Place your elbows on the inside of your knees. Lean forward gently, simultaneously pressing the knees toward the ground.

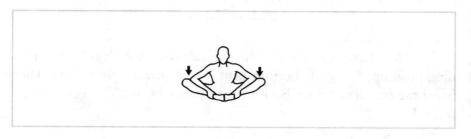

Running Form

Running is natural. Right? For the most part that's true. If there is something to teach in running, however, Cliff Held believes it is good form. He sees the biggest problems in most runners in their upper body form. Held does not alter lower body form. "To change lower body form is too unnatural and too highly technical for the average runner," he believes. In addition, "It is almost impossible, even on an elite level, to change foot plant without extensive retraining. You practically have to teach someone to walk in an entirely different way." Therefore, he advises, "Let your feet alone, and concentrate on your upper body."

Can improving upper body form make a difference? Here's Held's analogy. "I ask my students, 'How many times do you swing your arms back and forth in a 10K race?' Thousands of times. If every arm swing were more efficient, and thus could result even in a hundredth of a second improvement, if you add up all those hundredths, you could improve your overall time by seconds, even minutes."

Held is not alone in his belief in the importance of proper upper body form. Coach Tom Fleming, for one, recommends that his athletes work on upper body strength by using lightweight dumbbells. Fleming also claims that just the act of running itself will aid in developing form.

Can upper body form ultimately make a difference in performance? Relates Fleming, "If you were to ask Emil Zatopek, who had horrible form, he would probably say no. And he won five Olympic gold medals. The point is, I'll take a great engine with a beat-up-looking body any day." Despite exceptions like Zatopek, however, Fleming agrees that the average runner can benefit by improving upper body form.

The upper body ultimately affects what runners do from the waist down. Improper upper body movement during running results in improper leg lift. Since he believes that it is unreasonable to expect a person to correct all mechanical errors at once, Cliff Held focuses on improving one aspect of form at a time.

The biggest form problem is improper use of the shoulders and arms, says Held. The shoulders are too high and the arms are too low or too high. This creates inefficient use of the upper body. According to Held, proper upper body movement consists of two elements:

1. Proper arm swing. Bend the elbow at a right angle, but do not lock it in this position. Always keep body parts relaxed and fluid. When swinging the arm, the hand should brush the area just below the side of the running pants' waistband.

2. Shoulders. Tight shoulders cause tension in the neck and upper back. To make sure shoulders are relaxed, take a deep breath and exhale hard. The shoulders will automatically drop. While running, they should remain in an upside-down "U" shape, not in a "T" shape. In addition, the shoulders should not move during running.

To relax your upper body, think of something soothing. For example, some people visualize running in a serene forest or near tranquil water. This takes the focus away from the running effort.

Cliff Held points out that many runners on all levels have weak upper bodies. He believes that weight work can improve upper body efficiency, and thus running. He has invented what he calls the "THI" system of weight training. The letters refer to the shape the body makes when doing the exercises. "I call it the working person's weight training system for upper body strength," says Held. He explains that he keeps it short yet effective because most runners have many other obligations, and can't spend a great deal of time and money going to fancy gyms.

As Held pointed out earlier, a runner swings his or her arms thousands of times in the course of a run. "You need strength to do that," says Held. With the exercises below, he guarantees that in six weeks you'll notice a significant difference. "I've had tremendous results with this program," he emphasizes.

To do these exercises, you will need two simple dumbbells, from three to six pounds. Test the proper weight by going into a sporting goods store's free-weight department. Hold the dumbbells at your sides: If they are too heavy, they will pull you down. If they are too light, you'll be able to raise them with no effort. "You want something that feels like a weight, but is not oppressively heavy," says Held.

Held suggests doing the following exercises no more than three times a week, for 15 to 20 minutes, preferably on the days of your easy runs. Held also recommends that you do *not* do them in conjunction with your run; do them any other time of day, a minimum of one hour before or one hour after a run, in front of a mirror if possible.

Exercises

1. Sit on the floor with your back straight and your legs straight out in front of you. Put the weights in your hands and swing them in the running motion. Count to 15 maximum (right hand up and back, left hand up and back is one). Take a deep breath, and repeat. (Fifteen repetitions is Held's own workout. In the beginning, you may want to do less. Start with three or five—whatever necessary—and build up slowly.)

   Using the running motion while sitting guarantees that the mechanics of the arm swing are correct. If the arms fall too low, the weights will hit the floor, and you can't bring your hands up too high or you won't be able to move.

2. Standing up, do the same exercise, watching that the weights do not fall below hip level. (You may choose to do both #1 and #2, or only one of them.)

   Now you're ready for the "THI" series. Go through each movement once, completing the T-H-I for one set, up to a maximum of fifteen repetitions.

3. "T": With the weights at your sides, bring both hands up sideways simultaneously, reaching shoulder height, so your body looks like a "T" shape. Then bring them down. Pay attention in this and all exercises not to let the weights fall back down with gravity. You should slowly bring them down, maintaining control.

4. "H": Bring your arms out straight in front of you (Frankenstein style) and open them to your sides, then close again, as if you were playing the accordion.

5. "I": Hold the weights resting on the front of the thighs, so you see the backs of your hands. Raise them in front of you to shoulder height (Frankenstein style). Bring them back down.

Ultimate Strength and Flexibility Exercises

Buddy Stretching

When coach Tracy Sundlun, who has guided the career of 2:10-marathoner Pat Petersen, was an assistant coach at the University of Southern California, he designed a series of exercises, which he encourages all of his athletes to do religiously—regardless of their performance level. Sundlun feels buddy stretching, or resistance stretching, is more thorough and specific than the standard static runner's stretching.

Buddy stretching should precede the fitness drills described in the next chapter. Ideally, the stretches should be done two to three times per week—at a minimum, once per week. They can either precede or follow a training run, but Sundlun believes they are best as part of the warmup, as they have certain injury-prevention qualities. As with all new programs, allow yourself approximately three weeks or six sessions to acclimate to the stretches.

When doing buddy stretches, teamwork, trust, and relaxation are the key. Good communication between partners will ensure that the exercises are done effectively, but safely.

Exercises should be preceded by a warmup jog (until you break out in a sweat) and followed by sprints, the drills that follow, or your own personal drills (if you do them), and then your run.

Your partner should provide enough resistance over the full range of movement to make the exercise tough, but not impossible. He or she should provide slightly less resistance throughout the exercises than you have strength. The amount of that resistance will vary from exercise to exercise and even within each exercise, depending on your position.

All of these exercises are done lying on your back, unless otherwise indicated. Exercises are preferably done in the order listed. Where a number of repetitions is called for, do seven to ten.

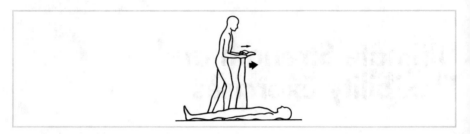

Hamstring Stretch. When being stretched, lie back, close your eyes, breathe deeply and evenly—in through the nose, out through the mouth. Concentrate on the area of stretch as your partner pushes gradually. With your leg raised straight toward the sky, your partner stands and, once you are relaxed, gradually pushes the leg in the direction of your head every time you breathe out. Spend about two minutes on each leg. Try to keep your knees as straight as possible, but under no circumstances should your partner ever attempt to hold or lock them straight for you.

Hip Rotators. Lie with one leg straight while your partner works on the other. Relax and let your partner do the work. He/she should move your leg in any way he/she desires, manipulating and stretching the hip, knee, and ankle joints until he/she is satisfied that you are sufficiently "noodle-like." Then switch legs and repeat.

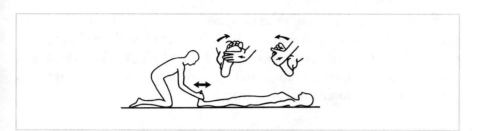

Ankle Work with Resistance. With your knees straight, move your toes up and back seven to ten times, then in and out, also seven to ten times, against resistance provided by your partner. In this exercise, you are working the muscles in your shins and your inner and outer thigh muscles. Toe raises, preferably done by standing on a curb, should take the place of a down segment.

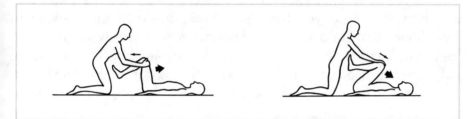

Knees to Chest with Resistance. Begin with your feet on the ground and your knees slightly bent. Bring your knees to your chest, working against the resistance of your partner. When you can bring them no further on your own, with or without resistance, your partner should then help you by pushing your knees to your chest while you continue to pull. This helps educate your stomach muscles to do this movement more efficiently.

Scissors with Resistance. Lift your leg against your partner's resistance, angling it just slightly in front of your midline. There's a notch in the hip joint which facilitates this movement.) When you can lift no higher, with or without resistance, your partner should lift the leg a bit more and then provide resistance as you bring the leg back down. You'll find your adductors (inner thigh muscles) are likely much stronger than your abductors (outer thigh muscles).

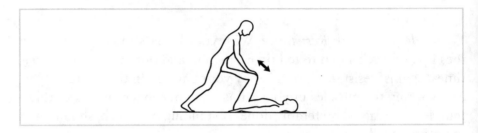

Body Weight Squat. With both legs extended, your partner leans against your feet as you bend your knees toward your head; then straighten them. For balance, your partner should do this by spreading his/her legs and then place his/her hands on your shins or knees. The emphasis here is on stretching and strengthening knees, hips, and lower back—not on developing power.

Hamstring Pulldown. Beginning with one leg raised 90 degrees or more from the ground, pull the heel down to the ground against your partner's resistance, keeping the leg straight. This exercise deals with the hamstring, and thus you perform the down motion only. After seven to ten repetitions, you'll notice how much more flexible your hamstrings have become.

Groin Stretch (Resistance in and out). Lie, or sit, with your legs bent and the soles of your feet facing each other. Your partner places his/her hands on your knees, creating additional weight, which you must lift as you close your knees and resist as you open them back up.

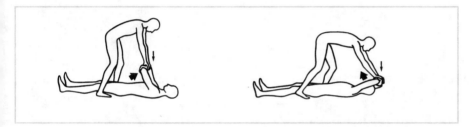

Shoulder Stretch (Resistance in all directions). Grasp both of your forearms, forming a triangle perpendicular to the ground. Your partner stands above you, also grasping your forearms. He/she constantly pushes straight down as you first lower your arms to the ground over your head, then lift them up to the perpendicular, then lower them to your hips, then lift them back up to the perpendicular again. This process is repeated seven to ten times.

Running and Fitness Drills

Tracy Sundlun has designed a set of drills that he has prescribed for his athletes for the past 20 years. He has found them particularly useful among those who do not have the benefit of a general sports background, especially many women. Sundlun designed the drills for sprinters as assistant coach at the University of Southern California, but they are applicable to any runner. Sundlun's top marathoners do them, and Olympic middle-distance champion Sebastian Coe favored similar exercises. In addition to superb conditioning, the drills add fun and variety to any running program. Although they require concentration, Sundlun says his athletes especially enjoy the camaraderie of doing the drills together.

Sundlun stresses the total fitness that his drills develop. They focus on general strength and coordination by working around the center of gravity and with the supporting or supplemental muscle groups that surround those used in running, but that don't get much conditioning through normal running and training.

"Most distance runners have good cardiovascular ability," says Sundlun, "but are lacking in overall athletic ability. Making a better athlete will automatically mean making a better runner." Sundlun gives the following example of how this works. If improving one's vertical jump, knee lift and generally increasing power—results of doing the drills—can improve a runner's natural stride by a quarter or a half inch, it can save between 40 and 80 yards in a 10k. In addition, the drills develop better coordination, flexibility, and abdominal strength—all of which improve running form. The better the form, the more efficient the runner. The more efficient the runner, the faster he or she can go with less effort and energy.

These drills exaggerate various aspects of the running motion, as well as isolating and working the specific muscles involved. Sundlun points out that in dissecting and developing the running motion, a person can develop and improve.

Drills should be done approximately twice a week and in the order listed, but no more than every other day, especially as they stress areas most runners have not used.

Take it slow and easy; if the exercise or the amount of the exercise is too difficult, cut back. You need not do every drill perfectly in every session. Says Sundlun, "If they lose their balance, or if they don't do the drill perfectly, some runners will say, 'Let me try that again.' Don't. You'll get it with practice, but to avoid overstressing the body, drills should not be repeated in one session." For some, these drills will be a workout in and of themselves. More advanced runners will want to use them as a warmup preceding a training run, or better, preceding a speed workout or interval session.

Warm up for the drills by jogging until you break out in a sweat.

Exaggerated Skipping. Swinging the opposite arm to the leg being lifted, drive each knee up as high as comfortably possible. Use the arm swing to help generate higher lift. As you drive off the ground, feel complete extension through the toe of the bottom leg. Avoid swinging the arms across the body, so that you travel in a straight line. Skip 100 yards up and 100 yards back. This exercise emphasizes body alignment and coordination, and works the feet and ankles.

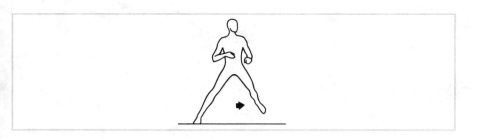

Basketball Slides. If you ever played basketball, you probably had to do this exercise. This is like a sideways skip, but without bending the knees. Face perpendicular to the direction you intend to go. If you're going to your left, step out with your left foot, shift your weight onto the left, and pull/propel yourself with your adductors (the muscles of your inner thigh). Bring the right, or trailing, leg to meet the left. Land on the right foot and repeat. (Do not cross your legs. The heels meet the heels, and the toes meet the toes.) Keep the arms bent in running position. The height achieved while sliding is unimportant. Slide-hop 100 yards, and slide back *facing the same direction.* That is, you should see the same scenery. This guarantees you work both sets of muscles in both legs. If you must look, look in the direction you are traveling, be sure not to twist your feet as well. The feet should remain parallel. This exercise works the adductors and abductors (inner and outer thigh) and is particularly useful for those with a history of groin problems.

Frankenstein. Extend your arms straight out in front of you. With feet flat on the ground, walk slowly, keeping the knees straight and raising one leg at a time as high as comfortably possible. Keep the trunk erect. It is not important to maintain a long stride. Eventually you want to be able to raise your feet high enough to meet your hands, but do not bend over or drop your rear end in an attempt to reach your hands. This exercise works the stomach muscles and quadriceps (top of the thigh). Walk 100 yards minimum.

Kick Butt. Bend at the waist so your upper body is parallel to the ground. (You'll look like Groucho Marx.) Rise onto your toes so your weight is on the balls of your feet. Glancing only slightly in front of you, with your arms bent or loose at your sides (whatever feels comfortable), run with your feet kicking up in back, trying to kick your butt. The steps should be quick. This exercise will likely feel uncomfortable in the beginning because of the forward body lean. "Many runners sit too far back when they run," Sundlun points out. "Getting used to putting the weight forward will promote better running form. The object in running is to do as little work as possible. A slight forward lean while running allows gravity to work for you." This exercise works on flexibility, coordination, and body position.

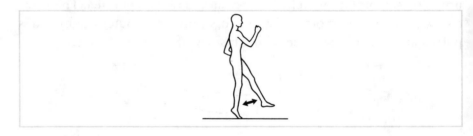

Stiff-Legged Running. With arms bent in 90-degree angles at your sides, rise up on your toes. Keeping the knees locked, run as quickly as possible. Maintain a slight forward lean. The strides will be very short. Do this for a minimum of 100 yards. This exercise works the feet, ankles, quadriceps, and hamstrings.

High-Knee Walking. This is another difficult exercise, so take it slowly. You may lose your balance in the beginning, but ultimately, the drill will aid you in developing better body control. High-knee walking is an exaggerated sprint motion done in slow motion. Rise up on your toes, lock the ankles, and lean slightly forward, as if a helium balloon were attached to your sternum. Maintaining an erect posture, raise your leg in an exaggerated walk, pawing the air like a show horse, before bringing it back to the ground. Concentrate on lifting the knees as high as possible without losing form. The lift comes from the use of your lower stomach muscles. Do not drop your rear end in order to lift your knees. Eventually your stomach muscles will gain strength and your knees will come up more easily. Only a small distance is covered with each step, and overall, while doing this exercise. If you stay on your toes and don't drop your rear end, keeping your center of gravity under control and up as high as possible, each step will be very short. The strain on your feet, ankles, Achilles tendons, and hips, as well as the concentration required, doesn't permit you to go more than 30 to 40 yards at a time. After doing this drill, shake your legs out and walk back. Do no more than 100 yards total in one training session.

High-Knee Jogging. This is the same exercise as high-knee walking, only jogging. It is still done in slow motion; however, the ankle is locked, but the heel does not touch the ground. The foot strike is quick, though again, the overall motion will feel slow. It will look like you are prancing.

Concentrate on the hips and trunk being lifted up. Says Sundlun, "If you're 5'6", think of being 5'10"." Cover the same distance as in the drill above.

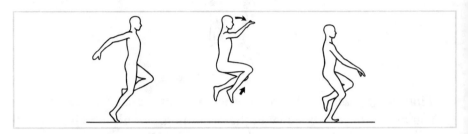

Triple Jump Bounding (optional). This is probably the most difficult drill, so you may want to attempt it only after building strength by doing the other drills for a while. Standing on one foot, hop up quickly, bringing your bent jumping knee up under your body, then extending it again to land on the ground. Use the arms in a counterclockwise circular swing to help lift your body, emphasizing the forward and upward motion. The nonhopping leg aids balance and thus can be held in any position. Focus on hopping high. Don't worry about going forward; it will happen naturally. Eventually you want to be able to hop 100 yards with each leg. Work into this exercise slowly. "It's more important to do ten hops properly than 100 of them with bad form," says Sundlun. This exercise works all the muscle groups while developing coordination.

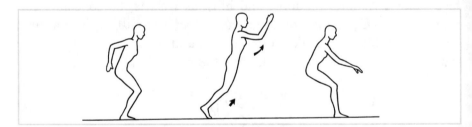

Standing Long Jumps. Starting with feet placed together flat on the ground, jump forward with feet together, extending the legs from your hips to your toes. Use your arms to help propel you. Do this for 30 yards forward and 30 yards back. This works all the muscle groups, especially the hips.

Swedish Drills. After doing the above exercises, Sundlun recommends a set of 10 to 14 100-meter sprints. In nicer, more accommodating weather, he suggests the second half of the sprints be aimed at developing acceleration. For this second half, begin the run very slowly. On every fifth step, accelerate the pace as much as possible in one step, as if shifting to the next gear. Maintain the new level of speed for five steps. No matter how slowly you start, you will quickly find yourself at top speed. Build speed until you are going as fast as possible, and then *still* keep trying to accelerate. As you accelerate, take a breath with each step, trying to keep the primary muscle groups relaxed. This is particularly the case at higher speeds, when in order to accelerate you must find additional measures to relax your body. Taking a breath tends not only to aid relaxation, but works like putting in the clutch of a car. The aim is to "learn how to find another gear."

Cross Training

11

Why cross train? Why engage in other sports? Why expend time and energy swimming and biking when running seems sufficient to promote well-being? According to writer Peter Gambaccini, who elaborates on cross training options in this chapter, complementing or even partially replacing running with some other form of workout can make sense for every level of footracer. The injured runner, forced to forsake the weekly road mileage, can choose from a wide array of cross training activities to work muscle groups and tax cardiovascular capacity. Many cross training options require low or even no impact; they offer a welcome respite from the pounding of the pavement.

> I think a current fallacy is the use of cross training to achieve success in running. You can't replace the need for higher-mileage running with another sport. However, I don't consider light weight work, such as with dumbbells, to be cross training. That is part of a runner's overall training.
>
> Cross training is great when you're injured, during an off-season, or for general fitness, but I don't believe in it as an integral part of a running program. I definitely believe that an athlete is a good runner because he or she runs.
>
> I'm not a big believer in extensive cross training to prevent injury, even if athletes claim to have injury problems that can be solved by it. For example, if an athlete comes to me with chronic muscle soreness, I examine the previous phase of training and probably discover that training wasn't done properly.

If you want to be a better runner, you've got to run more—it's as simple as that. To prove this point, I cite as an example those who are best succeeding in distance running: the Africans. The day I walk into the home of any runner in any African city, town, or village and find a StairMaster, rowing machine, or wet vest near a swimming pool, I'll be proved wrong. Until that day, I stick by my belief in the need to concentrate on putting in the running miles.

—Tom Fleming

Cross training can also prevent injuries caused by a muscular imbalance or other physical irregularities. A knee injury, for example, can be an alignment problem traceable to the relative power and weakness of adjacent muscle groups. Pure long distance runners tend to have mighty hamstrings and feeble quadriceps. However, muscle groups that work together need to be compatibly strong. It is risky to overdevelop one set and neglect the other. There are cross training solutions to this potentially disastrous problem.

Wisdom and purpose should guide your cross training. There is probably a cross training option for whatever particular weakness plagues your running. The more specific that cross training is to your needs, the more benefits you'll reap.

In addition to preventing future injuries and alleviating the stress of current ones, cross training can also make you a superior runner. Swimming enhances flexibility and even lengthens the running stride. Reasonable weight workouts give the upper body strength and tone that will keep running form intact. Bicycling fortifies the quadriceps needed to attack the tough hills. And cross-country skiing, if done properly, produces an even greater oxygen intake capacity than does running.

There's also the matter of diversion. Running is supposed to be fun. A second or third sport can alleviate monotony and inject a little joy into training.

I believe in cross training now, although I did not cross train for the first ten years of my running career, except for some water running and cycling when I was injured. But now I am using cross training on a more regular basis, such as doing a bit of skiing. I meet a lot of other athletes from other sports who cross train. I met the cyclist Connie Carpenter. She told me her husband (also a top cyclist) always skis in the winter. They need the change, she told me. It rejuvenates them.

The Swedish women masters runners are progressing, and it may be partly a result of the fact they probably do alternative sports, like skiing in the winter. In other words, they don't necessarily run 12 months of the year. I'm beginning to think that's a good idea—to do something different, like skate skiing or cross-country skiing, or whatever gives you the results.

Other forms of training revitalize you. You can get tired just doing one sport all the time. The body loves variety. The body is the same as the seasons: It likes change.

—Priscilla Welch

Runners on all levels report greater success and fewer injuries by reducing their mileage and cross training to make up the difference. Each runner will need to experiment, but it may be reasonable to cut running by 20 percent and substitute another sport for what's being omitted. And by alternating two aerobic activities, it virtually guarantees that all of the muscle groups are brought into play.

When embarking on a new regimen to supplement running, remember that cross training should not be an added excuse to exhaust oneself. Trying to handle a regular run and some cycling in one workout, for example, is just a hybrid form of overtraining.

Finally, start doing some serious stretching before your cross training. Your musculature will be working in entirely new ways; don't ask tight, cold, untested muscles to do new tricks.

Cycling

Bicycling has become one of the most popular and beneficial cross training options for runners. Like many runners, Dan Glickenhaus says, "I had always looked on cycling as a form of transportation, not really a way to train. I had no idea what RPMs (revolutions per minute by the bike's pedals) were." Glickenhaus has learned and then some. He's a former president of Team Red Line, New York's talented triathlon squad, and he won the Central Park Triathlon in 1989, 1990, and 1991.

Glickenhaus tasted victory as a frequent winner in New York City road races. He took up bicycling as a break from the impact of running while his injuries healed.

In the same way that many running injuries can be traced to incorrect form, cyclists will suffer if they aren't properly fitted to their bikes. Too many beginners ride with bike seats that are too low or too high, or with handlebars at an improper angle, which can cause back pain. Get an expert to fit your bike to your needs.

I cross train with bike riding. My recommendation is pretty simple. I take about 40 percent of my current aerobic training, and this includes a weekly two-hour run, and convert it into biking. For example, the two-hour run is sometimes replaced by a three-hour bike ride. However, this conversion does not include the anaerobic running: my twice-weekly interval training. The reason I have made this adjustment to biking is to relieve the stress of the pounding. Biking helps one avoid injuries because it allows more recovery time between running workouts and puts less overall stress on the body.

It's the cumulative stress that causes injuries. I believe that it's not so much that you're more prone to injury as you get older, it's that the amount that you've done builds up. Everybody has a certain saturation point. Then you get hurt.

Ask [top masters runner] John Campbell. He started running when he was 38. He was accumulating stress at the same rate and in the same way as if he had been 24 when he started. He had the same four or five years of exceling without major injury problems, and then he got hurt—just like someone in his 20s would in the same situation.

The other aspect of biking for me is that I participate in the multi-sport events. It's another way to have a training goal, and an area in which I can still improve. The frustration for me, and perhaps for many others, is that at some point, we cannot improve our running times. The guy who ran 2:36 for the marathon at age 32 is likely running about three hours when he's over age 40. Maybe if he starts to ride the bike now, and he enters biathlons, he can

> feel he's improving. He gets better on the bicycle, and that's a way
> to improve his training and competition goals.
>
> —Frank Shorter

Is cycling strenuous enough for athletes accustomed to running's rigors? Glickenhaus often wears a heart rate monitor, and has found that some of his highest heart rates are at the end of hill climbs on the bike. But Glickenhaus, who once ran 80 miles per week, warns that an equivalent cycling regimen takes a lot of miles. For example, Hawaii's Ironman Triathlon includes 26.2 miles of running and 112 miles of cycling; that four-to-one ratio between the two disciplines is fairly common. Therefore you can assume that the effort of a 10k run is equal to that of a 25-mile bike ride. So cycling is definitely the sport for people who wish to train a lot and don't care about investing the time.

Cycling complements running quite well. The effort of long distance athletes in both sports is similar to a degree; they are both essentially dependent on lower body strength. However, cycling is a more thorough muscular workout than running. The quadriceps drive most of the cycling stroke, but the calf muscles are working as the pedal is pulled back up. In the tuck position assumed by serious cyclists, the lower back is conditioned as well. In hill climbs, the arm and shoulder muscles do a great deal of the pulling. For variety use a light bike ride as a warmup before a run.

Although the sports go well together, a cycling workout shouldn't be too intense if you plan to run hard the following day. Conversely, a serious track session might be followed the next day by an easy spinning bike ride with no intervals or challenging assaults on hills.

Runners who start cycling should have some concept of what a workout is, states Glickenhaus. Bike computers and watches can help calculate pedal revolutions. It's wise to start with an easy warmup loop before following with a tough one. On the flats, a cyclist may, as runners do, sprint hard for the space between two telephone poles, ease off, and then speed up again.

Hills can be a real challenge. "When you're climbing a hill, you still want to maintain 60 to 80 RPMs in lower gear," warns Glickenhaus. The urge to stand up on the pedals should be avoided. It's more efficient, and more athletically beneficial, to remain seated. It's no secret that biking, in which legs encounter resistance as they rotate, and with the knee driving higher than it does in running, will help a runner's leg rotation.

It is even possible to do a type of interval training on bicycles. In a low gear, increase the RPMs of your pedaling. If normal is 60, try 80 for one minute. A cyclist can alternate 60 RPMs and 80 RPMs for one, five, or six sets, and then finish off with a slow ride home. Both in running and cycling, speed is a product of increased turnover. This kind of bike workout will do wonders for the quadriceps, helping to balance the overdeveloped hamstring from running.

The injury-free runner will still want to do his or her serious long runs and speed workouts. But to lessen the impact and add variety, the 30- or 45-minute "easy" recovery run can give way to, for example, a two-hour bike ride.

For the more serious athlete, cycling requires extra concentration. An opponent's surge in a road race may seem like a decisive move, but Dan Glickenhaus suggests, "In cycling you have to watch even more closely. If someone makes a break, he can be gone in a matter of seconds." It's also important in bike racing to be extra attentive for safety reasons. Taking an elbow in a crowded pack of runners is one thing. In a throng of cyclists, the same thing at high speed can cause a massive collision and serious injury.

Cross-Country Skiing

Cross-country skiing is a cross training option to which many runners quite sensibly turn in winter—and even in summer, with skis mounted on roller-skate wheels. Cross-country skiing is an excellent fitness substitute for road running. It's a long-distance sport that enhances cardiovascular fitness and utilizes many of the same muscle groups as distance running. Not surprisingly, good long-distance runners very often tend to make outstanding cross-country skiers.

As time goes on, I am more into alternative training. Biking—and mountain biking—and skiing have been my main activities in addition to running. Cross-country skiing is a way of life for many

Norwegians, and I have done it recreationally for years. I have also done the Nordic ski machine as an alternative workout when I was injured from running.

During injury, you can stay very fit with alternative sports, but be aware that resuming running still requires some adjustment. When you start running after a layoff, even if you are fit, your "tires are flat." You have to take time to get your legs used to running again. When I started running again after a period of alternative training, I wasn't breathing hard, but my legs were aching. To use the analogy of a car, it was like the engine was tip-top, but the tires were without air.

Since I retired from serious competition, I have really enjoyed doing other sports. I've had some "marathon" cross training sessions. For example, in December of 1991, I took a holiday vacation with my husband Jack. In three weeks in Austria and Germany, we covered a lot of miles: 250 skiing, 100 running and 100+ walking.

—Grete Waitz

Cross-country skiing has been traced back at least 27,000 years to Siberia. Later, it was a big asset to the Vikings in their eleventh- and twelfth-century conquests. And it can be the biggest boon of all to the cross trainer. Tests have shown that cross-country skiers have oxygen intake capabilities surpassing those of long-distance runners.

The rudiments of cross-country skiing are not difficult to master. I the beginning, it is quite like walking on skis. Going straight ahead, be advised not to lift the ski tips; keep them in contact with the snow at all times. This is facilitated by keeping your weight slightly forward.

More advanced, quicker skiing approximates the motion of running. The thrusting leg has a stronger push or kick, and the steps and the glides are longer. The weight can be well forward, and although the backs of the skis come out of the snow, the angle between the lower leg and the front of the ski should never exceed 90 degrees.

On uphill climbs with poles, the arms and shoulders get plenty of work. For going up steep, seemingly insurmountable slopes, switch to a "herringbone" technique, in which a V-shaped wedge is formed with the backs of the skis together and the fronts wide apart. For this, the poles are positioned behind the skis.

Two world-renowned Norwegian distance runners, Ingrid Kristiansen and Grete Waitz, have many years of cross-country ski experience; Kristiansen even won skiing titles before becoming a top runner. Waitz recalls that all the years that she lived in Oslo, she went skiing as part of training in winter months. She estimates that of every 12 distance workouts she would do, three or four were on skis. "That was one of the reasons I stayed injury free. Runners who have the opportunity should try cross-country skiing," she concludes.

On skis, Waitz discovered, "You get tired in a different way. You spend more time out there." She calculated that to get the equivalent exercise value, she would have to spend two minutes on skis for every one minute she'd run. "A ten-mile run would be like two hours skiing," she figured. Cross-country skiing, in which legs tend to be closer together and the body is less erect than in running, sometimes left Waitz with soreness in her inner thighs and lower back, strengthening those areas in the process. Skiers who use their poles to propel themselves can strengthen the upper body and firm up their abdomen. To regain her running form, Waitz would not ski during the week of an important race.

Much of the United States gets enough snow for you to try this sport in winter months. A mere two or three inches on the ground in a local park or woods is enough to merit giving cross-country skiing a try.

Skate Skiing

In recent years, a form of skating has been incorporated into cross-country skiing technique. Skate skiing is more or less what the name suggests. The push with the skis is more to the sides than straight ahead, and more extensive use of the poles is required. As a "skating" skier, you'll use more muscles and build more power than with the conventional technique. The quadriceps will be strengthened, and the abdominal and back muscles will also be conditioned.

Downhill Skiing

Downhill skiing isn't usually considered a valuable form of cross training, but if you've seen Alberto Tomba or A. J. Kitt whooshing down a slope at 60 miles per hour for over two minutes, you begin to perceive that this is physical work. Two of cross training's greatest benefits, a break from pounding and a chance to enhance flexibility, are features of downhill skiing. And few sports are as exhilarating as skiing. In training, skiers do an exercise in which, from a frog-like posture, they leap up and down repeatedly. The goal is to develop "explosive" quadriceps.

In general, I just try to stay active. Other than running, my sports of passion are climbing, hiking, fly fishing, and tennis—although I've never mastered tennis. I ski quite well, and sometimes I do in-line skating.

In addition to running, I also work out in a gym at NBC. About two years ago, G.E. [General Electric] put in an excellent gym. It has StairMaster, weights, computerized systems, and counselors, and attendance is good. I don't always work out twice a day, but I definitely go to the gym if I don't run. I do the ergometer, or I may do the StairMaster. If I run, I also go to the gym some of the time. I do both workouts when I feel I need to get in better shape. Right now, I'm trying to get in very good aerobic shape for a winter climb with world-class climbers.

When I have to miss a run, I just have to make the decision to let it go. The last time I was in Moscow, for example, I didn't run nearly as much as I wanted to. By the time I did my work I was simply too exhausted. It was raining, and not terribly inviting to go out. In cases like that, I'll do things like go to the front desk of the hotel and ask where the stairwell is. Then I'll do a workout like running up 13 flights. In fact, I run six flights of stairs from my office to the studio every evening before I go on the air.

—Tom Brokaw

Weight Training

Runners are not advised to "pump up" their bodies with heavy iron weights, but weight training with moderate weights and numerous repetitions is often recommended. Some people are now recommending heavier weights and fewer repetitions for runners. A coach or an observant running partner may be able to point out a flaw in your form that is traceable to weakness in a particular muscle group. Training with weights can alleviate such a weakness.

Many runners who do no other exercise have underdeveloped upper bodies; these athletes often overlook the fact that what happens from the waist up also matters in running. Arms are steering mechanisms; they provide balance, and prevent toppling over or veering to one side. In addition, vigorous arm motion is part of a powerful finishing kick. So strengthening the upper body by weight training can contribute to better running performance. Toning and strengthening muscles with weights can assist in preventing injuries. Weight training has its cardiovascular benefits, too.

While lifting weights, concentrate on regular breathing, really filling your lungs with oxygen. Breathe deeply during the easy part of lifting/lowering, and expel the air during the effort. A comprehensive weight workout can become even more strenuous and aerobically beneficial if you move very quickly, or literally dash, from one weight station to another, not pausing to rest and completely catch your breath. Triathlete Bill Noel goes through his series of 17 separate Nautilus exercises in under 30 minutes.

Bench presses, or overhead presses with free weights, will not only give the arms and shoulders strength but will also add tone and coordination. Rather than striving to lift your absolute maximum, as a runner you're better off working with about two-thirds of what you can lift. If 150 pounds is your best press, you should try sets of 100-pound lifts, perhaps four to six lifts per set. Make it feel like an effort, but don't strain yourself and risk injury.

There are specific weight exercises which condition each muscle group. With "squats," the bar of weight is placed on the shoulders behind the neck, and the weight is taken down by bending the knees and then raising up again. The quadriceps provide most of the upward thrust. Experimentation will determine what's comfortable, but it's unwise to bend until the thighs dip below a 90-degree angle; to do so may put undue strain on the knees and negate the positive effect on the quadriceps. Runners can also try "lungers," again for the quadriceps. In this exercise, with the weight on the shoulders, the athlete steps forward nearly as far as possible with the left leg, then steps back, and does the same maneuver with the right.

Several recently published studies and books have shown that strength training (weights) can increase leg strength and time to exhaustion without a corresponding increase in maximal oxygen consumption. This is according to an article in *American Athletics*, which says that there is evidence that increased strength will also reduce the incidence of injury in endurance athletes. Furthermore, the data from these studies do not demonstrate any negative performance effects from adding heavy-resistance training to ongoing endurance training programs. However, the article cautions that a running/resistance program combination must be fashioned so as not to result in overtraining.

—Fitness Features

Pull-downs are one of the most dependable exercises for developing all of the major upper back muscles and the biceps. From a sitting position, the weight is pulled from over the head down behind the neck to the shoulders, and raised up again. Leg curls are the best weight routine for the hamstrings. Lying on the stomach on a bench, the athlete places his or her feet behind the weight apparatus, and "curls" it by pulling the weight up toward the hamstrings.

It's not unusual to see runners or walkers carry weights in their arms as they stride down the road. This makes some sense, but only if proper form is maintained, and heavy weights are not recommended. Alternating left and right arm curls with light dumbbells in synchronization with your natural running motion is fine. But those athletes who run while weights dangle at their sides, with elbows virtually locked and little arm movement at all will be rewarded for their efforts with nothing but strained elbow and shoulder joints.

Stair Training

At New York's Downing Stadium, the site of the 1991 TAC/USA Track and Field Championships, onlookers watched admiringly as a pair of hardy athletes ran up and down the concrete stairs in every one of the stadium's 50-odd sections.

One needn't be quite so ambitious, but stair training is highly recommended. It can tax your aerobic capacity every bit as much as hills do, and like hills, stair training puts special emphasis on the quadriceps. It also requires a slightly higher than usual knee lift to reach the next stair, thus serving to extend the hamstrings. Stair training can help erase the tendency to run with a shuffle, too close to the ground.

Stair climbing is now a major activity in health clubs. Maybe it was partly inspired by the Empire State Building Run-Up, a race we started in 1978. Who could have guessed that what seemed then like such a "kooky" idea (and still does to many I suppose) would become a mainstream form of exercise.

In the late 1970s, someone from one of our public relations companies came to us about holding a race up 86 flights of stairs in the Empire State Building. I immediately loved the idea. In the beginning, we limited it to only ultramarathon runners. I thought those were the people who could best ascend the 1575 steps. I was actually wrong. A miler could probably do better. Eventually, we opened it up to about 100 qualified athletes from various sports, but mostly runners. The Run-Up has spawned similar events in places like Melbourne, Australia, and Chicago. In fact, every year the winner of the Melbourne event is awarded a trip to our event. The Run-Up has even created talk about having a Grand Prix of stair climbing races in buildings.

Traditionally, there has been an Empire State Building Run-Up for the staff preceding the main event. I've done it about eight times. To train for it, about a month before, I regularly run up the 20 flights of stairs in my building.

This is one event in which experience is key. Every athlete who does the Run-Up for the first time can make the common and critical error of starting too fast. My record for the Empire State Building is 15:59. That would actually put me in the middle of the pack in the main event.

This event is probably one of the hardest things I've ever done. There's no air in the stairwell, so it's tough to breathe. Afterwards, you cough like a smoker. It sounds a little gruesome, but it's really a great event. The Empire State Building is one of the most charismatic buildings in the world. It wasn't built for runners, but the fact is, the event has become a permanent feature, just like King Kong, who has also taken part (as a runner in costume). And people come from all over the country, and the world, to run this race.

After my illness, I knew I was taking back my life, and my fitness, when I resumed my stair climbing. For years, I walked up the ten flights of stairs to my apartment every day. Actually, I used to run them, and once got as fast as climbing those stairs in 39 seconds. For awhile after getting sick, though, I didn't even walk the stairs. It's so solitary in the stairwell, I was afraid I'd expire and no one would find me! Now I do those stairs every other day in a minute and a half. It's a lot slower than my record, but the important thing is, I do it.

—Fred Lebow

There's a key difference between hills and stairs, however. When running up stairs, only the toes and the forefoot need to strike the ground. The heel is out over the edge of each step, with only air underneath it. Stairs may be a training antidote to regular running, which can aggravate heel, Achilles tendon, and plantar fascia woes.

Stair training requires that the entire body's weight be lifted to ascend each stair. It's tiring. A session on stairs is not a long-distance haul; these should be short, intense workouts, done after a sufficient warmup.

Recently, the equivalent of stair training has been made possible by variously named products that are essentially platforms set at different heights to approximate a single step on a flight of stairs. These devices are portable and require very little space. On these platforms, you can step up and step down repeatedly, deriving the benefits of a moderate-paced run with only a fraction of the usual impact to the lower body.

The height at which you set these platforms determines the difficulty of the workout, particularly the amount of work the quadriceps, hamstrings, and gluteals have to do. Runners with certain injuries to the knee joint find that the afflicted area can be strengthened with this regimen. Doing the stepping in conjunction with light hand weights can create a more complete workout, doing wonders for the deltoids, triceps, and biceps as well.

Realize, of course, that just walking up stairs will have a positive effect on running form. You will still reap the benefits of a moderate aerobic workout, strengthen the quadriceps with each step, and stretch the hamstring and gluteal muscles in a manner that will loosen and lengthen your running stride.

Swimming

The attraction of swimming as cross training is obvious on several counts. Swimming is a zero impact sport, a total respite from pounding the road. The most severely stressed running muscles get a bigger break in swimming than in cycling or cross-country skiing. The aerobic and anaerobic effects of running can be virtually duplicated in swimming, if training distances are properly selected. And swimming utilizes many muscles neglected by runners—the shoulder and arm muscles, to be sure, but also other key groups, such as hip flexors and hip abductors, which are needed to propel a swimmer through the greater resistance of water. Well-trained swimmers also have a more complete range of motion in their joints than runners. Their shoulders and ankles are looser.

For the healthy, injury-free runner, swimming may be ideal as the second sport of a single day's exercise. Legs that are too weary to contemplate pedaling a bicycle can still handle a half hour in the pool or a swim at the beach.

There are also psychological reasons to swim. While swimming, an athlete is quite literally in another element. The water is calm and quiet; a form of sensory deprivation transpires. In this regard, swimming can be a more relaxing and contemplative endeavor than running.

"The pool is fantastic. We've had tremendous results," states John McDonnell, who directs his champion University of Arkansas cross-country and track athletes off the road and track and into the water. "We simulate an interval workout in the pool, the same effort as on a run." The basis for a swimmer's interval workouts is similar to running's training techniques. McDonnell says, however, "If the kid is a good swimmer, we make him swim, but not if he's swallowing water and he's just trying to survive. If that's the case, we give him an aqua vest." The athlete then runs in water, buoyed by his apparel.

Doug Stern, whose program for deep water running appears in this book, conducts special classes in New York for runners whom he tries to turn into superior swimmers—and, therefore, superior runners. "Runners come in with handicaps," Stern has found. "They have very inflexible ankles; they can't point their toes out as if they were ballet dancers." It's crucial to increase ankle flexibility, he says, "to get on top of the water." Moreover, according to Stern, "Runners have no upper body strength. They have no upper body localized endurance. Breathing patterns go down the tubes." Unless they adapt to water, even well-conditioned runners tire quickly, and swimming is of little use.

Why is the bendability of ankles important to runners? After a foot has landed on the ground, better ankle flexion increases stride length and frequency by making the push off that foot more forceful and powerful than it would be if the ankle were tight.

To aid ankle flexibility, which diminishes after childhood, Stern himself walks around barefoot almost all of the time at home. When seated, he places his toes as far behind himself as possible, pushing the tops of the toes down on the floor and forcing his heel and calf closer together. As a result, Stern, who is in his late 40s, has greater ankle flexion than most people.

If a runner moonlighting as a swimmer doesn't have a kick in the water, Stern suggests using fins. After the fins come off, kicking should be easier, and so should swimming. A strong kick elevates and stabilizes the swimmer's body. A freestyle sprinter will ride almost atop the water; as a consequence, the arms turn over faster. One difficult drill, in which, while kicking, the head is up and looking straight ahead and the hands are held together with arms extended, helps the novice swimmer master the desired high position in the water.

There are techniques for directing the physical conditioning of swimming toward a particular muscle group. A "pull buoy" stuck between the legs, rendering them less mobile, isolates the arms and requires them to provide 100 percent of the thrust through the water. Conversely, a kickboard, a floating device held in front by fully extended arms, requires that the legs do all the work.

As in other cross training options, swimming workouts can be geared for local muscular endurance. The huge sweep of the butterfly stroke, in which the arms move in a circular motion away from the shoulders, may be the most aggressive way of training the chest and shoulder muscles. Kicking while laying on one's back, on the other hand, is the most efficient way for a swimmer to condition the hamstrings. And enough freestyling with the correct form—as near to hydroplaning as is feasible—will strengthen the lower back. The runner-cum-swimmer may emerge from freestyle with improved posture and less of a swayback, which means more erect running form.

Since the water through which swimmers glide is far heavier than even the thickest air through which runners stride, swimming can be more taxing to the cardiovascular system The equivalent of a running session in swimming is easy to calculate. It takes four times as long swimming to cover the same distance running. For repeat 400s on the track, substitute repeat 100s in the pool. Instead of a six-mile run, do a mile and a half swim.

Circuit Training

When he was at his peak, winning three New York City Marathons and a Boston Marathon, Alberto Salazar merely supplemented his running with situps and pushups. Pushups and situps are often part of an ingenious supplement to a runner's training that goes by a variety of names, but is commonly known as a par course (also called circuit training). The par course shares some of the particulars of the obstacle courses that military boot camp recruits are required to traverse. In essence, the course is a series of exercise stations set along a runner's outdoor trail. Within a half-mile or mile loop, these exercise stations can be staggered at 50- or 100-yard intervals; the precise layout is largely contingent on the available space. The running and the exercises can be fully integrated into a single routine, akin to a cross-country race with miscellaneous obstacles, or perhaps an extremely daunting steeplechase.

The particulars of a par course can include situps on a negative incline platform (on which the head is lower than the feet), chinup bars (at different heights, to accommodate runners of various sizes), a pushup station, a balance beam, and a horizontal ladder, which an athlete crosses hand-over-hand. There is often a platform (or, for rural tastes, an evenly planed tree trunk) on which to step up and down as many times as possible within 30 seconds. Include this par course as part of a run to work the abdominals, shoulders, and arms, and lift knees higher than on a normal run. This is serious cross training. In fact, if you have a running-related injury, it's worth doing the par course all by itself.

The name "par course" comes from Europe, where Oregon native Steve Prefontaine, the 1972 U.S. Olympian at 5000 meters, first encountered it. A par course was later incorporated into one of the fabled saw-dust running paths of Eugene, Oregon, that is now known as Pre's Trail. Variations of the par course abound; some large corporations, such as IBM, even have them in their headquarters' parking lots.

Rowing

Rowing doesn't require a sylvan river or neighborhood pond. Good health clubs have rowing machines that very closely approximately a real rowboat. These devices can be purchased for in-home use as well. Rowing can be done as languidly or as feverishly as suits the cross train-er, but proper form is crucial to avert injury and reap rowing's benefits. A rower should keep the back straight, and make sure to push with the legs to make progress rather than pull with the back. Rowing indoors is a perfect alternative in foul weather, and it's a low impact method of strengthening quadriceps and calf muscles. Sprint intervals can even pro-duce an anaerobic workout. In general, a cross trainer should row two miles for the exercise effects of a one-mile run.

Basketball

Basketball, believe it or not, can be a valuable complement to road running. In addition to the obvious running up and down the 30-yard court, there's a chance to add spring to one's step. Comedian Joe Bolster is co-host of cable TV's *Sports Monster*, where his guests have includ-ed Bill Rodgers, Frank Shorter, and Mike Powell. At Denison University in Ohio, Bolster was a 1:53 half-miler, but he was also a guard on the varsity basketball team. He would often run a track meet and play in a basketball game on the same day. Obviously, the track meet, where any amount of fatigue would be a curse, had to come first in the order.

"The basketball really provided the speedwork," explains the come-dian. "You do sustained bursts at sprint level," says Bolster, whose coach had him do baseline-to-baseline sprint repeats in practice. After those practices, Bolster would go out and run ten miles. Basketball gave Bolster a little extra training that didn't hurt his running, and the aspect of play and camaraderie were added benefits.

Merrell Noden, who ran at Princeton and Oxford and now covers track, cross country, and other sports for *Sports Illustrated*, concurs that basketball has benefits. He explains, "When I try to get a rebound and

I go up for the ball three times in five seconds, I think I'm helping my running."

Volleyball

If rebounding in basketball helps a runner, it follows that volleyball would also be a boon. The constant vertical leaping from a poised and crouched position is clearly helpful to the quadriceps and the calf muscles. Games like basketball and volleyball, pitched team battles, can also help hone a runner's competitive edge.

Tennis

"You don't play tennis to get in shape; you get in shape to play tennis." That old adage is stressed by Peter Sikowitz, a former editor at *World Tennis* and current editor of *Men's Fitness*. Sikowitz is an athlete who began jogging to become a better tennis player. He became a "born-again runner at 30," and tennis was reduced to a secondary concern.

To sharpen himself for tennis, Sikowitz would do a four- or five-mile jog, and some side-to-side drills. "I found it really did help my tennis," says Sikowitz. "I'm sort of an endurance athlete anyway. I could stay out on the court all day."

Tennis training and a runner's training can indeed overlap. "A runner who wants to play tennis would be well advised to do some 200-meter intervals," says Sikowitz, since in tennis you go from a stationary position to a full sprint.

A runner not used to playing tennis will feel a bit of stress in the buttocks muscles, which get the conditioning, and Sikowitz figures tennis is half an upper body workout, particularly when a player is stretching to fire a fierce overhand serve.

For a runner, says Sikowitz, the benefits of tennis are mostly psychological and social. "Those are very important benefits. You're still outdoors; you're able to hang out with people of different ability." The latter is not true, of course, during a training run.

A runner's schedule can probably accommodate two tennis sessions weekly, an hour apiece for singles or two hours each for doubles. On the court, the runner is able to concentrate on another activity. "It's a mental vacation from running," explains Sikowitz.

Squash

Squash may be a more reasonable alternative to tennis, especially for urbanites. In a crowded metropolis, squash requires less space than tennis. It tends to be less expensive, and even a half-hour can be a useful workout. Having a less talented playing partner is less of a problem than in tennis; keeping the squash ball in play with easy volleying is simpler.

Like tennis, squash is a racket game, with smaller implements: a hard rubber ball and a playing surface in which all four walls—including the one behind you—are part of the game. It may require quicker reflexes and a better sense of geometry than tennis. But both games reward sharp, precise, intelligent shotmaking, and an athlete who excels at one game is often an ace at the other.

In squash, players are on their toes, ready to move in any direction in an instant. There is a lot of short sprinting involved, and the quadriceps are taxed.

Typically, a 60-minute squash game is equal in energy expenditure to a five- to eight-mile run.

Depending on your purpose, and that of your partner, squash and tennis can be played with ferocity or quite lackadaisically. It should be easy to fit in a game of whatever intensity is appropriate for your training.

In-Line Skating

At the dawn of the '90s, it often appeared that runners and reckless daredevils on in-line skates were competing for the same premium recreational space on American roadways. Runners didn't appreciate these new athletes, who career down hills in near kamikaze fashion, apparently expecting the runners to get out of their way.

By 1992, more and more avid runners had sheepishly revealed a little secret. They also fancied Rollerblades. The proper appellation for this new sport, which features boots with a single row of hard wheels from front to back, is "in-line skating." Skating shouldn't hurt runners, and can actually be a useful exercise respite.

In-line skating has already become a serious competitive sport. For example, the International In-Line Skate Association sponsors a 50K Championship in Central Park in New York; their most prestigious event is the Athens to Atlanta 85-Mile Marathon in Georgia in October.

Steve Novak, the president of the New York Road Skaters Association, submits that in-line skating is an excellent cross training activity for running as well as a literal change of pace. "And as opposed to running, in-line skating permits more of a sense of freedom," says Novak.

The muscles that drive in-line skaters are similar to the ones brought to bear in cycling. "You use a little more of the quadriceps. You are generally bent over, supporting your upper body weight with your back," Novak explains. The necessary arm swing, from the elbow forward, resembles what one strives for as a runner.

On in-line skates, the hips are behind the arms. An in-line skater's knees are bent for a lower center of gravity to improve balance and make it easier to recover from stumbles. People in a more upright posture will be flailing their arms wildly to keep from crashing.

Because of the single line of wheels, the motion of in-line skating is closer to ice skating than to traditional roller skating, which uses four wheels. In fact, the story goes that in-line skating was developed by hockey skaters in the mid-1970s.

As for stopping—the preferred method is to turn the hard rubber heel brake towards the pavement. Another option is "T-stopping," in which one foot turns sideways at a 90-degree angle to the forward position.

Sprint races of 200, 400, or 800 meters for in-line skaters are not unknown, but a more common and popular distance is 10,000 meters. Good 10k times are under 17 minutes, corresponding to a good runner's expectations for 5k. In-line skaters will not charge from the start as quickly as runners, but it is easier for them to maintain racing speed once it has been reached. The quality of the pavement will have an effect; ripples and bumps will slow down a competitive in-line skater. Pack drafting, with tactics and strategy similar to cycling, will also cause a variance in racing times.

A no-impact sport, in-line skating generates few if any knee injuries, shinsplints, or Achilles tendon ailments. A talented in-line skater will compete at distances from 5k to 150k. To handle that range, a day's training could include intervals, long distance at medium exertion, and sprints.

"Technique is so critical," stresses Steve Novak. "You can be in aerobic shape, but if you don't have technique, you can be defeated easily. Therefore," suggests Novak, "it is sometimes advisable to skate slowly or moderately and concentrate more fully on form."

Novak observes, "When you skate, it's not like running. You push straight out to the side. Keep the knees bent all of the time. The more bent the knee, the more you can push out to the side with your legs." Keep your body weight on the back of your heels. The ideal knee bend forms a 90-degree angle between the upper and lower legs, with the upper body bent slightly forward for wind resistance. A beginner should merely start by standing on the skates to practice balancing. Begin skating on a flat, smooth area, free of foot traffic and other obstructions.

Novak concedes that running "is a more concentrated exercise. You would have to skate for a longer period of time to equal running effort. In skating you have the opportunity to cease exertion, because you're rolling. In running, you're either running or you're not." Still, in-line skating can be a tonic for the runner's spirit. One of the primary attractions of the sport is that skating harkens back to our youth, concludes Novak.

Roller Skating

Long before in-line skating became a recreational phenomenon of the '90s, Irene Jackson's Central Park Track Club teammates would see her weave in and out of their midst on more traditional four-wheel roller skates. Jackson, a medalist at the Colgate Games and in the women's masters race at the Fifth Avenue Mile, suffers periodically from knee problems. Skating is not a high impact sport, but the impetus of forward force exercises the quadriceps. Jackson also discovered that with roller skating, she uses her upper body a lot.

With all forms of skates and skis, the foot is essentially stabilized; there's no forefoot or heel striking, and far less stress on the arch. Skating and skiing may be an alternative training method, then, for runners whose Achilles tendons or plantar fascia are ailing.

Ice Skating

Particularly if you can find a rink that isn't overcrowded, ice skating is a pleasant complement to running. Again, the thrust comes from the quadriceps, and the arm swing required for balance can loosen upper body muscles. This is a sport where form counts, so concentration is key. And concentration—so essential as the mind wavers in the fourth and fifth miles of a 10K—is a quality worth practicing.

Peter Downs, a 34-year-old New York businessman, once called himself "a conservative in terms of my athletic options." He used to laugh at people who sought exotic alternatives to running. "I'm someone who's really hard to convince about cross training. I'm a running purist. I just want to be a runner. But after 17 years…."

After 17 years, Downs cleared the snow off the frozen pond near his country home and found that anyone who's skied can ice skate. "If you have any athletic ability, you'll feel like I did. Within an hour, I was flying around the pond like Eric Heiden. And it's a great workout on your butt muscles and your legs. Within five or seven minutes, you feel winded from skating. I was out for a half-hour. I feel I got the equivalent of a three-mile jog." Ice skating is also relatively inexpensive. At a rink, you can rent skates, and Downs acquired a pair of Chinese blades for $40.

Snowshoes

The list of winter alternatives goes on. Janis Klecker, the Minnesotan who won the 1992 U.S. Olympic Marathon trials, customarily included two four-mile sessions on snowshoes in her weekly training regimen. The meshed snowshoes often sink three or four inches into frozen snow. With that kind of resistance, a step out of the snow must be a high and wide step. Any such exaggeration of a normal step taxes the muscles in a new way. The quadriceps feel the weight as they pull out of the snow, and the hamstring and buttocks muscles are exercised by the necessary high knee lift. Snowshoeing, which could be considered a type of winter hiking, is also another respite for runners with foot and lower leg ailments. The wide, flat surface of the snowshoes disperses the impact of each footstrike.

Boxing

Any exercise that doesn't hurt a runner is likely to help. The great jazz trumpeter Miles Davis trained for decades as a boxer. He wasn't going to risk his embouchure by getting pummeled in the ring, but he did punch the light and heavy bags, utilizing his fast on-the-toes footwork as he did so. Listen to any of his albums and you can hear that he was cardiovascularly fit. Punching the bags develops the shoulder and arm muscles so often neglected by runners, as well. In fact, a number of New York runners also work out with boxing.

Hitting the bags with a regular cadence requires coordination, the same coordination a runner prays for when his/her form is going to pieces late in a race. Because coordination is such a prized commodity, another bit of a boxer's training, jumping rope, can also help runners. The wrists and forearms, which should drive a racer forward in pistonlike fashion, get plenty of work as they turn the rope, and the jumping itself does wonders for the calf muscles. This is another form of training in which an athlete can alternate slower, leisurely segments with the equivalent of speed sessions. A 30-second interval in which you swing the rope as quickly and jump as lively as you can certainly has the anaerobic benefits of a 200-meter run.

To burn calories, get fit, add variety to your running—why not jump rope? Here are a few tips on the activity from *Running and FitNews*. To be sure the rope is the right length, stand on the middle of it and raise the ends up the sides of your body. The handles should reach your armpits. When jumping, don't grip the handles too tightly. Also, use your wrists, not your arms, to turn the rope. Your shoulders will get sore if you use your arms too much. Jump lightly and only as high as you need to clear the rope. Maintain good posture and keep your knees slightly bent. Try to jump for one to five minutes, working your way up to a total of 20 minutes for a good aerobic workout. Vary your workouts. Learn to jump using one and two feet, alternating feet, skipping, jumping double time, and crossing over the rope.

—Fitness Features

Undoubtedly, you can conjure up even more physical endeavors that can serve as complements and alternatives to running. The only requirement is: Always keep in mind that cross training should be aimed at preserving and protecting your body, and conditioning it in ways that the running motion is not able to do.

Deep Water Running

Doug Stern began teaching deep water running in 1970, when one of his high school students was forced off the track due to injury. That student was Steve Williams, who went on to become a world-class sprinter. To date, Stern, an avid NYRRC member, has instructed thousands of athletes who have gone through his various swim programs.

Following the New York City Marathon in 1990, Stern began conducting deep water running classes for runners in the New York area, initially to aid marathoners' recovery. Since then, he has taught hundreds of runners the deep water system. The benefits of deep water running and a do-it-yourself workout are described in this chapter by Stern.

"As a swimming teacher and coach, I've been surrounded by water all my life. I have always been a believer in the general power of water. Water is our most natural environment. It is where we are initially reared, in the womb, and it remains the most supportive and relaxing medium in which to be," Stern explains. "Water takes the stress off the body. When I am in the water, I feel I'm being cradled, held there. Therefore, it makes sense to use water to bring us back to health (in the case of injury) and to develop strength and stamina, while simultaneously benefiting from this sense of being nurtured."

Water has certain characteristics that make it ideal for nonweight-bearing resistance training. The most obvious is its buoyant effect. Because you float at, or near, the surface of the water, you can run suspended in the water without pounding or jarring your feet or joints. Second, water is viscous, or thicker than air. As you move your arms and legs through the water, you encounter tremendous resistance. This resistance can be used to strengthen both muscles and joints. The faster you move your arms and legs, the greater the resistance, and therefore the harder the workout and the greater the strength gain.

Deep water running is exactly what the name says. It is not aqua jogging, nor is it aqua aerobics. It is a system meant to most accurately simulate and enhance the act of running. It provides all the benefits of the land activity, yet with the safety and ease of an exercise performed in liquid.

The attributes of deep water running are many. Not only does it allow you to run without the stress of pounding, but it also enhances flexibility and helps speed the blood flow to the heart. That's because on land, gravity concentrates the blood in the lower body. Because of more efficient blood flow to the heart, all water activity promotes faster recuperation from bouts of intense exercise.

Another advantage of water is its cooling effect. On land, the body temperature rises more quickly; thus you are forced to intersperse hard running with jogging or walking, largely to allow for cooling of the body. In water, because body heat is more quickly dissipated, one needs a fraction of the time to recover. It's also a lot safer in regulating body temperature during critical times—such as in the hot summer months or during pregnancy. (Pregnant women can also avoid stress on muscles and joints by doing light deep water running.)

The properties of water afford an excellent opportunity to work on running form. On land, how can you stop in mid-stride to check your form? Impossible. But in water you run as if in slow motion, facilitating a better examination and development of running form. Better form means more efficient running. This translates to longer and faster running.

The benefits of deep water running are many. It increases range of motion and builds strength and cardiovascular conditioning. It enhances muscular endurance and flexibility—all of this without the risk of injury.

Stern says three types of runners are well served by water running.

1. The injured, who can use water to recuperate from biomechanical or overuse injuries. Runners with every type of injury have been represented in deep water running classes, including sufferers of Achilles tendinitis, stress fractures, metatarsal problems, and shinsplints. They have often been referred by physicians,

chiropractors, and physical therapists—or they hear about the classes through NYRRC publicity or by word of mouth.

In the water, those who would normally be forced to stop running entirely can allow injuries to be repaired by a break from running on land and simultaneously continue uninterrupted cardiovascular fitness activity. One of the additional benefits of deep water running is that muscles, joints, and their supporting structures are strengthened, thus protecting the body from future injury.

2. The beginner, who because of obesity or a sedentary lifestyle, is not yet able to run on land. Water running allows this category of runner to develop ability in a more supportive medium. In moving their legs at their own pace, these people don't tire as easily as they may be inclined to do on land. Some people come to running by testing themselves first in the water.

3. The fit athlete, who wants to intensify speedwork and fitness, yet avoid injury. The benefits of water running for fit athletes were noticed immediately after a series of classes was first begun—the day following the 1991 New York City Marathon. This system of active rest resulted in much quicker recovery for marathoners.

Instead of spending seven days running on land, a runner may want to replace one day with deep water running, for example, to recover from a harder effort. Not only does this lessen the stress of continuously running day after day, but a change in the training environment also adds variety.

Equipment

Although it is possible to do deep water running without a flotation device, Stern believes it is best to use one. This is especially true in the beginning, when learning proper technique. A flotation device keeps you above the water with little effort, which enhances the supportive nature of the water. There are many flotation devices on the market, from vests to belts.

The Workout

Stand in shallow water, about four feet deep. Begin by swinging the arms in a pendulum fashion, as you would for running. Emphasize pushing the elbows back and keeping the pendulum close enough to your body to graze the thigh with the thumb on the back swing.

When you are comfortable with the arm swing, begin moving your feet in high stepping fashion, coordinating the stepping with the arm lift (opposite arm and leg, just like in land running). Do this for one to five minutes, working your way down to a shorter time in future sessions after you have perfected the exercise.

Begin moving forward while doing this motion, slowly progressing to deep water until your feet can no longer touch the bottom.

Concentrate on running tall, but with no tension. To do this, keep the chest up and forward and the hips under the shoulders (that is, do not let the buttocks stick out). The facial muscles should remain relaxed—chin dropped and mouth open. Breathe naturally.

As you perform the workout, you may naturally move about, but even if you remain in one place, it is not important. Warm up by gently running for five minutes.

Strength Development

Arm Crossovers. While running, extend arms to your side, elbows straight, palms facing forward. Pull arms until they cross over in front. Then turn the palms outward and push the arms back as far as possible. On each crossover, alternate which arm finishes on top. Repeat for two minutes. This exercise strengthens chest and back muscles and develops shoulder flexibility. (Remember, in this and all water exercises, the faster you move, the greater the resistance, thus the more strength required and developed.)

Crunches (Situps). With hands paddling (sculling) at your sides to keep afloat, lie on your back and bring your body in a "V" position (that is, buttocks toward pool bottom). Flex toes upward as if pulling water

toward your chest. Pull your knees as far to the chest as possible, then return to original position. Be conscious of the feet pulling the water in and pushing it away on each movement. Do these crunches for two minutes at a comfortable pace. This exercise strengthens the abdominals.

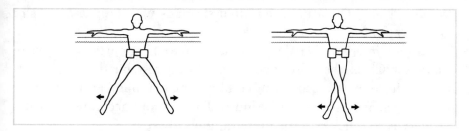

Abductor (Outer Thigh)/Adductor (Inner Thigh). Run to the pool wall. With your back facing the wall, extend your arms straight to the sides and hold on to the side or gutter of the pool. Extend the legs to your sides in a split position. Knees should be straight. Pull both legs together like scissors and cross them, alternating left and right legs in front. Push legs out to return to original position. Do this exercise for two minutes. This exercise strengthens inner and outer thighs, which help stabilize and give balance to the leg, and improves biomechanics.

Leg Crossovers. Maintain the same position as above, with your hands holding the sides of the pool. Point your legs straight under you, toward pool bottom. Pull the right leg across your body, bringing it as far as possible toward the left hand. Rotate the hips to facilitate this movement. Returning to starting position, reverse legs, with the left leg swinging toward the right arm. Do one swing per leg at a time, alternating right and left legs. Do this exercise for two minutes. This exercise strengthens quadriceps and inner thigh, and stretches hip flexors and shoulders.

Running

Now you're ready to do a deep water running workout. Begin with three minutes of gentle running, concentrating on form and building speed. Remember to continue to drive the arms, so that the elbows are swinging back. The arm swing often shortens with fatigue or loss of concentration.

Fashion interval or fartlek running of 20 to 25 minutes, with appropriate rest. Check the pulse at your neck during rest, but do so by counting only for only ten seconds and multiplying that number by six to get the number of beats for one minute. This is more accurate, as water recovery is so quick that the pulse rapidly slows.

Cadence is leg turnover. According to Doug Stern, it is an important aspect of deep water running. Cadence is also stride frequency—that is, the speed at which your legs are moving, coupled with stride length. Cadence improves by increasing range of motion, which is developed with deep water running.

Check cadence by counting one leg turnover for 15 seconds. Every minute you run, count cadence for 15 seconds to make sure you are continuing to run at the same pace, or faster. As a basis of comparison, and to check progress, it is good to check cadence while running on land as well.

It is good to be aware of the cadence of your legs during fast water running. Checking cadence helps keep you focused, since it can be easy

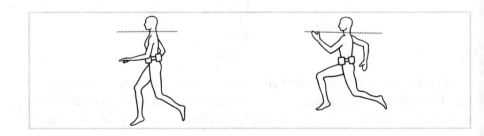

to space out in the water. In addition, good cadence will develop quicker running on land.

After hard running time has elapsed, spend five minutes cooling down with slow running.

Post-Workout Stretch

Do this gentle and comfortable stretch by facing the pool wall, and with your arms extended straight out in front of you, hold on to the side or gutter. Start with your feet under the water on the wall, knees bent. Keeping the knees bent, slowly walk your feet up the wall, stopping every few feet to straighten the legs and stretch. Finish when you have walked your legs all the way up to your hands. The entire cycle should take two minutes.

This stretch serves the same purpose as touching your palms to the ground on land. It stretches the hamstrings, calves, and Achilles tendons.

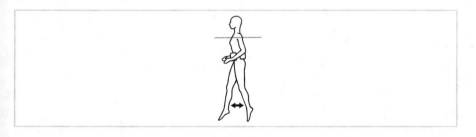

Finish the entire workout by gently shaking your legs out under water.

Power Yoga
Workout

Beryl Bender Birch began teaching yoga to ten runners a decade ago. Today, between 500 to 1000 people per week are enrolled in her course, which enables them to incorporate yoga techniques into their fitness and running programs.

"Everyone knows running is great for the cardiovascular system. However, it's also a fact that the sport dramatically tightens certain muscle groups while doing nothing for others." According to Bender Birch, "The Power Yoga Workout solves this problem by bringing a balance of strength and flexibility to a running program. When you follow the Power Yoga Workout, there's little need for any other type of training besides running. You don't need to lift weights, do calisthenics, or take stretch classes."

Bender Birch's exercises are intended to develop strength, flexibility, and mental concentration. They are also designed to ensure that muscles are worked efficiently and safely. As a companion training program to running, they comprise a fitness system that aids injury prevention and is therapy for rehabilitation from injury. According to Bender Birch and other experts, this efficiency and safety is something often greatly lacking in runners' random stretching exercises.

In addition, these exercises work the upper body, which running alone does not do. However, since the exercises below are an abbreviated form of a complete program, two exercises commonly performed by runners—pushups and situps (crunches)—will help develop additional strength and biomechanical balance.

The three laws of the Power Yoga Workout, which Bender Birch says are also applicable to any stretching program, are as follows:

1. *Be hot to stretch and stay hot while stretching.* Hot means from the inside out—sweating. Trying to stretch a cold body is like a glassblower trying to shape cold glass—it shatters. This is the risk when a runner typically slaps a leg onto a fence and struggles to bring his/her head to the knee in a futile effort to warm up for a run.

   The prerun routine outlined below is a versatile aerobic warmup, good for running or any other sport. The entire series of warmup movements is choreographed. They are coordinated with deep, controlled breathing through the nose, referred to here as yogic breathing.

2. *You must be properly aligned according to biomechanical integrity.* To prevent injury while stretching a muscle, correct alignment is mandatory. Stretching injures you only if you do it improperly, while cold, or without static contraction in the muscle opposing the muscle being stretched. Although the alignment must be precise, the exercises described here allow for an individual degree of flexibility.

3. *You must stretch intensely and in concurrence with strengthening in order to stretch safely and effectively.* These exercises offer an alternative to passive stretching, in which a person hangs down, hoping for gravity to do all the work. Contrary to the Power Yoga Workout, this passive stretching does nothing for the development of strength, flexibility, and concentration.

In order to gain the full benefit, an athlete must stretch with vigor. But to do so without injury, one must be aligned, must be hot and stay hot.

The Power Yoga Workout routine below is adapted from Beryl Bender Birch's class at the NYRRC. Although it is generally done indoors and preferably with bare feet, it can be done outdoors with running shoes on as well.

Pre-Run Routine

Don't worry about getting the breathing sequence exactly right until you have mastered the positions. Once you perfect the positions, then work on the breathing and do this as a dynamic, continuous routine—

that is, do it in one flowing movement. Unlike other forms of yoga, there are no rest periods between poses. Start by repeating the pre-run routine three times. As you progress, move up to six repetitions. In several months, when your arm strength in particular has improved, you may do the routine as many as ten times. All postures that call for a tightened, or contracted, thigh muscle prevent overstretching the hamstring, a common mistake that may lead to injury.

Position 1. Stand with feet together and arms at your sides. Do yogic breathing (through the nose) to quiet the mind and get yourself centered. This is called the readying position.

Position 2. Inhale. Bring arms up over your head, palms together. Tilt head back and look toward your thumbs. Tighten the thighs and buttocks. Do not arch back.

Position 3. Exhale. Bend your knees slightly, bringing your palms to the floor alongside your feet. Tuck your head into your knee.

Inhale. While maintaining position, raise your head, look up and lift your chest.

Position 4. Exhale. Walk your legs back, making your body straight like a plank. Drop down into a pushup position. (Beginners: Do a modified pushup, with the knees touching the ground.)

Position 5. Inhale. Place the tops of your feet flat on the floor. Push your torso off the ground with your arms, raise your head, and look up at the ceiling. Make sure to lift your buttocks off the ground. (Note: Keep knees on the ground if you have lower back problems or weak arms.)

Position 6. Exhale. Turn toes under so soles of feet are facing the floor. Lift yourself up into an upside-down "V" position, supported by your arms, hands on the floor. Push buttocks toward the ceiling. Hold this position for five breaths. Push down on the heels and flattened palms. (This is a perfect pose for runners. It stretches the hamstrings, calves, heels, feet, Achilles tendons, shoulders, and lower back.)

Position 7. Inhale. Bend knees, step feet forward until they are between hands, look up in front of you, lift chest (same as position 3).

Position 8. Exhale. Tuck head into slightly bent knees with palms on the floor next to feet (same as position 3).

Position 9. Inhale. Bring arms straight overhead, palms together. Squeeze buttocks, tighten thighs. Look up (same as position 2). Return to readying position.

Post-Run Routine

Between each of the positions below, you may insert a full sequence of the pre-run routine. Since you naturally cool down after a run, doing the pre-run routine will keep you hot throughout your post-run exercises. Exercises that include the option of touching shin, ankle, or floor allow for the extent of individual flexibility. The contracting of muscle groups is for strengthening and illustrates the meaning of the "hard" of Hard & Soft.

Triangle Pose. With legs three feet apart, turn right foot out 90 degrees; turn left foot in 30 degrees. Inhale, extend arms straight to the side. Hold your right thigh contracted. Exhale. Without bending your knees, bend at the waist to your right, placing the right hand on your right ankle (or shin). Hold your right thigh contracted. Look up at your left hand. Take five to ten yogic breaths. Come up, reverse feet, inhale,

and do the exercise to the opposite side. Don't forget to hold the left thigh contracted as well. Reverse and do to other side. This exercise stretches the hamstrings, hips, iliotibial band (side of hip), side of calf. Good for low back pain, tight hips, and hamstrings.

Inverted Triangle. Turn right foot out 90 degrees; turn left foot in 45 degrees. Inhale, extend arms to your side. Exhale, turn torso to the right and bring both arms down to shin, ankle, or floor. Do not bend knees. Make sure right thigh is contracted. Reverse and do to other side. This exercise is good for lower back, tight hips and hamstrings, and iliotibial band tightness.

Extended Side Triangle. Stand with feet four feet apart. Turn the right foot out 90 degrees, the left foot in 30 degrees. Inhale. Extend arms to the side. Exhale, bend right knee directly over the right ankle, bringing the right palm to the floor next to the inside arch of the foot. Extend left arm straight up toward the ceiling (arms and shoulders should form a straight line). If you are not comfortable with your hand coming to the floor, use a phone book or similar object to raise the level of the hand. Hold for five breaths. Reverse and do to other side. This exercise stretches hips, groin, lower back, ankles, and shoulders and strengthens thighs, arms, and back. Good for low back pain.

Warrior Pose. Stand with feet three and a half feet apart. Turn the right foot out 90 degrees, the left foot in 30 degrees. Twist upper body, turning hips to the right. Hold back leg straight. Bend the right knee directly over the right ankle (don't lunge). Raise the arms straight over the head, with the palms together. Hold this position for five breaths. Reverse and do to other side. This exercise stretches ankles, calves, hips,

and shoulders and strengthens thighs, ankles, arms, and shoulders.

Single Leg Forward Bend. Sit on floor, extend left leg straight in front, with toes of left foot flexed upward, pointing toward ceiling. Bring the right foot to the inside of the left thigh. Bend down the left leg until your hands reach the knee, shin, or foot. Tighten the left thigh. Grasp the leg and pull gently with arms while concentrating on tightening the left thigh. Take five breaths. Reverse and do other leg. (Note: Do not allow back to round. Keep chest lifted and head up. Extend back and spine. Work toward eventually bringing the chin to the shin.) This exercise stretches hamstrings, lower back, and groin and strengthens shins, quadriceps, and biceps.

Overtraining, Overracing

Life, says exercise physiologist David E. Martin, can be seen as an energy pie—no matter how you cut it, there are only so many slices. In the section below, Martin explains the crucial principles of rest and regeneration, and how runners must account for the energy spent not only on running, but also in their daily routines. "Stress plus training equals straining," he concludes.

Running is primarily a volume-oriented sport. That is, the more you run, the fitter you get—within limits, of course. And there's the rub: How much is enough, and how much is too much? There's probably not a serious runner who hasn't at some time come down with a case of the blahs. What caused it? Too much mileage? Poor coaching? Too much stress?

Back in the 1930s, the famous Harvard physiologist Walter B. Cannon coined the term "homeostasis" to define "those dynamic self-regulating processes that keep the body's internal environment constant." As this definition is viewed in the context of training, it's easy to see how we get more fit if the training stress is just right. The breakdown caused by the hard work stimulates adaptive processes in the body to help it tolerate more of the same. Scientists call this homeostatic adjustment; runners call it getting fit. It is a system that creates more blood volume, greater numbers of enzymes for fuel metabolism, increased stored fuel in the working muscles, stronger tendons and ligaments, and more.

How can you suddenly end up with tendinitis, a bad cold, or a big-time case of the training blues? Is it really a case of too much stress? Is it the inability to differentiate between good stress and bad stress? Or is it something you're leaving out of the training plan?

> I try to find new goals and challenges, but in order to take them on, you have to know when to take a break. I meet many triathletes around Boulder, where I live, and some of them are really smart. They tell me, "You've got to know when to go 'eyeballs out' for what you want, but you've also got to know when to take a rest in order to come out again." It's like a wave. You're on the seashore and a big wave comes in and that's you on a high, doing well. And then the wave recedes a little bit and then you back off and take a rest. You build yourself up again for the next surge. That's the way running is. You can't go up, up, up all the time. You find if you go up too high, you crash, and you may never come back.
>
> I was a little insensible in the first ten years of my competitive career. I think during that time I went "eyeballs out," and then I should have receded, like the wave. It's taken that wave ten years to come in, in order for me to know to back off a little. I call this next decade "my new decade, not decayed." I'm treating it as if I've been reborn into the running world. It's like 1983 all over again. It's not a bad way to go.
>
> —Priscilla Welch

Training is a two-step process. There is breakdown and recovery. Runners often are so caught up in the reps and sets and weekly mileage totals—the discipline and hard work or breakdown—that the recovery is forgotten. *Not* training is a part of training, because during the non-training period regeneration occurs. Without the easy days to permit regeneration, without the high carbohydrate diet to replenish fuels, without relaxing and therapeutic massages to help the sore muscles recover, profound tissue adaptation never occurs to permit better performance.

It is also essential to factor into your training program stresses from other activities. Consider your whole life as an energy pie, which contains the sum total of life stresses. You can slice that pie any way you desire, but the pie isn't going to get any larger. If the slice for the workaday job gets larger as the job becomes more stressful, try to reduce the size of other stressful slices to compensate. Excess stress can bring about a breakdown of bodily function as much as physical training. The pie is only so big, and unfortunately, high-achieving, active athletes often eliminate recovery slices to take on more stresses. Soon there are no slices to provide for the stress of sleepless nights, taxing business trips, or a few missed meals. Then fatigue, staleness, some bad race times, or an inability to keep up the training pace *forces* you to relax. So stress plus training equals straining.

Below, in outline form, are typical symptoms of overtraining. These symptoms don't necessarily surface all at once, but combinations of two or more are common.

Symptoms of Training-Related Overtraining

1. Lack of desire to train; thoughts of skipping sessions that aren't even particularly difficult.
2. Inability to complete training sessions that had been well within your grasp a week or two earlier.
3. Unusual muscle soreness following training, with recovery taking much longer than usual.
4. Performance plateau, or even lowered performance decrement, despite increased training loads.

Symptoms of Life-Related Overtraining

1. Increased tension, anger, complaining, negativity.
2. Decreased enjoyment of life.
3. Poor quality of sleep.

Symptoms of Health-Related Overtraining

1. Increased incidence of illness.
2. Decrease in body weight and appetite.
3. Constipation or diarrhea.
4. Swelling of lymph nodes.
5. Increased morning pulse.

Overtraining often is as much a result of attitude as it is a result of training. In the typical psychological stimulus/response paradigm, if schedule overload is the stimulus, overtraining is the response. So often runners look to their training diaries for the answer to their staleness and become frustrated when they see no telltale signs that training is the culprit. They see no sudden increase in weekly mileage, no increase in the number of hard sessions. It is not the running but the approach that has broken the training link of breakdown and recovery.

Awareness of the need for regeneration, coupled with understanding the inherent risks of overachieving, should prompt you to program downtime into your training. Taking a day off training each week is an example. Periodizing your running activities is another. This means, perhaps, creating a cycle of a buildup (training), competition (racing), and regeneration (downtime) over a period of several months.

Other training options may help. If you plod a few early-morning miles and then hope to blast some intervals later in the day, try instead training once a day, but making it meaningful. A fairly quick late-afternoon session of several miles pays off in time economy as well as in improving aerobic stamina. In terms of nutrition, ample liquid and carbohydrate replenishment immediately following training sessions will help keep energy levels adequate.

This still leaves the approach problem. Try mixing training activities with family life. How about doing stretching exercises with the children? Organize a warmup or cooldown routine as a family activity. Clearly, the best way to ensure that the energy pie is best sliced is continually to assess where to cut it.

My typical week ebbs and flows since I turned 40 in 1987. Sometimes I'll go as high as 120 miles per week when I'm training for a marathon, but usually in the summer I drop down to 80 or 90. I don't train for marathons in the summer anymore, and I don't run as many marathons. I don't want to train full-time for the marathon. I did that for 18 years. I realize now that with all the other demands on my life—with children, business, race promotion—I just can't do it anymore. I think that was why I eventually broke down physically, why I developed plantar fasciitis.

For 15 years as a marathoner I was pretty consistent. I never missed more than three days of training. When I turned 40, I started to experience injuries. I think it was because I didn't adapt to the circumstances of my age and the wear and tear factor. That's why the plantar fasciitis developed. I was trying to race and train and do travel and promotion. There's only so much physical energy and resilience in the body. If you go beyond a certain point, you're in trouble. And runners are famous for pushing themselves—that's what our sport is all about. What can you do, physically and mentally, over a set distance, in a set time? That's the test. To do that takes a lot of energy. When the string gets broken, your weakest point will go. The sole of my foot has always been my "Achilles" area. That's why my particular injury developed. It took six or seven months before I felt I had finally gotten it under control to the point I could start doing a little speedwork again.

Every athlete knows it's very hard to maintain consistency. We're dealing not only with competition, but with a host of vagaries. Just consider nature. You race in 30- to 40-degree weather, or colder, and then in 80 to 90 degrees. How can you constantly be able to recover and train through that, and maintain a high level of fitness?

That was the problem with what we did in the past. We raced year round—no rest, no vacations—and in all different weather conditions. Sooner or later, your body forces you to stop. It says, "I'm going to give you the flu," or "I'm going to give you Achilles tendinitis." One way or another, you're going to slow down.

—Bill Rodgers

Racing entails risk. The most common mistake in addition to overtraining is racing too much too soon. Once novices get a little taste of competition, which is very positive, they may start racing every week. If they don't outright break down, people in this category wonder why they can't run faster. It's because they never recover from one race to another, never build any peaks. It becomes just one big plateau

Ever notice how some people are always injured, and some people never are? What's that all about? The uninjured are either lucky, they've got a genetic gift, or they know how to strike the right balance. Sure, some inherited good biomechanics help, but largely, the uninjured remain that way because they are running smart.

Conversely, it's unlikely that the chronically injured have bad genes or are simply unlucky; it's more likely they're paying the price for constantly overdoing it.

—Tom Fleming

Fred Lebow on Overracing and Overtraining

Training is like putting money in a bank. You deposit money, and then you can take it out. When you train, you deposit your daily miles. The more training you put in, the more money you have in the bank. But you can only expect results based on the training you put in. In other words, you can't take money out of the bank that you don't have. You can't overdraw. That's what overracing is about. A lot of us have had that experience.

I know what overracing is about. I once ran 13 marathons in 12 months. During one of those periods, I ran three marathons in two weeks. The only recovery I had was on the airplane. My third marathon was a 4:03. If I had had at least a few weeks in between, I am sure I would have done better by at least a few minutes. I'm just lucky I didn't get injured or ill.

You can get into this overracing cycle, and it drives you crazy. You almost get addicted to the ritual of racing, and everything it represents. There's a guy who has run a marathon every single week for an entire year. I think he's crazy, but at the same time, I admire him.

Like so many enthusiastic runners, I have fallen into the temptation to overtrain. Now I've learned to undertrain, as opposed to overtrain. I recently ran a 20k, and I took off running for three days before to rest. I would have never done that before. When you've been sick like I've been, you learn your limits. And believe me, it's the ultimate lesson.

Part 2: Racing

Why Race?

15

Why run a race? You race to test yourself, for the ritual, the camaraderie, and for the adventure and discovery. If you didn't compete as a child, the race offers another chance. Once you've raced, the challenge and accomplishment are motivation to continue. Few experiences allow such a range of personal satisfaction, and even fewer are as symbolic. When you race, your effort is singularly your own. In your sparest clothing, and with the power of your own body, you confront the challenge of the race. In a race, no one else and nothing else can do for you what you must do for yourself.

> If I do well in a race I'm to the moon. If I do exceptionally well, I've jumped over that moon. What I find most exciting is when I decide to go for something, and take up the challenge. I can see the possibility of a door being opened at the other end, going for it, and actually getting there. That is the most rewarding. The publicity that comes after that, the "razzmatazz" I call it, is nothing, is worthless. It's that initial feeling of achieving what you set out to achieve that's so satisfying, and that only comes in the first two or three minutes after succeeding. Then, of course, you're already asking yourself the question "What next?"
>
> —Priscilla Welch

Racing appeals to millions of people. In fact, according to TACSTATS/USA, four million people in the United States are currently running races. Both the number of finishers in the country's 100 largest races and participation in all races increased by 6 percent in 1990 (com-

145

pared to 3 percent and 4 percent, respectively, in 1989). While the largest growth is in shorter distances (5k increased the most), marathon participation was up also, in a continuation of a steady rise since 1985. In fact, in 1989–90, marathon growth approached the peak popularity of the boom years in the early 1980s.

Fred Lebow has often pointed out that the beauty of the road race is the opportunity it presents for all comers and world-class athletes to share the same experience. In this regard, running is unique. In so few other endeavors in life can those of all levels of ability undertake the same task and gain the same sense of achievement. "Imagine being able to run for that long," Bill Rodgers once remarked in admiration of four-hour marathoners.

Over the years, I've done races at every distance, from one mile to 50 kilometers. I began by trying to run a mile all out, and died toward the end. A week later, I ran the same time, but by doing an even pace, with a lot less energy and a lot more satisfaction.

Running hasn't always been easy, particularly in the beginning. I especially recall my first marathon, which like a lot of people in the early days, I probably ran on too little experience. But there weren't many races of varying distances back then, and not so much training know-how, either.

It was the Cherry Tree Marathon in the Bronx in 1970—the race that was replaced by the New York City Marathon later that year. There were about 60 people entered, and it was freezing cold. In those days, there were no water stations. After the first six-mile loop, Harry Murphy, one of the great fixtures on the New York running scene, offered me a cup of whiskey. I gulped it down not knowing what it was, and although I'm not a drinker, I was so cold that it felt great. After the next six-mile loop, I happily downed another cup of whiskey. On the third loop, someone gave me a cup of water. I was so disappointed!

My good friend Brian Crawford—also part of the running scene since the early days and currently the director of administration at the NYRRC—was driving a car alongside me, yelling, "Drop out, Fred, drop out!" My girlfriend was in the same car, repeating the advice with a smile on her face. Between the whiskey and the encouragement to quit, it wasn't easy to finish. What's more, I got outkicked by Kurt Steiner, running his 99th and final marathon.

—Fred Lebow

If you have never raced, don't hesitate to try. People of every level of ability run races for a variety of reasons. And you may surprise yourself. As Grete Waitz has said, "There is something about the ritual of the race—putting on the number, lining up, being timed—that brings out the best in us."

If the idea of a race looms a bit large, consider an event that puts the emphasis on fun and participation. Fun runs, held almost everywhere, are a good introduction to racing. Races with unique themes are also popular.

One of my favorite events we conduct is the Breakfast Run. It's a July fun run limited to about 1,500 people who run two, four, or six miles. They come to the race with a suit on a clothes hanger, so they can be ready to go to work afterward. There's a special section at the breakfast site, Tavern on the Green, where they can check their clothes. They run, have breakfast, and change into their work outfits. Actually, some of them run straight to work from the race.

It's a great event. People come all the way from New Jersey just to run it, and then head back home. Although we have to limit registration to NYRRC members, and we don't give out T-shirts, it's still one of our most popular runs.

There's just something special about the atmosphere of this event. First of all, this elegant spot, Tavern on the Green, is open just for us. There's something wonderful about seeing waiters in black tie serving sweaty runners.

I like it because it's so social. I don't know why, but it's the only race we put on in which we get more women (55 percent) than men. I know a couple at this event who had breakfast at the same table, and they ended up falling in love.

—Fred Lebow

For example, the NYRRC conducts the Alamo Alumni Run, one in a national series of five-mile races, in which runners compete for their college alma maters and are scored as teams. The race is a good challenge, but the reunion of college buddies is an even better motivation! The *Runner's World*/New Year's Eve Midnight Run—complete with costumes and fireworks—is another festive event. The Backwards Mile (that's literal, by the way) is a novel approach to racing, to say the least. There are also races run for a cause—for example, the NYRRC's Race for the Cure, part of a national series for women that promotes breast cancer awareness and education.

> My attitude on racing is an extension of the Kenneth Cooper philosophy, with which I agree. Anybody who is out there more than 30 minutes at a time three times a week is running for some reason other than physical health. Most runners fall somewhere on the continuum of that minimum amount all the way up to working out 13 times a week, running 140 miles.
>
> I'd say for anyone on that continuum who is running beyond three times a week for half an hour there is a probably a psychological need to set a goal for their training. It helps to have a certain number of times it can be reinforced, and improvement can be seen. Racing is a good way to do that.
>
> —Frank Shorter

Elite marathoner Gordon Bloch points out that while some runners choose never to race, most are inspired to test themselves in some type of competition, be it a short distance fun run or a major marathon in a distant city. And the variety of reasons for racing are reflected in the variety of racing opportunities offered across this country and internationally. Bloch says if you're on the fence about running a race, consider what racing offers—on and off the course:

Fun. For most runners, racing is primarily a social event. It's a chance to meet people and participate in the running scene. Benji Durden, a 1980 Olympian, coach, and a runner for 25 years, says the fun of road racing is what keeps him participating.

Education. Many races are preceded or followed by clinics at which elite runners, doctors, physiologists, or other experts speak on a variety of topics related to running. These events are usually free and open to all. Expos are offered at larger races, displaying everything from running shoes to the latest carbo-loading beverages.

Motivation. "Knowing that I've got a marathon down the road is what gets me to lace up my shoes and head out the door each morning," says Julie Dworschack, a 32-year-old interior designer who completed the 1991 New York City Marathon in 3:53. If you have already met the goal of becoming fit through regular running, congratulations. You may find committing to a race motivates your continued training. After one race, see if you aren't inspired to improve your time in another race, or alter your training for a different type of running contest.

Challenge. Racing provides the satisfaction of taking on a hard task and finishing it, of meeting a challenge at your own level as well as against the clock and other individuals.

> Given the nature of running, certain things will never be altered. That's one of the beauties of our sport. There is no judge; it doesn't matter how you look. If you have reconstructive surgery on your nose, for example, you're not going to get the gold medal instead of the silver, like it may be in some other sports. It's still simply training-based, and the only judge is the clock.
>
> —Bill Rodgers

Are You Ready to Race?

Ready to try a race? Before you do, read this section to help ensure that your first race isn't your last.

Pick a Race You Can Handle

A good rule of thumb is that the race distance should be no greater than one-third of your weekly mileage. That means you can try a 5k (3.1 miles) if you run at least nine miles a week, a 10k if you're logging at least 18. Remember, your goal at this stage is to *complete* the distance, not to *compete*. Avoid longer races your first time; you can try them later. If you enter a race that's over your head, you will probably survive, but may struggle to finish, feel sore, and possibly get injured. Do *not* race if you have never run before or have been sedentary for a month or longer, especially if you smoke, have diabetes, are overweight, or have a family history of heart disease. (As you'll read in the marathon section, it is not a good idea for anyone to try a marathon as a first race.)

Give Yourself Time to Prepare

Even if you are in shape, don't jump into a race on a whim. Instead, pick one at least a few days away to give yourself time to prepare mentally and logistically. Think about the details: a good pair of shoes and the right clothes for the weather, where and when to register, etc. Then on race day you'll be able to relax and have fun. If you're out of shape, pick a race at least a few weeks or months away so you have time to prepare properly. (See the training programs in other chapters.)

Forget Time Goals

Run your first race for the experience, with a goal of making it to the finish line, not setting speed records. Dave Tanke's first race was a 10k that started on the George Washington Bridge and ran into Manhattan. It was held on a hot Fourth of July, with thousands of people entered. Between the heat and the crowds, and with his inexperience, a fast time was the last thing on Tanke's mind. "I don't even remember my time," he says. "I had entered the New York City Marathon in the fall and knew I needed to find out what racing was all about. My goal was to put forth a hard effort, but to feel strong the whole way."

You will have many chances to run fast later, so take this time to learn things about yourself: Were you nervous? Did you get thirsty or hungry? Did you talk to other runners, or keep to yourself? When did you feel tired—at the beginning, somewhere in the middle, or at the end? Did you have trouble concentrating at any point? Did you run progressively faster, slower, or stay at about the same speed throughout? Did you ever want to stop? Did you have fun?

Notice things around you: What was the start like? Could you get water along the way? Could you follow the course? What was your time at various points? (Most races have mile markers, often with digital clocks or someone calling out the time. Or you can set your watch at the start to record your time.)

Runners of all levels learn something from every race they run. Pat Petersen, multitime NYRRC Runner of the Year, got lost in his first race, a high school cross-country event. "I learned not to take the lead if I wasn't sure where the finish line was," he says.

Take It Easy Afterward

Intentionally or not, you will probably run your race faster than your normal training pace, thanks to the excitement around you. So take it easy for a few days, even after a short race. Run easily or do something else, such as biking or swimming, to let your muscles recover. Pat Petersen rarely runs hard for four or five days after a race, and for at least a month after a marathon.

Strategies for Better Racing

You've run one or more races, and you're hooked. Now your goal is to improve race performances through training and motivation. In creating your racing program, Gordon Bloch advises that you be prepared. Following are her tips for better racing performance:

Plan Your Schedule

Some runners race every weekend, others only a few times a year. Most elite runners divide the year into two or three seasons and aim to race their best at the end of each season. Then they rest, and build up again. For example, Pat Petersen usually runs one marathon in the spring and one in the fall. He chooses these races first, then plans others leading up to them to gauge his fitness and prepare himself mentally and physically for the marathon.

Top runners usually have the advantages of coaching advice and the pick of races all over the world. But any runner can plan a season. Many running clubs have long-range schedules of local races. You can check magazines such as *Runner's World* and *Running Times* to find races farther afield.

Dave Tanke divides his year into two seasons, culminating in a couple of fast 10k races in the spring and a marathon in the fall. Pick your big race or races first. They should be at least three months away so you can prepare properly. Then pick at least one or two races between now and then; run these races to evaluate your fitness and to gain strength and experience for the big ones.

Champion miler Eamonn Coghlan believes planning races is the key to racing success. "Following a carefully thought-out plan of buildup, sharpening, racing, recovery, and rest allows runners to perform at their best," he says. Exercise scientists call this seasonal approach to running (or any endurance sport) *periodization*. Periodization means using a planned program of base training, buildup, sharpening, racing, rest, and recovery to produce fast times without burnout or injury. Even if you don't care about racing fast, planning races lets you organize your life, especially if you travel to races.

Plan Race Strategies

Top runners often say they win races without having a strategy. Don't believe them! It's rare that a runner has no idea how he or she might reach the finish line first. Some go out fast from the start, hoping to build up an insurmountable lead. Others prefer to hang back, then come on strong in the end. Three-time World Cross Country champion Lynn Jennings is famous for this "sit and kick" racing strategy.

Your race strategy depends on many things: your strengths as a runner, your personality, the course, the competition, even the weather. For example, it is not a good strategy to try to run your fastest marathon in 75-degree heat with high humidity. A better strategy is to go out conservatively and hope to pick off the fast starters in the end. Good cross-country racing strategy involves moving to the front early to avoid getting trapped behind slower runners on narrow trails.

Race strategies don't always work, so make fallback plans. "My strategy for the 1992 Olympic Marathon Trials was to run with the lead pack through 20 miles, then assess how I felt to see if I could continue with the leaders," writes Gordon Bloch. "But I felt very tired at 18 miles, and knew I had to back off at that point in order to have the strength to finish." "To a large extent, you have to let the race unfold. Anything can happen," says Pat Petersen. "Don't waste energy worrying that things aren't going exactly as planned."

Taper and Peak

These skills are part of both race planning and strategy. Tapering, or to taper, means to cut back on running in the time before a race; peaking, or to peak, means planning your training and racing to produce your best possible performance in one or a few races. For a marathon, you should taper for at least two weeks, cutting your mileage at least 20 to 30 percent two weeks before the race, and 50 percent (the marathon mileage not included) one week before. Tapers for shorter races, from a mile to a half marathon, are shorter.

> The main thing is to orient your training, preparation, and goal-setting in a way that peaks. The other important aspect is focus. If you're going to do something with a goal that is significant, you have to be training for a significant period of time.
>
> Average runners often use racing as one of the goals in their training. Maybe it is to help them continue through their training, maybe it motivates them to get out there on a consistent basis.
>
> The focus for the average runner should be on consistency; that's all you need to shoot for. It's not necessary to try to achieve an ultimate goal. Consistency is more important than any particular training you do. Of the person following a very rigid program for two weeks a month and the person who just goes out and runs 45 minutes five days a week most of that month, the person with the longer, more generally consistent approach is getting better training.
>
> —Frank Shorter

There are many different strategies for tapering, but it's a good idea for all runners to do it in some form. Eamonn Coghlan says that no matter what the distance, you should either not run the day before a race, or just jog easily for a couple of miles to feel fresh and loose.

> I am one of many advocates of having both a training season and a racing season. The latter should be approximately three months in length. You should not do more than two races a month if you want those races to be key, maximum efforts. I do believe you can use a race as part of your training, in other words, "run through the race," if you have the self-control to do it at your training pace. Many people just like the act of participating in the event, which is fine, as long as they don't give a maximum effort every week. Otherwise, staleness and breakdown may occur.
>
> —Cliff Held

You may hear about runners who also "run through" races, that is, who do not taper. The race thus becomes more of a training run. While an extensive taper isn't needed for races early in your season, remember that racing is both an emotional and a physical experience. No matter what speed you run, a race will get the adrenaline flowing. Why not savor that experience? Pat Petersen doesn't favor running through races because he likes the confidence a good race gives him, and knows running through it means he won't race well. "When you taper, you can't log as many miles for that week, and that can make people nervous, especially when they're training for a marathon," he says. "But you gain so much more from a good race. Don't become a mileage junkie. You can run light and easy the day or two before a race, and you should take it easy afterward."

Focus and Concentrate

What do you think about during races? Even though your body is doing the work, your mind can help you run faster. Joan Samuelson, Olympic Marathon gold medalist, has talked about the "cocoon" of concentration she enters before a race. Gordon Bloch writes, "I was so focused at the 1992 Olympic Marathon Trials, I couldn't remember the name of a close friend who wished me luck before the start." You don't have to concentrate quite so hard, but focusing helps performance.

> I tell my athletes, "When you compete, concentrate on yourself. Don't focus on anger against a competitor." Living on that negative emotion may work for one or two races, but it is not the habit of someone who is consistently a winner. To be consistently good, once you're in your own lane, you run your own race. For racing, this is the best way to take your nervous energy and turn it into positive energy.
>
> —Joe Douglas

Before the race, stretch and warm up with friends, but be sure to take a few minutes to be alone. Talk to yourself about the race, reminding yourself that you have worked hard for this, the big day. Think about the course, review your race strategy. If you are nervous, that's fine. The adrenaline will help you run faster.

During the race, concentrate on your breathing, your pace, the weather, and your place compared to other runners. As you gain racing experience, you will develop an ability to know when you can run a little harder and when you should hold back. There is no magic to doing this, but it cannot happen without focus and concentration. That's why you shouldn't use the race to plan your dinner menu, wonder whether you locked the door, or muse on your neighbors' running attire. Dave Tanke focuses by coaching himself through each section of a race. He tells himself something like "relax and flow" on the downhills, "keep it steady" on the flats, and "shorten your stride, lift those knees" as he goes uphill.

From facing the experience of ultradistance triathlons, I have learned that athletics is about being able to stay relaxed and be patient. Racing is pain, and that's why you do it, to challenge yourself and the limits of your physical and mental barriers. You don't experience that in an armchair watching television.

In any race there are the moments you feel great, and the moments you feel you're not going to make it. You've got to be willing to breathe hard, sweat, and still stay relaxed. You hear it over and over again—a television announcer saying, "Watch that guy, he looks so relaxed." It's a rare athlete who wins who doesn't look relaxed.

I think the point is not to be afraid of the challenge. Fear is probably the thing that limits performance more than anything—the fear of not doing well, of what people will say. You've got to acknowledge those fears, then release them.

When I was a swimmer, I did all the wrong things. I would see the competition pull away, and the fear would grip me. I learned you can't hide from yourself or your ability. You have to accept what you have and be patient with yourself.

—Mark Allen

The longer the race, the harder it is to keep concentration throughout and, for most runners, a random thought or two will not ruin your race. Let the thought occur, then gently shift your attention back to the moment. You may want to try using imagery to concentrate. Visualize a string between you and the runner in front of you. See yourself winding the string into a ball as you pull closer. You can repeat a word or phrase in time with your breathing or footsteps: "Stay loose" or "I can do it" are some you might try.

As you practice focusing, you will learn to use your body's feedback to adjust your pace and plan how you will run the rest of the race. When you are well focused, you can pull up your level of performance. When you are having a bad race, focus on things that will inspire you—for instance, the crowds that cheer as you run by. Think back to a hard workout you did and remember how you pushed through the fatigue. Envision the finish line and think how proud you will be to cross it. Focus and concentration keep your mind sharp and your body working to finish the race as strongly as you can.

Pace Yourself

How fast should you run races? That is something you will learn by racing. However, the process will be quicker, and racing more enjoyable, if you practice running at race pace or faster in workouts. This is what speedwork is for.

"Thanks to speed workouts, when I feel discomfort in a race, I can tell myself, 'You've been here, stay with it,'" says Dave Tanke. Speedwork can also bring down your race times dramatically, as Tanke discovered when he started doing interval workouts with the NYRRC running classes in 1986. By timing yourself in speed workouts, you learn how fast to pace yourself in races. Finally, doing speedwork with others gives you a sample of the adrenaline rush of a race, although it is not a good idea to get in the habit of racing in speed workouts. You want to save your best performances for race day.

A word of caution: Don't lock yourself in to performing at a predetermined pace. Pat Petersen's best 10k was a leg of a relay in which he had no idea how fast he ran until days later. "I was in good shape and felt great," he says. "I let instinct take over."

Rest and Recover

A race taxes your body and mind more than your daily training, including speed workouts. You must rest afterward, no matter how you feel. "This is hard for many runners," says Eamonn Coghlan. "If they have a good race or season, they are pumped up, and want to train hard again right away. If they did poorly, they want to train hard to redeem themselves." Coghlan always forced himself to take a month off after each season, doing little or no running. "For the first week, I felt great. Then I'd get an itch to run, but I'd hold back. At the end of four weeks, I'd have such an appetite for running, I could scarcely contain myself. I really believe that forced rest lengthened my career." Pat Petersen never has a problem taking it easy after a marathon. "Racing, especially the marathon, takes so much physical and mental effort that the break is very welcome," he says. After running a marathon in late October or early November, he won't resume formal training until mid-December, and he avoids racing until the end of January.

Dave Tanke believes many runners pay lip service to the idea of rest. He himself used to rest for a month after the New York City Marathon, then run four or five races in December and January. Because he was still fit from his marathon training, he would often run personal best times. However, by February and March, his times worsened—just when he wanted to build up for some good 10k's in the spring. "Now I rest for four weeks at the end of a season, then build up my mileage, not racing at all for eight weeks, then doing a couple of low-key races, and only then starting to look for fast times."

A Checklist of Racing Do's and Don'ts

1. Even if you're not racing seriously, it pays to choose a well-organized race with a good reputation. Time and accurate distance may not be important to you, but adequate water stations are.
2. Read the race entry blank carefully and note the date, time, and location of the event. (You'd be surprised what nervousness makes you forget!) If you don't know directions, bring a map and the entry blank with you (often the blank includes directions).
3. If possible, scout the course and the location beforehand. It helps to know where that steep hill is, and the location of a friendly neighborhood gas station or restaurant—so you can use the rest room and avoid the long lines at the race site facilities if necessary.
4. The night before the event, pack your bag and check several times to make sure you have everything (even Carl Lewis has forgotten

his running shorts). Make sure you have your race number (pin it to your shirt ahead of time), that your shoes and clothing are broken in, and that you have all other necessary or emergency items: a bottle of water, adhesive bandages, petroleum jelly, toilet paper, safety pins, sunscreen, change of dry clothes, etc.

5. If you're planning to meet a friend to run with, select a spot ahead of time—preferably one that is away from the crowded starting area.

6. Stick to your tried-and-true methods of what to eat and drink—or what not to eat and drink—the night before and the morning of the event (avoid alcohol, don't eat too close to the race, don't drink coffee or other caffeinated beverages if you are not used to them).

7. Don't arrive so early you expend excess energy nervously waiting and suffer the elements, such as cold or heat. (Would you believe that at least one lone runner arrives every year at about 3 a.m. at the New York City Marathon starting area? The race starts at 10:45!) Once at the race site, try to find shelter from either winterlike conditions or direct summer sun. Do not sunbathe before a race.

8. Don't arrive so late that you can't find parking, or that the lines for the toilets are long. Arriving late exacerbates nervousness and cuts into precious warmup time.

9. Arrange to stash your warmup clothing in a car, baggage check, or with a friend. Especially if it's very cold, keep your outer gear on until the last possible minute.

10. Continue to drink water, even small sips, until race time.

11. After the race, don't forget your crucial cooldown routine. While it's nice to bask in your achievements and share in the camaraderie at the finish, novice runners often make the mistake of standing around after the race and chatting. Elite runners almost never do this—much to the dismay of the media, who often seek out a missing athlete who is off running a cooldown.

When Is It All Right to Drop Out of a Race?

One of the things running teaches us is to push ourselves, even when body and mind would rather call it a day. But sometimes dropping out of a race makes sense, and in very rare cases, it can be a matter of life and death.

> I'm conscious of every little pain and discomfort, from constipation to a side stitch I get while running. I have a new relationship to that pain. I don't fight it anymore; I respect my pain. In addition to living through cancer, I'm also getting older. I used to fight to push myself beyond pain, like while running a race. But I don't do that anymore. If it hurts, I just walk until I finish. This might not be what many runners do, but I think that after years of experience, there are runners who come to a similar philosophical stance. They still push themselves, but not recklessly. There's pushing to challenge your limits; then there is a kind of reckless pushing (left for young runners and the elite!). Experienced runners learn to respect the changing needs of their bodies. That's the wisdom that comes with time, and—for good or bad—with age.
>
> —Fred Lebow

Cliff Held, in an article in *New York Running News*, offers the following advice:

Drop out if you feel acute pain. This will most likely be in the hips, legs, or feet, and can signal an injury to muscle, connective tissue (tendons and ligaments), or bone. Sometimes it's hard to tell injury-related pain from the muscle fatigue that's normal when you work hard. Simple fatigue usually causes a burning sensation that lessens if you slow down. Pain caused by a muscle pull or tear, a sprain, or a fracture will likely get worse with every step.

Stop if you feel dizzy, disoriented, or if you stop sweating. These symptoms of heat exhaustion usually strike in hot, humid weather, but can occur anytime. By the time you feel them, you are at risk for heat stroke, a life-threatening condition caused by very high body temperature. Stop running, summon help, and get water in and on yourself as quickly as possible.

Attempt to finish, but you may have to forget it if you get a side stitch. It may hurt like crazy, but chances are it'll go away. Many people just run through the pain, taking deep, relaxed breaths. You also can try slowing down slightly and pressing your fingertips into the area. If that doesn't work, walk a bit, breathing deeply, then ease back into running.

The same is true of stomach problems. This is a tough call. Grete Waitz's 1985 New York City Marathon effort, during which she had diarrhea, proves that it's possible to finish in world-class form with severe abdominal distress.

You should not drop out just because you're not running a good time. This is the worst reason to stop. You can always salvage something from a race. If you stay in it, you'll approach the next race feeling stronger.

"I've dropped out of many marathons," says Fred Lebow. "I'm not proud of it. I feel terrible dropping out, but if I have to, I do. It's part of the game, and often gives you the impetus to do better in the future."

Part 3: The Distances

The Mile

The lights are dimmed every year for the highlight event at the venerated Millrose Games. In a solemn voice, the announcer intones, "Ladies and gentlemen, the Wanamaker Mile." A rumble, then a roar rises from the crowd at New York's Madison Square Garden.

Fred Lebow was inspired by the Wanamaker spirit. Imagine taking this race out of the arena and into the outdoors? Why not make this spectacle—which ignites the cheering of 18,000 fans—available to thousands more (even millions with television) by bringing the mile race to the roads?

"Would you run a mile on the road?" Fred Lebow asked Eamonn Coghlan after he won one of his seven titles in the Wanamaker Mile. "As long as we can run it on Fifth Avenue, so it finishes in front of the Irish Tourist Board," he answered. That's where Coghlan worked at the time, and he felt the promotion would be great.

Lebow ran into Coghlan at the Bislett Games in Oslo later that year. "What about that Fifth Avenue Mile?" Coghlan asked. "You're serious, aren't you?" Lebow replied.

In 1981 the club staged the first road mile, appropriately enough on one of the world's most elegant thoroughfares, Fifth Avenue. This event, broadcast on network television, has featured some of the world's fastest times run for the distance (although those times are unofficial, since they aren't run on a uniform track). And this racing format has been adopted worldwide.

Over the years, the Fifth Avenue Mile has expanded to allow racers of various abilities and in different divisions—not just the elite—to compete. High school, masters, and top local divisions are now included in the event. In keeping with the "everyone included" spirit of the NYRRC, in 1991, Lebow and the NYRRC created an "all comers" division in the race. Heat after heat of various groups of runners took off, giving everyone who participated an opportunity to experience what Eamonn Coghlan calls "that sheer exhilaration" of running the mile.

The Magic Mile

Many road runners think of a mile as one section of a longer race. The idea of running a single mile for time, let alone on a track, is absolutely foreign. However, this test of both speed and endurance need not be reserved only for the elite milers. In addition to being a distance worthy of racing by anyone, training for and running a mile can translate to running well at other distances.

Running writer and coach Cliff Temple points out that you may know your best time for 10k, or the marathon, yet you likely have no idea of your ability over the magic mile. In his hometown of Hythe in Kent, England, although there is no track, there is an accurately measured, straight seafront mile, complete with permanent markers. This means that local runners can time themselves over the distance when they feel like it—either in the middle of a training run or in a special time trial. Some runners try it once; others spend all year using it as a training gauge, trying to improve their times.

Across the United States, various running teams and clubs have marked out mile runs on paths, roads, and in parks. Contact those groups to find out where "the milers" head on the roads. If you don't have a spot nearby, seek the aid of your local running club or other group to help mark a mile in your area for everyone's use.

You might also want to check out an all-comers track meet—the introduction to running the mile (and various other distances) for many a runner. Either way, the mile can be a good indication of your current conditioning and your progress.

I do love to run indoors. I love the tightness of the track. I love the fact you're going around 11 times for a mile on a short straightaway and a tight turn with a bank. The crowd is right on top of you. I can get a tremendous feeling of exhilarating speed indoors that I don't get outdoors, because you can get the centrifugal force effect from the bank turn. That turn catapults you down the straightaway, and before you know it, you're back into that bank turn again. I enjoy that feeling. The sound of your footstrike on each stride hitting the board, and the speed you get back from that, give you a great uplift. Some runners sink in it. Some runners feel as if they lose their sense of balance on the turns. I don't. All the elements of indoor running I get a high out of, and as a result of that, I excel.

—Eamonn Coghlan

The Magic—and Mind-Set—of the Miler

"In certain ways, the feeling of running a mile in 3:49 is exactly the same as when I ran my first marathon in 2:25 in New York in 1991. And that sheer exhilaration that you experience is the same for a world-class runner as it is for a jogger," says Eamonn Coghlan of the mile.

The more complex the situation, the more disciplined you must be to go through it, the more you absorb the feedback and responses while going through it, the deeper the feeling of success. Coghlan believes that in the inner mind, this experience is equivalent in all realms of life—be it in sports or education and learning. "When I run a world record in the mile, and I get that feeling of sheer speed and invincibility, it is exactly the same feeling, psychologically speaking, that somebody else gets from running a personal best time," Coghlan explains.

"Running a fast mile feels almost like you're flying like a bird, in complete control of everything that's going on, physically and mentally. You feel absolutely fantastic, like a runaway express train that could effortlessly go on and on forever. There's just no pain. You feel as if you could run forever without anybody behind or in front of you. When I do it, it's as if I've gone through a wall. That's the optimal psychological experience.

"I think everyone should try running a mile. People can relate to the mile. That magical four-minute mile barrier has set a universal standard. To run under that time is a phenomenal achievement. For the average runner, to see how close that person can come to the 'almighty' gives them an indication of where they really stand."

Cliff Temple's Training for the Mile

To train for the mile, you need to develop your speed endurance. As a distance, the mile is too far to sprint, but if you are looking for significant improvement, it is not far enough to cover at a comfortable aerobic pace. This means you need to rehearse running at a pace that makes you fairly breathless but that is still some way short of sprinting.

Finding that ideal pace may require several attempts. If you push too hard you will go into oxygen debt. This means using oxygen faster than the lungs can send fresh supplies to the working muscles. In this case, you will simply have to slow down until a balance is restored. On the other hand, if you don't push hard enough, you may find when you are close to the finish that you still have a lot left, and will end up making a mad sprint for the line, knowing that you could have run faster earlier. This is not efficient pacing either.

So to start with, you can look for time improvements simply by correcting your pacing. When you can run at a speed you can just about sustain for most of the distance without going into oxygen debt, you will be close to your current potential. Once you feel you have reached that point, the way forward is through improved training, although don't feel you have to get your pacing absolutely perfect before you start specific training.

> The mile is also a key component in training. If you go out and run quarter-mile repeats, even though you get benefit, you don't get the same feedback as you get from running mile repeats. I can run quarter-mile after quarter-mile all day long, yet I can try to use that training to run a 5000-meter race, and bomb. But if I change my training repeats to three fourths or one mile, I'll be spent after two of them, because I have to extend my body and mind over four full laps of the track. For a quarter-mile, you don't have to concentrate that long, and the physical pain is over fairly quickly. Mile repeats, on the other hand, provide you with the physical and mental ability to withstand the longer distances in a race.
>
> —Eamonn Coghlan

A typical training session would involve running one or two miles steadily to warm up, and then running hard for 60 seconds. At the end of that, you should walk for 60 seconds, then jog for two minutes, by which time your breathing should return to near normal. Then you run hard again for 60 seconds, walk 60 seconds, and jog two minutes. A first attempt at this session should include a total of four hard runs. As you get used to it, increase the number of repetitions to six or eight, or even divide them into two blocks of four, with a 10-minute jog between the two sets.

Eamonn Coghlan has composed a training program based on a six-week period of four 10-day training cycles. "So many people get caught up in seven-day cycles," he says, "but that can be a trap. Most of us are just too busy or tired to get it all done in that time frame. A 10-day cycle allows more leeway and helps keep a person out of the 'compulsion trap.'"

Coghlan's schedule is designed to be undertaken only after a thorough level of fitness has been achieved (if you are not ready, follow the first 12 weeks of the Tom Fleming program outlined in Chapter 3) and is geared specifically for a runner who may have been racing 10k's or marathons and would like to attempt to break five minutes for the mile. A training program to attempt to break six minutes follows as well. To customize the program for your own racing goals at any other level, a calculator or a little math can help you easily adjust the workouts.

Training for a Five-Minute Mile

Warm up before all hard efforts and finish with a cooldown.

First 10-Day Cycle

Day 1: 4 × 3/4 mile on rolling hills, like a golf course (fast time is not important here, but try to do all the segments in the same time)

Day 2: five miles

Day 3: eight miles easy; 6 × 100-meter strides

Day 4: 6 × 400 meters at goal race pace (if your goal is five minutes, do each one at 75 seconds); jog/walk 400 meters' recovery between efforts

Day 5: five miles

Day 6: five miles

Day 7: 10 × 200 meters in 35 seconds; jog/walk 200 meters' recovery between each

Day 8: rest

Day 9: ten miles

Day 10: five miles, 6 × 100-meter strides

Second 10-Day Cycle (Repeat First Cycle)

Third 10-Day Cycle

Day 1: 2 × 3/4 mile on the track, 80 seconds per lap if possible; complete rest between

Day 2: five miles

Day 3: five miles easy, 6 × 100-meter strides

Day 4: 6 × 400 meters in 73 seconds, 400-meter jog/rest between

Day 5: rest

Day 6: six miles

Day 7: 8 × 200 meters in 35 seconds; 200-meter jog/rest between

Day 8: five miles

Day 9: five miles

Day 10: five miles

Fourth 10-Day Cycle

Day 1: 1 × 2000 meters (five laps of the track); 85 seconds per lap

Day 2: five miles

Day 3: five miles

Day 4: 4 × 400 meters (73 seconds each); 400 meters' rest; 4 × 200 meters (33 seconds each); 400 meters' rest

Day 5: rest

Day 6: five miles

Day 7: 2 × 800 meters (two minutes, 33 seconds each); complete rest between efforts

Day 8: five miles

Day 9: three miles; 10 × 100-meter strides

Day 10: five miles

Rest two days with light jogging, then race.

Training for a Six-Minute Mile

First 10-Day Cycle

Day 1: warmup jog 15 to 20 minutes, 4 × ³/₄ mile on rolling hills, like a golf course (fast time is not important here, but try to do all the segments in the same time)

Day 2: five miles easy

Day 3: eight miles easy; 6 × 100-meter strides

Day 4: 6 × 400 meters at goal race pace (if your goal is six minutes, do each one at 90 seconds); jog/walk 400 meters for recovery between efforts

Day 5: five miles

Day 6: five miles

Day 7: 10 × 200 meters in 42 seconds; jog/walk 200 meters' recovery between each

Day 8: rest

Day 9: 10 miles

Day 10: five miles; 6 × 100-meter strides

Second 10-Day Cycle (Repeat First Cycle)

Third 10-Day Cycle

Day 1: 2 × ³/₄ mile on the track, 96 seconds per lap if possible; complete rest between

Day 2: five miles

Day 3: five miles easy; 6 × 100-meter strides

Day 4: 6 × 400 meters in 87 seconds; 400-meter jog/rest between

Day 5: rest

Day 6: six miles

Day 7: 8 × 200 meters in 42 seconds; 200-meter jog/rest between

Day 8: five miles

Day 9: five miles

Day 10: five miles

Fourth 10-Day Cycle

Day 1: 1 × 2000 meters (five laps of the track); 1 minute, 42 seconds per lap

Day 2: five miles

Day 3: five miles

Day 4: 4 × 400 meters (87 seconds each); 400 meters' rest; 4 × 200 meters (40 seconds each); 400 meters' rest

Day 5: rest

Day 6: five miles

Day 7: 2 × 800 meters (three minutes, four seconds each); complete rest between efforts

Day 8: five miles

Day 9: three miles; 10 × 100-meter strides

Day 10: five miles

Rest two days with light jogging, then race.

The Mile and Track and Field

Any discussion of the mile would be incomplete without mention of the New York Games, sponsored by Mita and one of the NYRRC's crown jewels. The club has made a difficult but significant commitment to the revitalization of track and field in the United States by conducting what has become one of the most successful outdoor meets in this country. First held in 1989, the Games revitalized local interest in track and field (New York had gone without a comparable competition since 1966) and has spurred a national revival as well.

Track and field is the basis of running, the nurturing ground for road runners. There is hardly a good marathoner who hasn't first been a successful track runner—Grete Waitz, Rod Dixon, Frank Shorter, and Alberto Salazar, to name just a few. For developing elite runners, it's important that track is maintained and developed.

"I think it's worthwhile to promote track and field even though it isn't the 'in' sport of the 1990s," says Fred Lebow. "It can only help road running."

"Track and field is a show on a stage," according to Joe Douglas, "and unless a track meet gives the public a good show, it can't thrive. To put on a good show, it needs the financial support to bring in the stars. The New York Games is the only meet in the country that manages to attract stars. New York has been the leader in the world of road running. Now it is trying to have some success with track and field."

Fred Lebow on Running the Fifth Avenue Mile

A highlight race for me was the Fifth Avenue Mile in October 1991. I woke up the morning of the event and looked out the window. It was a beautiful day. I wanted to run that race so badly, but I was suffering one of the many minor physical ills that have plagued me since getting cancer.

I got to Fifth Avenue and walked up to the race start. Hundreds of runners were gathered: fat, thin, slow, fast. Seeing them all, I said to myself, "I can even walk this if I have to." Once the gun went off, my adrenaline did, too. I sprinted the first quarter mile in one minute, 40 seconds. I had gone out too fast, but I still hit halfway in 3:50. "I'm going under eight minutes," I realized. I looked ahead and saw Billie Moten, one of the cheeriest and kindest members of the local running community. Billie always has an encouraging word for everyone, and many a time she's made me feel up. But not today. She was my challenge! "I have to catch her," I thought. I couldn't do it, but in trying I came across the finish line in 7:44, the fastest mile I had run since getting sick.

The 5K

The 5k (five kilometers; 5000 meters; 3.1 miles) is the most popular running distance in the United States today. According to Linda Honikman of TACSTATS, "The shorter distance is more attractive to women and younger runners than the marathon." A majority of those who run the 5k, says Honikman, "want to participate and to have fun."

The 5k represents a challenge on every level—from simply completing the distance to catching the bug and training to run the distance well. In addition, the 5k offers a manageable alternative to thousands of runners—many of whom have run marathons—who are not able or willing to run longer distances on a continual basis. And the 5k provides racing experience at a less taxing, thus safer, distance than the 10k race or marathoning, especially in hot and humid summer months. Running the 5k also builds speed, an advantage for longer-distance races. A top track runner might do two or three 10k's all season, preferring to race mostly distances in the 5k range.

A Race of Strength and Speed

Like all good training and racing, doing well in the 5k requires balance. In this case, the balance is between strength and speed.

According to Eamonn Coghlan, the tactics for running the 5000 meters are exactly the same as for the mile. The key to running a smart 5000 is to relax, sit, and kick. For most average road runners, the 5k is a short distance. "It sometimes makes people panic," says Coghlan. "To do it well takes an ability to get into the proper pace and rhythm over the first quarter mile, then relax and settle down."

It's important then to concentrate on everything that's happening in the race. "Try not to focus on yourself, particularly on negative physical sensations," Coghlan advises. "Try to forget about yourself (that prevents panic), trust your instinctive ability, and focus on everything that's going on around you. Allow the environment to carry you along. Focus on other runners or spectators rather than worrying about your fatigue, a pain in your legs, or a stitch. Of course you're aware of yourself to a degree, but use your surroundings to help you through."

According to Coghlan the 5k on the track allows you to focus easily because of the repetition: 12½ laps. He suggests starting in control, then moving into contention with 2½ laps to go. "Because winning is almost always the objective (as opposed to running fast), I've always had a tendency to forget about the race, as long as I was being pulled along," Coghlan explains. "Then with those 2½ laps remaining, I focus more on the task at hand. Concentration is also tiring, and saving that intense focus for a while assures you'll have it when you need it." The same can hold true of running on the roads. If you save something for that final half-mile, you'll probably pass a few people on your way to the finish.

It takes the strength of a marathoner and the speed of a miler to run a good 5k, Coghlan contends. A lot of milers moving up to the 5000 get caught up in doing too much speedwork. "I truly believe that you have to do an incredible amount of strength work to be able to get to the latter stages of the 5k and still have enough speed to be able to 'kick it in,'" he says. Strength work in this case means training that consists of repeat 800 meters and one- and even two-mile repeats.

Most milers concentrate on their 200-, 400-, and 800-meter speed to get their times down, while 5000-meter runners should concentrate on 800-meter through mile speed. As a result, Coghlan believes, those who do typical mile training often don't have the kind of strength it takes to get to the last 400 meters in a 5000 with the necessary speed. "If you do too much short speed training, you won't have the strength to be able to 'kick off' at the end. Whereas I believe if you have the strength to be able to get to the last quarter mile, you will have the speed. That final speed has to be saved, so it's essentially like icing on the cake. The mistake is to put too much icing on the cake by speeding up too early.

"I never had basic sprinter's speed. I was never a good quarter- or half-mile runner. My ability to run a quarter mile all-out is only 50 seconds, yet at the end of a 5000-meter race I can run 50 seconds for a quarter. At the end of a mile race, I can run 50 seconds. However, if I warmed up and ran only a quarter mile all-out, I'd still only run 50 seconds. What I did have was tremendous ability to 'kick off' the final turn and win my races."

I learned to understand my strengths and weaknesses the hard way. In the 1976 Olympic Games 1500-meter final, I went against the truth of my experience. The night before that particular race, my coach, Jumbo Elliott, said to me, "There are a lot of fast half-milers in the race. If the pace is too slow going through the quarter, you're going to have to take it out, and run the speed out of these people." So for the first time in my life, I changed my tactics. I took the lead after the quarter mile. Instead of sitting behind John Walker (the eventual winner), which I had planned to do, and hopefully blowing by him with 150 meters to go, I became the sacrificial lamb. The fast half-milers in the race ended up beating me, and I came in a disappointing fourth place. I think the only reason that happened was because I took the lead from one quarter mile into the race as opposed to hanging in there and letting my strength get me to the last 100 meters, and then kicking by the other runners.

—Eamonn Coghlan

Training for the 5K

"I think the average runner focuses too much on mileage and not enough on speed," says PattiSue Plumer of training for the 5k. "To achieve maximum performance—no matter what the goal—you need some speedwork, or faster-paced running, whether it be fartlek or interval training. Either way, this training should be done at least once a week, at an effort quicker than race pace."

"To race a good 5k, run at least 40 miles per week. If you're currently running three to four miles per day at a comfortable pace and you're looking to improve your 5k, add some speedwork. For example, if your goal is a 20-minute 5k—a 6:30-per-mile average—you should run at least once a week at a six-minute pace—that is, 30 seconds faster than race pace—or as much under goal race pace as possible. Schedule at least one speed session per week; two or three faster-paced sessions are ideal."

PattiSue Plumer's 5K Training Program

If I were to train a group of average athletes who want to maximize potential but who, like most people, have jobs and responsibilities and do not train full time, I would fashion a five-day-per-week training schedule, which I have done here. In my opinion, the truth is that most busy people cannot sustain a seven-day-a-week schedule. There are too many other stresses and responsibilities in their lives.

The biggest mistake in this country is that we discount the stresses of outside life. A training program is no good if you are so beat you can't function in other aspects of your life. The mistake is that runners often don't modify their schedules when necessary. They don't take into account stresses such as staying up until all hours with a work project, or with a child who has the flu.

I train with a group of people that includes runners from every walk of life—masters, parents, those with full-time jobs. That's why in prescribing a training program, I take into account all aspects of life. I've seen my coach do this with our group of runners as well.

Often I am approached by athletes of various caliber who ask me whether to rest—to take a day off running. I take rest days. I tell them that an extra day of rest hurts a lot less than the risk of doing an extra day of training.

The Program

The following program includes parts of PattiSue Plumer's own training at one particular point in her season, which she has adapted for athletes in "decent shape, but new to hard running."

Monday: warm up and cool down: 10 minutes each of jogging. Fartlek: run hard for one minute, jog recovery for six to 10 minutes—a total of 40 minutes. Total running time: one hour. Track equivalent: quarters in 60 seconds

(Plumer's workout is the same, except she runs hard for one minute and jogs recovery for three minutes.)

Tuesday: easy run of 30 minutes to one hour, "depending on your goal and what you're used to doing."

Wednesday: same as Tuesday

Thursday: similar to Monday (if you have access to a track, use it for variety); eight to 12 times 200 meters, close to "all-out"; jog 200 meters' recovery at any pace, "the slower, the better."

(Plumer's workout: 12 to 20 times 200 meters, 27 to 31 seconds (depending on time of year and if "I'm running with the guys"); jog 200 meters for recovery between each.)

Friday: day off

Saturday: long run—at least one hour, up to 1½ hours, at "conversation pace."

Plumer's Comments on Her Program. There is nothing magical about one-minute or 200-meter repeats. They are just illustrations of one long-distance speed session and one short-distance speed session. I do the longer intervals in the first part of the week because, personally, faster speedwork breaks me down quicker than longer speedwork. And since I want to do speedwork at least twice a week, my program gives me a sufficient number of rest days between each session.

If, for some reason, you don't recover from these workouts—say, you are not ready to do a Saturday long run after a Thursday speed session—don't do it. Remember, I'm a believer in rest! Also, those with families or who want their weekends freer may want to adapt the schedule to do the Saturday run on Friday.

The 10K

The 10k (10 kilometers; 6.2 miles; 10,000 meters) is a road running standard. Even if you're a beginning runner, you've likely heard about the 10k. The popularity of this distance is indisputable. Seven of the country's 20 top largest road races in 1990—representing every possible distance—were 10k's.

Do you want to become a versatile runner? Do you want to run a good marathon? Then take a cue from the elite. Alberto Salazar is the former American record holder in the 10,000 meters (27:25), the 5000 meters (13:11), and the marathon (2:08:13). He held those records simultaneously, and each performance contributed to the other. Says Salazar, "I believe that to run your fastest marathon you should be as close as possible to your fastest 10,000-meter shape a few months before."

Everyone knows Frank Shorter won the Olympic marathon in the 1972 Games. But not many recall that just a few days before that race, he ran the Olympic 10,000 meters, coming in fifth in what was then an American record time of 27:51.

For the novice, a 10k is a good challenge. The distance is long enough to give the feeling of distance running, yet not as demanding as 10 miles or a half marathon. Running 45 to 60 minutes for a 10k will not require the extensive recovery a longer race does. Thus you'll be able to resume regular training and racing fairly quickly after running a 10k. However, it is not advisable to run 10k races more than once every two to three weeks to allow proper mental as well as physical recovery.

How Fast Can You Run?

You can factor your ability to run various distances by using the 10k as a gauge. The examples of two top runners' personal bests at 10k and the marathon, for instance, reveal that there is a pace variance of about 25 to 30 seconds per mile between 10k race pace and marathon race pace. Alberto Salazar's 27:25 is 4:25 per mile, while his marathon record of 2:08:13 averages a 4:53 pace. The difference is 28 seconds. Frank Shorter's 10k best is 27:45, a 4:28 pace. His marathon best is 2:10:30, a 4:59 pace, a 31-second difference.

Using about 30 seconds per mile as the average 10k-marathon differential, you can assess your 10k or marathon race time. If you want to run a 3:00 marathon, which is a 6:52 pace, using the above formula, you'd need to run a 10k at a 6:27 pace, or 40:00.

It is clear from the elite that quick 10k times equal marathon success. Almost every good runner will testify that performing successfully at various distances is related to the combination of strength and speed needed for 10k running. Therefore, the key to racing success at a range of running distances is based on 10k training. That's why many of the training programs and philosophies that appear in this book are based on performing well at 10k. The programs are then only slightly adapted for running the marathon.

Running the 10K

Grete Waitz offers a series of tips for the 10k, from emotional preparation to physical training:

1. First of all, don't panic. Ten kilometers is about six miles, and most people can walk that distance comfortably at four miles per hour. Therefore, even walking all the way, you could do it in one and one half hours. Think of it this way: Any improvement on an hour and a half is progress!

2. Make a commitment to train with a friend and perhaps do the race together. When motivation is low and excuses are easy to find, that commitment will help get you through the rough times and to race day.

3. During your training, "hurry slowly,"as we say in Norwegian. Gradually and progressively increase your training, rather than

try to cram it all into the last few days (as you might try to do for an exam).

4. If you cannot handle the increase in training sessions, simply ease back a little and put in more walking sections. Take it easy.

5. Don't let inclement weather keep you from training. If the weather is hot, cut back a little or walk more often, and drink plenty of fluids. If it is cold, dress appropriately and be sure to warm up well.

6. When jogging, you should be able to talk to your partner. So run at a conversational pace.

7. In the event of illness or other health setbacks, be aware that you cannot make up lost time in training by pushing yourself hard the following week. Let your body recover; step back one week in your schedule, and regroup. Change your goal if necessary.

Training for the 10K

Grete Waitz's 10K Program for Beginners

This program was developed by Grete Waitz for beginning runners, those who may have a base of fitness from another sport or who have been jogging and would like to participate in a 10k race.

Week 1

Sunday: alternate walking and jogging in one-minute intervals for 12 minutes

Tuesday: alternate walking and jogging in one-minute intervals for 14 to 15 minutes

Thursday: alternate walking and jogging in two-minute intervals for 16 or 17 minutes

Saturday: do alternate aerobic exercise (e.g., walking, cycling, swimming, aerobics, tennis)

At the end of this first week, you may experience more difficulty with your lungs than with your legs. Your legs are in use every day; however, your lungs probably haven't been worked so hard in a while. This discomfort will soon pass.

Week 2

Sunday: alternate walking and jogging, one minute walking and two minutes jogging, for 20 minutes (if you have a regular training partner, one can check the jogging time interval, the other the walking interval)

Tuesday: alternate walking and jogging at the same intervals as on Sunday

Thursday: alternate walking and jogging at the same intervals as Sunday for 26 minutes

Saturday: alternate exercise

The most difficult part of the program is over. You have survived the novelty of the activity as well as the first couple of training sessions, and have likely adapted to the discipline of regular exercise. Most people who give up their training usually do so in the second or third week.

Week 3

Sunday: jog for five minutes, walk for one minute. Repeat four times. Then jog for three minutes, walk for two minutes to finish. Total: approximately 29 minutes.

Tuesday: walk for two minutes. Jog for 10 minutes. If the 10-minute jog is achieved, then repeat it after another two-minute walk. If it proved too difficult, then cut it down to five minutes and repeat twice more with a two-minute walk interval. Finish with a two-minute jog.

Thursday: five-minute jog, two-minute walk; 10-minute jog, two-minute walk; five-minute jog, two-minute walk; three-minute jog, two-minute walk

Saturday: alternate exercise

Unless circumstances absolutely prevent it, try to vary your training venue. Footpaths in parks are probably the most pleasant, but playing fields, towpaths, country footpaths, and even the local track can all help to vary the scenery and maintain interest. All the training in this program is designed around time periods, not distances, so knowing the distance you have covered is not really important. Believe it or not, the hardest weeks are behind you. Disciplining yourself to go out training may have been difficult, the early stiffness may have been unpleasant—

but you have made it. Keep some structure to your program, and don't become impatient.

Week 4

Sunday: 12-minute jog, two-minute walk; five minutes running a little faster (but not racing); two-minute walk; 12-minute jog, two-minute walk; five-minute jog, two-minute walk

Tuesday: 15-minute jog, two-minute walk; 15-minute jog, two-minute walk; five-minute jog, two-minute walk

Wednesday: alternate exercise

Thursday: 17-minute jog, three-minute walk; 15-minute jog, three-minute walk; 10-minute jog, three-minute walk

Saturday: alternate exercise

Try to cut out, or at least cut down on, the walking stages in your training, and step up to four sessions per week.

Week 5

Sunday: 25-minute jog; try not to walk if possible

Monday: alternate exercise

Tuesday: 25-minute jog; 6 × 100-meter strides, with walking breaks between each (striding means stretching out, but not flat-out sprinting)

Wednesday: rest

Thursday: 25-minute jog

Friday: rest

Saturday: 20- to 27-minute jog, including 3 × 1-minute run at a faster pace (not a racing pace); walk for one minute after each one-minute faster section; resume jogging; when you feel ready, pick up your jogging pace and go for another one minute of faster running

This fifth week is tough. Don't be despondent if you needed to walk a bit. Remember, the training needs to be progressive to keep raising your level of fitness.

Week 6

Sunday: 30-minute jog, very easy—conversation pace!

Monday: alternate exercise

Tuesday: 30-minute jog, plus 6 × 100-meter strides (walking breaks between)

Wednesday: alternate exercise or rest

Thursday: 10-minute easy jog; 4 × 1-minute faster-pace runs with 2 minutes of rest/walk between; then 5 to 10 minute of easy jogging

Friday: rest

Saturday: 5-minute very easy jog, then either do a 5k fun-run, or approximately 3-mile training run in which you push yourself a little; check your time

Think back to your condition eight weeks ago and be proud of yourself!

Week 7

Sunday: 20-minute very easy recovery run

Monday: alternate exercise

Tuesday: 25- to 30-minute even-paced run (a little quicker than a jog)

Wednesday: alternate exercise

Thursday: 15-minute easy jog

Friday: rest

Saturday: 35-minute run

By now you should be enjoying the benefits of fitness: good sleeping pattern, healthy appetite, weight loss, etc.

Week 8

Sunday: 35-minute run

Monday: alternate exercise

Tuesday: 30-minute run, plus 8 × 100-meter strides (with recovery)

Wednesday: rest or 15-minute easy jog, if you're feeling really keen

Thursday: 15-minute jog, then 4 × 2-minute efforts, with 2-minute recovery; 10- to 15-minute easy jog to finish. Choose a nice circuit in your local park if you can.

Friday: rest

Saturday: 10-minute easy jog, then try out your 3-mile route again from two weeks ago; 5-minute easy jog to finish. Any improvement in time?

Only one more week of progressive training (the last week of the program is spent easing off to conserve energy for the race day).

Week 9

Sunday: 45-minute jog; walk a little, but only if necessary

Monday: alternate exercise

Tuesday: 35-minute run, plus 6 × 100-meter strides

Wednesday: rest, or 15-minute easy jog

Thursday: 15-minute jog; 8 × 1-minute quicker runs, with a 3-minute walk or jog for recovery; 15-minute easy jog

Friday: rest

Saturday: 25-minute easy jog

You've made it. The next week is spent easing down so you are ready for your big day.

Week 10

Sunday: 1-hour jog, with walking intervals as necessary

Tuesday: 20-minute jog

Thursday: 15-minute jog

Saturday: rest

Sunday: 10k race

Nerves are a part of racing. The nervousness will not hurt you, and the adrenaline your body releases into your bloodstream will help your running. However, try not to get carried away and start too fast. And don't forget, it's okay to walk for short spells if you feel like it. Don't eat a large breakfast before the race, but do try to eat something light at least two and one half hours before the start. Don't wear any gear (including socks) for the first time in the race. Make sure it's all well worn and laundered a few times before the big day. Can you imagine 10 weeks of hard work spoiled by a blister?

Week 11

You may be stiff the day after the event. Soaking in a hot bath helps ease the aches away, but so does exercise! Go for a short jog, 15 to 20 minutes, two to three days after the race, and maybe another one two days later. Keep at it—you have worked hard to get fit. Stay in shape. There are always other races and fun runs to enter.

10K for the Intermediate and Advanced Runner

I believe one of the keys to running a good 10k is to develop speed at shorter distances. The first time I ran 10k was in the Women's Mini Marathon in 1979 (31:15, a world best). I did this coming from my track background, where the longest distance I ran was 3000 meters. (At that time, that was the longest race distance generally available to women.) The smartest way to do well at 10k is to develop ability at shorter distances, like 5k. In my case, after I did a good 3000 meters on the track, I knew I was ready for a good 10k.

The biggest mistake I think people make in running 10k is going out too fast. The 10k's in which I haven't done particularly well are the ones in which I've started out too quickly—almost dying in the end. This is a particular risk when you're trying to run a good time. That's how it's usually been for me anyway, and why I eventually emphasized running for the victory rather than time. Although it's okay to try for a good time on selected occasions, that goal is just too draining to attempt all the time. While as a beginner you may naturally experience continual improvement, as you level off, try not to put pressure on yourself to run a personal best every time out.

To avoid starting out too fast, you have to "have eyes in your stomach," as we say in Norwegian: a good gut instinct of control. You can hone that instinct by doing your homework. Know the course, take into account the impact of the weather, and have the self-control that comes from self-confidence and experience. Even if you see the split time at the first mile, and it's slower than what you expected, you can be confident you'll catch and pass people by the end.

On the other hand, because a 10k isn't really that long a distance, you can't let your competition get too far ahead of you, or stray too far from your time goal if you have one. Proper pacing is a balance. It's something you have to learn to judge. You do hear runners who have waited too long say that if the race had been a mile longer, they could have caught their competition or run their goal time. But they made their move too late.

Another thing to be diligent about is the warmup. You start a 10k much faster than, say, a marathon, and often, with the adrenaline and crowd effect, much quicker than you may have expected or are used to. Therefore, warmup is crucial. I spend a good 30 minutes warming up for a 10k, unless, of course, it's in hot weather. Then I warm up less, and concentrate on staying cool but ready.

A 30-minute warmup may be too much for those not running competitively. However, some warmup is necessary. The point is to make sure your body is prepared to handle the initial quicker pace.

For a 10k, I taper my training the last five days before an event. If the race is on a Sunday, I'll do two easy days on Tuesday and Wednesday, a short interval workout on Thursday for sharpening, and take it easy again on Friday and Saturday. You may be "edgy" from tapering, but that's part of the process, and a sign you are ready to run.

—Grete Waitz

Fred Lebow on the NYRRC Bagel Run

The second biggest NYRRC 10k race (after the women's Advil Mini Marathon) is the Sheraton New York Bagel Run. It doesn't draw a world-class field, but it does provide some world-class fun.

The race starts and finishes at the south end of Central Park by Seventh Avenue, conveniently near the Sheraton, where over 2000 runners relax after the race, sitting at white-clothed tables to enjoy hot chocolate or coffee, bagels, lox, and cream cheese. The Bagel Run is also popular because in addition to the Sheraton-sponsored breakfast, the winners are crowned with an oversized bagel.

Among the various NYRRC races, the 10k races always draw large fields. It's longer than a mile but shorter than the marathon; people who run it feel like real distance runners.

Ten Miles to the Half Marathon

Some distance runners don't seem to be able to get going until about four or five miles into a 10k—when the race is nearly over. For these runners, the 10 miles to the half marathon is often an ideal range. Besides, this distance range is a good test of endurance—without the training investment and risks of a marathon. This range is also good preparation for the marathoner. As marathon practice, races in this range allow runners extensive experience on the road, usually from one and a half to two hours on average, requiring taking water, learning patience in pacing, etc.

> My favorite distances are 10 miles to the half marathon. On the shorter end of the competition scale, the 10k has become such a speed event. On the longer end, the marathon takes too much out of you. The reason I've been successful in longer events like the marathon is because I don't do them often. The other reason is because I like aspects of the training. I get a lot of enjoyment from my weekend long runs, in which I go with a group of men, run hard, and feel good. I mostly stick to the relatively longer distances because the shorter races are more difficult for me to train for. I can't keep up with the necessary track work because of my mechanics. I tend to get injured.
>
> —Joan Samuelson

If you've run 5k and 10k races, you'll likely feel a measure of physical comfort in events in this range. You'll be running 10 to 20 seconds slower per mile than in the shorter distances (as long as you don't make the mistake of going out at your 10k race pace, that is!). In addition, you'll also find that your next 10k will feel pleasantly short by comparison.

One drawback, however, is that there are fewer races of this distance available. It may be because there is a sizable participation gap. Of the top 20 largest road races in the United States in 1990, not a single one was in the 10-mile to half-marathon range. Runners seem to gravitate either to the shorter events or to the marathon.

Ten miles and half marathons are usually run in the fall and spring, when the weather allows for better and safer performance. One of the NYRRC's most popular events is the Trevira Twosome—a 10-mile couple's race, which began in 1979. The first race of its kind, it involves a twosome—a man and a woman—who each run their own pace (or they can run together) but are scored as a couple. (Because the distance is relatively long, a two-mile twosome race was eventually added.) The novelty aspect of this race takes some of the fear out of "going the distance" and relieves the pressure to perform well, allowing participants to focus instead on the fun of the racing experience. Undoubtedly, the focus on fun is key to the Trevira Twosome's enduring popularity.

Fred Lebow on the Half Marathon

When I was ill with cancer, I never could have dreamed I'd run as long as a half marathon again. In fact, I have done two half marathons since my illness, and they were very significant. One of them was in conjuction with the Indianapolis 500 car race in the spring of 1991. I had no intention of attempting to run that far, as I was in no way prepared after a year of illness and chemotherapy. But as I was a guest of the event, I entered just to complete a few miles. When 10,000 other runners took off, and I managed to make it through a few miles—with hundreds of people behind me (at least I wasn't last; since getting sick I had become used to that!)—I was so excited I went the entire way. Hoping just to break three hours, I came onto the race track to finish in 2:40. There were thousands of people cheering the thousands of other runners with me. It was a superb feeling. I felt I could do anything after that.

To top it off, the following day I was part of the Indy 500 parade. I rode in my own car with my name on the side. When my name was announced, I was amazed how the crowds cheered. I met the dignitaries on hand, Vice President Dan Quayle and General Norman Schwarzkopf. Together with having run the race, it was all a very "high" experience. This was one event during which I had the strong feeling that life certainly is worth living.

The Marathon

21

In the late 1970s and 1980s, the marathon captured the spirit of a nation in search of the ultimate personal challenge. Today the marathon is no longer an esoteric Mount Everest; it defines the goals of even the average distance runner. It's a sure bet that if you tell someone you're a runner, that person's immediate response will be, "Have you run a marathon?" Take Frank Shorter's word for it: If you want to legitimize your running in the eyes of your peers, tell them you're training for a marathon.

> Running a marathon is a tremendous accomplishment. I never understood why people ran them until I did it. Crossing the finish line of my first marathon gave me that "first-time glow"—a sense of accomplishment that I have not felt since. I love the event, and feel that my future is in it as far as Olympic competition is concerned. It's an intermediate goal, though. I don't foresee running marathons at age 50. I don't think a person can indefinitely do the kind of training required to be competitive in the marathon.
>
> Then, again, everyone is different. Grete [Waitz] did it for 10 years. Cathy O'Brien seems to be doing well in terms of marathon longevity, but the jury is still out on how it will affect her future. Maria Trujillo is someone who runs a marathon so frequently, it's like doing long training runs. I run my marathons few and far between. I didn't run one until 1986, and the next one two years later. I've only done four in all.
>
> —Francie Larrieu Smith

Marathon participation is on the rise. According to TACSTATS/USA, 263,000 people ran a marathon in the United States in 1990. That's up from 246,000 in 1989. There are marathons everywhere: from the streets of the world's major cities, up and down mountains, to the Great Wall in China. But for many, the best one is still the New York City Marathon.

New York has been the inspiration and model for many of the world's other marathons. This is particularly the case for races run through the streets of major cities. For many years, officials of the NYRRC have traveled the world advising on how to conduct a marathon. Some of the fledgling races with which they have helped have grown to world-wide prominence. These include such events as the London and Los Angeles Marathons, and scores of others.

Whether you prefer a small, quiet 26.2-miler in a rural area or the experience of the rush of running through a big city, the spirit of New York defines the meaning of the marathon race. In many respects, it is a symbol for the entire running movement.

What is the great appeal of the marathon? This is something I continually ask myself as nearly 50,000 requests for entries pour in every year for the New York City Marathon. I see the local hopefuls stand in line to turn in their requests, snaking almost a mile through Central Park. I multiply that by the thousands heading to post offices and mailboxes around the world, and realize we will have to turn away nearly half of them. I contemplate what could lead so many "ordinary" people to do something so extraordinary: run 26.2 miles.

But in my heart, I understand. Not only because I watch in wonder every year how this event unfolds, but because elsewhere, in every corner of the globe, I, too, have run marathons: 68 of them, to be exact. The event is so appealing to me, a middle-of-the-pack runner, that at one point I ran one every month for a year.

I can only say that of all of them, one stands out: New York. Even though I have not run it in its current form, I've lived with it long enough to know what it is like for those who do. I have run my own marathon only once: the first one. And my goal is to someday run it again, perhaps for my 60th birthday, when this book comes out.

—Fred Lebow

What is so compelling about running a marathon? That's hard to understand if you haven't done one, and sometimes the most difficult to comprehend when you're in the middle of one!

George Sheehan on the

Uniqueness of Running a Marathon

Nearly thirty Aprils ago, when I ran my first Boston Marathon, the racers were little more than an informal club. Of the 225 of us who ran, many were present only on a dare or as a joke. Others were overweight, out of shape, and attired in gym suits and sneakers.

That first year, I finished 96th in 3:07 and, because of this, considered myself one of the top 100 marathoners in the United States. Fifteen years later, at age 61, I ran a slightly faster time in the New York City Marathon. I didn't crack the top 2,000. As one of only 126 starters in the first New York Marathon in 1970, I have seen its field grow to more than 25,000.

Someone on the outside of these events might well ask, "What is going on?" Back in 1970, America was already interested in getting fit: Dr. Kenneth Cooper's aerobics book, for instance, had already sold hundreds of thousands of copies. However, though an emphasis on fitness was on the rise, only a handful of people—and few, if any of them, women—ran races. And only the hard core ran marathons.

My son, who is both a runner and an observer of this scene, had his own explanation for the marathoning boom: "Fitness is out, experience is in." Running has gone beyond fitness. The jogging movement, which began as a pursuit of health, has become an experiential quest. Runners are no longer content with fitness but are seeking a new awareness of the self in the total experience of running—and more often than not they are culminating that quest by experiencing a marathon.

The desire to run comes from deep within us—from the unconscious, the instinctive, the intuitive—and the runner's progression to a marathon is a natural one: how to train, what to do before a race, what shoes to wear, what pace to set at the start, when to accelerate, how to achieve the proper attitude. I have become ready for the part of the marathon that is pure body.

The marathon, however, is more than that. It is, to use Yeats's description of poetry, "blood, imagination, and intellect brought together." The marathoner comes to be the total person running the total race.

When I run a marathon, I put myself at the center of my life, the center of my universe. For these hours, I move past ideas of food and shelter and sexual fulfillment and other basic drives. I bring my life and its meaning down to this struggle, this supreme effort that I must make.

The music of the marathon is a powerful martial strain, a tune of glory. It asks us to forsake pleasures, to discipline the body, to find courage, to renew faith, and to become one's own person utterly and completely.

The athletic experience can be divided into three parts: the preparation (training the body), the event (challenging the self), and the aftermath (creating in the mind). For the runner, the marathon is the ultimate athletic experience, taking training and challenging and creating to their absolute limits.

Running has been described as a "thinking person's sport." The reference is to the predominance of middle-class, highly educated people who have taken up this activity. But it also refers to the fact that it is a sport requiring considerable study of the workings of the body. Runners in training acquire detailed knowledge of how the body operates best: One must have a working knowledge of exercise physiology and nutrition to come to a peak.

Training is the science of running. The application of that science is sensual. Runners have an expression, "Listen to your body." They understand that biofeedback machines merely amplify messages that should be heard without technology. They develop what Maslow called "biological wisdom." They become experts in their own bodies. They become good animals.

This listening and learning are often done by working at the edge of self-inflicted pain. Training on hills and with speedwork means repeatedly pushing the limits of tolerance to oxygen debt. At other times, however, training can be a pleasure; there are days when I get tremendous enjoyment out of the effort and the sweat and the competence I feel. Like Thoreau, I occupy my body with delight.

In training for a marathon, I grow in physical wisdom. I learn how my body works best. I read the texts, of course, but then I take those lessons and test them on the road. I filter the theories on exercise through my exercising body and come up with my own truth. I remake my body to my own image. I prepare myself for an exploration of my outer limits.

The marathon is the focal point of all that has gone before and all that will come afterward. "The distance race," wrote Paul Weiss, "is a struggle that results in self-discovery. It is an adventure involving the limits of the self." It is William James's moral equivalent of war—that theater for heroism where the runner can do deeds not possible in day-to-day living.

"Life," said James, "is made in doing and suffering and creating." It is all there in the marathon: the doing in training and the suffering in the race and finally the creating that comes in the tranquillity of the aftermath.

James spoke of the peace and confidence that come from every muscle of a well-trained body. Taking that body through a grueling 26.2-mile race improves one's self-concept and self-esteem immeasurably. Even more, it provides the material for the creative acts to follow.

Robert Frost once said that to write a poem you first must have an experience. To do any creative act, you must have an experience. To make your life a work of art, you must have the material to work with. The race, any race, is just such an experience. The marathon is that experience raised to the nth degree. It fills the conscious and unconscious with the sights and sounds, the feelings and the emotions, the trials and accomplishments of the event.

All That Matters Is Going the Distance

After I had finished the New York City Marathon, my daughter asked me if I had relived my past while running through the familiar streets. Surely, she thought, those miles must have brought back memories of my early life in Brooklyn and New York City.

Other spectators thought I must have been inspired by the spectacle at the start of the race, the helicopters hovering like fish in a giant mobile. And hadn't I been filled with emotion, they asked, when we passed through the enormous crowds lining the route, shouting encouragement?

In truth, none of these things happened. A marathon is not a city, nor is it a crowd. It is not a sense of nostalgia or one of the wonders of the world, whether man-made or natural.

The vista during the marathon is of no consequence. Degree of difficulty is what inevitably concerns me. Weather and terrain are my considerations. Other athletes view their playing areas similarly: not by the aesthetics but by what controls and influences performance.

The golfer looks at a famous hole on a famous course and sees only where the pin lies and what the wind is up to. The baseball player cares nothing about the history of a ballpark or about the classic games played there; he wants to know the distance down the foul lines and what the infield does to a ground ball.

It is a matter of what is important. Yeats once wrote that the English had too many flowers in their poetry. "Scenery is fine but human nature finer" is the way Shelley put it. I try not to let the flowers or the scenery distract me from the task at hand.

To me, a marathon is a marathon is a marathon. There is nothing else, just the matter of taking my body—five-feet-nine, 136 pounds, 9 percent body fat, and 60 percent slow-twitch fibers—a distance of 26 miles, 385 yards. Everything that affects this accomplishment is important; everything else, irrelevant. Worse than that, it is distracting and therefore ultimately defeating.

I will not deny, however, that each marathon imposes itself on my memory. The finish of every one I have run—more than 50 of them since that first one in Boston—will stay with me the rest of my life. Coming down the plaza at Boston's Prudential Center is not something easily forgotten, nor is the last mile through New York's Central Park.

There is nothing to compare to the feeling I get on completing a marathon. But I must not think of that until the end comes. There are, you see, only two concerns in a marathon: pace and form. Each step, each stride, must be made in a perfect form and at the perfect speed.

This sounds simple. Running is, after all, a reflex act. Nine-year-olds do it perfectly. There is no reason why an adult with sufficient discipline should not develop an effortless technique that requires no thought of the action. And since the body perceives exertion as efficiently as any instrument yet invented, it can be depended upon to pick that perfect tempo as soon as I settle down to serious running.

Unfortunately, once the marathon begins, what seems so simple becomes unbearably complex. The body loses the rhythm and harmony I know on the practice runs, and the messages that determine so accurately my pace in training are garbled and indistinct.

There are 26 miles, 385 yards to go, and I must focus not on scenery or on memories but on the basics of marathon survival.

Why Run? Who Knows for Sure?

Near the 23-mile mark of the New York City Marathon, I ran along in the grip of the inexpressible fatigue that comes at this stage in the race. I once again engaged in a struggle between a completely exhausted body and a yet-undefeated will.

As I ran past a group of onlookers, one of them recognized me and called out, "Dr. Sheehan, what would Emerson have said now?" I had to laugh, even in that pain. It was a particularly deft shot at someone who had used other people's words to express his own truth—and I was now in a situation that clearly no one else could describe. But the question also went to the heart of why I ran marathons.

The case for distance running cannot be stated simply, even by its adherents. No matter how often I am asked—usually in more favorable circumstances than at the 23-mile mark of a marathon—my answer is always inadequate.

This inadequacy is not only mine. At one race, a New York Road Runners Club questionnaire was distributed to the entrants, asking them why they ran. The list of suggested answers had been made by scientists of both the body and the mind, and there were 15 possible choices, the last one being, "Don't really know." The range of possible answers suggested that the researchers knew the runners would have trouble putting a finger on their personal motivations.

I think it suggestive, however, that only three of the answers— "Improving physical health," "Improving sexual capacity," and "Acquiring a youthful appearance"—had to do with the body. All the others (except the final disclaimer of not knowing at all) were about psychological benefits. Runners apparently take it as given that physical health is a by-product of, but not the real reason for, running.

I, too, am aware of that. I am my body. What I do begins there. But I am much more besides. What happens to my body has enormous effect on my heart and mind. When I run, I become of necessity a good animal. But I also become, for less obvious and more mysterious reasons, a good person. I become, in some uncanny way, complete. Perhaps it has something to do with a sense of success and mastery over this art of running.

The scientists tried to express this in their suggested answers. Do I run, they asked, to relax, to relieve boredom, or to improve my mental health? Is it possible, they inquired, that I do it to achieve recognition or to master a challenge or to find an additional purpose in life? Was running perhaps something I do for companionship and a sense of belonging, or because I am unhappy or unfulfilled without it?

What we were being asked was cast in the familiar "either/or" form. Is it process or product that pushes us? Is it what happens while we run, or what we achieve through running that motivates us? Is running for the body or the spirit?

Runners Are Different

My running is not an either/or activity. It is done for all these reasons and more. The product—the ability to run a marathon, the having done it—is indeed important, but so is the process. Training is not only a means, it is also an end in itself. The achievement is not the sole reason for running. There is also what goes on before the mastering of the challenge, what goes on while finding an additional purpose in life.

My running is both process and product. Sometimes it is all meaning and no purpose. Other times it is all purpose and no meaning. Sometimes it is work, other times play, and there are even times when it is an act of love.

We who run are different from those who merely study us. We are out experimenting what they are trying to put into words. We know what they are merely trying to know. They are seeking belief, while we already believe. Our difficulty is in expressing the whole truth of that experience, that knowledge, that belief.

So I wish Emerson had run that marathon, and that somewhere around the 23-mile mark a friend had asked him, "What's it all about, Waldo?"

Public Spectacle, Interior Drama

James Joyce took 10 years of Homer's *Odyssey* and compressed it into a single Dublin day. He looked into the mind and heart and body of the hero Ulysses, and created Leopold Bloom, who is Everyman. Joyce took those inner and outer events that happen to everyone and put all of them into the waking-to-sleeping day of his Irish Jew. It takes 18 hours.

The marathon does it in three. Like many sports events, the marathon is a microcosm of life. The marathoner can experience the drama of everyday existence so evident to the artist and poet. All emotions are heightened. Agony and ecstasy become familiar feelings. The journey from start to finish reveals what happens to a person who faces up to the self and the world—and why he or she succeeds or fails.

The successful runner is the one who endures, taking life as it comes and saying yes to it. This trait is so commonly displayed in the marathon that it seems universal. I believe every human must have this endurance capacity.

The truth is that every runner in a marathon is a survivor or nothing, including the winner. Winning is, in fact, unimportant.

"Brief is the season of a man's delight," sang Pindar in his ode to an Olympic winner. Tomorrow is another race, another test, another challenge. And then there is another race, and another.

In my profession, it's unique to run marathons. The marathon makes a statement for me. I'm used to seeing models lifting these little weights on their legs and saying, "This is how I keep in shape." Then they go off and smoke a cigarette. This isn't true of all of them; some truly are in shape. But even so, you don't hear about models running marathons and doing strenuous pursuits.

The marathon is something that appeals to me. Mind over matter. It has a parallel with a lot in my life because it's about not giving up. Another thing about the marathon, it proves you can do what you set your mind to do.

People respect you for running a marathon. They say things like, "I ran one mile; I can't imagine going 26!" Also, physically I'm a big person. I can't run much faster than I do, so I figure I'll go farther.

I'm very competitive, but I can be content with my running. I know a 3:51 marathon is fine, even when the women's winner ran 2:27. You can't be on the top of every hill.

Sports round me out. It's one thing to be good in one aspect of life: to be a good mom, good in a career, a good person, to run marathons. But to do them all, and do them the best you can, makes you a whole person.

—Kim Alexis

The New York City Marathon

Among the hundreds of races and programs created and conducted by the NYRRC, the New York City Marathon is the crown jewel. The marathon (and New York in particular) is more than just a footrace, it's an event. For a single Sunday every November, millions of people from all over the world come together for a challenge and a celebration in one of the most complex and grandest cities in the world. They call New York the Big Apple, and at least for a day, these people make it shine. And they make themselves shine—by running, or cheering, by volunteering to hand out water or put adhesive bandages on blisters.

My first NYRRC race was the 1974 New York City Marathon. The course was very tough—multiple loops of Central Park—and the weather was hot. I ran a stupid race. I went out too hard and beat myself. I should be a five-time winner of New York instead of four.

I remember the first time I talked with Fred. It was in Boston, before New York became a big race in 1976. I remember going to an NYRRC gathering in Boston and seeing Fred, Joe Kleinerman, Kurt Steiner—some of the stalwarts from the club. It was in that same year, at the Falmouth road race, that Fred came up to me and Frank Shorter and asked us to run the first five-borough New York City Marathon. We said we would like to run.

> The 1976 New York City Marathon signaled a critical change in the visibility of the sport, and visibility is the lifeblood of an event. The Boston Marathon has had great fame because of its heritage over the years. But New York has had television. What would Wimbledon or the Indy 500 be if they weren't on television? They'd be big in England or Indianapolis, but nowhere else. Boston should be on television, but New York has taken over. New York is the leader. It is the first to give open prize money; first on national television; first in professional race management. Those developments have been very important to the sport.
>
> —Bill Rodgers

What's more, the marathon represents a perfect human journey, a 26.2-mile odyssey through New York's neighborhoods. It is a journey that changes lives—from the disabled who prove something to themselves and others, to the dedicated, yet perhaps unknown athletes who will cross the finish line first, and in so doing, change their lives forever.

> I have been asked everywhere I go: Why do people run the marathon? Sure, there is a sense of status we gain among our peers. But I think the real reasons are more personal. I think it is because we need to test our physical, emotional, or creative abilities. After all, in practical life we cannot all "give it our all." We can't grow wings and fly. We can't sing without a great voice, or dance when we aren't dancers. Most of us won't perform on a stage. But whether a person is a world-class athlete or a four-hour runner, the marathon gives us a stage. In this case, it's the road, where we can perform and be proud, while millions of people applaud. It's like being on Broadway and getting a standing ovation!
>
> For another thing, in an unequal world, in this one endeavor people of vastly differing abilities share something in common: the act of going the distance. Whether it's two hours or four or five, the effort and achievement are similar.
>
> —Fred Lebow

The New York City Marathon is currently the largest race in the world. Next year it might not be. "It doesn't really matter," explains

Fred Lebow. "We're not reaching for the numbers—to be the biggest. We aspire only to be the best. In fact, we don't even want to be the fastest marathon. We want to have the most *competitive* marathon. What has always been most important above all, however, is to make sure that every single runner—not only the elite, but even the six- and seven-hour finisher—is treated with dignity and care."

> After nine times across the New York City Marathon finish line in first place—three of them in world best times—and six times a victor in the Women's Mini Marathon, in which she also broke the world record, I remain in awe of Grete Waitz as an athlete and as a person. Grete has been a big factor in the growth of women's running and the evolution of the New York City Marathon. If anyone had to choose a queen of the road, it would be Grete Waitz.
>
> —Fred Lebow

"It makes me feel good when people come up to me and say things about the marathon like, 'It changed my life.' Just to share the feeling of satisfaction people get is one of the reasons I always stand near the finish line to greet the four- and five-hour finishers. That's why I've always known that the marathon is more than just a 26.2-mile footrace; it's a life experience. It has always been that way for me, and over the years, I've seen that's true for the other runners who do it."

"This is not to downplay the vast importance of the world-class level of competition. Every winner of the race has thrilled and inspired millions of people, from television viewers to back-of-the-pack marathoners in the same race."

Fred Lebow's Marathon Adventures

I have been fortunate to run a total of 68 marathons. They have been held in 32 countries and on every continent except Australia. Various organizers around the world would invite me to give advice on creating or improving their events. To get a true feel for what they were doing, I would run the race. I began running the races as part of my work, but quickly got hooked on it for my own personal running.

The most difficult marathon I ever ran was Bermuda. The course is on very hilly terrain. The only tougher marathon I know of is Yonkers, in New York—the oldest marathon in the country, by the way. I've run races that are memorable for the unexpected, like the Moscow Marathon, where they passed out hot cherry soup, and the Finland Marathon, which featured pickle barrels—not with water, but with actual pickles.

I haven't done well-known marathons like those in Amsterdam or Lisbon, or the five-borough New York City Marathon, but I love the London Marathon, probably because it so resembles New York's. It's got the people, the numbers, the quality, and the organization. That's what it takes to make a great race. But it's not just the city that makes the race, it's also the people and the individual experience. I had those kinds of experiences in places like Cairo, Egypt, and Aruba, which I describe in the travel section of this book.

The most memorable marathon I ever ran was in Marrakesh, Morocco, in 1987. Marrakesh is a fascinating city, and the way the marathon course was laid out, you really got a feel for the place. The course covered a mix of sights, through the olive groves of the countryside to the streets of the city. People were out cheering boisterously all along the way. Even though the race suffered from a common problem—not enough water—it was still very exciting. The only thing that turned me off was at the finish. Trays of cigarettes were being passed out. It turned out the cigarette company was a race sponsor. I told the organizers that I, for one, would never return until they dropped that sponsor. They finally did.

One of the worst events I ever ran, actually a half marathon, was in Istanbul. At least I was not alone. I ran it with my friend Paula Fahey. It was extremely hot, and there was not one water station with any of the precious liquid left. Every time we came to a table, all that was there were empty bottles. It turns out the spectators had helped themselves to a drink. By the time the runners came by, the stations were dry. Finally we found a place to buy water. And at the finish, it was being sold.

One of my most dramatic marathon experiences was in 1983, in Shanghai. I described it in my first book. I had trained hard and was in great shape. I even thought I might run my personal best time, 3:29, which I had done in Syracuse, New York, in 1970. Shanghai had a small field of about 500 runners. The Chinese treated me as an honored guest and insisted, over my own objections, that I line up with the fastest runners in the very front row, where they had even painted on the road a number "6," matching my running number.

At the same time the starting gun went off, I was distracted trying to set my stopwatch. I got knocked down by runners behind me and landed hard on my shoulder. Everybody trampled over me, as there was no way to avoid doing so in the beginning surge. I was hurt, but I wasn't about to drop out right at the start. So I walked a little, then began running.

The entire pack of runners was far ahead. Crowds along the way were laughing at me—this Westerner running dead last, way behind the field. After 15 kilometers I was in such agony from my shoulder pain that I pulled off to the side. The course at this point was in farmland, and I saw this old guy carrying two pails of water on a bamboo pole over his shoulders. I waved him over and tried to indicate that my shoulder hurt and that I wanted him to dump a refreshing pail of water over me. But he got behind me, grabbed my shoulders, and pushed his knee into my back. There was a brief moment of tremendous, sharp pain, then magically my shoulder was better.

I ran okay until about five kilometers from the finish, and then the agony returned. I just about collapsed, but managed to finish in 4:28—dead last. They took me to the hospital, X-rayed me, spread something that looked like plum jelly around my shoulder and arm, and gave me mysterious but extremely potent pills to take. The pain didn't return until I ran out of the right combination of pills a few days later. Back in New York, the doctor said I had probably suffered a slight shoulder dislocation, and he put my arm in a sling. Examining the last of my Chinese pills, he said they were not something he could prescribe but that I could sell them for a lot of money on the street.

I've done a lot of marathons—too many, the experts would probably say. I was crazy. They invited me, so I ran. Even I have trouble believing my most ambitious series of races. It began in Greece, during the European Championships in 1982. On Sunday I ran a half marathon on the marathon course there. On Monday I flew to Tel Aviv, where I ran the Tel Aviv Marathon the following day. On Thursday I flew to Cairo. I spent the day looking over the Cairo Marathon course with a group from the British Embassy. On Saturday I flew to Rome. On Sunday I ran the Rome Marathon.

I may have been ambitious, but I was also tired. I had forgotten my running shoes at the hotel in Cairo, so I had to buy a new pair in Rome.

I didn't want to run the race in new shoes, but I was too tired to take them out on a run to break them in. I asked race director Bob Bright to help me out. He wore them on a one-hour training run.

My fatigue started to catch up with me while running the Rome Marathon. I stopped to go in a bar and get a soft drink. I lay down to rest for a few minutes in the grass. I finally finished the race, in 4:50.

But it doesn't end there. On Monday I flew back to New York for two days of meetings. On Thursday I got on a plane for Seoul, Korea, where I arrived on Friday. On Sunday I ran a marathon, testing the course that became the 1988 Olympic race route.

Korea provided another dramatic experience. The race had 7000 runners, all Koreans except for a few invited runners, including Allison Roe and Bill Rodgers. I got up on a ladder to look at the start. I remember the vision of 7000 heads of black hair. It looked like a black carpet, except for the two blondes standing in the front row: Rodgers and Roe.

This was another race with too little water. I remember a woman spectator came out with a kettle of water, and the runners flocked to her like locusts. It was so hot, it was hard to run very quickly. When I got to the 35-kilometer point, everyone suddenly started to sprint. It turned out that those who had not reached this point by three hours weren't permitted to continue. Sure enough, I missed the cutoff. But I had come all this way to run a marathon, and I wasn't going to quit. So I ran through anyway. The police came after me yelling, but fortunately they didn't catch me. I got to the finish, which closed off at four hours. Much to my anger and frustration, I was again cut off. I finished in 4:02, using my own watch to time myself.

Water: It's the most important part of a marathon. And so many times there isn't enough. I have gotten into the habit of always asking the organizers if they have adequate water and water stations. In Korea they told me, "No problem; it's taken care of." But never trust any race director. They're not being deceptive, but sometimes they just don't understand the logistics of providing sufficient water. I understand that in Korea, the problem was taken care of the following year. Then they were granted the Olympics.

By the time I finished that race in Korea, in a period of two weeks I had run three marathons and one half marathon. That was definitely the most outrageous thing I had ever done in my running life.

Would I change something about my marathon career? If I could change something, I wouldn't have raced as much as I did. I used myself up, to a degree. I'm using what's left, but it's impossible to reach the top level with the amount of training I'm doing now. And the demands of promotion are almost as fatiguing as the demands of training and racing. In general, I think there's no consciousness of how hard a professional runner trains. Even race directors often don't have the faintest idea. Sure, top distance runners are born with talent, but it takes a tremendous effort to develop that talent.

—Bill Rodgers

The New York City Marathon is truly grand. Exactly how big and how grand is it? Here are a few facts that shed light on the marathon's stature.

The New York City Marathon is:

1. The largest marathon in the world, with 25,797 finishers in 1991. (The second largest is London.)

2. The largest women's marathon field in the world.

3. The largest spectator sporting event in the world. (According to the New York City Police Department, nearly 2 million people line the streets at various times during the race.)

4. The site of three women's world records, one men's world record, and ten sub-2:10 times for men.

5. The only non-Olympic marathon with complete, live network television coverage.

6. The largest field of international runners of any marathon (8000 from 91 countries). The international contingent alone would rank as the fifth-largest marathon in the country, outranking the Boston Marathon.

7. Other "world records" include the world's longest carpet (one mile by three feet wide on the Queensboro Bridge), the world's longest urinal (328 feet), and the greatest number of volunteers for any mass sporting event (an estimated 13,315).

Marathon Training and Racing

If you've been running for at least a year, have done some shorter races, and have been running 20 or more miles a week for the past three months, you may be ready to begin training for the marathon. If you need to build up to 20 miles a week, remember to do so gradually; don't add more than 10 percent of your current mileage per week. You need to pick a race to work toward. The training program here allows for six months of preparation (or less, if you're a more advanced runner).

A successful training program follows the principle of adaptation to progressive stress. Research and experience show that all progress is made by stressing the body, allowing it recovery time, then stressing it again. Many helpful changes take place when the body is in a recovery period. For beginning runners, recovery means taking a day off. For those training for a marathon, recovery also takes place on easy running days. You will improve by respecting this cycle.

Marathon training must balance endurance and speed stress with recovery. The priority for first-time marathoners is to concentrate on endurance, because you need to increase your overall mileage and also the distance of your weekly long run. So the core part of your program will be building for the long runs. As you can see on the training schedule (see table), the stress levels are changed from day to day and from week to week.

More or less, my training weeks mirror each other. A typical training week for me is one medium-long run (15 miles) and one 18- to 22-miler. I fit everything else in between. That includes one eight-miler and one 12-miler. I am somewhat restricted in my training both because of my inability to handle track workouts and my priority of spending time with my children.

In preparing for a marathon, I begin two to three months before the event. My training intensifies a little; I add two "longish" runs, and if my body mechanics can handle it, I train on the track. I just hate the last week before the marathon. I hate the tapering. It's hard to let go of peak fitness. When I feel anxious about tapering,

> I think back to the 1984 Olympic Trials marathon and remember that I won despite having had a long layoff before the race.
>
> —Joan Samuelson

Those who run 25 miles a week can join the schedule at week 5. Those who run 40 miles a week should adjust their program until they are doing a long run of 12 miles a week for three weeks and then move into marathon training for a minimum of three months.

How fast should you go on your everyday runs? Most people try to train at a pace that's too fast. Don't. Pushing it will promote injury and fatigue and will work against your completing your first marathon. Instead, put yourself at a cruise pace—don't push, yet don't go so slow you feel like you're not doing anything.

> The tendency with marathon training is to overdo. The big mystery is how much mileage you can handle and still maintain a certain amount of intensity as well. For most top runners, I think that's about 105 miles per week. I've done more; I've done less. For my first marathon, I did much less. I've been trying to find the key mixture. I know what I need and what I like. I like long runs of 18 to 22 miles, and one 25-miler. I like one hard-paced run a week, 12 to 15 miles; one speed session of fartlek, 1 to 1½ hours, or intervals of 1 to 3½ minutes. (During marathon season, my coach and I formulate a buildup based on doing longer intervals.)
>
> Now that I'm a marathoner I've realized that you've got to be careful with marathoning. It can kill you off quickly. It's a matter of being able to handle doing what you must to prepare properly for the event. While I enjoy the challenge of the marathon, I don't enjoy the feeling of being dead-legged all the time. It's not fun to be tired. My advice to other runners is to stay with the shorter races, and maybe do the marathon at most once a year.
>
> —Francie Larrieu Smith

The mileage amounts on the training schedule are guidelines. The emphasis should be on gradually building the length of the long run and the total mileage per week. You need to build to 40 miles per week and hold that for eight to 10 weeks, then taper down the last two to three weeks leading to race day. Remember, your overall increase in mileage should not average more than 10 percent a week, and it's beneficial if your mileage increases for several weeks, then levels off—or even decreases—for a week. This allows for recovery time to adapt to the new stresses.

If you have a running background of several years and have more time to prepare for your marathon, you may be able bring your mileage up to 50 to 55 miles for eight to 12 weeks. This mileage gives you a different marathon experience. Your pace may be the same, but you seem to retain more flexibility in mind and body during the race. At 50 to 55 miles, many weeks can contain a 10-miler in addition to the long run. The training effect from handling more runs seems to make the difference.

Now check the training schedule against your work and social schedule for the next six months. Check the days in each week to schedule in your runs. You can write your schedule on a calendar or in a small book with blank pages. This will become your running log or diary. Plan time now for your five or six runs a week. Include time for stretching. Do you have a training partner? Coordinate schedules. Do you want to use a weekend morning for the long run, or would you be better off doing it during the week?

As you complete your runs, you can record them into the log. You can write in insights and feelings as you go. Document energy levels experienced on your long runs; write down when you start breaking in new shoes.

You are embarking on a long-term goal. Any perks that keep you motivated are healthy. The diary is one of them and helps you build confidence when you look at it and see how far you have already come.

In *The New Competitive Runner's Handbook,* author Bob Glover states that the long run of the week is "the single most important ingredient to marathon success." It is also the biggest challenge.

Before the marathon race itself, taper down your training for two to three weeks so you'll be rested. After the marathon, you have a recovery period without limits. But your long runs happen right in the middle of your training—with only a day or two of recovery. Respect the distance, as it will make you a marathon runner.

You don't need to run longer than 20 miles in training. Running too many miles at one time not only increases the chances of injury but also produces a state of fatigue that lingers and interferes with training.

The long runs, done at a relaxed and even pace—for most people, a little slower than the everyday training pace—make you energy-efficient. They teach your body to utilize fat as well as glycogen as fuel to produce muscular energy. As exercise continues into hours, glycogen levels drop and a physiological fatigue sets in. This is known as "hitting the wall." But by doing these regular long runs, our bodies become efficient at utilizing more fat energy and less glycogen energy. This helps keep sufficient energy reserves for the latter stages of the run.

Usually you'll find your stride will shorten on longer runs. This is energy-efficient and will help you relax. Even if you take more steps per mile, each step takes less energy. Monitor yourself as you tire. Try to keep up a regular rhythm. Your arms should not work harder. Your shoulders may begin to tighten, and that may give you a headache. Try dropping your jaw, arms, and shoulders at the same time. This will relax the shoulder and neck muscles.

There's no question you need all-around consistent, successful, long-term training to run a good marathon. This also means that 8 to 10 percent of that training should be anaerobic—race pace or faster. And you need the long runs of 18 to 22 miles about once every 10 days.

Racing is completely based on your training. There are no illusions. Cheerleaders can't help you. The outcome is based on what you've done in the months before. Success results from months and months of consistent training, and then by honing it, like with a series of races leading up the big one. The key is to get to the starting line—after those months of training and several weeks of tapering and rest—in peak shape.

I think the number one mistake the average runner makes is overextensive training and racing, and racing beyond one's training. I know people out there who are doing four-hour runs on weekends and they've got regular, full-time jobs. Those of us who run for a living spend a lot of time running, but those with other full-time jobs may do just as much.

The main problem is that most people simply don't know how to train properly, and therefore they're breaking down with injuries left and right. They don't know what shoe is right, either. Let's face it: A lot of places that sell running shoes still don't know how to advise the running customer properly.

—Bill Rodgers

Speedwork is any running done faster than your everyday training pace. It helps improve your running form and leg strength. Through this work, you'll learn how to pace yourself while in the discomfort of oxygen debt, how to recover from it, and then how to go back into it. From speed training, you gain the ability and confidence to push yourself a little harder in workouts and in races.

If you haven't done much speedwork in the past, you may need to wait until you've gotten used to the stress of higher mileage. If you try speedwork and it tires you so badly that your mileage suffers—hold it off longer. Even without speedwork, if you follow the training schedule, with its built-in stress/rest cycle, you may find your pace picking up.

After you've adapted to the higher mileage, though—as tolerated—you can give speedwork a try. Increase the pace of some of your runs. You can run over hillier courses or pick up the pace near the end of a run, even on your longer runs.

Speedwork for first-time marathon training does not need to be run faster than 10k pace–and even work at this pace should be limited to once a week and should not total more than 7 to 10 percent of your total weekly mileage.

Some sample speed workouts you can do on a track are eight to 12 440s (a 440—or 440 yards—is once around the track), with slow jogs—lasting 220 to 440 yards—between each fast run for recovery; and four one-mile runs (a mile is four times around the track) with 440- to 660-yard recoveries. The warmup, the cooldowns, the fast runs, and the recovery jogs are added together to make the day's mileage total.

Races are part of the larger training picture and can be goals in themselves. They can be fun and can help you mark your progress. Even if you've not done speedwork, you are likely to see improvement at a race because of your added mileage.

Shorter races can be handled as a speedwork day; longer races—10 miles to 25k—can double as long runs, but limit them to one a month. In the long races you'll learn the importance of starting slow enough, you can practice drinking water on the run, and you get great feedback on your pace because the elapsed time is usually called out or displayed at each mile marker.

You are unique and your training program should reflect your individuality. Your age, weight, athletic background, and biomechanical, physiological, and psychological processes are special to you and coordinate best when your training plan is designed to meet your needs. The following tips may help.

Compare Sensibly. When you admire the performance of another runner, don't think that if you follow the same training program you can run like her or him. Consider age, build, lifestyle, and running experience. Then learn how the runner trained when she or he was at your level, and adapt that information into your training program.

Don't Overlook Running with Others. This can add variety and fun to your training. It's good to agree on pace and distance in advance. However, sometimes you still end up running harder or longer than you planned. If so, run easier than planned the next day or so. Doing speedwork with others is a powerful way to train and is very different from doing it alone. Be sure that you don't get caught up in racing on each repetition.

Be Consistent But Flexible. Having a long-term schedule really helps here. If you miss a few days or a week because of illness, injury, vacation, or unexpected events, there is time to get back on schedule. But gradually ease back into it; it may take several weeks to catch up.

Flexibility pays off, but use caution. You can miss sleep occasionally and get away with it, for instance, but if cutting sleep to get in planned mileage becomes a habit and the result is a lower energy level, you may need to re-examine your goals.

Beware of Overtraining. This problem—and it's a concrete physical and mental problem—comes from too much mileage, too much intensity, or just too much too soon. The results: chronic fatigue, working harder to stay on your usual training pace, a loss of interest, restless sleep, possible cold symptoms, and possible injury.

What to do? Cut back mileage by at least a third, and cut down the intensity. Sleep late, enjoy a dinner out or a movie. It's truly the only solution. When you're feeling more yourself, resume training gradually–and train easier!

Stretch. And do it on your rest days as well as your running days. After a long or hard run, stretch, then gently stretch again about an hour later.

Watch Your Running Shoes. You may be thrilled by how comfortable your shoes are midway through your training program. But will they still be in good condition 12 weeks later? Unless the shoes were brand new when you started the program, the midway point may be a good time to buy and break in a new pair. *Do* buy good shoes.

Respect the Weather. In winter weather, stay off icy surfaces. Running on them increases your chances of injury by slipping or by altering your running style. Also, head into the wind on those cold days so you'll have it at your back on the way home. This is especially important on your long runs, because in the latter stages you produce less heat and can get chilled too easily. Always bring a hat and gloves on the long runs. Tuck them away in your pockets or waistband, if you find you don't need them.

Hot weather slows the pace and dehydrates the body. Drink lots of liquids during the day and during your runs. Try to run early in the morning or in the evening, when it's usually cooler and you're out of the sun's most intense rays. Training classes for the Honolulu Marathon teach that you must drink enough so that your urine is clear of noticeable color at least once a day.

Don't Change Your Habits the Days Before the Race. Don't eat strange foods or stuff yourself. You can carbohydrate-load just by changing the proportions of your diet; eat less protein and more complex carbohydrates. Stay off your feet as much as possible. Standing is the worst thing you can do. Don't go shopping or to exhibits. Eat a simple early dinner the night before.

Eat a light breakfast at least three hours before the race. Don't wear any new clothes to run in. You need proven comfort more than appearance. Pin your number on your race shirt before you leave home. Drink liquids and put petroleum jelly on your friction areas. Warm up just a little and stretch gently before the race.

During the race itself, you want to run as effortlessly as possible for the first 10k (6.2 miles) at least. It should feel as if you're holding back some; if you're pushing the pace to reach a projected mile time, you're going too fast too early. Slow *down.* Burn your fat, not your glycogen. If it's an unusually warm or cold day, readjust your time to a slower pace.

In terms of psychological and energy reserves, the first half of the race is 16 miles and the last half 10. Remember form and rhythm. Keep your stride economical. Don't push hard up or down the hills. Just run.

If you have to run an uneven stride because of any pain that develops and persists, seriously think about dropping out; otherwise you risk greater injury. Slow down or walk if you have cramps or a stitch or just feel that you have to. Every step counts.

Drink liquids often. If you've learned to drink a diluted carbohydrate drink or eat orange slices in practice races or on training runs, this will help you, especially in the last half. Try to drink some every 20 minutes. The carbohydrates really help keep you alert, and research shows that they help performance when running over 1½ hours.

You are well prepared for this event. That makes it possible, if not easy, to finish. Sometimes it's not so easy: In the last 10k you may be going along okay, then suddenly be uncertain if you can run two more steps. This is where you begin to dig deep and find reasons for going on. Spectators help with words of encouragement. Watch how little children will look at you in wonder.

You *are* a wonder. Just keep up your form and rhythm. The choice in every step is yours and becomes a big decision. You can go faster, slower, shuffle, walk, or stop. And you trained for six months—for this? Yes, it really is a glorious journey. Congratulations.

Anyone who runs more than two marathons a year, given the physical stress, has to be doing it mainly for some psychological reason—one that's even beyond the reason I run. It must have to do with a reinforcement of accomplishment, rather than a reinforcement of performance.

Anybody who runs more than two marathons a year is not going to run his or her best marathon in that year, unless it's the first or second one. If they say they ran harder in their third, my answer to that is: "You must have been holding back because you knew you were going to run another one."

The point is the recovery aspect. I ran the Honolulu Marathon easy, just as a training run, and three weeks later I was just getting back to the point where I could train again. And my recovery is pretty good. So I can't understand the people who run many marathons. Perhaps they have a talent for running more, easier—and that's how they get their reinforcement.

—Frank Shorter

First Marathon: The Six–Month Training Schedule

Week	Mon.	Tues.	Wed.	Thurs.	Fri.	Sat.	Sun.	Total Miles
1	—	4	5	3	—	3	7	22
2	—	4	5	4	—	3	7	23
3	—	4	5	4	—	3	9	25
4	—	4	5	4	—	3	7	23
5	—	4	6	3	—	3	9	25
6	—	4	6	4	—	3	10	27
7	—	4	6	4	2	4	10	30
8	—	4	6	4	3	3	12	32
9	—	4	6	4	—	4	12	30
10	—	4	7	5	3	4	10	33
11	—	4	7	3	4	3	12	33
12	—	5	8	5	3	4	10	35
13	—	4	7	4	6	4	12	37
14	—	5	7	4	5	4	15	40
15	—	4	6	4	6	4	12	36
16	—	4	8	4	6	4	15	41
17	—	4	8	4	7	5	12	40
18	—	4	10	4	6	4	15	43
19	—	5	8	4	7	3	18	45
20	—	6	10	5	7	3	12	43
21	—	4	8	4	7	3	20	46
22	—	5	7	5	9	4	12	42
23	—	5	10	5	—	4	20	44
24	—	3	6	3	8	3	15	38
25	—	4	8	4	—	4	12	32
26	—	4	6	4	—	2		

Fred Lebow's Marathon Checklist

1. A pretty course is nice, but it's meaningless if efficiency is not an event's top priority. Make sure the course is properly measured. (It should be advertised that the course is "certified.") Also, the event should have frequent mile or kilometer markers, or both, and clocks or split timers.

2. Water, water everywhere. The race should include lots of water stations: at the start, along most every mile or kilometer, and at the finish.

3. Location of the start and finish. It is best that either of these are close to the place you are staying. I personally don't like to travel 30 minutes to an hour to get to the start, unless there are sufficient amenities. For example, since 1991, our New York City Marathon buses that take runners to the start are equipped with rest rooms. And although it's about a 30-minute trip to the start, when the runners get there, there are rest rooms, and a light breakfast, including hot drinks.

4. It's preferable that race registration include an expo (exposition)—a type of fair—with exhibits, demonstrations, and services relevant to runners. I think this is an important part of the ambience, and part of the social aspect of the event. In that vein, it's also nice if the race includes a pasta party and/or reception. It doesn't have to be a big race to feature these things. I've been to small events that have all the right ingredients, like the Oslo Marathon in Norway.

5. If you're going to travel to the race, it should be a place to which you can fly directly. If getting to a race is a chore, it drains a lot of mental and physical energy better used to run.

Grete Waitz's Marathon Advice

Before the Race

1. Be truly motivated to train for a marathon. Do it for yourself—not on a bet or a dare, or because "everyone else does."

2. Be well trained. Maybe some people will feel this is unfair, but I personally do not feel that a normal, healthy younger person needs six hours to finish a marathon. Others must agree, as there is a time cutoff in some marathons.

3. To begin the racing experience with the marathon is to start at the wrong end. Take a couple of years to build a running base and try shorter distance races. You may even discover that 26.2 miles is not your ideal distance.

4. Be sensible about your expectations. If you want to run three or four hours and just enjoy the scenery, fine. If you are running

competitively (even on a relative level), however, be prepared not only for the physical rigors but also for the effort of enormous concentration.

5. Marathon training is no great mystery. Don't throw your current training out the window in search of that "magic" marathon program. My marathon training is fundamentally the same as my training for shorter distances, except the mileage is higher. I still do speedwork, but add a long run once a week leading up the race, about 15 to 18 miles. The importance of maintaining quality training for a marathon is illustrated by the fact that most of today's top marathoners have also been top track runners.

6. You should build up your long run slowly, the same way you build all mileage, and make sure to get used to running on asphalt if you aren't already.

7. The hard/easy rule still applies for marathon training. Intersperse rest/recovery after hard efforts. If you're running fairly low mileage, allow for some days off. At 40 miles a week, you might try taking off the day before the long run. It's often not how many miles you run, but how they're distributed that counts.

8. Do some shorter races leading up to the marathon. They are important as intermediate goals, for achievement and confidence, and to prepare you for the big day.

9. Be especially careful to avoid overtraining and injury. The bigger the event, the more we tend to push ourselves in training. For marathon training, the basic warnings still apply: When in doubt, do less rather than more. Be even more conservative as you approach the race. First and foremost, get to the starting line healthy.

10. Practice drinking fluids in training. If you plan to drink anything other than water, such as a sports drink, try it in training as well.

11. Eat a balanced diet, including the foods that best supplement training and racing efforts. I already eat a high-carbohydrate diet, so I don't deliberately change what I eat before a marathon. I just add more food according to my hunger. I never eat a big meal the night before any race, as it usually just gives me trouble the next day. I find it better to eat a bigger lunch and lighter dinner the day before a marathon.

During the Race

1. Respect the distance. Think ahead, past the great feeling in the early miles. Twenty miles is where the race really begins.

2. Take the race one mile at a time, being flexible enough to adapt to the unknown and the unexpected—including weather and/or course conditions and your personal biorhythms on race day.

3. The last half hour of the marathon is always difficult for me. I often use relaxation techniques at this point. I tell myself to relax each specific part of my body: neck, shoulders, arms. Then I may repeat some words like "steady, push" to keep up the pace and my confidence.

4. Drop out if you have to. I believe in sticking with an effort, and I have never dropped out of any road race but a marathon. When I did drop out of those two marathons, I knew I had to. Because of the length of the race, there's a much greater potential for serious problems. The race is not worth risking illness or injury. There's a difference between difficulty and danger, and you will have to learn to judge for yourself what would necessitate stopping. Major marathons have aid stations at each mile, so if in doubt, consult a medical expert.

After the Race

1. A full and careful recovery from a marathon is extremely important. Recovery measures should begin the moment you finish. Keep moving, get warm, and drink water. The days following the race I maintain a state of "active rest." I walk or jog and get a massage within a day or two if my legs aren't too painful to be touched. Most runners are concerned about loading up with carbohydrates before the race, but fail to replenish afterward. I eat the same diet after the race as I do before. More people probably get injured from insufficient recovery measures than from the marathon itself. My own motto is: It's a waste of time to train to be a better runner for at least two weeks after a marathon.

2. No matter how the run goes, remember that every marathon is a learning experience; you can never learn too much about the event.

Ultramarathon

22

Running an Ultra—Can You Go the Distance?

There is a "beyond" for a distance runner. It's called the ultramarathon, which is any run farther than the 26-mile, 385-yard marathon. What does it take to run an ultramarathon? Ted Corbitt, one of the most renowned and accomplished pioneers of the sport of long distance running, was also a master at ultramarathon distances. Corbitt, namesake of the Ted Corbitt Award presented annually by The Athletics Congress to outstanding American ultramarathoners, has also written extensively on the subject, and offers the following advice:

If the thoroughly trained marathoner has courage, patience, and a willingness to keep moving in the presence of deep, monotonous fatigue, that person can run up to 50 miles based on marathon training. Sergey Popov of Russia, and later Abebe Bikila of Ethiopia, world record holders in the marathon, both expressed the feeling that they could have run for another 10 kilometers.

The biggest mistake to avoid when running ultras—and all races, for that matter—is to run too many. When you are running well, there is a temptation to do too much. You feel invincible. Even if you don't verbalize it, it's there subconsciously. But especially in the long distances, it can truly shorten your career.

Beyond 50 miles puts a runner into another world. Longer training runs—up to 30 miles at a time—and weekly distances of 100 to 200

223

miles for extended periods of time, integrated with judicious rest periods, prepare a runner for any ultramarathon challenge. However, not all runners thrive on this level of training.

In addition to patience, to run ultramarathons one must possess the ability to suffer, both physically and mentally. Ultras last for hours! Another ultra runner once called it "monotonous agony." However, ultramarathoning can give you the same sense of achievement and self-esteem that all running provides. With ultras, you don't have to be a champion; it is gratifying just to finish. But like all running endeavors, you have to keep going when it gets rough. You've got to be a fighter—seeking to overcome a new form of fatigue.

> Not everyone has the type of mind for it. With all my success and satisfaction, I have suffered. I recall at 17 hours into my 24-hour run, I turned to my handler and said, "I can't go through this for another seven hours." But I did, and although I set an American record, I was led to conclude that in a sense, you can drop out of a race without really dropping out. That's how I felt.
>
> —Ted Corbitt

Stu Mittleman, a multitime American and world record holder in ultra distances from 100 miles to six days, is also an exercise physiologist. It sheds light on the magnitude of his achievements to consider that for his 1000-mile record, he ran 85 miles a day for nearly two weeks. And on the way to completing his 100-mile run in a time of 12:56, he averaged 7:40 per mile and went through the marathon distance in 2:56. Mittleman is also an accomplished triathlete, having competed in the Ironman World Triathlon Championship, and he finished second overall in the Ultraman Triathlon, a double Ironman distance.

Stu Mittleman reveres the act of running for long distances, and well he should. For him, long, endurance running is a natural extension of the human condition. "I put it in historical perspective," he says. "This is our heritage; our evolutionary gift, dating back to our days as hunters and gatherers." Mittleman contends that while our anaerobic "fight or flight" capabilities always existed, they were not enough to challenge a world that was generally bigger, stronger, faster, and capable of greater individual violence. "Humans," Mittleman maintains, "could act in groups and had the capacity for tremendous feats of endurance." In fact, he believes, "If done intelligently, the human body may derive more healthful benefits from a moderately paced six- to 12-hour run than by trying to hammer a hard marathon."

And in fact, so immersed did Mittleman become in his ultra running that he claims the difficulty was not so much to perform his achievements but to adjust to a world where he didn't run. "I used to joke that 'it only hurt when I stopped,' and to some extent I really meant it. My training was based on the belief that I could condition myself to the point where my main objective was to move. When the race ended and moving forward was no longer the primary objective, I felt the most uncomfortable."

On paper, Mittleman's achievements would seem to exact grueling and debilitating outcomes. Yet he approached his races with a unique philosophy. "An ultra is not something to be conquered, or to emerge from victorious. It cannot be viewed as something to overcome by gritting your teeth and bearing it." In fact, while Mittleman claims to have watched a number of his competitors grind to a hobbling finish, he says, "If I planned it right, and was optimally healthy and fit, I would actually get stronger as the race went on."

Stu Mittleman's Training Philosophy for the Ultramarathon

Ultra training should be based on achieving optimal health and fitness. The initial part of training, Phase I, focuses on establishing fundamentally sound health practices (nutrition and rest); proper equipment selection (most importantly shoes that fit and provide support); and achieving a good level of fitness (a balance of flexibility, strength, low body fat, and aerobic base training).

Once Phase I is accomplished, Phase II is geared to improve the body's ability to burn fat. The Aerobic Threshold (AT), the point at which your body moves from predominantly *aerobic work* to predominantly *anaerobic work*, is the crucial factor in this phase since the ability to burn fat is significantly impaired when training is based on running regularly above the AT. Thus the two primary objectives in Phase II are to:

1. maximize the body's ability to burn fat when working aerobically—below the AT;

2. increase the total amount of work that can be performed aerobically—raise the AT as close to maximum effort as possible.

Ultra running should be based on establishing the Most Efficient Pace (MEP), which is just at or just below the AT.

Establishing your AT is the first step. General formulas can be helpful if you are unable to get tested at reliable fitness evaluation centers. Your AT is approximately 40 to 50 beats below your predicted maximum heart rate. (To determine this formula, see Chapter 4, Heart Rate Monitor Training.) A training target zone between the AT and 10 beats below is ideal.

Establishing your initial MEP is next. After a sufficient warmup of 10 to 15 minutes of low-intensity walking or running, record the distance you are able to cover while running for 20 minutes in the target zone. (Ideally this should be done on a track or relatively flat, marked surface.) Your pace in the target zone represents your MEP.

The next eight to 12 weeks of training should be centered around increasing your MEP. This is accomplished by two to three MEP workouts per week. These workouts can be arranged in the following way:

Warmup: 10 to 15 minutes at 55 percent of predicted maximum heart rate

Target zone: 20 to 45 minutes at 40 to 50 beats below maximum heart rate

Cooldown: 10 to 12 minutes at approximately the same as the warmup heart rate

The best way to organize your fat-burning workout is to allow plenty of time to warm up. This should be accomplished by doing "preliminary exercise." This is simply a very low intensity of the mode of exercising in which you'll be training. If you're running, then walk first or run very slowly.

Preliminary exercise should ideally be done for 10 to 15 minutes. This enables you to mobilize fat and put it into the blood for use as energy when you are training. Without this "mobilization," your body will be less likely to burn fat and more likely to burn glycogen (which is stored in the working muscles) or blood sugar. Fat is not stored in the muscles and must first be mobilized, put into the blood, and finally pumped to the working muscles before it can be burned.

Finally, what you eat affects how well you burn fat. For the most part, you should avoid refined sugars (candies, cakes, ice cream) and hydrogenated fats. Your body does need high-quality sources of fat to burn fat effectively. (Physiologists call this the law of mass action: Your body needs fat to burn fat.)

Ideally, as you progress, the pace you are able to sustain while staying in the target zone will begin to increase. At some point, generally after four to six weeks, your progress will begin to level off. At this point, changes may be made in training that may include some out-of-target zone training (anaerobic work). However, it is very important that aerobic efficiency is maximized by improving fat metabolism prior to the onset of anaerobic training. If you begin to focus on anaerobic work prior to these improvements, you will gain anaerobic benefits at the expense of your endurance potential.

Sample Training Program for an Ultra of Six Hours or Longer

Phase I, Months 1 to 6

1. Focus on basic fitness and health.

2. Establish sound nutritional practices.

3. Develop an aerobic base (LSD—long, slow distance).

Phase II, Months 7 to 10

1. Focus on MEP training three times a week.

2. Do two three- to four-hour runs per month.

3. Do one above-AT time trial or race per week (10k to marathon distance).

4. Take one recovery day (45 to 90 minutes—easy!).

5. Phase II begins and ends with a 10-mile run on the track in the target zone (compare evenness of pace between them).

Phase III, Months 11 to 12

1. Focus on MEP training two times a week.

2. Do three three- to four-hour runs per month.

3. Do one above-AT time trial or race per week (10k- or 10-mile distance).

4. Have one pickup or interval session per week—total distance, three to four miles, with recoveries of half of interval distance.

5. Have two recovery days per week (45 to 90 minutes).

6. Phase III ends the week prior to the ultra race (skip long runs for two weeks).

Fred Lebow on Ultramarathoning

When I first got involved in the running scene, I didn't quite understand marathoning, let alone ultras. But particularly after conducting ultra events at the club, the ability to run such long distances fascinates me.

I did my first ultramarathon in the middle 1970s, a 50k in Vermont. It was very slow, but I finished. I ran one more ultra in Central Park. What it took was not so much ability (especially if you're trained to run marathons), as patience.

For years, the NYRRC conducted a 100-mile race, and then we put on a six-day run. I had read about a six-day run held in the early 1900s in Madison Square Garden. People used to pay to watch the runners. I began to read old archives on the subject, and about ultras in Ted Corbitt's book. We put on the first six-day run in 1983 on the track at Randalls Island. We got tremendous press coverage. ABC television's *Nightline* came out every day to focus on Stu Mittleman. What most captivated people, I think, was exploring the unknown. How could people run 100 miles every day? We brought in the best ultra runners in the world for the event. In 1984, Yiannis Kouros of Greece broke a decades-old six-day world record with 635 miles.

Ultramarathoners are very special people. As a rule, they are different from other runners. This kind of running is very total and very meditative. They are often very intelligent, introspective people. Many ultra runners are loners; several are authors or poets.

Ultras put other distances into perspective, like the marathon. To many people, the marathon is the ultimate distance. But that's not really true. There is the 100-mile, the 1000-mile, and the six-day runs. Those are the ultimate distances.

Cross Country

Cross country is the original and most challenging form of distance running. Many of the world's most accomplished distance runners, past and present, have a strong base in cross-country running. They stress the quality and variety of this form of running—for all levels of ability.

Some of the best and most famous cross-country running is done in New York City, in Van Cortlandt Park in the Bronx—one of the nation's oldest and most venerated courses. The NYRRC conducts cross-country races for all ages and abilities there. Many national cross-country championship races are also held at Van Cortlandt Park.

The NYRRC has long recognized both the value and the excitement of cross-country running. In the early 1980s, the club began a campaign to host one of the most prestigious events in the sport: the annual World Cross Country Championships. It took four years of hard work and extensive lobbying to be granted that meet by the IAAF (the world governing body of the sport). When the race took place in New York in 1984, it marked the first time the event had ever been held outside of Europe or North Africa.

Cross country is my first love in running. Like anyone's first love, I remember it with great sentimentality. It was my first experience in the sport, at age 14. In fact, in high school, I was a member of the boy's cross-country team.

Winning my first World Cross Country title made me feel invincible. Winning my second one made me feel even more that way.

229

> If I can win a third, I feel like I can run through a brick wall. [*In March, 1992, Jennings did, in fact, win her third title.*]
>
> —Lynn Jennings

Fred Lebow admits that one of the purposes of bringing the World Championships to the United States was to popularize cross country among the masses, much in the way road running has blossomed. Although that did not happen on a large scale after staging the championships, the NYRRC continues to endorse and promote the sport. To this end, not only does the club conduct events, but also for many years club officials have attended National and World Cross Country Championship events.

The strongest cross-country tradition belongs to the British, for whom the sport has been the focal point for runners for over a century. Many British runners hone their abilities during winter seasons of well-organized cross-country running and competition.

Cliff Temple reports that cross country was for a brief time part of the Olympic Games, but following the collapse from heat stroke of a number of runners at the 1924 "Chariots of Fire" Games in Paris, in record 45-degree Celsius (113 degrees Fahrenheit) temperatures, it was dropped.

Among Americans, no one runs cross country better than Lynn Jennings, who in 1991 became the most winning American woman in history by taking her sixth national cross-country title. She has also achieved the high honor of winning the world title three times. "I love the feeling of cross-country running," she says, "because it's done in the elements. The footing is tough and you're running against nature. Cross country is like being a mountain goat, picking your way over roots and rocks, leaping over logs. It's grueling; it takes a lot of heart. But the rewards are great."

"For an experienced runner, cross country is important as the basis for excellence on the track," says Jennings. "Cross-country running makes you tough, your legs strong." A change in running surfaces, such as in cross country, also offers a good variety of training. "I think all young children in the sport should run cross country, even if they are half- or quarter-milers. It's great for building an endurance base for future track running," Jennings says. "What's more, cross-country training develops various muscles and saves the legs by absorbing some of the shock that the pavement doesn't. Cross country is also helping me prolong my running career. It is part of maintaining a variation that keeps me interested. It's so different from the track or the roads. One of the reasons I stay healthy and uninjured is that I run according to seasons. I'm so consistent because I divide it up. Then I can attack each season with renewed vigor."

In terms of racing strategy, cross country is basically the same as any race but for the terrain. Competitors might make a move going up a hill, or create a gap after leaping over a log or turning a corner. If you want to try cross country, head to one of the all-comers meets. If you feel intimidated by racing, try cross country by training on trails and through woods to get the feeling.

Training for Cross Country

British cross-country expert Cliff Temple believes that training on the ground, as opposed to the roads, is a good investment, even if you never plan to race cross country. Its gains are similar to resistance training, with the degree of that resistance created by mud or thick grass. This often serves to build strength in the same fashion as hill running or running on sand dunes. Therefore, while the going might be slower than on the road, the strength developed may result in better results on the roads.

> To avoid injury, I have corrected some mistakes I used to make. For example, after my first two years in triathlon competition, which I spent on the verge of being injured, I began running on trails instead of roads. At first I thought it would throw my legs off, all the twisting and wobbling from the uneven surface. But the opposite is true. It has strengthened and protected my legs. Road running works just certain muscles. Negotiating the trails—with the rocks, stones and tree roots—seems to work the entire leg, and in addition, gives relief from the pounding. If you get on the trails, you'll experience quicker recovery and not get so torn down. That's why I now do 70 percent of my running on trails. When you read about an athlete running 110-mile weeks, what you often don't read is that the person is doing 90 percent of that running on trails.
>
> —Mark Allen

The reason, he explains, is that the changing ground composition gives you less in return for the effort expended. You don't get the same slight "bounce" you normally feel when road running in well-cushioned shoes. To compensate, you are forced to work harder with the lifting muscles of the thighs (quadriceps), to traverse the thick grass or heavy mud.

Cliff Temple's Training Tips

In order to acclimatize to cross country, run casually for about 30 to 40 minutes your first few times out. Then alter your sessions to include speedwork.

In a typical speed session, cover two to three miles in warmup, then run a series of eight 60-second efforts at faster than race pace, with a steady, two-minute recovery jog in between. These 60-second bursts should be run over anything (within reason) that comes in your path, whatever the terrain. The faster runs may even seem easier than running steadily through long grass, and they will certainly produce a higher pulse rate and greater mobility than running on the road!

Alternatively, devise a loop of between 600 meters and 800 meters using natural paths and obstacles, and run a series of four to six repetitions of the full distances, with a four-minute recovery. Alternatively, break the loop up as naturally as possible into, say, four sections of about 200 meters; run the first and third sections comfortably. Run continuously, lapping the circuit for a predetermined time—say, eight minutes. Then, after a five-minute rest, repeat it.

This is, in essence, interval training in a cross-country form and setting. You can fashion any form of distances, repetitions, or recovery. "But somehow, when executed in a pleasant setting (such as loops of a quiet lake), it never seems such a soul-destroying business as it is on a track," offers Temple.

When running cross country, don't expect:

1. To feel quite as comfortable or rhythmic in your running as on the road.

2. To set a personal best, whatever the distance. Don't compare cross-country times with road times.

3. To keep your shoes clean. Wear old shoes, but preferably shoes

that have a bit of grip on mud. Unless you are racing seriously, spiked shoes are not essential, but they are a great help on exceptionally muddy courses.

Expect:

1. To enjoy a change of running environment, and a new running experience.
2. A physical benefit from the effort you expend. You may ache a little the day after your first race because your running action will probably have been different on the uneven ground.
3. An initial feeling of relief when you've finished, then a lasting feeling of satisfaction, and finally the desire to try it again.

Fred Lebow on Cross Country

When I began running in the late 1960s, I started with cross country on the famous trails of Van Cortlandt Park in the Bronx. "Vanny," as it is affectionately known, is surely one of the toughest cross-country courses. Many a future running champion has cut his or her teeth on those trails, particularly the section called Cemetery Hill, which actually seems steep enough to get you to heaven!

I usually ran cross country with very few partners or by myself. I like mass events, but it is nice to enjoy the solitary aspect of the sport, too. Eventually I got out of the habit of running at Van Cortlandt, though, and discovered the ease and convenience of running in Central Park. Road running boomed. Then, shortly after the 1991 New York City Marathon, I got an invitation from Bill Apfelbaum, the head of Transportation Displays Incorporated, to run in the woods of Rockefeller State Preserve in Pocantico Hills, located in Westchester County in suburban New York. (Bill's company is responsible for all the great marathon bus posters around the country.) Bill is an avid and able runner, one among a few in our area who have kept the secret of a most incredible running site.

I'd heard a lot about "Rockies," mostly from Eamonn Coghlan, who trained there regularly while living in Westchester. But obviously not a lot of people have heard about this place. By the time Bill and his friend Jeff and I had completed our one-hour-plus run, I had seen just three other runners, four walkers, and a few cows. Of course, I never saw a vehicle. Central Park—where as many as 500 runners circle the reservoir path at peak time—it was not!

I can't say enough about that run. It rejuvenated me. It was a classic example of the peace, beauty, and challenge that cross-country running offers. Apart from the beauty of the landscape and the undulating terrain, it was my longest training run of the year to date. Bill claimed we did over seven miles, but I didn't feel any of it! All I remember was running over a carpet of fall foliage and hearing the crunch my feet made on the leaves.

Part 4: The Psychology of Running

Motivation

The running boom produced abundant testimony to the physical and mental benefits of the sport, testimony that motivated people of all ages and circumstances to pursue running for health and well-being. New runners today find motivation in the achievements of dedicated runners, not only the elite, but also the social runners who've literally gone the extra mile in their lives. But how and where do the old guard find motivation?

> Sustained motivation is essential to achieving your potential. To keep your motivation high, use mental stimuli. Find what gets you psyched, and surround yourself with it: posters, sayings, photos, running magazines, videos. The more you see it, the more you remember it. For example, you might put up a sign on your wall, or a note on your mirror or desk reminding you of your goal time. One runner I know uses his goal marathon time as his access number for an automatic bank machine.
>
> —Grete Waitz

Nearly two decades after the running boom, the majority of regular runners have been at it for over a decade. According to Harvey Lauer's American Sports Data, Inc., in 1990 a total of 7,731,000 runners said they had practiced the sport for 10 years or more—a significant number, considering that Lauer also estimates that 8.5 million Americans run on a regular basis (two to three times a week). At the NYRRC, long-time participation is also documented. Ten years ago, most New York City Marathoners were going the distance for the first time. In 1991 a total of 69 percent of the 25,797 finishers had previously run a marathon.

> Overracing makes people stale. I've found that overracing is particularly common when people start to improve and they don't want to miss the feeling of doing well. But they find they can't race every week, either the mind or the body will tell them that. Another category of people puts the problem of a personal crisis, like a divorce, into their running, until they stop caring about the running. Runners have to adjust their training to accommodate life stress. Running should be a relief from stress, a way to help cope with it, not another added stress.
>
> Another cause of running staleness is setting unrealistic goals, or not accounting for external factors like weather conditions and how they affect performance. I spend half my time reminding disappointed runners they have to consider factors like heat and humidity. Often these people will go out and run hard the day following a disappointing race out of anger and frustration. They want something so badly that they don't want to pay attention to all the variables.
>
> —Bob Glover

But after long years of hard work and challenges met, running can get a little stale. If anyone understands the need to keep running fresh, it's Amby Burfoot, for whom running has been both vocation and avocation for three decades.

Amby Burfoot's Motivation Training

During the 30 years that I've been running, as both a Boston Marathon winner and a midpack recreational runner, I've had plenty of time to think about the key ingredients of a training program. I've thought about long runs and hills, speedwork and tempo training, stretching and strengthening, cross training and circuit training, nutrition and psychology. And the more I've weighed and analyzed the contributions of each of these, the more I've leaned toward a conclusion that might surprise you: None of them is important.

The only thing that's important in your training program is motivation. And yet every year most runners spend hundreds of hard, sweaty hours planning, executing, and improving their training elements. The same runners spend almost no time planning, executing, and improving their motivation—despite the fact that motivation is the foundation on which all training is built. Without motivation, the benefits of a couple of great track workouts slip away faster than the high tide. Without motivation, the best stretching program grows boring, and the boredom leads to quitting, and quitting stretching leads to injury, and the injury leads to unfulfilled dreams.

All successful runners have recognized the critical role of motivation. What they haven't recognized, however, is that motivation is a skill. It can be learned and practiced. You may not be very good at motivating yourself right now, but you can get better at it. All it takes is a little bit of time and a lot of creativity.

I succeed based on my own personal motivation, dedication, and commitment. I know a lot of women want to beat me. I'm not going to let them. My mind-set is: If I'm not out there training, someone else is. I train to race. I love to train, but I love to race even more.

Can you build the motivation to be competitive, or is it something to which you're predisposed? I don't know. But I believe it's okay just to race for the social aspect. I found that out after attending a race to cheer for a friend, a recreational runner. "Kick, kick!" I yelled to her at the end. "You should feel the adrenaline," I told her when it was over. I felt she shouldn't want to let people pass her, but she didn't care. That lack of interest in being competitive isn't just the case for women; I've known men that way, too. They just want to be fit, maybe run against the clock.

—Lynn Jennings

Twenty-five years ago, while training for Boston, I motivated myself in the most primitive manner—with thoughts of my opponents. On those mornings when I was tempted to roll over and fall asleep again, I imagined my racing rivals leaping out of bed and roaring out the front door on a ten-mile workout. The thought so terrified me that I was generally lacing up my shoelaces within five minutes. All other elite runners, I'm sure, have used more or less the same tactic to get themselves going. For the elite, fear of losing a race is often the most powerful motivator.

It doesn't work, however, for everyone else. Midpack runners know that they will never win a race, that no one will ever hand them a $10,000 check for their weekend road-race performance. They have to find other less material motivations to help them stay the course. I learned this eight years after I finally did win the Boston Marathon in 1968. In 1976 I decided I no longer wanted to run for the laurel wreath. Other things in my life—family, job—had grown more important. At the same time, I did want to continue running. The fitness, the friends, the stress relief, even the occasional race—these were still important to me. Since I would no longer be winning anything, I would have to find new ways to keep myself motivated.

I now measure my running career by a far more significant milestone than my 1968 Boston Marathon win. On each of the past 29 Thanksgiving days, I have completed the annual five-mile race in Manchester, Connecticut. I have won Manchester nine times, but I'm much prouder that I'm still running it every year even though I finish far back in the pack. My Manchester "streak" has become one of the most sacred things in my life. It's an annual celebration at which I renew my membership in the human race and my involvement in healthy, vigorous sport.

As I have aged, my running times and goals have changed, and so have my inspirations. I used to idolize the Olympic greats—the Paavo Nurmis, the Emil Zatopeks, the Abebe Bikilas, the Frank Shorters. Now I have a different hero—"Old John" Kelley, who has run the Boston Marathon 60 times. I have had the good fortune to know Kelley since I first started running 30 years ago, and I have always been struck by the high energy and good spirit that seem to infuse every pore of his body. Kelley has been able to keep running, I believe, by treating each mile as the best and most important he has ever run. He could idly reminisce over the years when he won Boston and other great races, but he doesn't. Kelley concentrates on the mile he's running right now. And perhaps the next one. He keeps shuffling forward, and the wind seems always at his back, the road always rising up to meet him—not because he's Irish but because he treats every mile as the most challenging and exciting of his life.

In many ways I now try to model myself after Kelley. I've developed a set of motivational tricks that I'm constantly reviewing and redefining. They have only one purpose: to keep me running. They've worked for 29 years, and I think they'll work for another 29. I present them here with brief explanations and an advisory note. One man's (or woman's) motivation is another's black hole. These ideas will work best if you adapt them to your own needs and personality.

Don't Lock Yourself In

Don't strive for perfection. Most running programs are full of all the do's you have to follow to achieve success, and there is some truth to all these lists. Surely, improved running and racing do not occur haphazardly. But beyond a certain point, many of these do's become jailers. They prevent you from experiencing the full variety that running has to offer. They become dead ends rather than open doors, paths you follow blindly and without seeing all the opportunities to change and try something new. The result is burnout.

In fact, you don't have to *do* anything. You don't have to run long every Sunday. You don't have to run speedwork twice a week. You don't have to run hills. You don't have to run the same course every day, and to run it faster today than yesterday. Running is not an all-or-nothing proposition.

Success does not come to the most righteous and rigorously disciplined runners but to those who continue running. And the surest way to keep running is to maintain a high level of motivation by refusing to see running as a series of rigid rules. To get to the finish line, you'll have to try lots of different paths.

Be Spontaneous

Fitness takes many forms. Running happens to be one of the best and most efficient, but there are many other activities that can increase your strength, flexibility, and aerobic conditioning.

I didn't realize this as a youngster, but the most important factor for motivation is goal setting. You should always have a goal. For some people, that's staying fit and healthy, running a few times a week for 30 minutes. For me, it's competition and having time goals.

I made a conscious decision in 1980 to shift from concentrating on track running to road running. I used that new focus in 1984, when I sustained an injury. I set my sights on the Women's Mini Marathon in New York, because it is the largest women's road race in the country. It was like a cookie I held out for myself.

My goals are both intermediate and long range. An example of a long-range goal is the marathon. As far back as 1974, I had a goal to run a marathon. I did one 12 years later. When I turn 40 in November 1992, my goal is to run at least one more marathon, and set an age group record. I will continue to pick my races carefully in order to give my best possible effort.

What's kept me motivated is not having reached the goal I have always had: to win an Olympic medal. But I'm realistic enough to know there are other goals.

The average runner can sustain long-term interest by keeping running fun. There are all kinds of possibilities. I do a workout every Friday that's one of my favorites. I jog a mile and a half to the local high school track. I take off my shoes and do 8 to 10 strides barefoot on the grass. Then I put my shoes back on and I jog home. That's the entire day's running. I love it. You don't have to be a slave to a particular program. A lot of people think that even if they stop during a workout, it's not a workout. But every session is different. Just because you slow down, or even walk, it's still a workout.

I won't say I'm always motivated, although overall I like what I do. I never dreamed at age 13 that I'd still be running now. I thought I'd grow up, get married, and have children. In a way, I have an abnormal life. I'm not doing what society dictates. I have no children. I run for a living.

—Francie Larrieu Smith

While running was the first exercise to make a dent on America's fitness consciousness, many others have since followed. With bicycling and swimming came the triathlon boom, father to cross training. This mixing together of many forms of training is the healthiest trend to hit runners in two decades. Cross training now includes everything from in-line roller skating to mountain biking to hiking to weight training to Nordic skiing.

In its well-known advertisements, Nike has caught the spirit of cross training: Just do it. This should also be a slogan for all runners. Don't think too much about some new activity. Don't try to analyze whether it will improve your 10k time. If it's fun and sweaty, just go out and do it. In the long run, you'll be much better off for having a wide variety of aerobic activities in your repertoire. Everyone should do more than just run.

Break the Rules

Once upon a time, Dr. Ken Cooper, the Sir Isaac Newton of fitness, established the first law of aerobics, which reads: You must do at least 30 minutes of aerobic exercise at least three times a week. Millions of Americans lived and breathed by this rule, and their lives improved because of it.

Naturally, running soon developed other major rules. For example, when doing intervals, always run 400s on a track; always follow a hard day of training with an easy day; never run in a snowstorm. Millions of American runners followed these rules, and in general they prospered. But along the way, some things were lost—things such as creativity and inspiration and spontaneity, the very things that inevitably lead to the best runs that life has to offer.

The best run of my life took place on a beautiful spring day 12 years ago. I decided to spend the whole day running. My brother and I boarded an early-morning train and rode 55 miles to the west. When we got off, we started the long run home. I use "run" loosely. What we did that day, traipsing along the balmy Connecticut shoreline, was to run for 15 minutes, walk for 5 minutes, run for 15 minutes, and stop at every McDonald's along the way (there were plenty).

I had never run that far before. Or walked during a run. Or stopped at McDonald's for Cokes and apple pies. I had never taken a whole day off from work to do nothing but run. Having broken so many rules, I felt completely liberated, and I never enjoyed a run more.

A final caveat on rule-breaking: Despite what I've written above, there is one rule you should never, ever break. Follow this rule at all times: Always run during a total eclipse of the sun!

Simplify

Don't measure your pace or the miles you've covered. Too many runners have become slaves to their training logs. The 1990s are a good decade for taking a less-is-more approach to your running. When you quantify every part of your running, you steal much of the magic.

If you still want to keep a record of your running, do everything in minutes. You can even set yourself daily or weekly goals in terms of minutes run. But don't burden yourself with the need to run five miles at an eight-minute pace on a 100-degree day in July, or force yourself to run ten miles in January when the mercury is hiding below zero.

You can even construct a slimmed-down but effective training program I call the "20-20-60 plan" by logging your minutes of running. Every week, take one or more easy runs of 20 minutes. On another day, do a "tempo" run: a warmup and warmdown with 20 minutes of hard, sustained running sandwiched between. Also include a weekly long run of 60 minutes. You can get into reasonably good shape—or maintain your present condition—with this simple 20-20-60 approach.

Set Completion Goals, Not Time Goals

You can't beat the clock, at least not for long. Eventually all runners reach the point where they can't and won't get any faster. Unless these runners begin to cultivate other reasons for running, they'll soon grow discouraged with the sport and quit.

Because of the opportunities in age-group competition, many runners challenge themselves against others of the same age. And I know at least one runner who has figured out a way to compete with himself and nearly always win. George Hirsch, publisher of *Runner's World* magazine, wipes the slate clean at the beginning of each year. He pretends every race is his first effort at the distance, so he sets a "PR for the year" with each race early in the season. Then he spends the rest of the year trying to improve on his PR, or personal record. This is but one of the dozens of mental tricks veteran runners often play to keep their running fresh, challenging, and new.

Midpack runners often envy those up front, but they shouldn't. Elite runners, by definition, have no choice but to try to get ever faster. When they don't, they lose. Racing has no meaning for them outside winning. Midpackers, on the other hand, can invent dozens of different ways to have fun and succeed during a race. I have seen runners dance at every band along the course, sit down on the sidewalk to enjoy a fluid stop, and run in big, chatty social groups. And why not? All these options seem fun to me.

Find New Challenges

After a while, merely finishing 10k road races, no matter how much you allow yourself to play along the way, becomes old hat. Every runner needs new challenges. So concentrate on the marathon one year, the mile the next; then return to the marathon, only this time with a whole new training program. In recent years, increasing numbers of runners have been leaving the roads and taking to the trails. Here, they say, they get back in touch with what they liked most about running in the first place—the outdoor environment, smaller crowds, and a new adventure. While some trail races cover 100 miles or ascend rocky mountaintops, many are much more accessible. The average runner can manage them with just small amounts of special preparation—investing in a slightly sturdier pair of shoes or taking a refresher course in reading topographical maps.

Road relays are another fast-growing alternative to the weekend ho-hums. Many of the best road relays cover fascinating parts of the world—Mount Hood to the coast in Oregon, Jasper International Park in British Columbia, the lakes region of New Hampshire, the beaches of Long Island—and allow groups of runners to cover distances they could never do as individuals. Teams may include only men over 50, mixed men and women, and women only, and nowhere else does running's famous sense of camaraderie shine through so brightly. Every member must truly help every other member, and when the team finally reaches the finish line, you know you wouldn't have gotten there without everyone's contributions.

Remember, Running Is a State of Mind

This is the most important of all my motivation guidelines. If you can train your mind for running, everything else will be easy. Always remember that how long you stick with your conditioning program is much more important than how long and how hard you train today. It used to be said of baseball pitchers that the legs always go first. This is rarely the case with runners. With us, the mind always goes first, and then everything else falls to pieces. So stretch your mind before your hamstrings, and strengthen your creativity before your stomach muscles.

"The Rut"

Author and coach Cliff Temple calls running staleness "The Rut." He says part of the problem is being torn between two conflicting feelings: not wanting to stop running, but feeling like a record stuck in a groove. Here are suggestions adapted from his writings for getting out of "The Rut":

Find New Pastures. Most people run from the same place, on the same route. Once or twice a week, you might consider driving (or taking public transportation) to a different area and running from there. Just remember to pack the necessities, like a change of dry clothing and a drink. If you're normally a city runner, try the suburbs or country—and vice versa. If you're in unfamiliar territory, don't forget to take or make a map if necessary, or make the course an easy one so you won't get lost.

Bare Your Wrist. Running a new course can help break the often self-imposed pressure of timing every run, a habit that can also lead to "The Rut." Try just running how you feel, and don't compare it to other workouts. That means leaving your watch at home and letting the sunshine get to that thin strip of unexposed skin around your wrist.

Find a New Direction. Direction in this case is not north or south, but where your running career is heading. You may have started out to lose weight, to complete a fun run or even a marathon, and once achieved, those goals were suddenly behind you rather than in front of you. Perhaps aiming to better your race times or participate in a specific event some months ahead may help spark your motivation.

Change the Time of Day You Run. Is there a reason you always run at the same time or day, or is it just habit? This may be another potential cause of "The Rut." In the same way that you may try different routes, trying a different time of day on certain occasions may help. You may, in fact, discover that you are more of a morning (or an evening) person.

Don't Become a Running Bore. If every conversation seems to revolve around your personal best times or your various aches and pains—particularly among nonrunning family and friends—then chances are you've become a running bore. This may be alienating you from others. Balance is important in every aspect of your running, including avoiding "The Rut." So try to mix normal domestic and work life with the demands and desires of running.

Find Some Company. If you do most, or all, of your running on your own, then running in company can sometimes help you out of "The Rut." It may only be once a week, when you can meet with one particular running partner or a group, but it can be a great help. Is there one particular session or day on which you feel more vulnerable to "The Rut" than others? If so, that is the day on which to find company.

Midpack Motivators

You probably aren't motivated to run by tangible dreams of Olympic success or world records. Yet if you stop to give it thought, you have sources of inspiration. What motivates other runners to get out the door, particularly on days when they just don't feel like it? Here are some examples from average runners.

Rewards

Ana Da Silva, a good cross-country runner in high school, is still a runner at age 22. She now runs only recreationally. "I still use a watch occasionally, promising myself some treat if I beat a certain time. For added motivation, at times I listen to some good, hard rock music right before I go out. Sometimes, on days I'm truly not motivated, I use errands to make me run. I carry a plastic bag or small backpack and run to the store to shop, or I run to buy something really special, like a ticket to a Guns N' Roses concert."

Rewards are motivators in a more literal sense, too. "When I started running at 62," 76-year-old runner Adrienne Salmini explains, "it was a fight to find a race with a 60+ award category. Now, nearly 15 years later, the race directors have finally realized that 'we' are still out there. When I moved recently, I unpacked my 295 trophies and medals and put them up in the garage. Now I'm trying to figure out where to put my 150 running T-shirts."

The rewards of good self-image also serve to motivate. "My inspiration involves musculature. Most male runners have a muscular area on the outside of their upper leg, right where running shorts split. But most women—unless they are very serious runners, or body builders—don't have it." So explains Joan Rose, who, on examining a set of vacation photos, noted the beginnings of that musculature in a picture of herself. "It gave me a feeling of power, and yet it is really a very private part of me. When it is really cold or hot outside, and I'm having trouble getting motivated, I look at that picture, and then look at myself naked in the mirror. The reality is never as dramatic as the photo, but it gets me out the door."

Joan Twine, a 48-year-old runner, also finds rewards in improved body image. "With work, continuing my education, and having two children and six grandchildren, I need a lot of energy," she explains, "but what gets me out there a lot of the time is that I have a fear of being obese! Running is my sunshine. I get out every day with the strict habit of using an alarm clock. And every morning before I run, I say a prayer—giving thanks to God."

Just feeling good is reward in itself. According to veteran Stuart Witt, "I have been pretty committed to running for a long time. When I was 45, 12 years ago, I ran a 3:02 marathon. But on days when I'm not motivated, I reason that I'd rather put in one hour of drudgery to gain 23 hours of bliss. Bliss means that for the rest of the day, I'm not guilty about drinking a beer, watching a football game, taking a nap. And, too, there's my fantasy life. I once read that the actress Darryl Hannah runs in Central Park sometimes in the morning. I just know if she sees me out there running in my tights, she'd fall for me immediately."

Imagination

Like Stuart Witt, many runners use imagination as a motivator. Bruria Ginton, a 41-year-old massage therapist, keeps company with the elite. She treats every level of runner, from jogger to world-class. "When I'm reluctant to go out, I make use of my top clients. I conduct imaginary conversations—mostly monologues! I get automatic inspiration. I also tell myself how much easier it is for me to run than for them to run, how much less pressure there is. It's so much more of a luxury than an obligation. If I fear I'll cut my run short, I bring pictures of my clients, take them out to look at them, and tell myself, 'They'd just be beginning a workout now. Who am I to complain?'"

"I keep a very comprehensive training diary," says Lenny Grodner. "To get motivated, I visualize filling it up, each day listing all the details. I love October 1991, because out of 31 possible entries, 20 are filled. For inspiration, I can look to my diary of ten years ago, when a typical run was between 45 and 85 minutes long. No doubt about it, it's very tough trying to get up at 6 a.m. after having only six hours' sleep. Not only do I try to think of how many times I've conquered that feeling over the last 13 years, and how it has paid off, but I'll think about a top runner I know in the neighborhood—how he's probably getting up to run at that very same moment."

Inspirational Reminders

"For precisely the purpose of motivation, I have pictures and sayings hung in the central parts of my house: near my alarm clock, in the bathroom, and on the refrigerator," explains Hermine Higgins. "Three of them say: *Training—Everything else can wait; Just do it; You can run, but you cannot hide.* The best is a Nike ad with a picture of a really beautiful girl with beautiful legs, which I cut out, framed, and hung next to my bed so that I can see it when I get up in the morning before going out for my run. It says, 'Just because you have evil legs doesn't mean you can't be a nice girl.' I know this seems really silly, but it works for me!"

Health and Well-Being

Most runners find inspiration from other runners—either running partners or competitors. "I average 70 miles a week, so I take my running fairly seriously. But not too seriously," explains Tom Allen. "It's also a social outlet. I have managed to create a network, so that 90 percent of the time I train with a partner or group. To really keep things light, at times I prefer silly running. I find a friend of similar temperament and we plan what I call bozo runs—like running with jingle bells on during Christmas season or costumes at Halloween."

For others, running for the sake of good health provides the push. "My motivation is the need for stamina," explains Michelle Grodner, 41. "As I get into my 40s, the hardest thing for me is to get through the day. The other motivating factor is that I'm a college professor in nutrition and fitness. I tell my students they have to be physically fit. It wouldn't make a lot of sense if I wasn't myself!"

The Mental Edge

25

How much of what runners achieve is determined by the mind? Some say it's as much as half mind and half body, and that you can't maximize one without the other. According to Priscilla Welch, peak fitness brings about peak mental attitude. "When I took a break," she explains, "and lapsed with my fitness and diet, my mental approach declined as well."

Who knows what percent of athletic success is mental ability? We hear everything. A well-known sports psychologist, Keith Henschen, once said to me, "Ability is 90 percent physical and 10 percent mental, but let me talk to you about that 10 percent." Some people are driven harder than others. I think the good ones are different, maybe because of self-confidence. Fundamentally, they see themselves as successful people.

Consider someone like Rob de Castella, whom I admire. Deek's body? He has a good set of wheels; obviously he was born with innate ability. But his desire and his scientific approach to training and racing are what make him stand out in my mind. He's smart and methodical. Grete Waitz is a great talent who found her greatest ability at a slightly older age. When she developed the confidence from winning and doing well, she was impossible to beat. Bill Rodgers probably has more physical talent than anyone I've ever met, but his relaxed attitude under pressure is what distinguishes him.

As two examples of sheer willpower, I think of Steve Moneghetti of Australia, who is actively competing now, and Alberto Salazar, who was at his peak in the early 1980s. These are two people who have an absolutely incredible desire to be successful at the sport of running, and who will do whatever it takes to be good. If it meant having a limited time at the top and then burning out, like Salazar, I still admire that, because at least he went out and did it. That indescribable drive we call guts, will, desire—that's what makes someone go to the top.

—Tom Fleming

Good running psychology or "mental edge" comes from, among other things, focus, confidence, and concentration. Unlike physical ability—determined more or less by birth—mental edge can be learned, then honed through experience and sheer will. To exercise the body, then, is only part of the formula for success. You can exercise your mind, perhaps your most underdeveloped muscle. Consider the following techniques to help you achieve peak mental edge:

Relax. When you're too uptight for a race, no matter how well trained you are, you won't run your best. To run well, you've got to be relaxed. Tension causes your muscles to contract. Proper relaxation allows your body to perform. And when you're relaxed, you can concentrate on the mental aspects of running. So before a race or hard effort, relax. Take slow, rhythmic breaths. Jog slowly. Shake out your limbs. Roll your head. Practice your own personal form of meditation and centering.

Deep down I always believe I can win. That's hard with road racing, because everyone is in a different peak cycle, so you might not know exactly who your competition is. It's terrible to say, but even when I go up against Liz McColgan or Ingrid Kristiansen—true superstars—I always feel deep down that I can beat them. But the best thing that ever happened to me was when I learned not to worry about them. I learned to be proud of my performances, and the fact that I did the best I could do. It was very difficult when I started getting beaten on the track on a regular basis, and my American records got broken. At least I used to be able to say I was the best in the United States; suddenly that wasn't so. But I learned I could still run well, even if I did not win every race.

—Francie Larrieu Smith

Think Positively. To succeed, you must believe you can succeed. So think positively. When you train, visualize yourself achieving a goal, whether it be losing weight or running a good time in a race. Close your eyes and see yourself through each step on the way to your goal. Focus on details. The more you think positively, the more confidence you'll possess and the better prepared you'll be to succeed.

Some running should be different mentally just the way it is different physically. On my easy runs, I may use the time to relax and let my mind wander, but I never do that in hard workouts or races. At those times, I always focus on the task at hand. Spend at least some of your training time, and other parts of your day, concentrating on what you are doing in training and visualizing your running success.

—Grete Waitz

Concentrate. Block out distracting details when you run. Training and racing are not times to contemplate shopping lists or tomorrow's appointments. Great competitors are able to concentrate precisely on the task at hand, to block out distractions, and focus on their goals.

When I was a running coach in the NYRRC classes, I worked on helping students develop the toughness needed to be competitive and meet their goals. I emphasized focusing in a race, and not losing consciousness of what you are doing. Concentration is part of the discipline of racing. So, for example, saying hello to someone in the middle of a serious race is against the rules. You can say hello before or after, but during the event, you should be mentally focused on your goal. That doesn't mean it's not perfectly acceptable to run a race for the social aspect. That's why my first question to someone who is planning to race is always, "Exactly what do you want to achieve?"

—Cliff Held

Get the Feeling. The feeling is that sense of being "on" or of being completely ready. While running, it is a sense of ease or invincibility. Being "on" is part of what many call "runner's high." Try to recapture the feeling from a good race or workout. Then you can re-create it for future events. Who knows the feeling? Watch runners finish a race. Those who have won, excelled, or achieved their goals raise their arms, punch the air, or even shout with joy, triumphant with the feeling.

If you want to achieve a high goal, you're going to have to take some chances. Going into the 1992 Olympic Trials marathon, when I decided to give it one last push, people like my college coach Bill Dellinger asked me how much I was going to train. I answered: 100 miles a week, and that I'd try to work on my quality. That was all I needed at that stage, I said. Then all of a sudden I realized, who am I kidding? When I looked at what all the top marathoners are doing, and what I used to do, I knew that my commitment wasn't enough. I used to do 120 miles a week with tremendous quality. After a long layoff and running poorly, how could I possibly think that with much less volume and less quality, I was going to be able to come close to what I did before, or close to what the best are currently doing?

I reasoned I could run 100 miles a week, and not get injured, but there's no way I could be competitive. The only chance I had of making that Olympic team was to be running 120 miles a week. If I got injured, so be it. Dellinger would then say to me, "I told you so." And I'd say, "You're right, Bill. But if I'd have run 100 miles a week I would have gone in there and gotten killed. I would have run 2:15, and I wasn't going to do that."

[*In that race, Salazar was one of nearly half in the field who dropped out due to hot and humid weather.*]

There's also a mental risk. A lot of people don't do everything possible they can in terms of fine-tuning their training, really making their training quality—no matter how much or little it is—because they are constrained psychologically. I believe that a lot of the time it's because of the fear of really giving it everything they've got. They are constrained by the fear of failure, of coming up even a little short. If they don't give it everything, they've always got an excuse. It's frightening for a lot of people to make the maximum effort and then fail.

Is taking the risk worth it? That depends on your philosophy of life. You realize that striving and giving it your all, but falling a bit short, is going to help you more than never having taken that risk.

—Alberto Salazar

Plan and Study. As you condition your body, strive also to understand your running—from training principles to competition. Read books, keep a training diary, and attend clinics to learn how to understand your running. Experience itself—running and racing—will best help you determine your individual needs and goals.

The Psyching Team

Harold Selman, M.D., and Maryellyn Duane, Ph.D., share a unique insight into the psyche of distance runners. In addition to being marathon runners themselves, they are captains of the New York City Marathon Psyching Team. The team, which began its work in 1983, is composed of a group of 80 to 100 volunteer psychiatrists, psychologists, and social workers who are on hand at the marathon to deal with the many entrants who suffer psychologically oriented problems, such as anxiety over finishing the race or suffering too much pain. Because these anxieties are exacerbated by the long wait at the race start and the extreme fatigue at the race finish, the volunteers staff both these locations. The psyching team is a unique feature of the New York City Marathon. New York's marathon is the only event of its kind with such a team.

The following tips are distributed to runners before the marathon, but are relevant for all running and racing.

1. *Don't worry about worrying.* Concern over an upcoming event such as the marathon is perfectly normal and desirable. If not out of hand, it can even enhance your performance.

2. *Say all your fears out loud.* To help bring your unconscious worries into your conscious awareness, say them out loud. Once they

become conscious, you can begin to exert control over them and even use them to your benefit.

3. *Go over all prerace and race details in your head.* Control what you can, and make sure there are no big surprises on race day. Keep a sense of humor about your obsessing—if nothing else, it will help you stay busy when there is nothing else to do.

4. *Body scan.* Imagine your body as being a finely tuned machine. Think of your senses as the gauges, with the rest of your physical being as the well-oiled part. Check the gauges from head to toe often. See how well the machine runs.

5. *Decide what to wear in advance.* Make sure you look marvelous, but be comfortable at all costs. Plan to bring different outfits with you to the race to suit changeable weather. For those who can stand the attention, your name strategically placed on your outfit will undoubtedly bring extra attention and cheering from the crowd.

6. *Imagine yourself having a great run.* Use all your senses to visualize yourself in vivid detail enjoying every minute of the race. Go to sleep dreaming of what a thrill it is to run the race.

7. *Plan to take music breaks during the race.* Play a few of your favorite tunes the night before, and you'll be sure to get a music lift when you remember them during the race.

8. *Do some relaxation exercises at the start.* Make use of your time while you are waiting to begin the race. Close your eyes and direct yourself inward. Regulate your breathing. Imagine a scene that is pleasant to you, and relax all your muscles.

9. *Plan to affirm yourself during the race.* Negative thoughts creep into every marathoner's mind. Combat them by consciously telling yourself that you are doing a great job. Be your own cheering team.

10. *Enjoy fellow runners' company at the start of and during the race.* There is nothing like a sense of camaraderie to move you along. Be friendly and share this great experience with others. Don't be afraid to speak to your cohorts.

The Use and Abuse of Running

The physical benefits of running are well known, and the psychological benefits are touted as well. This fact is confirmed by those who study the sport, as well as those who engage in it. However, running can change from a positive pursuit to a negative one. And for many runners, this is a common shift, at least to some degree.

According to Selman and Duane, running abuse shares characteristics of other obsessive-compulsive disorders, including alcoholism and drug abuse, and is defined as running at the expense of health, relationships, and work performance.

How to Handle Eating Disorders

Advice for Coaches, Friends, Parents

If you think that an athlete is struggling with food issues, speak up! Anorexia and bulimia are self-destructive eating behaviors that may signal severe underlying depression and can be life-threatening. Here are some tips from Nancy Clark for approaching this delicate subject.

Heed the signs. Anorexic behavior includes extreme weight loss (often emaciation), obsessive dieting, compulsive exercise, Spartan food intake despite significant energy expenditure, distorted body perception (i.e., frequent comments about feeling fat despite obvious thinness). Anorexics commonly wear layers of baggy clothing to hide their thinness and may complain about feeling cold.

Bulimic behavior can be more subtle. The athlete may eat a great deal of food and then rush to the bathroom; you may hear water running to cover up the sound of vomiting. The person may hide laxatives and display other secretive behavior. Petty stealing of money for food is common among teammates. The bulimic may have bloodshot eyes, swollen glands, and bruised fingers (from inducing vomiting). Some even speak about a magic method of eating without gaining weight.

Approach the athlete gently. Be persistent, saying that you're worried about his or her health. Share your concerns about the athlete's lack of concentration, lightheadedness or chronic fatigue. These health changes are more likely to be steppingstones for accepting help, since the athlete undoubtedly clings to food and exercise for feelings of control and stability.

Don't discuss weight or eating habits. The athlete takes great pride in being "perfectly thin" and may dismiss your concern as jealousy. The starving or binging is not the important issue, but rather a smoke screen over the larger problem. Problems with *life* are the real issue.

Focus on unhappiness as the reason for seeking help. Point out how anxious, tired, or irritable the athlete has been lately. Emphasize that he or she doesn't have to be that way.

Be supportive and listen sympathetically. Don't expect the athlete to admit he or she has a problem right away. Give it time. Remind the athlete you believe in him or her. This will make a difference in the recovery.

Provide a list of sources for professional help. Although the athlete may deny there's a problem to your face, he or she may admit despair at another moment. If you don't know of local resources, two likely national organizations are included in the Resource List at the back of this book.

Don't deal with it alone. If you feel you're making no headway and the athlete is becoming more self-destructive, seek help from a trusted family member, medical professional, or health service. Make an appointment with a mental health counselor and bring the athlete there yourself. Tell the athlete that you have to involve other people because you care about him or her. If you're overreacting and there really is no problem, the health professional will simply be able to ease your mind.

Talk to someone about your own emotions. Remember that you are not responsible and can only try to help. Your power comes from using community resources and health professionals, such as a guidance counselor, registered dietitian, member of the clergy, or eating disorders clinic.

—Nancy Clark

How to Spot Running Abuse

Answer the following questions composed by Harold Selman and Maryellyn Duane. They say, "If you answer 'yes' to five or more, you need to examine your running closely. It would be a good idea to discuss your situation with a friend, coach, or counselor."

1. Do you weigh yourself before and after your runs?
2. Do you repeat the same running routine regardless of physical condition or weather conditions?
3. Do you keep running until you "round off" miles, even if you are tired or late for another activity?
4. Are you enjoying your runs less than previously?
5. Do you have running injuries?
6. Do you continue to "run through" your injuries?
7. Are you disappointed if you don't usually better your race performances or training runs?
8. Do you binge or eat junk or fatty foods, then increase your mileage to work off weight gain?
9. Do your friends and family tell you that you run too much?
10. Is running your only social outlet?
11. Do you get especially depressed when you are injured?
12. Do you often feel exhausted before you begin your runs?
13. Does your running schedule interfere with your work life?
14. Do you run marathons or ultras "back-to-back"?
15. Do you actually run more than you tell others?
16. Do you think about running when your mind should be on other issues?
17. Is recording your running in a log or diary a central part of your day?

18. Would you consider injuring yourself to continue a running "streak"?

19. Do you continue to run despite your doctor's recommendations to the contrary?

20. Do you some times run in isolated or dangerous areas?

Running and Recovery: The Don Imus Story

Radio talk show host Don Imus can bring the most powerful to their knees with the mere touch of a finger. That's when he pushes the bomb button, the sound of an explosion that blasts off the air whatever or whomever he doesn't want to hear. As his 1.5 million weekly listeners to WFAN in New York can testify, Imus spares no one, "bombing" even the best. He also airs scathing parodies of everything and everyone—from Mike Tyson to the Catholic church. Although he regularly abuses his callers, it seems the exposure on his massively popular show is worth the risk. United States senators, governors, and prominent newspaper columnists are regulars on "Imus in the Morning."

Despite his usual venom, on one subject Imus speaks with complete reverence: running. Exercise and a healthy lifestyle are the crux of his life—a life that was once governed by alcohol, drugs, and cigarettes. In the 1980s, Don Imus succeeded in rerouting his extreme and destructive addictions to positive, disciplined exercise and diet.

His office looks like a shrine to good health, from the several pairs of running shoes placed neatly under a table to the stacks of bottled water and vitamins the size of horse pills. In a perfect display of the Imus irony, a plastic Jesus sits atop a can of powdered sports drink.

"Before I started running in 1978, I didn't do any kind of exercise," Imus explains. "I rode my motorcycle. I had run track in high school—the 100 and the 220 yards—and played football. But I was never a star athlete.

"For some reason, I wanted to start running," he continues. "It was in Cleveland, where I had returned for a year from New York to work doing radio. There weren't many people running in Cleveland then. I remember that I had trouble finding a store to get running shoes. The first pair of shoes I had was Adidas Country, the ones made of leather.

"When I first started running, I had arthritis, and both my ankles swelled up. I used to have to take a cane out running every night. If it was snowing in Cleveland, I'd be out there running in the snow with that cane. Finally, after a couple of months, the swelling went down. Then I gradually increased the running; I'd jog a quarter-mile and walk a quarter-mile. Eventually I got to the point where I could run for three miles, then five miles. I continued to run on and off. But I didn't really start seriously running until some years later."

Imus started drinking when he was about 30 years old. He went through periods when he would drink and take drugs, then forgo the drugs and switch from hard liquor to wine or beer. "I considered drinking wine or beer not drinking. When I began running, I was drinking, but I wasn't doing any drugs," he says.

"I had been smoking all my life—a couple of packs a day. When I came back to New York in 1979, I stopped smoking. I continued to run and drink. Then I started doing a little cocaine, and I started smoking again. I smoked and ran for years. I got into cocaine heavily in 1980–81. I wasn't into it that long, but I did a lot in those couple of years. I still ran, but not while I was on cocaine; it's a debilitating drug. I would go through periods when I would run, then I'd go for a month without running. By this time, I was doing cocaine, drinking and smoking.

"Because of all the stuff I was doing, I never progressed to running much below 11-minute-mile pace," Imus continues. "The first three or four minutes of running were horrible, because I couldn't catch my breath. My chest was so tight. Then after those few minutes, I was fine. I could run for quite a while. Then, of course, when I stopped running I would start coughing. I used to run a lot in Riverside Park in Manhattan. Lots of times when I'd stop, and start coughing, other people would stop to ask me if I was okay.

"By 1987, I was in pretty bad shape. I went to rehab, because I thought I had no other choice. I wasn't going to make it. In Alcoholics Anonymous, they talk about high bottoms and low bottoms. Physically, I was in as bad shape as you can possibly get and still be alive.

"I stopped drinking on July 17, 1987. Quitting drinking made a huge difference, emotionally and physically. I stopped doing cocaine in June 1983. I stopped smoking in the middle of 1989. After I stopped smoking, I started running a little faster. Before, I couldn't talk when I ran. I had difficulty breathing. I quit smoking because it just started to be a pain."

During all the years of doing alcohol and drugs, Imus ran on average three days a week. While in rehab, he started running every day. "It replaced the drugs and alcohol," he explains, "plus I just liked it. I liked the way I felt after I'd run for 45 minutes or an hour every day.

"When I got out of rehab, I went to the Sports Training Institute in Manhattan. That's where I first started running on treadmills. In 1986 I bought two treadmills. I also did some weights back then, but I didn't have a serious program."

Is Imus addicted to exercise? "Actually, I do the running even more intensely than I did drinking and drugs," he says. "I was an episodic drinker and drug user. I wasn't a daily drinker or drug user. I can't imagine not running, though. In fact, I once wanted to see how long I could do it without taking a break. In 1990 I decided to see if I could run every day for a year. I ran every day for 375 days, averaging four miles a day. My streak ended in August 1991. There are days in a year—this is true for any person—you're not going to feel well. So there were obviously days throughout that year that I felt horrible. I had a couple of colds. I was on the road. I still ran—in Boston, in Texas. That streak gave me a great sense of accomplishment.

When asked to compare the addictions—drugs and alcohol versus running—Imus says, "I guess the difference is that running makes me feel good, and the other stuff kept me from feeling bad."

Perspective

Successful running—like most all endeavors—is about balance. This is true mentally (psychologically and emotionally) as well as physically. The downside in running is caused by a loss of perspective.

"One can't be too one-sided," says triathlete Mark Allen. "Athletics should reduce stress, not increase it. Obviously there is the stress before races or in serious training. That's part of the challenge, and challenge is okay. But if your training is like pulling teeth, or you fight with your spouse before heading out the door, you need to evaluate your athletic goals within the framework of the reality of your life."

Alberto Salazar believes that "struggling with my running for the past six or seven years has been the greatest thing that ever could have happened to me. It's made me a much tougher and more resilient person, one who is more ready for whatever life might throw at me in the future. I'm just so much better equipped for adversity, for not having things turn out the way I want them to."

What is the source of my success? I think it's a combination of consistency and balance. I know I haven't succeeded as an athlete merely because of my physical gifts. I found that out as a competitive swimmer. I think it is my mental ability. The key has been to strike a balance between training and the rest of life. Most people see my racing success, but they don't see what is really behind it. The only reason I have gotten here is because of the balance I have kept—with my wife, friends, healthy lifestyle—all the aspects of life.

—Mark Allen

"I think my attitude is key," explains Eamonn Coghlan. "I try not to get caught up thinking about the task ahead. I just do what has to be done. I have the belief in myself that what I am doing is right. Then I let the rest happen. A lot of athletes get caught up. They focus so much on the goal, the end result, rather than the process of getting to that point. As a result, they waste an awful lot of nervous energy. They get so caught up that as the event nears they crack up from nerves. They can't handle it; they lose all their self-confidence.

"Sure I get nervous about competition. But I differentiate between being nervous and being uncontrollably nervous," Coghlan continues. "I try to eliminate obsessing over the goal while I'm training for months on end. I know what my goals are; I know what I have to do; I visualize my race, then I forget about it when I'm not running. I don't become a hermit because of my running. I socialize with my friends.

"Of course I had those times of thinking about an event and feeling the butterflies in my stomach. On the day of a race I'd wake up with my stomach in knots. But rather than get sick from that, I learned to love that feeling. I'd be nervous but happy. That was the adrenaline working for me. What I try to do is harness the nervous energy, not allow it to worry me, and try to preserve it until the gun goes off. Then that energy goes into my race."

Fred Lebow on the Psychology of Running

Psychology is definitely part of running. I remember a lawyer—and quite a good runner. His wife hated running. So he used to do things like go to run the Boston Marathon with his briefcase, as if he had work there. After they got divorced, his wife took up running.

I think it's one thing to go through a period of business or personal problems, and pour extra energy into running. Once the problem is solved, you gain perspective and cut back on the running. It's another thing, however, to have crazy streaks—like 20 years without missing a day of running. These people run through illness, even while on crutches.

I know a lot of people who are negatively addicted to running. I see it in particular among single men. Running is their date. It's more important for them to add one or two miles to their training diaries than to be with a beautiful woman.

Every time I meet overly dedicated runners, I sense that in a year or two they won't be running. From what I've seen, I think I'm right about 50 percent of the time.

A lot of runners like to brag; some don't. The flip side of the runner who obsesses and talks about running all the time is the equally devoted yet quieter runner who may not be deriving all the social benefits from the sport. For example, one of the positive side effects of our fundraising campaign among runners in the New York City Marathon is that some runners finally come out in the open about their sport. One person wrote me, "Raising money did a lot of good things for me. Until I circulated my pledge form, my fellow employees at work didn't realize I was a runner. I got a lot of respect."

Part 5: Nutrition

Physical Fuel

26

A car can't run without gas, and a runner can't run without fuel. Like any other machine, the higher the quality of fuel used, the better the performance that will result. Unfortunately, runners don't come with owner's manuals, outlining optimal fuel choices. So what should a runner eat? What vitamins and minerals promote peak performance? And when should runners load up and on what types of foods?

Runners tend to be very health-conscious, more aware perhaps than the general public of the importance of a healthy diet and good nutrition in maintaining fitness. Yet every runner—from beginner to elite—seems to have a question about optimal eating.

According to scientists at the Gatorade® Exercise Physiology Lab, runners typically burn between 100 and 150 calories per mile, or 2600 to 3500 calories per marathon. To replace those calories—basic nutritional needs aside—a runner would need to eat 2 to 3 dozen bagels; 35 to 47 peaches; 11 to 15 servings of regular yogurt with fruit; or about 2 pounds of plain cooked pasta. At 100 calories burned per mile, a total of 67,588,140 calories were burned by the 25,797 finishers in the 1991 marathon.

—Fitness Features

What Are Healthy Foods?

Sports nutritionist Nancy Clark knows what runners need—a sound diet based on healthy foods. "When you're training hard—juggling work, exercise, and family—and eating on the run, you may have little time or opportunity to eat the proverbial three square meals a day. Yet, you can maintain a healthful diet," says Clark. "The trick is to eat a variety of wholesome foods that will protect your health, invest in your muscular strength, and contribute to your exercise program."

Healthy Eating Tips (from *World Class*)

1. Eat as much raw food as possible.

2. Use nonfat or low-fat dairy products like ricotta, cottage, or farmer's cheese, instead of cream cheese or full-fat hard cheese. Or cut the heavier variety with the lighter, using a mixture of the two in sandwiches and cooking.

3. Cut mayonnaise, sour cream, or other such dressings or sauces with yogurt, broth, milk, or lemon juice (in tuna fish or potato salad, for example). Change the proportions gradually if you need to acquire a taste for the lighter version. Eventually, you may be able to do without the heavy stuff entirely. If the dish seems too dry, add more of the liquids.

4. Cut salad dressing with lemon or vinegar. Try eating salad with only lemon or vinegar, emphasizing herbs and other seasonings for taste.

5. Use soy products in place of conventional protein sources. Soy flakes or soy grits can be used instead of meat or cheese in such dishes as casseroles, spaghetti sauce, lasagna, Mexican food, and stew. (Presoak the soy flakes or grits, or add extra water and/or tomato sauce to the dish if unsoaked.) Tofu goes nicely with noodle or rice dishes or whipped in the blender with lemon juice, yogurt or water, and herbs as salad dressing.

6. Avoid oil by using water to cook vegetables in recipes that call for them to be sautéed or fried. Use a steamer for other cooked vegetables, and bake rather than fry such vegetables as eggplant and potatoes.

7. Use water in which potatoes or vegetables have been cooked or steamed—for sauces, in bread, to cook rice, or in any other recipe that calls for liquid. If there is no immediate use for this water, refrigerate or freeze it (in premeasured proportions if desired).

8. If you use white flour, add some bran to it.

9. Rinse or drain tuna fish or canned vegetables or fruits, even if packed in water, to reduce the salt or sugar in the water. Don't hesitate to rinse any food (even prepared) that contains excess salt or fat.

10. Dilute juice or soda with as much water as possible.

11. Cut out up to half the sugar called for in baking recipes, or replace sugar with frozen fruit juice or mashed ripe fruit, like bananas or pears. Make desserts with a fruit base rather than with such things as chocolate, cream cheese, or whipped cream.

12. For healthy snacks, keep raw vegetables on hand or freeze berries, orange slices, or juice in ice-cube trays. Freeze flavored yogurt to satisfy ice-cream cravings.

—Grete Waitz

Because time and convenience are primary factors, the following are Nancy Clark's top choices to stock at home. They are available in small corner markets or sandwich shops and salad bars; they offer a significant amount of nutritional value for a reasonable amount of calories, and they are protective foods that guard health and optimize nutrient intake. Since none of the foods listed is nutritionally perfect, choose a variety of them to get a balance of the vitamins, minerals, and protein you need for good health and top performance.

Food	Importance	Comments
Low-fat milk	Calcium, protein	Calcium is important throughout your life.
Yogurt	Riboflavin	To maintain strong bones.
Broccoli	Vitamins A, C	One stalk cooked has 100% RDA for vitamin C.
Spinach	Vitamin A, folic acid	Preferable to pale lettuce in a salad.

Food	Importance	Comments
Green peppers	Vitamin C	Half a pepper offers 100% RDA for vitamin C; a healthful addition to pizza and salads.
Tomatoes	Vitamins A, C, potassium	Add sliced tomato to sandwiches; choose foods with tomato sauce—pizza, spaghetti.
Baked potato	Potassium, vitamin C carbohydrates	Eat the skin, which has 75% of the vitamin C. Add milk (not butter or sour cream) for moistness.
V-8 juice	Vitamins A, C, potassium	An easy way to get the nutrients from 8 veggies without cooking or preparation.
Orange juice	Vitamin C, potassium	Frozen is nutritionally similar to fresh; 6 oz. offers 100% RDA for vitamin C.
Cantaloupe	Vitamins A, C	Half a small melon offers 100% RDA for vitamins A, C.
Chicken	Low-fat protein	Dark meat has more iron than white meat.
Turkey	Iron, zinc	Remove skin to reduce fat, calories, cholesterol.
Fish	Low-fat protein	Broiled is better than fried. Salmon, sardines, and albacore tuna have a health-protective fish oil.

Food	Importance	Comments
Bran cereal	Fiber, iron, carbohydrates	Bran is one source of fiber that best promotes regular bowel movements. Select "fortified" cereals for extra B vitamins and iron.
Muffins (bran, corn, whole wheat)	Carbohydrates, B vitamins, fiber	More nutritious than doughnuts and pastry. If desired, top with jam rather than butter.
Bread (whole wheat)	Carbohydrates, B vitamins, fiber	Any dark breads (rye, pumpernickel, oatmeal) are preferable to refined white flour products.
Pizza	Calcium, protein, vitamin A	Pizza (without sausage, pepperoni; with thick whole-wheat crust and low-fat cheese) is nutritionally preferable to greasy burgers.
Popcorn (unbuttered)	Carbohydrates, fiber	A wholesome, low-calorie "munchie" that's preferable to potato chips, candy, or cookies.

General Guidelines for Eating Out

More and more people—including busy runners—are eating meals away from home. It's important to consume a nutritious diet to fuel your body and stay healthy, but today's athletes need foods that are quick, easy, and convenient as well. If you eat out, you can still eat well—if you make the right choices. Mary-Giselle Rathgeber, M.S., R.D., has devised a checklist and a chart to keep you eating healthy—anywhere!

1. If possible, check out the restaurant beforehand to make sure that high-carbohydrate, low-fat meals are available, or that it will honor special requests.

2. Don't be shy! Inquire how dishes are prepared and request that they be made without added fat and/or sodium. Most chefs will honor such requests.

3. When browsing through the menu, look for the words broiled, baked, steamed, poached, grilled, in its own juice.

4. Go for extra breads, vegetables, rice, potatoes, and noodles, but hold the butter, margarine, cream sauces, and gravies.

5. Ask for dressing on the side. Use sparingly.

6. Restaurants usually serve oversized portions of protein (6 to 16 ounces). Eat about half to three-quarters and take the rest home or share it.

7. If there is an item on the menu that is not the healthiest choice, but you really want it, split it with a friend.

8. Trim visible fat off meat.

9. Remember that alcohol adds "empty" calories and can be dehydrating. If you want a drink, however, spritzers and light beers are the best choices.

10. Be adventurous! Try vegetarian, macrobiotic, and natural-food restaurants.

Meals

Recommended	Not Recommended
Fast Food	
Low-fat or plain small burger	French fries
Roast beef sandwich	Big special sandwich
Grilled chicken sandwich	Fried chicken/fish
Baked potato*	Barbecued ribs

*Watch sauces, dressing

Recommended	Not Recommended
Fast Food (continued)	
Salad*	Chicken nuggets
Orange juice, nonfat or low-fat milk	
Biscuits	
Diner	
Lean beef, turkey, ham, or chicken sandwich (ask for more bread)	Other cold cuts
	Grilled cheese
	Creamy soup
Broth or bean soups	Pastries
Broiled fish, seafood, chicken	
Fruit cup	
Greek salad	
Snack Machines	
Fig bars	Chips
Raisins, peanuts	Ice cream
Pretzels, juices	Snack cake
Deli	
Yogurt	Muffins
Low-fat milk, juices	Snack cakes
Fresh fruits, veggies, salads*	Cold cuts
	Salads with mayonnaise
Sandwiches (see Diner)	
Pizza Parlor	
Thick-crust pizza	"Extra cheese"
Veggie toppings	Meat toppings
Breakfast	
Juice, low-fat milk	Sausage, bacon, ham
Pancakes with syrup	Hash browns
Hot/cold cereal	Cheese omelet
Bagel, English muffin, toast, low-fat muffin and jelly	Croissants
	Pastries
Boiled eggs	

*Watch sauces, dressing

Recommended	Not Recommended

Ethnic Restaurants

Italian

Recommended	Not Recommended
Cioppino	Antipasto
Minestrone soup	Parmigiana dishes
Marinara and Marsala dishes	Alfredo/cream sauces
Red or white clam sauce	Lasagna, cannelloni
Chicken cacciatore	Stuffed shells
Pasta	
Fruit or fruit ice	

Chinese

Recommended	Not Recommended
Won ton soup	Egg rolls
Moo goo gai pan	Egg dishes
Steamed dumplings	Fried dumplings
Noodles and rice	Sweet and sour dishes
Brown rice	Duck
Vegetarian dishes	
Stir fry	

Mexican

Recommended	Not Recommended
Fajitas	Nachos
Plain, "soft" tortillas (not fried)	Quesadillas
Vegetable and chicken dishes	Cheese dishes
Burritos	Refried beans
Bean soup, rice and beans	Tostadas
Enchiladas	Taco salad
Seviche fish	Guacamole, sour cream

Indian

Recommended	Not Recommended
Tandoori	Malai (coconut sauce)
Vegetable curries	Samosas (stuffed fritters)
Naan, roti (breads)	Poori (bread)
Dahl	Fried appetizers
Seekh kabob	Muglai

Japanese

Recommended	Not Recommended
Sushi, sashimi	Tempura
Miso soup	Tonkatsu
Teriyaki, yakitori	
Tofu	

Recommended	Not Recommended
Middle Eastern	
Couscous, rice dishes	
Kabobs	
Tabouli	
Greek	
Greek salads	Gyros
Kabobs	Spanikopita (spinach pie)
Plaki (fish)	Moussaka (lamb casserole)
Souvlaki	

Some Special Concerns

In addition to questions about good nutrition and healthful eating, Nancy Clark provides answers and advice to runners with common concerns.

What If You Constantly Crave Sweets?

First, assess your meal patterns. Among many runners, breakfast and lunch are either nonexistent or insufficient because of lack of time, the desire to have eating not interfere with training, and just plain habit. Once you build up a calorie deficit during the day, you get too hungry. Sweets cravings may simply be a sign that you're physiologically ravenous. To prevent these cravings, as well as filling up on nutritionally empty sweets, eat more calories at breakfast and/or lunch (depending on when you train), and snack in the afternoon if you eat a late dinner.

Many women know all about premenstrual sweets cravings. According to the research, a complex interplay of hormonal changes seems to influence women's food choices. High levels of estrogen may be linked with premenstrual carbohydrate cravings. Women may, in fact, be hungrier. During the week before menstruation, a woman's metabolic rate may increase by 200 to 500 calories daily. That's the equivalent of another meal. But in an attempt to fight off the hunger and extra eating, women commonly crave sweets. If you feel hungry, give yourself permission to eat 200 to 500 extra wholesome calories a day the week before your period. That ought to tame the cookie monster, yet won't contribute to weight gain.

> Exercise speeds up the pace at which food passes through the stomach, so if you feel uncomfortably full after every meal, you may be able to walk off the discomfort rather than resort to medication. Doctors quoted in *Food and Nutrition Letter* (Rodale Press) studied the digestive systems of those who either stood around or walked for an hour after eating. Food went through the stomach nearly 40 percent faster for those walking than for those standing still.
>
> —Fitness Features

If you crave a sugar fix before exercise, you may be hypoglycemic (have low blood sugar) and consequently be fatigued. However, sugar taken during exercise can actually enhance performance if you're performing for longer than 90 minutes. Again, the safest way to avoid sweets cravings is to eat adequate calories throughout the day. If you haven't done that, and you are hungry and craving sweets, eat them within 10 minutes of exercise to avoid hypoglycemia. Be aware, however, that you may experience an upset stomach.

Finally, there's nothing wrong with a moderate amount of sweets if desired as part of your weekly intake. But keep sugar to a minimum—that is, 10 percent of your daily calories. If you crave cookies, choose the lower-fat brands, and if candy is your weakness, have a small piece as a dessert after lunch rather than as a dinner substitute.

How Can You Lose Weight and Still Have Energy to Train?

The overwhelming concern among sports-active dieters is how to lose weight and yet maintain energy for training. High-energy, low-calorie reducing is possible. The trick is to choose wisely what and when you eat.

Remember, carbohydrates are not fattening. Excess fats are the dietary demon. For example, one teaspoon of carbohydrates has only 16 calories; that same amount of fat has 36 calories. Your body can very easily store excess dietary fat as body fat. You're more likely to burn off excess carbohydrates. So don't trade a fat-free baked potato for fat-rich cottage cheese, or eat spoonfuls of peanut butter from the jar—thinking that's better than a handful of crackers.

Prebreakfast aerobic exercise may burn fat faster than exercise at any other time of day. Studies have indicated that although you burn the same amount of calories no matter what time of day you run, two-thirds of the calories burned in a prebreakfast run will come from fat, while in the afternoon, fat will account for less than half the calories burned. The other half comes from burning carbohydrates—glycogen and glucose.

—Fitness Features

Does it matter when you eat? It seems to. If you feast at night—a common habit among some runners—you may gain weight more easily than if you eat the same amount of calories earlier in the day. You can also easily overeat at night. The bottom line for dieters is that you should eat at least two-thirds of your calories during the day, particularly a good breakfast, and then the balance at night. You'll not only burn off the calories when you exercise and have more energy for training, but you'll also prevent yourself from getting too hungry and overeating. Remember, when you get too hungry, you may lack the energy to care about how much you eat.

To burn calories, try eating spicy foods. Using chili and mustard spices increases metabolic rate by 25 percent. Also, exercise in the evening. The energy required to digest food can be doubled with mild exercise after a meal.

—Fitness Features

Evaluate when, why, and what you eat—and correct any poor patterns. Eat slowly. Overweight people tend to eat faster than their normal-weight counterparts. Practice moderation rather than heavy denial. You're less likely to binge. Avoid temptations by avoiding too much time in the kitchen and the supermarket cookie aisle. Post a list of nonfood activities to do instead of eating when you're bored, lonely, tired, or nervous. Finally, think lean and fit. Being positive about yourself is important for successful weight loss and your well-being.

What About Vitamins?

Approximately 40 percent of Americans take supplements, and an even higher percentage of athletes take them. Among the nation's top female runners, 91 percent have reported taking supplements on a regular basis. But too many people believe that a vitamin supplement can replace a meal and fulfill 100 percent of their nutritional needs. They're wrong. It's food that supplies protein, minerals, energy, and fiber. No vitamin provides energy (calories) or compensates for a meal of junk food.

> It's not just women who have to be good to their bones. Men also get osteoporosis, a condition that weakens the bones. According to *Runner's World* magazine, researchers studied the effects of calcium and vitamin D supplementation on the bone-mineral densities of men. They hoped to find that an extra 1000 milligrams of calcium a day would slow the rate of bone loss. What they found, however, was that the men in their study, ages 30 to 67, experienced bone loss in both their arms and back despite the extra calcium intake. To reduce their risk of developing premature osteoporosis, men should do as many women already do: engage in regular weight-bearing exercise (which strengthens bones) and eat calcium-rich foods.
>
> A Dallas researcher has shown that a diet fortified with calcium lowers cholesterol in men with borderline-high cholesterol levels. According to an item in *Runner's World* magazine, Margo Denke, M.D., assistant professor of internal medicine at the University of Texas Southwestern Medical Center, suspects that calcium prevents saturated fat from being absorbed. She suggests a daily calcium intake of 800 to 1200 milligrams.
>
> —Fitness Features

True, you need adequate vitamins to function optimally, but an excess offers no competitive edge. No scientific evidence to date proves that extra vitamins enhance performance. You can get the fundamental nutrients required by the body to maintain good health by eating a variety of foods from the four food groups. (Two exceptions are iron and zinc.)

To clear up another commonly held misconception, exercise does not increase vitamin needs. Exercise doesn't burn vitamins, just as a car doesn't burn spark plugs. Vitamins are catalysts that are needed for metabolic processes to occur.

If you usually eat a well-balanced diet, a supplement is unnecessary for the occasional off day. Most athletes with a hearty appetite get plenty of vitamins from wholesome foods, making multivitamin supplementation necessary only for some individuals at risk of nutritional deficiencies. Supplements may be appropriate for the following: dieters who are restricting calories; chronic undereaters; food-allergic people; lactose-intolerant people; and pregnant women. All these cases, however, should be verified by consultation with nutrition or medical experts.

In general, get vitamins from food first, but if you wish to get psychological health insurance by supplementing your diet, take a single one-a-day-type multivitamin. Rather than taking megadoses of vitamins, which may cause toxic reactions, have your diet evaluated by a registered dietitian and learn what nutrients you are actually getting, and what, if any, you may be missing, and the best food sources from which to gain them.

How Do You Eat Well as a Vegetarian Athlete?

You can do fine as a vegetarian if you know your nutrition. Many athletes proudly declare they are vegetarians, believing that vegetarian means health-conscious. However, many of these vegetarian athletes consume inadequate protein to support their athletic program. They are simply nonmeat-eaters who have not subsequently adjusted their diets.

> Even low levels, two days a week, of aerobic activity can significantly compromise iron levels. But eating iron-rich foods is better than taking supplements to offset a deficiency, according to a study by Roseann M. Lyle, Ph.D., at Purdue University in Indiana. According to *Self* magazine, after 12 weeks, women who had ingested 12 mg. of "muscle" foods—meat, fish, and poultry—had equal if not higher iron levels than those who had ingested a 50 mg. supplement.
>
> —Fitness Features

Believing carbohydrates are the key to endurance success, some nonmeat-eaters fuel up on them and forget the protein. Adequate protein is essential to build, repair, and maintain your muscles. Long distance runners can burn some protein for energy. The other mistake some people make is to replace red meat with eggs and cheese for protein, unaware that these foods have far more fat and cholesterol than lean meats. In this respect, a grilled cheese or egg salad sandwich is worse than a lean roast beef sandwich without mayonnaise.

You need not be an expert in nutrition, nor spend hours in the kitchen preparing vegetarian specialties, to meet your nutritional needs adequately. Following are some meatless but protein-packed eat-and-run choices:

Grains + milk products: bran muffin with yogurt; cereal and milk; pasta and cheese

Grains + beans and legumes (such as peanuts, lentils, kidney beans, pinto beans, etc.): bran muffin with peanut butter; pasta and tomato sauce with canned kidney beans

Legumes + seeds: hummus (ground chick-peas with sesame paste)

Milk products + any food: milk, yogurt, or cheese (preferably non-fat or low-fat) added to any meal or snack

By eating a variety of different kinds of foods throughout the day, you'll get the most complete nutritional value. In addition, to boost iron intake, which may be lacking in nonmeat diets, cook in a cast-iron skillet, buy iron-enriched breakfast cereals, and eat lots of dark green vegetables.

What Should You Drink Before, During, and After Running?

The best pre-run choice is water. Eliminate the risk of dehydration by quenching your thirst, and then drinking some more, especially during hot weather or heavy training. You can tell you are properly hydrated if you urinate a clear-colored urine frequently throughout the day. Another way to monitor hydration is to weigh yourself before and after you exercise. For every pound you lose, drink at least two cups of fluid. In addition, assess how you feel. If you are always tired, headachy, or listless, you may be chronically dehydrated.

Consume fluids, ideally water—two to three cups or more—up to two hours prior to a hard workout or competition. Because the kidneys require about 60 to 90 minutes to process excess liquid, you'll have the chance to eliminate any excess before competition. Then drink one or two cups of water 5 to 15 minutes before your workout or competition. Contrary to what you may have heard, cold drinks do not cause stomach cramps. In fact, in hot weather, your best bet is to drink a cold fluid. It will not only cool you faster, but also may empty more quickly from your stomach.

During any sporting event you should drink fluids. In hot weather, drink as much as you can as often as you can. Ideally, this is 8 to 10 ounces for every 15 or 20 minutes of strenuous exercise. Always drink before you're thirsty. By the time your brain signals thirst, you have lost 1 percent of your body weight, which equals about three cups of sweat for a 150-pound person. A general rule of thumb is to consume about one quart of fluid for every 1000 calories you expend. But rather than count glasses of water, you should drink liquids with each meal and monitor your urine output. You're unlikely to drown yourself by drinking too much.

You don't have to drink only water throughout the day. Almost any nonalcoholic fluid will do, and watery foods such as oranges and cucumbers contribute significant amounts of liquid. After working out, replenish your losses with any fluids or watery foods that you enjoy. Be aware, however, that caffeine and alcohol have a dehydrating effect.

What Should You Eat Before, During, and After Running?

Pre-running or racing food has several functions: to help prevent hypoglycemia (low blood sugar), to stave off hunger feelings, to fuel your muscles, and to give mental assurance that your body is well fueled. Each person has food preferences and aversions, so no one food fits the bill for everyone. To determine what food is best for you, experiment with the following guidelines.

1. Eat high-carbohydrate meals daily to keep your muscles fueled.

2. Choose high-starch, low-fat foods—bread, crackers, and pasta—as they tend to digest easily.

3. Avoid sugary foods, such as soda and candy, within an hour before hard exercise.

4. Allow adequate time for food to digest. The general rule is to allow three to four hours for a large meal; two to three hours for a smaller meal, and less than an hour for a small snack, according to personal tolerance.

5. Allow more digestion time before intense exercise than before low-key activity.

6. If digestion is a problem, choose liquid foods, because they leave the stomach faster than do solid foods.

7. If eating before a race makes you nervous, don't do it, but be sure to eat extra the night before.

8. If traveling, take along any nonperishable food important to you, to make sure you have it. Examples are bananas, dried fruit, and bagels.

9. Always eat familiar foods before a race. Don't try anything new.

10. Drink plenty of fluids.

Nourishment during running is recommended for workouts lasting 90 minutes or more. In this case, it is always best to experiment in training with anything you intend to try in a race. Best choices are carbohydrates—most conveniently in the form of sports drinks. Hard candy, gummy bears, diluted juice, and defizzed cola are some other choices that runners report using to maintain their blood sugar.

Most fitness runners recover at their own pace because they don't deplete their muscles' glycogen, or fuel stores, with a typical 20- to 30-minute workout. Hard-core endurance athletes, however, should monitor their diets carefully to ensure proper refueling.

What you eat after a hard workout or race can affect your recovery. One priority is to replace the fluids lost by sweating as well as the carbohydrates you deplete. Initially, right after exercise, a glass of juice or other small carbo-rich food and water will do the job. Consume carbohydrate-rich foods and beverages as soon as possible, at least within one to four hours after your workout. Preferably, within two hours you should have consumed 300 calories of high-carbohydrate foods. Examples are one cup of orange juice and a bagel; two cups of cranberry juice; or one bowl of cereal with a banana.

High-carbohydrate sports drinks can also refuel your muscles. But be aware that these types of fluids generally lack the vitamins and minerals found in wholesome foods. Use them to supplement a healthy diet, not as a food replacement.

What If You Feel Tired All the Time?

Since there are both nutritional and nonnutritional causes of fatigue, here are some possible reasons to help determine why you may be feeling chronically run-down or ill.

Mental Fatigue Due to Low Blood Sugar. If you are among those breakfast- and lunch-skippers, the low blood sugar that results from this habit could have you feeling fatigued. If your reason for skipping meals is lack of time, it's worth it to take even a few minutes to eat, something easy. If it's that you don't feel hungry, try eating less at night and distributing your calories more evenly throughout the day.

Muscular Fatigue Due to Lack of Carbohydrates or Lack of Protein. If you eat high-fat meals, try making some of the following switches with these popular foods: use more bread dough, less cheese in thick-crust pizza; more rice with Chinese food instead of egg rolls; and carbohydrate-rich snacks such as pretzels, juice, fig bars, and dried fruit to supplement your meals—particularly if those meals are irregular or unbalanced. Fatigue can also relate to lack of protein, common in non-meat-eaters and runners who eat too many carbohydrates.

Fatigue Due to Iron Deficiency Anemia. The real key to getting enough iron is absorption. You can enhance absorption by drinking orange juice or ingesting other vitamin C-rich foods with iron-rich foods, and limiting caffeinated drinks, particularly tea, with iron-rich foods.

Fatigue Due to Lack of Sleep. You can be tired mentally—from an intense job or other pressures—and physically—from strenuous exercise. In addition, if you eat a large or late dinner, you may have trouble falling asleep. Again, try reversing eating trends—more during the day, less at night.

Fatigue Due to Overtraining. Rest or recovery days are essential parts of a training program; they allow the muscles to replenish their depleted muscle glycogen. There is a difference between being a "compulsive runner"—proud of long streaks of running or hard workouts—and a "serious athlete" who trains wisely.

Fatigue Due to Stress and Depression. Work or life stress can cause depression and the feeling of lack of control. But you can control one aspect of your life: your diet. This can make you feel better both physically and mentally.

Although chronic fatigue can be a symptom of a medical problem, fatigue caused by habits outlined above can be resolved with better eating, sleeping, and training habits. If you're concerned about lack of energy, your best bet is to get a nutrition checkup with a registered dietitian and a medical checkup from your doctor.

Should I Consume Beverages with Alcohol or Caffeine Before or After Running?

It seems the alcoholic drink of choice among runners is beer. Perhaps you've heard the myth that beer is a good sports drink because it contains carbohydrates and other vitamins and minerals. In truth, *beer— or any alcohol—is a poor sports drink for many reasons*. First of all, alcohol has a dehydrating effect that gets you running to the toilet, rather than replacing valuable fluids. Drinking beer before an event increases your chances of becoming dehydrated during the event. As for carbohydrates or other nutrition, beer is a poor source. The truth is that most of its calories are from alcohol, which your muscles don't store, so with beer you're more likely to get loaded than carbo-loaded.

A major problem with postexercise drinking is that runners are dehydrated and they drink on empty stomachs. Drinking quickly to quench thirst and drinking on a empty stomach cause one to be affected by alcohol's depressant effect quickly. Instead of consuming beer immediately after exercise, first quench your thirst with two to three glasses of water. Have a high-carbohydrate food, then stretch and shower. Then have a beer at mealtime if desired.

Will caffeine help you run better? Some say yes; some no. One reason drinking caffeinated beverages before exercise seems to help some people is perhaps because it stimulates the nervous system. But in some people, caffeine can cause the jitters, an acidic coffee stomach, and have a dehydrating effect. So when considering caffeinated beverages, be sure to evaluate your personal sensitivity to this stimulant. Experiment during training to determine the right amount, if any, that works for you.

What About Eating Junk Food?

Rather than looking at foods as either good food or junk food, it is better to consider the entire diet. After all, you could limit your diet to several good foods, excluding all others, and actually end up with a poor and unbalanced diet. Any food in moderation can fit into an overall wholesome diet. Gaining understanding of certain foods may help you gain a perspective on their place in your diet.

Sugar. Although sugar is reputed to be an evil that causes sugar highs and sugar lows, only some people are truly sensitive to its hypoglycemic effect. Most tolerate sugar just fine. However, refined sugar is a nutritional zero. But a sweet treat can appropriately fit into a meal plan without sabotaging a healthful diet.

Fat. Of all the nutritional culprits, fat is the most health-harmful. Low-fat diets, though, don't mean no-fat diets. Generally, athletes should consume 25 to 20 percent fat in their diet. For example, for an active woman who eats 2000 calories per day, that's 500 calories, or 55 grams of fat per day (the equivalent of about four tablespoons of oil or a cup and a half of premium ice cream). Learning to read food labels will help you determine the fat content of various foods and thus compute your daily total. Preferably you will select the more heart-healthful fats, such as olive oil, peanut butter, nuts, and other vegetable fats.

Low-fat Eating Tips

- Combine equal amounts of ground beef with shredded raw vegetables like carrots or zucchini.
- Blot the oil on pizza and burgers with a paper napkin.
- When eating chicken, stick to the white meat; it has roughly half the fat of dark meat.
- Use jelly or jam on toast instead of butter or margarine.
- Use mustard instead of mayonnaise.
- Put one slice of cheese instead of two on your sandwich.
- Order mushroom pizza instead of pepperoni.
- Use diet dressing instead of regular.

Here are other fat facts from *Glamour* magazine:
- The softer the cookie the higher the fat.
- The moister the cake the higher the fat.
- The cheaper the food the higher the fat.

—Fitness Features

Salt. Many athletes mistakenly think that salt causes high blood pressure. They go to great extremes to limit their salt intake, without understanding that salt does not cause high blood pressure. In fact, most athletes have low blood pressure, and since you lose salt during hard workouts, salt replacement can be an appropriate part of a sports diet. If you and your family members have no history of hypertension, go ahead and have those forbidden pretzels, salty peanuts, or canned soup.

When considering junk food, remember that there is a fundamental difference between poor dietary habits and a moderate amount of nutritionally questionable foods. Instead of categorizing good or junk, simply make sure you're eating an overall well-balanced diet that includes nutrient-rich powerhouse foods. These include whole-grain breads and cereals, orange and tomato juices, cantaloupe and bananas (which are nutritionally preferable to apples and grapes), dark-colored vegetables (spinach, tomatoes, and green peppers, superior to paler iceberg lettuce and cucumbers), and low- or nonfat milk and yogurt. By eating more of the best, you can include a few treats without sabotaging your health with one snack.

> I think nobody enjoys their food as much as runners and other people who work out. But you have to be very careful about what you eat, and I am more careful. I still like my bacon and sausage on Sundays, and cheeseburgers, but I don't eat them a lot, at least not as much as I used to. I have them sporadically.
>
> People believe I have a bad diet because in 1980 *The Runner* magazine did a dietary analysis of what I ate. I was training high-mileage the week they took the sample. I was traveling, and I probably ate more junk food than normal. I got a bad rap. But I look at it this way. I never had anemia from lack of iron; I never had a stress fracture from lack of calcium. My cholesterol isn't that high. It's 208 (it's never been under 200), but my HDL—the good cholesterol—is very high.
>
> —Bill Rodgers

Fred Lebow on Eating by Instinct

I believe nutrition is very important. As a runner, I naturally eat well. I have meat only two to three times a year. Right now, because I have to gain weight after my bout with cancer, I eat anything, including junk food. But a year after chemotherapy and radiation treatments, I still often don't crave food. Sometimes I don't care what I eat; I just want to gain weight.

I don't think everyone should live by that philosophy, but now that I have experienced it, I think there is a lesson in it. Restricting one's eating is part of good discipline, but I'm here to represent the other side, too: eating as a pleasure, especially a spontaneous one.

Prior to the 1991 New York City Marathon, I was walking down the street on the way to paint the blue line that runs along the course. I passed a pizza shop, and had a rare urge to indulge. It felt great. When it comes to food, I want to take advantage of every desire I have.

I have only eaten meat a few times a year for years. I once tried a complete vegetarian diet—no meat, no fish. I was so weakened, I realized I was making a mistake. I know one runner who tosses down 30 vitamin pills at a time, yet he looks so unhealthy, like a pale vegetable. You can't live off vitamins. You should eat a proper daily diet but be able to indulge. My current favorite is a fish cake and french fries at McDonalds. I top it off with a piece of poppyseed cake from the deli. I know it's terrible. But I only do it once a month. It's my indulgence.

Eating Elite—
Recipes

What do elite athletes eat? Chris Schlott gathered these recipes from top runners who have competed in NYRRC events in her *New York Running News* column, "Eating Elite." They provide a veritable smorgasbord of runners' food.

Honey Chicken

From the kitchen of Joan Samuelson, 1984 Olympic marathon champion:

3 lb. chicken, cut up
3 tbsp. butter or margarine
$1/2$ cup honey
$1/4$ cup prepared mustard
$1/2$ tsp. salt
1 tsp. curry powder

Remove skin from chicken pieces, wash, and pat dry. Melt margarine, add other ingredients. Roll chicken in mixture, coating both sides. Arrange meaty side up in pan. Bake in 375-degree oven for 45 minutes to 1 hour, or until chicken is tender and golden. Delicious with rice. Serves 4–6.

Nutritional analysis:
Good source of protein.
Calories: 3006, or 501–752 per serving

Protein: 280 gm., or 46–70 gm. per serving
Fat: 75 gm., or 12.5–19 gm. per serving
Carbohydrates: 171 gm., or 28.5–43 gm. per serving

Forester's Casserole

From the kitchen of Lisa Ondieki, 1988 Olympic silver medalist in the marathon and 1987 Women's Mini Marathon champion:

1 lb. boneless chicken breasts
3 tbsp. olive oil
1 large onion, chopped
8 oz. mushrooms
2 tbsp. flour
10 oz. unsweetened apple juice
4 oz. chicken stock
Salt and pepper, to taste
Parsley, chopped

Stir-fry chicken pieces in skillet with 2 tbsp. hot oil until golden brown. Remove from pan. Place mushrooms, onions, and 1 tbsp. oil in pan, cooking until tender. Add flour and gradually blend in apple juice and stock. Stir over gentle heat, add chicken, and continue simmering until sauce thickens, about 10 minutes. Serve with chopped parsley. Serves 4.

Nutritional analysis:
Good source of protein, potassium, and A and B vitamins.
Calories: 1180, or 295 per serving
Protein: 138 gm., or 34.5 gm. per serving
Fat: 41 gm., or 10 gm. per serving
Carbohydrates: 61 gm., or 15 gm. per serving

Chicken with Mushroom Sauce

From the kitchen of Mary Slaney, Olympian who at one time held every American record from 800 meters to 10,000 meters:

1 1/2 lb. boneless chicken breasts
1/2 cup evaporated skim milk
1 cup fine, dry, whole-wheat bread crumbs
2 cups fresh sliced mushrooms

2 tbsp. sliced green onion
1/2 cup dry white wine
1 tsp. lemon juice
1/8 tsp. dried thyme, crushed
1/8 tsp. dried marjoram, crushed

Flatten chicken breasts. Dip in milk, then in bread crumbs. Roll up jelly-roll style. Place in 8 × 8 × 2-inch baking pan. Bake covered in 350-degree oven for 20 minutes. Meanwhile, for sauce combine in skillet mushrooms, onion, wine, lemon juice, thyme, and marjoram. Cook until vegetables are tender. Spoon sauce into dish with chicken. Bake uncovered for 5 minutes more or until chicken is done. To serve, spoon sauce over chicken. Serves 4.

Nutritional analysis:
Low in fat; good source of protein and potassium.
Calories: 980, or 245 per serving
Protein: 31 gm., or 8 gm. per serving
Fat: 4 gm., or 1 gm. per serving
Carbohydrates: 15 gm., or 4 gm. per serving

Curried Chicken Salad

From the kitchen of Marcus O'Sullivan, top miler and Irish Olympian:
1/2 cup yogurt
1/2 cup light mayonnaise
1 tsp. curry powder
1 large onion, chopped
2 lb. cooked chicken, skinned, boned, and diced
1 cup walnuts
1 cup raisins
Chopped parsley

Combine yogurt, mayonnaise, and curry in large bowl. Add onion, chicken, walnuts, and raisins. Toss. Refrigerate 2 hours. Serve on lettuce with sprinkled parsley. Serves 4.

Nutritional analysis:
Good source of protein, iron, and potassium.
Calories: 2317, or 579 per serving
Protein: 149 gm., or 37 gm. per serving

Fat: 128 gm., or 32 gm. per serving
Carbohydrates: 160 gm., or 40 gm. per serving

Shrimp à la O'B.

From the kitchen of Cathy O'Brien, two-time U.S. Olympic marathoner:

1½ lb. medium-size shrimp
1 red pepper, sliced into strips
1 green pepper, sliced into strips
1 yellow pepper, sliced into strips
6 scallions, sliced
1 medium white onion, chopped
2 tbsp. olive oil
2 cloves garlic, crushed
Salt and pepper, to taste

Heat olive oil in skillet or wok over high heat. Add onions and scallions; stir and cook for about 1 minute. Add peppers. Stir and let cook for a few minutes, then take off heat and set aside. Add garlic (and a little more olive oil, if necessary) to pan and stir for about 1 minute. Add shrimp and cook for about 10 minutes, or until pink. Add cooked vegetables to shrimp and cook entire mixture together on medium heat. Add salt and pepper. Serve on rice with green beans as a side dish. Serves 3–4.

Nutritional analysis:
Low in fat and cholesterol; good source of vitamins A and C and protein.
Calories: 1100, or 275 per serving
Protein: 125 gm., or 31 gm. per serving
Fat: 35 gm., or 9 gm. per serving
Carbohydrates: 23 gm., or 6 gm. per serving

Vegetable Curry

From the kitchen of Priscilla Welch, 1988 New York City Marathon winner and masters world record holder:

2 carrots, about 1 cup, sliced to preference and partially cooked
Assorted other vegetables (about 2 cups), such as:

½ bunch broccoli flowers, about 1 cup
1 scallion, sliced
1 cup baby corn
1 cup water
1 tbsp. cornstarch
1 cube or packet chicken broth
Curry powder, to taste

Partially steam carrots and broccoli for about 5–10 minutes. Sauté vegetables about 3 minutes. Add curry, to taste. Mix cornstarch with approximately 3 tbsp. water and stir until smooth. Pour water into saucepan, add cornstarch and broth cube or packet. Heat until thickened. (Crumbled-up rice cakes can also be used for thickening.) Pour over rice or noodles. Serves 3–4.

Nutritional analysis:
Low in fat and an excellent source of vitamins A and C (vitamin content will vary with vegetables used).
Calories: 256
Protein: 13 gm.
Fat: 1 gm.
Carbohydrates: 39 gm.

The interesting aspect of the runner's diet is that it has become everyone's diet. What people in general are eating is not far removed from the Ronzoni Pasta Party before the New York City Marathon. We've gotten to the point that eating like a marathoner ready to race (and when you're training hard, you eat that way all the time) has become the prescribed diet for everyone.

—Frank Shorter

Pasta with Vegetables

From the kitchen of Bill Rodgers, four-time champion of both the New York City and Boston marathons:

2 oz. thin spaghetti
½ clove garlic, minced
2 tsp. olive or salad oil
½ small zucchini, cut into thin strips

1/2 small carrot, sliced thin
1/4 cup frozen peas, thawed
1/4 cup low-fat cottage cheese
Parmesan cheese, grated, to taste

Cook pasta as directed. Sauté garlic in oil until tender. Add zucchini and carrots and cook 1–2 minutes. Add drained pasta to vegetables. Add peas and cottage cheese. Toss well with pasta. Serve with grated cheese. Serves 1.

Nutritional analysis:
Excellent source of complex carbohydrates with vitamin A and protein.
Calories: 433
Protein: 21 gm.
Fat: 14 gm.
Carbohydrates: 100 gm.

Pasta Primavera

From the kitchen of Eamonn Coghlan, indoor world record holder in the mile:

1 lb. dry pasta or 2 lb. fresh
1/4 cup olive oil
1/2 cup chicken broth
4 tbsp. fresh basil or chives, minced
2 cloves garlic, minced (optional)
Salt and pepper, to taste
3 cups vegetables, about 1/2 cup each; choose from the following:
 Asparagus, cut in 3-in. pieces
 Red peppers, cut in strips
 Green peppers, cut in strips
 Carrots, sliced
 Zucchini, cut in julienne slices
 Broccoli florets
 Cherry tomatoes

Cook pasta until al dente. While pasta is cooking, plunge the vegetables in boiling water for 15 seconds. Rinse in cold water. Sauté garlic in olive oil, add broth, and heat through. Add all vegetables and herbs, season with salt and pepper. Toss pasta with vegetable mixture in large bowl. Add grated cheese if desired. Serves 4.

Nutritional analysis:
Excellent source of complex carbohydrates while relatively low in fat. Good source of vitamins A and C, depending on choice of vegetables.
Calories: 2317, or 579 per serving
Protein: 77 gm., or 19 gm. per serving
Fat: 66 gm., or 16.5 gm. per serving
Carbohydrates: 357 gm., or 89 gm. per serving

Here's some news about vegetables. The real nutrition stars are broccoli, spinach, green peas, white potatoes, and yams. Starchy vegetables like potatoes and lima beans are very high-fiber sources and contain five vitamins and two minerals. All dried beans and peas are equally nutritious and high in fiber. Ironically, claims *Environmental Nutrition* newsletter, the lowest fiber counts are for salad vegetables: cucumbers, lettuce, mushrooms and radishes. Salad is often consumed for fiber intake, yet an average salad has less fiber than one-half cup serving of cooked carrots.

Not all fruits and vegetables are created equal. In general, the deeper the color, the more nutrients they contain. Think red and green for the best nutrition. According to *Prevention* magazine, pink grapefruit has more than 30 times the vitamin A of white grapefruit, and anything that's red, like a tomato—or orange, like a carrot—has a lot of beta-carotene, which the body uses to manufacture vitamin A. It appears that a diet high in beta-carotene helps protect against most types of cancer. And the greener the greens, the better. Romaine lettuce, for example, has twice the calcium and iron, eight times the vitamin C, and more than ten times the vitamin A of the paler-green iceberg lettuce.

—Fitness Features

Lentil Soup

From the kitchen of Nancy Ditz, 1988 Olympic marathoner:

3 cups uncooked lentils
7 cups water (or stock)
2 tsp. salt
2 tsp. minced garlic
1 cup chopped onion
1 cup minced celery
1 cup chopped carrots
2 tbsp. butter or margarine
1/2 tsp. black pepper, or to taste
1 1/2 cups chopped fresh tomatoes
2 tbsp. red wine
2 tbsp. lemon juice
1 1/2 tbsp. molasses or brown sugar
1 tbsp. wine vinegar (preferably red)
Thyme, oregano, or basil, to taste

Simmer lentils, water, and salt 3–4 hours, covered. Sauté garlic, onion, celery, and carrots in butter. Add to lentils. After 1/2 hour, add remaining ingredients and continue simmering for additional 1/2 hour. Give to friends to eat up. Serves 6.

Nutritional analysis:
Low in calories; rich in protein, iron, and potassium.
Calories: 1201, or 300 per serving
Protein: 55 gm., or 14 gm. per serving
Fat: 28.5 gm., or 7 gm. per serving
Carbohydrates: 160 gm., or 40 gm. per serving

Bob Marley Pasta Casserole

From the kitchen of Pete Pfitzinger, two-time Olympic marathoner:

1 large onion
2 cloves garlic
1 cup spinach, fresh leaves
1 stalk celery
1 cup chopped broccoli
1 cup sliced mushrooms

2 cups chopped eggplant
2 tbsp. olive oil
1 lb. whole-wheat macaroni
6 oz. low-fat cottage cheese
3 oz. grated cheddar cheese
Black pepper, to taste

Place onion, garlic, spinach, and celery in food processor and chop finely. Sauté all chopped vegetables in iron skillet with 2 tbsp. olive oil. Boil 1 lb. whole-wheat macaroni. Drain and put in casserole dish. Add cottage cheese, cheddar cheese (save some to sprinkle on top), and black pepper, and mix in contents of iron skillet. (*Editor's note:* Cooking in an iron skillet greatly increases the amount of iron delivered to the diet.) Bake covered for 45 minutes at 350 degrees. Uncover for the last 15 minutes. "Fred Lebow could run a 2:11 marathon if he ate this," claims Pfitzinger. Serves 2–4.

Nutritional analysis:
High in carbohydrates and vitamins A, B, and C. Good source of iron, potassium, and fiber.
Calories: 2468, or 617–1234 per serving
Protein: 126 gm., or 31.5–63 gm. per serving
Fat: 55 gm., or 14–27.5 gm. per serving
Carbohydrates: 381 gm., or 95–190.5 gm. per serving

Vegetable Pizza

From the kitchen of Barbara Filutze, top masters runner:

1 unbaked pizza shell, usually found in supermarket freezer case
8 oz. pizza sauce
1/3 cup chopped green pepper
1/3 cup sliced scallions
1/3 cup sliced mushrooms
1/3 cup chopped tomatoes
1/2 cup part-skim mozzarella cheese
1 tbsp. Parmesan cheese

Stretch pizza dough on 12-in. pizza pan. Pour on pizza sauce to cover top of dough. Place all chopped vegetables in bowl and mix. Spread vegetables on top of sauce; sprinkle top with cheeses. Bake in 400-degree oven for about 15 minutes. Place in broiler for another 5 minutes, watching closely. Serves 2.

Nutritional analysis:
Contains very little fat; high in vitamins A and C and in complex carbohydrates.
Calories: 820, or 410 per serving
Protein: 33 gm., or 16.5 gm. per serving
Fat: 15 gm., or 7.5 gm. per serving
Carbohydrates: 139 gm., or 69.5 gm. per serving

Mom's Lasagna

From the kitchen of Jim Ryun, American mile star and multitime participant in the Trevira Twosome:

1 lb. lean ground beef
1 envelope dry onion soup mix
3 8-oz. cans tomato sauce
1 cup water
8 oz. wide lasagna noodles, 9 strips
8 oz. part-skim mozzarella cheese, grated

Brown meat in saucepan. Stir in onion soup, tomato sauce, and water. Cover and simmer for 15 minutes. Meanwhile, in large pot partially cook the noodles in boiling water for 5 minutes. In 2-qt. oblong baking pan, cover bottom with some of sauce mixture. Layer noodles on top, then half meat sauce; alternate another layer of noodles and remainder of meat sauce (save 1/2 cup for top layer); apply one more layer of noodles, lightly cover with sauce, then sprinkle with grated cheese. Bake in preheated 400-degree oven for about 20 minutes. Easiest lasagna ever and tastes great.

This recipe can be easily adapted for vegetarians or those limiting their intake of beef. Simply substitute all or part of the ground beef with any combination of slightly sautéed sliced mushrooms, cubed eggplant, or sliced zucchini. This would considerably lower the fat, protein, and calorie content but would significantly increase the complex carbohydrate and fiber content. Serves 6–8.

Nutritional analysis:
Excellent source of protein, complex carbohydrates, and B vitamins.
Calories: 2960, or 370–494 per serving

Protein: 213 gm., or 26.5–35.5 gm. per serving
Fat: 126 gm., or 16–21 gm. per serving
Carbohydrates: 255 gm., or 32–42.5 gm. per serving

Vegetable Lasagna

From the kitchen of Lisa Weidenbach, winner of numerous major marathons, and Bill Weidenbach:

1 28-oz. can whole tomatoes, chopped
2 6-oz. cans tomato paste
9 whole-wheat or spinach lasagna noodles (about 8 oz.)
8 oz. low-fat mozzarella cheese
8 oz. low-fat ricotta cheese
1 10-oz. package frozen chopped spinach
2 small zucchini, sliced
2 small carrots, grated or sliced
1 large onion, chopped
2 cups mushrooms, sliced
1 tbsp. basil
1 tbsp. oregano
2 tsp. sugar
2 tsp. black pepper

Cook noodles; drain. Blend the following ingredients in large saucepan: tomatoes, tomato paste, zucchini, carrots, onions, mushrooms, basil, oregano, sugar, and black pepper. Simmer for about 1 hour or whatever time you have available. Grate mozzarella cheese; set aside. Blend ricotta cheese and spinach, set aside. In a 9 × 13-in. baking pan, beginning with layer of tomato sauce, alternate with layer of noodles, half the ricotta mix, half the mozzarella, layer of sauce, and another layer of noodles; repeat and end with layer of noodles and layer of sauce on top. Sprinkle top with Parmesan cheese. Bake uncovered at 350 degrees for about 50 minutes. Let sit for 15 minutes before serving. Serves 4–6.

Nutritional analysis:
Rich in complex carbohydrates; good source of vitamin C, protein, and calcium.
Calories: 2416, or 402.5–604 per serving

Protein: 94 gm., or 15.5–23.5 gm. per serving
Fat: 66 gm., or 11–16.5 gm. per serving
Carbohydrates: 312 gm., or 52–78 gm. per serving

Tofu Lasagna

From the kitchen of Judi St. Hilaire, winner of the 1990 Women's Mini Marathon:

2 8-oz. pkgs. tofu, herb-flavored, soft-curd
1 tbsp. olive oil
1 medium onion, chopped
1 clove garlic, chopped
1 cup mushrooms, sliced
4 cups spaghetti sauce
12 lasagna noodles
8 oz. low-fat grated or sliced mozzarella cheese
1/2 cup grated Parmesan cheese

Boil noodles until just tender, and rinse in cold water. Heat oil in skillet and sauté onions, garlic, and mushrooms. Crumble tofu and add to skillet mixture; stir until steaming stops, about 5–10 minutes. Add 1 cup spaghetti sauce and simmer about 5 minutes. Spread 1/4 cup spaghetti sauce on bottom of 9 × 13-in. baking pan. Layer 4 noodles, 1 cup spaghetti sauce, then 1/2 of tofu mixture. Repeat and top with 4 more noodles, 1 cup spaghetti sauce, and cheeses. Bake at 350 degrees for 15 minutes or until cheese melts, browns, and bubbles. Serves 8.

Nutritional analysis:
Excellent source of complex carbohydrates and protein; relatively low in fat.
Calories: 2685, or 335.5 per serving
Protein: 165 gm., or 20.5 gm. per serving
Fat: 91 gm., or 11.5 gm. per serving
Carbohydrates: 293 gm., or 36.5 gm. per serving

Tuna Pasta Salad

From the kitchen of Gillian Beschloss, age group NYRRC Runner of the Year:

1 lb. tricolored pasta twists
3 tbsp. vinegar
3/4 cup olive oil
1/4 cup lemon juice
Pepper, to taste
1 head broccoli, cut into florets
2 yellow squash, sliced
2 zucchini, sliced
1 green pepper, diced
1 red pepper, diced
1 medium Bermuda onion, diced
16 1/2-oz. can tuna, drained (or shrimp or crabmeat)

Cook pasta, rinse in cold water, and drain well. With whisk, mix oil, vinegar, lemon juice, and pepper. In large bowl combine vegetables, pasta, and dressing, and toss gently. Add tuna and toss gently again. Place in refrigerator and chill for 1 hour. Quick and easy to make. Can be stored in refrigerator for a few days and is ready to eat at any time. Especially great for runners on the go. Serves 4–6.

Nutritional analysis:
Plenty of complex carbohydrates; good source of vitamins A and C, calcium, protein, and fiber.
Calories: 3573, or 595.5–803 per serving
Protein: 103 gm., or 17–26 gm. per serving
Fat: 358 gm., or 59.5–89.5 gm. per serving
Carbohydrates: 820 gm., or 136.5–205 gm. per serving

Easy Enchilada Stack

From the kitchen of Arturo Barrios, world record holder in the 10,000 meters, and Joy Rochester:

1 lb. ground turkey, or bite-size cooked chicken pieces
1 cup onion, chopped
1 8-oz. jar salsa sauce
1 8-oz. can diced green chilies
1 8-oz. nonfat plain yogurt
1 cup low-fat cheddar cheese, shredded
4 flour tortillas

Preheat oven to 350 degrees. Cook meat and onions until lightly browned. Add salsa and chilies. Mix and simmer covered, 5–10 minutes. Drain slightly if there is excess liquid. Alternate layers of tortilla, meat mix, yogurt, and cheese, finishing with a tortilla. Reserve a little of the salsa and cheese for sprinkling on top. Bake uncovered in oven for 25 to 30 minutes. Serves 2–4.

Nutritional analysis:
Good source of protein, B vitamins, and calcium. Relatively low in fat.
Calories: 1893, or 473–946.5 per serving
Protein: 183 gm., or 46–91.5 gm. per serving
Fat: 106 gm., or 26–53 gm. per serving
Carbohydrates: 52 gm., or 13–26 gm. per serving

Pasta with Beans

From the kitchen of Orlando Pizzolato, two-time New York City Marathon champion, and Ilaria Pizzolato:

1 lb. potatoes, pared and cut into 1-in. chunks
2 large onions, cut into eighths
1 28-oz. can tomatoes
2 stalks celery, sliced
3 cloves garlic, minced
1 tbsp. sage
1/4 cup chopped parsley
2 1/2 qt. water
1 1/2 cups short tubular pasta, uncooked
1/2 tbsp. cinnamon
1 large can cannellini beans (19 oz.), drained and rinsed
Salt and pepper, to taste
Parmesan cheese, to taste

Combine potatoes, onions, tomatoes, celery, garlic, sage, parsley, cinnamon, and water in large pot. Cook very slowly over low flame for about 2 hours. Add beans, salt, and pasta. Cook until pasta is al dente—about 20 minutes, stirring often so pasta doesn't stick to bottom. Pour soup into bowls and sprinkle with pepper and Parmesan cheese. Wait at least 5 minutes before serving. Great time-saver when cooked ahead and reheated at mealtime. Serves 6.

Nutritional analysis:
Rich in carbohydrates while low in fat; good source of potassium, protein, iron, and B vitamins.
Calories: 1462, or 243.7 per serving
Protein: 44 gm., or 7.3 gm. per serving
Fat: 12 gm., or 2 gm. per serving
Carbohydrates: 251 gm., or 41.8 gm. per serving

Ham and Potato Tart

From the kitchen of Lynn Jennings, six-time national cross-country champion and three-time world cross-country champion.

3 large baking potatoes, unpeeled and sliced very thin
Freshly ground black pepper, to taste
2 medium onions, sliced very thin
1/4 lb. Virginia, Black Forest, or other flavorful ham, sliced
1/2 lb. aged Gouda cheese, grated
3 small dots margarine

Set the oven at 425 degrees. Grease deep 10-inch pie pan with vegetable cooking spray. Arrange 1/3 of potato slices, overlapping in bottom of pan. Sprinkle with pepper. Layer with 1/2 the onions, then lay 1/2 the ham slices on top of the onions and sprinkle with 1/2 of the cheese. Repeat the layers of potato, onion, ham, and cheese. Finish with potatoes, arranging slices so they overlap neatly. Sprinkle generously with pepper. Dot margarine on top. Cover with foil and bake for 20 minutes. Uncover and continue baking for another 20–25 minutes, or until potatoes are very tender and top is browned. If vegetarian dish is desired, substitute thinly sliced zucchini for ham. (This tart has no crust and is baked without cream or eggs. The starch in the potatoes knits the ingredients together so the tart can be sliced into wedges for serving.) Serves 4.

Nutritional analysis:
Good source of potassium and protein.
Calories: 1775, or 444 per serving
Protein: 105 gm., or 26 gm. per serving
Fat: 77 gm., or 19 gm. per serving
Carbohydrates: 173 gm., or 43 gm. per serving

Turkey Burritos

From the kitchen of Dave McGovern, national 40k race walk champion:

4 large (10-in.) tortillas
1 lb. ground turkey
1/2 small onion, chopped
2 scallions, chopped
1/4 cup diced green peppers (optional)
1 tbsp. (at least!) chili powder
1/2 tsp. garlic powder
1/2 tsp. ground pepper
1/2 tsp. salt (optional)
1/4 tsp. hot pepper sauce (optional)
1 6-oz. can tomato paste or 2 diced tomatoes
1 cup shredded reduced-fat Monterey Jack or mozzarella cheese
1 cup shredded lettuce

(*Note*: If you want to add refried beans, get the kind made without lard, or make your own.)

Brown ground turkey; drain fat. Add onion, scallions, green pepper, chili powder, garlic powder, pepper, salt, and hot pepper sauce. Cook over low heat; add tomato paste or tomatoes and heat through. Place 1/4 of mixture into center of each tortilla and sprinkle with 1/4 cup cheese. Microwave on high for 30 seconds or heat uncovered in 350-degree oven until cheese melts, about 10 minutes. Remove tortilla from oven and add 1/4 cup lettuce and fold tortilla into something that looks like a burrito. Serve with rice. Makes 4 large burritos, or 1 burrito per serving

Nutritional analysis:
Relatively low in calories and fat; good source of protein and vitamin B6.
Calories: 1389, or 347 per serving
Protein: 151 gm., or 38 gm. per serving
Fat: 43 gm., or 11 gm. per serving
Carbohydrates: 102 gm., or 25.5 gm. per serving

To get the most vitamins out of steamed and boiled vegetables, cooking time is critical. Vegetables that tend to cook unevenly, such as asparagus and broccoli, will cook uniformly and much more quickly when the stalks are lightly peeled. Use a vegetable peeler rather than a paring knife so you remove only the top layer. Also, according to *Glamour* magazine, root vegetables such as potatoes, beets, and turnips will not cook faster if peeled and will lose vitamins if they are.

—Fitness Features

Broccoli with Garlic Sauce

From the kitchen of Ria van Landeghem, Belgian national record holder in the marathon, and Marc DeBleick, from Boulder, Colorado:

1 bunch broccoli, cut into florets, about 2 cups
2 carrots, cut in julienne strips
1/2 cup mushrooms, sliced
5 cloves garlic, sliced thin
4 scallions, cut into 2-in. pieces
1 tbsp. olive oil
Sauce:
2 cups chicken broth
6 tbsp. oyster sauce
1 tsp. olive oil
2 tbsp. low-sodium soy sauce
2 tbsp. rice vinegar
1 tsp. sugar
3 tbsp. cornstarch

Prepare all vegetables as directed, and set aside. Combine all ingredients for sauce, except for cornstarch. In a wok or fry pan, heat olive oil and add broccoli and carrots. Stir-fry about 5 minutes. Add remaining vegetables and cook 1 minute, stirring often. Mix cornstarch with 3 tbsp. water until pastelike. Stir into sauce ingredients and mix well. Add sauce to vegetables and simmer until sauce thickens slightly and broccoli is tender, about 5 minutes. Be careful not to overcook vegetables. Serve alone or over brown rice. Serves 4–6.

Nutritional analysis:
Excellent source of vitamins A and C; good source of calcium, potassium, and dietary fiber.
Calories: 597, or 99.5–150 per serving
Protein: 21 gm., or 3.5–5 gm. per serving
Fat: 25 gm., or 4–6 gm. per serving
Carbohydrates: 93 gm., or 15.5–23 gm. per serving

Yummy Granola

From the kitchen of Lynn Williams, Olympic medalist and former Women's Mini Marathon winner:

1/2 cup margarine
2 heaping tsp. honey
2/3 cup brown sugar
2 tsp. almond or vanilla extract
5–6 cups oatmeal flakes
1 cup shredded coconut
1/2 cup wheat germ
1/2 cup bran
3/4 cup slivered almonds (or chopped walnuts)

Melt margarine, honey, brown sugar, and extract in large pot. Add remainder of ingredients and stir thoroughly. Spread mixture on cookie sheets and place in 350-degree oven for about 8 minutes, or until toasted light brown. Remove from oven and allow to cool on cookie sheets. When cool, break it up into chunks and store in cool place. It keeps a long time. *Note:* Dry ingredients can be added in any combination you prefer. Makes 16 1/2-cup servings.

Nutritional analysis:
Good source of fiber, vitamin A, potassium, and iron.
Calories: 3460, or 216.3 per serving
Protein: 135 gm., or 8.5 gm. per serving
Fat: 189 gm., or 11.8 gm. per serving
Carbohydrates: 379 gm., or 23.7 gm. per serving

Honey and Banana Omelet

From the kitchen of Barry Brown, American masters record holder:

3 eggs

1/4 cup skim milk
4 tbsp. honey
Cinnamon, to taste
Nutmeg, to taste
1 banana
1 tbsp. butter

Melt butter and 2 tbsp. of honey in skillet. Cut banana lengthwise, then in half. Sauté banana in skillet until slightly soft. Set aside. Beat eggs and milk in a bowl. Pour into skillet. Cook over medium heat until semifirm. Sprinkle with cinnamon and 1 tbsp. honey. When eggs are set, place banana to one side of eggs, pour 1 tbsp. of honey over eggs, and fold omelet in half. Sprinkle top with cinnamon, nutmeg, and honey. Cook omelet until firm and honey starts to crystallize. Transfer to plate and enjoy! Serves 1.

Nutritional analysis:
Good source of potassium, protein, and vitamins A and B_{12}.
Calories: 786
Protein: 21 gm.
Fat: 30 gm.
Carbohydrates: 101 gm.

Whole-Wheat Soda Bread

From the kitchen of Nancy Tinari, 1988 Olympian from Canada:

2 cups whole-wheat flour
1 1/2 cups all-purpose flour
3/4 cup oat flakes, ground into a powder (use food processor or blender)
1 tsp. baking soda
1 tsp. salt
3 tsp. baking powder
2 tbsp. brown sugar
1 egg, beaten
2 cups buttermilk
1/2–3/4 cup raisins

Combine first 7 ingredients in large bowl. Beat egg with buttermilk, then stir into flour mixture with wooden spoon, making soft dough. Turn out on lightly floured board and knead gently, incorporating raisins. Form into round shape and place on greased baking sheet. Slash deep cross in top with sharp knife. Bake at 375 degrees about 45 minutes, or until bread sounds hollow when tapped. Serves 10–12.

Nutritional analysis:
Low in fat and sugar; good source of dietary fiber and complex carbohydrates.
Calories: 2235, or 186–223.5 per serving
Protein: 76 gm., or 6.3–7.6 gm. per serving
Fat: 18 gm., or 1.5–1.8 gm. per serving
Carbohydrates: 448 gm., or 37.3–44.8 gm. per serving

Beer Bread

From the kitchen of Liz Downing, biathlon world champion:

3 cups self-rising flour
1 can beer (light beer, nothing too heavy or the flavor of the beer is too prominent)
3 tbsp. sugar (optional)

Mix all ingredients together. Cover bowl with damp cloth for approximately 1 hour. Place in greased loaf pan and bake for 35–40 minutes at 375 degrees. Cool, then eat. Serves 4–6.

Nutritional analysis:
Rich in complex carbohydrates and no fat.
Calories: 1200, or 200–300 per serving
Protein: 13 gm., or 2.2–3.3 gm. per serving
Fat: 0 gm.
Carbohydrates: 87 gm., or 14.5–21.8 gm. per serving

Carrot-Pineapple Cake

From the kitchen of Kathy Pfiefer, national-class road racer:

1³/₄ cups sugar
1 stick margarine
4 eggs
1 tsp. vanilla

2 cups all-purpose flour
2 tsp. baking powder
2–4 tsp. baking soda
1 1/2 tsp. baking soda
2 cups lightly packed shredded carrots
1 8-oz. can crushed pineapple (drained)
1/2 cup raisins
Cream cheese frosting:
1/2 stick margarine
4 oz. low-fat cream cheese, softened
1 tsp. vanilla
1 1/2 cups powdered sugar
1 tbsp. milk (to desired consistency)

Preheat oven to 350 degrees. Spray bottom of 9 × 13-in. baking pan with a nonstick vegetable oil spray; set aside. Let margarine soften at room temperature, then cream with sugar. Beat in eggs, then stir in vanilla. Stir in flour, baking powder, cinnamon, and baking soda. Add carrots, pineapple, and raisins; stir just to blend, and pour into pan. Bake for about 45 minutes. For frosting, let margarine and cream cheese soften at room temperature; then cream together. Add vanilla and powdered sugar. Stir well. Add milk to desired consistency. Allow cake to cool before frosting. Kathy says, "A few calories, but well worth it." Serves 12–15.

Nutritional analysis:

Lots of carbohydrates, some vitamin A, potassium.
Calories iced: 4347, or 290–362 per serving
Calories plain: 2977, or 198.5–248 per serving
Protein: 87 gm., or 5.8–7.3 gm. per serving (iced)
Carbohydrates: 660 gm., or 44–55 gm. per serving (iced)
Fat: 183 gm., or 12.2–15.3 gm. per serving (iced)

Honey Bran Muffins

From the kitchen of Pat Porter, eight-time national cross-country champion:
1 1/4 cups all-purpose flour
3 tsp. baking powder

1/4 tsp. baking soda
1/2 tsp. salt
1 1/2 cups all-bran cereal
1 cup skim milk
1/3 cup canola oil
1/2 cup honey
1 egg
1 cup raisins

Sift together flour, baking powder, baking soda, and salt, and set aside. In mixing bowl, pour milk over bran cereal, add oil and honey, and let stand a few minutes. Add beaten egg and mix well. Add dry ingredients to cereal mixture, then add raisins. Stir well to combine. Grease 2 1/2-inch muffin pans (coated with vegetable oil spray) and pour batter until each cup is three-quarters full. Bake at 375 degrees for 20–25 minutes, or until firm to the touch. Serves 12.

Nutritional analysis:
Low in saturated fat; good source of dietary fiber.
Calories: 2364, or 197 per muffin
Protein: 48 gm., or 4 gm per muffin
Fat: 96 gm., or 8 gm. per muffin
Carbohydrates: 408 gm., or 34 gm. per muffin

Oat Chocolate Chip Cookies

From the kitchen of Kathy Hadler, 10,000-meter 1988 Olympic Trials qualifier, and Chip Hadler:

1/4 cup light corn syrup
1/4 cup brown sugar
2 tbsp. vegetable shortening
3 egg whites, whipped to stiff peaks
3 tbsp. water
1 tsp. vanilla
1/3 cup + 3 tbsp. sifted enriched all-purpose flour
1/4 cup nonfat dry milk powder
1/4 cup + 1 tbsp. reduced-calorie vanilla pudding mix
1/2 tsp. baking soda
2 cups quick oats (uncooked)
1/4 cup dry bran cereal

1/2 cup semisweet chocolate pieces
Nonstick vegetable spray

In 1¹/2-qt. bowl, cream corn syrup, brown sugar, and shortening with electric mixer on low speed until smooth. Add beaten egg whites, water, and vanilla. Mix on medium speed for 1 minute or until smooth. Stir together flour, nonfat dry milk, pudding, and baking soda. Add to dough and mix 2 minutes on low speed or until thick and fluffy. Stir in oats, bran, and chocolate pieces until well mixed. Place rounded teaspoons of dough 1 in. apart on vegetable-sprayed cookie sheet. *Slightly* flatten with fork. Bake at 350 degrees for 8–10 minutes. Makes 48 cookies.

Nutritional analysis:
Low in both fat and cholesterol; good source of dietary fiber.
Calories: 2208, or 46 per cookie
Protein: trace
Fat: 72 gm., or 1.5 gm. per cookie
Carbohydrates: 384 gm., or 8 gm. per cookie

Part 6: Fitness and Safety

Hydration

Water, water everywhere—that's the scene at well-organized running events, in parks and on paths. Yet no matter how much water there is, and how often runners are schooled on their need to consume the precious liquid, dehydration remains a widespread problem. "Of all the training errors contributing to poor performance in an athlete, improper hydration—or dehydration—is by far the most common," states Andres Rodriguez, M.D. He emphasizes his point by adding that dehydration is far more prevalent than other training errors, such as poor diet, improper training, or bad shoes. In Rodriguez's experience, "When you see runners after a race who look like hell, invariably they will tell you, 'I didn't drink enough water.'"

The problem of dehydration plagues even the most experienced runners. Joan Samuelson shuffled the final miles of the 1991 New York City Marathon and then was promptly treated for dehydration. And elite marathoner and medical doctor Ricardo Ortega of Spain, who has run 2:11:50 for the distance, was forced to drop out of two of his 26.2-mile races. When asked why, he merely replied, "I didn't drink enough water."

Proper Hydration

According to American College of Sports Medicine guidelines, endurance athletes should consume 12 to 16 ounces of fluid prior to a race. Along the marathon course, runners need to drink between four and eight ounces of fluid every 15 to 20 min-

315

utes. In addition to all those cups of water, New York City Marathon supporter Vermont Pure Natural Spring Water supplies a total of 120,000 12-ounce bottles of water for the race and its events.

—Fitness Features

Proper body fluid balance is vitally important to maximal physical performance. For this reason, dehydration is a major factor in limiting any work performance, says Andres Rodriguez. Water requirements are greatly increased in long distance running, especially in a warm and humid environment. Acute water loss through profuse sweating will cause dehydration. This, in turn, will produce a decrease in blood volume. The ability of the circulatory system to carry blood to the skin will be diminished, and the thermal regulatory mechanism of the body will be impaired. The need for proper fluid replenishment before, during, and after strenuous exercise cannot be overemphasized. Be properly hydrated before a race: Drink cool water frequently on the days preceding as well as on the day of the race—before, during, and after the event.

Watery foods also help hydration. Choose from nutritionist Nancy Clark's suggestions below.

Foods	% Water
Lettuce	95
Cucumber	95
Tomato	95
Orange	85
Banana	75

According to Rodriguez, you should take 300 to 400 cc (11 to 14 ounces) of cool water before training on a warm day, and drink repeatedly during a long distance race, even in excess of your perceived needs. Never allow yourself to feel thirsty, since thirst is a clear sign of dehydration. It is practically impossible to overhydrate yourself during a race. Do not be afraid to drink repeatedly; ample amounts of fluids will minimize the risk of circulatory and thermoregulatory impairments.

The body generates heat during exercise and elevates body temperature. The sweat that is produced during exercise evaporates from the skin and lowers body temperature. This heating-cooling mechanism will fail to function if the water supply is inadequate. Dehydration will therefore lead to heat injuries. If ignored by the runner, these can have serious or even fatal consequences.

You can easily tell when you are properly hydrated: You will feel the urge to urinate frequently; you will void large quantities of urine, and the urine will be clear.

Sports Drinks

Some runners hydrate with water and others with sports drinks. Sports drinks contain electrolytes and carbohydrates (glucose, sucrose, fructose, or glucose polymers). Although sweat can be substantial during prolonged exercise, the loss of electrolytes and minerals in sweat is really negligible, since healthy kidneys compensate by conserving the electrolytes and minerals, according to Rodriguez.

> Plain tap water is usually better than more expensive bottled waters, report researchers at Northeastern University quoted in the *Rodale Report*. Most bottled water is not refrigerated (particularly during the shipping process), and when stored at room temperature for 30 days, bacteria can increase anywhere from 100-fold to 10,000-fold. Although tap water also isn't refrigerated, these bacteria are usually killed when chlorine or ozone is added to local drinking supplies. Advice: If you drink bottled water, keep it refrigerated for several days before consumption.
>
> —Fitness Features

However, recent studies indicate that ingesting a 5 to 8 percent carbohydrate solution every 15 to 30 minutes during the race can significantly delay the onset of exhaustion in well-trained athletes, as well as in lesser-trained runners. But keep in mind that large amounts of carbohydrates, especially fructose, can irritate the stomach and cause cramps, nausea, and vomiting. These solutions should first be tested during training runs, and they should never be used for the first time during a competitive race.

Nancy Clark also believes that for most recreational athletes, water is sufficient, especially in combination with an appropriate diet. However, those who compete in high-intensity events such as marathons or triathlons, and who might want a special beverage, need not assume that only commercial sports drinks will do the trick. She points out that for years successful athletes have been drinking homemade sports drinks—containing sugar for energy– such as water bottles filled with cooled tea with honey or defizzed cola. Other possibilities include diluted apple juice or orange slices and water.

According to Clark's *Sports Nutrition Guidebook*, during a moderate-to-hard endurance workout, carbohydrates supply about 50 percent of the energy. As you deplete carbohydrates from muscle glycogen stores, you increasingly rely on blood sugar for energy. By consuming carbohydrates that help maintain a normal blood sugar level, you can exercise for a longer time. Also, much of endurance capacity depends upon mental stamina. Maintaining a normal blood sugar level will help you to concentrate.

What sports drink works best for you is probably best determined by experimentation. Clark points out that the best time to drink fluid replacers is during exercise, and not 20 to 45 minutes beforehand, when they might trigger a hypoglycemic reaction, and not afterward, when your muscles require full-strength, carbohydrate-rich beverages to replace the glycogen burned during the event and the minerals lost in sweat.

Fluid Loss and Dehydration

Scientists at Gatorade® have studied and documented the problems associated with fluid loss and dehydration: During physical activity, the body's internal controls constantly adapt to meet the demands of environment and exercise. The more strenuous the activity, the harder the muscles work. The constant contraction of working muscles produces heat and causes an increase in body temperature.

The symptoms of dehydration are:

- Muscle cramping (usually of large skeletal muscles) due to excessive loss of electrolytes through heavy sweating or because lost fluids are not adequately replaced.

- Sweaty skin.

- Infrequent urination and dark-colored urine.

- Weakness and nausea.

Here are some first-aid tips to combat dehydration:

- Move to a cooler location—the shade or an air-conditioned room.

- Massage, forcefully stretch, or extend cramped muscles.

- Replenish lost fluids with water or specially formulated sports beverages.

—Gatorade®

The body responds to this buildup of internal heat by activating thermoregulatory responses to reduce body heat. Heat produced by the muscles is carried by the blood to the skin's surface and then dissipated through evaporation of sweat from the skin; through radiation into cooler surrounding air; by convection as the body moves through the air; and through conduction, or contact, with cooler objects or surfaces.

Although sweating helps cool the body, sweat loss occurs at the expense of intra- and extracellular fluid volumes. As the level of fluids in the body is reduced, plasma volume also decreases, contributing to a higher heart rate and reduced ability to dissipate heat.

As a result, the body's temperature increases. This accelerates fatigue, reduces performance levels, and increases the risk of heat illness. Heat illnesses, including heat cramps, heat exhaustion, and heat stroke, occur as a result of dehydration and elevated body temperature. In extreme cases, heat illness can be fatal.

It's just as important, says Dr. [Andres] Rodriguez, to keep the body well hydrated when working out in the cold, as it is in the heat. Whether you are in a race or just out for a training run, you should drink water before and after the activity, and if it's a long run or race, you should drink along the way. Drink even if you don't feel thirsty; your body is still losing tremendous quantities of water, and if you don't replace what's lost and restore the balance of fluids, you will eventually feel the effects of dehydration. "The problem with winter races," says Dr. Rodriguez, "is that after the race, runners are interested in only one thing: getting warm. They should always stop and have some water as soon as possible, then go inside and warm up." He suggests drinking cool water in small sips, and keeping fluid intake high for the rest of the day.

You probably won't notice any severe effects of dehydration from not drinking enough on a cold day. You may, however, feel minor symptoms, such as light-headedness, muscle cramps, headache, and general fatigue and weakness.

—Fitness Forum

In addition, very old, very young, chronically ill, and overweight people do not adapt as easily to exertion in hot temperatures, making them more susceptible to heat illness.

Heat Cramps

Loss of water and salt from sweating that is not replaced, especially during exercise or physical labor outdoors during hot, humid weather, can cause muscle spasms or heat cramps. Usually in abdominal or leg muscles, heat cramps are often accompanied by weakness and nausea and are the first warning signs of dehydration.

To relieve heat cramps, massage cramped muscles and cool the body with cold tap water and wet towels. Slowly sip plain, cool water. If left untreated, heat cramps may lead to more serious heat illnesses.

Heat Exhaustion

Heat exhaustion is a more serious, systemic condition, often building up slowly over several days or weeks. It may appear after vigorous exercise or come on gradually from dehydration. Symptoms include: cool, pale, and moist skin; profuse sweating; dilated pupils; headaches; nausea; dizziness; and vomiting. Body temperature will be elevated.

Medical attention is necessary to treat heat exhaustion. First move the person to a cooler location and place in a shock position, lying on the back with feet up. Loosen or remove excess clothing and rehydrate with water or an electrolyte solution.

Heat stroke is a more severe and advanced form of heat exhaustion. It is a potentially fatal condition requiring immediate medical aid.

Experts estimate that approximately 200 deaths occur each year from heat stroke, but actual numbers are probably higher due to the number of incidents attributed to other conditions, such as heart attacks.

Heat stroke is triggered by profuse, prolonged sweating, leading to the eventual inability to sweat. Heat stroke can also lead to hyperthermia (high body temperature), hyponatremia (decreased concentration of sodium in the blood), and hypovolemia (low blood volume).

Heat stroke symptoms include cessation of sweating, hot and reddened skin, confusion, agitation and bizarre behavior (the most telltale signs), rapid pulse, seizures, and unconsciousness.

While waiting for medical assistance to arrive, move the individual to a cool, shaded area and loosen or remove excess clothing. Next, cool the body by fanning and immersing in a cool—not cold—bath or wrapping in wet sheets. Provide small amounts of fluids.

Heat illness is a serious medical condition resulting from inadequate fluid intake to replace fluid loss through sweat. To prevent dehydration, the main cause of heat illness, it is important to drink fluids before, during, and after physical activity in hot weather.

Fred Lebow on Hydration

Water was always important in our events; however, it didn't become a number one priority until the 1984 New York City Marathon. It was an extremely warm day. We had half a million cups of water for the 16,315 starters, but it wasn't enough. A 44-year-old Frenchman died during this race. It wasn't necessarily of dehydration (he had had a previous heart condition and was a smoker), but the lack of water and this tragedy were linked together. We were all shocked into action.

There are 30 water stations in the marathon. At each station, runners use more than one cup; they may pick up three or four, to drink and pour on themselves. Now we order 1.8 million cups for 25,000 runners. In cool weather, we end up with a lot of extra cups. But my motto is, I'd rather be stuck with 1 million unused water cups than end up one cup short.

We used to have problems with water distribution. It took us years to hone our water system. The issue isn't only having enough cups and enough water, it is having them properly laid out, so a passing runner can best get at them. That's why I tell anyone running a marathon to check out the organization, especially to make sure the water is sufficient. Lack of water isn't such a problem in most places these days, but when I ran the Boston Marathon in 1970, I don't remember passing even one water station.

Skin Care

Have you ever noticed a great paradox of many a seasoned runner: a fit athlete with the body of a teenager, but the face of an ancient? Fred Lebow was discussing this phenomenon some years ago with New York plastic surgeon and avid runner Dan Weiner, M.D., whom he ran into coincidentally on an airplane shuttle flight from Boston to New York.

Lebow told Weiner that some runners believed that their excess facial lines and sagging were due to the "bouncing" action of running. When Weiner explained the physiological reason, Lebow said he found it hard to believe someone had not created a skin product to prevent the problem. To answer Fred's challenge, Weiner and Mickey Lawrence, who works closely with the NYRRC throughout the year, developed Sports Proof—a year-round skin care product designed specifically for runners.

Runners Save Face

Runners and other exercisers once avoided sunscreens or other creams because sweat caused them to drip into the eyes, creating an annoying stinging sensation. Today, several companies make products specifically for use during exercise that do not run or drip.

Exercise is good for your skin. According to information from *Vitality* magazine, it boosts production of collagen, which keeps skin supple—plus, sweating increases the flow of nutrients to the skin's surface.

—Fitness Features

323

Dan Weiner believes runners no longer advance the "bouncing" theory as to why their skin does not "go the distance" as well as the rest of their bodies. He feels they are currently aware of their high-risk status regarding degenerative skin changes and the possibility of skin cancer. Mickey Lawrence, however, has her doubts about this raised consciousness regarding the problem. To emphasize the need for conscientious skin care, here's a review of the facts from Weiner, Lawrence, and other experts:

1. One major fallacy is that skin damage is caused only by the sun. While sun is the primary destructive agent, wind, cold, and dryness also contribute. What's more, sun is potent during unsuspected times. For example, sunlight gets through on cloudy days, as do up to 80 percent of the sun's damaging rays. In addition, temperature is not a gauge of sun danger. It is solar radiation that causes harm, and there's as much of that on a nice spring day in New York City as there is in the middle of a Florida summer.

2. Although millions of people will develop skin cancer in the next decade, many times that number of people will develop degenerative changes and experience premature aging of the skin. These changes include an initial dryness, scaling, and abnormal pigmentation, followed by premature aging with lines and wrinkles. Finally, in some cases, skin cancer develops. This is why year-round protection against all the elements is necessary. Runners are obviously at high risk as they engage in an outdoor activity on a regular basis.

3. Note the sun protection factor (SPF) of a sun care product. This is a guide to the length of protection, not to the amount of protection. Dan Weiner feels that, in general, sunscreens with an SPF of 12 to 15 are sufficient. Products are made as high as SPF 45 for those people with sun-sensitive skin, those exposed to the sun all day, and those who live in more intense sun areas.

4. Dan Weiner stresses the need for runners to apply skin care protection diligently all year long. Apply skin care cream or sunscreen at least 15 minutes before running, then reapply as needed. It is important to include sun-sensitive areas and those areas that receive greatest exposure: In addition to the face, apply to the ears, scalp, back of the hands, and shoulders. In terms of clothing, the general rule

is that if you can see through it, the sun can get through. Sunlight penetrates light clothing, so apply protective cream under a singlet for maximum protection. In addition, sunscreen should be used even if a person is already tan.

5. Summer running sense includes running at low peak sun hours—particularly avoiding the hours between 10 a.m. and 2 p.m. (3 p.m. if possible)—and wearing protective clothing such as T-shirts and hats or visors.

Applying vitamin E to the skin may help thwart skin cancers caused by exposure to the sun, according to researchers at the University of Arizona quoted in *Nutrition Action Healthletter* in 1991. According to Helen Gensler, the head of a study using vitamin E on the skin of mice, adding vitamin E to sunblocks and suntan lotions is a good idea. Aside from protecting against skin cancer, Gensler claims vitamin E prevents sunburn. In addition, it accumulates in the skin, so you don't have to worry about it washing off. It's too early to say how much or which kind of vitamin E is best. Gensler's study used the active form, di-alpha-tocopherol, but it degrades at room temperature. Skin creams use alpha-tocopherol acetate, which is stable at room temperature. But Gensler doesn't yet know whether the acetate form protects against UV radiation.

—Fitness Features

6. In the next decade, 40 million people will contract skin cancer. In fact, more people contract skin cancer than all other types of cancer combined. Due to an increase in outdoor activity and a depletion of the ozone layer, skin cancer is on a rapid rise.

Who gets skin cancer? Just ask some of those most vulnerable: runners who hit the road during the noonday sun, many of whom enjoy the freedom of going shirtless. In fact, according to the Centers for Disease Control, more men are dying of skin cancer (malignant melanoma) than of any other cancer. Maybe that's because it seems men have a greater difficulty maintaining diligent skin care. Their rationale is often that women have a history of applying creams and cosmetics, while it is harder for men to become accustomed to the habit. In addition to being diligent about skin protection while outdoors, Dan Weiner recommends moisturizing and conditioning of the skin on a regular basis. Professional facials are good, he adds, even for men.

7. Know the signs of skin cancer, which are: a skin growth that increases in size and appears pearly, translucent, or any shade of brown, black, or multicolored; any change in a mole or birthmark, or one that is irregular in outline; a spot or growth that continually itches, hurts, scabs, erodes, or bleeds; and an open sore that does not heal for more than one month, or heals and then reopens. Any suspicious signs should be checked by a physician immediately.

Massage

Since 1980, the NYRRC has been providing massage to runners, administered by volunteer massage therapists. Major events such as the New York City Marathon, the New York Games, the Fifth Avenue Mile, and the Advil Mini Marathon feature massage.

Massage captain Marilyn Frender says the biggest job by far is at the marathon, where 100 massage therapists serve the field of 25,000 runners, both at the race start and finish.

Massage for athletes has been part of the worldwide sporting scene for many years, says Frender. Most professional and amateur runners alike are aware of or are using sports massage as a regular part of their training program. In fact, many teams or clubs retain a massage therapist to aid their athletes.

Benefits of Massage

According to Frender, with massage, a runner can run better, longer, and more easily, raising the level of performance and at the same time lowering the level of stress that running can cause to the body. Massage can serve as a warmup—and warming up is a vital part of any athlete's training program. Warming up involves the gradual and coordinated preparation of the muscles, along with the joints, lungs, and heart, for the increased stress of exercise. Massage literally increases the blood circulation—in essence, heats the blood. The blood then carries that heat throughout the body, just as any other warmup would do.

Massage

- •Increases blood circulation, thus allowing muscles to function more efficiently;
- •Relaxes muscles and relieves cramps;
- •Increases flexibility;
- •Decreases nervous tension;
- •Reduces post-run soreness; and
- •Gives a sense of general well-being.

Massage also serves as a warmdown activity, says Frender. It slows down the breathing and pumping of the heart, cools the muscles, and then soothes and relaxes those muscles, relieving cramps and any other post-running physiological stress. In reducing muscle tension, spasms, and cramping, massage greatly promotes general relaxation and rapid recovery.

Although a post-event massage is similar to a pre-event massage, the state of the body is entirely different. After a race or hard workout, the muscles are in a state of fatigue and congestion; the tissues are filled with waste products. In increasing the blood circulation in this case, massage assists the blood in eliminating this tension and debris.

Massage is also a great benefit psychologically. After a massage, an athlete feels relaxed, rested, and ready to go. In addition, athletes benefit from the knowledge that they are better prepared and protected because of being massaged. The bottom line for most athletes is that massage serves as a reward for their discipline and hard effort.

Massaging Runners

Marilyn Frender has done her craft on every level of runner—from the novices to world-class sprinters and marathoners. In Frender's experience, the difference between the elite and some others is that the elite will tell her exactly what they need and where. This is because they are usually well accustomed to being massaged.

It should be taken into consideration, as Frender points out, that she is dealing with a large number of people on a short-term basis, most of whom she does not know. Her job is to provide short but effective pre- and postrace massage. The following details Frender's massage philosophy and approach:

A runner's feet and legs are probably the most important part of the body to be massaged. However, paying some attention to the lower back, shoulders, even the neck muscles and the jaw, can be a great help. Frender likes to give a 15- to 20-minute up-tempo light massage over the entire body. Up-tempo means it acts to stimulate, rather than sedate, the runner. She does not use ice, nor does she do any deep, specific, or trigger-point work. This avoids the need for the athlete to go through any period of muscle breakdown and recovery. Incidentally, oil is usually not used in this type of sports massage, but rather for full body massage.

Not all runners want a massage before a race, preferring one only afterward. If runners do not prefer a pre-event massage on their legs, Frender works on their abdomen, in an effort to loosen the *hara*. She explains that *hara* is a Japanese word and concept that refers to the area between the rib cage and the pelvis. All vital organs, excluding the heart and lungs, are in this area. Oriental belief is that this area of the body represents the center of life. It is the site of energy and force.

Although massage is an excellent post-event treatment, it is not begun until a runner has thoroughly cooled down. Massage therapists at NYRRC events do not use heat; however, if an athlete is cold, that person will be wrapped in a blanket. NYRRC massage therapists also do not work on sprains, cuts, bruises, or blisters, or on those with thermal problems (hypo- or hyperthermia) or dehydration. The club is fortunate to have on hand a highly skilled medical staff to which these runners are referred.

All things considered, there is no more effective way to prepare an athlete's body for total commitment than by giving that person the added opportunity for freer motion. Regular massage keeps the body in better physical condition; helps prevent injuries; and can reduce pain, help cure, and restore mobility in injured muscles. Sports massage gives runners extra protection and betters their performance—per event and for the length of their career.

How to Find a Massage Therapist

Although you can look in the yellow pages of the telephone book or call a massage school for referrals, Marilyn Frender still believes word of mouth is probably the most effective way to find a good massage therapist. Most massage therapists are able to do sports massage, but some have special training or even certificates in sports massage. For general information, you can contact the American Massage Therapy Association (see the Resource List).

The cost of a massage varies widely, depending on the experience and reputation of the therapist and in what part of the country that person works. Average rates in 1992 are $35 to $70 per hour. Most therapists also have half-hour rates.

Partner and Self-Massage

Massage is not new, nor is it the exclusive practice of professionals, explains Frender. It is part of the theory of the healing and calming power of touch. "Touching and rubbing is something people do instinctively," says Marilyn Frender. "When you have a bump, you rub it." Massaging a partner doesn't take a lot of skill, she adds; it just takes patience. "Giving a partner a massage is like giving a nice pat on the back."

A runner's muscles can derive enormous benefit from regular, properly administered self- or partner massage. You can safely and effectively massage your feet, ankles, legs, buttocks, shoulders, and neck—or have a partner do it. The following is taken from an article by Frender on self-massage, which can also be done by a partner. It previously appeared in *New York Running News*.

Self-massage is most effective if done regularly: after every run (or at least every speed workout) or at some other time during the day when you can relax. It's crucial to know that while massage can help relieve fatigue and soreness, it cannot cure an injury. If you feel persistent pain in your muscles or joints, see a medical specialist. Here are some guidelines to self-massaging various parts of the body:

Foot Massage

This is the most important, and often neglected, area to massage. Start by soaking your feet in warm-to-hot sudsy water for about 30 minutes. Towel dry. Sitting up, massage one foot at a time. Work the toes, too, since stiff, unrelaxed toes can cause pain on the run. You may want to use creams or petroleum jelly, especially if you tend to develop calluses or blisters. After massaging the feet, keep them elevated for about 20 minutes.

Heel Massage

Running's constant pounding may produce low-level pain here, known as jogger's heel. Use your thumbs to apply direct pressure to the tender area, pushing hard for up to 15 seconds at a time. You might also want to try deep friction massage: Move your thumbs back and forth with strong pressure across the heel in the sore spots. Again, if pain is severe, see a doctor.

Achilles Tendon Massage

It is easiest to massage this area if you sit up with your legs crossed. Work one leg at a time, feeling with fingers and thumbs around and behind the ankle bone. Apply direct pressure up and down the length of the tendon.

Calf Massage

It's common to feel tightness and soreness in the calves and behind the knees. For relief, sit down and cross your legs so you can comfortably reach the sore areas. Massage with kneading or compression, probing for sore areas.

Kneecap Massage

To soothe minor pain in the front of the knee, apply pressure with thumbs around the kneecap, rubbing gently anywhere you feel a tender spot. Circle the kneecap with your thumbs, with legs outstretched.

Thigh Massage

Both the hamstring and the quadriceps muscles (back and front of thigh) can benefit from self-massage. Lie face down (or on your back) and apply firm pressure up and down the leg, working tender spots with thumb and fingers, using deep friction to increase circulation.

Lower Back and Buttocks Massage

You should be able to reach these areas comfortably either standing up or lying down. Standing, place your hands on the hip bones and move in small circles with your thumbs; run your fingers and thumbs firmly down the gluteus medius muscles on the sides of the buttocks and across the gluteus maximus muscles on the cheeks.

Neck and Shoulder Massage

Use finger and thumb pressure and light friction up and down the muscles in the back of your neck and across the shoulders to relieve tension and stiffness. Move your head from side to side and shrug your shoulders to work out the kinks.

Fred Lebow on Massage

Massage is probably one of the most important medical aspects of my running life. I always have a massage a day or two before a marathon. I don't do it as regularly afterward because I don't often have the opportunity. I did have a massage after my first Boston Marathon, and I can still remember how wonderful it was.

Although massage therapists are available to elite runners at our major events, they are there for everyone at the New York City Marathon. Our massage therapists at the marathon are one of the "finer touches" of the event.

I'll never forget, though, how a massage once did me in. I was at the TAC National Championships in New York in 1991, getting a wonderful massage. While I was enjoying it, Leroy Burrell broke a world record in the 100 meters. Such a feat in my own backyard, and I missed it—but it was a great massage!

Hot and Cold Weather Running

The beauty of running is that you can do it year round. Temperature extremes are no reason to halt your routine. However, you should follow certain guidelines and precautions. In addition, be aware that it takes about two weeks to adjust to climatic extremes. Therefore, you may want to go easy at first if you are not accustomed to the weather conditions.

Cold Weather Running Tips

Here are some cold weather running tips adapted from a NYRRC brochure written by Bob Glover. These tips should help you prevent injuries and get through the doldrums of the long, dark winter:

Poor Footing

The main weather-related cause of injuries is poor footing during winter months. These injuries most often come from being tight when trying to guard against slipping on snow- or ice-covered running surfaces. Tense muscles, whether consciously or unconsciously tightened, are more prone to strains and other overuse injuries. The runner usually alters his or her running form to increase traction, which leads to further problems. Lateral foot slippage often occurs on icy spots, causing a pulled muscle or tendon. The most common winter running injuries are groin and hamstring pulls caused by slipping and sliding through

333

the snow. These nagging injuries often require rest, or they will still be with you when the snow has melted. Of course, you may also slip and fall. If you do, try to land lightly and then immediately stop your run and ice the injured area to reduce swelling. Running in a few inches of snow forces you to work muscles normally not taxed. If your quadriceps become fatigued, knee injury could result. Limit your running in snow and slippery conditions to 30 to 45 minutes at a time to minimize injuries.

Training must go on with or without dry surfaces if you intend to keep reasonably fit. The best prevention against injuries in the winter is to make sure you warm up well (start with brisk walking or a slow jog), maintain good flexibility (cold weather runners are less flexible) with regular stretching exercises, and run relaxed, not allowing yourself to tense up out of fear of falling. When running on slippery surfaces, shorten your stride slightly and shuffle along, maintaining good balance. Be especially careful on downhills and turns and when running in the dark. Don't attempt fast running under slippery conditions. Studded shoes that aren't overly worn are the best in the snow—just like the snow tires you put on your car for better traction. Adjust your pace. It takes more effort to run with extra clothing and with difficult footing, so don't be obsessed with trying to maintain the same training pace you can hold in warmer, drier conditions.

Frostbite

To prevent frostbite, keep covered, keep dry, keep moving. Frostbite usually occurs to ears, face, fingers, and toes. Frostbitten skin is cold, pale, and firm to hard to the touch. The first step in treatment is to warm rapidly without excessive heat. It is recommended that immediate medical attention be given. Prevent frostbite by keeping the extremities and face well protected in extremely cold weather.

The danger of frostbite greatly increases with wind, which when combined with air temperature produces the "windchill factor." Running into the wind worsens the windchill factor, while running with the wind may speed you along and produce a sweat. Therefore, begin your runs into the wind on out-and-back courses. Otherwise you'll build up a good sweat with the wind at your back and then turn into a biting wind for the return, which may cause frostbite or at least extreme discomfort.

Hypothermia

Hypothermia is the lowering below normal of the central or core temperature of the body. As the temperature falls, the body responds with shivering, which is the muscles' attempt to produce heat. If not attended to, the runner could next become incoherent and then lapse into a coma and even die.

Hypothermia usually strikes when you are wearing wet clothing. If your clothes are soaked from getting splashed with slush or if you sweat too much from overdressing, you should change right away rather than keep running. Take off your wet clothing immediately after running, or hypothermia may strike you.

Clothing

Dress in layers that can be easily adjusted. If you get too warm, you can always remove a layer and tie it around your waist. The key is to trap the heat naturally produced by the body. Wear up to three layers, four if it is extremely cold. Two layers are enough for most racing conditions. The innermost layer should be absorbent and nonirritating, such as a cotton T-shirt. A preferred inside material is polypropylene or similar fabrics that are very lightweight and transmit your moisture away from the body, allowing you to remain dry and warm. The second insulating layer is usually a long-sleeved turtleneck or a hooded wool sweatshirt. The outer shell is usually designed to break the wind. A nylon windbreaker or Gore-Tex® fabrics, which "breathe" better than nylon and repel water as well as wind, are preferred by many runners.

The legs need less protection, as they are generating the most heat. One layer of clothing is usually enough. Tights, or nylon or Gore-Tex bottoms, usually suffice. Polypropylene or wool liners can be worn under pants to add warmth on very cold days.

The extremities must be kept covered. The most important area to keep covered is the head. As much as 50 percent of body heat is lost through the head. In extremes of cold, a ski mask may be used to keep the face and nose warm. Coating your face with petroleum jelly will also help. Ears should be protected by a ski cap or wool headband. Mittens are warmer than gloves. An old pair of wool socks will do just fine, but you can purchase polypropylene liners and Gore-Tex mittens.

For the feet, a single pair of wool or polypropylene socks are all you need. If you keep moving and don't get too wet, your feet won't get cold.

If you get hot when running or racing, first remove your hat (tuck it in your waistband), then your mittens, then unzip your outer layer, and then remove it and tie it around your waist. As you cool, replace this clothing in opposite order.

Be prepared—dress properly. Be flexible. On a single run the conditions may change several times. Don't toss away any articles of clothing when you are running or racing unless you are positive you won't need them again. Remember that there is danger not only in underdressing and getting too cold, but also in overdressing and getting too warm. You should open your clothing as soon as sweat starts to build up. You can develop heat injuries when running overdressed. Additionally, drink fluids when racing or doing long runs in cold weather, or you risk dehydrating.

Alternative Training

You don't have to run every day all winter no matter what the weather. On the other hand, don't just quit and get out of shape. A good method is to cut back on your mileage during the winter and make some of it up—especially on bad weather days—with alternative training. Basically 30 minutes of biking or swimming indoors is an aerobic training equivalent of a 30-minute run. So, too, is an aerobics class, using a rowing machine, and other forms of alternative exercise. The most natural way to exercise when snow clogs your running paths is to ski cross-country.

Keep Running Enjoyable

As much as possible, run during the daytime rather than at night. Daylight running is much more cheerful in the winter, and it is warmer when the sun is out. Make a date a few times a week with other runners to keep winter running from becoming too dreary.

Here are some more cold weather tips:

- Although some people fear that running in cold weather can damage their lungs, this is not possible. That's because the lungs warm air sufficiently as it enters. If the cold air is uncomfortable to breathe, though, a face mask or hat that covers the nose and surrounds the mouth may help.

- Several parts of the body are most vulnerable to frostbite, such as toes, fingers, the nose, and ears. Bring a handkerchief or tissue to dab your eyes and nose often. If you feel pain or numbness in these areas, wiggle and move them, but don't rub. This can damage the blood vessels if the skin is in fact frozen. Don't blow warm breath on the skin either. The best way to warm these areas is with other parts of your body, such as putting your hands in your armpits.

- If the thought of that initial hit of biting cold makes it hard to get outside, try warming up indoors first to get the blood flowing. If the thought of going out at all is just too chilling, but you don't have access to equipment for alternative training, work out by repeatedly climbing or running up flights of stairs, jumping rope, or running in place.

- While icy surfaces can be treacherous for running, snow is usually no problem. If you are worried about the quality of your training, remember that a slower pace in more difficult conditions can equal a tougher workout under more ideal conditions.

- In extreme cold, coat your face (or at least your nose and cheeks) with a layer of petroleum jelly. Don't forget year-round skin care. (See Chapter 29, "Skin Care.")

- If your hands are especially sensitive to cold, wear a double layer of covering—such as combining a pair of gloves and mittens. The same goes for the ears—another likely spot to suffer most from cold. Try a headband covered with a hat for double protection.

Runner and *New York Running News* contributor Kay Denmark has come up with some tried-and-true tips on surviving the winter season.

- Dry, awful winter claws—be gone! Let the cold weather work for your hands by giving them a hot mitt treatment while running. Glob on the petroleum jelly, then tuck those fingers into mittens or cotton socks. No matter how hot your hands get while running, try not to take off their coverings. The heat helps the jelly soften your skin.

- For those too macho to wear gloves in the winter, an old washer-woman trick can help. Before going out, briefly soak your hands in vinegar, and let them thoroughly air-dry. This helps to keep your hands warmer. It doesn't last forever, so it's best for short runs—or hanging out the laundry to dry, as originally intended.

- I don't know about you, but I can't run with my mouth shut. After enduring bone-chilling weather outdoors, when my teeth reach the warm air of my apartment, I experience a painful sensation. If you can relate, never fear, because there is a solution. Try placing a dry towel or washcloth in your mouth upon crossing the threshold. It works. It also proves delightfully entertaining to any eyewitnesses!

- Winter is not especially kind to hair. Those precious locks need some protection from the drying effects of wind and cold. Before running, pour some conditioner into the palms of your hands and work it through your hair.

- Ginger tea is great for warming up after a run. I learned about this magical liquid from an elderly woman in the tropical rain forest of Dominica, and it's the best winter brew of which I know. It helps break up congestion, and the subtle, hot kick of ginger warms a cold winter body. Simply place four or five thin slices of fresh ginger in a cup and add boiling water. Allow the brew to steep a while. Then let it seep its spicy warmth into icy you.

- Winter noses are often frozen, chapped, and unattractive. Rather than walking around with greasy-looking, petroleum-jellied nostrils, a simple solution is to apply some Chap Stick. Hey, it works on your lips, so why not?

- Here's a tip you likely associate with summer, but it applies equally to winter. Sunblock protects against winter sun and wind, which can be extremely destructive to your skin. (For more information on this important subject, see Chapter 29, "Skin Care.")

- Wind can propel every bit of available dust into your eyes. By the time your run is over, your eyes may be red, irritated, and even puffy. Try a remedy often attributed to Ethel Merman. Put a small amount of witch hazel on cotton balls, close your eyes, and put the cotton on your eyelids. This soothes abused and tired eyes.

Summer Weather Running Tips

Running during the summer months can be quite enjoyable with extended daylight hours and the warmer weather. But running in hot weather can be trouble; and racing in it can be dangerous. Summer heat and humidity can cause muscle cramps, blisters, fatigue, heat exhaustion, and heat stroke. Symptoms that you should be aware of include headache; dizziness; disorientation; decrease in perspiration; and pale, cold skin. At the first sign of any of these symptoms, stop, walk, or rest. A precautionary plan to assure safe, healthy running is outlined in an NYRRC brochure written by Bob Glover:

1. *Wear cool clothing.* Light-colored, loose singlets are best. In direct sunlight, provide your body with shade—a light-colored hat to protect your head and a light-colored, loose shirt that covers your shoulders.

2. *Drink plenty of fluids.* On very hot or humid days, the body's natural cooling process of sweating and evaporation can stop. So drink before you get thirsty—one to three quarts a day—and make frequent stops, at least every two to three miles, for fluid replenishment during your runs.

3. *Avoid the heat.* If you don't plan to race in the heat, don't train in it. Run during the cool of the early morning or late evening. Look for running paths that are shaded, and run on the shady side of the road.

4. *Adjust your pace.* Start out more slowly and run a steady pace in both training runs and races. You may need to slow down as much as a minute per mile and make further reductions in pace along the way.

5. *Adjust your distance.* In hot weather, shorten your planned distance. If you have planned a long run for a particular day, and it's too hot, postpone the long run for a cooler day.

6. *Keep your body wet.* During training runs and races, pour water over your head. Use sponges to douse your body with water. Wear a light-colored running hat and put ice in it.

7. *Heat-train for races.* If you anticipate running a race in hot weather, give yourself from 10 to 14 days of progressive heat training. A few times a week, run at a time of day that is hotter.

8. *Replenish your body's supply of minerals.* Magnesium and potassium, in particular, are lost through sweating. Fresh fruits and vegetables, especially bananas, watermelon, cantaloupe, carrots, and tomatoes, contain these essential elements. Or you may try one of the commercially produced electrolyte replacement drinks made for runners.

9. *Most important, use common sense.* If you feel dizzy, overheated, *or cold*, stop and walk. Get out of the sun. Don't race hard in hot weather. Remember, heat exhaustion and heat stroke can affect any level of runner, seasoned competitor and novice alike.

One easy way to speed up adaptation to hot weather is to take hot baths every day for a week. Heating up your body will help prime your sweat response to work faster. After about a week of this, your body will better adjust to high temperatures, and you'll sweat faster, aiding evaporation and cooling.

Exercise on a hot day and you need as much cooling power as you can get. But what doesn't do the trick is the drip-off, trickle-down of your neck sweat. What is cooling is just the opposite, according to experts quoted in *Vogue* magazine: a thin film of all-over-your-body perspiration. This is because it's the evaporation of sweat off the skin that's cooling, not the sweat itself. In other words, sweat that drips, not evaporates, is a wasted cooling effort. If you normally sweat heavily when you exercise, lightly dab off excess sweat, but be sure to leave a thin layer behind.

—Fitness Features

Safety

In April 1989, a young woman runner was attacked, brutally beaten, raped, and left for dead by a gang of youths in New York City's Central Park. This incident brought the issue of running safety into international focus.

For years, the NYRRC has held educational forums on safety for runners, and lobbied to improve conditions to facilitate safety in Central Park and other areas. After all, violence against runners was not unheard of before. *New York Running News* editor in chief and NYRRC director of media and public affairs Raleigh Mayer had written an emotional editorial in the magazine prior to the Central Park jogger attack about her own attack and rape while running through Central Park. The crime against Mayer happened in the same location as that of the Central Park jogger. She was subsequently interviewed on network television, radio, and in the newspapers, calling for a more enlightened view and treatment of rape victims.

> *Attention women*: Runner and rape survivor Shelley Reecher of Eugene, Oregon, created and manages Project Safe Run, a highly successful service that lends women trained dogs to run or walk with. To find a Project Safe Run chapter near you, or to help start one, contact Reecher at Project Safe Run, 2226 Fairmount Blvd., Eugene, OR 97403; tel. (503) 345-8086.

In response to the jogger attack, the NYRRC Safety Office was instituted, which is overseen by a full-time staff member. The club also finances gatekeepers in a kiosk in Central Park, and works with the Central Park police precinct in a crime watch effort.

Contrary to what people often believe about big cities, and New York in particular, this city—which has the largest concentration of runners anywhere—happens to be one of the safest places in which to run. It's a little-known fact, but the Central Park precinct has long had the lowest crime rate in the city. That's in part because various organizations, including the NYRRC, have lobbied to provide better safety services.

The following runners' safety information is adapted from a brochure distributed by the NYRRC, as well as NYRRC safety clinics given by now retired detective Lucille Burrascano of the New York City Police Department.

Safety Tips

1. There's safety in numbers, so don't run alone. Although this is the cardinal rule of running safety, a majority of runners do their running solo. Find a partner or a group to run with. A local runners' club is a good place to start. If you must run alone, go where there are other people.

2. Whenever possible, run during daylight hours. If you must run at night, wear light-reflecting or light-colored clothing and avoid running in deserted areas. Whenever possible, choose courses that enable you to avoid running in the street.

3. Be thoroughly familiar with your route. Know the location of phones, call boxes, police stations, fire houses, hospitals, 24-hour businesses, etc.

4. Listen to your instincts and be willing to vary your route if you sense that you are in danger. If you are alone, wait for another runner if possible.

5. Avoid running in deserted or poorly lighted areas, or adjacent to dense foliage or places from which you can be set upon without warning. Be especially alert at blind corners or when you are crossing intersections.

6. Run against traffic whenever possible. Move first when a vehicle is coming toward you. Do not expect vehicles to move for you.

7. Run relaxed and confident, yet be aware of your surroundings and who is around you at all times. Run defensively—watching for and avoiding cars, bikes, dogs, etc.

8. Don't acknowledge or respond to verbal harassment.

9. Carry a whistle or alarm device to summon emergency assistance.

10. Don't wear jewelry (chains, medallions, rings, expensive watches, etc.).

11. Tune into your surroundings, not out.

12. Avoid wearing headphones. In recent years, it has become common practice among many people to run with headsets. It is generally unsafe to do so, as the runner is usually unaware of his or her surroundings, and cannot hear outside noise well. In 1991, the NYRRC attempted to ban the use of headphones in its races. So many loyal runners/headphone users complained that the club rescinded the ban. However, NYRRC policy states that wearing headphones while running is an unsafe practice. For runners who still insist on using them, the club recommends they pay careful attention to their surroundings, keep the volume as low as possible, and perhaps use only one of the earphones.

13. Always carry some form of personal identification while running (including medic alert ID if applicable) in case of emergency. It's also a good idea to carry a small amount of paper money. Write personal information and blood type on the inside of your shoes.

Henley Gibble, runner and executive director of the Road Runners Club of America (RRCA), is a strong safety advocate who has published an extensive number of safety bulletins. For information on organizing community safety, call Gibble at the RRCA (see the Resource List).

When Dogs Are Not Runners' Best Friends

Like the long hounded mail carriers, it is not uncommon for runners to be confronted by dogs. What should you do if you're confronted by a dog during a run? According to Mimi Noonan, D.M.V., a veterinarian at the Animal Medical Center in Manhattan and a member of the NYRRC, it depends on the dog. A lot of times the animal will just come up and smell you, and then it will go away. However, some dogs are inherently aggressive, she points out. The best thing to do is just to stop and be nonthreatening. If you run away, they usually will chase you. If you try to throw something at them or hit at them, they'll try to bite. Just be as nonthreatening as you can. And if you can't, you should yell, "No! Go away!" and "Down!" or "Sit!"

If you have a squirt bottle of water, Noonan says use it, but she does not recommend spraying Mace in a dog's face because the dog may then chase you. Concludes Noonan, "What you don't want to do is get into a chase with a dog because almost every dog in the world is faster than any person."

If you do get bitten by a dog, go to a hospital immediately. If possible, find the owner of the dog to determine whether the dog has been vaccinated against rabies.

7

Part 7: Health and Medicine

Run Healthy

33

To run healthy means to run using common sense. So if you have been inactive for more than a few months, or have any health problems, consult a qualified physician for a thorough medical examination before undertaking a running program. Dr. Andres Rodriguez also advises that you do the following:

Avoid the "invincibility syndrome." Don't take the "must go on" or "must win" attitude to extremes. If you're not feeling well, especially during an acute viral infection or when suffering from a systemic disease, stay off your feet.

> What kept me relatively injury-free throughout my career was sound training and racing. My career had a sensible sequence: from shorter distances on the track to longer distances on the roads. Nothing I have done was on an impulse. Admittedly, my first marathon in 1978 was sort of run on a whim, but to a degree I was well prepared by having a strong running background. In those days, however, the amount of marathon training knowledge and widely available information wasn't even a fraction of what it is today.
>
> This doesn't mean I didn't make mistakes along the way in my career. Looking back, I regret that very often I didn't cut back on my training when I felt something was wrong. I made the common mistake of thinking I could run through it, that it wasn't as bad as it was. I think this sense of invincibility is what all we runners have in common. And we learn the lesson the hard way, believing we

> are the exception. Much of the time, we're good at giving advice to others, but when it comes to ourselves, we don't follow the rules.
>
> So don't be afraid to take a day off. Don't be afraid to use alternative training. I think that's why so many people get injured, because they don't cut back when they hear a message from the body.
>
> —Grete Waitz

Get a good night's sleep before a race. Do not take any sedatives. Have a light meal three or four hours before a race. Carbohydrates such as toast, crackers, and fruit are best. Avoid heavy meals containing fats, proteins, and sweets. Avoid all alcoholic beverages before a race, and definitely do *not* take any drugs that serve as stimulants.

Watch the weather. Adjust your race or training goal if it's hotter or more humid than usual. Do not overdress. Clothing should feel comfortable and should be loose-fitting. Wear clothes you've worn running before; new clothes could chafe or cause other discomfort. Light-colored clothes will help reflect heat. Remember that you heat up as you run. If you feel comfortably dressed at the start of a race or training session, you are probably overdressed.

Wear proper running shoes. Shoes should fit well and should feel comfortable. New or badly worn-out shoes could cause discomfort and injury.

Do warmup exercises before a race or training session and cooldown exercises after. Follow your normal stretching routine after these exercises.

Watch the condition of the road as you run to avoid accidents. Gravel, curbs, grates, and potholes can be dangerous if you don't see them.

Run at your own pace. Do not push too hard too soon. This will invariably lead to early exhaustion. If you develop a leg cramp, slow down or stop running. Massage and slowly stretch and relax the involved muscle. If the cramp continues, ask for assistance.

When racing, avoid all sudden sprinting, especially at the end. If you've been regularly practicing speedwork, your body will be used to accelerating. But even in trained runners, sudden sprints may lead to leg muscle injuries. It is imperative that you withdraw from a race if you have a fever, chills, generalized malaise, cold or flu, nausea, vomiting, or diarrhea. If there is the slightest doubt, stop at a first-aid station or ask advice from medical personnel before or after the race.

> What I've learned over the years is that you really have to tune into your "denial mechanism" quickly if you want to stay active. In other words, everybody gets to a point where they start to overdo it, and break down or get hurt. And almost everybody denies it when it first hits.
>
> Staying healthy is a question of how quickly you can get beyond the denial and deal with the reality. You then have an opportunity to back off that little bit you need to recover. And it doesn't take much adjustment, because what I've also found is that you don't have to back off a lot if you can recognize the potential problem soon enough.
>
> It's really very simple to recognize. It's accepting that you're limping. My test is, any time you get to the point where something is truly interfering with your running gait, back off and let it heal. Don't keep going simply because you *can* keep going.
>
> —Frank Shorter

IMMDA's Ten Medical Commandments

The following health tips from Dr. Andres Rodriguez and Yolanda Rodriguez are distributed to international race directors and entrants in major NYRRC races. They are, in fact, the Ten Medical Commandments of the International Marathon Medical Directors Association (IMMDA) for the prevention of injuries in marathon or long distance running:

1. Make sure you are physically fit for the running activities that you're undertaking.
2. Train properly.
3. Follow guidelines for proper nutrition.
4. Maintain adequate hydration before, during, and after the race.
5. Perform warmup and stretching exercises before the run, and cooldown and stretching exercises after the run.

Working out *first thing* in the morning may not be good for you, warns an article in *Self* magazine. When you lie down for a long period of time, the disks in your spine expand with fluid, making them tighter, tenser, and more likely to become irritated, according to August A. White III, M.D., of Harvard Medical School. Dr. White recommends an hour or so of everyday activity after rising, before you work out.

—Fitness Features

6. Dress properly, according to the weather.

7. Use proper, comfortable shoes—not a new pair.

8. Watch the condition of the running surface or road.

9. Do not overdo it; run at your own pace.

10. Listen to your body: Slow down, or even stop, if you do not feel well.

Injury Prevention and Cure

As every athlete, coach, and medical professsional can verify, if you've been running long, hard, or far enough—you've likely experienced some type of injury at one time or another. In fact, witnessing the medical care network for just one event, the New York City Marathon, is proof. From runners eagerly seeking guidance on injuries at the Marathon Expo and clinics, to those being cared for on race day by 1500 medical volunteers, no single subject seems to concern—and often obsess—a runner more than injury.

Injury seems to have little relevance until it hits you personally. Then, no matter what level of runner you are, it can be devastating. For the elite athlete, it represents the loss not only of personal identity, but of a job and a livelihood. For the serious athlete, being forced to take off from running is like losing a dear friend. Even for a beginner, it can be like having a (new) rug pulled out from under. You will never realize how much you cherish your running until—even temporarily—it is no longer yours.

Almost everybody gets hurt. That's because you're trying to get the best out of yourself, and in order to do that, you're training to the limit, approaching that very fine line. A lot of us go over that fine line and get injured. You have to be highly in tune with your body. You have to be able to reach that fine line but not go over it.

As a masters runner, people often ask me if injuries have to do with aging. Injuries can occur with overtraining and some dietary deficiencies, but I don't think they have to do with age. To run on an international level, to be the best masters runner, or any level runner, you must train extremely hard. You try and keep one eye on the body, as best as you can.

We're seeing now through those like myself that the higher risk of injury doesn't necessarily happen for someone just beginning to run seriously. You begin very gradually, and it can possibly be a three- to five-year buildup before those injuries begin to occur.

—Priscilla Welch

That's the bad news. The good news is that injuries heal, and with the injury experience comes wisdom. Coping with injury (or illness) is one of the many aspects of running that, as George Sheehan has articulated so well over the years, shows us that running is often a metaphor for life, including personal adversity.

Why all the heavy philosophy? Because putting things in perspective is not always one of the great skills of the injured runner. Over the years, a great number of telephone calls to the NYRRC (often characterized by desperate pleas for help) have been from injured runners. The club keeps a directory of area health care professionals for just this purpose—many of them discovered and referred by the staff, veteran injured runners themselves. And to illustrate the yin and yang of the sport, other than participation in the club's major races, the best-attended functions are the injury clinics.

An Ounce of Prevention

Certified sports chiropractor Dr. G. Thomas Kovacs notes that overuse injuries are obviously due to factors such as running on hard, nonshock-absorbing surfaces, overstriding, downhill running, and improper shoe selection. But other factors, he explains below, will also affect your musculoskeletal system.

Flexibility and Stretching. Be sure you are flexible enough and that your stretching routine concentrates on the muscles used for running, such as lower back, hamstrings, and calves.

Most sprains and strains should be treated with ice, at least for the first 48 hours. Ice, best applied in a plastic bag or wrapped in a towel, dulls the pain as well as decreases blood flow, lessening internal bleeding and swelling. After icing, wrap an elastic bandage snugly but not tightly around the sore area, and elevate it above the heart. Stop ice treatments as soon as the skin is numb, usually after 15 or 20 minutes. Ice is not the remedy for blisters or open wounds, or if you have circulatory problems. Heat, meanwhile, is used once the swelling is gone in order to relax muscles, decrease pain, and speed recovery.

Here's a first-aid idea for pulls and sprains that need cold applied to them immediately to keep swelling down. Instead of fumbling with ice cubes, use a bag or two of frozen vegetables—corn, peas, or other small items. They're handy, and can be easily shaped to fit around whatever it is you've damaged. Or you could fill balloons with various amounts of water and freeze them. This way you can make custom-fitted cold packs.

—Fitness Features

Strength. Do you have adequate strength in your quadriceps, shins, and abdominal muscles to make it through your workout, or do you ignore strengthening those "opposing" running muscles?

Diet. Does your diet consist of candy bars, or vegetables and whole grains? Sixty-five percent of your diet should be in the form of complex carbohydrates, while proteins and fats each should be about 15 percent of your diet. Remember, you are what you eat.

Rest. Do you allow your body adequate time to rest and recuperate?

Vigilance. Do you monitor key factors of overtraining, such as resting heart rate, body weight, and number of hours slept per night? Did you know that an increase in resting heart rate of 10 points has a high correlation to injury within three days? An unexpected weight drop of three pounds will also have the same effect.

Equipment. Are you wearing a pair of shoes that even your dog shunned? Do you know the various running shoe features, such as straight lasted and curve lasted? Did you know that flat-footed people need motion control in a running shoe?

Warmup. Do you make the same mistake as numerous runners by assuming that warming up is the same as stretching, or do you warm up properly by first running slowly so you can stretch farther and perform better? A one-degree increase in muscle temperature during warmup will make your muscles 13 percent more efficient. This translates into more power!

Program Planning. Do you suddenly increase your weekly mileage by as much as 50 percent, or do you increase properly—by 10 percent per week? Do you end your workouts by racing someone to the finish line, or do you cool down properly so that your heart can relax slowly?

Hydration. Are you the type of person who has a beer or two before you go out for a run, rather than hydrate yourself with water?

What to Do When You Can't Run

Athlete and M.D. Norbert Sander—winner of the 1974 New York City Marathon—advises that you avoid the pitfall of giving up entirely—not exercising, overeating, and getting into a general depression—when sidelined by an injury. "As the years and injuries come and go, the experienced runner usually begins to appreciate the personal benefits and positive feelings derived from good fitness and day-to-day running," he explains. "The temptation to push close to the injury edge in the hopes of greater performance becomes less appealing, and thus the amount of downtime usually decreases."

If you exercise to the point that your muscles hurt the next day, you might think the best way to ease this discomfort is to work through the ache. But research outlined in *Vogue* magazine indicates that exercise slows, not speeds, muscle recovery, and may even lead to injury. A Massachusetts research team had a group work their arm muscles to exhaustion, then put one arm in a sling for three days. Although both arms stayed sore for the same number of days, the immobilized arm regained its strength more quickly. Another group of researchers tested whether exercising with sore muscles increased the risk of injury. They found muscle soreness in runners caused them to stiffen their lower bodies, thus making them poorer at absorbing shock, causing a greater risk of injury. Researchers now have this advice for the sore: Give your muscles a rest, at least for a day or two.

—Fitness Features

If you can't work out the standard minimum of 20 to 30 minutes, don't give up on working out at all. A study quoted in *Runner's World* magazine found that multiple short bouts (three 10-minute sessions, for example) of moderate-intensity exercise resulted in significant training effects—nearly the same as those produced by a single 30-minute bout. This just proves how simple achieving fitness can be.

—Fitness Features

Sander writes that most world-class marathoners have relatively short periods of extraordinary performances due to the tightrope walk necessary between record-breaking runs and physical breakdown. The risk at the top is quite high, although worth it at least for short periods. "I myself had two periods of high-level running—one for four months after I graduated from college and won 14 of 15 races, culminating in a time of 61:40 for a 20-kilometer race. Predictably, my penultimate run was followed by a year-long ankle injury that effectively killed off any chance of progressing on to the next level, which I thought, at that time, would be national-class. Ten years later I had a resurgence, but without my former speed, going up in distance to the marathon. I won Yonkers in 1973, New Orleans and New York in 1974, and placed second, fourth, and fifth in three other international marathons," Sander explains.

According to Sander, getting back to high-level competition after injury can take a very long time—mentally and physically—especially in terms of the spiritual resolve to press deeper and deeper into oneself. Today there are a good number of conditioners to help keep you in shape when running is impossible: Stationary or outside cycling, cross-country ski machines, treadmill running, and pool running all can help to maintain a level of fitness and avoid the depression that often goes with injury.

Fred Lebow on Injury

I've had a bad knee for years. I tried wearing an elastic brace; I put a lift in my shoes; I was given orthotics—some of this made it worse. It got to the point where I would start running, and it would begin to swell up. Finally, I went to see Dr. Norb Sander. He told me I had to have it operated on. In 1986, I had arthroscopic surgery (just like Joan Samuelson, except I didn't win the Olympic Trials marathon 17 days later). It was better, but it didn't completely disappear.

I tried swimming (I didn't know about water running then, or I would have done that); I joined a health club to do some exercises, but I found it extremely boring.

In retrospect, I think I babied my knees too much. Sometimes now I'll have a little pain even when I walk, but I start running and it goes away. While you can't ignore your aches and pains, I think you can't be too oversensitive about them either.

The bottom line is common sense. Unfortunately, that sense isn't so well developed until you experience the entire injury cycle—beginning, middle, and end. No doctor, no coach can truly replace personal experience. They may try to help you, but even if you listen to them, you don't totally comprehend.

Usually, one day, the problems are gone. You have to give it time, but not planned time. No matter what the guidelines say, everyone heals at a different rate. You can't decide when you will be healed.

Since my brain cancer, I have no knee problems. My chemotherapy and radiation must have had some effect. I don't know how, and my doctors don't believe it. Maybe it's a year's worth of medication having had some effect on my knee. Maybe it's the cutback in running.

I've encountered every type of runner, from sprinters to marathoners, and every one of them has been injured at one time or another. They all treat it very differently. The most difficult are the sprinters. When they hurt themselves, it's often much more serious than injury to a long distance runner. It's probably the explosive nature of their event.

Generally, a long distance runner can incur injury and come back much faster than a sprinter.

What have I learned from years of watching top athletes suffer injury? There is one universal aspect of injury among elite athletes. If I'm injured, I can still work. They can't; their work is running. I've learned that I can get hurt and still live a normal life.

What really distresses me is that some runners don't renew their NYRRC membership because they're injured. They don't realize that injury itself is not the end. No matter how badly you're injured, you can eventually overcome it.

34

Sports Medicine and Modalities

Sports Medicine

According to Norbert Sander, M.D., medical problems in runners are essentially injuries, though a whole gamut of illnesses, such as fatigue syndrome, exertional blood in the urine, chest pain, shortness of breath, anemia, and exertional headaches may occur as part of training. Those are less prevalent, but nonetheless do occur.

Joe Weisenfeld, Norbert Sander, and Margaret Dessau offer their insights into the runner's body, from the ground up. Weisenfeld, a podiatrist, tells you what to do for your aching feet. Sander, a sports medicine expert who has treated more than 20,000 runners in the New York area for every conceivable athletic injury since he founded the Preventive Sports Medicine Center in1976, alerts you to the needs and modalities of your body parts, from your ankle to your head. Dessau, also an M.D., describes that essential running function, breathing.

Blistered, Bruised, and Smelly Feet

Blistering, black toes, or bad-smelling runner's feet are usually minor surface foot problems, explains Weisenfeld.

Treatment:

- A post-run soak in warm (not hot) water with salt to help prevent infection. Salt removes sweat and oils and keeps the skin properly dry. For perspiring, smelly feet and blister prevention, soak in a diluted solution of tea (warm, not hot). Use real tea, not herbal (it's the tannic acid that does the trick)—two tea bags to a quart of water. Do this soak once to twice a week. Both soaks can be done for five minutes, twice per day.

• Remember, socks can reduce injury. Socks are now made with heel or toe pads and arch supports. Others are made for blister prevention. There are also a variety of over-the-counter foot and arch supports in the form of shoe inserts.

Shinsplints

Shinsplints, explains Sander, is a general term used for any pain in the shins. Pain in the shins can be muscular, which is short-lived; involve soft tissue if the lining of the bone is inflamed; or, more seriously, indicate a stress fracture of the bone itself. It is crucial to determine the difference by examination and sometimes by X ray.

Tenderness along the inside of the shin over the muscle and not the bone is usually due to a strain of the tibialis posterior muscle (on the inside of the knee and extending to the arch).

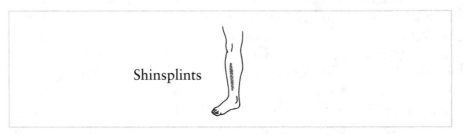

Shinsplints

Possible causes:
• overtraining
• too-rapid increase in training
• biomechanical (specifically, pronation or flat arches)
• training surfaces (hard or hilly ground; sharp turns on indoor tracks)

Treatment:
• rest (usually one week to one month), ice, anti-inflammatories, and, in some cases, the correction of excessive rolling in of the

arch (pronation) by a good antipronation running shoe, an over-the-counter soft arch support, or a custom-made orthotic.

Stress Fracture

Sander explains that a stress fracture is the most serious cause of shinsplints. If the pain is pinpointable and on the bone, if it is present on weight-bearing (e.g., getting out of bed in the morning), and if it comes on relatively rapidly, it may represent a stress fracture. Though a simple X ray may prove this after approximately two weeks of pain, in 10 to 20 percent of cases the only way to be really sure is by a bone scan, which is diagnostic.

Stress
Fractures

Possible causes:
- same as for shinsplints

Treatment:
- total rest from any weight-bearing activity, for six to eight weeks. No other treatment is indicated. During this time, pool training, stationary bicycling, and swimming are good ways to stay fit. An air cast is seldom necessary, but hand crutches sometimes are useful for added relief and support.

My worst cycle of injuries started off with a stress fracture in my shinbone in 1982. After being out for six weeks and missing the indoor season that year, the very first step I took—literally—I got an Achilles tendon strain. From February to September I was out of action. I went to scores of doctors in an attempt to have my problems remedied—physical therapists and chiropractors among them.

Eventually, at the suggestion of world-class runner Dr. Thomas

Wessinghage, I went to West Germany and had cobalt radiation treatments on my Achilles tendon. Within days, I was jogging. Within a week, the pain had completely gone, and I started training for the 1983 indoor season and the World Championships. The injuries returned in December of '83 with another stress fracture in my shinbone. I had two stress fractures that year, one in each shin. I missed the 1984 Olympic Games as a result. In 1986 I didn't run well because I went on a special diet, and inadvertently lost a lot of weight. Then I had another stress fracture in '87 and again in '88.

It was terrible, particularly missing the Olympics. Years later, you look back on the times of injury and the intensity of it has dimmed. But when you realize what you actually went through, it seems overwhelming. It's difficult to describe the frustration, day after day. My wife, Yvonne, had to live through this with me—a pain in my shin, a pain in my Achilles, not being able to do the thing I wanted to do. The only thing on your mind 24 hours a day is, "How do I get rid of it?" And 24 hours a day, in an attempt to calm me down, Yvonne is saying, "Leave it alone. Don't be touching your shin and your Achilles. Forget about it."

It was a terrible thing. I'll never forget it, particularly in 1982. I'd get out of bed in the morning and I'd put my foot on the floor and I'd feel the pain. It started and ended my day. It was as if it would never, ever go away. I used all sorts of electronic devices. At one point, I wrapped my shin in one device for 14 hours a day. It was a cast that sent electronic waves to the bones to try to speed the healing process.

That's why I say you can't forget about it. It's there all the time and it just won't go away. You don't see any light at the end of the tunnel. But all of a sudden, it seems, the injury is gone. How does it seem to go away overnight? I don't know.

Eventually I became very philosophical about injury, because what else could I do? I'm not bitter that I missed the 1984 Olympics. I'm not bitter that I missed running in the outdoor European Championships, even though I should have been a favorite to win. A negative attitude is not going to help you overcome the frustration. But a positive attitude will. It will also help you to enjoy other things during that 24-hour daily cycle of obsession, as opposed to letting the injury dominate your life.

If I had it to do over again, would I change anything in my career? Yes, I'd be more careful about injuries. I think there's a very fine line—most runners know about it—between staying healthy while maintaining top shape and getting injured. The intensity of some of the training I did was too much, particularly in 1980 before the Moscow Olympics, and even in 1983, my good year. I did some incredible sessions day after day. There was probably no need to do that. I didn't practice what I preach. I think all runners fall victim to that.

—Eamonn Coghlan

Calf Muscle Strains

Calf muscles tear or are strained suddenly, but can heal quickly and effectively if healing measures are instituted immediately, explains Sander.

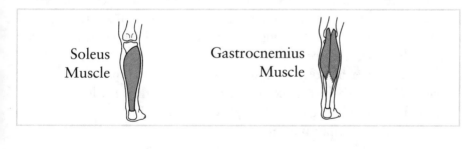

Soleus Muscle

Gastrocnemius Muscle

Possible causes:
- overtraining
- too much distance
- too much speedwork
- lack of flexibility
- improper warmup
- improper footgear

Treatment:

- rest, ice, and, most importantly, expert physiotherapy and/or deep massage to restore healing and prevent contracture or shortness of the affected muscles. Anti-inflammatories are not too successful with this problem. Also, an acutely inflamed muscle should never be stretched.

Many runners are sore at one time or another, notes Ann Rugh, a physical therapist and former longtime coach with the NYRRC running classes. Sore quadriceps (the muscles in the front of the thigh) and hamstrings (back of the thigh) are especially common. "Soreness doesn't necessarily mean you're injured, but it can make running uncomfortable, slow you down, and may increase the risk of injury," says Rugh. Fortunately, there are several things you can do to combat or avoid the problem.

Doing as much of your running as possible on soft surfaces, such as grass or dirt, can be a big help. It's worth it to walk, bike, or drive to a suitable area. No matter where you run, you should warm up your legs with a few minutes of walking or light jogging, then thoroughly stretch, holding each move for at least 10 seconds. Stretch after you run, too, when you can often get a fuller extension because the muscles are warm and loose. Rugh also recommends icing the legs immediately after a run, concentrating on spots that feel sore. "I advise people to freeze water in a paper cup, then peel the top of the cup away and stroke up and down the entire area of both legs. Spend five to eight minutes on each leg." This can help reduce the inflammation that leads to soreness. Keep the legs elevated to prevent pooling of blood, which can aggravate inflammation.

Another post-run strategy is implementing weighted knee extensions, which are best done with a weight machine or a light weight bound to the front of the lower leg. "This is not a strength exercise," Rugh stresses. "You should use less than half the maximum weight you can lift, and move each leg smoothly for just a few minutes to gently stretch it out." As with any running-related exercise, the decisions of whether, when, and how much to do should depend on your body's response. If these strategies don't work, or if severe pain or joint discomfort develops, consider cutting back your mileage and seeking professional attention, perhaps from a physical therapist or doctor familiar with sports medicine.

—Fitness Forum

Knees

Sander describes knee pain as the most common running injury, comprising up to 40 percent of all injuries according to some studies. Well over half of these can be attributed to patellofemoral syndrome, or simply put, injury to the workings of the kneecap as it functions with the area of the leg above and below it. Pain from this injury occurs anywhere outside, in, or around the kneecap.

Sander says wear and tear from this malfunctioning (left treated) can lead to softening and cartilage damage on the inside surface of the kneecap, a condition called chondromalacia patella. The pain from this injury is underneath the kneecap.

The pain in both of these conditions, patellofemoral syndrome with or without chondromalacia, is in the front of the knee, which is sore to the touch. Usually, there is no swelling, locking, or giving way of the knee. The pain is often worse after running and when the knee is flexed for long periods, such as in a car, theater, or in an airplane.

Sander cites a 1991 study from the Bowman-Gray School of Medicine, Wake Forest University, as helpful in understanding patellofemoral syndrome and how to treat it. The study was composed of 20 uninjured runners and 16 runners with this injury. While the study is limited, it does touch on several important points.

The findings were predictable, but in some cases surprising:

1. Anatomy of the injured group varied. Those runners had, in general, a structural deviation: Their infrapatellar tendon was pushed excessively to the lateral side.

2. Pronation, or rolling in of the arch, did not seem to differ in frequency between the two groups. This is a surprising result, indicating that the injury may not be caused by pronation alone, which in the past was believed to be its main source.

3. Quadriceps muscle strength seemed weaker in the injured group.

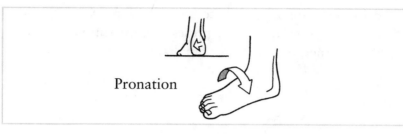

Pronation

4. Training mileage made little difference; the injured group actually trained 30 percent less than the uninjured group.

5. Surface was a major factor. Curve running increased injuries, as did running on a curved road. Flat running produced the best results and least injuries.

Possible causes:

- running surface (uneven or hilly)
- weakness in the supporting muscles (i.e., quadriceps)
- improper biomechanics (excessive pronation possibly a contributing factor)
- overtraining

Treatment:

- rest, change of surface, isometric quadriceps strengthening, ice, and possibly anti-inflammatory medication for a short period (ibuprofen, 7 to 10 days)

Sander says that "Despite the above study's findings on pronation, other specialists in the field, as well as myself, feel that correcting pronation also reduces kneecap stress and may be helpful. It may also serve as a preventive to further patellofemoral injuries. Correcting pronation can be accomplished in the simplest case with a good antipronation running shoe, many of which are well constructed and already on the market, by an over-the-counter soft orthotic, and by fitted, custom-made orthotics fashioned by an experienced sports medicine podiatrist.

"At our clinic over the years, there have literally been thousands of runners with patellofemoral syndrome who have responded in the end only to correctly made orthotics that have stabilized their knees and made their running enjoyable and pain-free."

Quadriceps Exercise

Here is a simple exercise to strengthen the quadriceps. Sit on the ground with the legs extended. Keeping the knee locked, lift one leg at a time briskly, and then slowly lower it. Do this for one set of 25 repetitions while leaning the trunk of the body slightly forward, and then do one set of 25 leaning slightly backward. Change legs and repeat, for a total of four sets. Do this exercise once a day.

—Norbert Sander

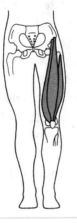

Quadriceps
Muscle

Lateral Knee Pain

Sander describes pain on the outside of a knee that does not swell or lock and that comes on after intense races or increased training as usually being tendinitis of the iliotibial band (a band of tissue that begins high on the side of the leg and extends to the outside part of the knee). This injury is a particular nuisance, since the rate of healing is highly variable from one runner to the next. Often the pain will completely disappear with rest, only to occur suddenly at an almost foreordained point in the run each time, be it two miles, four miles, or as little as 400 yards.

Possible causes:

- almost always overuse and not mechanical. Therefore, this injury is less common than those knee injuries outlined above, which can result also from biomechanical problems.

Treatment:

•rest, ice, anti-inflammatories, and deep friction massage by physical therapists. Orthotics are usually not helpful, although some runners look to them in desperation. Sander personally feels they are not a solution to iliotibial band syndrome.

At the Nike Marathon in Eugene, Oregon, in 1980, I attended a special session on iliotibial band syndrome and was relieved to see others just as frustrated as I by its quixotic nature. The moderator told of a runner who suffered from it for over a year, trying every possible remedy before insisting that he be referred to a podiatrist for orthotics. The physician agreed and was surprised to get a call three weeks later from the patient, saying that the orthotic had miraculously done the trick and the injury was totally healed. He asked to see the magical inserts and the runner happily appeared at his office. He hadn't even bothered to go back to see the podiatrist, he said, because of the immediate results. When the physician looked down into the running shoes, he found the orthotics were inserted upside down and on the wrong side!

—Norbert Sander

Internal Knee Injuries

These injuries are marked by a more subtle, deep pain that continues over a long time, despite conservative measures such as rest and reduction in training, Sander writes. They may result in swelling, locking, or giving way of the knee, and an inability to extend the leg.

The most common in this category of running injuries are tears of either the medial or lateral cartilages. While the act of running itself rarely produces these tears, the constant pounding or even a misplaced step can turn a small infracartilage defect into a complete tear that passes from the cartilage out into the joint space and produces characteristic swelling, locking, and instability. These are potentially quite serious injuries and may require surgery to heal properly.

Possible causes:

•unlikely from running itself. This category of injury is often caused by prior contact sports knee injuries or skiing accidents. Often forgotten, the residual effects of these injuries may set the stage for cartilage tearing while running years later. If a runner continues to train on a torn cartilage, the resulting friction between the unprotected femoral and tibial bones may lead to early irreversible osteoarthritis of the joint.

Sander writes that today, when the index of suspicion is high and further studies are clearly necessary, the radiologic test of first choice is the Magnetic Resonance Imaging (MRI) scan of the knee. Though very expensive, it can, if negative, save the runner from undergoing an unnecessary diagnostic arthroscopy and point treatment in a more conservative direction. Since the MRI resolution is exceptionally good, even a small tear can be visualized and the possible decision to go ahead with arthroscopy can be made.

Hamstrings

There is no muscle more fickle for the runner than the hamstring, says Sander. Stretching from the ischiotuberosity (the point we sit on) in the pelvis, the hamstring passes down the back of the leg and inserts just across the back surface of the knee. Running parallel to the hamstring is the sciatic nerve; thus many chronic hamstring strains are mistaken for sciatic nerve damage.

According to Sander, "The hamstring takes the brunt of almost every step and tends to overdevelop and tighten as the years of running pass. A physiotherapist from Metropolitan Hospital in New York was the first to show me how the tightening of all posterior muscles—neck, back, and calves—is related in a chainlike reaction to chronic hamstring strain. Others have postulated a relative weakening of the antagonistic muscle, the quadricep, as the cause of hamstring muscle strains. In all cases, the symptoms are similar: a chronic, at times spastic, toothache-like pain found anywhere along the muscle from the lower buttocks to down behind the knee, usually made worse by fast running or sitting (on the origin of the muscle at the ischiotuberosity)."

Possible causes:

- •overuse
- •excess speed training
- •poor warmup

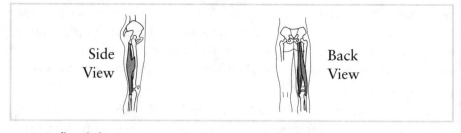

- inflexibility
- temporary or chronic fatigue syndrome
- running when injured

Treatment:

- varied, with the logic not always consistent. Sander says, "Stretching in my experience, may make the hamstring strain worse if it is in the acute phase, although a good program of preventive stretching is helpful when the muscle is pain-free. Stopping running completely also does not usually work, with the pain still there after even prolonged periods of rest. I have found the most successful approach to be a conservative but active one, including slow, short running at distances of one to three miles daily; deep, vigorous muscle massage; physical therapy two to three times weekly; the judicious use of anti-inflammatories (ibuprofen 400 mg. one daily at supper); and a strength program for the quadriceps if they are found to be weak, which can be determined by a qualified physician or physical therapist. Weight training for the hamstring is usually not successful and can worsen the condition.

"In the case of this injury, alternative training can help maintain fitness and at the same time strengthen the opposing muscles, the quadriceps. For example, stationary biking for 30 minutes a day does this, while sparing undue stress on the injured hamstrings. The most moderate approach is running in water, which increases quadricep strength and stretches the hamstrings—all without the risks and results of impact.

"The basic philosophy with the injured hamstring is to regroup training and slowly present an increasing work load to the hamstring, allowing it to redefine its balance with the uninjured side as well as with its antagonists, the quadriceps muscles. Pressing on with high levels of training despite pain only causes more microtears in the muscle with resulting scar tissue and the risk of permanent disability."

Sciatica

When is leg pain—which passes down the back part of the upper part of the leg, sometimes extending to the foot—a sign of sciatica? Sander explains that true sciatica is usually due to pressure on the last lumbar nerve segments of the spine. The pressure is caused by slippage of a cartilage disk out onto the nerve or by the effects of degenerative arthritis of the lumbar spine on the nerve roots found there. Runners, in this case, will experience generally more pain than with hamstring muscle strains, with the pain additionally radiating below the knee and even extending to a numbness of the foot. Along with numbness, loss of power on the affected side and absence of normal knee and ankle nerve reflexes may also be present. Occasionally, a piriformis muscle (located underneath the large buttocks muscle) strain deep in the buttocks can also impinge on the sciatic nerve and give all of the above symptoms. A CAT scan or an MRI scan can well determine the source of the problem.

Possible causes:

- In Sander's experience, true sciatica is not caused by running but rather is usually due to a structural problem in the spine, such as arthritis of the spine, a herniated disk, or acute muscle spasm in the lower spine.

Treatment:

- Interestingly, very few cases of sciatica ever come to surgery. In over 95 percent of cases, rest, anti-inflammatories, physical therapy, and the "gentle passing of time" are the best healing agents. When symptoms persist, however, usually for several months or more, back surgery in the form of a diskectomy may be necessary.

The Groin

According to Sander, "Muscle injuries to this area are usually due to strains of the adductor muscle (groin muscle located on the inside of the leg extending to the knee) or the iliopsoas muscle (higher groin muscle that extends from the lower part of the pelvis to the upper part of the groin), or sometimes both. An inguinal hernia needs to be ruled out by a proper examination. Strains of these muscles can be serious injuries resulting in months and even years of disability. Slipping on a wet floor on only one occasion resulted in a three-year groin strain in a runner patient of mine."

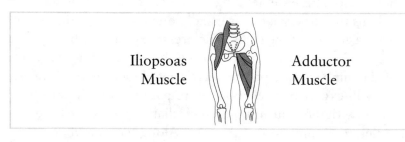

Iliopsoas
Muscle

Adductor
Muscle

Possible causes:

- usually overuse (excessive long runs or speedwork). Often the injury is made worse by continuing to run despite growing pain, until virtually all training is impossible. A significant amount of damage is done during the period of continued running, especially if races are run.

Treatment:

- Rest away from running is the best measure. Physical therapy can help somewhat, but has its limitations in the groin muscles. Anti-inflammatories are temporarily useful, but may mask the pain and encourage false confidence.

In the case of this injury, all strength training for the legs should be discontinued, as well as situps, until the pain is absent. A slow return to training is necessary on flat, level surfaces that have no give. Sand, gravel, ice and snow, or even loose dirt only place more stress on the groin. Lighter running shoes also help.

In women, the possibility of a pelvic stress fracture should be considered when groin pain is severe, is made worse on standing, and remains despite rest. Stress fractures in the pelvis in males are rare. Sander has not seen one in over 15 years. A bone scan will confirm the diagnosis. The rest period for a pelvic stress fracture is in the range of 12 weeks but can last up to a year.

The Hips

Sander observes that women seem to suffer more strains of the gluteal muscles than men, especially the outer hip muscle and the connection of this muscle to the hip joint.

Possible causes:

•probably mechanical, simply because of wider hips

If you're a runner who's ever feared for your bones and joints, here's some good news. According to *American Health* magazine, running has been shown to increase bone density without wearing down knees, hips, and ankles. A Stanford University School of Medicine study determined that runners had 40 percent greater bone density than a nonrunning control group. This change is particularly good news for women, who have a high chance of losing bone mass as they age. But if your bones are better, how about your joints? Both the Stanford runners and another group, from the University of Florida, showed no greater signs of osteoarthritis, a degenerative joint disease. Joint pain, swelling, and other such complaints among runners were comparable to nonrunners' problems.

—Fitness Features

Treatment:

•Injuries here usually respond to limited rest as well as to a reduction in training, anti-inflammatories, occasionally physical therapy, and running on a flat surface. Surprisingly, by increasing the tempo of running and shortening the distance, the gluteal muscles seem to heal faster. Long, slow running only seems to aggravate the condition.

As in the pelvis, severe, sudden pain in the hips, worsened by weightbearing, may represent a stress fracture of the head or the neck of the femur, which should be looked for immediately to avoid further damage.

The Low Back

Contrary to general belief, Sander writes, running does not put a great deal of stress on the back. One study actually showed more tension in the low back from coughing, bending, pushing a broom, or standing up than occurs during running. For this reason, muscular strain of the low back is generally improved with running as long as, determined by a medical professional, a significant derangement does not exist in the spine itself in the form of a herniated disk or severe degenerative osteoarthritis.

Back pain, which affects 80 percent of people at some point, has many causes, so you should probably see a medical professional for a definitive diagnosis. Norbert Sander, M.D., gives the following general advice on how runners can avoid and treat back pain:

- *Strengthen the abdominals.* Because the spine is supported by the muscles of the abdomen, back problems can result if abdominal muscles are allowed to weaken. Running, while it puts pressure on the lower back, does nothing to strengthen the abdominals, and as a result, many runners develop lower-back strain. Situps, pushups, and leg raises are all good exercises for strengthening the abdominals. Using a rowing machine or cross-country ski machine can help, too; start off slowly if you aren't used to these activities.

- *Stretch out.* Stretching your back muscles before and after you run can help prevent tightness and back spasm, a seizing up of the muscles that can be extremely painful. One good exercise is to grab a doorknob with both hands and bend from the hips, arching the back slightly and holding for 10 to 30 seconds. You should feel a stretch in the lower back and hamstrings. You can also sit with one leg straight out in front, bend the opposite leg, placing the foot on the outside of the straight knee, and twist your upper body toward the straight leg, pushing with the opposite elbow against the bent knee. Hold for 10 to 30 seconds, then switch sides.

- *Don't train through pain.* If back pain is severe, especially if it comes on suddenly and/or radiates down the legs (a sign of sciatica), running can aggravate the condition. Most back pain is muscle-related and often disappears with a few days of rest, taking over-the-counter anti-inflammatory drugs, and using a heating pad. But it's a good idea to see a specialist to rule out nerve and disk problems. "People with bad backs very rarely have to give up running completely, but by pushing through pain you may make things worse by changing your gait and throwing other muscles out of balance," says Sander. In many cases, a few days of rest will have you back to your normal routine.

—Fitness Forum

Sander advises that professional help should be sought for persistent back pain that does not respond to rest and/or stretching and strengthening exercises and anti-inflammatories.

Possible causes:

• usually not running-related

Treatment:

• temporary rest

• physical therapy

• prescriptive exercises (e.g., curls, a form of situps)

In most cases, even before an X ray or a scan is done, a competent examination by a physician can pinpoint the problem as centered either in the supporting muscles, spinal bone, or due to nerve impingement. Suspicion of nerve damage or a herniated disk should, of course, lead one to temporary rest, a proper scan, and eventual progressive physical therapy to strengthen low back muscles.

The most effective means of stabilizing muscular low back strain is temporary rest followed by progressive physical therapy with a strong emphasis on learning a home program of low back exercises that should be done daily as a preventive measure.

While manipulation and massage can be palliative, back exercises performed by a runner at home or in the office can provide much more mileage and make one more independent than time-consuming treatment by health professionals.

Medical Problems in Runners

While runners are generally healthy, any persistent complaint should be investigated thoroughly, since exercise does not make one immune to general disease, writes Sander. Since the well-trained are used to a level of well-being generally above the sedentary, real disease may surface in many subtle ways early in its course.

Most commonly seen in my office, writes Sander, are the following.

Abdominal Pain

Kidney stones create abdominal pain as they begin in the outside abdomen and in some cases move to the front of the pelvis.

> No one is absolutely sure what causes stitches or cramps, but they are most likely an abnormal contraction or cramp in the diaphragm, the large muscle used in breathing that separates the lung and abdominal cavities and is attached along the bottom of the rib cage. *Runner's World* advises that the treatment of any acute muscle cramp is stretching the muscle. To stretch the diaphragm during exercise, take a big breath, hold it as long as possible, and then force the air out against puckered lips.
>
> —Fitness Features

Possible causes:

- slightly more common in runners due to the dehydrating effects of training

Treatment:

- copious post-training hydration, especially with water and juices, is necessary. In general, back pain and bloody urine are hallmarks of a stone, although pain alone is possible.

Exertional Hematuria

Bloody urine that occurs during or just after running and that clears rapidly (exertional hematuria) is generally benign. It is seen more in summer months and occasionally is accompanied by a very slight burning. If the dark, bloody urine continues or remains unchanged even after training and throughout the day, a medical consultation should be undertaken to rule out more serious problems. Urinary infections are not more common in runners.

According to Andres Rodriguez, M.D., blood in the urine, known as hematuria, sometimes results from physical trauma to the body caused by strenuous exercise such as running. It's been known to occur in some people after a particularly hard workout or race (such as a marathon). A contusion to the kidney area can likewise cause blood to appear in the urine.

Hematuria caused by physical exertion usually clears up by itself within a few days. There is nothing you can do to prevent it or speed its passing. (Staying hydrated while you work out or race and drinking plenty of fluids afterward, however, do prevent dehydration and help keep your kidneys functioning normally.)

The only time to be concerned about hematuria is if it lasts longer than three or four days, or is accompanied by pain or difficulty in urinating. If either of these things happens, you should see a urologist immediately. The doctor will examine you, test a sample of your urine, and order further necessary tests before prescribing a treatment.

Chances are, however, that the problem will pass quickly—and, after giving your body time to rest, you will be ready for your next challenge on the road.

—Fitness Forum

Possible causes:
- thought to be related to dehydration

Treatment:
- hydration (two to three quarts of fluid throughout the day it appears). One is safe if the condition clears by the next day. If it persists, seek medical attention.

Diarrhea

Abdominal pain and cramping with diarrhea are sometimes seen during or just after running.

Possible causes:
- If the symptoms persist, stool analysis for parasites should be done as well as an examination of the bowel for various types of coli-

tis. Occasionally, runners with gluten (wheat products) sensitivity may experience abdominal pain, especially if there is a family history of adult celiac disease (chronic diarrhea secondary to poor absorption of nutrients). Simple dietary changes can in some of these cases be very helpful.

Treatment:

• Eliminating all caffeine (coffee, tea, chocolate, and beverages) and milk products (in the case of possible lactose sensitivity) from the diet may help, but occasionally Imodium or Kaopectate is necessary prior to running, for short periods.

Chest Pain

Pain in the chest, especially during running, is one symptom that should *not* be ignored, writes Sander. Chest pain occurring during exercise is a serious medical signal and should be attended to immediately by a physician.

"It was upsetting for me to appear on the television show *Nightline* to discuss heart disease in runners the day Jim Fixx died. It is impossible to be sure what the outcome would have been had Fixx acted on the chest pains he had been experiencing in the weeks prior to his death. Many patients have come to my office with just the same symptoms in my 20 years of practice, and were sent for the necessary tests, receiving what in many cases was life-saving intervention," Sander says.

According to exercise expert Dr. Gabe Mirkin, it's usually all right to exercise with a cold, provided you don't have a fever and your muscles don't hurt. There is no evidence that mild exercise aggravates a cold, but occasionally colds can affect your heart. *Running & FitNews* cautions that if you notice irregular heartbeats during exercise, stop the activity. Be aware that most cold medications won't help you exercise with a cold. Since you breathe through your mouth when you run, decongestants, which unstuff your nose, aren't necessary. And antihistamines, which stop runny noses, also dry up mucous membranes. These same membranes are needed to moisten air as it passes to and from the lungs during exercise. It's better to take cold medicine after exercise rather than before it.

—Fitness Features

Treadmill stress testing, thallium stress testing, and cardiac angiography when appropriate can pinpoint the area of heart involvement and direct the physician toward a solution, Sander explains. "Running through chest pain is dangerous until the cause of it is found. However, not all chest pain is cardiac. Over the years I have seen several cases of pulmonary embolism (clots passing through the lungs) caused by stasis or pooling of blood in the calves during a long trip, either in a car or in an airplane, just following a long run or a training session. In this case, a lung scan and immediate use of anticoagulants in a hospital setting are necessary."

Most often, chest pain is simply muscular, either from lifting, sprinting, hyperventilation, or even coughing. Tenderness over the muscles of the chest wall is a hallmark, and the use of anti-inflammatories over a few days alleviates the pain.

Headaches

Minor headaches from running may be common and are usually caused by dehydration. Severe headaches can occur with exertion, Sander explains, and in some cases can last for several hours. Since this is distinctly uncommon, close attention should be paid to ruling out the most serious causes if these headaches persist.

Possible causes of severe headaches:

- the vascular type such as migraines, which can be precipitated by pressure on the venous sinuses of the brain during exercise and occasionally by hypoglycemia and mineral depletion secondary to strenuous training
- tension headaches secondary to scalp muscle contraction
- organic, due to an aneurysm or neoplastic (tumor) growth within the brain

Due to the seriousness of vascular aneurysm and brain tumors, an MRI or CAT scan of the brain should be part of the medical workup.

Treatment:

- Treatment of chronic benign headaches consists of appropriate medication or biofeedback training to relieve stress. Thermal and electromyographic (EMG) types of biofeedback also have, in certain cases, proved successful.

Chronic Fatigue Syndrome

One of the most common medical problems in endurance runners is periodic fatigue, Sander points out. In over 90 percent of cases of chronic tiredness and lackluster running, however, a direct organic medical cause cannot be found. Despite this, there is almost always an overuse syndrome involved, both physical and mental. This may result from simple overload in professional, home, personal, or athletic life that insidiously wears down a runner who continues to train at a high level. Often in these cases there is a fair degree of denial with runners, disappointed that no clear medical problem is present. With patience, time, and reduction of overload, however, normal levels of energy slowly return.

> During my years of not running well, I had biomechanical problems, blood problems, and I knew that if I could solve those problems, I should run well again. I never believed in this mystical "burnout syndrome," or chronic fatigue syndrome. I believe there's a specific physiological reason, and that you can always break it down to an actual deficiency or biomechanical problem.
>
> You can be so overworked that your system doesn't work well, if you want to call that burnout. But then, you figure out how to get your system to work well again, and you're not burned out. It's like a car overheating. What do you do to fix it? You fill it up with water, change the oil, so it runs normally again.
>
> A lot of my problems were that I had surgeries that laid me up for a long time. I had nerve damage after one of those surgeries. That took 2½ years to heal. That brought me up to 1988, and physically, since then, I really haven't had any major biomechanical problems.
>
> Then it was a matter of trying to come back slowly and surely. I started at a young age and did something very successfully for 10 years. Then I didn't do it at all well for six years. You think that in a couple of years you'll be right back where you were. But it doesn't work that way. I had a long, gradual buildup. All of a sudden to jump back in, it's hard.
>
> —Alberto Salazar

This is not to discount the other 10 percent of cases where true depression may be present as well as a host of disorders ranging from anemias, chronic viral syndromes, and mononucleosis to more subtle hormonal imbalances. The search for causes may lead one to diagnoses such as Epstein-Barre virus, which still has not been proven to cause any specific disorder. In fact, over 80 percent of the normal population tests positive for Epstein-Barre virus. However, the presence of this virus does not mean it is the cause of fatigue. Lately, however, researchers have recently been getting promising results with the use of antiviral medication in some cases of significant fatigue syndrome.

The proper approach to fatigue syndrome is to take it seriously, seeing a physician for a complete medical history, physical examination, and laboratory screening, including a complete blood count, a survey of all electrolytes, liver function tests, a kidney function and glucose test, a mononucleosis screening, a Lyme screening, and even in some cases an HIV test. Thinking over one's daily routine and training schedule is also very important in coming to grips with the cause of chronic fatigue syndrome when no organic cause is found.

Breathe Easy—A Runners' Respiratory Review

In an issue of *New York Running News*, Margaret A. Dessau, M.D., examined the whole spectrum of runners' breathing issues.

"Breathing is normally an unconscious process, but when people run, they suddenly become very aware of their breathing and may worry about their lungs' proper functioning. I am frequently asked certain questions on this subject and I would like to give you some answers."

Labored Breathing

"Runners often ask me whether it's normal to have labored breathing during an all-out effort, such as a sprint. Actually, difficulty catching your breath, or dyspnea, on exertion is normal; the point at which it happens, however, depends on your level of fitness and on your individual central nervous system controls. Many complex factors, especially your competitive drive, can influence your perception of dyspnea."

What is really happening when you find yourself gasping for breath? You are hyperventilating, which is a healthy physiologic response to the demands of exercise. Ventilation is the process of breathing oxygen in and carbon dioxide out. The more rapidly and vigorously your muscles are contracting, the greater the demand for oxygen, and the greater the need for clearing metabolic waste products. Increased lactic acid and carbon dioxide would cause fatigue and weakness if they were not removed. How does your breathing adjust to this situation? Chemical sensors in the brain recognize these changes, and the brain then sends signals to the lungs, which "rev up." You begin to ventilate more frequently and deeply. Your diaphragm and muscles of the chest, shoulders, and abdomen work even harder, while the muscles in your legs and arms continue to pump away. It may feel uncomfortable, but it is definitely not dangerous.

What You Can Do to Control Your Breathing

Is there anything you can do to make the mechanics of your breathing more efficient? Here are some suggestions:

1. If you start to gasp for breath, relax and drop your shoulders.

2. Breathe through an open mouth, with deep, slow, regular breaths, rather than shallow panting.

3. Ease yourself into a calm frame of mind. Knowing that breathlessness isn't necessarily a danger sign, but is usually a normal response to increased energy demands, you may find it easier to overcome any anxious, panicky feelings.

Are there any safety precautions you should keep in mind when running? Here are some important ones:

1. When running aerobically, you should have sufficient breath to carry on a conversation with a companion. It's true that during all-out sprints or races, you will push yourself to your anaerobic threshold for limited periods of time. It is normal to feel quite breathless and uncomfortable under those conditions. But you should be able to recover your more comfortable breathing level within a few minutes of slowing your pace, getting a "second wind."

2. Occasionally you may develop a "stitch," a sharp pain in your lower chest that seems to cut off your wind suddenly. Stitches, which probably result from diaphragmatic spasm, are not dangerous, even though they can stop you in your tracks. Here's a

maneuver that is often successful in breaking a stitch: Take in a very large breath, hold it for a few seconds, and then blow it out as forcefully and rapidly as possible, while grunting.

3. One very important word of caution: If you have coughing spasms, palpitations, chest pain or pressure, or persistent shortness of breath after slowing down, stop running immediately. These symptoms are not normal, and you should consult your physician. You must make certain you are not suffering from any lung or heart condition that might make exercise dangerous until your condition is treated.

> Ozone gas in our breathing space is especially a problem in the summer months. There's more sunshine, less wind, and trees hold pollutants underneath their leafy canopies. As a result, there are more frequent summertime air-quality warnings—essentially ozone alerts. According to *Longevity* magazine, studies show that people who exercise vigorously for more than an hour when the ozone level is high can experience lung irritation; shortness of breath; shallow, rapid breathing; and coughing. It is therefore best to pick cloudy over sunny days and to exercise in the early morning, before pollution accumulates. The hours of 11 a.m. to 4 p.m. are particularly hazardous. Runners should opt for park paths instead of highways.
>
> —Fitness Features

Runners must be alert to the external environment, especially to extremes of temperature and humidity. Cold air will not freeze your lungs, but it can irritate the trachea and bronchial tubes, causing an aching chest or even asthma or bronchial spasm, with cough and abnormal shortness of breath. You may prevent these problems by wearing a loose wool muffler over your nose and mouth to warm up the air you breathe in. In addition, to prevent exercise- or cold air-induced asthma, you may require prescription medications.

Also, very hot, humid air may irritate sensitive lungs and so may high levels of air pollutants, including carbon monoxide from traffic exhaust. On days with high pollen counts, runners with allergies may find breathing more difficult due to blocked, inflamed nasal and bronchial passages. By selecting the environment you run in, and also by using prescribed inhaled medications, you can run symptom-free.

Special Breathing Problems

How do certain special respiratory illnesses and conditions affect runners? How cautious should you be, for instance, when you have a common cold, a viral upper respiratory condition? Frequently, the "bug" can impair normal ventilatory function due to inflammation of the airways of the nose, throat, and lungs, causing cough and undue shortness of breath. Therefore, it's wise to cut back on your training for a few days until you recuperate. If you don't, the infection may last longer, and may even progress to pneumonia.

What about exercise and smoking? Even former smokers may still have some degree of residual lung damage from chronic bronchitis or emphysema. The extent to which this impairment will interfere with exercise can be assessed by a breathing test called spirometry. Generally, "tincture of time" heals mild cases, and running helps former smokers become nonsmokers permanently.

If you have asthma, is it safe to exercise? Some runners with dyspnea and wheezing just assume it's asthma and neglect to check with a physician. Some even figure it is okay to borrow a friend's inhaler, which may contain a prescription medication. Obviously, either of these can lead to serious trouble. Most asthmatics under proper treatment can even compete safely and successfully.

Finally, is exercise advisable for people whose breathing capacity is limited by structural conditions such as osteoporosis, scoliosis, or arthritis? It cannot undo the damage that exists, but it may help prevent further deterioration, and may even improve breathing efficiency through respiratory muscle training.

Medications, Procedures, and Medical Modalities

With the running boom in the 1970–80s also boomed the field of sports medicine. Many of the treatments runners commonly undergo today were, not long ago, considered new and radical.

What's on the cutting edge in the 1990s? The medical modalities described below range from the well known to the relatively obscure. Although they represent a wide range of treatments being used by today's runners, there are likely many others that fall into this category.

Anti-Inflammatory Medication

Dr. Norbert Sander writes that anti-inflammatory medications are nonsteroidal agents that diminish pain and reduce microswelling around injured tissues. Minor inflammation due to injury should respond with the use of these medications in three to four days. More serious inflammation will not sufficiently respond. Any prolonged use (longer than one week) of these medications should be monitored by a physician.

"These medications are available over-the-counter, and stronger doses are available by prescription. I generally recommend using ibuprofen as opposed to aspirin. It takes a much greater number of aspirin to be effective, and aspirin seems to irritate the stomach more frequently.

"The short-term use of anti-inflammatories is generally safe as long as there is no allergy to them and one is without a history of gastritis or stomach ulcer. They are best taken with foods. I prescribe them in two ways: as a short course taken for seven days, to calm an acute injury (e.g., ibuprofen at 600 mg. three times daily); at the same time, to determine how serious the injury is, I monitor its response to the anti-inflammatories.

"Secondarily, anti-inflammatories can be used in very small doses, such as ibuprofen at 400 mg. once a day at supper with the intention of diminishing the lingering effects of trauma or a stubborn injury, as the medication works overnight and allows return to training the next day. I never suggest the use of anti-inflammatories, including aspirin, before training or racing, or for an injury such as a stress fracture, since serious injuries can be masked or made much worse. In addition, it should be pointed out that unexpected side effects can strike from any medication and are sometimes serious.

"Just before the Marathon to Athens race in 1975, I found myself with a swollen hand, red and infected, standing in a pharmacy in Athens attempting with the remnants of my Jesuit school Greek to negotiate a bottle of penicillin and some liquid iodine to cover my fingers. I had been taking Butazolidin, a since abandoned anti-inflammatory, for a chronic sciatica condition, and suffered an acute decrease in my white cell count because of it. Luckily, the penicillin was effective and I was able, with difficulty, to finish the classic course. However, to this day I keep the bottle of iodine, labeled in a somewhat exotic Greek lettering, in a place of honor in my medicine cabinet. Its use has been, thankfully, limited.

"The decrease of white cell count can be a serious side effect of anti-inflammatory medication, and for this reason, periodic laboratory work should be done if a runner is taking anti-inflammatories over an extended period of time."

> Taking aspirin with a caffeinated beverage such as coffee, tea, or cola may increase the aspirin's effectiveness as a pain reliever, according to a recent study published in the *Archives of Internal Medicine* and quoted in the University of California at Berkeley *Wellness Letter*. Scientists have long known that caffeine has an analgesic effect (which is why it is added to some pain relievers), but this is the first published study to demonstrate that caffeine can boost the effect of aspirin.
>
> —Fitness Features

Arthroscopic Surgery

According to Sander, arthroscopic surgery is reserved only for those infrequent cases of cartilage tear inside the knee. During this surgery, a small incision is made below the kneecap and a scope is pushed inside to observe the cartilage. At the tip of the scope is a device to sew the cartilage tear. This procedure has a good rate of success in runners when done by an experienced surgeon.

After arthroscopic surgery, aggressive physical therapy is essential to ensure an excellent result and rapid return to full training.

Physical Therapy

Running injuries that are especially receptive to physical therapy treatments are calf muscle strains, hamstrings, and gluteal muscles of the hips and buttocks as well as low-back syndromes, explains Sander. What does physical therapy and one of its modalities—deep muscle massage—actually do? Since the time of the ancient Greeks, athletes have treated their muscles by deep stimulation and stretching and strengthening. This has been an important step in preventing muscle injuries. Muscles are especially well vascularized (have a good blood supply), while cartilage, ligaments, and tendons have a relatively poor blood supply. By increasing blood supply to muscles while breaking up microscar tissue, the injured areas heal faster.

Ultrasound, electrical stimulation, massage, range of motion stretching exercises, specific strengthening exercises, and newer techniques such as ionophoresis (absorption of cortisone applied across the skin locally to muscles) are all tools that are very effective in the hands of a certified physical therapist, Sander concludes.

Physical therapy is a popular medical modality with runners. The treatment is usually undertaken after an M.D. referral, when a physical therapist evaluates the cause of dysfunction. Physical therapy is both preventive and rehabilitative—a system of working with muscles, soft tissue, and joints.

Some of the physical therapy techniques include: manual mobilization to increase range of motion; several types of massage: friction (particularly used for injuries such as tendinitis); regular sports massage (to increase circulation and flexibility); also used is muscle energy, a manual technique that strengthens and stretches the soft tissue. Strengthening exercises are done with free weights or machines such as isokinetic machines. Other modalities include electrical stimulation and ultrasound.

Tzvi Barak, P.T., Ph.D, O.C.S., points out that over the past few years, various specialties in the field of physical therapy have been established. He recommends that runners seek out either orthopedic or sports clinical specialists. To find a qualified physical therapist in your area, see the Resource List.

Chiropractic

The word "chiropractic" comes from the Greek *cherios* (hand) and *practos* (done by). Chiropractors' work includes joint mobilization or adjusting procedures to reestablish normal ranges of joint movement by correcting misaligned or subluxated vertebrae. Chiropractors adjust vertebrae to reestablish normal nerve supply to organs, glands, muscles, joints, and skin by relieving pinched or compressed nerves. Since every function of the body depends on the brain's and spinal cord's normal functioning, ensuring proper nerve flow via the spinal nerves is of utmost importance to chiropractors.

Dr. G. Thomas Kovacs evaluates runners statically and dynamically, sometimes watching them run on a treadmill or even outdoors. Work with athletes is not confined to evaluating one particular area of injury. "We must realize that structure determines function and we must look at the body as a whole," says Kovacs, "from the feet all the way up to the head."

To find a qualified chiropractor in your area, see the Resource List.

Body Work

Marcus Daniels, body work practitioner, believes that his theories are on the cutting edge and that many of them won't become commonly used running modalities for another 5 to 10 years.

The focus of the modalities described below, he explains, is threefold: injury repair, health/fitness maintenance, and optimal efficiency. To Daniels, however, these three are inseparable. "Once an injury occurs, the entire body weakens and recompensates," he explains. "After healing of the injury, an inherent weakness still exists and the entire structure has to be realigned to permit biomechanical efficiency. For elite runners, this is particularly important."

Movement with efficiency means movement starting from the internal "intrinsic" muscles. In injury or compensation, movement usually starts from external "extrinsic" muscles. The result is more effort and tension, hence the body tires more easily.

Daniels recommends some of the following treatment/therapies, which can be undertaken primarily for prevention and structural reorganization. These include the deep tissue systems such as Rolfing and Postural Integration. There are also movement therapies such as Feldenkreis and the Alexander Technique. You may also find a practitioner who deals with sports injuries.

Another category of treatment Daniels recommends is acupuncture, a medical specialty originating in China and used for 5000 years. In terms of acute injury, acupuncture reduces swelling and pain very quickly. In terms of optimal racing efficiency, acupuncture points activate the energy "chi" points and bring extra energy to the body. This practice is very common in Japanese running circles, especially the day of a race.

Concludes Daniels, "Depending on the needs of the individual runner, these modalities can serve many functions. In addition, they can be used in combination with other sports medicine treatments."

Neuromuscular Therapy

One of the most enthusiastic proponents of neuromuscular therapy is also one of the most prominent members of the running community. David Welch, husband of world-class master Priscilla Welch, is a neuromuscular therapist by profession and treats many runners, mostly in the British couple's adopted American home base of Boulder, Colorado. Welch points out that he works cooperatively with other area professionals, including medical doctors, a chiropractor, and a physical therapist: elite runner Mark Plaatjes.

The following excerpt from the St. John Neuromuscular Pain Relief Institute reflects Welch's approach:

"Neuromuscular Therapy, St. John Method, is the science by which homeostasis is brought about between the nervous system and the musculoskeletal system. There are numerous applications for runners, since this is a therapy that specifically treats pain and soft tissue (muscles, tendon, ligaments, fascia) dysfunction. A certified neuromuscular therapist is well trained in evaluating the physiological principles of:

1. dysfunctional biomechanics;

2. postural distortion;

3. ischemia (lack of blood);

4. nerve entrapment/nerve compression;

5. trigger points.

"Injury prevention is by far the the best way for serious runners to operate so that they can achieve optimum performance and maintain peak levels of biomechanical efficiency. Many of the conditions that plague runners can be easily avoided by evaluating the body for the above physiological principles (i.e., numbers 1 through 5) and treating soft tissue for any imbalances found. Neuromuscular Therapy (NMT) is a very precise form of manual deep tissue therapy. Should injury occur, NMT is an excellent form of rehabilitation. In addition to aiding healing, it addresses the actual cause of the injury rather than just treat the painful effect."

World-class marathoner Mark Plaatjes (2:08:58 best time) was felled in the 1989 New York City Marathon by an injured hamstring. He managed to make it to the 20-mile-mark aid station, where the tight muscle was massaged. He then made it another mile before turning back to the aid station. Plaatjes, a physical therapist by profession, then spent five hours working at the aid station on other runners.

Part 8: Aging and Exercise

Aging
and Exercise

Ironically, in Western society growing old is usually dreaded, while at the same time, medical advances continually prolong life expectancy. However, as Margaret Dessau, M.D., sees it, aging need not be an inexorable path to disability and dependence. Older people can continue to lead active, productive, and independent lives, provided they maintain proper diet and exercise programs. Dr. Dessau knows this from the example of her active octogenarian parents, in whose honor she shares her ideas:

"Although the incidences of cardiovascular disease and cancer increase with age, individuals can minimize their risks by regular exercise and prudent diets. A healthy lifestyle can prevent atherosclerotic heart disease and even reverse the damage done by fatty deposits already narrowing coronary arteries. Unfortunately, there are no data that exercise reduces the risk of cancer, although the better the overall condition one maintains—together with specific therapies—the better the prognosis for cure and survival."

There are many physiologic changes in all the organ systems that occur with aging; however, significant declines are not inevitable. That's because these changes result more from physical inactivity and disuse than from the aging process itself. In fact, many of the declines in function can be prevented, or greatly minimized, by moderate, and even mild, regular exercise.

Not only can the cardiovascular system be protected from atherosclerotic disease, but also from the typical signs of aging such as excess

391

fatigue (loss of stamina) and breathlessness. Contrary to previous thought (that deconditioning results from aging itself), new studies show that aerobic capacity can be maintained with age if moderate exercise is continued (moderate meaning in intensity and duration). This requires doing physical activity for a minimum of half an hour at an intensity that raises the heart rate to 70 percent of its maximum rate (see Chapter 4, "Heart Rate Monitor Training," for the formula to determine this figure) at least five days a week.

However, a December 1991 study by Dr. John Duncan of Cooper Aerobic Institute in Dallas, Texas, published in the *Journal of the American Medical Association (JAMA)*, showed that even lower levels of physical activity benefited women who walked only three miles five days a week at a pace of 20 minutes per mile after gradually building up over three weeks. Although the subjects didn't improve aerobic fitness or lose weight, their protective HDL cholesterol levels rose after six months. More vigorous walking, at a 12-minute-per-mile pace, did improve cardiorespiratory fitness as well, and decreased body fat in addition, without causing any exercise-related injuries.

Musculoskeletal fragility (bone weakening) and osteoarthritis (joint stiffness) are the common degenerative changes found in joints, cartilage, and bone. They can also be prevented by appropriate exercises and stretching. Bone density can actually be increased, resulting in fewer fractures. Frequently with age, muscles need longer periods of slow stretching to warm up before exercise to prevent muscle strains or tendinitis.

Obesity and depression, often associated with aging, also are not inevitable, but again, are primarily results of inactivity. The loss of muscle bulk and power, together with increased percentage of body fat, can be minimized by continued exercise, while improving overall mood and vigor.

I've been asked if it's mental or physical ability that declines with age. I think it's mainly physical ability that changes, as opposed to any mental "burnout" that occurs from being at it for years. My physical ability has been affected, in the sense that wear and tear has knocked me back. This is not so much specifically in terms of injury or my ability to recover from it, but there's a general wearing down—almost as if it were bone-deep—from year after year of intense running. In my case, that means nearly 20 years as a marathoner. It's very different if you are older but still relatively new to the sport, like masters runners John Campbell or Priscilla Welch, who got into running in their 30s. It takes years to develop the kind of fatigue I'm talking about.

Unfortunately, this wear and tear is exacerbated by the reality of our sport. We train and compete year round, and running is worldwide. Running is very different from other sports in this regard. If we compete in the USA in the Boston Marathon in the spring, for example, then we might go in the fall to the Berlin Marathon or in the summer to the Stockholm Marathon. That's the way it has evolved.

In the early 1970s, that wasn't so. There were fewer competitive opportunities, and because that was the case, runners tended to focus more on their training, and therefore weren't as worn down from competition and travel. Today, runners get worn down from the combination of travel, racing, and promotion.

Perhaps I could have saved myself a bit early on. In retrospect, I might have made some changes, like not running some of the hot-weather marathons. However, I think you compete somewhat according to your personality and what is standard practice at the time. Back in the 1970s, people like Frank Shorter ran only one or two marathons a year. I ran three or four. I liked competition. It wasn't that I was paid, because at that time I wasn't. It was exciting: to travel to places like Japan, and to represent the USA.

—Bill Rodgers

Another benefit of exercise is its versatility. As one ages, exercise may be modified according to specific needs. If arthritis is causing pain in the weight-bearing joints, such as the knees or hips, an exercise such as running can be replaced by brisk walking, biking, or swimming. Exercise in a pool is helpful, where the buoyancy alleviates stress. Exercising in a warm pool is helpful in specific cases, especially in alleviating spinal disk problems. Exercise is adaptable on many levels. If vision or hearing is a problem, for example, indoor exercise with a companion is a safeguard.

If aging is viewed negatively, we will only fulfill our low expectations of quality and length of life. For inspiration, we can look to other societies in which people remain healthy and vital into later years, like the Hunza in Pakistan, who often live over 100 years. Significantly, their lifestyle is grounded in physical activity and good diet.

Whether we live longer or not by exercising is yet to be confirmed conclusively in studies; however, the mental and physical benefits of exercising are clearly evident and widely acknowledged. Life is a cycle, and as such, goes through various predictable biological changes. Some we can avoid; some, which are natural, we cannot. Overall, exercise can reward us with a fuller, more vital, and more spirited life—no matter what the length of that life.

Role Models

Lois Scheffelin

Lois Scheffelin is 80 years young. In the 1991 New York City Marathon, she ran her best marathon time of 6:27, winning the Abel Kiviat award for the oldest female to complete the race. And at age 80 Lois had *improved* her athletic performance by a remarkable 25 minutes. "I don't feel myself slowing down," she says confidently. In fact, after that '91 race, she "got the marathon high" and ran a 10k race in celebration only one week later.

Scheffelin's athleticism dates back to her youth, when she was a competitive tennis player who qualified for the National Championships at Forest Hills (now the U.S. Open). She always ran a little then to keep in shape. When she contemplated taking up the sport seriously at age 50, she thought she was too old. She put the idea on hold. It wasn't until Scheffelin turned 75 that she ran a marathon. The impetus was the plan to make the run a three-generation family affair, in which her son (age 50) and her grandson (age 23) participated with her in their first 26.2-miler. Since then, the 5'6" 115-pound athlete has run a slew of races at all distances, including six marathons.

Running has also helped Scheffelin through some tough times. Her husband had just been diagnosed with cancer when she took up the challenge of her first marathon. Running carried her through his death in 1987. "When my husband was sick, it was a godsend to run." It was the only time of the day during which she was relieved from caring for her ailing spouse.

Like so many exceptional people who defy the odds with their athletic achievements, Scheffelin met with some resistance when she began. "The first time I told my doctor about my running, he threw up his hands in disbelief." But perhaps times are, in fact, changing. Says Scheffelin, "My new doctor thinks it's great." Scheffelin makes an important point about understanding the risks of running—and it is true for any age. Like everyone who exercises—and more, who go to the extent of running marathons—athletes learn to realize their limits. Scheffelin's feats are remarkable, but she knows when to scale back. Of her daily training she says, "I know myself. If I ever get a headache, or feel ill or tired, I stop."

A sufferer of arthritis, Scheffelin is both a member and a volunteer for the Achilles Track Club for the disabled. She largely credits her running career to this single source. "Getting to know them is so inspiring. Without Dick Traum and the Achilles Track Club, I don't know if I'd still be at it."

A good deal of Scheffelin's motivation and personal gratification come from the attention she gets. "I think it's an ego trip. I'm a show-off. If I had done all this at age 50, no one would have paid any attention," says Scheffelin, who has been the star of tabloids and national television for her marathon accomplishments.

She even humbled David Letterman on *Late Night*. Of her interview she says, "I know he can give people a hard time. But he was perfectly nice and respectable to me."

Al Gordon

Al Gordon has a lot in common with Lois Scheffelin. A lifelong athlete who has benefited from good genetics and positive family role models, it seems he has been blessed with everything: a long life, good health, talented children, and material wealth. The 90-year-old tells how his athleticism began.

"My father never drove an automobile, and we took many long walks together. He lived until age 87. I was always athletic. In high school, I was on three or four teams. I was an average college runner, competing in the quarter-mile (in 51 to 52 seconds) and the low hurdles. I was a long way from setting the world on fire, but I got a lot of third places."

Although running was something Gordon always did, he didn't start pounding out the longer distances until he was 40 years old. Still, he was far ahead of his time. Relates Gordon, "This was in 1955, and people thought I was nuts. But in those days, the people weren't the problem. The greatest danger was the dogs!"

His first road race was a 10k in Central Park in 1976. After his wife—who was also very athletic—died, he started running even longer distances, and decided to do a marathon. In 1983, he ran his first marathon in London, and was the oldest finisher in that race. He ran the 26.2-mile race one other time. Today he walks on a treadmill, or bikes, and does daily calisthenics. Gordon, who has also done several five-hour walks and still plays golf (without the use of a golf cart, he stresses), still maintains an active working life as the honorary chairman of Kidder, Peabody—a New York securities firm.

Gordon, who together with his three sons is a graduate of Harvard University, is known for having paid for the building of that school's indoor track, one of the most heralded state-of-the-art facilities in the country. He is also a NYRRC board member emeritus and club benefactor. The Al Gordon Library at the club is named for him. In addition, when Fred Lebow faced medical insurance problems during his illness with cancer, it was Gordon who came through to finance some of his treatments.

But Al Gordon's success story only begins with his own athletic achievements and philanthropy. He has five children, whom he inducted into the exercise and fitness ranks when they were young. At each child's 16th birthday, for example, their father took them to Holland for a four-day walk totaling 100 miles, in which 15,000 people participated. He also took each one of them mountain climbing.

Running is in the family, too. His oldest son sought to make the U.S. Olympic team in the 400 meters, and all three of his boys still run. His oldest daughter, a vice president at Chase Manhattan Bank, ran the Boston Marathon—her first—15 years ago at age 35 in 2:57. His other daughter was a professional dancer.

"I have always believed in physical fitness," says Gordon, who has also played tennis and skied. "If people are physically fit, they are better adjusted for life. Running is the greatest anodyne. It's mental therapy. While running, one develops a rhythm—the mind becomes detached.

"Let's face it, exercise is an addiction. The body wants to do it. It's just like having a dog who gets excited when he senses it's time to go out for a walk and run. Since having a knee operation, I do certain exercises. Now they're an addiction. It's as if I wake up and I'm compelled to do these damn exercises!"

Gordon's prescription for a long and healthy life is obviously one to which his experience attests. "Short of abusing your body, I think genetics has a great deal to do with it, no matter what you do. But I think if you do reasonable physical exercise, eat less, and you're conscious of your health, you'll feel better." It doesn't come without effort, he adds. "You have to push yourself."

Anna Thornhill

Unlike Lois Scheffelin and Al Gordon, 52-year-old artist Anna Thornhill did not grow up athletic—in fact, far from it. Raised in various locations around the world, but mostly in Malaysia and England, Thornhill spent her youth trying to avoid the two things she hated most: math and physical education.

One thing she knew she loved, however, was art, which has been her calling since she was a young child. In fact, it was her art that got her running, and lead to the discovery of her athletic talent.

"I used to devote my entire life to art," she relates. "I would sleep only four hours a night. There were weeks I would never go out of the house." Her success culminated in a sold-out show in 1975. However, by then her skin had turned yellow, and her health began to suffer. "What we didn't realize then is that the art materials were toxic. Twenty-five years later, of course, there are warning labels, but meanwhile, a lot of artists are dead."

Thornhill sensed that she had to get outdoors, and get moving somehow. Her husband, Simon, had grown up playing soccer, and hated running, but she had a running neighbor who one day took her along. His loop was four miles, and on her first try, she ran that extraordinary distance. "I took to it like a duck to water," she says.

She began running in May 1977, at age 37, and entered her first race in October: the New York City Marathon! Since then she has run over

30 marathons, with a best of 2:57, and one 100-miler, while logging 80 to an astounding 155 miles a week in training. She also ran a world road best for her age, 50, in the one mile, with a time of 5:24. Thornhill, who is usually in the top five women finishers overall in her races, regularly goes head to head with women 20 and 30 years her junior. She also frequently trains with her husband, who eventually got hooked on running as well.

To see Anna Thornhill, with the compact, muscular body of a 20-year-old, is to understand why she believes that there is not necessarily a lessening of speed and strength with age. "I ran my best times in my early 40s, and they are still the same times I run now. I don't believe in erosion. Invariably, the loss is due to a lessening of training."

Perhaps the most inspiring of her experiences, however, is Thornhill's two-year battle with menopause. "Some women breeze through menopause," she says. But Thornhill was not one of them. Always one who suffered heavy, painful menstrual cycles, the cessation of those cycles was even tougher.

Thornhill's body signaled menopause with a series of extremely heavy menstrual cycles. In the summer of her 49th year, she pushed through one marathon while bleeding so heavily that she finished "white as a sheet." By October of that year, she had suffered four major hemorrhages. Each doctor she consulted sounded an alarm. One told her she was so low on electrolytes, she could suffer a heart attack. In fact, she was so weak that at one point she literally didn't even have the strength to walk.

That's when the talk of a hysterectomy came up. Thornhill adamantly refused. "I was afraid of the possibility of severe side effects from a hysterectomy. And I didn't want to be cut up." However, after the fourth hemorrhage, she finally did agree to take danazol, an anti-estrogen hormone that stops ovarian function.

Of her troubles she says, "Initially I was in shock. Deep down, you believe if you're in good shape, it can't be happening to you." Once she was over the crisis, however, she was overcome by new feelings of joyousness. Says Thornhill, "Once I was on danazol, I started experiencing hot flashes. I had always heard they were terrible, but I loved them. They were an affirmation that I was alive.

"I believe that being in good physical and mental shape helped pull me out of the trouble. And now, to feel so great is quite a surprise.

On reflection, I am astonished, considering what I had read about menopause—that you're depressed. I find the reverse is true.

"Running has enormous psychological and physical benefits, especially for women in the older age categories. It celebrates your age and your ability. As you get older, you set new goals.

"Some women pretend; they try to hide their age. I say: nonsense. Why hide it? Celebrate it!"

Toshika D'Elia

Toshika D'Elia began running at age 44. At 50 years old, she covered the marathon distance in 2:57:20, a world record at that time for her age. She has won her age category at the annual NYRRC Awards night 10 times—more than any other runner. At age 62, she is still competing, and won the NYRRC award again for 1991. Perhaps it is no wonder that despite the fact D'Elia still appears to compete with the athleticism of a woman four decades younger, her coach says initially she had a difficult time accepting that her running times were slowing.

"I think you begin to truly accept the aging process more gracefully when you are over 55 or 60," she says. "At age 50, you still have a lot of energy. I think that it's actually life goals, or what you emphasize, that changes slightly. I am very involved with my grandchildren now, which means so much to my pleasure. I am happy to adjust my training regime to spend time with them. This has helped me to accept my aging as it relates to my running.

"I run a half hour slower for the marathon than I did at age 50, and three to four minutes slower for 10k. I can accept that I am slower, as long as I'm in good shape."

Dan Hamner, M.D.

Dr. Dan Hamner not only practices what he preaches, he also does both on a superlative level. A top masters runner who at age 52 has run a 1:17 half marathon and 10 marathons with a best of 2:51, he also heads a Manhattan sports medicine practice and is the author of a book on the subject of health and exercise.

As a high school senior in his native Kentucky, Dan Hamner competed in the quarter mile and long jump, winning the AAU long jump title. He hung up his running shoes after that though, until he put them on again 30 years later, in 1986. He began again at age 47½ by running laps around the track at Emory University in Atlanta, where he was doing his professional training in cardiac rehabilitation. But it wasn't like the old days. After all, he had never run over two laps, even as a youthful competitor.

But something immediately clicked for him. "It hit me how much I used to like to run. I remembered that instant gratification you get from sprinting." Hamner began to get serious, reading up on exercise physiology to educate himself on his running.

By November 1986, Hamner had moved to New York. That's when a friend took him on a three-mile run. Four weeks later he ran his first race, a five-miler, in a time of 37:40. From a couple of training runs to a five-mile race is a huge leap, but, Hamner admits, he's a "type A runner."

"I was hooked, crazed. I started beefing up my mileage. After that first race, I raced every weekend." He joined the NYRRC running class, and nine months later ran a 1:20 half marathon. He went on to rediscover track, of which he says, "I love it more than I ever did." He has since participated in the half mile at the World Veterans Games.

A heavy drinker who quit the habit in the early 1980s, Hamner has reason to be thankful for rediscovering running. "It's like a gift from a higher power," concludes the Alcoholics Anonymous adherent. "I had wrecked myself with alcohol. Now I am rejuvenated. I feel young for my age, like a 25-year-old. I work 12 hours every day."

Yet Hamner has learned his limits. "I'm older; I'm not a kid. I know myself. I've been careful and listened to my body. I watch for signs of overtraining, physiological markers. I have gone through every injury and come through nicely. Nothing lasted more than two to three weeks."

But this cautiousness did not come naturally. Hamner has been forced to learn to temper his reborn running enthusiasm. "Because I was training hard day in and day out, I was operating at a high anaerobic threshold. My training runs used to be no slower than 7:15 to 7:30 per mile. Now I'll back off to a more leisurely eight-minute pace, particularly after a hard track workout."

Hamner has a definite belief in one's ability to improve with age. "I don't see any limits," he states. "We can all break the rules. I believe the only thing we can't escape are those illnesses that seem to lurk behind the bushes, like prostate cancer and lymphoma."

Despite his general optimism, Hamner admits there are facts of aging we cannot avoid. "Cells die. Connective tissue gets old. That's aging," says Hamner. "We all break down."

Precisely when that happens, however, is the question. Hamner says that although it is still unproven, he doesn't believe there are any significant physiological changes until the middle 40s. But he does point out that aging is surely influenced by the many extraneous aspects of life—such as family or job stress.

However, although we may deteriorate for a variety of reasons, Hamner feels there is a lot we can do to improve ourselves along the way. He preaches various vitamin and nutrition regimes, in addition to his own personal love: exercise.

"Exercise opens you up to oxygen, and cleans out your arteries," says Hamner as he bounces up yet again from his chair to attend to one of his many patients. Dressed in running shoes and jeans, he exudes a joy and energy like the 25-year-old that he does, in fact, seem to be.

Fred Lebow on Aging

You change perspective as you age. I've had to realize that I probably won't break seven minutes a mile anymore. I have to be satisfied with breaking nine minutes a mile. Not only am I older, I'm less healthy, so I have to accept that I cannot run as fast as I once did. But I get the same pleasure, if not more so, from what I can do. In fact, I'm delighted by what I can do.

You can come to believe that when you reach 60, you're not old. Even when you reach 70 and 80, there's no limit. Your body has more power, more resources, than you can imagine. You don't have to sit in a rocking chair; you can be out running.

I remember a runner in her 80s from Florida who ran some of our races, Ruth Rothfarb. She used to run down a major avenue, and pass people sitting on the porch in their rocking chairs. This woman was a tremendous revelation and insight to those people. "Do you know how many people I got out of those rocking chairs—going for a walk, maybe someday going for a run?" she said to me. It's encouraging to realize that the older you are, the more others will benefit just by seeing you run.

There are a couple of people over age 90 in the New York City Marathon. They're so energetic; they've got great life stories. They've been successful professionally. One's a doctor who still practices part-time. There are some amazing "older" people in the New York City Marathon: Josef Galia and Paul Spangler—the over 90s; Mavis Lindgren (84); Robert Earl Jones (the father of James Earl Jones) (81); John Petroff (82). It's no wonder the press gives them so much attention during marathon time.

One of the greatest inspirations to me, and others in the New York running community, is 89-year-old Max Popper. Popper is a tremendous runner who has won his age category repeatedly at our annual NYRRC Awards Banquet.

Popper, who runs almost every race, used to beat me. Now I feel lucky to beat him. Max has shown me that there is no reason to give up. He is proof of what I honestly believe: that your mental state dictates much about how you live. I look at Max and understand that having a positive outlook makes you vibrant.

Since I got cancer, this has taken on even added meaning. I was never depressed much in my life, but every once in a while at the club, there is a setback. We lose a sponsor, an event doesn't come off right. I don't get dragged down by this like I used to. Why bother? I've been through a lot, and now is the time to enjoy myself. Besides, what are these little setbacks compared to the troubles of the rest of the world?

Frankly, I used to fudge my age—lie about it to state it more directly. I'd make myself a few years younger than I actually was. Now I never do. I'm proud to be exactly who and what I am. When this book comes out, I will have just turned 60 years old.

Aging has taught me about all of these things. And I have learned to watch, and be inspired, by the spirit of the older runners who participate in NYRRC events. They are true role models for us all.

36

Masters Running

Dr. Margaret Dessau gently reminds us of an unalterable fact—from the moment of birth, we age. However, the effects of exercise and physical fitness on the aging process are less certain than the fact of aging itself. And what is still yet to come is an examination of competitive athletes and the aging process. As masters world record holder Priscilla Welch points out, the sport of running for those over 40 is just "too new to know."

A handful of prominent pioneers in various sports have prompted society to question its assumptions about aging and competitive athletes. Yet very few sports have provided an arena of competition for athletes over age 40. Running has—and it's called masters running.

Masters running is for running superstars—and anyone else ambitious enough, and with perhaps a bit of latent talent, to aspire to success in age-group competition. Even for us not on, or even near, the world-class level, role models such as Priscilla Welch and Bill Rodgers inspire us to maximize our athletic potential and to enjoy it far longer than it was previously believed possible. And this is just by staying at it. Who is to say how far we can go when the science and technology that have been devoted to general sports psychology are focused on those over 40? Like women, aging athletes face an unknown world, one filled with both challenges and social barriers.

The New York City Marathon is an example of how untested the limits of masters performances are. While the age records in this race leveled off years ago and remain static for ages 16 to 38, dramatic improvements can be seen in the past few years from those in the masters (and near masters) ranks: ages 38 through 44. Greater participation and encouragement and incentives (including financial) for older runners undoubtedly account for this improvement. When one considers that running times are measured in seconds, and that a minute in a marathon is significant, the following contrasting times (showing improvement by as much as 12 minutes) take on even greater meaning.

1987 Age Record		1991 Age Record	
	Men		
39	2:28:09	39	2:25:01
40	2:17:30	40	2:16:15
41	2:21:04	41	2:14:34
42	2:19:09	42	2:15:44
43	2:22:44	43	2:18:18
44	2:27:39	44	2:20:51
	Women		
39	2:40:34	39	2:39:32
40	2:35:30	40	2:35:30
41	2:39:11	41	2:39:11
42	2:43:10	42	2:30:17
43	2:40:50	43	2:40:50
44	2:48:13	44	2:36:15

The Three A's

Acceptance. Accommodation. Adjustment. These are "the three A's" of masters running—and of aging in general. Coach Bob Glover says he tries to get masters to do two important things. The first is to adjust running times to the aging process. He says that while as a runner you can likely still improve to a point, it is best to compare yourself to your peers—not to performances you achieved when you were younger. Obviously, improvement will be more dramatic if you are just taking up the sport, but at some point that improvement levels off.

The second adaptation for a master, Glover suggests, is to allow for more recovery time. If you normally did two speed sessions per week, it might be better to adjust to aging by doing just one—and allow more days after a hard training run or race to recover. For beginners in this age bracket, Glover—who teaches all beginners regardless of age to intersperse running and walking—prescribes even more walking.

In terms of adjusting your goals, he points out the example of one of his athletes, running phenomenon Toshika D'Elia. While it was initially hard for her to accept running slower times, D'Elia has been buoyed by the fact she has been nominated for an award in her age group every year for the entire 12 years of the NYRRC Awards Banquet. She has won ten times. "The beauty of masters running," says Glover, "at least in New York, is that you can change age categories in competition every five years."

With the right perspective and the right training, as a master your running can be, to quote Priscilla Welch, "so new to know." Welch says, "I don't think we know how far we can go. Masters running is so young, particularly for women. I don't think there's enough of us out there really pushing ourselves to be able to judge our limits. The Swedish woman Evy Palm has improved her times since she was age 45. She's now 49, and she's still running 32 minutes for 10k on the track, and 1:12 for a half marathon. She's one example, and there're several other Swedish masters women on the rise."

Welch continues, "I don't believe in an age decline. Maybe you lose a bit of speed, but that's inevitable. Yet, there again, do we have to lose speed? Is it just something we've been brainwashed to believe happens? Eventually, with age, you must lose some speed, but I don't think it's necessarily at age 40. I think it happens much later than we previously thought. This is my opinion; I haven't consulted any experts. As an older runner, however, I do almost believe you have to work harder at your quality workouts than a younger person. And possibly it takes a little longer to recover."

Masters Training

Can you improve as a master? Yes, you can, says Frank Shorter, but you have to keep personal records so you can judge your relative performance. "The way I gauge it is: I know what training intensity is, and I know the feeling of competition. I've developed a sense of how close I've been able to come now to my maximum. What I've found is, I can reach about 95 percent of 'all out.' The last 5 percent is very hard for me because I know that no matter how much I get out of myself, I'll never run a 2:10 marathon again; I'll never run under 28 minutes for 10,000 meters; I'll never run under 13:20 for 5k. There's just something about realizing that which makes it hard to go absolutely all out in a competitve situation. The way I view it, you just have to get the satisfaction somewhere else.

I don't think training need vary with age. Everyone's training is a bit different because he or she responds differently to various systems; each body is different. It takes a long while to find the recipe that suits you, and then it's tough to hold on to it. You're influenced by others you meet who may be doing better than you are, and you want to improve, so you think maybe that person's training would help you do so. It's not necessarily so. You should stick with the recipe that works. You can head for a lot of pitfalls trying to change what already works.

I think I'm still capable of running a personal best marathon time of 2:25. The real question is not my ability to do it, but whether I want to do the training required to achieve it. I think there are a lot of people over 40 capable of exceling, it's a question of if they want to, whether they really want to put in the training. I think people stop themselves before they possibly have reached their potential. When you're running against those in the open category (under age 40), it's as if you're all one age group. Sometimes when I stop to think about it, I realize, "My God, I could be this girl's mother. When I was doing so-and-so, she was in her crib." But I don't think about that until it's right under my nose.

My experience is different from, say, Bill Rodgers', because I didn't start running until I was 35. I started blooming when I was 40. Bill Rodgers, and a lot of others, have been running for years; they remember other competitions in younger bodies.

—Priscilla Welch

"But people don't need to perform well in order to be able to run," Shorter concludes. "I run because I like the motion. I like being out there. In that way I'm like any average runner."

I went to Cooper's aerobic center in the summer of 1991, when I was 43. I had all the tests done. They showed I had pretty much maintained all of my fitness. My VO$_2$ max had gone down very little. They predict about 1 1/2 percent drop after age 30, which would total about 18 percent for me. However, mine went down only 7 percent. I went in at the same weight I was in 1975: 134 pounds.

I think that athletes believe that if they maintain the same body weight, they maintain the same conditioning. But although my weight hadn't changed, my body fat had gone up 4 percent. It doesn't take a rocket scientist to figure out that if your body fat goes up 4 percent and you weigh the same, there are that many pounds of muscle that are no longer there. Based on that alone, I think logic would indicate that the more of that muscle one can maintain, or get back in my case, the more it will help.

—Frank Shorter

Frank Shorter believes there are specific adaptations to training as a master that will help maintain conditioning. One thing you can do is maintain a weight training routine. "I think you lose a certain amount of muscle mass and strength with age, and while it's only a percentage, it's enough that if you've been very active as a younger person, it has a significant impact on your performance. That's why now I do a 30-minute weight routine several times a week, to build and maintain muscle."

Shorter also stresses the aspect of recovery. "As you get older, you still maintain the same daily goal as to how much training you'll do. You lock into a certain amount that you feel is a day's exercise. If you maintain that amount from age 30 to 45, and you've been losing muscle mass, in essence you've been slightly overtraining as you age. You're aiming to reach your daily quota, but you've had less strength to do it. You're going to be taxed more, and obviously it will take you more time to recover."

> I still love the sport just as much as I always did. Each person can always seek and find what is important for him or her. For me, it has always been being fit, trying to break records or doing my best in a race. It is gaining everything one gets from competition—all the cliches.
>
> —Bill Rodgers

Masters Competition

Is competing as exciting as it once was? "Quite honestly, no," says Bill Rodgers, "largely because of the buildup of fatigue. I'm fighting that, and it's very frustrating. I still love to compete in masters-only races, for example, where I can get the same feelings I used to have in open competition of being out in front. Some people think I'm not racing anymore, but the fact is, I'm still racing just as much as I ever have, and as hard as I can. I'm not winning Boston, New York City, or any marathons right now, but I'm one of the top masters runners in the world. I have been for a while."

> I can't speak for men, because I can't put myself into their shoes. But it's possible that women of this age have begun to participate in greater numbers because they have more leisure time. Also, it's accepted, whereas years ago it was looked down on.
>
> It's been proven that you can run, and run well, at age 40 and beyond. It's not merely a younger person's sport. In masters competition, there's a few of us who have shown the way—that we can run as well as the younger ones—and for those who are competitive, there's a little bit of money. That's encouraging women to take it up.
>
> —Priscilla Welch

Fred Lebow on Masters Running

The great thing about masters running is it gives everyone a goal. When I look at my age category results, and see, for example, that I came in 16th, I want to do better. I want to aspire to come in the top 10.

If I look at the 10k world record—in the 27-minute range—and I realize how far from that I am, it is not very encouraging. But if I look within my age group, I realize that the record is not so far away. That's another advantage of age group competition: You seem to gain time. You can afford to run slower and still do relatively well.

Another great aspect of masters running is that it spurs people to resurface. I think of a top local competitor, Hugh Sweeney, who did well in our races as far back as the early 1970s. Then he dropped out of sight for a long time. All of a sudden he's back, doing well as a master.

Photo: Ken Levinson

Ultramarathoner Stu Mittleman, his shoes cut open to relieve pressure on his feet, gets a massage during a 6-day run.

Photo: Kathryn Dudek

Carl Lewis winning the 100m at the New York Games in 1990.

Photo: Michael DeVito

The Start of the Chemical Corporate Challenge.

Tom Brokaw running in Central Park.

Anne Marie Letko training with coach Tom Fleming.

Photo: Michael Tighe

Norb Sander winning the New York City Marathon in 1974.

Photo: Kathryn Dudek

Eamonn Coghlan on his way to the World Indoor Mile record of 3:49.78 in 1983.

Photo: Victah Sailer/Agence Shot

PattiSue Plummer winning the 1990 Fifth Avenue Mile.

Photo: Nancy Coplon

Kathrine Switzer and Nina Kuscsik holding relics from the early days of the Women's Mini Marathon.

Lynn Jennings wins her third World Cross-Country Championship in 1992.

Photo: Victah Sailer/Agence Shot

Juma Ikangaa winning the 1989 New York City Marathon in the course
record time of 2:08:01.

Nine-time New York City Marathon champion Grete Waitz.

Frank Shorter, *Runner's World* publisher George Hirsch, Bill Rodgers, and Fred Lebow.

Photo: Nancy Coplon

Some of the one million paper cups needed to hydrate runners in the New York City Marathon.

Photo: Nancy Coplon

Achilles Track Club member Linda Down after a race.

NYRRC races sometimes have a Pee-Wee division.

Part 9: Children's Running and Fitness

Children's Running and Fitness

As road running and the fitness movement blossomed in the 1970s and 1980s, the NYRRC staff, as well as other experts in the field of sports and fitness, noticed that something was missing. While adults were striving, and succeeding, to improve their health and fitness, the nation's children were falling behind. From one decade to the next, those who measure children's fitness have found that it has been declining.

The statistics are disheartening: Thirty percent of school-age boys and 50 percent of girls can't run a mile in less than 10 minutes. Forty percent of children ages 5 to 8 show at least one risk factor for heart disease, such as obesity, high blood pressure, or elevated cholesterol. These early risk factors make them more likely to develop heart disease later in life.

Nationwide physical fitness tests show that youngsters over age 10 are becoming less fit. They have declined in cardiovascular endurance and increased in weight, according to an ongoing study highlighted in *Working Mother* magazine. The study, which involved about 9.7 million schoolchildren, shows that kids take about a minute longer to run a mile and have gained 3.6 to 8.3 pounds over the decade the testing was done.

As many as one in five U.S. children may have high cholesterol—and current recommendations for selective testing would miss half of them. A two-year screening project publicized in 1991 adds to growing evidence that guidelines urging tests only for kids

413

with a family history of heart disease or high cholesterol may not be strict enough. According to *USA Today*, the study found that about half with excess blood fats had neither family history nor parents with known high cholesterol levels. But some doctors say the cost, benefit, and safety of mass screening are questionable. As of early 1991, a National Institutes of Health panel was considering new childhood testing recommendations. High cholesterol in children is associated with a sedentary lifestyle, which often includes the combination of television-watching and junk-food consumption.

—Fitness Features

The ideal amount of exercise instruction for children recommended by experts is a minimum of 30 minutes a day for elementary-school-age children and 45 for those in secondary school. Unfortunately, at this time we can't look to schools to get the job done. Only one state in the country, Illinois, requires daily physical education instruction in its schools.

In addition to the poor state of children's fitness, a trend in the running movement prompted the NYRRC to develop children's programs. A significant change in the nature of the running demographics was noted at the club. The majority of the club's members—as well as others in the running movement—who had previously been single people in their 20s, were now becoming parents in their 30s and even 40s. Their lifestyles were changing, as were their needs and interests. Running was not merely a solitary activity, but something they wanted to share with their families. To serve the changing needs of these people, it became a club priority to educate and expand fitness—making it a family affair.

When it comes to children and sports, there is often a fine line between parental pressure and support. This is especially the case when the parents themselves are very interested and/or active in the sport. Without the proper guidance, children often get discouraged for a variety of reasons, and eventually lose interest.

Adults very often direct sport for their children based on adult models. This isn't necessarily the wrong approach, but it happens quite often that the child's needs and wishes are not exactly the same as the adult's. It is not the coach's or the parents' ambitions that should be the basis for a child's sports program.

Teenage years are crucial in maintaining a sports program. This is the time during which youth tend to drop out of sports participation. To help your child stick with it, consider what I have learned in my experience as a teacher working with young people. The following is a list of reasons I have found as to why youth quit sports participation. You can use some of the positive steps outlined in this chapter to keep these things from happening.

- boring and/or monotonous training
- the perception that the expectation for good performance and results is too great
- lack of parental interest in the child's activity
- too little encouragement
- too great a feeling of defeat
- lack of a sense of security in training
- failure of adults to realize and/or be sympathetic to what children want from the sport
- adults' inability to distinguish children's varying capabilities
- neglecting and/or failing to develop the social aspect of the sport

—Grete Waitz

The third factor in the move to develop children's fitness was community involvement. The club has always sought to be a vehicle for improvement in the quality of life of the community, particularly of the inner city population. As part of this effort, the NYRRC conducts an extensive running and fitness program for children and youth. It began on Father's Day in 1981 with the first Pee Wee run, and later with the creation of the Urban Running Program (URP), which focused on running for New York's inner city children. Out of the URP grew other programs.

Currently, the club conducts three highly successful children's running and fitness programs. One is City-Sports-For-Kids, coached by Bob Glover, which is held on Sunday afternoons and includes a staff of trained NYRRC coaches. Although it is in its early stages, this program is growing by leaps and bounds. It has expanded by at least one-third in each of its first two years. In 1992, over 1000 children ages 5 to 12 years old will have participated.

The goals of City-Sports-For-Kids are as follows: to enhance physical fitness, to develop self-esteem through success-oriented sports, and to build bridges of understanding through play for boys and girls of various races and religions. The program provides instruction in a variety of sports skills, including basketball as well as track and field activities such as high jump, sprinting, long jump, and shot put.

The second children's program is the NYRRC Junior Road Runners Series. It offers fun runs and races for young runners. There are approximately six noncompetitive races held per year as part of this program. Each race includes warmup exercises, Pee Wee runs (distances of one block to 1/4 mile) for 2- to 6-year-olds, and one-mile runs for ages 6 to 17. These runs are extremely popular, with over 300 participants per event. The significance of these runs is that they are held in conjunction with adult races, which achieves two of the NYRRC's major goals: to bring out all generations, and to make running and fitness a fun family affair.

The third program is the New York City Junior Marathon. This event, held the week before the New York City Marathon, is for boys and girls ages 5 to 12. It consists of runs of quarter- or half-miles, ending at the marathon finish line. All participants receive a special Junior Marathon Medal.

The goal of the NYRRC programs, writes Bob Glover, is to create a lifelong pattern of fitness among families by encouraging everyone to share the experience of getting fit and healthy together. Together, Mom, Dad, and the kids—grandparents, too—create the best support for maintaining a healthy diet and regular aerobic exercise. This, in turn, fosters a closeness and harmony that strengthen the family. Healthy eating and making family exercise part of your weekly schedule are essential ingredients for a successful family fitness program.

The State of Youth Fitness

The following information is adapted from an NYRRC brochure on children's fitness written by Bob Glover.

Studies by the President's Council on Physical Fitness and Sports and the American Alliance for Health, Physical Education, Recreation, and Dance (AAHPERD) demonstrate that the youths in this country need to improve their fitness levels.

Do physically fit children have more efficient immune systems than couch potatoes do? James M. Rippe, M.D., director of the Exercise Physiology and Nutrition Laboratory of the University of Massachusetts in Worcester, believes the answer is yes. Says Dr. Rippe in *Working Mother* magazine, "The link is there, in some yet-to-be-determined way. For one thing, the body temperature rises slightly during exercise, and the immune system may interpret this as mild fever and marshal infection-fighting cells."

In fact, a study done at Loma Linda University in California showed that moderate exercise strengthens the immune system by triggering the release of antibodies that attack viruses and bacteria. What's more, endorphins, the mood-elevating brain chemicals released through exercise, may also signal the immune system to work harder.

—Fitness Features

The AAHPERD'S "Shape of the Nation" survey of school physical education programs revealed that children are not getting enough exercise in school, partly due to budget cutbacks that affect school physical education programs. The AAHPERD recommends at least 30 minutes of daily vigorous exercise for children in grades K–12. (However, as mentioned above, only one state in the United States, Illinois, requires daily physical education classes.) The AAHPERD also recommends that schools place more emphasis on lifelong fitness activities such as running, swimming, and walking, in addition to team sports.

The major responsibility for the fitness of our children rests with parents. They can work to help improve fitness programs in schools and community groups. Parents can be a great inspiration for their kids by being good fitness role models and by making fitness a fun, lifelong family activity.

Here's what parents can do to help their children become more physically fit:

1. Join them in walking or biking more often as a means of transportation—for example, to or from school.
2. Encourage vigorous physical activity over sedentary activities, such as the excessive watching of television or playing of video games.
3. Spend some time each week participating together in fun physical activities such as running, hiking, cross-country skiing, or playing tennis.
4. If you are an athlete, you can be a role model for your child. If you're not athletic, you can steer your child toward someone who is. Find a program like the ones at the NYRRC, or a running group or friends who run. Children's fitness classes and programs are also conducted by the Ys in every state.

Children and Running

It's good to expose your children to running at an early age—but don't force them to run. While most adults run for fitness, kids run because it's fun.

As a runner, you can motivate your child by being a fun running companion. A good way for parents to introduce children to running is to make it a natural part of their play. Youngsters have short attention spans, so break up their runs with walking, skipping, singing, or exploring. Let them run after you while playing baseball, or run up and down hills while playing hide and seek in the park. Very young preschoolers often enjoy brisk walks with a few dashes in between. The key is to integrate running into your child's play.

Older children, like adults, enjoy talking during the run to pass the time. A good conversation on the run is a great way to communicate—and both of you will be surprised how fast the time goes by.

Let your children decide when and how often they want to run. Don't push them. Make the early experience positive, successful, and fun. They may want to run for several days and then move on to other activities, returning on and off to running. The important thing is that they are exercising and having fun.

An important safety note: The American Academy of Pediatrics recommends that children, as well as their parents, should be screened by a physician before starting a sports or fitness program.

Preschool Running Tips

For kids age 5 or under, running is just playtime activity. Parents should encourage fun running and not stress competition at this age. The NYRRC Pee Wee running program is designed to develop an awareness and joy of running. Think of it this way: prefitness for preschoolers. Pee Wees should be encouraged to sprint short distances, not run long distances.

Praise the kids for running, no matter how fast or how slow they run, or how many times they stop or even fall down. The goal is to begin to establish in their minds that running and exercise are not only good for them, but also fun for the entire family. Sometimes a good storybook helps to reinforce this. Ask at a library or bookstore for a list of titles on the subject.

Elementary-School-Age Tips

Attitudes and habits about fitness and exercise tend to be firmly established in this age group. By adolescence it is already very difficult to change one's style of living, so this is a crucial stage for developing good fitness habits.

Two important factors for fitness development between the ages of 6 and 12 are having a parent who exercises as a role model and a good physical education program at school that stresses aerobic fitness, not just sports.

Fitness running, as opposed to competition, should be emphasized for most kids of this age, and the distance should be limited to one to four miles. There are numerous ways to get your kids involved. Have them accompany you while you run. Go at their pace for whatever distance they can maintain interest. That might be around the block, or a loop of a nearby park. You can also encourage your children to participate in activities in which they do a lot of running without realizing it, such as soccer or tennis.

At the school where I teach, kindergarten-age children are led in running and fitness games (see below). I find that by first grade (age 6), the time is right to get kids interested in more structured fitness activities, like organized sports. Age 5 is still a bit young for this, unless a child shows particular interest. By the first grade, our students are playing soccer. However, the ball we use is softer than a regulation soccer ball. They also play basketball and softball. These activities help develop hand/eye coordination and motor skills.

I believe two to three physical education classes per week are enough in terms of a structured class. Children in our school may also opt for a one-hour after-school program of sports such as kickball or floor hockey. On Friday, an early dismissal day, these activities are also held between 1 and 3 p.m.

Other movement activities can be done in daily free play sessions. Kindergarten and first grade are when children automatically want to play tag and climb, both good physical development activities.

After training specifically to do so, two times a year the students run various distances in Central Park as a school activity. They are not timed. We advise them that if they can't make it jogging or running the entire way, they can walk and jog.

In the upper grades, it is a greater challenge to get kids active. We are trying to get the older students more physically active, particularly in the second to fourth grades, by offering three structured sports per term—like soccer and basketball. As the school year progresses, we add sports such as swimming and ice hockey.

Some parents take their children to run in Central Park. I have noticed that having active parents in running or sports definitely does give a psychological push to the kids to be involved.

—Bob Wynn

Biking, skating, dancing, jumping rope, and swimming are other activities you can do together at this age, when the children can build a good aerobic base of fitness. Many kids enjoy riding their bikes to accompany parents on the run. This can be a great way to get in your run while chatting with your child.

The NYRRC encourages children age 12 and under to compete in age-appropriate events. The emphasis is on providing the experience of the joys of running for fitness and fun, as well as participating in a variety of sports and aerobic fitness activities.

The NYRRC endorses the guidelines established by the American Academy of Pediatrics: Preadolescent children should not run long distance races held primarily for adults. If kids want to try competition, they should run against each other, not adults. Younger children should be encouraged just to take part. This can best be accomplished in low-key fun runs, like those conducted by the NYRRC.

Tips from a Running Mom

- Children are never too young to begin running. Toddlers can benefit by being included in the fitness activities of parents and older siblings. Bring them along and encourage their participation (e.g., my 2-year-old daughter Shira runs and walks near her sister, Yael, who is instructed to go in circles or up and back).

- Learn to understand the difference between encouragement and pushing, and be sensitive to it. Support your children's exercise or fitness activity, but don't force them. If they are especially tired, or unwilling, scale down the activity.

- Select and promote "active toys" that enable children to develop fitness or coordination skills—like jump ropes and balls.

- Set challenging and exciting fitness-oriented goals. This is particularly useful during breaks from structured activity. I trained with my 5-year-old every day during a two-week school vacation with the specific goal of running the final mile to her school together (walking breaks allowed, of course!). Not only did the activity provide daily inspiration and structure, it also was something mother and daughter shared together on their own.

- Give equal time, interest, and enthusiasm to physical education. In discussing the school day, for example, show your child that physical education and sports is as of much interest and importance as "the three r's." Inquire enthusiastically about physical education class, or even who ran fast during recess.

- If you're on the PTA, work toward improving fitness in addition to other aspects of the curriculum. If one does not already exist, work toward setting up a school fitness network.

- Encourage girls with the same intensity as boys. In fact, you might want to give an extra measure of support to girls. Although you may personally feel enlightened in this regard, you are working against a society that stresses the "Go for it!" attitude in sports and exercise more for boys than girls.

- Take your child on a "training run" at the most convenient time, after your own run. Our daughter is dressed and ready for the returning parent. It's a good plan on all fronts: as a nice sharing activity, to ensure your child gets the necessary dose of exercise, and also as a good warmdown for parents after a workout.

- If you run races, bring your children to watch you. It greatly impresses and inspires them to see the focus and effort their parents invest in competition. What's more, they learn to understand healthy competition—in which Mom or Dad likely doesn't finish first, but still "wins." Even if you don't race, have the kids attend events anyway, and get them involved by cheering or passing out water. It is never a problem in our family to inspire the children to run after they see a race.

- Incorporate fun and meaningful movement into all aspects of life. Be creative. For example, don't just stand around waiting for the school bus. Our family holds informal "mini-relays" and hopping and skipping sessions with both our children and the others who are waiting. It keeps everyone occupied, warm in chilly weather, and starts the day off right. This goes for any waiting, or "dead" time. Fill it with movement. We use games and challenges: "Let's see who can hop a long time on one foot," "Let's see who can run a circle around the house," or "Let's see who can skip to the store" are examples.

- Don't lose momentum during inclement weather. It is a lot more challenging to keep up an exercise program for those who live in climates in which outdoor exercise may sometimes be impossible. Children don't enjoy suffering through bitter cold or intense heat, and with reason. Both physically and psychologically, it is harder on them than for adults. In summer heat, focus on fitness activities such as swimming or evening bike riding.

In cold weather, again be creative. Try indoor fitness. Roll up blankets or use pillows and create a hurdles course in a large room or in a hallway. Move furniture around for an obstacle course. Children enjoy the challenge of covering these courses for time. Background music also spurs them on, and when it's over, they can continue to exercise by dancing to the music.

- Try to get a church or community center to allow you and others the use of its space during the winter months. Children will have more room to run and play. If it works successfully, consider pitching in with other parents to donate balls and toys for the space, and doing cooperative supervision or baby-sitting.

- In better weather, running relays and obstacle courses can be done outdoors. Encouraging the neighborhood children to join in gives the added benefit of the group and makes your children feel proud to have their parents initiate and lead the activity.

- Make fitness a part of children's general activities, such as play dates and birthday parties. You can go from the elaborate to the simple: ice skating parties to backyard birthday relays. Even sedentary activity can promote fitness, like finding library books on sports and doing art projects on the subject.

- Advocate, educate, participate. Bring running and fitness into your children's world any way you can. Volunteer to help lead recreation or free play activities. Copy this section of the book to distribute to schools or other groups.

—Gloria Averbuch

Children age 10 and up can qualify for a Presidential Physical Fitness Award in a total of 58 fitness and sports categories. Among them are "running," "jogging," and "marathon." Also, you can help your children's schools institute the President's Challenge. For further information on any of these programs, contact the President's Council (address in the Resource List), or telephone (202) 272-3427.

One-Mile Running Program for Children

The following is a program to build up to running one mile in six weeks, adapted from *Children's Running* by Don Kardong and Jim Ferstle. (For age guidelines, see advice from Grete Waitz near the end of the chapter.)

Week 1: 10- to 15-minute jog/walk on Monday, Wednesday, and Friday

Week 2: 12- to 18-minute jog/walk on Monday, Wednesday, and Friday

Week 3: 15- to 20-minute jog/walk on Monday, Wednesday, and Friday

Week 4: 20-minute jog/walk on Monday, Wednesday, and Friday, and 3 to 4 long (200 to 400 meters) runs at one-mile pace

Week 5: same as for Week 4

Week 6: 20-minute jog on Monday and 10-minute jog on Tuesday, with 4 to 5 sprints at the end

This is just a sample program. Many others can work just as well. Whatever the plan, though, remember to increase gradually. You might encourage children to keep a training log (diary).

Running Games for Young Children

Duck, Duck, Goose (from Bob Wynn)

This can be done with any number of children. I have had from five to 22 play. Children sit in a circle. One child (the tagger) walks the outside of the circle, touching the head of each child, naming them "duck, duck,"… When he or she decides to proclaim a child "goose," the goose must get up and chase the tagger around the circle, trying to tag him or her before he or she goes around one full time and sits down in the goose's vacated spot. If the goose cannot, he or she sits in the middle of the circle for one turn. Each unsuccessful goose sits in the middle of the circle for one turn. The tagger starts the process again, and keeps the job until he or she is tagged. Play the game until everyone gets a chance to be a goose. With fewer children, you may want to run the circle more than one time, or choose another designated out-and-back distance.

Steal the Bacon (from Bob Wynn)

Designate two bases. In a gym, for example, this can be two opposite walls. The children stand in the middle against, or near, the two bases. A ball is placed on the floor, and two or four children at a time from each team stand near it. Each team attempts to pick up the ball and run to their respective base without being tagged by the other team. The object of the game, particularly with older children, is to try to "fake out" the opponent, gesturing to go for the ball but not touching it, hoping to trick the opponent into picking up the ball at an opportune time for tagging. With four children, the ball can be picked up and moved toward the base by passing to a teammate. Call two to four children to the center until everyone has had a turn. This game not only develops running ability, but skills such as those used in basketball.

Runner's Leapfrog (from Bloomsday)

Get three or more friends or "training buddies." Line up single file. Start running in a straight line, one person in front of the next. All of you should run at the same pace. Now you can start "leapfroggin'." The runner in front of the line raises his or her hand. When the last runner in your line sees the front runner raise that hand, he or she will sprint to the front of the line. Repeat this until each runner has gone through the line twice.

Palm Springs (from Bloomsday)

Start jogging. Stretch your arms out in front of you. Point your fingers so your hands are flat and the palms of your hands point to the ground. Now raise your knees while jogging so they touch the palms of your hands. Do this for one minute. Try to raise your knees really high!

High Five! (from Bloomsday)

Start jogging. Begin to run so your heels kick your rear end. Do this for one minute. Jog for two minutes. Do the "high five!" for another minute.

Get three friends or "training buddies" together. One person will be the "general." Everyone start jogging forward. When the "general" gives the command "about face!" everyone turn and jog in the opposite direction. Continue jogging forward and backward as the "general" gives the "about face!" commands.

Competition

Children run so naturally and gracefully that it seems they were born to do it. However, there's a big difference between a child's spontaneous running and running for competition. As has been pointed out earlier, the NYRRC encourages children to participate in age-appropriate events and discourages young children from competing in events designed for adults. In particular, the New York City Marathon first adopted an age minimum of 16, which was eventually raised to 18. This standard had previously been in existence in other countries.

According to author Cliff Temple, "When children undertake training and racing over long distances on the road (e.g., marathon), it can create many problems for the developing body. The growth of the bones around the heels and the knees particularly can be disrupted by excessive training loads, which can lead to problems in later life. The fact that physiologically children can run marathons must not be confused with whether medically they should. It is clear they should not."

Inappropriate training or competition in running (or, for that matter, any sport) is potentially damaging not only physically, but also psychologically. How many child running stars become adult running stars? It is tough to find even one. The theme of this book is the same for children as it is for adults: to make running essentially an enjoyable, lifelong activity.

Grete Waitz, who began running for fun at age 12 and appropriately progressed to serious competition as she got older, provides the following guidelines, a compilation from conferences in which European coaches presented their views on youth running:

1. Specializing in middle distances (800 meters to the mile) should not take place before 13 to 14 years of age; long distances (up to 10k), not before 15 to 16 years of age.

2. Young runners should have well-rounded training before specializing (e.g., at one time, I competed in the high jump, sprints, and even the throwing events).

3. Aerobic, or endurance, training is important for young runners, but it should only be done easily.

4. Young runners should be careful with anaerobic training. Hard anaerobic training should be avoided before puberty, and once begun, increased only in small doses from year to year.

5. Strength and sprint training are good for young runners.

6. Long-term planning is crucial to prevent early peaking and burnout.

Fred Lebow on Children

Unfortunately, children are not fit. In fact, it seems clear children are less fit now than they were 20 years ago. They watch more television and eat more junk food now than ever. I don't think this speaks well for their future, and it speaks even worse for our society.

If kids are into sports, it's baseball, football, and basketball—not track and field. And if track and field for young people isn't available or promoted, all running is going to be hurt.

Children used to participate more regularly in track and field. But there aren't many youth track and field programs in existence anymore. Most schools don't have any specific programs, and even some colleges have dropped them.

I think the New York Games is a step in the right direction in bringing track and field to the attention of the public, and specifically to children. It's the only new track and field event in this country in the last ten years. And a large part of the stadium audience is kids—hundreds of them who have been given free tickets to encourage youth attendance. The network television broadcast of the event helps, too. But we need more, much more, to bring children and this activity together. It's such a perfect combination.

Part 10: Women's Running

The Early Years

The 1991 New York City Marathon, informally dubbed the "Race of the Mothers," boasted a field of moms among the top contenders—Liz McColgan, Lisa Ondieki, and Joan Samuelson. These runners symbolize the evolution of the sport from a predominantly male pursuit to an activity enjoyed by all people of all ages. The women's running movement continues to this day to gain dramatic momentum.

Alice Schneider, the NYRRC's director of computer operations, notes a significant and dramatic increase of women runners in the past few years. While membership statistics show no growth and even decline among men, women of all demographic descriptions are signing up, particularly in the older age groups. Women are also becoming more involved in running teams and, as a result, running teams are increasingly female.

The NYRRC is a leader worldwide in promoting women's distance running. The club conducts several nationally and internationally prominent women's-only road races, including the Advil Mini Marathon, and the Race for the Cure (to promote breast cancer research and education). The Mini Marathon is the largest all-women's race in the country and the most prestigious of its kind in the world. In addition, the New York City Marathon has long boasted the largest women's marathon field in the world (currently about 5,700). NYRRC events have set the stage for dramatic achievements among women runners, including world best times for the 10k and 10 miles and landmark sub-3:00 and sub-2:30 times in the marathon. And to support women's participation in the sport, the New Runner/New Racer clinics, pregnancy clinics, masters clinics, and the Mother's Day Tune-Up run for women and little girls are also conducted by the club.

> The Mini has been unique in its ability to generate excitement about ancillary events. One is the Mother's Day Mini Tune-Up and Pee Wee run. The other events are the Mini clinics. These clinics are a natural outgrowth of the Mini's success. The most enduring and popular is the New Runner/New Racer Clinic. Fifteen hundred women take part every year in this clinic, which features elite athletes, nutritionists, and running and exercise instruction. This is one of the most effective clinics the club conducts. I need only watch it every year to realize that, and to chat with some of the participants. Eight years ago, for example, I met a woman at the New Runner Clinic. She was on the chubby side, and awed that people could run a few laps of a hotel conference room. Since then, her life has radically changed. She has had a couple of children, and she's also run three or four marathons, breaking four hours for the distance.
>
> —Fred Lebow

The impact of women's running is felt off the roads as well and is now a part of the consciousness of changing times. Prominent women runners such as Nina Kuscsik, Kathrine Switzer, and Grete Waitz have been instrumental in effecting athletic and social change. After winning the 1979 New York City Marathon, Grete Waitz was the subject of a *New York Times* editorial calling for equality in women's running. The fact that she made the editorial as well as the sports pages illustrates the social significance of her achievements.

Where (and When) It All Began

By 1971, the second year of the New York City Marathon, women were making dramatic inroads into the male-dominated world of road running. That year, the first two women to finish the race, Beth Bonner and Nina Kuscsik, also became the fastest women in the world, and the first to break three hours. (In the 1979 New York City Marathon, Grete Waitz became the first woman in the world to break 2:30.) However, in 1971 women were not officially permitted to compete in distance races with men. The irony, and the disparity, became too great. It motivated Fred Lebow, Kathrine Switzer, Nina Kuscsik, and others to launch a women's-only race. Lebow and company recruited in schools, bars, and even among Playboy bunnies. The first Women's Mini Marathon (named for the miniskirt, which was then in vogue) drew 78 women— a huge turnout for the time. The Playboy bunnies didn't run the distance, but they generated much-desired publicity. Controversial—and sexist—as this might seem now, Fred Lebow understood even then the need for media exposure to advance the sport. And if the bunnies were an insult, real injury was added when, at a press conference for the event, Kuscsik and Switzer were asked by the media to pose with their dresses hiked up over their knees. They refused. Today, the Advil Mini Marathon, a world-renowned event, is broadcast on network television. Bunnies and miniskirts have long been superseded by a gripping athletic competition.

> The New York Road Runners Club was the first organization to allow women to participate legally in a marathon. But it didn't happen easily, or with even a fraction of the numbers of participants we have today. Once a few women showed the world what they could do, women's running really caught on.
>
> In the early 1970s, Johnson Wax made a women's shaving cream called Crazylegs. The company telephoned me, wanting to promote its product with a women's marathon. "But there are only two women who run the marathon!" I explained to them.
>
> How about a Mini Marathon? I suggested. The word "mini" was in vogue then. But even with the distance shortened to six miles (it later became 10k, 6.2 miles), it took every bit of creative energy we could muster just to recruit 78 entrants in the first Crazylegs Mini Marathon. Kathrine Switzer and I went to bars—the only places we knew to meet women—and handed out race fliers.
>
> When Bonne Bell got involved in the Mini in 1974, the event grew dramatically. It went from hundreds to thousands. To this day, the question comes up: How can we get thousands of women to run this race, when only hundreds come out for a mixed race at the same distance? I think it's because for many women there is a special camaraderie that is part of the Mini. It is their exclusive event. They feel it is their showcase, and rightfully so.

> At the time we first held what is today the Advil Mini Marathon, women in sports, including running, were not accepted. That means socially, as well as politically—by the governing body of the sport. Today women's running is both socially and commercially viable. Major sponsors support the Mini, and network ABC-TV broadcasts it around the country. Partly as a result of women's mass participation in road races like the Mini, the first women's Olympic marathon took place in the 1984 Games.
>
> —Fred Lebow

In 1972, the six women in the New York City Marathon, led by Nina Kuscsik, staged a sit-down strike, protesting a ruling by the Amateur Athletic Union (AAU), the governing body of the sport, that required their race to begin ten minutes before the men's. When the ten minutes elapsed, the women got up and ran with the men. The AAU added 10 minutes to their finishing times. Kuscsik launched a lawsuit against the AAU. Simultaneous starts for men and women soon became legal. In addition, the Trails End Marathon in Oregon also filed suit against the AAU for requiring that women, but not men, have a physical exam before running that race.

Back in 1967, Kathrine Switzer symbolically heightened the struggle for women's equality—both as athletes and as human beings. Switzer signed up for the Boston Marathon as K. V. Switzer, got a number, and attempted to run—until she encountered race official Jock Semple, who tried to pull her off the course. Switzer went on to finish that race, win the New York City Marathon, and make a career in women's running and sports.

> I began running when I was 13, as part of an effort to make the school field hockey team. The truth is, I wanted to be a cheerleader, but my parents wouldn't stand for it. My father told me, "Life is to participate, not to spectate." He suggested I play field hockey, and military man that he was, he recommended I get in shape by running. I began doing one mile a day, every day.
>
> Immediately, I learned a basic rule of this sport—and of any endeavor—some days are good, some bad. I had to persevere.
>
> Running became my secret weapon. I breezed through team

practices with abundant energy. I reasoned that if one mile was good, three miles must be better. Eventually I became disappointed with team sports and decided to quit and focus on being a runner. When a coach at Lynchburg College saw me circling the track, he asked if I would serve as a last-minute substitute for a male runner on the team. I caused pandemonium at the small Virginia school. . . a prelude to the incident with which I will forever be associated.

I had heard of the Boston Marathon; Roberta Gibb had run it. With the help of coach and friend Arnie Briggs, who had run the race 16 times, I prepared myself by training 10 miles a day, and even once ran the entire marathon distance to convince a then-skeptical Arnie that "even though I was a woman," I could go the 26.2 miles. To this day, the event is prominent in my mind: The shock and fear when race official Jock Semple attempted to pull me off... the course and my boyfriend fending him off. Fortunately I was able to complete the race.

—Kathrine Switzer

"I first heard about Kathrine Switzer the way most people did: through the famous Boston Marathon story," Fred Lebow recalled. "At that time, women's running—not to mention women running a marathon—was just not part of the general consciousness."

Kathrine ran one of the NYRRC's early Women's Mini Marathon races, and came in the top five. She went on to win the New York City Marathon in 1974 by the widest margin of any victor (man or woman) in the history of the race: 27 minutes, 14 seconds.

"I remember that Kathy ran that race in a tennis skirt, and that she was part of the first television coverage ever broadcast of the New York City Marathon. She was interviewed by Donna DeVarona. Today they are both part of the three-hour network ABC-TV broadcast of the race," Lebow explains.

After winning the New York City Marathon, Kathrine established herself as a spokesperson for running, and in 1977 became head of the (now defunct) Avon International Running Circuit.

In 1978, the first Avon Marathon, with 124 women, was held in Atlanta. By the end of the circuit in 1985, events had been conducted in 27 countries with over 1 million women. In one race alone, a 1983 event in São Paulo, Brazil, 11,000 women ran. At that point it was the largest women's race ever held.

"Particularly in non-Western countries, the Avon races went against local culture, where women competing in a running event was not deemed socially acceptable. But women did participate—and with great joy,"saya Switzer.

"Avon's involvement in organizing events with so many foreign federations gave us the power to finally negotiate with the International Olympic Committee (IOC) and the International Amateur Athletic Federation to open running events to women competitors," Switzer says. "I think the Olympic women's marathon would eventually have happened, but I believe it was hastened by the Avon women's running circuit."

The Avon Marathon in London in 1980 fulfilled all the Olympic requirements set by the IOC for inclusion of an event in the Olympic Games at the time. Those requirements specified that a sport be practiced in 25 countries and on three continents. In this one race, 27 countries and five continents were represented. This event—which became the prototype for the London Marathon—was ground-breaking in yet another way. It was the first time in history that the streets of London were closed for a sporting event. Switzer recalls the race with satisfaction. "When I watched the women running across the Westminster Bridge, and realized the London streets were closed to accommodate them, I knew we were going to see the first women's Olympic marathon in 1984."

Over the years, Kathrine Switzer has also worked closely with the NYRRC. "After all," she says, "the women's running movement would never have happened without Fred Lebow. The Boston Marathon was certainly a catalyst, but the truth is, the core of the women's running movement was based in New York, with the initiative and support of the NYRRC."

In 1971, Kathrine Switzer collaborated with Lebow and Nina Kuscsik to make women's running "official." They dispelled the myths that prevented women from taking up the challenge—that running would, as Switzer says, cause overly muscular legs, body hair growth, and even infertility!

Like Switzer, Nina Kuscsik ran against the odds in her pursuit of the sport.

"My first marathon was Boston in 1969," she explains. "I entered just like the other 'illegal' women at that time—by jumping out of the bushes near the start at the last minute and by hiding among the men runners. I used to fantasize about a legion of women runners in pink T-shirts bearing the slogan 'Long Island Garden Club.' Women could and should be runners and still be able to drink tea at the Garden Club."

In the early 1970s, with the help and encouragement of Vince Chiappetta and Aldo Scandurra, Kuscsik read the running rule books and attended AAU meetings. "This was the beginning of the era of NOW (the National Organization for Women) and women's consciousness-raising," she explains. "For me, it was the beginning of a 20-year-long fight to rewrite the rules of running."

> Several years ago, the Women's Mini Marathon was run on a horribly hot and humid day. There were nearly 7000 women in the field. At the medical area at the finish, we treated 300 women. One of the members of the press asked me, "Should the race have been called off?" "Why?" I answered. "Because we treated a mere 300 women? That means that 6700 knew what to do."
>
> —Joe Weisenfeld, D.P.M.

In 1972, Kuscsik helped organize the sit-down strike at the New York City Marathon. All the runners, including men, supported the protest, and signed a petition on the starting line arguing for a common start. There were two victories that day: Kuscsik's winning time of 3:08:42 and an announcement from the parks commissioner in New York City saying that races from then on would be started with the command "Ladies and gentlemen, on your marks."

A major turning point for women's running was in 1976, when the men's and women's national championships were combined for the first time, claims Francie Larrieu Smith, "The women stole the show. The women's races were the most competitive. Women broke records. In addition, we looked good in our 'bun huggers'!" she says.

> There are so many levels to the development of women's running. In those early days, women got together maybe to play bridge, but they didn't get together and talk about their feelings or their problems. Now this is commonly done, but it wasn't back then. But

running was a special opportunity to do that. Just as it is today, it was a way of getting together. You had miles to go, and you could talk. You made special friendships over the miles.

I remember running a 50-mile race in 1977, and thinking that if I had a different girlfriend to escort me on a bike for those 9.5-mile loops, it would be like having separate telephone conversations with friends. Actually it was good thing I didn't try that, as I needed my concentration to run an American record, and I didn't want to be accused of being paced!

—Nina Kuscsik

Are women runners more equal with men now? "Yes," says Kuscsik, "but men have had to come a long way, too. In the early days, male runners were simply considered weird. So the sport didn't just open up for women, it also changed for all runners."

Is a woman different from a man? Of course, that's physiology. But there's more to an athlete than physiology. Since I've been fortunate to coach a good group of female runners, I have noticed other differences between them and the men I coach.

I'm a fairly new coach, so I'll speak here as an athlete as well. In terms of attitude, at least among the athletes I encounter, a top woman runner is without a doubt more driven and focused on what she wants to achieve than a male. People may argue with this, but thus far this is true to my experience. This is true as well of the women who come into my store who are overweight or have just had a baby. Once they make a commitment to train, they are amazingly dedicated.

As a male and an athlete talking, I can testify that we runners know about pain. But women are incredibly tough; they can stay at it. Perhaps I'm overstating it, but over the past three years, I have seen that my most dedicated athletes are women. What makes them tougher? Is it the dedication, pain threshold, the psyche of a woman? It's not just one of those traits; it's probably all of them.

—Tom Fleming

But women have come to the sport and train for the sport in different ways than men. For instance, Nina Kuscsik believes the aerobic dance movement of the early 1970s indirectly promoted jogging to improve appearance, thus legitimizing women's running. More directly, the first Women's Mini Marathon, and the first women's marathon, the Avon Marathon in Atlanta in 1978, offered women runners from all corners of the earth their own special events. And, of course, money has changed the sport, Kuscsik points out. Women can actually earn a living by running—albeit very few. And for the casual runner, the exposure of top women runners has placed running among legitimate female pastimes—perhaps like bridge and mah-jongg for generations before.

"There are so many reasons why people run," says Kuscsik. "My advice is to go into it with an open mind. You go to school to get an education, but you can end up getting more of an education from the people you meet than the books you read. The same is true in running. There is untold fulfillment to be gained from the sport, even beyond the exercise angle."

Women's Health

Women's Health Issues and Concerns

Based on personal and professional experience, Mona Shangold, M.D., offers the following information on the variety of health issues and concerns of women runners.

Exercise is even more important for women than for men. This fact runs contrary to the social conditioning women once received long ago—the same conditioning many are still receiving today not only in developing countries but also in the United States. Fortunately, many girls and women have accepted the scientific evidence that exercise is positive. As a result, more women are exercising today than ever before, and the number of exercising women is increasing steadily. The girls who were once labeled with the unflattering term "tomboy" are now addressed with the complimentary term "athlete."

Although more women are exercising now than ever before, an even greater number should be exercising. Regular exercise decreases susceptibility to osteoporosis and obesity—two conditions that are more common among women than among men. Both aerobic and resistance exercise strengthen bones, and both types also help to prevent fat accumulation. Aerobic activities include running, brisk walking, biking, and swimming. Resistance activities include weight training with free weights or machines.

441

Osteoporosis

As humans age, muscles and bones shrink and weaken. This change occurs in both men and women, but the consequences are more serious in women. At any age, the average woman has thinner and weaker bones and smaller and weaker muscles compared to the average man. Losing bone density puts many women into the danger zone in which bones break easily. Although both men and women lose bone with aging, bone loss is greatly accelerated after menopause, when women lose the supply of estrogen that previously protected their bones. Although exercise helps to strengthen bones, it is not as effective as estrogen. (That is why the bones of athletes shrink and weaken if they stop menstruating at any age, as will be discussed later.)

> Women runners are at a definite advantage over their sedentary counterparts. The average sedentary woman in her 30s has 33 percent body fat; in her 60s, 42 percent. By contrast, women runners in their 40s average 22 percent body fat, while those in their 60s average only 26 percent.
>
> —Fitness Features

Weight Gain

Humans get fatter with age, and exercise is the best way to minimize a growing girth. Fat accumulates for several reasons, but mainly because the metabolism slows down. Resting metabolism depends on muscle tissue mass. Aerobic and resistance exercise add and strengthen muscles, speeding up resting metabolism and total metabolism. As a result, more calories are burned, even while sleeping! Because the average woman has less muscle tissue than the average man, and because she usually does less to maintain her muscles, she has a more dramatic decline in her metabolism and adds fat with increasing ease. Most women don't realize that adding muscle will both speed the metabolism and make it easier to do routine chores (e.g., carrying groceries, packages, or luggage).

> When I entered my first race, the 1977 New York City Marathon, I had a chance to chat with a lot of women runners at the starting

area. Many were discussing gynecologic problems that had developed during training. When I revealed that I was a gynecologist, I was overwhelmed with questions about personal problems. I realized that very little was known or discussed about gynecologic problems in runners. Very few doctors had written about these issues prior to that time, and very few women were discussing such problems. The small numbers of women who had been exercising before that time had aroused relatively little interest and promoted few scientific investigations.

I devoted most of my fellowship in reproductive endocrinology to studying the effects of exercise on reproductive function. Some of my studies included questionnaires I distributed to women entering the 1979 New York City Marathon and measurements of hormone concentrations in women runners. (Although I had run the New York City Marathon in 1977 and 1978, the work connected with my study prevented me from entering in 1979.) We were the first to report that luteal phase deficiency, a condition associated with infertility, is more common among runners than among the general population.

Doing more research and speaking to more women stimulated further interest and other questions to answer. Thus, I embarked upon a career in a new field that has grown appreciably since then: sports gynecology. Several hundred doctors now belong to the Sports Gynecology Society of the American College of Obstetricians and Gynecologists, all of whom provide gynecologic care to women who exercise and encourage sedentary women to exercise.

—Mona Shangold, M.D.

Menstrual Irregularity and Amenorrhea (Absence of Menstruation)

Any woman who bleeds more often than every 23 days or less often than every 35 days needs to be evaluated and probably treated for menstrual irregularity. Menstrual irregularity and amenorrhea are higher among women athletes than among the general female population for various reasons, including weight loss, fat loss, alterations in diet, nutritional inadequacy, physical or emotional stress, and changes in hormonal balance. However, despite the higher prevalence of menstrual dysfunction in athletes, it is dangerous to assume that exercise is the culprit. Athletes develop the same conditions that cause menstrual dysfunction in nonathletes, and some of these are serious. Although most athletes with irregular periods or amenorrhea will be found to have no serious condition responsible, a thorough evaluation—including blood tests—is needed to determine whether the cause is serious.

After completion of this evaluation, *all* who have the problem more than a few months (four to six months) should be treated with hormones to replace what their bodies are not making. Of course, they should continue to exercise.

Although many athletes seem to have an aversion to taking hormones, women who are deficient in estrogen have been found to lose bone mass at an increased rate and may lose a significant amount of bone when they have this condition. For this reason, treatment is recommended before six months have passed. Any athlete who has this condition for three years or longer will have lost more than she can regain.

Delay of Menarche

Athletes tend to experience menarche (the first menstrual period) at a later age than sedentary girls. Delayed menarche isn't harmful unless it occurs after age 18. Any girl who hasn't begun to menstruate by the age of 16 should be evaluated and possibly treated. Treatment should definitely be started by the age of 18, if menstruation hasn't started by that time. Although exercise and delayed menarch are related, it isn't clear which is cause and which is effect. It is likely that heavy exercise delays menarche and that delayed menarche improves athletic success.

Pregnancy

Much has been made over the years of a woman's ability to continue running—even training—during pregnancy. It began nearly a decade ago with the case of Ingrid Kristiansen, who, not realizing she was pregnant, continued to train and race for the first five months of her first pregnancy. She even ran a marathon. However, Kristiansen later claimed she never would have done so if she had known she was pregnant.

Once upon a time, pregnant women were advised to avoid exercise.

It is now known that this recommendation was based on fear and lack of data. It now appears that it is safe to continue exercising throughout pregnancy as long as the pregnancy is normal and uncomplicated.

Kristiansen made a quick return to top form shortly after giving birth. Other women, such as Liz McColgan, the 1991 world champion at 10,000 meters and 1991 New York City Marathon winner, did so as well.

My philosophy is based on two basic truths about exercise and pregnancy. The first is that we are all an experiment of one. It hasn't been long since pregnancy has been considered a healthy condition and not an illness during which one should remain inactive. And it hasn't been long since a generation of athletic women has been testing this new style of life during pregnancy. The second truth is that you should listen to your body with new and more rigorous intensity. Fatigue and pain mean different things now. They may come from hormonal changes, or muscles and tendons that you never knew existed before. And you're a different person in other obvious physical ways—with a belly growing in front of you. Remember that for nine months, your body is not your own. You have given it to someone else.

You have spent a good many years teaching yourself the discipline of pushing through pain and discomfort to achieve your athletic goals. Now you have to reverse that thinking. Being disciplined during pregnancy isn't pushing through pain and fatigue but forcing yourself to stop, do less, rest.

Some people feel good running up to the day of delivery, and others, like me, reach a point where it doesn't feel right. That doesn't mean to stop exercising. For instance, I combined swimming, race walking, stationary cycling, and light weight lifting, alternatives I had prepared for well in advance.

Gestation takes nine months, but childrearing is forever. One of the unexpected pleasures of my child's development is her identification with running. She knows that when Mom or Dad are out in the morning, they are "running." When she sees pictures of runners, she says "Mommy" or "Daddy." And when she runs, as all children do, and I run along with her, I realize the legacy I want to give her. It's not necessarily to run a sub-40-minute or even a sub-32-minute 10k—although that's fine, if she wants to—but an appreciation of being physically active; of an ability to use her body while more fully experiencing the elements of sun, rain, and wind. And it is this message I want to give her: that if I am fit and strong on the outside, I strive to be fit and strong on the inside—of heart, soul, and mind.

—Gloria Averbuch, 1988

These women illustrate the results of one study that suggests that physically fit women may actually be able to carry out the added work load of pregnancy, labor, and delivery with greater ease to both themselves and their fetuses than sedentary women.

Below are important considerations for pregnant exercisers.

1. *Blood Distribution.* Although as yet unproven, blood is less likely to be diverted away from the fetus when exercise is kept at low intensity. Thus, women planning to exercise during pregnancy should attain a high level of fitness prior to becoming pregnant, and to remain fit throughout the pregnancy, because exertion is relatively easier for a fit woman. Training should not begin for the first time during pregnancy. Since high-intensity exercise is more likely to divert blood flow from the pregnant uterus, it is safest to avoid intense exertion (like speedwork). A proper cooldown after exercise is also important, and safer than stopping abruptly. This will help to maintain adequate blood flow to the baby during this risky time.

2. *Temperature.* In the absence of definitive data, it is wisest for pregnant women to avoid excessive heat accumulation during exercise. High temperatures have been shown to be harmful to the fetus, principally in animals, but probably in humans, too. Keeping a close watch on body temperature is particularly important for fetal development during the first trimester. Heat accumulation can be avoided by such measures as exercising at cooler times of day, exercising for shorter durations in each session, wearing lighter clothing, and maintaining adequate hydration. A pregnant woman should exercise at a comfortable intensity, based on perceived exertion and disregarding heart rate.

Check rectal temperature immediately at the end of exercise. It should be 101 degrees Fahrenheit, or less. The maximum safe temperature limit has not yet been determined.

3. *Nutrition*. Pregnant women who continue to exercise must provide enough calories and nutrients for themselves, their exercise, and their pregnancy. Pregnant women require more protein, more calories, and more of many vitamins and minerals than non-pregnant women. However, only thiamine, niacin, riboflavin, and pantothenic acid are needed in higher quantities because of exercise. A balanced diet supplying sufficient calories will provide enough of these vitamins and minerals. All pregnant women need more calcium, more iron, and higher amounts of many vitamins than they do when not pregnant. Most of them will benefit from prenatal vitamin supplements, as well as additional calcium and iron supplements to meet these needs. It is also important for pregnant exercisers to drink extra fluid to replace losses and to prevent excess heat accumulation.

According to *Running & FitNews*, one study showed that calcium absorption from kale is higher than that from milk. Other calcium-rich vegetables include broccoli, collard greens, mustard greens, and turnip greens. Other nondairy sources of calcium are tofu, canned salmon, and sardines with the bones. Although dietary calcium is preferable to supplements, Tums is also a source, as is calcium-enriched orange juice.

If you're taking your calcium and iron supplements at the same time (or within about one hour of each other), you could be reducing the absorption of the iron. Take calcium before bedtime, or take half the dose between breakfast and lunch and the rest before you go to bed.

Iron is best absorbed when taken on an empty stomach along with vitamin C—from orange juice, for example. However, many people experience stomach pain when they take iron supplements on an empty stomach. They are often advised to take iron with their meals.

If you're a woman who can't stand the cold, you may not be getting enough iron. A woman's ability to regulate her body temperature may depend on the amount of iron in her diet. This is the conclusion of a Department of Agriculture study quoted in *Environmental Nutrition*. The effect of iron depletion on temperature regulation occurs before iron deficiency and anemia are diagnosed. Six women were tested in a temperature-regulated chamber, a cool 64 degrees, before and after iron supplementation. It was found that before supplementation, the women's internal temperature and external skin temperature were much lower than when tested after supplementation.

—Fitness Features

Although most obstetricians usually advise pregnant women to gain 30 to 35 pounds, they do not know whether this recommendation is appropriate for exercisers. Until more precise recommendations are established, this amount seems reasonable. No one knows if pregnant exercisers should gain more, less, or the same amount as sedentary pregnant women. The amount a woman should gain probably depends on many factors, including the change in her exercise habits, and when, during pregnancy, this change takes place. Women who stop exercising during pregnancy will gain more weight and have heavier babies than they would have if they had continued exercising throughout pregnancy.

When I discovered I was pregnant, I made a decision to take almost a complete break from running. I don't agree with training hard or racing during pregnancy. I don't believe it is good for the fetus. I only ran when I felt like it; mostly I went for walks. I didn't bike or swim. In fact, I didn't exercise much at all. I gained 33 pounds during my pregnancy. I had never weighed more than 107 pounds.

Our daughter was born in October 1990. The birth was surprisingly easy. Four and a half hours after I got to the hospital, Emma arrived, weighing seven pounds, three ounces. I took my time getting back to running. I wanted to get used to having her—and get enough sleep.

A couple of weeks after the birth, I started jogging. That means I would jog 200 meters and then walk. It really hurt. That shocked me. Also, I felt uncoordinated. Because of the weight difference, my center of gravity was off. I took it easy, because I wanted to give my body time to adjust.

I'd love to have a few more children. After competing in the Olympics in 1992, I'll run one or two marathons, and have another baby. Meanwhile, taking the time off running helped me mentally. I was getting stale. Now I'm a lot more focused. I have a strong desire to compete, to get out there and go up against the best women runners.

—Lisa Ondieki

Hunger is not always a good guide because pregnancy may cause reduced appetite. Pregnant exercisers should eat more than they ate prepregnancy. A consultation with a nutritionist and an obstetrician is a good idea.

It is reasonable for pregnant women to continue exercising in their customary aerobic sports at the same *perceived* level of exertion practiced prior to pregnancy. This will require a slower pace and perhaps a shorter session, since the pregnant woman is doing more work merely by being pregnant. If she exercises at her normal pace with the added weight of pregnancy, she will be doing even more work.

It is unwise to initiate an aerobic exercise program during pregnancy. Walking is as vigorous an activity as a woman should undertake during pregnancy if she was not previously an exerciser. After giving birth, a woman can probably resume exercising as soon as it can be done without pain. After a vaginal delivery, this may be as soon as one to three days for light exercise and five to seven days for heavy exercise. After a cesarean delivery, this may be as soon as 7 to 10 days for light exercise and 21 days for heavy exercise.

I ran throughout most of my pregnancy. During the second trimester (the fourth, fifth, and sixth months), running caused uterine contractions that began earlier in each run as the pregnancy advanced. By the end of the sixth month, I stopped running altogether, partly because dressing for winter running took longer than the duration of each running session that was interrupted by contractions, and mainly because I didn't know whether the contractions were significant or dangerous. (I wanted a healthy child and wasn't willing to do anything that might jeopardize my chance of having one.) In retrospect, the contractions probably were not of significance, but I had no way to know that at the time. My son was born by cesarean delivery, primarily because of his large size (nine pounds at birth). Fortunately, he was and has continued to be very healthy. I resumed lifting weights eight days after his birth and resumed running 10 days after his birth.

—Mona Shangold, M.D.

Weight training may safely be practiced by all pregnant women with normal, uncomplicated pregnancies, even if they have not previously done it. The gains in muscle and bone strength from weight training may offer many benefits. In addition to bone strength, stronger muscles will suffer less from the strain of the added weight of pregnancy and the altered center of gravity, theoretically decreasing the risk of low back pain and other types of muscular aches and pains. There is no evidence that weight training, when practiced with proper form, is dangerous for pregnant women. In fact, some women runners have chosen to concentrate on weight training while pregnant, preferring to maintain muscle tone, which cannot be achieved as well with the light amount of running done during pregnancy. Some also find it more comfortable during pregnancy than running. Another benefit is variety. Pregnancy may be a good time for a woman runner to experiment with cross training, and weight training falls into that category.

I struggle with the decision to sacrifice training for my children, particularly when I want to run a full marathon. I know I need to rest more, but I don't want to give up time with the children. When I'm training hard, I'm a bear. My disposition changes; I get more irritable. So I vacillate.

You gain all kinds of strengths with motherhood. I lost mental strength when motherhood was new to me. Now that strength is back. I'm always on a fine line, trying to balance my career with my responsibilities as a mother. But I know what I want in the end. Jimmy Connors once said he wishes his children could have seen him in his prime. I hope my children remember me being in my prime as a mother, not as a runner.

—Joan Samuelson

Breast Protection

Smaller-breasted women may prefer to run without a bra, while other women may prefer to exercise with a bra that provides good support. The breast is subject to considerable motion during vigorous exercise, and while uncomfortable, this movement is not harmful to women with large breasts.

Dysmenorrhea

Menstrual cramps can be a bother to an athlete, interfering significantly with performance. However, these days, and in most cases, disabling pain is totally preventable. Several medications are available, by prescription and over the counter, but aspirin and ibuprofen should never be taken together. Ibuprofen is more effective for this pain than aspirin. For severe pain, a woman should try ibuprofen first. If this does not alleviate the pain, she may want to see her gynecologist for a prescription, such as Anaprox. Medication is usually required for only one or two days (at the onset of menstruation). Some women experience less dysmenorrhea during exercise, and some report less since they have been training regularly. Explanations for this remain mostly speculative.

Premenstrual Syndrome (PMS)

In one study, increased exercise was shown to decrease PMS, with greatest improvement noted in breast soreness and fluid retention. Athletes who are significantly inconvenienced may benefit from consulting a gynecologist for evaluation and treatment. Several drugs have been shown to be effective for this condition, but all of them have side effects.

When it comes to women and exercise, sports medicine specialists generally focus their concern on amenorrhea. Needless to say, there's another group of female athletes who also deserve special attention—the athletes who do menstruate regularly. Approximately 30 percent of these women suffer from PMS (premenstrual syndrome) and experience one of several of the nineteen identified PMS symptoms.

Fatigue, hunger, and intense cravings for chocolates and carbohydrates in any form are very common PMS symptoms. Many women can tell the time of the month by their low energy levels and wild eating habits. Premenstrually, they may boost themselves up by devouring bagfuls of candy and dozens of cookies, in addition to bran muffins, bread, and bagels. A woman's dietary intake can certainly vary throughout the month!

In *Physiology and Behavior*, Stephanie Dalvit-McPhillips verified this pattern, reporting that a complex interplay of hormonal changes seems to influence food choices. Premenstrually, high levels of estrogen may be linked with carbohydrate cravings that result in greater carbohydrate consumption. Her subjects ate about 500 more calories per day during the 10 premenstrual days, as compared to the 10 days postmenstrual—with most of the calories derived from carbohydrate foods.

Women may crave carbohydrates not only because of hormonal fluctuations, but also because they are physiologically hungrier. Hunger tends to create sweet cravings. Premenstrually, a woman's metabolic rate may increase by 200 to 500 calories—the equivalent of an additional meal! However, most women athletes—being very weight-conscious—try to cut back on calories, since they are feeling fat from premenstrual bloat and water weight gain. The result: double deprivation (higher caloric needs plus restricted caloric intake), and the craving for sweets becomes overwhelming.

To control the premenstrual cravings, a woman can experiment with adding more carbohydrate-calories at breakfast and lunch. For example, by eating an additional bran muffin at breakfast, she'll curb the nagging hunger that she'd otherwise resolve with candy that afternoon. She'll abate the PMS sugar splurges as well as other symptoms such as irritability, headache, fatigue, depression, and mood swings. She'll have more energy for exercise and better enjoy her training buddies, rather than being cranky with them.

—Nancy Clark, M.S., R.D.

Many runners believe that running will protect them from the undesirable effects of aging and menopause. Although regular exercise can retard several aspects of the aging process, it cannot compensate for the estrogen deficiency that follows menopause.

Menopause—a woman's final menstrual period—occurs when the ovaries run out of functioning eggs. For approximately five years before her last period and about five years afterward, she passes through the *climacteric*—a time when her hormone levels are different from the levels before and after. During this transition time, many women have bothersome hot flashes. Estrogen is the most effective way to treat hot flashes. Exercise has no effect on these symptoms.

After menopause, a woman's estrogen levels are lower than they were during her reproductive years. This reduced estrogen level accelerates bone loss, the most serious problem that follows menopause. Although running has a beneficial effect on bone density, it is not beneficial enough to compensate for an estrogen deficiency—in both young amenorrheic athletes and in older menopausal women. Many studies have shown that athletes with low estrogen levels lose bone density at any age, and the bone loss is proportional to the duration of estrogen deficiency.

Low levels of estrogen also cause many menopausal women to experience vaginal dryness. Some may have no symptoms, but others are greatly bothered by vaginal irritation, burning during urination, and/or pain during intercourse. Estrogen therapy is the most effective treatment for this problem. Again, exercise has no effect.

Exercise may reduce your risk of some female cancers. Rose Frisch, Ph.D., a researcher at Harvard University, has found that women who exercise are generally leaner than their sedentary counterparts. Says Frisch in *Runner's World* magazine, "Leaner women tend to produce a form of estrogen that is less potent and less likely to stimulate uterine and breast cancer cells to divide actively." Translated, this means less risk of cancer.

—Fitness Features

Two other menopausal problems may receive benefit from both exercise and estrogen: cardiovascular disease and depression. After menopause, women have a higher risk of heart disease (compared to their risk before menopause), partly due to estrogen deficiency and partly due to the aging process and the cumulative effects of an adverse style of life. Because most runners probably have a reduced risk of heart disease compared to sedentary women of the same age, they may be less in need of estrogen for this particular indication.

Similarly, both estrogen and exercise may cause mood elevation in some women. In fact, some depressed runners may be treating themselves unknowingly. While some are no longer depressed because they run regularly, some who are depressed despite regular running may get additional benefit from estrogen. Anyone with suspected heart disease or suspected depression should consult a physician before considering exercise or estrogen as therapy.

It is unfortunate that so many runners have an aversion to taking medication, even when that treatment is advisable. It is also unfortunate that some runners believe they are indestructible and immune to disease. The estrogen deficiency that follows menopause increases every woman's risk of developing osteoporosis. To reduce this risk, most women should take estrogen, unless they have a strong contraindication (e.g., breast cancer, endometrial cancer, certain clotting disorders, previous thrombophlebitis, or active liver disease). Any woman who has a uterus and takes estrogen should also take progesterone, to protect her endometrium (the lining of her uterus). Women who have had a hysterectomy may safely take estrogen alone.

Don't view estrogen as an enemy. It is much more likely to be your friend. Estrogen deficiency is much more dangerous than estrogen treatment, which will probably reduce your risks of several diseases and improve the quality of your life.

Nutrition

Although women athletes have nutritional needs similar to those of male athletes of the same size, they are more likely than men to require calcium and iron supplementation.

The average woman's diet is deficient in calcium. Women require at least 1000 mg. of calcium daily; women deficient in estrogen (as reflected by amenorrhea or menopause) require at least 1500 mg. of calcium daily. Inadequate dietary calcium hastens bone loss, which may progress to osteoporosis. Most women need supplementation to obtain the proper amount of calcium.

The average woman's diet is also deficient in iron. Since women lose iron in the process of menstruation and often ingest inadequate amounts in their diet, many women are iron-deficient. Iron deficiency can impair athletic performance, even in the absence of anemia. The blood test that detects anemia does not measure iron stores. The iron stores in one's liver, spleen, and bone marrow can be deficient (the adequacy of iron stores is assessed by measuring blood ferritin), even though a woman has a normal amount of iron in her red blood cells (detected by measuring hemoglobin or hematocrit). Because of the prevalence of iron deficiency among women, it is reasonable for women to take iron supplements.

The only nutrients athletes require in greater quantities than sedentary women are thiamine, niacin, riboflavin, and pantothenic acid. These requirements can usually be met from a balanced diet supplying enough calories.

Part 11: Walking

11

Walking for
Health, Fitness,
and Competition

You've got to walk before you can run. That's how it is for toddlers, and for some adults as well, including beginners, injured runners, and converts to this road-related activity.

Sports journalist and champion race walker Elliott Denman knows just about everything there is to know about walking—for recreation, fitness, or competition. His advice follows:

One step at a time. There is no other way to go. Aspiring walkers of whatever motivation—health, fitness, recreation, competition, or any combination thereof—may start off with the left or the right foot. But the benefits are only there for those who do it the right way from that point on. That means going slowly before learning to go quickly. That means finding a way to make walking a central phase of an active style of life. And that means persevering. In walking as in other aspects of life, very few positive developments result from short-range planning.

While there is no such thing as "the right way" to walking success, there certainly are many options. Many walk only for the sheer health of it or to feel good about themselves by losing weight or managing stress. Some walk for adventure. And some others may want to compete. A handful actually plunge into serious training programs, with such major goals as the walking events in the Olympic Games, World Championships, and World Cup serving as inspiration.

Health and Fitness Walking

One of America's greatest testaments to "wellness through walking" is Henry Laskau of Coconut Creek, Florida. As a younger man, he literally walked out of Hitler's Germany and built a new life in the United States. He went on to represent the United States in walking at three Olympic Games, win the incredible total of 42 national championships, and walk to a heap of records.

Since his retirement, and moving from New York to Florida, Laskau has spent much of his time spreading the gospel of health and fitness walking. His clinics and lectures on walking have developed a large following in the Sunshine State, and Florida has become one of the nation's most walker-friendly states.

"While walking is certainly a basic skill that is part of our daily lives, walking for fitness is very different from recreational walking," Laskau emphasizes. According to Laskau—now in his mid-70s but still in the best of shape—it's all in learning proper technique and continuing to work on it.

"Technique is the single most critical element in learning a new sport or exercise program," he says. "Proper execution of technique guarantees achievement of total personal potential, maximizes walking's benefits, and prevents injuries. Technique is knowing what is supposed to happen during the activity and mentally projecting the physical movement while performing it." Walking, to Laskau, is "a learned, coordinated movement." Basically, it involves "synchronizing your body to achieve close coordination of your heel/toe activity, while utilizing your arm positioning and swing to generate propulsion."

"It's a smooth, gliding motion; when performed properly it's an effortless, well-timed, synchronized movement." Once you've "got it," you'll soon be hooked, Laskau nearly guarantees.

California chiropractor Paula Kash echoes virtually all of Laskau's statements. She's seen walking do so many positive things for those who do it, and do it properly. "Get your technique down," she says, and walking will "increase cardiovascular health, burn calories, and firm muscles. Enhance posture and coordination by walking tall and creating an overall feeling of well-being." What to wear? It begins at the bottom. Most important, says Kash, are "comfortable shoes with good support. The key word is comfort, for freedom of movement."

A particular advantage of walking is its low injury rate. Bob Carlson of Denver is a veteran walker, walking coach, and walking activist. Among the points he continues to stress is that walkers break down far less frequently than runners.

> Walking may pose less of an injury risk than running, but surely running provides a better workout. Or does it? The Institute for Aerobics Research recently performed a six-month study of more than 100 young women to find out. What they discovered was that 12-minute-mile aerobic walkers, speeding along with an arm-swinging, hip-swaying gait, improved fitness as much as joggers. By covering three miles a day, five days a week, they boosted their fitness levels by 16 percent—almost twice as much as brisk walkers and four times more than strollers.
>
> But according to *Vogue* magazine, the researchers were especially encouraged to see that all walkers, at whatever pace, showed about the same increase in HDL ("good" cholesterol) levels. Counts went up by as much as 6 percent.
>
> —Fitness Features

"I estimate from my own experience of never having the slightest injury from walking, but several hamstring and calf pulls from running, that there is a great difference in the injury potential of the two—maybe by a factor of six to one," says Carlson.

"A running injury can be traumatic," he continues, "causing a lay-off from training for a fair amount of time. A walker, even if he or she twists an ankle, is far less likely to have an injury bad enough to disrupt training for more than a few days.

"With excellent form and technique, a walker does not have to be in quite as good shape as a runner at the same level to be competitive as he or she gets older. A lot of this has to do with the pounding and mechanics of running, and the energy necessary to lift the body off the ground.

"These points should give heart to aging runners (and that's all of us). Maybe there is still hope for them if they are forced to hang up their running shoes for one reason or another."

Longevity

Harry Drazin of Interlaken, New Jersey, exemplifies the agelessness of walking. He is a walker for all seasons, a man who consistently leaps the generation gap. For many years, Drazin took excellent advantage of the network of boardwalks that dot the north New Jersey Shore area. He'd take regular walks through such towns as Asbury Park, Ocean Grove, and Belmar, breathing the invigorating salt air and delighting in an ever-changing variety of seaside vistas.

His outlook on walking changed dramatically about a decade ago. By this time he was a widower in his late 60s. Whereas walking once served as conditioning for his golf game, now he needed it as an activity he could plunge himself into.

"Walking benefits the mind as well as the body. You can start out pretty glum, from some episode the day before perhaps, but after a good walk, you can feel like a new person. When you're out walking, you can savor the sunrises, the sunsets, the oceans, the mountains, the scenery, the people. Runners may not have time for all that. They go by so quickly.

"A most thrilling day for me was the day I got started walking," said Drazin. "I'd played golf a lot and done some other activities, but I'd never done a sport like walking. After a two-, three-, or four-hour walk, not only do you meet so many other nice people, you also get the cardiovascular benefits. I'm 78 now, but I feel as good or better than I did in my 40s and 50s."

Harry Drazin has become a folk hero of sorts to other walkers. When he was knocked over by a stray bicyclist at the 14-mile mark of the New Jersey Waterfront Marathon several years ago, he refused to count himself out. Three weeks later, after a brief hospital stay and some extensive recuperation time, there he was, back on the course, completing the remaining 12.2 miles of the marathon on his own.

Like Drazin, Britisher Tebbs Lloyd Johnson—Lloyd, as he was known—is a legend in longevity. Johnson competed in the 50k walk at the 1948 London Olympic Games and placed a very strong third. He was 48 years old at the time. He set a British 50k record back in 1936 that took 20 years to beat. He was one of walking's greatest advertisements up until his death at 84 in 1984.

Competition and Camaraderie

New Yorker Nick Bdera has taken "that extra step," into competition walking. "When I was 30, I weighed 225 pounds and had a 40-inch waistline," said Bdera, an employee of the New York Road Runners Club. "I hated all sports. My idea of exercise was getting up to change channels on the television set."

But once he ran into Walkers Club of America director and East Side Track Club coach Howard Jacobson, Bdera's life began turning around. When he won the 1989 national 40-kilometer walking title, Jacobson said, "Nick's a product of our New York clinic program. He just got tired of his old self and decided to do something about it. He got on a fitness program and now he's a mainstay of our team." Now in his early 40s, Bdera continues to be a frequent race winner.

But competition isn't for everybody. There are many who choose not to run, or chase other walkers, either. Speed is never one of their aims, and racing is definitely not their thing. There is no great hurry to their walks. They take it all "in stride." Among them are the Volksmarchers, the mall walkers, the wellness walkers, and the adventure walkers.

Volksmarching—or "people's walking"—is of European origin but is making steady inroads throughout the United States. It is the ultimate mass participation event. Speed is no object, only enjoyment of the exercise. Distances are usually moderate, in the range of 10 to 20 kilometers (6.2 miles to 12.4 miles). Medals are given to all who complete the distance within modest time limits. Past and present military personnel are Volksmarching's most frequent enthusiasts. The recreation office at your nearest military installation is a good place to acquire more information on Volksmarching.

Your nearby shopping mall may be the newest "Main Street." The emergence of shopping malls for this new function has led to the creation of mall walkers' groups everywhere. Most frequently, the mall walkers are invited to stride out before the start of normal shopping hours. Some mall walking groups are highly organized, while others are more individually oriented. Check with your mall's management office for more information.

"Wellness" is the newest buzzword in the health-care industry. The message is finally being circulated that it's far better and more effective to do what's necessary to prevent illness than to attack a health problem after it's already developed. Walking has become one of the wellness field's mainstays. Hospitals, rehabilitation centers, and private health clubs all have their "wellness" walking groups. Again, check your local listings for more information on these programs if you're interested.

Another of walking's beauties is the way it fosters family togetherness. Avram and Marcia Shapiro of Adelphia, New Jersey, are good examples. Avram Shapiro, a distance runner in his mid-50s, got into walking for cross-training purposes. Now he's a nearly full-time competitor in walking events of all distances, and his running has taken a backseat.

His wife, Marcia, also took to the sport quickly, and now joins her husband on the starting line of walking events everywhere. They walked the 1990 New York City Marathon, and The Athletics Congress's 40-kilometer national championship race at Fort Monmouth, New Jersey.

After walking down the aisle, many couples keep right on walking together. The lesson is clear. Walking can serve as the cornerstone of a happy marriage. The sport of walking is populated by many couples. Leading U.S. competitive racers include Debbi and Don Lawrence, Holly and Paul Wick, and Michelle and Mike Rohl, all of Wisconsin; Tracey and Bobby Briggs of Washington, D.C.; and Wendy and Ray Sharp of Colorado. At the 1991 40K Nationals, Jeanne and Gerry Bocci of Michigan, Dorothy and John Sholeen of New York, and Marcia and Avram Shapiro of New Jersey walked their way to medals.

Walking into the Future

Walking is a growth industry. That's evident from the National Sporting Goods Association, whose numbers show that walking is positioned to make some very important strides through the 1990s. NSGA statistics revealed that in 1990, a total of 71.4 million Americans counted exercise walking as a major fitness activity and stepped out regularly. This was a huge advance from the 41.5 million walkers reported in a similar survey just five years earlier. Swimming (with 67.5 million participants) and bicycle riding (with 55.3 million) ranked second and third respectively.

Walking's Summit Meetings

The Olympic Games remain walking's ultimate summit. Two races for men, 20 kilometers (12.4 miles) and 50 kilometers (31 miles), and one for women, 10 kilometers (6.2 miles), are on the program of the quadrennial global spectacular. Walking has been an Olympic event for men since 1908, which means it predated now-established events such as the 5000- and 10,000-meter runs, the 4 × 100- and 4 × 400-meter relays, the decathlon, and the entire women's program.

In the early Olympic years, walking's racing distances changed frequently. The 50k has been a Games event since 1932, and its adherents call it the longest, toughest Olympic event of them all. Their arguments are persuasive. It is nearly five miles longer than the marathon run and usually takes at least an hour and a half longer than the marathon to complete. The 20k has been on the Olympic program since 1956, while the women's 10k made its Olympic debut in 1992.

What's Legal and What's Not

Judging has always been a major subject of discussion in walking. "Legal" walking has had many different definitions over the years. At the moment, TAC rules define walking as "a progression of steps so taken that unbroken contact with the ground is maintained." There are two major stipulations. First, "during the period of each step, the advancing foot of the walker must make contact with the ground before the rear foot leaves the ground." In other words, no hopping, skipping, or jumping, which constitute the walking offense of "lifting."

Second, "the supporting leg must be straightened (i.e., not bent at the knee) for at least one moment when in the vertical upright position." In other words, no "creeping." The judges are empowered to enforce these rules, and they do so by a system of warnings that can lead to disqualification if a walker persists in violation in the view of at least three members of the judging panel.

Of course, these calls must be made by well-trained officials. But even qualified judges are far from perfect. That's why some people believe that it's time the event got away from the requirement that judging calls must be made "as seen by the human eye," and venture into the technological age.

One such person is Dr. Dennis Furlong of Canada, who proposed an electronic shoe for judging purposes to the IAAF Walking Committee in 1990. While the committee expressed interest, use of the shoe does not appear imminent.

The Challenge to Americans

In recent years, American male walkers have lagged internationally. Not since 50k man Larry Young's outstanding third-place finish at the 1972 Munich Olympic Games has an American won an Olympic walking medal. In the 1992 Olympic year, U.S. women—led by Debbi Lawrence and Lynn Weik—were closer to the world's top than the U.S. men.

Bruce Douglass of Mystic, Connecticut, the TAC National Walking Committee chairman, has called for implementation of a 10-year plan to bridge the competitive gap. "First, efforts to educate and monitor the development of current national-level athletes must continue," says Douglass. "Second, the work of the youth and junior subcommittees must be formalized and expanded. The third emphasis is on the continuation of our attempts to promote walking across the United States."

Douglass firmly believes that "it pays to advertise," and so has ordered the mass printing of instructional brochures and other promotional materials. "We are trying to capture an audience," says Douglass. "We must encourage a strong base of grass-roots walkers to gain the few outstanding individuals who will propel our program forward."

Walking as a Spectator Sport

There's nothing like some hot competition to warm the hearts of walking's would-be friends. Two of the grandest races in U.S. walking took place at the 1990 Goodwill Games in Seattle. The men's 20-kilometer and the women's 10-kilometer races were staged, in their entirety, on the University of Washington Stadium track and were major successes in every aspect. The men covered 50 laps and the women 25 as large crowds roared their approval of both races. These games built some of the best goodwill walking has ever had.

Walking and running are part and parcel of the same internationally recognized sport form, known everywhere but in the United States as "athletics." As proof that walking and running are connected, consider the case of Nadezhdsa Ryashkina, who posted a world record time of 41:56:21 with her Goodwill Games 10k win. Just 2½ years earlier, she had been a struggling middle-distance runner with a most uncertain future in track and field.

High-Level Help

Encouragement for those seeking to reach top-level performance comes from the highest sources. The London-based International Amateur Athletic Federation has two excellent publications, "The Organization of Race Walking Events" and "Coaching of Race Walking," available by mail order. The Athletics Congress of the United States publishes a rule book that tells everything you ever wanted to know about race walking, a directory listing names and addresses of principal figures of the sport in this country, plus some excellent promotional and instructional brochures. And there are a wealth of other publications on walking available. Just check with your local library or bookstore, or the contacts listed in the Resource List at the end of the book.

One of running's most celebrated figures is one of walking's strongest supporters. "It [walking] complements our own sport [running]," said Fred Lebow, New York Road Runners Club president, back in 1988. Virtually every major NYRRC race has included a division for race walkers.

"We have been doing this for years now," said Lebow. "There are prizes and awards for everybody. Sometimes the walkers are more enthusiastic than the runners."

The Bottom Line

The hikers, the ramblers, the strollers—they're all there, out in force, virtually everywhere. Many a lifetime walking advocate got a start in the Boy Scouts and Girl Scouts. A 14-mile hiking achievement can easily be the spur to many years of walking delights.

Henry David Thoreau may have said it best a century ago: "I think that I cannot preserve my health and spirits unless I spend four hours a day at least—and it is commonly more than that—sauntering through the woods and over the hills and fields, absolutely free from worldly engagements.

"When I am reminded that the mechanics and shopkeepers stay in their shops not only all the forenoon, but all the afternoon too, sitting with crossed legs, so many of them—as if the legs were made to sit upon, and not to stand or walk upon—I think that they deserve some credit for not having committed suicide long ago." And to quote yet another famous figure, Thomas Jefferson once said, "Of all exercises, walking is the best."

But just thinking about it won't do. In the words of former National AAU walking chairman Charles Silcock, "Off your seat and on your feet."

Fred Lebow on Walking

I don't race walk. I admire people who do, though. It's hard. I enjoy watching competitive race walking, like in indoor competition in Madison Square Garden or when the club hosted the IAAF International Race Walking Championships. We have always endorsed race walking. Howard Jacobson, a competitive race walker and coach, got walking going in this area in about 1975. We've always had a good turnout for both our open walking and running classes every Saturday morning. A lot of the participants in running and walking have shifted from one activity to the other. Eventually the participation and level of walking influenced us to create a walking division with prizes awarded in our races.

I think the fitness walking movement is great. It really reaches people for whom running is so far removed. Often it doesn't make sense to tell people who've been completely sedentary to go out for a run, but you can tell them to go out walking. Walking makes sense. Once they realize how easy and beneficial walking is, they start running. And many people who start out as walkers eventually join running clubs.

In early 1992, Jack Rudin, a member of the Rudin family, one of the original New York City Marathon sponsors, started walking in our races. His son Eric and nephew Bill have run the marathon, but Jack had never done anything like this before. We were thrilled. In fact, we put up a special finish banner for him in his first race.

12

Part 12: The Running Lifestyle

Running and Travel

One of the most appealing aspects of running is how portable it is. Where you go, it goes. With a bit of planning and experience, not only is running a convenient travel companion, it is a wonderful adventure.

The NYRRC is truly an international organization in this regard, and travel is one of its major areas of expertise. Over the years, the club has coordinated travel and accommodations for the thousands of international runners in its events (8000 from 91 countries in the New York City Marathon alone). The club covers every detail, including the recruitment of 350 volunteer translators for the international marathoners.

In addition, the NYRRC is an active AIMS (Association of International Marathons) member, and has programs for fitness vacations. Many of the NYRRC staff have attended and/or participated in races all over the world as part of their work.

Many runners are travelers, for business or pleasure. Having traveled extensively around the world on running business, often as the guest of marathon race directors, Fred Lebow is an expert in this area. He gives his advice below, followed by tips from other traveling runners.

On the Road with Fred Lebow

During my tenure at the NYRRC, I have been fortunate to travel all over the world. At last count, I have run races and roads in over 50 countries, putting in the miles on every continent. Some of the techniques I have developed over the years for travel and running may seem a bit unorthodox, but they work for me. At the very least, you can adopt (and adapt) some of these methods to suit your needs.

Speaking of suits, I used to travel with one. I arrived at the 1977 Boston Marathon with my two suitcases, one of which contained a suit, tie, and dress shoes. Eventually, after significantly more travel experience, I worked my way down to one soft bag, which must have a shoulder strap. Instead of a suit, if necessary I take just a jacket and tie. And I never check a bag. Everything is in a carry-on. The point is, I have found it easiest and wisest just to pack enough to get by, and to take it with me on the plane.

I never make a big deal out of what I wear while I'm away (nor, frankly, do I make a big deal about my clothes at home, either!). But that required breaking a habit I had going all the way back to my youth. When I was young, my family used to go to great lengths to have us bathed and always dressed in clean, fancy clothes. Even when we were hiding from the Nazis during the war, we dressed up nice. Crazy.

However, I always pack my all-weather running gear. Even though I prefer singlets in hot weather, I also pack long-sleeved shirts and long pants, depending on where I'm going. I have been to places such as Istanbul, Morocco, and most Arab countries where it isn't appropriate to dress without having my arms and legs covered (not to mention that one can't get into various sight-seeing spots without being dressed this way).

Having proper clothing is probably even more important for women. There are many countries where it is not advisable for women to run in shorts. Unless you are familiar with the site, it is probably wise for every runner to take long, lightweight running pants. And in all cases, it is also advisable to check with one of the locals about the proper customs before going out to run or tour. In my experience, this doesn't just apply to the Third World. It includes places in some European countries as well.

When I travel, I never worry about jet lag. I have found that the best way to approach any trip is to go out for a light run after arriving. (I take a shower beforehand if I'm feeling especially groggy.) I learned this from many of the elite runners who come to our races in New York and do the same. In addition, according to an article in *New York Running News*, experts on jet lag recommend that travelers begin following the schedule of the new place—meals, sleep habits, etc.—as soon as possible. It's especially helpful to engage in an outdoor activity like running, so the body is exposed to sunlight, which seems to send a time signal. This is particularly true if you arrive somewhere in the early morning, having flown from a place where it's late in the day.

Even though I always run upon arriving, I take my running very easy because of the stress of travel. Going for a run may sound rough when all you feel like doing is lying down. My feeling is, experiment; try to run anyway. You can always stop and walk, or take a rest. When I've been tired mid-run, I go with the feeling. I just stop and take a break. I've even taken a short rest in the middle of a marathon. Beware, however, of doing it in a strange place. Taking my shoes off for a relaxing catnap in Chicago, I awoke to find they had been stolen. I had to make my way back to the hotel in my socks.

Before you take off for a run in a strange place, get a general understanding of where you are, and how and where it is most appropriate to run. You can do this by asking a cab driver, someone at your hotel, a native, or a friend who has visited the place. I remember arriving in Teheran, and I was so anxious to run, I went out immediately. And just as immediately, Iranian soldiers stopped me. I never saw another person running in Iran.

Once you get acclimated to your surroundings, running can be wonderful. It's new, it's fresh, and it's adventurous. But beware of getting carried away in a new location, which is very common. On a beautiful day in Barcelona, I found myself about 13 miles out, having left my map in a pocket back in my hotel room. My mind went blank; I couldn't even remember the name of my hotel. I went to a police station for help. After a dozen calls, they finally located my hotel and drove me back. Imagine seeing a guy walking out of a police car wrapped in a blanket! To assure everyone I wasn't a criminal, I did what I always do: gave out race T-shirts. I always carry a stock of those as souvenirs.

Most travel veterans advise running early in the morning. However, I think this depends on where you are. Surely it is easiest, and in busy cities, it makes sense in order to avoid crowds and traffic. But I have had great runs in spots like Chicago at sunset, where the light casting its reflection on the water is a beautiful sight.

Where are the best locations to run a race? There are so many places that are good for different reasons. Many feel the place, rather than the race, is most important. I have run a half marathon in Cairo in terrible conditions for a good time, but the course—run down roads and past buildings that haven't changed in 2000 years—was amazing. Early mornings in China were fascinating, passing other runners and those practicing t'ai chi. I've always wanted to experience running the marathon in California through the redwoods.

But for me, it's not just the city, it's the people that make the race. I ran the first Oslo Marathon about ten years ago, and the crowds were incredible. I ran the very difficult (and lonely—there were no spectators) Aruba Marathon, which had the potential for being a disaster, until I met some friends (animal and human). There were no spectators, only goats. I actually have a special feeling for goats, as we used to have them at home when I was growing up. But they don't make for a great cheering section. Fortunately, I was spotted by coach and running administrator Tracy Sundlun, who paced me and gave me encouragement over the entire final 10 miles. Aruba was a very memorable race, and place.

I've spent a large percentage of my work life on the road over the past few years. I've run all over the world. When I'm in Moscow I run along the Moscow River. I've run in Lhasa, Tibet, all over China and Russia, in Nairobi, Cairo, and Paris.

My favorite places to run are Hyde Park, in London, and the Bois de Bologne, in Paris. I cherish New York's Central Park in a way I almost can't describe. But I love to run in the clean air of the Midwest, with the horizons, and I love to run through the streets of San Francisco.

When you run in places you visit, you encounter things you'd never see otherwise. I remember sites like Esfu, Egypt, during a river cruise on the Nile. We were running in the early morning to look at ancient pyramids, while the Egyptian elders, smoking their big pipes, were staring at us—these Americans wearing baseball caps.

I'll never forget running years ago in Warsaw, and seeing the stunned look on the faces of an older couple. Of course, I didn't understand what they said to each other, except for one word I'll never forget: "chogging." I kept right on going, laughing to myself.

I've had quite a few unique experiences and adventures on the run, as well. The first time I ran in China, I tried to join up with a group of local runners. How must it have looked, a Westerner trying to run up to them, particularly at a time when not many of them had been to China? They ran away from me! And during guerrilla warfare in 1981 in El Salvador, I ran right into an army patrol.

—Tom Brokaw

Running can make for some great sight-seeing. One of the nicest features of travel running is going through famous parks in places like Vienna and London. And running can also be a great challenge, or a way to experience history. I once ran in the Colorado Rockies, where it started out hot and we ended up in high altitude with snow. In Greece, I ran the original marathon route, and in Rome I began a run from the Vatican.

Unlike the "old days," now there's a lot of good help and advice on travel running. Some major hotels, particularly in big cities, have running maps. In the United States, you can check on locations, running groups, or races by contacting local running clubs, by calling the YMCA or YWCA, or the Road Runners Club of America. There is even a road running club in Paris. If you're taking a trip, check the Resource List in the back of this book in addition to reading this chapter. Feel free to call the NYRRC library for any other travel information.

Lebow's Rules of Travel

1. Get away with as little clothing as possible. A nice running suit doubles for me as leisure wear. You might want to bring two of them.

2. You don't have to dress up while traveling. Why get all done up just to get all sweated up? I've been to Paris, Rome, London, New York—and I've realized you can dress down and still be acceptable in all those places. What's most important is to be comfortable, and you can do that with a moderate amount of style, too.

3. Ask a hotel concierge (or other local) where to run. Take with you a map and the telephone number and address of where you are staying. You can use the business cards most hotels keep in their rooms or at the front desk. During your run, look for landmarks

to navigate by along the way. And be precise. After getting lost, one friend of mine told a Casablanca resident, "I remember my hotel; it was a white building." The gentlemen replied, "Do you realize what 'Casablanca' means? Every building here is white."

4. Try laundering your running clothes the easy way: while you're in them. I learned this trick through rather unpleasant circumstances—after I stepped in animal "waste" in Marakesh, Morocco. I couldn't bear to touch my shoes, so I took a shower in them. Now I take a shower with all my running clothes on. At least in summer gear, I know of a number of other runners who do this, even at home.

If a certain nonperishable food is part of your pre-race preparation (bananas or bagels), bring it with you to be sure you'll have it. Sometimes, this isn't just to have some extras. You may not like the local fare, or in some cases, even have access to it. One NYRRC staffer toed the starting line of an eastern European marathon hungry, after spending days on scant rations of tea and rice. Rather than standing in long lines during limited hours for questionable results, he ate what his host had on hand.

Tips from a Running Travel Agent

Travel agent Thom Gilligan tempts New York City Marathoners at the Expo with running tour packages. Gilligan urges runners to consider using a travel agent, who represents all airlines, hotels, car rentals, and other companies that offer services to travelers. "Their service is free," he says, "and if you know one who is a runner, all the better." Here are some of his inside tips on travel.

Special Travel Gear

Woolite. A small pack, or travel-size bottle, of Woolite is a good idea. It works in cold water and can be used not only on wool but also on cotton and synthetics.

Water Purifiers. The tap water in many countries is unsuitable: either it is not palatable or contains bacteria that can cause all types of illness. You can purchase a water purifier that filters out any impurities for about $30 in most camping equipment stores. They are lightweight and can just about slide into a running shoe.

Airline Flights

Nonsmoking Seats. While nonsmoking planes are now a feature of travel within the United States, international flights are another story. Gilligan has found that the biggest problem for runners on these flights is arranging for a nonsmoking seat. If all nonsmoking seats are taken at check-in, flight attendants must create a new nonsmoking row. "If you get into an argument," says Gilligan, "throw the book at them." That book is *Fly-Rights*, available free from the U.S. Department of Transportation, Office of Consumer Affairs, Room 10405, 400 7th Street, SW, Washington, D.C., 20590.

Upgrades. There's nothing like the luxury of first-class or business class. Even if you do only a small amount of air travel, it pays to join every possible frequent flyer program. That's because when seats are full in regular coach, you may get "upgraded" to first or business class. Priority is given to those passengers who have a frequent flyer number in their reservation record. In addition, frequent flyers also receive periodic mailings of special discount certificates, two-for-one fares, etc.

Carry-on Luggage. Pack your running gear in your carry-on bag. This not only keeps you on the road if your luggage is lost, but in some countries running gear is quite valuable and is often stolen from checked luggage. Running shoes, shorts, Gore-Tex suits, and other gear are "hot commodities." Always lock your bags. Buy small locks even for your gym-type bags.

Hotel Rooms

Nonsmoking Rooms. Many hotels now offer nonsmoking rooms, which should be requested when making a reservation.

Secret Deals. Most city hotels offer special weekend rates that are only available if you are smart enough to request them.

Running Maps. Special running maps are now produced by some hotels, such as the Park Lane in London and the Park Plaza in Boston. Many Hyatt hotels also provide them.

Plastic Bags. Plastic laundry bags most often located in hotel room closets are a convenient place to stuff wet running gear when you pack your bags.

On my bulletin board is a postcard I sent to myself from a faraway country. "See the world; it matters," the card says. And one of the greatest ways to see the world is by running, a sport you can practice anywhere. Whether just to maintain fitness, as a unique mode of transportation or sightseeing, or to take part in a race, running in new territory makes you realize just how universal the sport is, and how unique it can be as a travel companion.

I have been fortunate to visit nearly 30 countries, and to run in many of them. Here are some tips based on what I learned while running around the world.

1. Be flexible. The stress of travel and sight-seeing will likely necessitate a reduction in training. It's important to accommodate this added stress, both to prevent illness and injury and to enjoy your trip. During travel it's especially important to practice a runner's cardinal rule: listen to your body.

2. Find a travel agent sympathetic to your needs as a runner. If it's someone who specializes in running, ask about races, clubs, or running areas. In addition, for general running or race information in different countries, you can write to that country's Sports Federation (the equivalent of The Athletics Congress in the United States); or in major American cities, check the local Road Runners Clubs (also see the Resource List at the back of this book).

3. Try to run before you fly, even if it means getting up with the sun. That way you won't have to attempt to overcome fatigue and the challenge of a new spot immediately after arriving because you feel compelled to get in a run.

4. During airplane flights, walk around, stretch out, eat lightly, and drink plenty of water.

5. Bring versatile running gear that's easily washable and quick-drying. Carry shoes and clothing in plastic bags so you have a place to repack the gear when it's wet. Take the insoles out of running shoes to speed drying time. If you pack wet gear after a run, remember to remove it first thing on arrival.

6. If you fear the absence of your runner's diet, bring some of your staples along as insurance. Cereal and powdered milk are lightweight and portable, as are whole-grain crackers or pretzels. When eating out, don't be shy to ask for your food prepared "light." Just be polite.

7. Speaking of bringing things along, running paraphernalia makes great gifts. I learned from Fred Lebow—who takes running presents everywhere—that running T-shirts, patches, and pins are unique and greatly appreciated "thank you" items for people who show kindness or do you favors. In a crunch—so to speak—American candy and gum are good gifts in many countries.

8. You'll probably be better off running in the morning. Business or sightseeing often present unexpected scheduling and fatigue, and mornings are the best time to avoid pedestrians and traffic in major cities. Early morning runs are also a great way to really see a city.

9. Allow for jet lag, especially for races or hard training. The general rule is that it takes about a day of adaptation for each hour of change in time zone.

10. Allow time for your total workout, including proper warmup and cooldown. Many people compromise important warmup and cooldown routines when time is short or when it's inconvenient to do them. To make it more convenient, adapt exercise routines to hotel rooms. For example, instead of the fence or tree you normally use to stretch, try bedposts or staircases. The same adaptation holds true if you can't run. Warm up and run or walk flights of the hotel stairs instead.

11. Be especially alert to cars and traffic lights. As an American running in England for example—where traffic travels in the opposite direction than in the United States—my first, and last, lapse in concentration nearly proved fatal!

12. Carry identification, including the name and telephone number of where you are staying. If you're setting out to run alone, tell someone where you're going and when you plan to return. Take money, and if you're running more than 30 minutes—especially if it's hot—don't stray from accessible water, or a place to buy a drink if necessary.

13 If you're on business, try breaking up meetings with a run. In fact, this can be smart business sense, as runners are generally respected for their discipline. In addition, a run with business associates often creates a refreshing new rapport.

14. Learn important words and a few pleasant greetings in the native language.

—Gloria Averbuch

International Marathoning

Michelle Jordan, Janet Nelson, and Carl and Renee Landegger are all true international marathoners. Their combined total of 69 marathons called for training the equivalent of running 3.3 times around the world, or about 84,000 miles.

The New York City Marathon quickly became the Mount Everest of the running boom that began in the mid-1970s. Much to their own surprise, these New Yorkers in their 30s, 40s, and 50s, who had previously prided themselves on walking a mile and a half from their apartments to their offices at most, were suddenly finding themselves running up to 10 miles a day to bring their bodies into shape to finish the marathon: Here's their account:

In the late 1970s, a few of us living on or near East 72nd Street in Manhattan formed a group that ran every morning from 7 to 8 a.m. around the 6-mile Central Park loop. Gradually we fell into the routine of running a few of the many races put on in Central Park by the New York Road Runners Club. At some point, we decided to run the 1978 New York City Marathon. One or more of our group has run in every New York City Marathon since then.

Sometime after our first marathon we decided that we couldn't continue referring to ourselves simply as "the group." After many hours of animated debate, all while running around the park, unanimity was achieved and we swore eternal allegiance to the "72nd Street Marathoning and Pasta Club."

In accordance with the precedent established by King Henry VIII for the Knights of the Garter, twelve expensive and unique T-shirts were created, and the appropriate resolutions were passed ordaining that no more could ever be produced. In addition, existing shirts could only be awarded by the unanimous consent of all shirt-holders.

Among the prouder boasts of the club is that Fred Lebow, who lives on East 72nd Street, has requested a T-shirt, but after many hours of discussion, it was decided that while all honor and gratitude remains due to Fred, the fact that he does not regularly run with us excludes him from membership and a T-shirt. Besides, it makes a much better story to be able to say that Fred Lebow wanted to join and we wouldn't let him in, than to say that Fred is, in fact, a member.

In 1980 the first London Marathon was organized with the assistance of the New York Road Runners Club. The 72nd Street Marathoning and Pasta Club at once decided that it was essential for our prestige and honor to run it. That is how we became "experts" in international marathoning.

I DID IT reads the sweatshirt that each member of the 72nd Street Marathoning and Pasta Club has somewhere at the back of the closet. The back also reads: New York, London, Rome, Vienna, Copenhagen, Budapest, Shanghai, Prague—a list of our various marathon odysseys.

London has the best crowds, equaled only by New York. Londoners really appreciate the ordinary runner and remain along the route for hours, cheering every effort. It is wonderful to have such enthusiastic support from start to finish. Even an average runner feels like a star, and being a woman adds an additional feeling of excitement. When we ran through lower-middle-class areas, rotund middle-aged women cheered the female 72nd Streeters with a primitive chauvinistic pride, spurred by seeing women in their own age group ahead of thousands of younger, yet obviously weaker, male runners.

In its early days, Rome was not the best organized or the flattest course, nor was it run in the coolest temperatures, but it certainly was unbeatable for scenic beauty. How can one not feel exhilarated finishing at the magnificent Colosseum? What a background for the finisher's photo.

Fred Lebow immortalized himself in this race. He and Allison Roe, former marathon world record holder, seemed to have found the only bad restaurant in Rome the night before the race. Roe was so ill that she could not start the race the next morning. Fred, to uphold the honor of the New York Road Runners Club, did run, but became famous when he stopped at about mile 15, lay down by the side of the road, slept for half an hour, and then got up and—peacefully, comfortably, and very self-satisfied—finished the race.

Copenhagen came next and was only agreed upon, after very vociferous debate, on the sound scientific basis that it was guaranteed to be run on an absolutely flat course.

Copenhagen is a small and friendly marathon, and the Tivoli Gardens is a first-rate place for a postmarathon celebration. A real Scandinavian smorgasbord is well worth the trip in itself, but trying to get the Danes to make a traditional pre-race breakfast of American-style pancakes failed completely, as did the efforts of our pit crew to purchase plain water at any local bar along the route.

Then came Vienna, very flat, and arguably the best organized first-time marathon that anyone had ever produced. Among its truly wonderful and distinctive features was the way that the various refreshment tables along the route were marked by large balloons suspended 12 to 15 feet above each table, a technique adopted by New York in 1991.

Nineteen eighty-six found us in Budapest. The beer lived up to every expectation, the food was outstanding, and the people couldn't have been friendlier and more cooperative when, somewhat to their surprise, a group of New York runners appeared for their marathon. We didn't get any T-shirts, which was a major disappointment, but we were given towels instead.

Conflicting schedules forced the club to limit itself to the wonders of the New York City Marathon for the next few years, but 1991 found the club colors flying proudly in Prague, where the delegation was headed by one of our female members, a Czech national by birth. The opportunity to return to the country of her birth after it established its independence and participate in the Prague Marathon proved irresistible. Prague is full of history, and the course is great. It starts on a downhill and finishes in the most historic square, built in the 12th century, in the center of town.

The Prague Marathon is well organized, offering a variety of drinks, sponges, wet towels, etc., at frequent intervals. The undisputed highlight of the finish line was the ability to buy unlimited quantities of Pilsner Urquell, which the club's beer expert identified as the world's greatest beer, in quart-size paper cups at five cents a cup.

As of this writing, members of the club (who now range in age from 40 to 70) continue to run their daily routes in Central Park and are in serious debate on the location of the next marathon. Paris in the spring seems to be winning.

What has the club learned in 12 years of marathoning that may be helpful to other runners? That runners welcome other runners all over the world; that the more you train the less you suffer; that no matter where the race, training and marathoning as a group creates deep and lasting friendships; and that there is nothing easy about marathoning, but there is nothing else that brings such genuine exhilaration.

Guidelines for International Marathoners

1. Decide what you want to get out of your international marathon experience, then choose the city accordingly. "The fastest" course may not be in the most "entertaining" city.

2. Don't expect all international marathons to be conducted with the slick efficiency of New York or London. Be prepared for the odd snafu and roll with the punches.

3. Don't underestimate the effects of jet lag. Leave early enough to give yourself sufficient recovery time. On arrival you may feel fit enough to trot around the museum, but running a marathon is something else.

4. Check out the likely weather and temperature ranges for the race and take several combinations of clothing.

5. Pack a personal care kit that includes the basics you need, e.g., petroleum jelly, aspirin, granola bars, moleskin. Some of these may be tough to find abroad.

6. Check out the foreign visa requirements long before departure. Some countries won't let you in on just a passport, and you can't make it to the starting line unless you can first get on the plane.

7. If you need an inoculation before you go as part of an overseas health requirement, get it done well in advance to avoid any stiffness or allergic reaction too close to marathon day. (See the Resource List for further information.)

8. If you want to run an international marathon with other runners from the United States, check out whether a group trip is being organized. This may save you some money too.

9. If you want to run abroad but don't feel up to a marathon, check out the half marathons and 10ks. Many marathon events incorporate these and other shorter races.

10. Take some time to check out the course beforehand. If it isn't well marked, learning the way ahead of time may help you feel more secure. You'll also learn about the terrain in the process, such as where the uphills are, to plan your pacing.

11. Eat prudently the night before the race and stick to familiar foods. By all means experiment with the local fare, but wait until after the marathon.

12. (For Women Only) Don't be intimated by the "macho antics" of some local male runners at the starting line. You'll run most of them into the ground by midway!

13. Don't be fooled by women runners who wear makeup at the starting line. Particularly in Europe, they have mastered the art of looking gorgeous and running fast!

14. Be prepared for water stops that don't exist, or have run out of water. Carry your own bottle if in doubt.

15. Watch out for ankle-twisting surfaces. Cobblestone streets or uneven paving is not unusual.

16. Talk to local runners along the route. Few situations offer such a great opportunity to enjoy a friendly and informative exchange. It's amazing how much you can learn about your "host" country—even with minimal language skills—from a local marathoner.

17. Watch out for cavalier drivers and cyclists. Sideswiping marathoners is still an accepted sport in some countries.

18. For encouragement from the crowd, wear a T-shirt with your name and country written on it. Both translate into most languages, and the crowd will root for you.

19. Standards of fair play can vary, so don't get thrown if you see a local runner get a bit of help from a friend on a bicycle. Consider it all part of the local experience.

20. Unless you're in it for a winning place, make time to take in your surroundings as you run. Marathon courses often go through neighborhoods and locations off the tourist track. This will give you a real feel for the country.

21. Carry the name and address of your hotel or where you are staying with you. If you get stuck far from the finish line, you may

be better understood showing someone the address than trying to pronounce it.

22. Take enough money for a cab or bus or train fare back home.

23. Be courteous to local marathoners. Be careful, especially in a crowded start, not to shove or push.

24. Wash your souvenir international marathon T-shirt with care. It may well run and fade faster than you did!

25. Make up your mind to have fun. The actual race is only one part of the entire international marathon experience. If you're only interested in the race itself, it's cheaper and more convenient to stay home.

26. Start training for the next one as soon as you get home.

Running U.S.A.

Peter Roth, a NYRRC original, has been involved with the club and the running movement for many years. Part of his contribution has been to travel around the country to locate the best running sites. He has updated his version of where to hit the roads (and parks, trails, and tracks) in various cities around the country from his book *Running U.S.A.* and has included a list of possible contacts in those places.

Atlanta

Atlanta Track Club (404) 231-9066; Phidippides Running Store, Ansley Mall (404) 875-4268

The famous Peachtree Road Race course is close to most Atlanta hotels and the downtown area. Many local and visiting runners ply back and forth along Peachtree Street, testing the course as well as getting to and from Piedmont Park, just 2 miles from downtown. For a more direct route to the park, head out Piedmont Avenue. The Grady High School track is adjacent to the park and is used for speed workouts on Tuesday nights. To be closer to the park, stay at hotels in the midtown Colony Square area.

Atlantans desiring more serious workouts head for the Kennesaw Mountain trails about 20 miles northwest of town. Also, Stone Mountain, 15 miles east, is a favorite for its 5- and 8-mile loops.

Boston

New England Athletics Congress (617) 566-7600; Boston Marathon (BAA) (617) 236-1652; Bill Rodgers Running Center (running store) (617) 723-5612

With the tradition of the Boston Marathon and the large universities throughout the city, Boston has many excellent courses to satisfy its active running population. Close to the downtown hotels and offices is the Charles River. Its riverbank pathway gives you many distance options, depending on which of the 11 bridges you want to use. The longest loop can take you 16.78 miles, although if you want a shorter 3.79-mile loop, use the Charles River Dam to the east and the Harvard Bridge to the west. For a shorter run of 2.82 miles, use the Longfellow Bridge to the east, instead of the dam.

To the west of Boston, in the Brookline/Newton area, you can run around the popular Cleveland Circle Reservoir next to the marathon route. The reservoir is close to 2 miles around but has very little shade. Many runners hop over the fence to run closer to the water. You can extend the run onto Commonwealth Avenue and challenge the famous Heartbreak Hill. This is a series of four medium-sized hills covering about 3 miles on the marathon route.

In Cambridge, many runners congregate at the Fresh Pond Reservoir's parking lot before heading out for the 2¼-mile paved loop around the water. Every Saturday morning at 10:30 a.m. you can find a small race of 2½ or 5 miles here. You don't need to register in advance. If you are looking for group workouts, try calling the BAA office.

Chicago

Chicago Area Running Association (CARA) (312) 666-9867; Chicago Marathon (312) 951-0660

The answer to finding great runs in Chicago is simply to head east to the lakefront. Its beauty and accessibility make this the foremost place to enjoy your workouts in Chicago. Surprisingly, the water in Lake Michigan is pure enough to attract throngs to its downtown beaches. Many local running clubs schedule their workouts here, and you are bound to find runners congregating in Lincoln Park to the north of downtown along the shoreline. The best spot is a few blocks north of Fullerton Avenue, where you will also find a bulletin board with notices of local races.

Lincoln Park is about a 5-mile strip, yet you don't need to be confined to its boundaries. If you head south, the Gold Coast covers 1½ miles to Navy Pier, and you can go another 7½ miles to Jackson Park where there's a 2.2-mile loop adjacent to the University of Chicago and its excellent track. There are a few other small parks around the city.

About ½ mile east of the O'Hare Airport hotels is the heavily wooded Des Plaines Forest Preserve. Here you will find a 5½-mile long dirt trail along the east bank of the Des Plaines River. Most of the trail will be south of where you will probably enter the preserve.

Cleveland

Cleveland West Road Runners Hotline (216) 228-6031

This lakeside city offers some convenient downtown running, although weekend activity is in outlying parks. The lakefront, known as the Marginal Area, has miles of flat, unremarkable, shadeless terrain. You will have some good views of the Cleveland skyline. An old warehouse and steel mill area, known as the Flats, lies next to the Cuyahoga River and provides another downtown running opportunity. There are several little bridges to run over, and the streets are winding and confusing, but you can always work your way back along the river to where you began.

At a minimum of 8 miles from downtown, the Emerald Necklace is an unbroken chain of parks that is also known as the Metroparks System. It runs in an arch from east to west around Cleveland for a distance of about 100 miles. Different clubs use different parts of it, the largest of which is the Cleveland West Road Runners, which uses the Rocky River, Lakewood area. They have a group run every Saturday morning at 7:30 a.m.

Dallas

Cross Country Club of Dallas, White Rock Marathon (214) 596-9002; Lukes (Running Store), Oak Lawn (214) 528-1290

Running in this city is focused on two locations, Bachman Lake, 6 miles from downtown, next to Love Field Airport, and White Rock Lake, a bit farther away, northeast of town. On weekends, a large group meets at White Rock Lake at 7 a.m. and starts running 11 minutes later. They call themselves the 7-11's. The grand meeting place here is Big Thicket Cabin on East Lawther Drive along the northeast side of the lake. One loop around the lake is 9 miles. Other runners meet here informally throughout the mornings. Bachman Lake has a smaller but popular 3.1-mile loop.

Running downtown is complicated, with no easy route to follow. The hotels near and along the Stemmons Freeway offer some opportunities to follow service roads or run on the Trinity Riverbed Levee. It is recommended that you do not run in this area alone.

The Cross Country Club of Dallas puts on races the first Saturday of every month. Lukes on Oak Lawn is a well-known resource for local information.

Denver

Rocky Mountain Road Runners Hotline (303) 871-8366; Runners Roost (303) 759-8455; Gart Bros. Sportscastle (303) 861-1122

This is an easy city to run in, with beautiful vistas of the Rocky Mountains and long, even flat, unimpeded routes. Weather is seldom a problem, but the high altitude can slow you down, especially if you have just arrived. There are a number of popular areas in town. The lunch crowd can be found at Cheesman Park, where a wood chip trail offers views of the capitol dome. One loop is a little less than a mile. Washington Park, a couple of miles to the southeast of downtown, gets the early, late, and weekend crowds. Here, a shaded, mostly flat road loops around for 2.2 miles.

Cherry Creek Trail is a beautiful course that runs along Speer Boulevard and out to Cherry Creek Reservoir after about nine miles. This is a paved trail with no intersections to interrupt your run. The reservoir attracts many runners as well. The Platt River Greenway connects to the trail and can add many more miles to your run.

For mountain runners, there are three great courses close to downtown. The most challenging is Lookout Mountain, which goes 5 miles uphill. The most interesting is Genesee Park, which contains an animal preserve, including buffalo. The closest is Red Rocks Park, only about 7 to 8 miles west.

Detroit

Detroit Free Press Marathon (313) 223-4769; Motor City Striders (313) 544-9099; Michigan Runner (313) 227-4200; Downtown Runners (Tom Henderson) (313) 357-8300

This is a friendly running town that takes advantage of a large forested island in the Detroit River. Belle Isle is a 2½-mile run from downtown, and once you are over the bridge, you can use a perimeter road of 5½ miles or use trails through the woods. You will see a lot of natural wildlife here. A large group of Downtown Runners sets out every Tuesday at 5:30 p.m. The meeting place changes every week, so you need to call ahead.

The beautiful Elmwood cemetery lies just off Jefferson Avenue before you get to the Belle Isle Bridge. It was designed by Robert Olmstead, who also designed New York's Central Park. Here you can run a 1½-mile loop and wander over dirt paths on the only hills (man made) in the city.

Local runners feel this is a safe city to run in, and a lot of old crime-ridden neighborhoods have recently become gentrified. Only 20 minutes to the west are wonderful rural areas for your long weekend runs.

Houston

David Hannah, Director, Houston-Tenneco Marathon (713) 757-2700; Memorial Park Tennis Center (713) 861-3765

Houston is one of those few cities that has a favorite running spot where everyone likes to meet. Memorial Park is said to attract as many as 10,000 runners on weekend days. Many begin their workouts at the Tennis Center, doing their warmups and socializing in the parking lot before heading out on the crushed granite 3-mile trail. A big campaign succeeded in funding night lighting for 24-hour use of the trail. The Tennis Center also has information on local clubs, races, etc. The closest hotel is the Houstonian, and there are other hotels in the nearby Galleria area in uptown Houston.

From downtown, you can run west through the greenbelt along the Buffalo Bayou River. After 2½ miles you'll reach a residential area, and after another 2½ miles west you'll be at Memorial Park. A loop from downtown to the bridge at Sheperd Drive and back on the other side of the river will give you a 5-mile workout.

Kansas City

Kansas City Track Club Hotline (816) 471-5282; Mid-America Running Association (816) 746-1414

This busy running town has three parks that attract local runners. Liberty Memorial Park, the most convenient, lies adjacent to Crown Center. This is a small park, but you can do about 1½ miles without repeating yourself. Mill Creek Park, also small, is located in the Country Club Plaza Area. Here you will find an undulating .8-mile loop.

The most popular, Loose Park, is located about 3½ miles south of downtown. Runners usually park and meet at the tennis courts on the west side. Although the park only has a 1-mile paved loop, extra miles are covered in the neighboring residential communities.

The Kansas City Track Club has probably the oldest consecutive weekly group run in the country. Its Wednesday Night Run (WNR) includes from 25 to 60 members each week. During standard time they meet at 6 p.m. and during daylight savings time they meet at 6:30 p.m. Call ahead to find the meeting place, which changes. A potluck dinner follows the run.

Los Angeles

David Anton, Los Angeles Marathon (310) 444-5544

This spread-out city has no central running courses, and the favorites are hard to reach except by car. Run early and you will avoid the poor air quality Los Angeles is known for. About 5½ miles north of downtown, Griffith Park has a vast 53 miles of trails that zigzag in seeming disarray. The 15 miles of paved roads are easier to follow, and you'll find many runners working their way along them. If you run up to the observatory, you'll appreciate the spectacular views below. Only 3 miles from downtown is Elysian Park, but the roads there are hard to follow. It's best to go there with someone who knows the way.

A favorite local route is San Vicente Boulevard for a pleasant run to the ocean in Santa Monica. To avoid more traffic, you can also run a parallel course three blocks south on Margarita Avenue past many palatial homes. Once at the ocean, you can head south along the beach and if you have the time and endurance, you need not turn around for about 30 miles. Los Angeles Airport lies along this waterfront course. To find the most runners at any one time in any one place here, head out to Balboa Park in Encino, where you will have a choice of flat routes from 3 kilometers to 7 miles.

Miami

Miami Runners Club 1-(800) 9404-RUN

This warm, mostly flat city has an active running community, and the Miami Runners Club puts on frequent races. There are two very popular routes that local runners use, and they are worth the short trip to get to them. To run from downtown, there is easy access via Biscayne Boulevard to the Venetian Causeway, which will give you a pleasant 2½-mile run over to Miami Beach.

Southwest of the city at Tropical Park you can find a 5-kilometer and a 5-mile out-and-back course that is in constant use. This is the busiest spot, except on Saturday mornings when hundreds of runners gather at 6:30 a.m. at Parrot Jungle for a long workout. They take Old Cutler Road and the Rickenbacker Causeway to get to Crandon Park in Key Biscayne. One way is a mostly shaded, well-marked 13.1 miles. Of course, you can turn back at any point. There is plenty of water supplied by volunteers along the route.

Minneapolis

Minnesota Distance Running Association—Race Line (612) 925-4749; Twin Cities Marathon (612) 673-0778

The Minnesota Distance Running Association is a venerable and active running club that can get you plugged in to whatever local events are going on. This is a busy running community, although with 22 lakes in the city, everyone is spread out enjoying the beautiful neighborhoods near their homes. Winter running is a challenge here, but the elements have nurtured many local world-class runners. The joy of toughing it can be seen in the popularity of the springtime Mudball Run, held when the terrain is particularly sloppy.

Most hotels are situated in downtown, and the best routes are out at the three lakes southwest of town. Loring Park is on the way to the lakes, with a loop that is close to 1 mile around. The first lake you'll reach is Lake of the Isles—2.8 miles around on a flat, paved path. Next, heading south, is Lake Calhoun's 3.2-mile circumference, and last is Lake Harriet's 3-mile loop.

Native runners also use the River Road loops along both sides of the Mississippi. This course starts 3½ miles from downtown, and distances vary according to which bridges you use.

New York

The New York Road Runners Club (212) 860-4455

New York has some of the best and most convenient running sites in the country. Central Park is the gem of the city, and from the dark hours of early morning until the late hours of night it is flooded with runners over the myriad routes that its 840 acres provide.

Of course, in New York, as well as most other cities, you must run with caution, especially at off-hours. The favorite meeting places in the park are at the Engineer's Gate at 90th Street and Fifth Avenue, near the reservoir (a block from the NYRRC headquarters at 9 East 89th Street), or at 67th Street on the West Drive, next to Tavern on the Green, where the marathon finishes. At the Engineer's Gate there is a gatehouse that is staffed part-time by an attendant. In addition, brochures on NYRRC events and programs are on display and available at all times. Numerous hotels are within a short jog of the park, which features a 6-mile loop, although shorter routes taking the 72nd Street or 102nd Street cutoffs are available. In the center of the park is a 1½-mile loop on a flat dirt path around the reservoir. On Saturday mornings, a group run with stretching instruction is conducted for the public at 10 a.m. at 90th Street and Fifth Avenue (Engineer's Gate).

The New York Road Runners Club holds races just about every weekend year round. The club also sponsors a safety program in Central Park that provides a patrol throughout the day and evening. You can usually find running partners by stopping at the club building at 9 East 89th Street, and there are chaperoned group runs conducted each weekday evening at 6:30 and 7:15 p.m. It's a great place to pick up the club's magazine, race fliers, and other running information. The club also has a store that sells gear (not shoes) that features the club and the marathon.

Although not as convenient to out-of-towners, there are other great places to run in New York. Riverside Park begins at 72nd Street along the Hudson River and extends up to the George Washington Bridge about 5$1/2$ miles to the north. Most runners stay within the promenade areas between 72nd and 120th Streets where an up-and-back route is about 4.8 miles. In Brooklyn, Prospect Park is a popular running site that offers a pleasant, rolling 3$1/2$-mile loop on the Park Drive.

Philadelphia

David Brier, Middle Atlantic Road Runners Club (215) 545-4400; Finish Line Sports (215) 569-9957; Joe Cook, Dept. of Recreation (215) 685-0150; Northeast Road Runners (215) 535-6092

This city has one of the biggest urban parks in the country, Fairmount Park. Only a short distance from Center City, you can find some natural trails here that seem to have distant rural settings. The main route, though, is along the Schuylkill River, just north of the Philadelphia Art Museum. Here, runners meet at Plaisted Hall, the southernmost building along Boat House Row. They run up to Falls Bridge and come back on the other side of the river and around the Art Museum. This is a safe, flat, 8.4-mile loop.

A couple of miles north of Falls Bridge, you can reach a gravel bridle path, Forbidden Drive, which runs close to Wissahickon Creek. It's called "Forbidden" because no vehicles are allowed. This will take you through scenic wooded and flat terrain until you come to the end at the northwest border of the city, 5$1/2$ miles away.

About 15 miles north of Center City lies Pennypack Park, which is well utilized by the Northeast Road Runners. A paved path runs east to west for about 11 miles over gentle terrain until the west end becomes very hilly. If you can get to Valley Forge National Park, 25 miles from town, you'll enjoy some beautiful, hilly runs through its 2255-acre terrain. Local runners meet at the Covered Bridge on Route 252.

Phoenix and Scottsdale

Runner's Den (602) 277-4333; Arizona Road Racers (602) 954-8341; Star System Arizona Marathon Festival (602) 246-7697

Running is hot in this city—literally and figuratively—due to the desert environment and the easy access to unimpeded routes. There is no central location at which to meet other runners, but there are frequent events put on by the Arizona Road Racers. Most mileage is tread along the Arizona Canal's 23.67-mile length. Recently the pathway has been reconstructed to pass under intersecting roads and allow you a nonstop workout. Downtown running is limited to fairly busy streets and small Encanto Park.

A new running path has been built along a dry creek bed called Indian Bend Wash. Its 15-mile length starts in North Phoenix and runs right through the heart of Scottsdale, ending at Arizona State University in Tempe. The pathway goes under most cross streets.

Phoenix contains the world's largest park within a city. At the South Mountain Preserve, 7 miles south of downtown, you can enjoy many trails within its 15,357 acres. If you head 7 miles north of downtown, you can reach the North Mountain Preserve for interesting runs that include Squaw Peak Park. Both preserves have well-marked trails, and maps are available at the gates.

Pittsburgh

Pittsburgh Citiparks (412) 255-8983; Pittsburgh Marathon (412) 765-3773

At the confluence of three large rivers—the Allegheny, Monongahela, and Ohio—sits the Golden Triangle, with its downtown office complexes. Numerous bridges cross the rivers and runners enjoy looping over them in many configurations. Point Park at the Triangle, Roberto Clemente Park, and Three Rivers Stadium can be included in these loops.

The most popular venue in town is Schenley Park. Close to downtown and adjacent to Carnegie-Mellon University, its 456 acres offer a 10-kilometer cinder and dirt trail and a perimeter sidewalk. East of Schenley Park, you will find the 499-acre Frick Park, with many nature trails that wind through ravines, along creeks, and over hills. North

Park is also a popular hangout, where a mostly flat 5-mile bike trail circumvents a lake. This park is 14 miles out of town on Route 19.

There is a lot of street running in Pittsburgh. The downtown is quite flat, but once you are in the suburbs there are hills galore. These are long hills, and when you get on top of them, you can stay there for a flat run. Of course, intersecting streets can be a distraction.

San Francisco

San Francisco Marathon (415) 391-2123; Golden Gate National Recreation Area (415) 556-0560; The Schedule (415) 472-7223; City Sports Magazine (the "Source Section") (415) 546-6150; Fleet Feet Store (415) 921-7188

Few cities have the dramatic climate and terrain that you can find here. The ocean, bay, bridges, and hills offer exciting vistas and venues for a variety of opportunities. Local runners gravitate to the Marina Green and the adjacent Golden Gate Promenade, which take you along the bay and up to Fort Point, under the Golden Gate Bridge. You can also run up to the bridge and then across it to Marin County. A run from Marina Green to Marin County and back is a little more than 7 miles. Not far from the Green, on Chestnut Street, is the Fleet Feet Store, which is a good place to stop for local running information.

Most local clubs use the magnificent Golden Gate Park for their regular group workouts. You will find it about 3½ miles southwest of downtown. There are many different meeting places and complex routes, although an easy course would be to follow the North and South Drives, which form a loop. The park is about 3 miles long. Kezar Stadium, just outside the park, has been rebuilt with a new 400-meter track which is open to the public.

St. Louis

St. Louis Track Club Hotline (314) 781-3726; St. Louis Track Club (314) 781-3926

Although two major rivers flow together just north of town, there are no decent courses that put you close to either the Missouri or the

Mississippi. There is a small park at the Gateway Arch where you can get a few miles in if you are limited to that part of town. Local hotels have maps that will facilitate your needs.

Six miles from the arch, at the western edge of downtown, is a large, wonderful 1400-acre park that was the site of the 1904 World's Fair. Forest Park is the major focus of running here, and its well-marked paths give you a perimeter run of 6.2 miles, with a .9-mile add-on through a wooded area. There are some interior paths available as well. There are many local tourist attractions at the park for you to enjoy. Runners meet at the Lindell Pavilion Fieldhouse along the northern edge of the park.

Shaw Park, a few miles farther west, offers a 2-mile loop. There are many corporations nearby, and at the lunch hour, it's a busy runners' thoroughfare.

Seattle

Super Jock 'N Jill Runner's Hotline (206) 524-RUNS; Seattle Marathon (206) 547-0885; Northwest Runner Magazine (206) 526-9000

This city lies on a strip of land between Puget Sound and Lake Washington. Many of the long routes can be found along the eastern edge of the city on the shores of the lake. Next to the sound, on the western edge, there is a downtown 2¼-mile waterfront run between the Aquarium and Pier 89. Across Elliot Bay you can run on the Alki Beach roads and enjoy their great views of the city skyline.

As great as these runs are, nothing beats the attraction of Green Lake, located a few miles north of downtown. Its 2.78-mile loop gets very crowded each morning, and often by 5:30 a.m. the parking lot is full. Many runners head south to the adjacent Lower Woodland Trails for extra mileage, zigzagging over its hilly, grassy fields.

An old railroad right-of-way has been recycled into a long, flat, traffic-free path known as the Burke-Gilman Trail. It begins along Lake Union, heads east through the University of Washington campus, and then winds toward the northeast, eventually hugging the lakeshore at the northern tip, a 16.6-mile journey. From here, a 12-mile extension on the Sammish River Trail will take you to Marymoor Park in Redmond.

Washington, D.C.

Montgomery County Road Runners (301) 353-0200; The *Washington Post*'s Friday Weekend Section; Marine Corps Marathon (703) 640-2225

Running in this city offers many important landmarks to enjoy as well as beautiful and convenient parks. The Mall, between the Lincoln Memorial along the Potomac River at the west end and the Capitol to the east, usually has a busy crowd of lunch runners seeing and being seen on this flat, open, grassy terrain. There are few intersecting streets along the 2-mile stretch. If you head west past the Lincoln Memorial and then south, you can run about a mile along the river in West Potomac Park, then make a 4-mile loop around the adjacent East Potomac Park. Running around the east side of the Tidal Basin can deliver you back onto the Mall near the Washington Memorial.

If you head north along the river, you will pass the Kennedy Center and wind up in Rock Creek Park. The park is a thickly wooded area along both sides of Rock Creek, which flows into the Potomac. A bike path will keep you close to the park roads as you wind your way about 9 miles northward to the Maryland boundary. The park extends another 10 miles into Maryland.

Workaday Running

Running becomes a lifestyle when it's no longer a chore, but an integral part of the day. Eventually it becomes like brushing your teeth; you no longer think about it, you just do it. And you *need* to do it, like you need to brush your teeth.

> Think of taking a shower. That's just the point. It's so natural, you don't even think about it. Do you think about what arm you wash first? Do you know if you washed your neck?
>
> The sound of the running water puts you in a secluded environment. It's meditative. Your thoughts come in, and go out. That shower may be the only private time you have all day. Are you truly dirty if you don't take a shower every day? No, but you feel that way. It's the same with running. Just like a shower, running is part of my daily life.
>
> —Nina Kuscsik

"I remember in my hardcore days 15 years ago," says Fred Lebow, "I'd get up at 5 a.m. and run in the cold, even freezing rain. Why? I had a need that running fulfilled, and the adversity of the conditions did not overshadow that need.

"Like so many runners, if I don't run, I don't feel right. I don't feel relaxed; I don't enjoy eating. Sure, running alleviates guilt, but more, it just makes you feel better. You feel good while you're running and you feel even better when you're finished."

499

Running, working, and living in New York City is definitely a balancing act, and it's hard work. I just have to pick time periods centered on more intense training and racing in which running is my first priority. I sometimes struggle to explain this to my employer: that, at the moment, my running is top priority. Currently I am writing chapters for a health and fitness book for *Reader's Digest.* I go into an office for 35 hours a week. I have made it clear that this is all the time I can give, but I meet that commitment, and make sure to schedule my time to attend an occasional meeting. I make sure I am not letting them down. Being in this particular job keeps me plugged into publishing, and working with people. Freelance writing is pretty solitary work, and together with the solitary aspect of running, I could probably go for days at a time without seeing anyone if I didn't make an effort to do so.

Although I am determined not to work full time, I feel I shouldn't say no to a job. That's the nature of my business. I have no trouble disciplining myself to run my mileage, do my speedwork, but I do have trouble disciplining myself to accept my limitations. You just can't do everything. And there are so many diversions in New York! I've been living in the city for eight years. We both really love it—personally and professionally. I have a lot of positive feelings about running in New York. After all, if you can do it here, you can do it anywhere. I think that's true for any big city, by the way.

At one point, I went to train for an extended period of time with other elite women in Boulder, Colorado. I went there with an open mind. If it worked out, I told myself, I could consider living there. I had a wonderful time; I loved the physical beauty, the good training. But I didn't click into the place. I found it a little monotonous and stifling. Maybe I've lived in New York too long.

—Gordon Bloch

Fred Lebow expresses opinions shared by many when he talks about running. The physical and mental benefits of the sport, as well as the sense of achievement and devotion to health and fitness it inspires, are common among all runners—elite and average. But for runners who don't run for a living, fitting in fitness takes some planning.

Time Management

There is a hardly a runner—no matter how dedicated—who doesn't wonder on certain days, "Just how am I going to fit it in?" Many of those who run took up the sport because it is the easiest and most convenient and effective exercise. However, with busy lives and responsibilities, even the easiest activity can become difficult.

Here are some helpful time management techniques, as practiced by NYRRC Leadership Council members.

Be Prepared

At the time delegate Herman Badillo helped lead the candlelight vigil at the strife-ridden 1968 Democratic National Convention in Chicago, he was a three-pack-a-day smoker. It was in the midst of this crisis that he decided to kick the habit. He went from three packs of cigarettes to one, and then he gave up smoking for good. To keep his weight down, Badillo took up running that same year.

But it was a decade later, in his role as Bronx borough president, during which time he helped establish the New York City Marathon, that he got the running bug. He decided to run that race in 1978, and 11 marathons later, he's still at it.

When you run in the morning, you gain time in a sense. It's like stretching 24 hours into 25. You may need to sleep less and get up earlier, but if you can get by that, running early seems to expand the day.

The way I see it, you have to view running time not as extra or wasted time, but as important, productive contemplation time. During a one-hour run, for example, I can accomplish more thinking than during any other time of day.

I get an idea on the run, then stop and write a note to myself with a twig in the dirt. I got an idea for the Fifth Avenue Mile while running in Central Park. I wrote "5" in the dirt. I didn't need to go back and look at it, but the act of writing it down made me remember the idea, and seemed to solidify it in my mind.

I think running to work is the best way to economize on time. It may seem a bit impractical, but I still think it is preferable to missing out on running altogether. True, to run to work you have to learn to "let go" and loosen up a bit in your style and habits. You also have to be creative about how to combine the two.

I used to run to work when I was employed in the "nonrunning world." I would take a backpack, with a clean shirt and small towel. If I had an appointment, I'd run into a lobby or phone booth, wipe off and change my shirt. I even remember taking a suit that way. I'd run in jeans, and carry a shirt, tie and jacket in my pack. I'd go into a telephone booth to change. I felt like I was Superman!

I've also been in situations where running is integrated into work life. Instead of going out for a martini lunch, we go for a run. I've done this in different places: Los Angeles, Chicago, San Francisco. In some circles, this is an accepted way of doing business. There have been times at the club, too, during which I'd talk business on the run with staff members.

Every time I have a personal or work problem, I go for a run. It doesn't cure anything, but it helps me to be able to think and to visualize. As other busy people have pointed out in the book, no FAX machines or telephones are around to bother you.

However, the other day I saw a guy running while talking on the telephone. I thought, "Gee, I hope this never happens to me. Running is one oasis I love, because I have no telephone." Eleven million cellular telephones were sold in 1991. I hope I don't start to see them on the roads!

—Fred Lebow

Those were the days when running was easy to plan, Badillo says. Even when he changed jobs and became deputy mayor of New York City, he'd get up early, at 5:30 a.m., and put in his long run of six to seven miles. However, during the eight years he served as a U.S. congressman, all that changed. "I couldn't run as much," he relates. "The hours were too long, and the commute between Washington and New York was also time-consuming."

But Badillo put in the miles; he still managed to average four to five per run. He did his runs on the capital's streets, until the police—who wanted to stop a rash of muggings of congressional members—told him about the canal in Georgetown, bordered by what he says is a beautiful gravel road.

Badillo didn't let all the traveling he did as a congressman stop him either. He ran on congressional tours: in the 110-degree heat of Indonesia in August—where "people were stunned to see me. They thought I'd collapse"—and in places like Paris, Rome, and Israel.

Life may have calmed down a bit since Badillo took up his Manhattan law practice in 1979, but he says it's still a problem to find time to run. "Lawyers get up early, for breakfast meetings. And because I'm still active in politics, I've got night meetings as well."

Here's how Badillo solves the problem. When he is under time constraints, he puts his running gear in the trunk of his car. When he finishes an evening meeting at 9 p.m., for example, he heads out for a run. In Badillo's case, that's usually in Central Park, which has a nearby restaurant where he can change his clothes, and has the safety features of being relatively well-lighted and having other runners at most times of day and night.

Often the key issue for busy people trying to fit their running in, says Badillo, is daylight. So when he can't find any in his neighborhood's Van Cortlandt Park, he takes an adjacent avenue which is well lighted. In the event he can't run at all, he tries to fit in his exercise with a home rowing or cross-country ski machine.

Badillo's advice to busy people is to be creative, flexible, and always prepared. Despite his ever-changing roles and schedules, that's how he makes sure to get his own running done.

Makeup Runs

When life for Valerie Salembier, the publisher of *Family Circle* magazine, gets so hectic she contemplates skipping her run, she repeats this mantra to herself, "Valerie, think about how you will feel if you *don't* do this." The tall, thin energetic executive also uses other thoughts to get her going. "Think about what you can eat for lunch," she tells herself. These reminders are followed by the same type of self-encouragement when she's finished her workout. "I'm so glad I did this," she tells herself. Salembier is clearly correct about the source of her motivation when she says, "I'm my own best cheerleader."

Sometimes it is difficult to train seriously in light of my work and my home life, but I make it work. I can't exercise when I work a 15-hour day, but I make it up by doing more the next day. It's important to me. In fact, sports is an extension of my work. It makes me feel good physically and mentally.

A lot of the time I have to incorporate my fitness with my family life. My older son Jamie, who is 6, sometimes wants to ride his bike with me while I run. He can make it about five miles. I put my second son, 3-year-old Bobby, in the baby jogger. Five wheels and my two feet, and we're off.

My training consists of 30 to 50 miles per week of running. I also sometimes do free weights, and in the gym, StairMaster on full blast for one hour. Sometimes I do step classes or stationary biking. When I can find a pool, I do a one-mile swim.

If I get tired, I'll slack off of exercising for a month. I do get worn out. It's from the children; it's from work. I listen to my body, but I don't use that as a cop-out.

My goal is to complete an Ironman Triathlon. That takes an amount of training I cannot currently do with my career. But I hope to do it in the future. Thank God I believe women get stronger in their 30s!

—Kim Alexis

There's no way to talk about slow, or even slower, periods of time in Salembier's life. When she wasn't working her current job, she was publishing *TV Guide*, or serving as president of the *New York Post*. Of her schedule, she says with a sigh of resignation, "It's awful, I get up too early. I work too many hours. I go to bed too late."

But she still gets her running in, at least four times a week. On weekdays she's up at 5:30 a.m. in order to put in nearly five miles, though she sometimes does a bit less depending on the time of her first appointment. In the summer, when there are more daylight hours, she prefers to run in the evenings. Like most of those profiled in this chapter, she tends to fit in as much exercise on weekends as possible. On Saturdays and Sundays, her runs increase to at least 6½ miles.

Salembier, who works 12-hour days, claims an intense work life is not exclusive to her job. "You have to work hard, no matter what you do, if you want to achieve." But when it becomes obvious she cannot do it all—work and running—how does she reconcile the conflict? "I've tried very hard to learn to be philosophical about it, but I've failed miserably. When I haven't run for a few days, I get feisty and difficult. It's terrible."

But she did plan to blend her two demanding passions more harmoniously in 1992. "Unfortunately, work has always come first. But I'm making a New Year's resolution that my morning winter runs will come first. I'll get in to work when I get there." Salembier points out she is very good at keeping New Year's resolutions. After all, that's how she started running, on precisely January 1, 1980.

Salembier, who knows it can be tough to fit running in, has some useful, concrete suggestions for doing so. "This sounds compulsive, but I make it an appointment, and write it on my calendar. It's like any other appointment. Unless I am deathly ill, it is not broken."

Many jobs include travel, Salembier points out. Hers is no exception. If she's gone more than one day, she makes sure to bring her running gear. Some opportunity to run usually presents itself. When she's back at her desk, she still keeps her running gear handy. That way, if there is a sudden appointment cancellation in the day, she knows just what to do with the precious extra time. Spontaneous training like this was made easier in past jobs that had shower facilities. As this isn't the case for most people, she suggests, if it is feasible, joining a nearby health club.

Another motivating factor that has worked well for Salembier is having a regular running partner. In her case, there are two, which means that 90 percent of the time she runs with company. One is her husband. The other, with whom she has trained for ten years, is her girlfriend. "Beth and I talk nonstop. That we can do that for 6½ miles is amazing. She is truly my sister." Salembier suggests finding a partner with flexibility. In her case in particular, this complements her schedule, which is quite rigid.

How do her vocation and avocation coexist? Salembier sums up the running/work equation this way: "It's about balance; some semblance of balance is so critical."

Make It Your Job

Paula Zahn knows what it means to be in serious training. When CBS Sports President Neil Pilson first confronted her and coanchor Tim McCarver with the 1992 Olympic task, he handed them a foot-thick briefing book and announced, "Now your Olympic training begins."

By the time Zahn appeared on the broadcast—smiling with casual ease, in the middle of the night (French time), and viewed by millions of people—she had reviewed the book, plus 200 athlete profiles, and had been additionally briefed for hours daily for half a year. This immersion in Olympic study took place on top of her regular duties as coanchor of *CBS This Morning*. Zahn admits about that time, "I didn't have much of a life, but I knew that going into it. But it was the most exciting thing I've ever done."

Even without the Olympics, Zahn pays a price for her success. Up at 4:30 a.m., she reads and is briefed on the news right up until she goes on the air live from 7 to 9 a.m. She returns home at 1 or 2 p.m., only to continue to read and study for the next day. It would seem she'd be used to it after five years on the job, but she quotes fellow CBS broadcaster Charles Osgood about the nature of her early-morning hours. "It's not a matter of feeling good; it's a matter of getting used to feeling lousy."

So where does running fit in? For the lifelong athlete (Zahn was a competitive swimmer and skier from childhood through college), it has to. "Finding an escape valve in this business is very tough. It is not a job you can turn on and off. Exercise has always been a great escape for me. It is one of the few times I don't have a beeper registering 20 calls a minute."

She used to go out routinely for a run after work, often with her three-year-old daughter Haley in a running stroller. "I'm not a fast runner. I usually get lapped, just poking along. But whatever the pace, it makes me feel better," she says. However, during her Olympic training, that changed. "I was working two full-time jobs," she says. "It was difficult to exercise. But when I didn't, I paid for it. My body immediately reacts to a lack of exercise. 'Take me outside; let me out' it cries.

"I lost that daily regimen for the first time in my life," she laments. She faced that philosophically: "I said to myself: this is a very short period of my life. It will pass, and I'll get back again."

Zahn did take steps to improve things when her regular running was not possible. She bought a set of free weights, which she often uses, even for a brief 15 to 20 minutes. "At least I feel like my circulation is going," she says. When the weather allows, she skips the cab ride home and walks two miles. And on weekends, she and her husband pack in heavier workouts, with five-mile runs and a half hour with the weights.

During the Olympics, she skied the women's Olympic downhill course, and as had been done at the 1988 Olympic Games in Seoul for other television broadcasters, she and coanchor McCarver requested that exercise bikes be installed in their hotel rooms. They managed to fit in their pedaling, despite a crazy schedule of broadcasting from 2 to 5 a.m. French time and sleeping 6 a.m. till noon.

When life makes demands that don't allow her to "have it all," Zahn has learned to let go. During her Olympic preparation, she found she needed more sleep. And if it became a choice between working out or spending time with her daughter, she never wavered. However, she acknowledges that, although being outdoors with Haley is a pleasure, "It does not replace exercise, either physically or mentally." But after the Olympics, she adds, "I didn't have to make that choice."

Zahn emphasizes that life does not remain static, and that we must be ready for its ebb and flow. She concludes, "Our lives continue to change. You have to make adjustments to see what feels right—mentally and physically."

Put It on the List

"I'm a list maker," proclaims George Hirsch, who for years has adhered faithfully to his routine of making nightly lists, then crossing out tasks as he completes them. "I get great pleasure from seeing things crossed off the list," he says. But while most runners who are so religiously governed by a list would surely need to include their daily workouts, Hirsch never does. He knows he will put in the miles. "Running is automatic. It's closer to something like washing my face when I get up," he concludes.

In the business world, George Hirsch is known for starting up successful magazines. He founded *New York* magazine and *New Times*—

the latter of which became *The Runner*. *The Runner* was merged into *Runner's World* in 1987, and since that time, Hirsch has served as publisher of *Runner's World*.

Hirsch is a busy executive, and as a runner, he's no slouch either. Although he puts in a relatively modest 40 miles a week for someone competitive, he managed to win the 1990 NYRRC Runner of the Year award in the 50-plus age category—which means in his age group he won the majority of New York races in which he competed.

Hirsch, who gets in his training any time of day during which meetings are not scheduled, admits that for doing his sport, being publisher of a major running magazine "makes my life easier." Wherever business travel takes him—from the magazine's headquarters in Pennsylvania to consulting with advertisers around the country—he can be assured of finding running time. In fact, he even conducts specific business agendas while racking up the miles with some of his co-workers.

Despite the fact that running is an integral part of George Hirsch's life, he is often compelled to sacrifice training time. In 1986, when he ran for the United States Congress from his East Side New York district, he had a hard time fitting in any running at all. One of the problems was being a novice at campaigning. "I've been a magazine publisher for 25 years. I know what I'm doing. But as a political candidate, I was learning every step of the way." During the 24-hour-a-day schedule of political campaigning, Hirsch would forego a run in favor of catnaps, which he took whenever and wherever he could. He claims he perfected the art of a 15-minute snooze during mid-Manhattan cab rides.

Hirsch says he learned most acutely that life often presents us with more tasks than we can possibly accomplish when he was a business student at Harvard, where he was inundated with work. "You understood you were not going to get every assignment read. I soon realized that was the philosophy: to give us more work than we could possibly do, to be faced with some tough choices. Just like the real world."

Even doing the familiar job in which he is comfortable, and within the supportive atmosphere of a running magazine, Hirsch is often forced to sacrifice his run. As he travels a great deal—traversing busy streets—he uses this analogy, "There are traffic jams in life, both literally and figuratively." Although Hirsch is a serious runner, he keeps the time and energy he devotes to the activity in perspective. "I don't make my living as a runner. I'm not training for the Olympics, so running is not my highest priority—although staying fit is."

Hirsch has recently come up with a solution to those times when he can't get out to run, which is made tougher at many hours because he must cross busy Manhattan streets for several miles until he reaches Central Park. The purchase of a low-impact treadmill has allowed him the opportunity to train comfortably in the evening and save his legs from some pounding at the same time.

But perhaps George Hirsch's real gift—which is often rare among serious runners, not to mention high-powered business people—is his ability to relax. "I'm pretty good at it," he says. "After days I've been busy, I will not set my alarm on weekends in order to get up and run. I'll sit in bed with the newspaper, coffee, and a bagel. I take it easy on myself."

Yet, when it's time to buckle down, he puts in the training time. When he takes on the marathon challenge, for example, he plans six weeks worth of long runs, with at least three 18 to 20 milers. But the real secret of his success is knowing exactly how and when to be serious. While Hirsch says he would never drop out of a marathon once he's started, if he doesn't find time to do the training, he'll change his plans and not toe the starting line. "Life is forgiving," says the man who has mastered perhaps the ultimate balancing act.

The Earlier the Better

Working as a nightly news anchor fills up a day. But for Tom Brokaw, a day is not complete without exercise—preferably running. He explains:

"I run 15 to 20 miles a week, five to six times a week. I always run in Central Park when I'm in the New York City. I also run regularly in Connecticut. I try to run in the morning, because I find if I don't do it then, it just keeps getting slipped on the schedule. I have a dog now in New York, and I take her with me. That helps to get me out.

"When I'm on the road, I always take my running gear with me. I'm not always successful at running as much as I'd like to while traveling, but I either try to run or swim. Most hotels now have health clubs, and that's very helpful.

"In a sense, at times my running and work life have been combined. For example, I ran with 1992 presidential candidates, like Senator Bob

Kerry—a very active runner—and Jerry Brown. They can get into little competitions when you run with them. The obvious question is about the president. No, I've never run with George Bush.

"As far as the effect of exercise on my work life, friends used to say to me, 'You have to be fit because you're on television.' I answer that I have to be fit because it makes me feel better. I'd do this no matter what my profession was. I'm mentally more alert, physically more able. I have a reputation of being able to work extra-long hours and maintain mental acuity. I don't know how well deserved that reputation is, but I really believe working out makes it possible to perform demanding work.

"I also use exercise to help me relax and unwind. On days of big events, I often run beforehand. When I did the Democratic presidential candidates debate in 1991, I ran that morning. I used the time to think about the flow of things, and how I felt I wanted the debate to go.

"Often I think about my daily agenda while running. I did the first interview with [Mikhail] Gorbachev that he ever granted in this country, and I ran beforehand. The weather was nasty, and the streets were icy, but I got out. I thought about him, and that interview."

Corporate Running

Work and running; real life and play—never the twain shall meet? Not so, if the largest running series in the world is held up as the example. The Chemical Corporate Challenge (formerly the Manufacturers Hanover Corporate Challenge) is a series of 3.1-mile runs for corporate teams. The series, which includes 125,000 people from 6000 corporations, is held in several countries abroad, and in 15 cities throughout the country. The largest version is conducted by the NYRRC in Central Park, which was also the site of the first Corporate Challenge back in 1977.

Barbara Paddock, vice president and director of event marketing for Chemical Bank Corporation and also a runner, oversees the series. She emphasizes how the event has integrated running into the workplace on every level. The Corporate Challenge isn't just a road race; it's nearly an institution. Through participation, publicity, or by word of mouth, says Paddock, "If you're part of the corporate world, you've likely heard of the Corporate Challenge."

Paddock explains the nature of the event: "The race is more about company camaraderie than athletic achievement. It is an opportunity for employees to have fun in a noncompetitive, nonworking atmosphere." A look at an overflowing Central Park on race day is testimony to her claim. Banners, banquet-style picnics, team uniforms and photos, cheerleading sections of fellow employees—all testify to the fact that running and work need not be isolated pursuits.

To see if there is a Chemical Corporate Challenge event held in your area, contact Chemical Bank Corporation: Event Marketing Department, 140 East 45th Street, 16th Floor, New York, New York 10017. Telephone: (212) 270-8100.

Business and Running

Can successful running be translated to business—and vice versa? One person seems to have made it very clear it can. Alberto Salazar— the former multi-event American and world record holder—was still in serious training when he delved into the restaurant business—immersing himself much in the way he had done in his running. In June 1987, he co-purchased a Eugene, Oregon, restaurant. During his tenure, the Oregon Electric Station became one of the most successful restaurants in the entire Pacific Northwest. In November 1991, Salazar brought his athletic and executive abilities together when he became a major player in the world of international road racing and track and field as an executive with Nike. Salazar says:

"I think there is a correlation between running and business success. In fact, sometimes I make too direct of a correlation. I tend to be a bit simplistic: Just work hard and it will result in success. In running, however, the rewards are much more directly related to the work you put in. You've got to train smart, but there is a much greater correlation between the amount of effort and the amount of success.

"In business, there are a lot of other variables. It's not quite so simplistic. At first I tended to think that running and business were both regulated by the same effort. But I realized that in business you've probably got to be even smarter, because you're dealing in various ways with a lot of other people. That's resulted in the hardest adjustment for me in the business world. I tend to be a little too confident, or to move a little too quickly.

"However, I think there is some similarity between the two in terms of overall philosophy. You have a job to be done and you do whatever it takes to accomplish it. You have to fight the inclination to be negative. That's one of the things I've noticed in the business world. You bring up an idea or a solution to a problem, and the first thing people think of is why it can't be done. I think the proper way is first to see why something *will* work, and then deal with the hurdles as you go along. Being optimistic can get you past a problem.

This aspect of running and business is similar. Good runners should be the same way. They should be optimistic, envision themselves winning or running a goal time. Then they go about doing the work to accomplish that goal. If you don't look to the ultimate goal—be it financial or otherwise—if you look merely at all the problems along the way, you'll never get it done. Sometimes you can be naive or simplistic and overlook what may become major problems later on, but overall, you're still better off having the same attitude in business as you have for successful running."

24 Tips for Environmentally Conscious Running

Welles Lobb, a free-lance writer from Allentown, Pennsylvania, points out that runners spend a large chunk of their lives outdoors breathing fresh air and bounding over land. Through their close contact with the natural world, many develop an appreciation of nature and sympathy for its well-being. So, as we stride through this age of vital environmental concern, here's Lobb's list of 24 new and recycled conservation tips from *New York Running News* for individual runners and clubs to consider. Although not every tip is practical for everyone, if we all do our share, we can make our world a better place for running.

Reduce Unnecessary Driving

1. Run from either your home or place of work instead of driving to a workout spot. If safety or training reasons require you to drive, try to combine this trip with others (for example, grocery shopping or banking) to consolidate use of your car. You can also run or walk to a nearby workout site for your warmup, if that's possible.

2. Measure your running routes by bicycle odometer, rather than by car.

3. Consider commuting to and from work by foot. With co-workers who are also runners, take an active role in installing a locker-and-shower facility at your workplace.

4. Clubs: Encourage members to carpool or use public transportation when traveling to races. Assign a member the job of organizing car pools for club members traveling to out-of-town races. Also, consider renting a van or bus for group trips to races.

Keep Training and Racing Sites Clean

5. Try to pick up at least one piece of litter at workout or race sites. Carry personal garbage home in your car and dispose of it properly.

6. Clubs: Organize a club "Cleanup Day" at a local park or popular running route. Combine it with a fun-run and social event.

Use, Don't Abuse, the Land

7. Run on established trails. Trailblazing and taking shortcuts can cause damaging erosion.

8. In an emergency, if no public toilet is nearby and you must relieve yourself, don't do so near an open water source or on fragile vegetation. Also, bury solid wastes.

Support the Cause

9. Support races that contribute to environmental causes like parkland acquisition, clean water, or clean air.

10. Write to your elected officials to express your views on the importance of clean air and public land acquisitions, especially the establishment of trails for nonmotorized traffic.

11. Clubs: Get political! Endorse pro-environment candidates for public office in your club newsletter. Also, include a conservation tip of the month in your newsletter.

12. Clubs: Organize a club environmental committee to brainstorm about running/conservation projects. Also, invite a public official, conservation officer, or environmental activist who is a runner to speak to your club about running and the environment.

Save Natural Resources, Reduce Waste

13. Bring your own supply of safety pins to races. This relieves the race director of potential shortages and expenses, and may ultimately reduce the demand for manufactured metal. Also, donate your accumulated collection of race safety pins to your club for future use.

14. Consider a "no shirt" option when filling out your race application. Chances are you already have a stockpile of race T-shirts at home.

15. Donate your old shirts, sweats, and shoes to charities. Clubs: Organize an old-clothing and running-shoe collection drive for charity.

16. Clubs: Print your newsletter on recycled paper.

17. Wear your running clothes two or three times before machine-washing them. Remove perspiration odors with a quick rinse after daily use. Air-dry clothes instead of using the dryer.

18. Carry your own water supply to races. This stretches the race director's supply and reduces the number of thrown-away cups.

Recycle

19. Share running magazines or newspapers with friends, then recycle them.

20. Buy sports drinks or bottled water in containers that your state accepts as recyclables.

21. Clubs: Raise funds by collecting and selling members' aluminum and glass recyclables to local buyers.

Eliminate Plastics

22. Request environmentally benign products at races: paper drinking cups, nonplastic awards, and paper bags for packets, for example.

23. Clubs: Provide ceramic, metal, or paper dishes, cups, utensils, etc., at socials.

Last But Not Least

24. Save water: Keep showers brief and use a water-saver head.

Fred Lebow on the Run-to-Work Movement

Since starting work at the NYRRC, I generally run everywhere: to work, to meetings, to receptions. In fact, by 1974, I began to realize I could get everywhere so much faster by running than by subway, bus, or taxi.

That's when we started the Run-to-Work movement at the club. But it really escalated for a time a couple of years later during a New York City transit strike. First of all, we set up a water station on the Brooklyn Bridge with a RUN TO WORK sign for people walking or running to work. To spread the message, we sent out press releases on how to run to work. People seemed to get the idea; they were running to work by the hundreds. We began to have conversations with various companies about accommodating runners, by installing shower facilities and changing rooms, for example.

Unfortunately, when the strike was over, the Run-to-Work movement lost momentum. But the health and fitness movement lived on and did help affect the management at many companies, which now have extensive gyms and workout and health programs.

The New York City transit strike and Run-to-Work helped popularize wearing running shoes to walk to work, or any other place. And some people still run to work. My goal is to revitalize this program, especially in New York, where transportation fares are always on the rise. In addition, in places like New York, it's very easy to run to work because the paths and distances are convenient.

13

Part 13: Running Equipment

Running Shoes

Running is easy, the common refrain goes, just lace up your shoes and head out the door. Just lace up your *running* shoes, that is. They're the only protection you've got from the impact of hard surfaces on long stretches of road.

How to Choose Running Shoes

According to Joe Weisenfeld, D.P.M., running shoes are like lovers. There is no one type for everyone, but when you find yours, you're set for life. Stick with it.

Once an elite runner and now an accomplished masters runner, Gary Muhrcke began selling running shoes in 1976 from the back of a van. Now he owns six Super Runners Shop stores in the New York metropolitan area, which, he emphasizes, specialize in the technical aspects of running shoes. In other words, says Muhrcke, "I stress shoes used by athletes, not just those that look good." The most important thing, echoes Muhrcke, is to stay with a shoe you've used successfully in the past. If the worry is that your favorite model has changed, or will do so in the near future, relax. Muhrcke says most of the good companies create shoes that evolve, and that it is this evolution that has produced the most successful shoes on the market. Therefore, if you need motion control, for example, you'll be able to fulfill that need with increasing effectiveness in future generations of shoes.

If the name or the look of a shoe changes, knowledgeable salespeople can determine which shoe is most like the one you currently wear. It's a matter of knowing the characteristics and the fit. "If you're wearing a shoe that rates an A− grade," claims Muhrcke, with evolving shoe technology, "a smart salesperson can offer you one that gets an A+."

If you are trying on a shoe at the Super Runners Shop, you are allowed to test that shoe by running outside the store on the sidewalk. Muhrcke claims that nothing will better reveal if the shoe is right than a true test run. What if your store doesn't allow it? "Tell them to change their policy," says Muhrcke. To help you find that perfect pair, look for durable, comfortable running shoes that will be strongest and give support where you are weakest or tend to have problems or injuries.

Before going to the store to buy shoes, determine what you need, advises Dr. Weisenfeld. Do you want a sturdier, more supportive, heavier training shoe or a racing shoe (also known as a flat) which is lighter, and has more flexibility? You may be tempted by a combination shoe, called a racer-trainer, but it is usually not as good as either one separately. Have a price range in mind and shop in a store that specializes in running shoes. Employees there should be able to recommend a few different shoes in your price range. In addition, they can assess which shoe might suit your build, your running style, and your running goals. They can also show you how to prolong the life of a shoe with proper care (e.g., using shoe glue products).

If the Shoe Fits

Don't overlook socks, Weisenfeld advises. If you don't wear them when running, fine. But if you do, bring them with you to try on with shoes. Another plus to a running shoe specialty store is that you can become acquainted with the various lines of sports socks and their properties (some of which are mentioned in this chapter).

A training shoe should be long enough to fit a thumb-width at the toe end of the shoe. A racing shoe can be snug; the toe can almost touch the end of the shoe. The width should be comfortable when standing. Keep in mind that feet tend to be larger later in the day.

Should Women Buy Men's Shoes?

Once upon a time, claims Muhrcke, there was, in fact, more variety and quality to men's running shoes than women's. "Years ago women thought their shoes weren't as good. Now I think women's shoes are superior for them and make more sense than buying men's shoes." Top companies make both men's and women's versions of shoes. Women's shoes are made lighter than men's, and thus serve women better. But if a woman has a wider or larger foot, says Muhrcke, she shouldn't hesitate to try men's shoes.

Although separate shoe models are made for men and women, a man with a narrow foot can try a woman's shoe and a woman with a wide foot can try men's shoes. Women should check the heel width though, as it may be too wide in a men's shoe. The shoe lacing can also help with width sizing, says Weisenfeld.

Do You Need More Than One Pair of Running Shoes?

"I don't know about you, but I can't put my foot into a wet pair of shoes," says Gary Muhrcke. So, if sweat or rain plague you as a regular runner, you need more than one pair of running shoes. Initially, however, Muhrcke and Weisenfeld suggest not buying two pairs of a new model at once. Try the shoes for at least a few weeks to make sure they work for you.

Do You Need Separate Racing Shoes?

The technology of training shoes has evolved to the extent that lightweight models may well serve for most runners' purposes, including races. "The biggest factor is weight," says Muhrcke. "You may save only two ounces in a racing shoe, but two ounces over 10,000 meters is a lot." Most would benefit from racing shoes, he concludes, if not for the physical aspects then for the psychological ones. It's the ritual. "Putting on racing shoes is the thing you do on race day that psychologically prepares the body to race."

Construction Details

Before buying your running shoes, consider the construction of the shoe as well as the fit. Weisenfeld recommends that you check:

Lasting. The last is what a shoe is shaped around. The type of last greatly affects the flexibility and stability of the shoe. Slip lasting allows for increased flexibility and characterizes lighter shoes. Board lasting increases stability and the integrity (resistance to deformity) of the shoe. Combination lasting includes the advantages of both methods. There are two shapes used in lasting—curved and straight. Most people find a slightly curved last to be most comfortable.

Flexibility. Flexibility refers to the bend of the shoe in the area surrounding the ball of the foot. Racing shoes should be very flexible while training shoes should be slightly stiffer. Most shoes can be made more flexible by bending the shoe across the ball horizontally.

Shock Absorption (Cushioning). The two parts to shock absorption are front (or forefoot) and heel (or rear foot). Generally, softer shoes (air shoes) exacerbate problems for runners with structural imbalances. People who have impact-related problems (e.g., heel bruises) benefit from soft shoes. If you have a specific problem, select a shoe that provides appropriate cushioning.

Insoles (Sock Liners). Insoles add to shock absorption. These are removable and replaceable and either come with the shoe or are purchased separately. Foam rubber or canvas insoles are unacceptable. Some, like antishearing insoles, can be purchased separately. These reduce friction to prevent blisters. If necessary, to prevent slipping, insoles can be glued into the shoe.

Heel Counters. The heel is cradled in a cup that is called a counter. It should be stiff, especially in a training shoe. The counter resists excessive heel motion. If you have any imbalances causing a problem, look for a strong heel counter, made of plastic.

Toe Box. If your toes are thick or slide forward, look for a high toe box shoe. If you still have toe problems after purchasing the shoes, the toe box can be cut to allow room. The cuts should be vertical, not horizontal.

Quality Control. The shoes must be balanced. They should not rock or tilt to the sides when placed on a flat surface.

Caveat Emptor. Gary Muhrcke advises that you can get the most from your purchase, and best protect yourself, by being on the lookout for shoe wear. Muhrcke's Law: Repair shoe heels as soon as necessary. The basic sign of the need for repair is if the outsole has worn down to the midsole. You should be able to bring your shoes into a running shoe store for repair.

> As part of its social action programs, the NYRRC has made collections of used running shoes to donate to homeless shelters or to those who have been a part of its various other programs. Why not find a good use for your shoes in your own community? Make a collection and bring them to a local homeless shelter or other charitable organization. T-shirts are also often coveted, particularly by children.

World Shoe Relief distributes running and athletic shoes to the homeless and the needy around the world. Simply tie shoelaces together and if possible, indicate the shoe size. Send them to World Shoe Relief, P.O. Box 423, Trabuco Canyon, CA 92678.

After one year, even if your shoes do not appear worn-out, they probably are. "The elements alone—heat, salt that melts snow, pavement—wear out shoes," claims Muhrcke. Even a shoe that still looks good can lose shock absorption. With one repair of the outsoles, a shoe that is used constantly should last 800 to 1000 miles.

There are two common mistakes that Gary Muhrcke has seen over the years that receive little publicity. The first is that people don't understand pronation: the act of the foot rolling inward on footstrike. Customers tell Muhrcke that they need antipronating shoes when many times they have normal footstrike. "To a degree, to pronate is to run normally," explains Muhrcke. "Pronation is part of foot function; the 'hit and roll' of the foot disperses energy, as it should." Runners continually point to wear on the outer shoe heel as a sign that they need special shoes. "The eventual wear of shoes on the outer heel is also normal," says Muhrcke. Obviously there are categories of runners who may need a more specialized shoe, for example, those who are large or heavy, or who increase their mileage and subsequently suffer injury. But generally this is not the case.

The other mistake is made by women who want to buy top-of-the-line shoes. They correlate price with quality, but pricier running shoes are those with more features, which add weight. However, as Muhrcke points out, women are lighter than men and don't need the heavier shoes. "They're doing themselves a disservice," he says and suggests that these women stay with a sparer, simpler model. "The bottom line," says Muhrcke, "is that running is a very simple sport. After all, even two-year-olds run. A lot of people try to complicate it." With today's technology and expert help, it should be easy to buy the appropriate running shoe.

Shoes and Injury Prevention

According to Tom Fleming, running shoe manufacturers now produce shoes not only designed to reduce the risk of injury but also to help eliminate the cause of (often chronic) injuries that may already exist.

True, much of injury-free running depends on biomechanics, but the correct choice of a running shoe is very important, especially for those prone to certain types of injuries.

Most running shoe designs emphasize either shock absorption (which provides mainly cushioning) or motion control (which provides mainly stability). Generally, the more a shoe is designed for motion control, the more rigid it is and the less it absorbs shock. Conversely, the better the shock absorption, the less motion control, says Fleming. The challenge for today's shoe manufacturers is to provide shock absorption and motion control in one shoe. Manufacturers today realize the importance of shock absorption, even for people who need shoes with good motion control, for example, people who have stability problems or flat feet.

So Fleming advises that you choose a shoe that will best accommodate your feet—and your potential foot problems. If you have supination (feet roll to the outside) and therefore tend to have bowlegs or suffer from iliotibial band syndrome, stress fractures, shinsplints and plantar fasciitis, choose a shoe that offers plenty of shock absorption. Look for a slip-lasted shoe with a soft midsole. If you have excessive pronation (rotation or torque to the inside), choose a shoe with good foot control. Choose a straight-lasted shoe with a firm midsole, particularly on the inner (medial) side of the shoe, which also may have a firm board last.

Monitor Your Shoes

From the beginning of shoe use, the wear of the outsole should be noted, and later midsole compression should also be monitored. Tom Fleming says that although most people incur injuries because of improper training, if an athlete becomes injured or sore in the first two to four weeks after changing shoe type, the shoe must be considered the likely cause. In this case, it is best to resume using the old shoe model.

The wear on the shoe pattern on the bottom of the sole (ridges, waffles, etc.) tells you about your footstrike and thrust (how your foot pushes off the ground). This is what a shoe dealer assesses when looking at your old shoes. Shoe wear can be valuable to discover what a normal pattern of shoe wear is for you and to determine which brands and models wear better or longer.

Wear on the sole of the shoe is not always the first indication of shoe deterioration. Some runners compress the midsole before they wear out the outsoles. Learn to assess compression. While outsole wear is more obvious, many runners don't check for compression (called "bottom-ing-out" by dealers). Thus many customers wonder why, although the shoes don't appear to them to be worn-out, they don't feel the same cushioning. Gauging the effectiveness of cushioning will help you from running in shoes past their prime.

Pronators wear out the midsole fast; also, the medial sides of the shoes compress quicker. Forefoot strikers (those who land first on the ball/toe of the foot) can also compress or compact the midsole materi-al more quickly, says Fleming.

Additional Shoe Tips

1. Shoes generally lose their shock-absorbing qualities anywhere from 500 to 700 miles, or about six months of running 5 to 10 hours a week.

2. Take your old pair of running shoes to the store with you to show the dealer.

3. When buying running shoes, ask to try on several different types for comparison. After buying a pair of shoes, wear them for casu-al walking for at least a few days before running. According to guidelines from the International Marathon Medical Directors Association, training with a new pair of shoes should be done slowly and gradually, and competing should be done only when you are absolutely sure that the shoes are trouble-free.

4. Choose shoes that are roomy enough. For one thing, your feet expand during running. As Joe Weisenfeld suggests, you should purchase shoes that have about a thumb-width between the longest toe and the front of the shoe, and make sure the toe box allows enough room to wiggle your toes. He also suggests buy-ing the shoes in the afternoon, when your feet are bigger.

5. You might consider treating your shoes with a protective coating, like Scotchgard, or some other product made specifically for this purpose.

6. Cliff Temple suggests that you carefully look at the inside of the shoes for rough seams or other possible causes of blisters.

7. Temple also has this advice for beginners: Don't buy cheap shoes—such as sneakers not specifically designed for running. But don't buy the priciest model to begin with either.

8. Tom Fleming says, "Look down at your feet. How are they shaped: long and narrow ('needle feet') or square and short ('thimble feet')? Now go for a shoe in that shape. People tend to buy shoes in the shape of their feet—even if they don't realize it."

Fred Lebow on Running Shoes

I remember buying my first pair of running shoes, in 1969. They were actually tennis shoes. I finally decided to buy a pair of *real* running shoes, so I purchased a pair of spikes. At the time, I figured that's what runners wear, right?

I'll never forget running on 53rd Street and Second Avenue in Manhattan in those spikes. After a lot of strange looks from other people, I finally got to soft ground on the reservoir in Central Park, but meanwhile I had killed all the spikes by running the two miles on concrete from my house. I didn't know better. It was embarrassing. I bought one of my early pairs of real running shoes from Europe, through mail order. Now, in terms of running shoe technology, I think there are no bad shoes anymore.

Eventually, I didn't need to buy running shoes because the shoe companies sent them to me for free. They knew I showed up absolutely everywhere in running shoes, so it was good exposure. Asics is a sponsor of the New York City Marathon, so the company provides me with a model of shoes I like, which is great.

For years, I've been in the habit of wearing running shoes everywhere and for every function. I even wear them with my tuxedo. There's only been a couple of times when wearing running shoes didn't go over so well. One of those times was my attempt to attend a meeting at the New York Athletic Club, which has a strict dress code. They wouldn't let me in, so Ollan Cassell of The Athletics Congress, who was with me for the meeting, took me around the corner and bought me a pair of acceptable shoes.

Running Apparel

"Just like running's world records, running clothes and accessories have evolved quickly," says Don Mogelefsky, managing editor of *New York Running News*. "And they continue to be improved upon with stunning frequency. In what has blossomed into a multibillion-dollar industry, the race to create the ultimate in functional and stylish running gear sprints on."

In this chapter, Mogelefsky offers his insights on running apparel for the 90s:

"The running attire catchwords for the 90s are simply these: Don't sweat it! And they're meant to be taken quite literally. The days of running in good old-fashioned sweats—as in sweatshirts and sweatpants—are woefully numbered, and for good reason. Although they've long been regarded as staple running equipment, sweats, in essence, accomplish everything you don't want as a runner. They cling to moisture, keeping you uncomfortably wet while you run, and actually become heavier as a result. Additionally, they offer no protection from wind, rain, or snow. In fact, running in sweats these days is the equivalent of using a rotary-dial telephone. Sure, it'll work, but why on earth would you want to use it?"

Fortunately, a huge assortment of highly efficient gear exists for the modern runner. This section focuses on the latest technological advances in running attire, as well as some of the more popular accessories available to consumers. Keep in mind that this is an overview; a comprehensive look into all the products available to runners today would require a book in itself.

527

Fall and winter present runners with the challenge of staying warm, dry, and protected from the wind without wearing so many clothes that they can't move or risk getting overheated. Diane Magnani, former running store owner and a 2:49 marathoner, frequently answers runners' what-to-wear questions. "A good rule of thumb is that you should dress to run as if it were about 20 degrees warmer and you were going out for some activity not designed to raise your heart rate," she says. That way, you may feel chilly at first, but you'll warm up considerably after the first 5 to 10 minutes.

You'll save yourself a lot of sweating if you remember to dress in layers—especially when the weather is unpredictable. For example, you might start an early-morning run wearing a polypropylene top under a long-sleeved cotton shirt under a nylon shell, with polypro tights and nylon rain pants on the bottom. As you warm up and the sun gets high in the sky, you can remove the shell, pants, and cotton shirt and tie them around your waist or carry them in a small pack.

You'll also be able to get away with fewer and less bulky clothes, says Magnani, if you wear a hat and mittens or gloves. At least 50 percent of the heat your body loses is lost through your head. If you get warm, just pull the items off and tuck them in a pocket.

If you're trying to run a fast time in a race, you may want to opt for a bit of shivering on the starting line in order not to be burdened with extra items in the later miles. If you can, have a friend with you to whom you can hand a sweatshirt and sweatpants just before the race starts.

It's a misconception, Magnani notes, that it's healthy to sweat excessively when you work out. People used to believe one of those suits that makes you sweat was a way to lose weight. All it does is make you dehydrated. Of course, you will perspire some, no matter how cold it is, and the best way to deal with that is to make sure the layer next to your skin is one that "wicks" moisture away from the skin, such as polypropylene. To keep moisture away from the outside, wear a fabric that also "breathes."

—Fitness Forum

Running apparel is available for warm weather and cold and rainy weather. Warm-weather clothing is meant to keep you cool and dry, cold-weather clothing to keep you warm and dry. As you may well imagine, winter wear is essential to the majority of runners. A persistent dilemma for the inclement-weather runner—and for companies producing activewear—has been to come up with a running suit that not only prevents moisture and wind from getting in but also allows moisture (i.e., sweat) to get out.

Until fairly recently, runners had the dubious choice of wearing jackets and pants that would either get soaked by rain or that were effective in preventing the flow of moisture onto the body, but not in wicking perspiration away. However, a virtual revolution in fiber technology has set the industry on its cold and soggy collective ear—and, in the process, made the elusive goal of moisture management a reality.

Probably the most well known and popular moisture-management fabrics currently in vogue are polypropylene and Gore-Tex. "Polypro," as it's called, is a lightweight, breathable, insulating fabric that is effective in wicking moisture away from the body. Gore-Tex is a waterproof (guaranteed 100 percent waterproof by its maker, W. L. Gore and Associates), breathable fabric that transports perspiration vapors outward while preventing precipitation from penetrating inward. Generally, polypro is used as an "inner shell" and Gore-Tex complements it as an "outer shell."

Practically every running wear manufacturer sells running suits made of polypro and Gore-Tex—or a similar combination of fabrics that produce the moisture-managing effect. The Asics DTX (Dynamic Technical Excellence) pants and jacket—to single out one such offering—are popular.

The amount of time you spend in the elements also figures into how you should dress. According to Gary Muhrcke, "If you're going to be out less than 45 minutes, you probably don't need Gore-Tex—you can get away with just having a nylon shell. The nylon shell will basically keep the hot air that your body generates in and the cold air out. For being outside beyond 45 minutes, we do recommend Gore-Tex. That's because it lets the initial body heat out, and therefore it works almost like having an extra layer of skin—so you don't generate as much moisture on your body, and you don't sweat as much."

As far as cutting-edge technology goes, Hind and Nike have been leading the way in implementing technological advances. Hind's Drylete fabric and Nike's FIT (Functional Innovative Technology) fabric are regarded as state-of-the-art in providing optimum moisture control. The Textile Fibers Group of Hoechst Celanese Corporation, among other research companies, continues to be instrumental in developing improved fibers for activewear. One of the Textile Fibers Group's latest innovations is a thermal polyester fiber called BTU, or Bio Thermal Underlayers. This fiber consists of a unique combination of cross sections and fiber lengths that wick perspiration away from the body without absorbing it. Small fibers on the fabric's surface actually lift the fabric off the skin and prevent chafing and irritation. Nike recently began using BTU, mainly in the manufacture of thermal underwear products.

Aside from polypro and Gore-Tex, a variety of other moisture-controlling fabrics are currently being used extensively. Among the best sellers are MFT, Thermax™, Coolmax™, and Supplex™. MFT, or Micro Flow Transmission, consists of billions of tiny pores that are too small to allow the penetration of outside moisture but large enough to allow the passage of perspiration vapors. MFT is extremely breathable and also windproof, waterproof, and lightweight.

Thermax, Coolmax, and Supplex are all made by DuPont. The Thermax fiber is one-sixth the diameter of a human hair and has a hollow core that traps body heat. Like the other leading fibers, it also transports perspiration away from your body. Coolmax, another wicking material, has 20 percent more surface area than other fibers and thus hastens the evaporation of perspiration. Supplex is an ultralightweight, supple fabric that is very breathable and water- and wind-resistant.

Now that you're familiar with the technological mainstays of the running wear industry, you can best assess some of the actual products on the market. It should be noted that once you've accumulated a small collection of running wear, you can mix and match outfits to your heart's content. Surprisingly, even jackets and pants of outrageously different designs very often can be worn together. (If anyone laughs at you, you can always go back to the drawing board.)

Jackets

For inclement-weather running, wear a waterproof, breathable fabric. If it's merely cold but there's no precipitation during your run, you may opt for a soft and cozy fleece jacket or pullover. If you're not going to be out for an extended period of time, any type of nylon windbreaker that's lined with polypro should do the trick. Added features to look for in a jacket include a ventilated mesh lining, a back or front vent, a raised collar, and reflective piping for night running. Note: Jackets, as well as all running clothing, are made by many companies, only a few of which are mentioned here. The best way to decide what's best for you, of course, is to comparison shop.

Tights/Shorts

If you don't wear a Gore-Tex (or similar type) running suit when you run in cold or wet weather, you may simply want to don a pair of tights and a breathable, waterproof jacket. Tights are usually made of Lycra™, which is a stretchy, supportive material, in combination with one of the wicking fabrics mentioned earlier, and often come with "gripper" elastic ankles and an elastic waist for a snug fit. If you prefer not-so-tight tights, they are also made with a cotton/Lycra combination in a stirrup style. (Cotton, naturally, is somewhat lacking in wicking action, however.)

> Manufacturers of Lycra running tights have raved that their product gives you a performance edge. Wearing tights, they say, will increase blood return in the lower extremities and thereby improve performance. But a study quoted in *Runner's World* magazine proves otherwise. Researchers at Wake Forest University showed that using tights has absolutely no effect— good or bad—on performance. So wear them to warm your legs, not heat up your racing.
>
> —Fitness Features

In warm or not-too-cold conditions, you may prefer to run in shorts, which offer you the greatest freedom of movement. The most efficient running shorts are made of Coolmax or Supplex and have ample splits on the sides to allow for a full stride. Furthermore, many shorts and tights are fluorescent or come with reflective piping, to be worn in the dark for safety.

Shirts

Turtlenecks are functional for winter running, as the neck is an especially vulnerable spot if left exposed. Most turtlenecks for runners are made with either Supplex, Thermax, or Coolmax—often in combination with Lycra—or with 100 percent cotton. As with all running attire, all-cotton garments are less expensive than moisture-controlling ones, which may be something to consider if you're on a budget. Some companies also offer cotton/Lycra shirts, usually as part of an ensemble with those not-too-tight cotton/Lycra tights.

Mock turtlenecks, T-shirts, singlets, and women's tops are also available in a slew of lightweight fabrics to suit whatever needs you may have. Of course, for men running in warm weather, the least expensive and most time-efficient option may be no shirt at all. (However, you risk the danger of extensive sun exposure this way.)

Gloves, Mittens, and Hats

The importance of keeping the extremities insulated while running in freezing weather can't be stressed enough; they are the primary places through which heat escapes from the body. Mittens are preferred over gloves simply because body heat allows the fingers to warm each other (the fingers are isolated in gloves). Many gloves, mittens, and hats are lined with polypro and made of a wool blend or acrylic. Insport sells an interesting product called the Soft Hood. This is a versatile garment composed of Supplex and Lycra, which can easily be converted into a hood, headband, or do-it-yourself turtleneck. If you'd like more information about the Soft Hood or other products made by Insport, write to Insport, 1870 NW 173rd Avenue, Beaverton, OR 97006, or call (800) 652-5200.

You can eliminate some excess perspiration altogether by shedding extra layers as you warm up during winter runs. But where are you going to put the scarf, mittens, and hat which all seemed essential when you first set out? Try creating a modern-day chatelaine. Tie a soft piece of sash cord around your waist (a leather belt will chafe). Add a few large safety pins to the sash. When you want to take off the scarf, just wrap it around the cord. Your gloves and hat can be pinned to the sash while you continue running at a cooler, less encumbered pace.

—Kay Denmark

Sports Bras

The Jogbra company is clearly tops in this field, offering a wide range of supportive, moisture-wicking sports bras. For women who participate in "low impact" activities such as tennis or aerobics, the Jogbra Coolmax Coolsport is recommended; the Jogbra Classic, made of cotton, polyester, and Lycra, holds up to higher-impact sports; and the Support Team Bra, which features an adjustable support band, is possibly the best bra you can wear for extremely active sports participation. For those women who are style conscious, the Lace/Lycra Bra is an option. For bigger-breasted women, the Jogbra Sportshape and the Super Sport Bra offer unparalleled support and come in sizes up to 40D. Note that almost all major bra manufacturers also make at least one type of sports bra. For further information about Jogbra products, write to Jogbra, P.O. Box 927, Burlington, VT 05402, or call (800) 343-2020.

Socks

Polypro and Coolmax, as well as a fabric called Orlon, are the most frequently used materials in creating running socks. (By now you're probably thinking, "Polypro from head to toe!"—and you've got the right idea.) In addition to keeping your feet warm and dry, some of today's running socks producers advertise an amazing product claim: No blisters! One such manufacturer is the Double Lay-R Sock Company. Selling socks constructed of twin layers of fabric that resist blistering and chafing, the company guarantees 1000 miles of blister-free running or they'll give you a new pair. They can be contacted at Double Lay-R Sock Company, 69 West State Street, Doylestown, PA 18901, or (800) 392-8500.

Thorlo is probably the best-known brand of running socks. Thorlo socks are known for their thickness and high-density padding in the heel and forefoot—and for their blister resistance. Inquiries regarding Thorlo products should be addressed to Thorlo, P.O. Box 5440, Statesville, NC 28677, and marked to the attention of Ms. Susan Graham. Or you can call (800) 438-0109.

Night Running Wear

The key to the nocturnal running scene is to *be seen*. To ensure that you are, 3M has created a variety of reflective materials that are being attached to jackets, shirts, shorts, tights, hats, vests, shoelaces, and even dog collars. When running in the dark, and especially in or near traffic, you should make an effort to help people see you.

Sunglasses

Running during the day has its share of hazards, too—namely, exposure to the sun's ultraviolet (UV) rays. Extended UV exposure can cause retinal and corneal problems, impair night vision, and lead to eyestrain due to constant squinting. To protect runners' eyes, manufacturers have created sunglasses that are not only effective in blocking UV rays but are also "sportsworthy"; they won't fall off your face. Most sports sunglasses come in a wraparound style to ensure maximum UV blockage. Many have shatterproof, antifog, scratch-resistant lenses and are set in lightweight, durable frames. Adjustable ear stems, interchangeable lenses, and adjustable frame angles are other options you may want to look into. As for the color of your lenses, gray is recommended for bright sunlight, brown or bronze for a hazy sun, and amber or yellow for cloud cover or fog. Some sports sunglasses also come with a removable foam strip on the top of the frame that absorbs perspiration and prevents the glasses from slipping or bouncing.

If you wear vision-correcting lenses of any kind (eyeglasses or contact lenses), it's important that you maintain your ability to see clearly when running, says Michael Fedak, M.D., a Manhattan ophthalmologist and accomplished ultra runner. This can be done easily, he says. Most people have little or no trouble wearing their corrective eyewear on the run, and doing so has a number of advantages.

The first is safety. "Especially running in the city, you need to be able to see traffic, obstacles, and other people," says Fedak. Some people get used to running without glasses because they find them inconvenient or uncomfortable, then are amazed at the difference in their perception when they wear them. Another advan-

tage is that glasses protect the eyes from airborne particles—
"another hazard of urban running"—as well as wind, insects,
branches, and other potentially damaging or annoying objects.

Runners have two main complaints about wearing glasses:
They can fog up, and the bouncing or slipping around can be distracting. The former problem gets serious only when running at
an all-out pace, claims Fedak, who wears glasses for protection
while running even though he doesn't need them to correct his
vision. "If you can, just take them off and wipe the lenses."

As for slipping and bouncing, there are several solutions. One
is to simply wear glasses that fit snugly. You can either get your
pair tightened or consider buying a pair of lightweight "sport"
glasses, many of which can be fitted with prescription lenses.
"That's what I wear, and I never even notice them," says Fedak.
Or if you can, try a strap that wraps around the back of your head.

Contact lenses are favored by many runners for their convenience, and, according to Fedak, all but the old "hard" types will
stay securely in your eyes under most conditions. "It's very rare to
have them fall out," he says.

Sunglasses are becoming increasingly popular among runners
because of concerns about the damaging effects of the sun. The
problem can even occur on overcast days, when Fedak suggests
wearing orange- or yellow-tinted lenses for improved clarity as well
as UV protection.

"You've got nothing to lose with sunglasses, as long as you use
a pair with maximum UV protection (they should be marked on
the label or hangtag). Shop around—they don't have to be that
expensive, even the ones that are specially designed for sports. I
just bought a pair of bright yellow ones for $9.95 that are protec-
tive and virtually indestructible."

—Fitness Forum

Heart Rate Monitors

Heart rate monitors, or HRMs, are ideal for runners who want to get the most out of their workouts yet not overexert themselves. By monitoring the heart, athletes can optimize the benefits of a workout by staying within their "target range" of performance. A quality HRM displays your heart rate while you run so you can maintain a safe and beneficial level of exertion. The top-of-the-line HRMs for distance runners are the Polar Pacer and the Polar Accurex. Both of these HRMs work by attaching electrodes to the chest (via an elastic strap), which then transmit signals to a wristwatch-style transmitter. See the Resource List for information on purchasing HRMs.

Sports Watches

Perhaps nothing matters more to the diehard runner than his or her watch. After all, it's often not whether you win or lose a race; it's how you time yourself! As with the other running products discussed here, deciding exactly which sports watch to purchase is largely a matter of personal taste, needs, and wallet size.

Some of today's computerized watches can perform practically any function, short of telling you in which stocks you should invest. The features that runners are usually concerned with are a countdown timer, stopwatch, and split-time recorder. The fairly expensive Seiko S129 is capable of timing up to 400 races or 100 split/lap times (it's meant primarily for coaches and race directors of small events) and can print results either during or after an event. Other sports watches, in an array of brands and styles, are available in running stores and through mail-order catalogs.

Jogging Strollers

Babysitting was never so much fun! Although jogging strollers are controversial when used in competitive races (they're banned from use in all NYRRC races) they're a wonderful way to spend time outdoors with your infant or toddler. Most strollers are three-wheeled carts that are lightweight but sturdy, have fold-up frames, and are amply adorned with safety features. Check ads in various runners' magazines for information on strollers.

Where to Find It All

No matter what type of running accessory you're interested in, excellent shopper's guides and reference sources are the many mail-order catalogs advertised primarily in the back of major running magazines. By perusing these publications, you can outfit yourself for the entire season without even leaving your home.

The NYRRC also has a mail-order merchandise department and a gift shop. An entire line of New York City Marathon and NYRRC activewear is the featured product, and shirts, tights, jackets, hats, gloves, and a variety of other competitively priced items are also available. To receive an NYRRC merchandise brochure, write to the Merchandise Department of the club. You can also visit the gift shop during club hours.

The days when a solitary road runner was viewed as "a nut running through the street in his underwear" now seem but a distant memory. Once considered a poor man's sport (after all, the only equipment you really needed was a pair of sneakers—and, of course, your underwear), running has surprisingly transformed itself into a sometimes costly venture. A quick glance at the back pages of *Runner's World* magazine provides a small sampling of the products currently available to the consumer: everything from a three-seated Jogging Kart (for the entire family on the go) to a Mini Stun Gun for Runners [dial (404) 320-STUN], presumably "aimed" at those who occasionally take a run on the wild side.

In this land of opportunity—and entrepreneurial frenzy—two words remain as clear and all-important as ever: caveat emptor! With the proliferation of products available to the consumer, it is sometimes exceedingly difficult to distinguish between gimmickry and usefulness. The only advice that seems clearly prudent is to do your research before spending your money. Read magazine articles about specific products, talk to your running friends about accessories they use, and most important, ask questions of the salespeople you deal with. Generally, runners do like to help other runners.

Fred Lebow on the Power of a T-Shirt

It seems T-shirts are a runner's most cherished possession. They certainly are a race director's! We started giving out T-shirts to several hundred entrants in the 1973 New York City Marathon. Now, for races alone, we make about 200,000 T-shirts a year, and we sell an additional 130,000 a year.

People ask me all the time how we get over 7000 volunteers for the marathon (not to mention the 6000 others along the course, and volunteers for our 100 other events). I answer: Never underestimate the power of a T-shirt. Even heads of corporations, who earn six-figure salaries, call me to ask for a T-shirt.

Perspiration stains make even the most beloved T-shirts look especially grimy. But that old faithful cleaning cure-all, borax, can often do the trick. Before laundering, soak the shirt for an hour in hot water with approximately a half cup of borax.

—Kay Denmark

For some reason, the rich and not-too-rich alike treat a T-shirt like gold. A couple of weeks ago, the filmmaker Spike Lee was directing a movie near the NYRRC. We met, and I gave him a shirt. He checked carefully to make sure he had the right size. He was really happy with it.

Sometimes people say they are tired of getting T-shirts in races, so at one point we tried something else. We tried giving out watches, shorts, hats, headbands, shoelaces —nothing worked like T-shirts. People complained, "Where are the T-shirts?" Even though many of the racers have dozens of T-shirts in their drawers, they always want more.

A T-shirt can be sort of a bribe, but it's a legal bribe. In 1976, the first year the marathon went through the city streets, a group of hoods from one of the neighborhoods paid me a call. It turned out part of the route was on their turf. I was nervous, to say the least. I handed them all T-shirts and made them the guardians of that part of the course. It worked. On the day of the race, there they stood, "on guard" in an organized line along the roadway, wearing their T-shirts.

We give T-shirts as goodwill gifts in other countries. I give them out at meetings with city agencies. I gave a shirt to the pope, to presidents. A T-shirt not only opens doors, it widens them.

Part 14: Resources

Resource List

Heart Rate Monitor Training

As of 1992, heart rate monitors range in price from about $110 to over $350—depending on model and dealer.

Polar Pacer
9701 Shore Rd., #4B
Brooklyn, NY 11209
Heart monitor; order from Cliff Held, $110 (includes postage and handling).

Computer Instruments Corporation
99 Seaview Blvd.
Port Washington, NY 11050
(516) 484-2400

Creative Health Products, Inc.
5148 Saddle Ridge Rd.
Plymouth, MI 48170
(800) 742-4478

Deep Water Running

Roth Hammer, International
P.O. Box 5579
Santa Maria, CA 93456
(805) 481-2744
1-(800) 235-2156
Belts under $10.

From *Runner's World* magazine
Bioenergetics
2841 Anode Lane
Dallas, TX 75220
(800) 433-2627
Wet Vest ($125; $140 for large)

AquaJogger
Excel Sports Science
P.O. Box 5612
Eugene, OR 97405
(503) 484-2454
(800) 922-9544
Belt ($50)

Hydrotone International
6125 West Reno Suite 900
Oklahoma City, OK 73127
(405) 948-7754
(800) 622-8663
Hydrobelt $40

Nutrition

Food and Nutrition Information Center
National Agriculture Library, Room 304
Beltsville, MD 20705
(301) 504-5414
Supplies answers to nutrition-related questions; has bibliographies on various subjects, including sports nutrition.

American Dietetic Association
216 West Jackson Blvd., Suite 800
Chicago, IL 60606
(312) 899-0040
1-(800) 366-1655
Referrals for qualified sports nutritionists, and other information.

Nancy Clark
SportsMedicine Brookline
830 Boylston St.
Brookline, MA 02167
(617) 739-2033

Suggested nutrition resources for runners, by sports nutritionist Mary-Giselle Rathgeber:

Books

Diet for a Small Planet by F. Lappe. New York: Ballantine Books, 1980.

Eating for Endurance by Ellen Coleman. Palo Alto: Bull, 1987.

Eating on the Run by E. Tribole. Champaign: Leisure Press, 1987.

Jane Brody's Good Food Book. New York: Bantam Books, 1987.

Laurel's Kitchen by L. Robertson and C. Flinders. New York: Bantam Books, 1976.

Newsletters

Environmental Nutrition
2112 Broadway, #200
New York, NY 10023

Tufts University Nutrition Newsletter
P.O. Box 50169
Boulder, CO 80321

Wellness Newsletter
University of California, Berkeley
P.O. Box 359148
Palm Coast, FL 32035

Nutrition Action
Center for Science in the Public Interest
1501 16th St., NW
Washington, DC 20036

Eating Disorders

American Anorexia/Bulimia Association
418 East 76th St.
New York, NY 10021
(201) 836-1800
(212) 734-1114
Send self-addressed stamped envelope—three stamps plus $1.
Offers a national referral service; self-help groups and information on eating disorders.

National Association of Anorexia Nervosa and Related Disorders (ANAD)
P.O. Box 271
Highland Park, IL 60635
(312) 831-3438
(708) 831-3438
Enclose $1 for postage and handling. Runs a nationwide system of free support groups and a referral list of psychotherapists.

Health/Medical

Massage
American Massage Therapy Association
1130 West North Shore Ave.
Chicago, IL 60626-4670
(312) 761-AMTA

Recommended reading by Marilyn Frender:
Sportsmassage by Jack Meagher and Pat Broughton. New York: Doubleday, 1989.

Sports Without Pain by Ben Benjamin. New York: Summit Books, 1979.

The American Orthopedic Foot and Ankle Society
1300 Cabrini Medical Tower
901 Boren Ave.
Seattle, WA 98104
(800) 235-4855; in Seattle, 467-7558
Information and referrals regarding foot problems.

Physical Therapy
American Physical Therapy Association
1111 North Fairfax St.
Alexandria, VA 22314
(703) 684-2782

Chiropractic
American Chiropractic Association
1701 Clarendon Blvd.
Arlington, VA 22209
(703) 276-8800

Neuromuscular Therapy
St. John Neuromuscular Pain Relief Institute
10950 72nd St. North, Suites 101–4
Largo, FL 34647
(813) 541-1800/1900

The Physician and Sportsmedicine
Attn.: Editorial Department
4530 West 77th St.
Minneapolis, MN 55435
The Sports Medicine Clinic Directory, a guide to sports medicine clinics around the country ($20).

Walking

(Referrals from Elliott Denman)

Appalachian Trail Conference
5 Joy St.
Boston, MA 02108

The Athletics Congress/USA
P.O. Box 120
Indianapolis, IN 46206

Boy Scouts of America
Rte. 1
New Brunswick, NJ 08903

Front Range Walkers
c/o Bob Carlson
2261 Glencoe St.
Denver, CO 80207

International Amateur Athletic Federation
3 Hans Cres.
Knightsbridge, London SWIX 0LN England

International Walking Society
P.O. Box 4307
Boulder, CO 80306

National Parks Association
1701 18th Street, NW
Washington, DC 20009

New England TAC Walking
c/o Justin F. Kuo
120 Riverway, #8
Boston, MA 02215

New Jersey TAC Walking
c/o Elliott Denman
28 North Locust Ave.
West Long Branch, NJ 07764

New Mexico Walkers and Striders
c/o Dr. and Mrs. Eugene F. Dix
2301 El Nido Ct. North
Albuquerque, NM 87104

North American Racewalk Foundation
c/o Viisha Sedlak
P.O. Box 18323
Boulder, CO 80308

The Ohio Race Walker
c/o Mr. Jack Mortland
3184 Summit St.
Columbus, OH 43202

Pacific Association TAC Walking
c/o Mr. Ron Daniel
1289 Balboa Ct. #149
Sunnyvale, CA 94086

Pacific Northwest TAC Walking
c/o Gwen Robertson
255 Mount Quay
Issaquah, WA 98027

Southern California Walkers
c/o Elaine Ward
1000 San Pasqual #35
Pasadena, CA 91106-3393

TAC National Racewalking Chairman Bruce Douglass
36 Canterbury Lane
Mystic, CT 06355

United States Armed Forces Sports
HODA (DACF-AFS)
Alexandria, VA 22331-0522

United States Olympic Committee
1750 East Boulder St.
Colorado Springs, CO 80909-5760

The Walkers Club of America
c/o Howard Jacobson
P.O. Box 210
Commack, NY 11725

Wisconsin TAC Walking
c/o Mike DeWitt
4230 27th St.
Kenosha, WI 53142

World Association of Veteran Athletes
c/o Mr. Robert Fine
4223 Palm Forest Dr. North
Delray Beach, FL 33445

YMCA of the USA
101 North Wacker Dr.
Chicago, IL 60606

YWCA of the USA
726 Broadway, 5th Floor
New York, NY 10001

Travel

Thom Gilligan
Marathon Tours
108 Main St.
Boston, MA 02129
(617) 242-7845
1-(800) 783-0024
FAX (617) 242-7686

To learn what vaccinations you may need for overseas travel, contact:
Centers for Disease Control, 24-hour hot line: (404) 332-4559

Bibliography

Books by or about Contributors

Corbitt: The Story of Ted Corbitt, Long Distance Runner by John Chodes. Los Altos, CA: Tafnews Press, 1974.

Cross Training: The Complete Training Guide for All Sports by Gordon Bakoulis Bloch. New York: Simon & Schuster, 1992.

Good Housekeeping Answer Book: Women's Medical Problems by M. M. Shangold and E. C. Gross. New York: Hearst Books, 1981.

Inside the World of Big-Time Marathoning by Fred Lebow with Richard Woodley. New York: Rawson Associates, 1984.

Marathon, Cross Country and Road Running by Cliff Temple. North Pomfret, VT: Trafalagar Square, 1990.

Marathoning by Bill Rodgers with Joe Concannon. New York: Simon & Schuster, 1980.

Mark Allen Total Triathlete by Mark Allen and Bob Babbitt. Chicago: Contemporary Books, 1988.

Masters Running and Racing by Priscilla Welch, Bill Rodgers, and Joe Henderson. Emmaus, PA: Rodale Press, 1991.

Nancy Clark's Sports Nutrition Guidebook by Nancy Clark.
Champaign, IL: Leisure Press, 1990.
In bookstores, or by mail: send $16.50 (includes postage and handling) to:
New England Sports Publications
P.O. Box 252
Boston, MA 02113

Olympic Gold—A Runner's Life and Times by Frank Shorter with Marc Bloom. Boston: Houghton Mifflin Company, 1984.

Peak Energy: The High-Oxygen Program for More Energy Now! by Daniel Hamner, M.D., and Barbara Burr. New York: G. P. Putnam's Sons, 1988.

Respiratory Anatomy and Physiology by D. E. Martin and J. W. Youtsey. St. Louis: The C. V. Mosby Company, 1987.

Running from A to Z by Cliff Temple. Los Altos, CA: Tafnews, 1987.

Running Tide by Joan Benoit. New York: Alfred A. Knopf, 1987.

Running U.S.A.: A Guide to Running in 125 American Cities by Peter Roth. New York: Simon & Schuster, 1979.

Stretching and Strengthening for the Long Distance Runner by Beryl Bender Birch. New York: Avon Books, 1981.

The Complete Sports Medicine Book for Women by M. M. Shangold and G. Mirkin. New York: Simon & Schuster, 1985; rev. ed., 1992.

The Family Fitness Handbook by Bob Glover and Jack Shepherd. New York: Penguin Books, 1989.

The High Jump Book, 2nd ed., by D. Stones, G. Joy, J. Wszola, and D. Martin. Los Altos, CA: Tafnews Press, 1987.

The Injured Runner's Training Handbook by Bob Glover and Dr. Murray Weisenfeld. New York: Penguin Books, 1985.

The Marathon Footrace by D. E. Martin and R. W. Gynn. Springfield, IL: Charles C. Thomas Publishers, 1979.

The New Competitive Runner's Handbook by Bob Glover and Pete Schuder. New York: Penguin Books, 1983.

The Runner's Handbook by Bob Glover and Jack Shepherd. New York: Penguin Books, 1978; updated ed. 1985.

The Woman Runner by Gloria Averbuch. New York: Simon & Schuster, 1984.

30 Phone Booths to Boston by Don Kardong. New York: Penguin Books, 1985.

Training Distance Runners by D. E. Martin and P. N. Coe. Champaign, IL: Human Kinetics Publishers, 1991.

Women and Exercise: Physiology and Sports Medicine edited by M. Shangold and G. Mirkin. Philadelphia: Davis, 1988.

World Class by Grete Waitz and Gloria Averbuch. New York: Warner Books, 1986; now available as *Grete Waitz' Guide to Running*. London: Stanley Paul & Co. Ltd., 1987.

Books for Runners

Books for Runners is the most extensive source in the country for running and fitness books and videos, listing 250 titles. As a service to readers of this book, they have prepared this bibliography. Some of the classics are hard-to-find books. The new titles present the very latest in sports theory and science. For a complete listing, please contact:

Books for Runners
The CAVU Company
60121 Sweetgrass Lane
Bend, OR 97702
(503) 382-0864

Classics

Acceleration by Randy Smythe. Ames, IA: Championship, 1988.

All About Road Racing by Tom and Janet Heinonen. Los Altos, CA: Tafnews Press, 1979.

And Then the Vulture Eats You edited by John L. Parker, Jr. Tallahassee, FL: Cedarwinds, 1990.

Athlete's Guide to Mental Training by Robert M. Nideffer. Champaign, IL: Human Kinetics, 1985.

Athletic Training by Thomas D. Fahey. Mountain View, CA: Mayfield, 1986.

Backwards Running by Robert K. Stevenson. Fullerton, CA: Stevenson International, 1981.

Basic Track and Field Biomechanics by Tom Ecker. Los Altos, CA: Tafnews Press, 1985.

Biomechanics of Distance Running edited by Peter R. Cavanagh. Champaign, IL: Human Kinetics, 1990.

Biomechanics of Running Shoes edited by Benno M. Nigg. Champaign, IL: Human Kinetics, 1986.

Boston—America's Oldest Marathon by Ray Hosler. Mountain View, CA: Anderson World, 1980.

Coaching Evelyn by Pat Connolly. Los Altos, CA: Tafnews Press, 1991.

Competitive Runners Training Book by Bill Dellinger and William Freeman. New York: Macmillan, 1984.

The Complete Book of Running by James F. Fixx. New York: Random House, 1977.

The Complete Marathoner edited by Runner's World. Mountain View, CA: Anderson World, 1978.

The Complete Middle Distance Runner by Denis Watts, Harry Wilson, and Frank Horwill. Los Altos, CA: Tafnews Press, 1982.

The Complete Runner, Vol. II, edited by Runner's World. Mountain View, CA: Anderson World, 1974.

Computerized Running and Training Programs by James B. Gardner and J. Gerry Purdy. Ames, IA: Championship, 1970.

Corbitt by John Chodes. Los Altos, CA: Tafnews Press, 1974.

Cross Country and Distance Running by Harry Groves. Ames, IA: Championship, 1981.

Cross Country for Coaches and Runners by Dave Long, Lynn King, and Bill Loeffelhardt. Ames, IA: Championship, 1981.

Cures for Common Running Injuries by Steven I. Subotnick. New York: Macmillan, 1979.

Diet for Runners by Nathan Pritikin. New York: Simon & Schuster, 1985.

Divine Runner by Earl Paulk. Decatur, GA: Kingdom Publishers, 1978.

Eat to Win by Robert Haas. New York: NAL (Penguin), 1985.

Encyclopedia of Nutrition by John Yudkin. New York: Penguin, 1985.

Endurance Running by Norman Brook. North Pomfret, VT: Trafalgar Square, 1989.

Exercise, Nutrition and Energy Metabolism by Edward Horton and Ronald L Terjung. New York: McGraw-Hill, 1988.

Eyes on the Gold by Stephen F. Tomajczyk. Jefferson, NC: Mcfarland, 1986.

Fast, Faster, Fastest by Dr. James Klinzing. Ames, IA: Championship, 1987.

Female Endurance Athletes edited by Barbara L. Drinkwater. Champaign, IL: Human Kinetics, 1986.

Fitness for Athletes by Dr. Terry Todd and Dick Hoover. Chicago, IL: Contemporary, 1978.

Fitness on the Road by John Winsor. Bolinas, CA: Shelter, 1986.

Food for Sport by Nathan J. Smith and Bonnie Worthington-Roberts. Menlo Park, CA: Bull, 1989.

The Four-Minute Mile by Robert Bannister. New York: Lyons & Burford, 1955.

Galloway's Book on Running by Jeff Galloway. Bolinas, CA: Shelter, 1984.

Give Us This Day Our Daily Run by Christian W. Zauner and Norma Y. Benson. Longmeadow, MA: Mouvement, 1981.

The Gold's Gym Book of Strength Training for Athletes by Ken Sprague. New York: Berkley, 1979.

Half a Mind: Hashing by Alice Johnson. Camden, ME: Yankee Books, 1989.

Happy Feet by Frank Murray. New Canaan, CT: Keats, 1990.

Health and Fitness Log by Marlin and Loris Bree. Chicago, IL: Contemporary, 1988.

Hidden Causes of Injury, Prevention, and Correction for Running Athletes and Joggers by John Jesse. Pasadena, CA: Golden West, 1977.

How Road Racers Train by Greg Brock. Los Altos, CA: Tafnews Press, 1980.

How to Keep Your Feet and Legs Healthy for a Lifetime by Gary Null and Howard Robins. New York: Four Walls Eight Windows, 1990.

How to Run Your First Marathon by Ardy Friedberg. New York: Simon & Schuster, 1982.

How Women Runners Train edited by Vern Gambetta. Los Altos, CA: Tafnews Press, 1980.

Improve Your Running Skills by Susan Peach. Tulsa, OK: EDC, 1988.

In Pursuit of Excellence by Terry Orlick. Champaign, IL: Human Kinetics, 1990.

Injured Runner's Training Handbook by Bob Glover and Murray Weisenfeld. New York: Penguin, 1985.

Inside Running by Dr. David L. Costill. Dubuque, IA: Brown Benchmark, 1986.

Inside Track by Carl Lewis with Jeffrey Marx. New York: Simon & Schuster, 1990.

Jogging by Shirley Zeleznek. Riverside, NJ: Crestwood, 1980.

Jogging by A. Garth Fisher and Phillip E. Allsen. Dubuque, IA: William C. Brown, 1987.

Jogging Everyone by Charles Williams and Clancy Moore. Winston-Salem, NC: Hunter Textbooks, 1983.

Jogging with Jesus by C. S. Lovett. Baldwin Park, CA: Personal Christianity, 1978.

Jogotherapy by Dr. Frederick D. Harper. Alexandria, VA: Douglass, 1979.

Johnny Miles by Floyed Williston. Tallahassee, FL: Cedarwinds, 1990.

The Joy of Running by Thaddeus Kostrubala. New York: Simon & Schuster, 1984

Knee Health by Vivian Grisogono. North Pomfret, VT: Trafalgar Square, 1989.

The Loneliness of the Long-Distance Runner by Allan Sillitoe. New York: Penguin, 1959.

Long Distances edited by Jess Jarver. Los Altos, CA: Tafnews Press, 1989.

Long Road to Boston by Bruce W. Tuckman. Tallahassee, FL: Cedarwinds, 1988.

Long Run Solution by Joe Henderson. Mountain View, CA: Anderson World, 1978.

Lyndon's Complete Pace Chart for Runners by Rick Selig. Topeka, KS: Lyndon Product, 1987.

Marathon: The Clarence DeMar Story by Clarence DeMar. Shelburne, VT: New England, 1937.

Marathon, Cross Country, and Road Running by Cliff Temple. North Pomfret, VT: Trafalgar Square, 1990.

Marathon Running by Jerolyn Nentl. Riverside, NJ: Crestwod House, 1980.

Masters Age Graded Tables edited by National Masters News. Van Nuys, CA: National Masters News, 1990.

Masters Age Records 1991 edited by Peter Mundle. Los Altos, CA: Tafnews Press, 1990.

The Masters Running Guide by Hal Higdon. Van Nuys, CA: National Masters News, 1990.

Maxing Out by Gordon Scoles. Ames, IA: Championship, 1985.

Meditations from the Breakdown Lane by James E. Shapiro. Boston: Houghton Mifflin, 1983.

Middle and Long Distance/Marathon and Steeplechase by Denis Watts and Harry Wilson. Los Altos, CA: Tafnews Press, 1985.

The Milers: A History of the Mile by Cordner Nelson and R. L. Quercetani. Los Altos, CA: Tafnews Press, 1985.

Motivation: The Name of the Game by Joe Newton and John Behan. Los Altos, CA: Tafnews Press.

Nancy Clark's Sports Nutrition Guidebook by Nancy Clark. Champaign, IL: Human Kinetics, 1990.

The New Competitive Runners Handbook by Bob Glover and Pete Schuder. New York: Penguin, 1988.

New Guide to Distance Running edited by *Runner's World*. Mountain View, CA: Anderson World, 1983.

Nutrition and Athletic Performance by Ellington Darden. Pasadena, CA: Golden West, 1975.

Nutrition for Fitness and Sport by Melvin Williams. Dubuque, IA: William C. Brown, 1988.

The Olympian by Brian Glanville. Tallahassee, FL: Cedarwinds, 1969.

Personal Best by George Sheehan, M.D. Emmaus, PA: Rodale, 1989.

Personalized Weight Training for Fitness and Athletics by Frederick C. Hatfield and March Krotee. Dubuque, IA: Rendall/Hunt, 1984.

PRE! by Tom Jordan. Los Altos, CA: Tafnews Press, 1977.

The Purple Runner by Paul Christman. Tallahassee, FL: Cedarwinds, 1983.

Risk! by Steve Boga. Berkeley, CA: North Atlantic, 1990.

Run Farther, Run Faster by Joe Henderson. Mountain View, CA: Anderson World, 1979.

Run Gently, Run Long by Joe Henderson. Mountain View, CA: Anderson World, 1978.

Run Log by John Cronin and Tim Houts. South Laguna, CA: Sports Log, 1991.

Runners and Other Dreamers by John L. Parker, Jr. Tallahassee, FL: Cedarwinds, 1989.

The Runner's Bible by Marc Bloom. New York: Doubleday, 1986.

Runner's Complete Medical Guide by Rich Mangi, William Dayton and Peter Jokl. New York: Simon & Schuster, 1979.

The Runner's Handbook by Bob Glover and Jack Shepherd. New York: Penguin, 1985.

Runner's Repair Manual by Murray Weisenfeld and Barbara Burr. New York: St. Martin's, 1981.

Runner's Training Guide edited by *Runner's World*. New York: Macmillan, 1987.

Runner's World Training Diary edited by *Runner's World*. New York: Macmillan, 1979.

Running and Racing After 35 by Allen Lawrence and Mark Schied. Boston: Little, Brown, 1990.

Running for Lifelong Fitness by Robert N. Girandola. Englewood Cliffs, NJ: Prentice Hall, 1987.

Running from A–Z by Cliff Temple. Los Altos CA: Tafnews Press, 1987.

Running Is for Me by Fred Neff. Minneapolis, MN: Lerner, 1980.

Running My Way by Harry Wilson. Los Altos, CA: Tafnews Press, 1988.

The Running Revolution by Joe Henderson. Tallahassee, FL: Cedarwinds, 1980.

Running: The Consequences by Richard C. Crandall. Jefferson, NC: McFarland, 1986.

Running Tide by Joan Benoit. New York: Knopf, 1987.

Running to the Top of the Mountain by John F. Durkin and Joe Newton. Los Altos, CA: Tafnews Press, 1988.

Running With Man's Best Friend by Davia Anne Gallup. Loveland, CO: Alpine, 1986.

Running with the Whole Body by Jack Heggie. Emmaus, PA: Rodale, 1986.

Running with Your Dog by John Sanford. Fairfax, VA: Denlingers, 1987.

Science of Sports Training by Thomas Kurz. Cypress, CA: Stadion, 1991.

The Self-Coached Runner by Allen Lawrence and Mark Schied. Boston: Little, Brown, 1984.

The Self-Coached Runner II by Allen Lawrence and Mark Schied. Boston: Little, Brown, 1987.

Serious Training for Serious Athletes by Rob Sleamaker. Champaign, IL: Human Kinetics, 1989.

A Six-Minute Mile by Jinny Beyer. McLean, VA: EPM, 1984.

Sport Speed by George Dintiman and Robert Ward. Champaign, IL: Human Kinetics, 1988.

Sport and Exercise Injuries by Steven Subotnick, M.D. Berkeley, CA: North Atlantic, 1991.

Sports Fitness and Training by Rich Mangi, William Dayton and Peter Jokl. New York: Random House, 1987.

Sports Illustrated Running for Women by Janet Heinonen. New York: Penguin, 1989.

Sports Injuries: A Self-Help Guide by Vivian Grisogono. North Pomfret, VT: Trafalgar Square, 1989.

The Sports Medicine Book by Gabe Mirkin, M.D. and Marshall Hoffman. Boston: Little, Brown, 1978.

Sports Nutrition by Walt Evans. New Canaan, CT: Keats, 1989.

Sports Psyching by Thomas Tutko and Umberto Tosi. New York: St. Martin's, 1980.

Sprinting and Hurdling by Peter Warden. North Pomfret, VT: Trafalgar Press, 1989.

Sprints and Relays by Frank W. Dick. Los Altos, CA: Tafnews Press, 1987.

Sprints and Relays edited by Jess Jarver. Los Altos, CA: Tafnews Press, 1990.

Strength Training for Runners and Hurdlers by John Jesse. Pasadena, CA: Golden West, 1981.

Stretching by Bob Anderson. Bolinas, CA: Shelter, 1980.

The Total Runner by Jerry Lynch. Englewood Cliffs, NJ: Prentice Hall, 1987.

Track and Field News' Little Blue Book edited by Track and Field News. Los Altos, CA: Tafnews Press, 1991.

Track's Greatest Champions by Cordner Nelson. Los Altos, CA: Tafnews Press, 1985.

Track's Greatest Women by Jon Hendershott. Los Altos, CA: Tafnews Press, 1987.

Train America! by George Dintiman Nase. Dubuque, IA: Kendall/Hunt, 1988.

Ultimate Sports Nutrition by Frederick C. Hatfield. Chicago, IL: Contemporary, 1987.

Ultramarathons by Nathan Aaseng. Minneapolis, MN: Lerner, 1987.

The Van Aaken Method by Ernst Van Aaken. Mountain View, CA: Anderson World, 1976.

Walk Jog Run for Wellness Everyone by Patricia A. Floyd and Janet E. Parke. Winston-Salem, NC: Hunter Textbooks, 1990.

Weight Training for Fitness and Sport by Thomas P. McHugh. Dubuque, IA: Kendall/Hunt, 1984.

The Winning Edge by Frank G. Addleman. New York: Simon & Schuster, 1984.

Women, Sport, and Performance by Christine L. Wells. Champaign, IL: Human Kinetics, 1991.

The Women's Stretching Book by Susan L. Peterson. Champaign, IL: Human Kinetics, 1983.

World Class by Grete Waitz and Gloria Averbuch. Boston: Little, Brown, 1986.

World Class Marathoners by Nathan Aaseng. Minneapolis, MN: Lerner, 1982.

Your Injury by Merrill Ritter, M.D., and Marjorie Akbohm. Dubuque, IA: William C. Brown, 1987.

New Releases

A Cold Clear Day: The Athletic Biography of Buddy Edelen by Frank Murphy. Kansas City: Wind Sprint Press, 1992.

Are We Winning Yet? by Mariah Burton Nelson. New York: Random House, 1991.

Beyond Winning by Gary M. Walton. Champaign, IL: Human Kinetics, 1992.

Bill Rodgers and Priscilla Welch on Masters Running and Racing by Bill Rodgers and Priscilla Welch. New York: St. Martin's, 1991.

Children and Sport by Vivian Grisogono. North Pomfret, VT: Trafalgar Square, 1992.

The Competitive Edge by Richard Elliott. Los Altos, CA: Tafnews Press, 1991.

The Complete Foot Book by Donald S. Pritt and Morton Walker. Garden City Park, NY: Avery, 1992.

Death Valley 300 by Rich Benyo. Forestville, CA: Specific Publications, 1992.

Eating for Endurance by Ellen Coleman. Menlo Park, CA: Bull, 1992.

Florence Griffith Joyner by Nathan Aaseng. Minneapolis, MN: Lerner, 1991.

Fundamentals of Track and Field by Gerry A Carr. Champaign, IL: Human Kinetics, 1991.

High Performance Training for Track and Field by William J. Bowerman and William H. Freeman. Champaign, IL: Human Kinetics, 1991.

The Hurdles edited by Jess Jarver. Los Altos, CA: Human Kinetics,1991.

Jackie Joyner-Kersee by Neil Cohen. Boston: Little, Brown, 1992.

Lore of Running by Timothy D. Noakes, M.D. Champaign, IL: Human Kinetics, 1991.

Middle Distances edited by Jess Jarver. Los Altos, CA: Tafnews Press, 1991.

Nutrition for Sport by Wilf Paish. North Pomfret, VT: Trafalgar Square, 1991.

An Orientation to Total Fitness by Vincent J. Melograno and James E. Klinzing. Dubuque, IA: Kendall/Hunt, 1992.

Peak When It Counts by William F. Freeman. Los Altos, CA: Tafnews Press, 1991.

Portrait of an Athlete by Bruce Durbin, Sr. Champaign, IL: Human Kinetics, 1992.

Power Foods by Liz Applegate. Emmaus, PA: Rodale, 1991.

Quality of Effort by Reggie Marra. New Rochelle, NY: From the Heart Press, 1991.

Recipes for Runners by Sammy Green. Garden City Park, NY: Avery, 1991.

Run Fast by Hal Higdon. Emmaus, PA: Rodale, 1992.

Runner's World 1993 Calendar edited by *Runner's World*. Emmaus, PA: Rodale, 1992.

Running for Fun and Fitness by George R. Colfer and John M. Chevrette. Dubuque, IA: Kendall/Hunt, 1992.

Sports Illustrated Track and Field Guide by Jim Santos. New York: Penguin, 1991.

Think Fast by Joe Henderson. New York: Plume, 1991.

Track and Field News' Little Blue Book edited by Track and Field News. Los Altos, CA: Tafnews Press, 1991.

Training Distance Runners by David E. Martin and Peter N. Coe. Champaign, IL: Human Kinetics, 1991.

Weight Training for Women by Thomas D. Fahey and Gayle Hutchinson. Mountain View, CA: Mayfield, 1992.

Young at Heart: The Story of Johnny Kelley—Boston's Marathon Man by Frederick Lewis and Dick Johnson. Waco, TX: WRS Press, 1992.

Videos

All VHS

Bill Dellinger's Championship Track & Field by Bill Dellinger.

Do It Better: Running by ESPN.

Highlights of the 1988 Summer Olympics by Bryant Gumbel.

How to Improve Speed by James Klinzing.

The In-Training Video by Roy Benson.

Marty Liquori's Runner's Workout by Marty Liquori.

1988 Olympic Videos: Men and Women by Bryant Gumbel.

Running Is Your Life by Lasse Viren.

Running Theory from Mile to Marathon by Paul Cummings.

Sebastian Coe: Born to Run by Sebastian Coe.

Speed and Explosion by George Dintiman and Robert D. Ward.

Sprint Training, Vols. I and II, by Loren Seagrave and Kevin O'Donnell.

Sprinting with Carl Lewis by Tom Tellez.

Sprints, Starts & Relays by John Smith.

The Supermilers: 4 Minute Mile and Beyond by Track & Field News.

Winning Sports Nutrition by Arizona Coop Extension.

Women in Sport by Joan Vickers.

Magazines

The following information is from the NYRRC library:

Athletics (Canada)
1220 Sheppard Ave. East
Willowdale, Ont., M2K 2X1
Canada
(416) 495-4057

Athletics Today (England)
2–6 High St.
Kingston-upon-Thames
Surrey, KT1 1EY
England
081 547-3922

Athletics Weekly (England)
EMAP Pursuit Publishing Ltd.
Bretton Ct., Bretton
Peterborough, PE3 8DZ
England
0733-261144

Atletica
Starlight Communication s.r.l.
Via Bassini
41-20133 Milano
Italy
02/70632266

Atletica Leggera
Via Dante 6
27029 Vigevano (PV)
Italy
0381/85340-87144

Corredores
Mexico
355-1268

International Amateur Athletic Federation (various publications)
3 Hans Cres.
Knightsbridge
London SW1X 0LN
England
071-581-8771

Jogging
P.O. Box 100 23
100 55 Stockholm
Sweden
08-667-19-30

Jogging International
24 rue du Sumelin
75020 Paris
France
40-30-00-44

Running (England)
67–71 Goswell Rd.
London EC1V 7EN
England
071-410-9410/250

U.S. Magazines and Newsletters

American Athletics
P.O. Box 1497
Los Altos, CA 94023
(415) 968-4419

American Health
28 West 23rd St.
New York, NY 10010
(212) 366-8900

California Running News
4957 East Heaton Ave.
Fresno, CA 93727
(209) 255-4904

Chicago Runner
459 North Milwaukee Avenue
Chicago, IL 60610
(312) 845-9123

The Competitor
214 South Cedros
Solana Beach, CA 92075
(619) 793-2711

Florida Running
8640 Tansy Dr.
Orlando, FL 32819-4529
(407) 352-9131

Footnotes
629 South Washington St.
Alexandria, VA 22314
(703) 836-0558

The Harrier
P.O. Box 41
Marlboro, NJ 07746
(908) 308-9701

Illinois Runner
P.O. Box 53
Fairbury, IL 61739
(815) 692-4636

Indiana Running & Racing News
503 East Main St.
Hartford City, IN 47348
(317) 348-4739

Inside Texas Running
9514 Bristlebrook Dr.
Houston, TX 77083
(713) 498-3208

Master Pieces
P.O. Box 14668
Lenexa, KS 66285-4668
(816) 746-1414

Master Runner
210 7th St., SE, Ste. C-23
Washington, DC 20003
(202) 546-5598

Metrosports
695 Washington St.
New York, NY 10014
(212) 627-7040

Michigan Runner
7990 West Grand River, Suite C
Brighton, MI 48116
(313) 227-4200

National Masters News
P.O. Box 2372
Van Nuys, CA 91404
(818) 785-1895

New England Runner
P.O. Box 252
Boston, MA 02113
(617) 899-0481

New York Running News
9 East 89th St.
New York, NY
(212) 860-4455

Northern California Schedule
80 Mitchell Blvd.
San Rafael, CA 94903-2038
(415) 472-7223

Northwest Runner
1231 NE 94th St.
Seattle, WA 98115
(206) 526-9000

Ohio Runner
P.O. Box 586
Hilliard, OH 43026
(614) 224-7500

Oklahoma Runner
P.O. Box 2008
Tulsa, OK 74101
(918) 581-8306

Oregon Distance Runner
2300 SW Hoffman Dr.
Portland, OR 97201
(503) 224-6020

Peak Running Performance
P.O. Box 128036
Nashville, TN 37212
(615) 383-1071

The Physician and Sports Medicine
4530 West 77th St.
Minneapolis, MN 55435
(612) 835-3222

Road Race Management Newsletter
2101 Wilson Blvd., Suite 437
Arlington, VA 22201
(703) 276-0093

Runner (New York Edition)
6-2 Steven Dr.
Ossining, NY 10562
(914) 961-2626

Runner Triathlete News
P.O. Box 19909
Houston, TX 77224
(713) 781-7090

Runner's World
33 East Minor St.
Emmaus, PA 18098
(215) 967-8956

Running Advice
576 Armour Cir.
Atlanta, GA 30324
(404) 892-1158

Running Commentary
441 Brookside Dr.
Eugene, OR 97405
(503) 683-2118

Running & FitNews
9310 Old Georgetown Rd.
Bethesda, MD 20814
(800) 776-ARFA

Running Journal
P.O. Box 157
Greeneville, TN 37744
(615) 638-4177

Running Research News
P.O. Box 27041
Lansing, MI 48909
(517) 393-3150 or (800) 333-FEET

Running Stats
1085 14th St.
Suite 1260
Boulder, CO 80302
FAX (303) 494-1362

Running Times
2022A Opitz Blvd., Suite 1
Woodbridge, VA 22191
(703) 491-2044

Southern Runner
P.O. Box 6524
Metairie, LA 70009
(504) 454-8247

Sports Illustrated
Time & Life Bldg.
Rockefeller Ctr.
New York, NY 10020-1393
(800) 528-5000

Starting Line
P.O. Box 19909
Houston, TX 77224
(713) 781-7090

TACSTATS
915 Randolph
Santa Barbara, CA 93111-1031
(305) 253-8448

Track & Field News
2570 El Camino Real, Suite 606
Mountain View, CA 94040
(415) 948-8188

Triathlete
1127 Hamilton St.
Allentown, PA 18102
(215) 821-6864

Ultrarunning
300 North Main St.
P.O. Box 481
Sunderland, MA 01375
(413) 665-7573

Walking
9–11 Harcourt St.
Boston, MA 02116
(617) 266-3322

Women's Sports & Fitness
1919 14th St., Suite 421
Boulder, CO 80302
(303) 440-5111

ORGANIZATIONS

American Chiropractic Association Council on Sports Injuries and
Physical Fitness
1916 Wilson Blvd.
Arlington, VA 22201
(703) 276-8800
Explains and promotes the role and participation of chiropractors in sports
medicine.

American College of Sports Medicine
1 Virginia Ave., Suite 340
P.O. Box 1440
Indianapolis, IN 46206
(317) 637-9200
An organization that promotes and integrates scientific research and practical
applications to sports medicine and exercise science to maintain and enhance
physical performance, fitness, health, and quality of life.

American Medical Joggers Association
P.O. Box 4704
North Hollywood, CA 91617
(818) 706-2049
Uses the medical community as a role model to encourage the public to main-
tain a more healthful and better lifestyle based on exercise.

American Running and Fitness Association
9310 Old Georgetown Rd.
Bethesda, MD 20814
(301) 897-0197
A membership organization for people interested in running and fitness.
Publishes the monthly newsletter *Running & FitNews.*

Association of International Marathons (AIMS)
137–141 Leith Wlk.
Edinburgh EH6 8NS
Scotland
31-554-9444
Fosters and promotes road running throughout the world; works with the IAAF
and exchanges information, knowledge, and expertise among its members.

Association of Road Racing Athletes
1460 Paulsen Bldg.
Spokane, WA 99205
(509) 838-8784
Seeks to organize economic opportunities for top road racers; includes a circuit of twenty major road races.

The Athletics Congress of the USA, Inc.
P.O. Box 120
Indianapolis, IN 46206-0120
(317) 261-0500
The national governing body for track and road racing.

Fifty-Plus Runners Association
P.O. Box D
Stanford, CA 94309-9790
(415) 723-9790
Distributes information on senior fitness.

Melpomene Institute
1010 University Ave.
St. Paul, MN 55104
(612) 642-1951
Nonprofit agency that disseminates information on physically active women.

North American Network of Women Runners
P.O. Box 719
Bala Cynwyd, PA 19004
(215) 668-9886
Addresses lack of resources that deters women from participating in running and other health, fitness and sports activities. Sponsors low-cost motivational women's fitness programs with child care.

President's Council on Physical Fitness and Sports
701 Pennsylvania, N.W., Suite 250
Washington, D.C. 20004
(202) 272-3421
The PCPFS serves as a catalyst to promote, encourage, and motivate the development of physical fitness and sports programs for all Americans.

Road Runners Club of America
629 South Washington St.
Alexandria, VA 22314
(703) 836-0558
An association of over 200 running clubs in the nation; telephone for local RRC organization near you, or to start a chapter in your area.

TACSTATS/USA
915 Randolph Rd.
Santa Barbara, CA 93111
(805) 683-5868
Keeps records for all age groups at all major racing distances.

U.S. Olympic Committee
1750 Boulder St.
Colorado Springs, CO 80909
(719) 632-5551
Guardian of the U.S. Olympic movement; it is dedicated to providing opportunities for American athletes of all ages.

NYRRC Race Results

New York City Marathon

Course record:

1989	Juma Ikangaa	2:08:01
1981	Allison Roe	2:25:29
1970	Muhrcke, Gary	2:31:39
	No female finisher	
1971	Higgins, Norman	2:22:55
	Bonner, Beth	2:55:22
1972	Karlin, Sheldon	2:27:53
	Kuscsik, Nina	3:08:42
1973	Fleming, Tom	2:21:55
	Kuscsik, Nina	2:57:08
1974	Sander, Norbert	2:26:31
	Switzer, Kathrine	3:07:29
1975	Fleming, Tom	2:19:27
	Merritt, Kim	2:46:15
1976	Rodgers, Bill	2:10:10
	Gorman, Miki	2:39:11
1977	Rodgers, Bill	2:11:28
	Gorman, Miki	2:43:10
1978	Rodgers, Bill	2:12:12
	Waitz, Grete	2:32:30
1979	Rodgers, Bill	2:11:42
	Waitz, Grete	2:27:33
1980	Salazar, Alberto	2:09:41
	Waitz, Grete	2:25:41
1981	Salazar, Alberto	2:08:13
	Roe, Allison	2:25:29
1982	Salazar, Alberto	2:09:29
	Waitz, Grete	2:27:14
1983	Dixon, Rod	2:08:59
	Waitz, Grete	2:27:00

1984	Pizzolato, Orlando	2:14:53
	Waitz, Grete	2:29:30
1985	Pizzolato, Orlando	2:11:34
	Waitz, Grete	2:28:34
1986	Gianni Poli	2:11:06
	Waitz, Grete	2:28:06
1987	Hussein, Ibrahim	2:11:01
	Welch, Priscilla	2:30:17
1988	Jones, Steve	2:08:20
	Waitz, Grete	2:28:07
1989	Ikangaa, Juma	2:08:01
	Kristiansen, Ingrid	2:25:30
1990	Wakiihuri, Douglas	2:12:39
	Panfil, Wanda	2:30:45
1991	Garcia, Salvador	2:09:28
	McColgan, Liz	2:27:32

Runner's World Midnight Run

Event record:

1981	Rod Dixon	22:33.4
1991	Lynn Jennings	26:13

Course record:

1987	Vince Draddy	23:18
1987	Wendy Sly	27:16

The course was 8k (4.97 miles) from 1980 to 1984. In 1985 the course was approximately 4.7 miles. In 1986 it was changed to 5 miles.

Previous Winners

1980	Rodgers, Bill	23:15.2
	McIntyre, Kathy	27:24.3
1981	Dixon, Rod	22:33.4
	McIntyre, Kathy	27:55.6
1982	Meyer, Greg	23:00.7
	Shields, Eva	28:43.3
1983	Meyer, Greg	23:14
	Schilly, Katy	27:02

1984	Murphy, David	22:52
	Malone, Anne Marie	26:39
1985	Kigen, Simon	22:23
	Sly, Wendy	24:15
1986	Draddy, Vince	23:45
	Borovicka, Carla	27:50
1987	Draddy, Vince	23:18
	Sly, Wendy	27:16
1988	McKeon, Jim	24:09
	Letko, Anne Marie	27:45
1989	Hudson, Brad	23:20
	Letko, Anne Marie	27:22
1990	Martin, Ken	23:19
	Jones, Kim	27:28
1991	Trautman, John	23:33
	Jennings, Lynn	26:13
1992	Bouazza, Abidi	24:09
	St. Hilaire, Judi	25:58

Fifth Avenue Mile

Event record:

1981	Sydney Maree	3:47.52
1986	Maricica Puica	4:19.48

In addition to the elite event, there are mile races for high school, masters, New York and metropolitan area, and open men and women.

Previous Winners

1981	Maree, Sydney	3:47.52
	Warren, Leann	4:25.31
1982	Byers, Tom	3:51.35
	Scott, Debbie	4:23.96
1983	Scott, Steve	3:49.77
	Sly, Wendy	4:22.66
1984	Walker, John	3:53.62
	Puica, Maricica	4:24.35

1985	O'Mara, Frank	3:52.28
	Williams, Lynn	4:25.03
1986	Gonzalez, José-Luís	3:53.52
	Puica, Maricica	4:19.48
1987	Elliot, Peter	3:53.52
	Wade, Kirsty	4:22.70
1988	Scott, Steve	3:53.43
	Slaney, Mary	4:20.03
1989	Elliott, Peter	3:52.95
	Ivan, Paula	4:28.25
1990	Elliott, Peter	3:47.83
	Plumer, PattiSue	4:16.68
1991	Yates, Matthew	3:56.75
	Hill, Alisa	4:31.57

Manufacturers Hanover Corporate Challenge Championships

Park Avenue, New York City; 3.5 miles

As of 1992, the event is called the Chemical Corporate Challenge.

Previous Winners

1986	Doherty, John	15:46
	Harford, Olive	18:43
1987	Simonaitis, Dennis	16:17
	Keenan, Ann	18:17
1988	Crabb, Steve	16:17
	Danity, Llian	18:40
1989	Martin, Eamonn	15:45
	Van Blunk, Elaine	18:01
1990	Ave, Steve	16:12
	Hutcheson, Karen	18:39
1991	Norris, James	16:21
	Donovan, Peg	18:57

Trevira Twosome 10-Mile Run

Event record:

1980	Herb Lindsay	45:59.8
1991	Jill Hunter	51:41

One of the foremost couples races in America, Trevira has made many matches. In 1982 Pamela Kekich and Neil Cook (couple 1500) were married on the finish line! Jill Hunter's time in 1991 is a world best.

Previous Winners

1979	Virgin, Craig	46:32.7
	Goodall, Ellison	55:37.9
1980	Lindsay, Herb	45:59.8
	Groos, Margaret	54:29.4
1981	Rose, Nick	46:07.3
	Catalano, Patti	53:41.3
1982	Centrowitz, Matt	46:39
	Urish, Carol	55:42
1983	Smith, Geoff	47:07
	Gross, Margaret	55:28
1984	Murphy, David	46:42
	Urish-McLatchie, Carol	55:15
1985	Murphy, David	47:18
	Waitz, Grete	53:19
1986	Hussein, Ibrahim	47:29
	Samuelson, Joan	53:18
1987	Rose, Nick	46:43
	Welch, Lesley	53:04
1988	Gregorek, John	48:31
	Waitz, Grete	53:48
1989	Thackery, Carl	47:40
	Moore, Barbara	55:13
1990	Sheriff, Brian	46:55
	O'Brien, Cathy	52:35

1991	Sheriff, Brian	47:17
	Hunter, Jill	51:41
1992	Akonay, Boay	46:42
	Appell, Olga	53:28

Advil Mini Marathon

Event record:

1980	Grete Waitz	30:59.8

Grete's time in 1980 was a World road racing best. The race was changed from 6 miles to 10k in 1975. This race was previously called the L'Eggs Mini Marathon.

Previous Winners

1972	Dixon, Jacqueline	37:01.7
1973	Shrader, Katherine	36:46.7
1974	Ennis, Doreen	35:45.6
1975	Lettis, Charlotte	35:56.6
1976	Shea, Julie	35:04.8
1977	Neppel, Peg	34:15.3
1978	White, Martha	33:29.7
1979	Waitz, Grete	31:15.4
1980	Waitz, Grete	30:59.8
1981	Waitz, Grete	32:43.1
1982	Waitz, Grete	31:59.2
1983	Audain, Anne	32:23
1984	Waitz, Grete	31:53
1985	Larrieu Smith, Francie	32:23
1986	Kristiansen, Ingrid	31:45
1987	Martin, Lisa	32:49
1988	Kristiansen, Ingrid	31:31
1989	Williams, Lynn	32:09

1990	St. Hilaire, Judi	32:36
1991	Asiago, Delillah	32:24
1992	McColgan, Liz	31:41

Empire State Building Run-Up

Event record:

| 1990 | Scott Elliott | 10:47 |
| 1989 | Suzanne Malaxos | 12:25 |

This is a race up the 86 flights (1575 steps) of the Empire State Building. Total distance is approximately one-quarter mile. Due to construction, the 1991 and 1992 running only went up 82 flights.

Previous Winners

1978	Muhrcke, Gary	12:32.7
	Schwamm, Marcy	16:03.2
1979	Rafferty, Jim	12:19.8
	Kuscsik, Nina	15:03.4
1980	Ochse, Jim	12:20
	Kuscsik, Nina	14:55
1981	Squires, Peter	10:59.7
	Kuscsik, Nina	14:46
1982	Ochse, Jim	11:41.1
	Evans, Mary Beth	13:34
1983	Waquie, Al	11:36.8
	Koncelik, Burke	13:40
1984	Waquie, Al	11:29
	Carmichael, Isabel	13:32
1985	Waquie, Al	11:42
	Aiello, Janine	13:14
1986	Waquie, Al	11:27
	Aiello, Janine	13:19
1987	Waquie, Al	11:56
	Wendle, Janet	15:12
1988	Logan, Craig	11:29
	Aiello, Janine	13:43

1989	Rishworth, Robin	11:09
	Malaxos, Suzanne	12:25
1990	Elliott, Scott	10:47
	Malaxos, Suzanne	12:27
1991	Case, Geoff	10:13
	Spencer, Corliss	11:32
1992	Case, Geoff	9:33
	Day-Lucore, J'ne	12:00

U.S. Marathon Calendar

Below is a list of marathons in the United States that were held in the months listed as of 1992 and adapted from the NYRRC calendar. For future dates, contact the individual sources or send a S.A.S.E. to the NYRRC with your request for future calendars.

January

Charlotte Observer Marathon, NC	(704) 358-KICK
Metro-Dade Miami Marathon, Miami, FL	(800) 940-4RUN
Englewood Reserve Marathon, OH	(513) 898-7015
Jacksonville Marathon, Jacksonville, FL	(904) 739-1917
Star System Arizona Marathon, Phoenix, AZ	(602) 246-7697
Tucson Marathon,Tucson, AZ	(602) 299-6731
Great Valley Marathon, Chambersburg, PA	(717) 263-5631
Houston-Tenneco Marathon, TX	(713) 757-2700

February

Las Vegas Int'l Marathon, Las Vegas, NV	(702) 876-3870
Tallahassee Marathon, Tallahassee, FL	(904) 574-1458
Winter Fun Run Marathon, Vandalia, OH	(513) 898-7015
Savannah Marathon, Savannah, GA	(912) 927-1490
Carolina Marathon, Columbia, SC	(803) 777-2456
Long Beach Marathon, Long Beach, CA	(213) 494-2664
Space Coast Marathon, Melbourne, FL	(212) 860-4455
Mid-Winter Marathon, Huber Heights, OH	(513) 898-7015
Lost Soles Marathon, Talent, OR	(503) 535-4854
Smoky Mountain Marathon, Townsend, TN	(615) 524-5040
Ohio River Runner's Marathon, Dayton, OH	(513) 225-4674
HMRRC Marathon, Albany, NY	(518) 474-1160
Blue Angel Marathon, Pensacola, FL	(904) 452-3922
Fort Worth Cowtown Marathon, TX	(817) 735-2033

March

City of Los Angeles Marathon, CA	(213) 444-5544
Hyannis Marathon, Hyannis, MA	(508) 778-6965
Last Train to Boston Marathon, MD	(410) 661-6099
Maui Marathon, Kahului, Maui, Hl	(808) 572-9620
Napa Valley Marathon, Calistoga, CA	(707) 255-2609
Music City Marathon, Nashville, TN	(615) 889-1306
Catalina Island Marathon, Avalon, CA	(213) 433-4557
Shamrock Marathon, Virginia Beach, VA	(804) 481-5090
Marathon of the Great Southwest, TX	(915) 677-8144
Jimmy Stewart Relay Marathon, L.A., CA	(213) 829-8968

April

Hogeye Marathon, Fayetteville, AR	(501) 442-4612
Arbor Day Marathon, Aurora, CO	(303) 979-4957
Longest Day Marathon, Brookings, SD	(605) 692-2334
Boston Marathon, Boston, MA	(508) 435-6905
Lake Powell Marathon, Lake Powell, AZ	(800) 835-4671
Drake Relays Marathon, Des Moines, IA	(515) 274-5379
Lake County Marathon, Zion, IL	(708) 317-1060
Big Sur International Marathon, Carmel, CA	(408) 625-6226
Toledo R.R. Glass City Marathon, OH	(419) 882-1674
Michigan Trail Marathon, Ann Arbor, Ml	(313) 769-5016
Yonkers Marathon, Yonkers, NY	(914) 377-6440

May

Wild Wild West Marathon, Lone Pine, CA	(619) 876-4444
Lincoln Marathon, Lincoln, NE	(402) 423-4519
Newsday Long Island Marathon, NY	(516) 542-4437
Nissan Buffalo Marathon, Buffalo, NY	(716) 437-RACE
Giant Eagle/City of Pittsburgh Marathon, PA	(412) 765-3773
YMCA Great Potato Marathon, Boise, ID	(208) 344-5501
Lake Geneva Marathon, Lake Geneva, Wl	(414) 248-4323
Spring Fling Marathon, Vandalia, OH	(513) 898-7015
Shiprock Marathon, Farmington, NM	(505) 326-2273
Sugarloaf Marathon, Kingfield, ME	(207) 265-2273
Capital City Marathon, Olympia, WA	(206) 786-1786
The Revco Cleveland Marathon, OH	(216) 487-1402
Andy Payne Memorial Foot Races, OK	(405) 424-3010
Bayshore Marathon, Traverse City. Ml	(616) 941-5743
Coeur D'Alene Marathon, Coeur D'Alene, ID	(208) 765-6019

Bank of Vermont Vermont City Mar., VT   (802) 658-1815
Marathon-Under-the-Lights, Rochester, NY   (716) 342-1533

June

Sunburst Marathon, South Bend, IN   (219) 233-6161
Ghost Town Marathon, Helena, MT   (406) 444-8983
God's Country Marathon, Galeton, PA   (814) 274-9109
Russian River Run, Ukiah, CA   (707) 463-4388
Steamboat Marathon, CO   (303) 879-0882
Nipmuck Trail Marathon, Ashford, CT   (203) 455-1096
Grandmas Marathon, Duluth, MN   (218) 727-0947
Mayor's Midnight Sun Marathon, AK   (907) 343-4474
Copper River King Salmon Marathon, AK   (907) 424-3277
Ridge Runner Marathon, Cairo, WV   (304) 643-2931
Park of Roses Marathon, Columbus, OH   (513) 898-7015
City of San Francisco Marathon, CA   (415) 391-2123

July

Salmon River Summer Marathon, ID   (208) 756-2995
Grandfather Mountain Marathon, Boone, NC   (704) 264-7528
Kilauea Volcano Marathon, HI   (808) 967-8222
Deseret News–KSL Radio Marathon, UT   (801) 237-2139

August

Union Terminal Marathon, Cincinnati, OH   (513) 898-7015
Summer Spree Marathon, Vandalia, OH   (513) 898-7015
Mammoth Mountain Marathon, El Sobrante, CA   (510) 841-1190
Pikes Peak Marathon, Manitou Springs, CO   (719) 473-2625
Chilkoot Charlies Snowgoose Classic, AK   (907) 561-7652
Sports Arts Festival Marathon, CA   (213) 458-8315
City of San Francisco Marathon, CA   (415) 391-2123

September

Scotty Hanton Marathon, Ml   (313) 985-9623
Tupelo Marathon, Tupelo, MS   (601) 842-2039
Black Hills Marathon, Rapid City, SD   (605) 348-7866
Virgil Trail Monster Marathon, NY   (607) 539-7229
Talent Harvest Festival Marathon, OR   (503) 535-4854
The Bismarck Marathons, Bismarck, ND   (701) 255-1525

American Odyssey Marathon, Marathon, WI	(715) 675-6977
Walker/North Country Marathon, MN	(218) 547-1313
Eriesistible Marathon, Erie, PA	(814) 899-4974
Dutchess County Classic, Wappingers, NY	(914) 635-2936
Portland Marathon, Portland, OR	(503) 226-1111
Duke City Marathon, Albuquerque, NM	(505) 888-2448
Clarence DeMar Marathon, Keene, NH	(603) 357-1215
East Lyme Marathon, East Lyme, CT	(203) 739-1564

October

St. George Marathon, St. George, UT	(801) 634-5850
Twin Cities Marathon, Minneapolis, MN	(612) 341-8400
Sacramento Marathon, Sacramento, CA	(916) 678-5005
Greater Johnstown YMCA Marathon, PA	(814) 535-8381
Finger Lakes Marathon, Ithaca, NY	(607) 272-3442
Columbus Marathon, Columbus, OH	(614) 433-0395
Lakefront Marathon, Milwaukee, WI	(414) 272-RUNS
Tayor Wineglass Marathon, Painted Post, NY	(607) 936-9971
Detroit Free Press/Mazda Int'l Marathon, MI	(313) 222-6676
Hilton Marathon, Hilton, NY	(716) 865-8723
Louisville Marathon, Louisville, KY	(502) 456-8160
Humboldt Redwoods Marathon, CA	(707) 442-6463
Richmond Newspapers Marathon, VA	(804) 649-6325
KAKE-TV/Wichita Marathon, Wichita, KS	(316) 267-6812
Tri-Cities Marathon, Tri-Cities, WA	(509) 545-5693
Chicago Marathon, Chicago, IL	(312) 951-0660
Cape Cod Marathon, Falmouth, MA	(508) 548-0348
Marine Corps Marathon, Washington, DC	(703) 640-2225

November

Omaha Riverfront Marathon, Omaha, NE	(402) 553-8349
New York City Marathon, NY	(212) 860-4455
Andrew Jackson Marathon, Jackson, TN	(901) 668-1708
Chickamauga Battlefield Marathon, GA	(615) 875-8367
San Antonio Marathon, San Antonio, TX	(512) 732-1332
Atlantic City Marathon, Atlantic City, NJ	(609) 822-6911
Jim Thorpe Marathon, Oklahoma City, OK	(405) 232-3060
Vulcan Marathon, Birmingham, AL	(205) 995-LEGG
St. Louis Marathon, St. Louis, MO	(314) 781-3926
Atlanta Marathon, Atlanta, GA	(404) 231-9064
Mississippi Beach Rotary Marathon, MS	(800) 237-9493
Seattle Marathon, Seattle, WA	(206) 547-0885
Cincinnati Holiday Marathon, Cincinnati, OH	(513) 898-7015

December

White Sands/Alamogordo Marathon, NM	(505) 434-5605
San Diego Marathon, San Diego, CA	(619) 268-5882
California Int'l Marathon, Sacramento, CA	(916) 447-2786
First Tennessee Memphis Marathon, TN	(800) 489-4040
Vandalia Holiday Marathon, Vandalia, OH	(513) 898-7015
Western Hemisphere Marathon, Culver, CA	(213) 202-5689
Dallas White Rock Marathon, Dallas, TX	(214) 596-9002
Almost Heaven Marathon, Charleston, WV	(304) 744-6502
WZYP Rocket City Marathon, Huntsville, AL	(205) 881-9077
Kiawah Island Marathon, Kiawah Island, SC	(803) 768-3400
Honolulu Marathon, Honolulu, HI	(808) 734-7200
Tampa Bay/Brandon Marathon, Brandon, FL	(813) 681-4279

International Marathons

Following is a list of international marathons that were held in the months listed as of 1992 and adapted from the NYRRC calendar. For future dates, contact the individual sources.

January

Tiberias Marathon, Israel	972-3-5616264
Marrakesh Grand Atlas Int'l Marathon, Morocco	2-313-925
ADT Bermuda Marathon, Bermuda	(809) 238-2333
Pyramids Marathon, Cairo, Egypt	(301) 320-3663
Osaka Int'l Ladies Marathon, Osaka, Japan	6-315-2601

February

Midwinter Marathon Apeldoorn-Holland	00-31-55-788-421
Marathon Popular de Valencia, Spain	6-369-2071
Beppu-Oita Mainichi Marathon, Tokyo, Japan	3-3546-2503
Tokyo Int'l Marathon (Men's), Tokyo, Japan	3-5245-7085
Ho Chi Minh City Marathon, Vietnam	(802)388-3818
Marathon Ciudad de Seville, Seville, Spain	54-33-2361

March

China Coast Marathon, Hong Kong	5-840-0059
Polytechnic Marathon, Windsor, England	071-225-0146
Marathon Catalunya-Barcelona 92, Spain	3-268-0114
Tel Aviv Int'l Marathon, Tel Aviv, Israel	3-561-3316

Marathon de Paris, Paris, France	1-42 7717 84
Bolognamaratona, Bologna, Italy	0039-51-37-34-31

April

Marathon Rotterdam, Rotterdam, Netherlands	10-417-2440
Aalborg Boulevard Marathon, Denmark	98-164-500
Mobil Canberra Marathon, Canberra, Australia	06-2318422
ADT London Marathon, London, England	44-81-948-8039
Maratona di Torino, Torino, Italy	39-11-53-00-70
Boston Marathon, Boston, MA	(508) 435-6905
Maratona Brasilia 92, Brasilia, Brazil	55-61-243-2504
Belgrade Marathon, Yugoslavia	11-44-44-333
Marathon Popular de Madrid, Spain	1-266-9701
Marathon Int'l des Hauts-de-Siene, France	1-47-29-34-62
Vienna Spring Marathon, Austria	0043-222-402 691712

May

Fletcher Challenge Marathon, New Zealand	064-7-34-88448
DB-Marathon Munich, Germany	89-652-081
Nature Made Vancouver Int'l Mar., Canada	(604) 685-5616
New Brunswick Heart Marathon, Canada	(506) 422-3086
Ibusz Marathon Budapest, Hungary	1-181-437
National Capital Marathon, Ottawa, Canada	(613) 234-2221
Johnny Miles Marathon, Nova Scotia, Canada	(902) 752-8209
Lakeland Runaway Marathon, Canada	(403) 853-8471
Hanse-Marathon Hamburg, Germany	40-615-020
Wonderful Copenhagen Marathon, Denmark	45-38-3414000
Stockholm Marathon, Stockholm, Sweden	46-8667-1930
Qantas Melbourne Marathon, Australia	03-429-5105

June

Det Norske Fjellmarathon, Beito, Norway	47-63-60999
Moscow Int'l Peace Marathon, Russia	(617) 646-6606
Post Marathon Bonn, Bonn, Germany	02-28-46-40-29
DB-Marathon Leipzig, Leipzig, Germany	N.A.
Leningrad White Nights Marathon, Russia	(408) 373-7506
Yukon Gold Midnight Marathon, Canada	(403) 668-4236
Int'l Marathon Enschede, Enschede, Holland	53-305-486
Nanisivik Midnight Sun Marathon, Canada	(416)869-0772
Maratona do Rio, Rio de Janeiro, Brazil	21-210-3237
Mount Kilimanjaro Marathon, Tanzania	01-320-3663

July

Midnight Sun Marathon, Tromsø, Norway	47-83-22583
Calgary Int'l Marathon, Alberta, Canada	(403) 270-8828
Prague Marathon, Prague, Czechoslovakia	0049-7531-580242
JAL Gold Coast Marathon, Australia	61-75-931616
Int'l Marathon—Night of Nuremberg, Germany	0911-264030
Friendly Voyageur Marathon, Ontario, Canada	(705) 8652671
Nova Scotia Marathon, Nova Scotia, Canada	(904) 637-3254

August

Siberian Int'l Marathon, Omsk, Russia	N.A.
Helsinki City Marathon, Helsinki, Finland	90-1581
Adelaide Daimatsu Marathon, Australia	08-213-0615
Hokkaido Marathon, Sapporo, Japan	011-232-0840

September

Saskatchewan Marathon, Canada	(306) 382-2934
Oslo Marathon, Oslo, Norway	47-2-565370
Twin Cities Marathon, St. John's, Canada	(709) 368-9234
Reebok Marathon Brussels, Belgium	32-2-511-90-00
Prince Edward Island Marathon, Canada	(902) 566-3966
Amsterdam City Marathon, Netherlands	N.A.

October

Toronto Marathon, Ontario, Canada	(416) 495-4311
Athens Marathon, Athens, Greece	(617) 242-7845
Int'l Eurasia Marathon, Istanbul, Turkey	(90-1) 522-8774
Gatorade Venice Marathon, Venice, Italy	(041)940-644
DB-Marathon Frankfurt, Frankfurt, Germany	N.A.
Dublin Marathon, Dublin, Ireland	(617) 242-7845

November

New York City Marathon, New York	(212) 860-4455

December

Barbados Marathon, West Indies	1-809-431-3385
Maraton Ciudad de Caracas, Venezuela	582-263-1182

FOR WOMEN ONLY

For Women Only, Great Road Races, and Running Camps are reprinted courtesy of *Runner's World* magazine. Information applies to 1992. Contact individual sources for updated information.

January

LADY TRACK SHACK 5-K
CLASSIC
Winter Park, FL
Track Shack Event Management
1322 N. Mills Avenue
Orlando, FL 32803
(407) 898-1313

CHARLOTTE OBSERVER 10-K
Charlotte, N.C.
Don King, *Observer* Promotion
P.O. Box 32188
Charlotte, NC 28232
(704) 358-5425

LADY TRACK SHACK 5-K
Orlando, FL Track Shack
1322 N. Mills Ave.
Orlando, FL 32803
(407) 898-1313

MOVING COMFORT 8-K
San Diego, CA
Chuck Pennell
2115 Craig Ct.
Lemon Grove, CA 91945
(619) 531-5282

February

MIAMI HEART INSTITUTE RACE
FOR LIFE 5-K
Miami, FL
Miami Heart Inst. Race For Life
4701 Meridan Avenue
Miami Beach, FL 33141
(305) 674-3060

SANTA CLARITA
RUNNER'S WOMEN'S 5-K
Santa Clarita, CA
Karen Callahan
Santa Clarita Runners
P.O. Box 800298
Santa Clarita, CA 91380
(805) 296-0138

GEA/SPAULDING 5-K
WOMEN'S CLASSIC
Glenpool, OK
Ken Spaulding
P.O. Box 1149
Glenpool, OK 74033
(918) 322-3285

STRAUB HAWAII WOMEN'S 10-K
Honolulu, HI
Allison Price
Straub Clinic
888 S. King St.
Honolulu, HI 96813
(808) 522-4479

March

WOMEN'S HOSPITAL 5-K
Houston, TX
Helen Varty
American Lung Association
3100 Weslayan
Suite 330
Houston, TX 77027
(713) 968-5800

HONOLULU WOMEN'S 10-K
Honolulu, HI
Paula Rath
888 South King Street
Honolulu, HI 96813
(808) 522-3795

BONNIE BELL 10-K
San Francisco, CA
Scott Thomason

P.O. Box 27557
San Francisco, CA 94127
(415) 681-2323

LADY AVIA 10-K
Baltimore, MD
Baltimore RRC
P.O. Box 9825
Baltimore, MD 21284
(301) 323-7860

April

ATLANTA'S WOMEN'S 5-K
Atlanta, GA
Atlanta Track Club
3097 E. Shadowlawn Avenue, NE
Atlanta, GA 30305
(404) 231-9064

YWCA WOMEN'S 10-K & 5-K
Spokane, WA
YWCA
West 829 Broadway Street
Spokane, WA 99201
(509) 326-1190

BALTIMORE LADIES
CLASSIC 10-K
Baltimore, MD
Baltimore RRC
P.O. Box 9825
Baltimore, MD 21284
(301) 323-7860

EMMA CREEK CLASSIC
WOMEN'S 5-K
Hesston, KS
Paula Patton
Box 2000
Hesston, KS 67062
(316) 327-4831

LADIES FOUNTAIN 5-K
(STATE CHAMPIONSHIP)
Chambersburg, PA

Ginger Zimmerman
889 Knob Hill Road
Fayetteville, PA 17222
(717) 352-3008

LADY WHITE ROSE 5-K
York, PA
Bobbi Kehr
386 Spartan Rd.
York, PA 17403
(717) 741-3836

WOMEN ON THE MOVE 5-K
Erie, PA
Laurel Swartz
Women's Health Connection
3330 Peach Street
Erie, PA 16508
(814) 870-6145

LAURA STEGMAN
MEMORIAL 5-K
Lompoc, CA
Bill & Mary Graham
1309 East Palmetto Ave.
Lompoc, CA 93436
(805) 736-2371

RACE THAT'S GOOD
FOR LIFE 5-K
Oak Park, IL
Jim Mathews
Oak Park RC, Box 2332
Oak Park, IL 60303
(312) 527-9870

May

FREIHOFER'S RUN
FOR WOMEN 10-K & 5-K
Albany, NY
George Regan
233 Fourth Street
Troy, NY 12180
(518) 273-0267

TOUCH OF CLASS 5-K
White Rock Lake
Dallas, TX
CCCD
P.O. Box 820414
Dallas, TX 75382
(214) 855-1511

WISCONSIN WOMEN'S 8-K
Waukesha, WI
Kris Clark-Setnes
P.O. Box 481
Germantown, WI 53022
(414) 255-1008

DAISY 5-K
Austin, TX
Joe and Denise Huerta
4411 Secluded Hollow
Austin, TX 78727
(512) 218-0414

MONTANA WOMEN'S
5-MILE & 2-MILE
Billings, MT
John Dorr
2714 Hoover Avenue
Bllings, MT 59102
(406) 248-4362

YWCA MOTHER'S DAY
5-K & 2-MILE
Duluth, MN
Kris Sheldon
YWCA
202 West 2nd Street
Duluth, MN 55802
(218) 722-7425

ATALANTA'S VICTORY
5-MILE & 2-MILE
Arcata, CA
Cathy Dickerson
Six Rivers RC
P.O. Box 214
Arcata, CA 95521
(707) 826-1512

MOTHER'S DAY 5-K
Yorktown Heights, NY
Linda Geppert
Taconic TTC
P.O. Box 99
Baldwin Place, NY 10505
(914) 628-9283

MOTHER'S DAY 5-K
Charleston, WV
Karen Frashier
Corporate Development
Charleston Area Medical Center
P.O. Box 1547
Charleston, WV 25326
(304) 348-6702

NA HOLO WAHINE 5-K
Wailuku, HI
Lani Perry
VIRR
P.O. Box 330099
Kahului, HI 96732
(808) 242-1992

NIKE WOMEN'S RACE 8-K
Washington, D.C.
Nike Women's Race
Box 134
Mount Vernon, VA 22121
(703) 780-3037

ADVIL MINI TUNE-UP
New York, NY
NYRRC
9 East 89th Street
New York, NY 10128
(212) 860-4455

SITKA WOMEN'S 3-MILE
Sitka, AK
Carol Hughes
215 Brady Street
Sitka, AK 99835
(907) 747-6317

WOMEN'S AMERICAN ORT 5-K
Salt Lake City, UT

Denise Doebbling
1406 Blaine Avenue
Salt Lake City, UT 84105
(801) 486-0493

WOMEN'S RUNNING RACE
5-MILE & 2.1 MILE
Pittsfield, MA
Kathy Korte
11 Cross Road
West Stockbridge, MA 01266
(413) 232-7173

GMAA SPRING
WOMEN'S 3.3-MILE
Williston, VT
Ruth Painter
688 Williston Road
Williston, VT 05495
(802) 878-3048

RIVER CITY
WOMEN'S 5-MILE & 5-K
Clinton, IA
Kathy Hand
Gateway YWCA
317 Seventh Avenue South
Clinton, IA 52732
(319) 242-2110

BAY CITY ALL WOMEN'S 4-MILE
Bay City, MI
Marlene Sundberg
400 North Lincoln
Bay City, MI 48708
(517) 892-3439

RUN FOR THE ROSES 5-K
Salisbury, MA
Ed Liebfried
WCRC
58 Columbus Avenue
Exeter, NH 03833
(603) 772-6396

SANTA CLARITA WOMEN'S 5-K
Santa Clartia, CA
Karen Callahan

Santa Clarita Runners
P.O. Box 800298
Santa Clarita, CA 91380
(805) 296-0138

MELPOMENE 5-K
St. Paul, MN
Melpomene Inst.
1010 University Ave.
St. Paul, MN 55104
(612) 642-1951

WISCONSIN WOMEN'S 5-K
Waukesha, WI
Kris Clark-Sentnes
P.O. Box 481
Germantown, WI 53022
(414) 255-1008

WOMEN'S GOLD COAST 8-K
Birch State Park, FL
Greater Fort Lauderdale RRC
P.O. Box 2512
Fort Lauderdale, FL 33303-2512
(305) 970-3482

YWCA MOTHER'S DAY 5-K
Duluth, MN
YWCA
202 W. 2nd St.
Duluth, MN 55802
(218) 722-7425

CAMC WOMEN'S 5-K
Charleston, WV
Karen Frashier
CAMC
P.O. Box 1547
Charleston, WV 25326
(304) 348-6702

SITKA WOMEN'S 3-MILE
Sitka, AK
Carol Hughes
215 Brady St.
Sitka, AK 99835
(907) 747-6317

YWCA WOMEN'S 5-K
Manchester, NH
YWCA
72 Concord St. Manchester NH
03101
(603) 625-5785

STRAWBERRY FESTIVAL 5-K
Vista, CA
Kathy Kinane
3633 Cerro Ave.
Oceanside, CA 92056
(619) 630-4980

WOMEN'S 5-K
Buffalo, NY
Tricia Ditmer
13882 Rt. 78
Wales, NY 14139
(716) 457-9425

June

ADVIL MINI MARATHON 10-K
New York, NY
NYRRC
9 East 89th Street
New York, NY 10128
(212) 860-4455

ALASKA WOMEN'S 10-K
Anchorage, AK
Larry Ross
3605 Arctic #AA
Anchorage, AK 99503
(907) 562-2161, ext. AA

BONNE BELL 10-K & 5-K
Minneapolis, MN
Race Elves
2035 Highland Parkway
St. Paul, MN 55116
(612) 698-1018

YWCA WOMEN'S 5-K
Manchester, NH
Helen Hamilton
YWCA

72 Concord Street
Manchester, NH 03101
(603) 625-5785

CHARLOTTESVILLE
WOMEN'S 4-MILE
Charlottesville, VA
Charlottesville Track Club
P.O. Box 5542
Charlottesville, VA 22905
(804) 293-6115

PIKE LAKE WOMEN'S 10-K
Duluth, MN
Pamela Solberg-Tapper
5978 N. Pike Lake Road
Duluth, MN 55811
(218) 729-9861

APTOS WOMEN'S 5-MILE
Aptos, CA
Santa Cruz TC
P.O. Box 1803
Capitola, CA 95010

PEACH COBBLER
WOMEN'S 5-MILE & 2-MILE
Grand Junction, CO
Bob Kline
2908 Bonita Avenue
Grand Junction, CO 81504
(303) 243-2531

WOMEN'S DISTANCE
FESTIVAL 5-K
Pawnee, OK
Theodore Morgan
Pawnee Warriors RC
314 Forest Street
Pawnee, OK 74058

FOR WOMEN ONLY 5-K
Ann Arbor, MI
Renee Rienas
241 Sunset
Ann Arbor, MI 48103
(313) 761-1165

WOMEN'S DISTANCE
FESTIVAL 5-K
Utica, NY
Joanne Rella
34 Bolton Road
New Hartford, NY 13413
(315) 733-9580

LADY FOOTLOCKER
COLUMBINE CLASSIC 5-K
Denver, CO
Sharon Klute
Colorado Columbines
3948 S. Jasmine Street
Denver, CO 80237
(303) 825-1313

DANSKIN WOMEN'S
TRIATHLON
White Plains, N.Y.
Gloria West
316 N. Appleton St.
Appleton, WI 54911
(800) 452-9526

FOCUS ON WOMEN 5-K
Worcester, MA
Central Mass. Striders
Greendale Station,
Box 2
Worcester, MA 01606
(508) 464-2608

July

LONG ISLAND
SUMMER 5-K WOMEN'S RUN
Jericho, NY
Barry Saltsberg
Women's Race
62 Sylvia Lane
Plainview, NY 11803
(212) 264-7558

GREAT LEGS 5-K
Lowell, MA
Christina Bellinger

3 Dexter Street
Newburyport, MA 01950
(508) 462-2715

WOMEN'S DISTANCE
FESTIVAL 5-K
Columbia, MD
Karen Harvey
Howard County Striders
4520 Alpine Rose Bend
Ellicott City, MD 21043
(301) 461-1772

WOMEN'S DISTANCE
FESTIVAL 5-K
Ukiah, CA
Ruth Powell
North Coast Striders
295 Oak Manor Drive
Ukiah, CA 95482

Niceville, FL
LeaAnn Hermsen
NW Florida TC
513 Juniper Avenue
Niceville, FL 32548

Belchertown, MA
Diane McNamara
Sugarload Mountain AC
34 Juckett Hill Road
Belchertown, MA 01007

Omaha, NE
Erin Sullivan
Omaha RC
5006 Cass Street
Apartment #1
Omaha, NE 68132
(402) 551-7230

Congers, NY
Ann McGrath
Rockland Lake Runners Assoc.
P.O. Box 132
Congers, NY 10920
(914) 268-0277

Chambersburg, PA
Merrilyn Kessler
Chambersburg RRC
1759 Crottlestown Road
Chambersburg, PA 17201

Colonial Heights, VA
Becky Wamsley
40 Brandywine Court
Colonial Heights, VA 23834
(804) 526-2770

Hopewell, VA
Earl King
Tri Cities RRC
2705 City Point Road
Hopewell, VA 23860

Newport News, VA
Denise Suits
Peninsula TC
6 Krause Court
Newport News, VA 23664

Norfolk, VA
Wendy Farnham
134 West Bay View Boulevard
Norfolk, VA 23503
(804) 480-0342

Richmond, VA
Nancy Jakubek
Richmond RR
5825 East Willow Oaks Drive
Richmond, VA 23225

Virginia Beach, VA
Rosemary Kalz
Tidewater Striders
3905 Jousting Arch
Virginia Beach, VA 23456

Parkersburg, WV
Norma Phillips
1114 39th Street
Parkersburg, WV 26104
(304) 422-4158

WOMEN'S DISTANCE
FESTIVAL 5-K
Westminster, MD
Linda Galinaitis
Westminster RRC
1796 S. Pleasant Valley Road
Westminster, MD 21157

Grandview MO
Peggy Donavan
Mid-Amereican Masters
6733 East 126th Street
Grandview, MO 64030

WOMEN'S DISTANCE
FESTIVAL 5-K
Sheboygan, WI
Ann Griffin
Shoreline Striders
2412 Camelot Boulevard
Apt. 201
Sheboygan, WI 53081

NJ TAC WOMEN'S
5-K CHAMPIONSHIP
Freehold, NJ
Jeff Decker
Freehold Area Running Club
P.O. Box 934
Freehold, NJ 07728
(908) 699-4119

WOMEN'S 5-K CLASSIC
Alton, IL
Betsy Knezevich
2912 Airport Road
Godfrey, IL 62035
(618) 466-1081

WOMEN'S DISTANCE
FESTIVAL 5-K
Huntsville, AL
Nancy Shephard
Huntsville TC
94 Scenic Drive
Huntsville, AL 35801

Springfield, IL
Sally Cadagin
Springfield RR
1204 Interlacken
Springfield, IL 62704

Annapolis, MD
Jenny Spivak
Annapolis Striders
P.O. Box 187
Annapolis, MD 21401

Sedalia, MO
Milene Mittelhauser
Sedalia Runners
905 West 28th Street
Sedalia, MO 65301

Albuquerque, NM
Pamela Grosvenor
Albuquerque RRC
2914 Morningside Drive, NE
Albuquerque, NM 87110

Clarksville, TN
Patti Marquess
Cumberland Valley TTC
1858 Patricia Lane
Clarksville, TN 37040

ROCHESTER WOMEN'S 4-MILE
Rochester, MN
Jeanne Block
4516 Avon Lane, NW
Rochester, MN 55901
(507) 289-8841

WOMEN'S DISTANCE
FESTIVAL 5-K
Kensington, MD
Anna Berdahl
Montgomery County RRC
P.O. Box 1703
Rockville, MD 20850
(301) 353-0200

Kingsport, TN
Hank Brown
State of Franklin

1548 Behmeade Drive
Kingsport, TN 37664

Corpus Christi, TX
Lupita Galvan
Corpus Christi RRC
1431 Brentwood
Corpus Christi, TX 78415

WOMEN'S DISTANCE
FESTIVAL 5-K
Napa, CA
Steve Zanetell
Napa Valley Marathon
1325 Imola Avenue West
Napa, CA 94559

Pueblo, CO
Marijane Matines
Southern Colorado Runners
117 Regency Blvd.
Pueblo, CO 81005

Tallahassee, FL
Barbara Yonclas
Gulf Winds TC
1816 Alantis Pl.
Tallahassee, FL 32303

Endicott, NY
Shelley Reynolds
Triple Cities RC
1874 Dutchtown Rd.
Endicott, NY 13760

San Antonio, TX
San Antonio RRC
10414 Dreamland
San Antonio, TX 78230

Hampton, VA
Denise Suits
Peninsula TC
18 Barron St.
Hampton, VA 23669

Kansas City, MO
Wilma Payne
4309 Hickory La.
Blue Springs, MO 64015

Lancaster, SC
Clude Sinclair
c/o Dept. Social Services
Hwy. 9 East
Lancaster, SC 29720

DANSKIN WOMEN'S
TRIATHLON
San Jose, CA
Gloria West
316 N. Appleton St.
Appleton, WI 54911
(800) 452-9526

WOMEN'S 5-K CLASSIC
Alton, IL
Betsy Knezevich
2430 Orchard La.
Godfrey, IL 62035
(618) 466-1081

August

WOMEN'S DISTANCE
FESTIVAL 5-K
San Luis Obispo, CA
San Luis Distance Club
P.O. Box 1134
San Luis Obispo, CA 93406
(805) 528-4059

Grand Junction, CO
Bob Kline
Mesa Monument Striders
2908 Bonita Avenue
Grand Junction, CO 81504
(303) 243-2531

Bethany, OK
Jeff Kiser
Bethany Striders RRC
7801 N.W. 23rd Street
Bethany, OK 73008
(405) 521-3161

Memphis, TN
Carol Chambers

Memphis Runners
1204 Chamberlain Drive, #10
Memphis, TN 38119

RUN FOR ROSES
St. Louis, MO
Gary Krosch
15 Southmoor
St. Louis, MO 63105
(314) 961-2647

WOMEN'S DISTANCE
FESTIVAL 5-K
Coal Valley, IL
Tom DeClerck
Cornbelt Running
9603 114th Street
Coal Valley, IL 61240

Baltimore, MD
Jerry Jurick
Baltimore RRC
3712 Beech Avenue
Baltimore, MD 21211

PICNIC RACE 5-K
Nashville, TN
Kibby Clayton
P.O. Box 110385
Nashville, TN 37222
(615) 833-4124

SUSAN B. ANTHONY
WOMEN'S 5-K
Sacramento, CA
Joanne Hollister
P.O. Box 19908
Sacramento, CA 95819
(916) 454-6131

WOMEN'S DISTANCE
FESTIVAL 5-K
Birmingham, AL
Mary Bryan
Birmingham TC
3608 Birchwood Lane
Birmingham, AL 35243
(205) 967-7160

Marshalltown, IA
Lynn Watlers
Iowa River Striders
2510 S. 6th Street, D-30
Marshalltown, IA 50158
(515) 753-0147

Lewisburg, PA
Martha Miller
Buffalo Valley Striders
107 S. 14th Street
Lewisburg, PA 17837

BROOKS WOMEN'S 10-K
Calgary, Alberta
Margaret Carlton-Grover
735 Alexander Crescent NW
Calgary, Alberta
Canada T2M 4B8

LEADING LADIES 5-K
Indianapolis, IN
Kathy Holloway
737 West Berkley Road
Indianapolis, IN 46208
(317) 926-6223

MAGGIE VALLEY
MOONLIGHT 5-K
Maggie Valley, NC
Wayne Abbe
P.O. Box 998
Maggie Valley, NC 28751
(704) 926-1630

WOMEN'S DISTANCE
FESTIVAL 5-K
Riverdale, MD
Ann Wass
Prince Georges RC
5903 60th Avenue
Riverdale, MD 20737

Abilene, TX
Laura Packer
1917 Westwood
Abilene, TX 79603
(915) 673-7744

ALICE FAY'S 5-K
Charlottetown, Prince Edward
Island
Myra Fraser
P.O. Box 3303
Charlottetown, PEI
Canada C1A 8W5
(902) 566-5096

WOMEN'S DISTANCE
FESTIVAL 5-K
Toms River, NJ
Ocean Running Club
15 East Drive
Toms River, NJ 08753
(908) 240-5916

PEACH COBBLER
WOMEN'S 5-MILE & 2-MILE
Grand Junction, CO
Sammy Burria
287 32½ Rd.
Grand Junction, CO 81503
(303) 434-0190

WOMEN'S DISTANCE
FESTIVAL 5-K
Champaign, IL
Second Wind RC
1912 David Dr.
Champaign, IL 61821

WOMEN'S DISTANCE
FESTIVAL 5-K
Spokane, WA
Lori Shauvin
Bloomsday RR
1807 E. 60th St.
Spokane, WA 99223

Tucson, AZ
Mike Hartigan
Southern Arizona RRC
4625 E. Broadway, #112
Tucson, AZ 85711

Nashville, TN
Patricia Nelson

Nashville Striders
1215 Stonewall Blvd.
Murfreesboro, TN 37130

Midland, TX
Mary Lou Hennessy
Permain Basin RR
3214 Cimmaron
Midland, TX 79705

DANSKIN WOMEN'S
TRIATHLON
Milwaukee, WI
Gloria West
316 N. Appleton St.
Appleton, WI 54911
(800) 452-9526

September

FOCUS ON WOMEN 5-K
Worcester, MA
Central Massachusetts Striders
Greendale Station
Box 2
Worcester, MA 01606

WOMEN'S DISTANCE
FESTIVAL 5-K
Washington, D.C.
Nina Trocky
Washington Runners
2929 Connecticut Avenue, N.W.
Washington, D.C. 20008

Adamstown, MD
Sharon Ford
Frederick Steeplechasers
5551 Doubs Road
Adamstown, MD 21710

San Angelo, TX
Anne Fish
San Angelo Road Lizards
7590 S. Country Club Road
San Angelo, TX 76904

Shasta, CA
Debbie Ridding

Trinity RRCA
Star Route, Box 170
Shasta, CA 96087

Augusta, GA
Amanda Gray
Augusta Striders
504 Waterford Dr.
Evans, GA 30809

Omaha, NE
Erin Sullivan
Omaha RC
5006 Cass St. Apt. #1
Omaha, NE 68132
(402) 551-7230

Media, PA
Rita Jordan
Delco RR
311 South Ave.
Media, PA 19063

San Angelo, TX
Anne Fish
San Angelo Road Lizards
7590 S. Country Club Rd.
San Angelo, TX 76904

Roanoke, VA
Sandra Andrew
Star City Striders
2101 Crystal Springs Ave.
Roanoke, VA 24014

WOMEN'S BIATHLON
New York, NY
Big Apple Triathlon Club
P.O. Box 20427
Cherokee Station
New York, NY 10028
(212) 289-4113

WOMEN'S DISTANCE
FESTIVAL 5-K
Denver, CO
Ann Burback
Colorado Columbines/CMRA

877 S. Nelson Street
Lakewood, CO 80236
(303) 988-2629

Cumberland, MD
Linda Yockus
Queen City Striders
836 Gephart Drive
Cumberland, MD 21502

NYRRC WOMEN'S
HALF-MARATHON
New York, NY
NYRRC
9 East 89th Street
New York, NY 10128
(212) 860-4455

WOMEN'S 5-K RACE
Dayton, OH
Clint Jett
Recreation Div.
451 West Third Street
Dayton, OH 45422
(513) 225-4670

WOMEN'S DISTANCE
FESTIVAL 5-K
Martinez, GA
Margaret Fornes
Augusta Striders
3657 Brannen Drive
Martinez, GA 30907

RUN JANE RUN 10-K & 5-K
Fort Wayne, IN
Women's Bureau
303 East Washington Boulevard
Fort Wayne, IN 46802
(219) 424-7977

GOLD LEAF WOMEN'S
5-K CLASSIC
Wichita, KS
Clark Ensz
121 N. River Boulevard
Wichita, KS 67203
(316) 267-6812

ROUND CHURCH WOMEN'S
10-K & 5-K
Richmond, VT
John Scheer
P.O. Box 572
Burlington, VT 05402
(802) 862-0122

WOMEN'S DISTANCE
FESTIVAL 5-K
Fort Myers, FL
Laura Jeffcoat
Fort Myers TC
1437 Dubonnet Court
Fort Myers, FL 33919

Humboldt, TN
Pam Chambers
Jackson RR
2667 Beau Beth Ln.
Humboldt, TN 38343

Alexandria, VA
Jennifer Thacker
Washington Runners Unlimited
492 Naylor Pl.
Alexandria, VA 22304

Winchester, VA
Cindia Stewart
Shenandoah Valley Runners
115 Shirley St.
Winchester, VA 22601

Gulfport, MS
Lindo Sullivan
Gulf Coast RC
1 Oakwood Court
Gulfport, MS 39503

FREIHOFER'S 8-K, 5-K & 3-K
Syracuse, NY
David Oja
213 Scott Avenue
Syracuse, NY 13224
(315) 446-6285

WOMEN'S COMMUNITY CLUB
5-MILE & 2.8 MILE
Longmeadow, MA
Walter Childs
P.O. Box 1484
Springfield, MA 01101
(413) 566-3145

WOMEN'S DISTANCE
FESTIVAL 5-K
Portland, ME
Ron & Susan Davenny
Maine TC
20 Curtis Road
Portland, ME 04103

CAROL WOLFE MEMORIAL 5-K
Kettering, OH
Robert Vilkas
Ohio River RRC
545 Kenwood Ave.
Dayton, OH 45406
(513) 443-3886

WOMEN'S DISTANCE
FESTIVAL 5-K
Deland, FL
John Boyle
W. Volusia RRC
140½ S. Brooks Ave.
Deland, FL 32720

WOMEN'S RUN
FOR HEALTH 5-MILE
Appleton, WI
Jane Curran-Meuli
1506 S. Oneida
Appleton, WI 54915
(414) 738-2623

WOMEN'S DISTANCE
FESTIVAL 5-K
Frederick, MD
Sharon Ford
Frederick Steeplechasers
5551 Doubs Rd.
Adamstown, MD 21710

Cape Girardeau, MO
Debbie Leoni
Cape RR
2823 Hildale Cir.
Cape Girardeau, MO 63701

WOMEN'S RIVER RUN
10-K & 5-K
Wenatchee, WA
Women's Resource Ctr.
P.O. Box 2051
Wenatchee, WA 98807
(509) 662-0121

DANSKIN WOMEN'S
TRIATHLON
Dallas, TX
Gloria West
316 N. Appleton St.
Appleton, WI 54911
(800) 452-9526

WOMEN'S DISTANCE
FESTIVAL 5-K
Portland, ME
Ruth Hefflefinger
Maine TC
20 Curtis Rd.
Portland, ME 04103

October

WOMEN'S 5-K
Nashville, TN
Kibby Clayton
P.O. Box 110385
Nashville, TN 37222
(615) 833-4124

ST. LUKE'S HOSPITAL
WOMEN'S RUN 10-K & 5-K
Kansas City, MO
Ginny Epsten
St. Luke's Community Relations
4400 Wornall Road
Kansas City, MO 64111
(816) 932-2258

WOMEN'S DISTANCE
FESTIVAL 5-K
Weaverville, CA
Carmen Brown
Trinity RR
P.O. 2461
Weaverville, CA 96093

BLUE MOUNTAIN
HALF-MARATHON, 10-K & 5-K
Missoula, MT
Sue Monk
715 Kensington
Missoula, MT 59801
(406) 721-1464

MOVING COMFORT 8-K
San Diego, CA
Chuck Pennell
2115 Craig Court
Lemon Grove, CA 91945
(619) 531-5282

WOMEN ON THE MOVE 5-K
Bethlehem, PA
Sandra Wiens
Northampton Community College
3835 Green Pond Road
Bethlehem, PA 18017
(215) 861-5350

WOMEN'S DISTANCE
FESTIVAL 5-K
Midland, TX
Permain Basin RRC
1017 W. County Road, #130
Midland, TX 79703

GBES WOMEN'S 5-K
Mystic, CT
Guido Brothers Escort Service
1037 Shewville Road
Ledyard, CT 06339
(203) 886-2809

WOMEN DISTANCE
FESTIVAL 5-K
Chillicothe, IL

Norman Astwood
Illinois Valley Striders
5224 East Marquette
Chillicothe, IL 61523

East Greenbush, NY
HMRRC
P.O. Box 12304
Albany, NY 12212
(518) 273-3108

TUFTS HEALTH PLAN 10-K
Boston, MA
Meg Crowley
Conventures, Inc.
250 Summer Street
Boston, MA 02210
(617) 439-7700

RUN FOR THE ROSE 5-K
Oak Ridge, TN
Cande Cseay
Methodist Medical Center
990 Oak Ridge Tpk.
Oak Ridge, TN 37830
(615) 481-1829

WOMEN'S ONLY 8-K & 3-K
Flint, MI
Bauman's Running Center
1453 W. Hill Road
Flint, MI 48507
(313) 238-5981

WOMEN'S DISTANCE
FESTIVAL 5-K
Minneapolis, MN
Kelly Kruell
Northern Lights
4225 41st Avenue S.
Minneapolis, MN 55406

RUN/WALK FOR
YOUR HEALTH 5-K
Wilmington, DE
Women's Sports Specialties
5335 Limestone Road

Wilmington, DE 19808
(302) 239-0838

TAC/USA ALHAMBRA
MOONLIGHT 8-K
Alhambra, CA
Elinor Fong
111 South First Street
Alhambra, CA 91801
(818) 570-5044

GOLD LEAF WOMEN'S 5-K
Wichita, KS
HCA Wesley Medical Ctr.
550 N. Hillside
Wichita, KS 67214
(316) 688-3310

WOMEN'S DISTANCE
FESTIVAL 5-K
Denver, CO
Lisa Page
Colorado Columbines
8779 S. Allison St.
Littleton, CO 80123
(303) 972-1619

Gettysburg, PA
Joanne Smith
Gettysburg YWCA/RRC
909 Fairfield Rd.
Gettysburg, PA 17325

SYRACUSE FREIHOFER'S 5-K
Syracuse, NY
David Oja
213 Scott Ave.
Syracuse, NY 13224
(315) 446-6285

NYRRC WOMEN'S
HALF-MARATHON
New York, NY
9 E. 89th St.
New York, NY 10128
(212) 860-4455

WOMEN'S DISTANCE
FESTIVAL 5-K
Carbondale, IL
Ann Knewitz
512 W. Oak
Carbondale, IL 62901

Richmond, VA
Becky Wamsley-Cornett
Tri Cities RR
3417 Spendthrift Dr. #518
Richmond, VA 23294

STRIDER X-C 3-MILE
Nashville, TN
Kibby Clayton
P.O. Box 110385
Nashville, TN 37222
(615) 833-4124

November

DREAM OF ROSES
10-K & 2-MILE
Salem, OR
Phidippides RC
P.O. Box 2315
Salem, OR 97308
(503) 399-7057

WOMEN'S DISTANCE
FESTIVAL 5-K
Sierra Vista, AZ
Myles Moss
Sierra Toyota
2596 Fry Boulevard
Sierra Vista, AZ 85635
(602) 458-8880

LADIES 5-K TURKEY TROT
Alexandria, VA
Pauline Landes
6601 Telegraph Rd.
Alexandria, VA 22310
(703) 922-9841

YWCA TURKEY TROT 5-K
Bristol, TN
YWCA
401 5th St.
Bristol, TN 37620
(615) 968-9444

December

BALBOA BOOGIE 5-K
San Diego, CA
Chuck Pennell
2115 Craig Court
Lemon Grove, CA 91945
(619) 460-3110

The following lists the Race for the Cure events, which raise funds to fight breast cancer. The Washington, D.C., race is a mixed event, while the other 16 are for women only.

January

Palm Beach, FL
Donna Miller
c/o Palm Beach Gardens Medical Center
3360 Burns Road
Palm Beach Gardens, FL 33410
(407) 622-1411

March

Austin, TX
Branden Kanepa
4307 Caswell, Apt. C
Austin, TX 78751
(512) 323-9419

April

Wichita, KS
Terry Burnett

1112 East James Street
Derby, KS 67037
(316) 788-4414

Indianapolis, IN
Junior League
644 W. 77th St., North Dr.
Indianapolis, IN 46260
(317) 848-8123

Des Moines, IA
Junior League
756 16th St.
Des Moines, IA 50314
(515) 243-3329

Detroit, MI
Jane Hoey
Prentis Cancer Ctr.
110 E. Warren
Detroit, MI 48201
(313) 833-0710, ext. 245

May

Peoria, IL
Junior League of Peoria
256 N.E. Randolph Avenue
Peoria, IL 61606
(309) 685-9312

Philadelphia, PA
Elaine Grobman
Breast Health Institute
1015 Chestnut Street
Suite 510
Philadelphia, PA 19107
(215) 627-4447

Minneapolis, MN
Charlene Plitman
Northwest Racquet, Swim & Health Club
5525 Cedar Lake Rd.
Minneapolis, MN 55416
(612) 546-3555

June

Plano, TX
M.A. Hanook
The Susan G. Komen Breast
Cancer Fund
3701 Knob Hill Drive
Plano, TX 75023
(214) 596-9002

Davenport, IA
Dianne Otte
St. Luke's Cancer Center
1227 E. Rusholme
Davenport, IA 53802
(319) 326-6797

Washington, D.C.
National Race for the Cure
1990 M Street, N.W.
Suite 310
Washington, DC 20036
(202) 828-7032

Decatur, IL
DMH Cancer Care Institute
2300 N. Edward Street
Decatur, IL 62526
(217) 877-2476

Arsenal Island, IL
Dianne Otte
St. Luke's Hospital
1227 E. Rusholme St.
Davenport, IA 52803
(319) 326-8000

July

Aspen, CO
Ann Hoover
P.O. Box 4151
Aspen, CO 81612
(303) 923-5334

September

Scranton, PA
Rose Broderick
700 Quincy Avenue
Scranton, PA 18510
(717) 963-2100

New York, NY
Cheryl Quinn
Race for the Cure
P.O. Box 2421
New York, NY 10108
(212) 245-3316

Atlanta, GA
Sandy Teepen
900 Charles Allen Dr.
Atlanta, GA 30308
(404) 874-1421

Birmingham, AL
P.O. Box 59205
Birmingham, AL 35259
(205) 599-3742

Orange County, CA Race for the
Cure
Orange County, CA
P.O. Box 11626
Santa Ana, CA 92711
(714) 953-2264

Amarillo, TX
Harrington Cancer Center
1500 Wallace Boulevard
Amarillo, TX 79106
(806) 359-4673

October

Houston, TX
Julie Thurber
11755 Cawdor Way
Houston, TX 77024
(713) 461-8547

Dallas, TX
Suzy Gekiere
5504 W. University
Dallas, TX 75209
(214) 352-3435

Atlanta, GA
Laura & Tom Pearce
2300 Peachtree Road North
Suite B109
Atlanta, GA 30309
(404) 350-9207

San Francisco, CA
Lynne Fox
2360 Pacific
San Francisco, CA 94115
(415) 929-1455

Portland, OR
Barbara Himmelberg
15541 N.E. Eilers Rd.
Aurora, OR 97002
(503) 295-8226

Nashville, TN
Margaret Groos
Minnie Pearl Cancer Foundation
230 25th Ave. N.
Nashville, TN 37203
(615) 342-1740

Great Road Races

January

CHARLOTTE OBSERVER 10K
Charlotte, NC
Don King, *Observer* Promotion
P.O. Box 32188
Charlotte, NC 28232
(704) 358-5425

Jackson Day Race 9K
New Orleans, LA
Chuck George
NOTC
P.O. Box 52003
New Orleans, LA 70152
(504) 482-6682

Super Bowl Sunday 10K
Redondo Beach, CA
Super Bowl 10K
Chamber of Commerce
1215 North Catalina Ave.
Redondo Beach, CA 90277
(213) 376-6913

February

Runner's Den 10K
Phoenix, AZ
Rob Wallach
6505 North 16th St.
Phoenix, AZ 85016
(602) 277-4333

Gasparilla Distance Classic 15K
Tampa, FL
Gasparilla
P.O. Box 1881
Tampa, FL 33601-1881
(813) 229-7866

Great Aloha Run 8.2-Mile
Honolulu, HI

The Great Aloha Run
P.O. Box 31000
Honolulu, HI 96849-0014
(808) 735-6092

Colonial Half-Marathon
Williamsburg, VA
Bonita Bates
P.O. Box 399
Williamsburg, VA 23187
(804) 221-3362

Cowtown 10K
Fort Worth, TX
Beverly Weiss
P.O. Box 567
Fort Worth, TX 76101
(817) 735-2033

March

Jacksonville River Run 15K
Jacksonville, FL
Doug Alred
3853 Bay Meadows Rd.
Jacksonville, FL 32217
(904) 739-1917

West End 5-Mile
Dallas, TX
Tom Short
c/o Athletic Supply
6921 Preston Rd.
Dallas, TX 75205
(214) 522-3960

St. Patrick's Day 10K
Torrance, CA
Elite Racing
1904 Church St. Suite B
Costa Mesa, CA 92627
(714) 548-4897

Azalea Trail 10K
Mobile, AL
Gerald Thomlinson

Port City Pacers
P.O. Box 6427
Mobile, AL 36660
(205) 473-7223

Heart Trek 10K and 5K
Atlanta, GA
Ben Barron
American Heart Association
P.O. Box 13589
Atlanta, GA 30324
(404) 261-2262

Carlsbad 5000
Carlsbad, CA
Elite Racing
2431 Morena Blvd. Suite 2H
San Diego, CA 92110
(619) 275-5440

Kansas City Ekiden Relay
Overland Park, KS
Bill Buchanan
8575 West 110th St. Suite 100
Overland Park, KS 66210
(913) 451-8094

April

Cooper River Bridge Run 10K
Charleston, SC
Mark Blatchford
Wellness Center
45 Courtney Dr.
Charleston, SC 29401
(803) 792-9196

Capitol 10,000
Austin, TX
Renet Presas
Austin American-Statesman
P.O. Box 670
Austin, TX 78767
(512) 445-3596

Cherry Blossom 10-Mile
Washington, DC
Phil Stewart

c/o Northern Telecom
P.O. Box 884
Middletown, MD 21769
(301) 371-5583

Redbud Classic 10K and 2-Mile
Oklahoma City, OK
Jane Politte
6488 Avondale Dr., Suite 184
Oklahoma City, OK 73116
(405) 272-6382

Sallie Mae 10K
Washington, DC
Jane Sisco
Sallie Mae 10K
1050 Thomas Jefferson, NW
Washington, DC 20007
(202) 728-6456

Crescent City 10K Classic
New Orleans, LA
Mac DeVaughn
8200 Hampson St.
Suite 217
New Orleans, LA 70118
(504) 861-8686

Get in Gear 10K
Minneapolis, MN
Jeff Winter
5115 Oliver Ave. South
Minneapolis, MN 55419
(612) 920-6886

Alaska Heart Run 5K
Anchorage, AK
Roy Reisinger
2630 Forest Pk. Dr.
Anchorage, AK 99517
(907) 277-7279

Cherry Creek Sneak 5-Mile
Denver, CO
Barbara Schirkofsky
Bank of Cherry Creek
3033 East 1st Ave.

Denver, CO 80206
(303) 388-4331

Icebreaker 5-Mile
Great Falls, MT
Scott Henderson
Parks and Recreation Dept.
P.O. Box 5021
Great Falls, MT 59403
(406) 727-5881

May

All-Iowa Festival of Races
Cedar Rapids, IA
Marcie Hosch
318 5th St., SE
Cedar Rapids, IA 52402
(319) 365-1458

Lilac Bloomsday Run 12K
Spokane, WA
Sylvia Quinn
Lilac Bloomsday Association
P.O. Box 1511
Spokane, WA 99210
(509) 838-1579

Run for the Zoo 10K and 5K
Albuquerque, NM
Gwen Poe
1723 San Cristobal, SW
Albuquerque, NM 87104
(505) 247-1533

Gum Tree 10K
Tupelo, MS
Johnny Dye
1007 Chester Ave.
Tupelo, MS 38801
(601) 842-2039

Old Kent River Run 25K
Grand Rapids, MI
Stuart Gillette

P.O. Box 2194
Grand Rapids, MI 49501
(616) 771-5261

Bay to Breakers 12K
San Francisco, CA
Examiner Bay to Breakers
P.O. Box 7620
San Francisco, CA 94120
(415) 777-7770

Revco Cleveland 10K
Cleveland, OH
Jack Staph
1925 Enterprise Pkwy.
Twinsburg, OH 44087
(216) 425-9811

500 Festival Half-Marathon
Indianapolis, IN
Josephine Hauck
P.O. Box 817
Indianapolis, IN 46206
(317) 636-4556

Big Boy Classic 20K
Wheeling, WV
Hugh Stobbs
P.O. Box 1046
Wheeling, WV 26003
(304) 243-3880

Bolder Boulder 10K
Boulder, CO
Bolder Boulder, Inc.
3285 30th St. Suite 106
Boulder, CO 80301
(303) 444-7223

Hospital Hill Half-Marathon
Kansas City, MO
Rich Ayers
Crown Center
2405 Grand Ave. Suite 200
Kansas City, MO 64108
(816) 274-3196

Shelter Island 10K
Shelter Island, NY
Cristine Clarke
P.O. Box 266
Shelter Island, NY 11964
(516) 749-7867

Garden of the Gods 10-Mile
Colorado Springs, CO
Nancy Hobbs
P.O. Box 38235
Colorado Springs, CO 80937
(719) 473-2625

Orange Classic 10K
Middletown, NY
Steve Paskewitz
40 Mulberry St.
Middletown, NY 10940
(914) 343-2181

Steamboat Classic 4-Mile
Peoria, IL
Joy Kessler
Running Central
700 W Main St.
Peoria, IL 61606
(309) 688-7313

Cascade Run-Off 15K
Portland, OR
Cascade Run-Off
P.O. Box 40228
Portland, OR 97240
(503) 226-0717

Peachtree 10K
Atlanta, GA
Peachtree Road Race
3097 Shadowlawn Ave.
Atlanta, GA 30305
(404) 231-9064

Chicago Distance Classic 20K and 5K
Chicago, IL
Lorna Brett
1440 West Washington Blvd.
Chicago, IL 60607
(313) 786-1900

Utica Boilermaker 15K
Utica, NY
Earle Reed
P.O. Box 4729
Utica, NY 13504
(315) 797-1310

Deseret News 10K
Salt Lake City, UT
Deseret News 10K
P.O. Box 1257
Salt Lake City, UT 84110
(801) 237-2135

Bix 7-Mile
Davenport, IA
Ed Froelich
2685 East Kimberly Rd.
Bettendorf, IA 52722
(319) 359-9197

Wharf to Wharf 10K
Santa Cruz, CA
Wharf to Wharf Race
P.O. Box 307
Capitola, CA 95010
(408) 475-2196

Asbury Park 10K
Asbury Park, NJ
Asbury Park 10K
P.O. Box 2287
Ocean Township, NJ 07712
(908) 922-9479

Parkersburg Half-Marathon
Parkersburg, WV

Dorsey Cheuvront
P.O. Box 718
Parkersburg, WV 26102
(304) 424-2786

America's Finest City Half-Marathon
San Diego, CA
Neil Finn
P.O. Box 3879
San Diego, CA 92163
(619) 297-3901

Falmouth Road Race 7.1 Mile
Falmouth, MA
Jon Carroll & Rich Sherman
P.O.Box 732
Falmouth, MA 02541
(508) 540-7000

The Crim Road Race 10 Mile
Flint, MI
Lois Craig
P.O. Box 981
Flint, MI 48501
(313) 235-3396

Maggie Valley Moonlight 8K
Maggie Valley, NC
Wayne Abbe
P.O. Box 998
Maggie Valley, NC 28751
(704) 926-1630

September

Park Forest Scenic 10K
Park Forest, IL
Bud James
Parks and Recreation Dept.
200 Forest Blvd.
Park Forest, IL 60466
(706) 748-2005

New Haven Road Race 20K and 5K
New Haven, CT
John Bysiewicz
P.O. Box 1893

New Haven, CT 06508
(203) 397-0214

Philadelphia Distance Half-Marathon
Philadelphia, PA
Philadelphia Distance Run
P.O. Box 43111
Philadelphia, PA 19129
(215) 953-8080

Al's Run 8K
Milwaukee, WI
Milwaukee Journal/Al's Run
P.O. Box 661
Milwaukee, WI 53201
(414) 224-2419

Virginia 10-Mile
Lynchburg, VA
Marilyn Reynolds-Straub
P.O. Box 3035
Lynchburg, VA 24503
(804) 525-5420

Bridge to Bridge 12K
San Francisco, CA
KNBR Promotions
55 Hawthorne St.
San Francisco, CA 94105
(415) 995-6868

October

Bowling Green Classic 10K
Bowling Green, KY
Rick Kelley
P.O. Box 1802
Bowling Green, KY 42102
(502) 782-3600

International Peace Race 10K
Youngstown, OH
Jack Cessna
P.O. Box 1320
Youngstown, OH 44501
(216) 743-6632

Arturo Barrios 10K
Chula Vista, CA
Elite Racing
2431 Morena Blvd., Suite 2H
San Diego, CA 92110
(619) 275-5440

Downtown 5K
Providence, RI
Charles Breagy
P.O. Box 40759
Providence, RI 02903
(401) 232-2622

Pleasant Run 5-Mile
Indianapolis, IN
Garry & Terri Petersen
179 South Home Ave.
Franklin, IN 46131
(317) 736-9500

Tulsa Run 15K
Tulsa, OK
Stan Austin
Tulsa Run
1 Williams Center
P.O. Box 2400
Tulsa, OK 74102
(918) 588-2850

November

Old Reliable 10K
Raleigh, NC
Butch Robertson
P.O. Box 1229
Raleigh, NC 27602
(919) 829-4843

Phoenix 10K
Phoenix, AZ
Harvey Beller
1201 East Jefferson St.
Phoenix, AZ 85034
(602) 229-1060

Vulcan Run 10K
Birmingham, AL
Birmingham Track Club

P.O. Box 360044
Birmingham, AL 35236
(206) 995-5344

Manchester Road Race 4.78-Mile
Manchester, CT
Manchester Road Race
P.O. Box 211
Manchester, CT 06040
(203) 649-6456

Run to the Far Side 10K and 5K
San Francisco, CA
David Shaw
California Academy of Science
Golden Gate Park
San Francisco, CA 94118
(415) 750-7142

December

Citrus Bowl Half-Marathon
Orlando, FL
Jon Hughes
Track Shack
1322 North Mills Ave.
Orlando, FL 32803
(407) 898-2425

Brian's Run 10K
West Chester, PA
Brian's Run
P.O. Box 2440
West Chester, PA 19383
(215) 251-5401

Fiesta Bowl 10K
Phoenix, AZ
Rob Wallach
6102 North 16th Ave.
Phoenix, AZ 85016
(602) 277-4333

Runner's World Midnight 5-Mile
New York, NY
NYRRC
9 East 89th St.
New York, NY 10128
(212) 860-4455

Current Sponsors of the NYRRC

New York City Marathon
Chemical Banking Corporation
Mercedes-Benz
John Hancock
ASICS
Rudin Family
Runner's World

Supporting Sponsors
New York City Marathon
Gatorade
Ronzoni
Hoechst Celanese
Seiko
Vermont Pure Natural Spring Water
Tiffany & Co.
American Airlines
ABC Television

Advil Mini Marathon
Advil

New York Games
Mita
Gatorade
The New York Times
American Airlines

WCBS Newsradio 88
Runner's World
Tiffany & Co.
TDI

Alamo Alumni Run
Alamo Rent a Car
Trevira Twosome
Hoechst Celanese

Chemical Corporate Challenge
Chemical Banking Corporation

Empire State Building Run-Up
Empire State Building

Sheraton New York Bagel Run
Sheraton New York

Race for the Cure
Susan G. Komen Foundation

Tavern on the Green Breakfast Run
Tavern on the Green

Backwards Mile
New York Health & Racquet Club

Carey Limousine Wall Street Rat Race
Carey Limousine

K-Rock Run for the Reservoir
K-Rock 92.3 FM

Running Camps

Arizona Track Camp
Prescott, AZ
July 12–18; all ages; $265
Features: Videotape analysis, training techniques, individualized workouts; well-planned recreational program, including golf, tennis, racquetball, soft-ball, swimming, and weight training; 5,400-foot altitude.
Contact: Mike Gray, 3358 West Starfall Pl., Tucson, AZ 85741; (602) 579-0360

Big Lake Fitness Vacation Camp
Sisters, OR
August 30–September 6; adults only ; $395
Features: Personal consultation with a registered dietitian; presentations in biomechanics, shoes, sports massage, sports psychology; personalized eight-week training program; footwear analysis; waterfront activities, mountain bik-ing, and horseback riding; located in the Cascade Mountains.
Contact: Bob Williams, c/o Big Lake Fitness Vacation Camp, P.O. Box 25601, Portland, OR 97225; (503) 643-6184

Brevard College Distance Camp
Brevard, NC
July 19–25 and July 26–August 1; all ages, $265 one week, $490 for two weeks
Features: Workshops on training, nutrition, stretching, sports medicine and psychology, weight training and racing strategy; team activities teach unity, leadership, and goal setting; rafting trip included in two-week session; located in the Blue Ridge Mountains.
Contact: Dave Rinker, Distance Running Camp, Brevard College, Brevard NC 28712; (704) 883-8292 or (704) 884-3762

Brianhead Running Camp
Brianhead, UT
July 30–August 2; all ages, $75 plus lodging and meals
Features: Workshops in biomechanics, sports psychology; spectacular trail running in Cedar Breaks National Monument Park; 9,000-foot altitude.
Contact: Tom Miller, Human Performance Engineering, 730S 1200E, #15, Salt Lake City, UT 84102; (801) 583-4710

Camp Fleet Feet
Lake Tahoe, CA

August 3–9; all ages; single, $125; family, $195
Features: Lectures and demonstrations, personalized training schedule; activities include swimming, hiking, mountain biking. Costs based on runners sharing a campsite and supplying their own food, but motel accommodations are available.
Contact: Camp Fleet Feet, 2407 J St., Sacramento, CA 95816; (916) 972-1119

Colorado High-Altitude Running Camp
Colorado Springs, CO
August 2–8 and 9–15; all ages; $280
Features: Workshops in sports psychology, altitude physiology, and training; trail running on Pikes Peak Marathon course; a visit to the U.S. Olympic Training Center is included; 9,500-foot altitude.
Contact: Alan Johnson, CHARC, 2170 Wickes Rd., Colorado Springs, CO 80919; (719) 578-0817

Craftsbury Running Camp
Craftsbury Common, VT
June 28–August 23; all ages; $385–$495; five– to seven-day packages
Features: Choose from eight different week-long sessions; running and multisports (weeks one and two), running and racing, running and sports medicine, New England runners, New York runners, running and sports medicine II, and Masters running. Offers video analysis, sports massage, and personal training.
Contact: John Brodhead, Craftsbury Running Camp, P.O. Box 31, Craftsbury Common, VT 05827; (802) 586-7767

David Mountains Fitness and Training Camp
Fort Davis, TX
August 9–16; all ages; $365–$575
Features: Videotaping, form analysis and running, cycling and swimming workshops; also offers saunas, hot tubs, tennis courts and a weight room; lodging varies from bunkhouses to deluxe cabins; 5,000- to 6,500-foot altitude.
Contact: Marta Robertson, 1135 Heights Blvd., Houston, TX 77008

Galloway's Vacations for Runners
Lake Tahoe, CA
July 5–11; all ages; $849–$1,149; July 11–15; all ages; $599–$899
Blue Ridge Mountains, NC
August 18–22 and 22–26; all ages; $399–$499
Feaures: Camp run by Jeff Galloway, 1972 Olympian and running author; offers scenic running trails, clinics, and demonstrations by expert staff members; individual consultations; luxurious suites.
Contact: Jeff Galloway, P.O. Box 76843, Atlanta, GA 30358; (404) 875-4268 or (404) 255-1033

Gary Tuttle Training Camp
Carpinteria, CA
July 26–31; all ages; $290–$325
Features: Videotaping and form analysis, seminars and demonstrations, personal training program; excellent cross-training facilities for swimming, biking, and hiking.
Contact: Gary Tuttle, 1410 East Main St., Ventura, CA 93001; (805) 643-1104

Gold Medal Camp
California, PA
August 2–7; all ages; $160
Features: One of the oldest running camps in the country. Offers videotaping and form analysis; workshops by college coaches on strategy, running form and training methods; train on a championship cross-country course and rubberlite track.
Contact: John Harwick, 48 Morris St., Clymer, PA 15728; (412) 254-2369

Green Mountain Running Camps
Lyndonville, VT
August 16–22; adults, $425; students, $365
Hanover, NH
August 23–29; coaching clinic, $250; students, $395
Features: Biomechanical analysis, videotaping and form analysis, seminars, individual coaching, drills on hill running, pacing and circuit training.
Contact: John Holland, RD 1, 333A Baptist Church Rd., Yorktown Heights, NY 10598; (914) 962-5238 or Roy Benson, 5600 Roswell Rd., Suite 355N, Atlanta, GA 30342; (404) 255-6234

High-Altitude Running Camp
Grouse Ridge, CA
August 10–14; all ages; $45
Features: Presentations on physiology, injury prevention, nutrition, shoe selection. Located in the Sierra Nevada, 7,700-foot altitude. Bring tent and provisions.
Contact: Nick Vogt, Christian Runners' Association, 1025 Grange Rd., Meadow Vista, CA 95722; (916) 878-0697

Jay Birmingham's Mesa Running Camp
San Luis, CO
July 5–August 15; all ages; $50, daily; $250, weekly
Features: Seminars on nutrition, sports psychology, and physiology; development of a year-round training plan; field trips to Great Sand Dunes; 8,800-foot elevation.
Contact: Mesa Running Camp, P.O. Box 543, San Luis, CO 81152; (719) 589-3560

Maine Running Camp
Bar Harbor, ME
June 21–27 and June 28–July 4; all ages; $495/week, residents; $225–$295, commuters
Features: Offers training on beautiful trails, challenging hills and track, nutritional counseling, videotaping and form analysis; room in residence halls of College of the Atlantic.
Contact: Andy Palmer, c/o Maine Running Camp, 450-C Main St., Saco, ME 04072; (207) 284-1550

National Triathlon Training Camps
Los Angeles, CA
July (TBA); 14 years and over; $275; August (TBA); 14 years and over, $185
Columbia, SC
August (TBA); 14 years and over; $160
Features: Audiovisual presentations on swimming, cycling, and running; seminars and demonstrations by certified coaches and top triathletes on racing strategy and transitions; personal training program.
Contact: Mark Wendley, National Triathlon Training Camp, 1015 Gayley Ave., Suite 217, Los Angeles, CA 90024; (310) 478-8304

Newport Running Camp
Newport, RI
August 2–8; all ages; $395
Features: Bill Dellinger, Peter Squires, and Ted Hersey direct this camp. Group training runs on sandy ocean beaches, wooded trails, country roads, and challenging hills; offers workshops, videotaping and form analysis.
Contact: Bernadette Squires, 89 Wood Pl., Bloomingdale, NJ 07403; (201) 838-6443 or Ted Hersey, St. George's School, Newport, RI 02840; (401) 847-6788

Next Step Running Camp
Ashland, VA
July 30–August 2; adults only, $250
Features: Seminars on injury prevention and rehabilitation, massage therapy, training in cycles and improving speed; personalized training plans.
Contact: Showers Sports Group, 5915 Waters Edge Landing Ln., Burke, VA 22015; (703) 250-1046

Park City Running Camp
Park City, UT
July 20–24; all ages, $125 plus special lodging and meal package
Features: Learn to run faster by improving your running style; train more effectively and develop racing skills; rent a mountain bike for some awesome trail riding; finish the camp experience by running in the *Deseret News* 10K.

Contact: Tom Miller, Human Performance Engineering, 730S 1200E, #15, Salt Lake City, UT 84102; (801) 583-4710

Princeton Triathlon Camp
Princeton, NJ
June (TBA); adults only; $495
Features: Videotaping and form analysis; world-class 50-meter pool; clinics on cycling techniques, group intervals; participate in mini-triathlon.
Contact: Peter Farrell, Conference Services, Triathlon Camp, Princeton University, 71 University Pl., Princeton, NJ 08544; (609) 258-3522

Smoky Mountain Running Camp
Asheville, NC
July 5–July 25 (three one-week sessions); all ages; $295–$395
Santa Cruz, CA
August 2–7; ages 10 and over; $350–$475
Features: Complete biomechanical analysis; educational and training work-shops; videotaping and form analysis; hill-running, pacing and circuit-training drills; special guests are Nike International athletes.
Contact: Roy Benson Running Camps, 5600 Roswell Rd., Suite 355N, Atlanta, GA 30342; (404) 255-6234

University of Winconsin Adult Running Camp
Stevens Point, WI
July 30–August 2; adults only; $100
Features: Biomechanical analysis, videotaping, and form analysis; seminars on nutrition, sports psychology, and physiology; health enhancement center pro-vides weight training and swimming facilities.
Contact: Rick Witt, Cross-Country and Track Coach, University of Wisconsin at Stevens Point, Stevens Point, WI 54481; (715) 346-3677

Vail Cross-Training Camp
Vail, CO
June 9–14; all ages; $945
Features: Personal exercise prescription; fitness assessment, body composition, and videotape analysis; learn proper use of a heart monitor; guest speakers include Frank Shorter and Ken Souza; offers deluxe accommodations.
Contact: Jim Davis, P.O. Box 3364, Vail, CO 81657; (303) 476-5968

Camps for Students

All-Star Cross-Country Camp
Indianapolis, IN
July 26–31; grades 7–12; $225, resident; $160, commuter
Contact: All-Star Cross-Country Camp, 4606 Brookside Pkwy., Carmel, IN 46033; (317) 844-8399

Appalachian Mountaineer Cross-Country Camp
Boone, NC
July 26–August 1; grades 7–12; $240, resident; $150, commuter
Contact: John Weaver, Track Office, Appalachian State University, Boone, NC 28608; (704) 264-1040

Appalachian Mountaineer Cross-Country Camp
Boone, NC
June 14–19; grades 7–12; $240, resident; $150, commuter
Contact: Al Fereshetian, Route 2, P.O. Box 590, Boone, NC 28607; (704) 262-2519 or (704) 264-7528

Arkansas Camp of Champions
Fayetteville, AR
July 5–10; ages 10–17; $275
Contact: John McDonnell, University of Arkansas Track Office, Fayetteville, AR 72701; (501) 267-2891

Blue Mountain Running Camp
South Sterling, PA
August 23–28; grades 7–12; $175
Contact: John Covert, 3426 Shelley Ln., Bethlehem, PA 18017; (215) 866-2973

BYU Cross-Country Camp
Provo, UT
August 5–8; ages 13 to 17; $185
Contact: See BYU Track & Field Camp

BYU Track & Field Camp
Provo, UT
June 29–July 3; ages 13–17; $185
Contact: Sports Camps, 155 Harman Bldg., Provo, UT 84602; (801) 378-4851

Camp Varsity
Madison, VA
August 9–15; grades 7–12; $190
Contact: George Watts, University of Tennessee, Track & Field, P.O. Box 15016, Knoxville, TN 37901; (615) 974-2240

Cornell Track All-Events Camp
Ithaca, NY
June 28–July 3; ages 12–17; $250
Contact: Laurie Updike, P.O. Box 729, Ithaca, NY 14851; (607) 255-7333

Cougar Track & Field Camp
Pullman, WA

July 5–10; ages 8–18; $150
Contact: Rick Sloan, WSU Athletics, Pullman, WA 99164; (509) 335-0311
Edinboro Distance Village
Edinboro, PA
July 26–31 and August 2–7; grades 7–12; $159 (team discounts)
Contact: Doug Watts, Edinboro University, Edinboro, PA 16444; (814) 732-2877 or (814) 734-1384

ESU Cross-Country Distance Camp
Emporia, KS
July 26–29; grades 5–12; $135, resident; $55, commuter
Contact: Mark Stanbrough, ESU, P.O. Box 20, 1200 Commercial, Emporia, KS 66801; (316) 343-5354

Fighting Illini Cross-Country Camp
Champaign, IL
July 21–25; ages 13–18; $225, resident; $125, commuter
Contact: See Fighting Illini Track & Field Camp

Fighting Illini Track & Field Camp
Champaign, IL
June 14–18; ages 13–18; $225, resident, $150, commuter
Contact: Linda Horve, Fighting Illini Summer Camps, 113 Assembly Hall, 1800 South 1st St., Champaign, IL 61820; (217) 244-0088

Foss Running Camp
Stratford, NH
August 16–22 and 23–29; grades 7–12; $245 (team discounts)
Contact: David Parker, RFD 1, P.O. Box 217, Barnstead, NH 03218; (603) 269-3800

Georgia Tech Track & Field Development Camp
Atlanta, GA
June 14–17; ages 13–19; $100
Contact: Wendy Truvillion, GTAA, 150 Bobby Dodd Way, NW, Atlanta, GA 30332; (404) 894-8220

High-Altitude Cross-Country and Track & Field Camp
Flagstaff, AZ
August 1–5; ages 12–17; $245, resident; $175, commuter
Contact: Ron Mann, High Altitude Camp, P.O. Box 15400, Flagstaff, AZ 86011; (602) 523-5646

Ithaca College Cross-Country Camp
Ithaca, NY
August 2–7; ages 11–18; $350, resident $220, commuter (team discounts)
Contact: Jim Nichols, Ithaca College, Ithaca, NY 14850; (607) 274-3745 or 273-5931

Jackrabbit Cross-Country Camp
Brookings, SD
July 19–24; ages 12–18; $170
Contact: Scott Underwood, Athletic Dept., South Dakota State University, P.O. Box 2820, Brookings, SD 57007; (605) 688-5625

Jayhawk Distance Running Camp
Lawrence, KS
July 19–24; grades 7–12; $200
Contact: Steve Guyman, Distance Running Camp, University of Kansas, 143 Allen Field House, Lawrence, KS 66045; (913) 864-3486

Jayhawk Sprint Camp
Lawrence, KS
June 21–26; grades 7–12; $200
Contact: Theo Hamilton, Jayhawk Sprint Camp, University of Kansas, 143 Allen Field House, Lawrence, KS 66045; (913)864-3486

Longhorn Track & Field Camp
Austin, TX
June 6–13; ages 10-18; $150–$375
Contact: Michael Sanders, Track Office, University of Texas, P.O. Box 7399, Austin, TX 78713; (512) 471-6042 or (512) 280-1157

Luther College Distance Camp
Decorah, IA
July 12–17; grades 7–12; $190
Contact: Kent Finanger, Distance Camp, Luther College, Decorah, IA 52101; (319) 387-1885 or (319) 382-2198

Marauder Cross-Country Camp
Lancaster, PA
August 2–7; grades 7–12; $195
Contact: Jeff Bradley, 824 Kingsway Dr., Lancaster, PA 17601; (717) 898-1905

The Mighty Burner Speed Camp
Pomona, NJ
June 21–25; ages 9–18; $325, resident; $160, commuter
Contact: Larry James, The Mighty Burner Speed Camp, Stockton State College, Office of Athletics and Recreation, Pomona, NJ 08240; (609)652-4876

Nebraska Track & Field and Distance Camp
Lincoln, NE
June 14–18; ages 13–18; $170
Contact: Dave Harris, Track Office, University of Nebraska, Lincoln, NE 68588; (402) 472-6461

New England Prep Cross-Country Camp
Northfield, MA
August 16–21; grades 7–12; $350
Contact: Patrick Mooney, New England Prep Camp, 251 Main St., Northfield, MA 01360; (413) 498-2894

Oregon Kids Track Camp
Eugene, OR
June 22–25; ages 8–12; $170
Contact: John Gillespie, Track Camp, Athletic Dept., University of Oregon, McArthur Ct., Eugene, OR 97403; (503) 346-4492

Oregon Track & Field Camp
Eugene, OR
July 13–18 and 19–24; ages 12–17; $220
Contact: Bill Dellinger, Track & Field Camp, Athletic Dept., University of Oregon, McArthur Ct., Eugene, OR 97403; (503)346-4492

The Paavo Running Camps
Paavo North Camp
Grand Marais, MI
July 5–11; grades 7–12; $325
Paavo West Gold Medal Camp
Rocky Mountains of Colorado and Wyoming
July 19-August 1; grades 7-12; $675
Paavo Regional Camps
Lupton, MI
June 8–12; grades 7–12; $185
Elvins, MO
June 22–26; grades 7–12; $185
Contact: Marshall Sellers, Paavo Running Camps, 801 Trout Creek Rd., Bristol, IN 46507; (219) 848-7141

Penn State Cross-Country and Distance Camp
University Park, PA
August 2–7; grades 7–12; $320
Contact: See Penn State Track & Field Camp

Penn State Track & Field Camp
University Park, PA
July 6–11; grades 7–12; $300
Contact: Penn State Sports Camps, Penn State University, 405 Keller Bldg., University Park, PA 16802; (814) 865-0561

Road Runners Cross Country Camp
Grove City, PA
July 26–31; grades 7–12; $180

Contact: Jim Longnecker, Grove City College, Grove City, PA 16127; (412) 458-2110

The Round Hearth at Stowe Running Camp
Stowe, VT
August 2–7; grades 6–12; $310
Speed Development Camp: July 15–18; grades 6–12; $195
Contact: Grady Vigneau, Summer Sports Festival, 39 Edson Hill Rd., Stowe, VT 05672; (800) 344-1546

Runner's Workshop
Lake Tahoe, CA
August 2–7; ages 12–18; $265 (team discounts)
Catalina Island, CA
August 26–31; ages 12–18; $290 (team discounts)
Contact: Bob Messina, P.O. Box 817, Huntington Beach, CA 92648; (213) 825-8699

Sam Bell's Track & Field Camp
Bloomington, IN
July 5–10; grades 7–12; $250
Contact: Sam Bell, 2310 Woodstock Pl., Bloomington, IN 47401; (812) 339-5978 or (812) 855-8583

Slippery Rock Cross-Country Camp
Slippery Rock, PA
August 2–7; ages 12–18; $200, residents; $165, commuters
Contact: John Papa, Track Office, Slippery Rock University, Slippery Rock, PA 16057; (412) 738-2798

Slippery Rock Track & Field Camp
Slippery Rock, PA
July 5–10; ages 12–18; $200, residents; $165, commuters
Contact: Gary Aldrich, Track Office, Slippery Rock University, Slippery Rock, PA 16057; (412) 738-2797

Spartan Cross Country Camp
East Lansing, MI
July 26–31 and August 2–7; ages 14–17; $240 for one week; $465 for two weeks
Contact: Bob Stehlin, Summer Sports School, 222 Jenison Field House, East Lansing, MI 48824; (517) 355-5364

Springfield Track & Field Camp
Springfield, MA
July 12–17, ages 10–18; $250
Contact: Jim Pennington, Springfield College, Judd Gym, 263 Alden St., Springfield, MA 01109; (413) 788-3351

Stanford Cross-Country Camp
Stanford, CA
August 15–19; ages 9–17; $400, resident; $300, commuter
Contact: See Stanford Track & Field Camp

Stanford Track & Field Camp
Stanford, CA
June 27–July 1; ages 9–17; $400 resident; $300, commuter
Contact: Betsy Riccardi, Stanford Running Camps, Stanford University, Stanford, CA 94305; (415) 725-0761

Steens Mountain Camp
Eugene, OR
August 2–8 and 9–15; ages 13–19; $299, single; $269, team
Contact: Harland Yriarte, P.O. Box 5433, Eugene, OR 97405; (503) 747-4501, ext. 4501

University of Iowa Cross-Country and Track & Field Camp
Iowa City, IA
July 5–9; ages 10–18; $215, residents; $165, commuters
Contact: Wayne Fett, Summer Sports Camps, University of Iowa, E216 Field House, Iowa City, IA 52242; (319) 335-9714

University of Michigan Cross-Country Camp
Ann Arbor, MI
July 26–31; ages 13–18; $265
Contact: Mike McGuire, Track & Field Office, University of Michigan, 1000 South State St., Ann Arbor, MI 48109; (313) 764-5320 or (313) 483-3475

University of Wisconsin Running Camp
Stevens Point, WI
July 19–24; grades 7–12; $195
Contact: Rick Witt, Cross-Country and Track Coach, University of Wisconsin, Stevens Point, WI 54481; (715) 346-3677

University of Wisconsin Running Camp
Stevens Point, WI
July 12–17; grades 7–12; $195
Contact: Len Hill, Track & Field Camp, University of Wisconsin, Stevens Point, WI 54481; (715) 346-4415

USAFA Track & Field/Running Camp
Colorado Springs, CO
June 7–12 and 14–19; grades 7–12; $275
Contact: Ralph Lindeman, Dept. of Athletics, USAFA, Colorado Springs, CO 80840; (719) 472-2173

Wolfpack Distance Cross-Country Camp
Raleigh, NC

July 19–26; grades 7–12; $240 (team discounts)
Contact: Rollie Geiger, P.O. Box 8502, Raleigh, NC 27695;
(919) 515-3959

Reprinted by permission of *Runner's World* magazine. Dates apply to 1992.
Contact individual camps for verification of future dates and prices.

Pace Chart (Kilometers)

1K	1Mi	5K	10K	15K	20K	Half	25K	30K	35K	40K	Marathon
0:02:45	0:04:26	0:13:45	0:27:30	0:41:15	0:55:00	0:58:01	1:08:45	1:22:30	1:36:15	1:50:00	1:56:02
0:02:50	0:04:34	0:14:10	0:28:20	0:42:30	0:56:40	0:59:47	1:10:50	1:25:00	1:39:10	1:53:20	1:59:33
0:02:55	0:04:42	0:14:35	0:29:10	0:43:45	0:58:20	1:01:32	1:12:55	1:27:30	1:42:05	1:56:40	2:03:04
0:03:00	0:04:50	0:15:00	0:30:00	0:45:00	1:00:00	1:03:18	1:15:00	1:30:00	1:45:00	2:00:00	2:06:35
0:03:05	0:04:58	0:15:25	0:30:50	0:46:15	1:01:40	1:05:03	1:17:05	1:32:30	1:47:55	2:03:20	2:10:06
0:03:10	0:05:06	0:15:50	0:31:40	0:47:30	1:03:20	1:06:49	1:19:10	1:35:00	1:50:50	2:06:40	2:13:37
0:03:15	0:05:14	0:16:15	0:32:30	0:48:45	1:05:00	1:08:34	1:21:15	1:37:30	1:53:45	2:10:00	2:17:08
0:03:20	0:05:22	0:16:40	0:33:20	0:50:00	1:06:40	1:10:19	1:23:20	1:40:00	1:56:40	2:13:20	2:20:39
0:03:25	0:05:30	0:17:05	0:34:10	0:51:15	1:08:20	1:12:05	1:25:25	1:42:30	1:59:35	2:16:40	2:24:10
0:03:30	0:05:38	0:17:30	0:35:00	0:52:30	1:10:00	1:13:50	1:27:30	1:45:00	2:02:30	2:20:00	2:27:41
0:03:35	0:05:46	0:17:55	0:35:50	0:53:45	1:11:00	1:15:36	1:29:35	1:47:30	2:05:25	2:23:20	2:31:12
0:03:40	0:05:54	0:18:20	0:36:40	0:55:00	1:13:20	1:17:21	1:31:40	1:50:00	2:08:20	2:26:40	2:34:43
0:03:45	0:06:02	0:18:45	0:37:30	0:56:15	1:15:00	1:19:07	1:33:45	1:52:30	2:11:15	2:30:00	2:38:14
0:03:50	0:06:10	0:19:10	0:38:20	0:57:30	1:16:40	1:20:52	1:35:50	1:55:00	2:14:10	2:33:20	2:41:45
0:03:55	0:06:18	0:19:35	0:39:10	0:58:45	1:18:20	1:22:38	1:37:55	1:57:30	2:17:05	2:36:40	2:45:16
0:04:00	0:06:26	0:20:00	0:40:00	1:00:00	1:20:00	1:24:23	1:40:00	2:00:00	2:20:00	2:40:00	2:48:47
0:04:05	0:06:34	0:20:25	0:40:50	1:01:15	1:21:40	1:26:09	1:42:05	2:02:30	2:22:55	2:43:20	2:52:18
0:04:10	0:06:42	0:20:50	0:41:40	1:02:30	1:23:20	1:27:54	1:44:10	2:05:00	2:25:50	2:46:40	2:55:49
0:04:15	0:06:50	0:21:15	0:42:30	1:03:45	1:25:00	1:29:40	1:46:15	2:07:30	2:28:45	2:50:00	2:59:20
0:04:20	0:06:58	0:21:40	0:43:20	1:05:00	1:26:40	1:31:25	1:48:20	2:10:00	2:31:40	2:53:20	3:02:51
0:04:25	0:07:06	0:22:05	0:44:10	1:06:15	1:28:20	1:33:11	1:50:25	2:12:30	2:34:35	2:56:40	3:06:22
0:04:30	0:07:14	0:22:30	0:45:00	1:07:30	1:30:00	1:34:56	1:52:30	2:15:00	2:37:30	3:00:00	3:09:53
0:04:35	0:07:23	0:22:55	0:45:50	1:08:45	1:31:40	1:36:42	1:54:35	2:17:30	2:40:25	3:03:20	3:13:24
0:04:40	0:07:31	0:23:20	0:46:40	1:10:00	1:33:20	1:38:27	1:56:40	2:20:00	2:43:20	3:06:40	3:16:55
0:04:45	0:07:39	0:23:45	0:47:30	1:11:15	1:35:00	1:40:13	1:58:45	2:22:30	2:46:15	3:10:00	3:20:26
0:04:50	0:07:47	0:24:10	0:48:20	1:12:30	1:36:40	1:41:58	2:00:50	2:25:00	2:49:10	3:13:20	3:23:57
0:04:55	0:07:55	0:24:35	0:49:10	1:13:45	1:38:20	1:43:44	2:02:55	2:27:30	2:52:05	3:16:40	3:27:28
0:05:00	0:08:03	0:25:00	0:50:00	1:15:00	1:40:00	1:45:29	2:05:00	2:30:00	2:55:00	3:20:00	3:30:58
0:05:05	0:08:11	0:25:25	0:50:50	1:16:15	1:41:40	1:47:15	2:07:05	2:32:30	2:57:55	3:23:20	3:34:29
0:05:10	0:08:19	0:25:50	0:51:40	1:17:30	1:43:20	1:49:00	2:09:10	2:35:00	3:00:50	3:26:40	3:38:00
0:05:15	0:08:27	0:26:15	0:52:30	1:18:45	1:45:00	1:50:46	2:11:15	2:37:30	3:03:45	3:30:00	3:41:31
0:05:20	0:08:35	0:26:40	0:53:20	1:20:00	1:46:40	1:52:31	2:13:20	2:40:00	3:06:40	3:33:20	3:45:02
0:05:25	0:08:43	0:27:05	0:54:10	1:21:15	1:48:20	1:54:17	2:15:50	2:42:30	3:09:35	3:36:40	3:48:33
0:05:30	0:08:51	0:27:30	0:55:00	1:22:30	1:50:00	1:56:02	2:17:30	2:45:00	3:12:30	3:40:00	3:52:04
0:05:35	0:08:59	0:27:55	0:55:50	1:23:45	1:51:40	1:57:48	2:19:35	2:47:30	3:15:25	3:43:20	3:55:35
0:05:40	0:09:07	0:28:20	0:56:40	1:25:00	1:53:20	1:59:33	2:21:40	2:50:00	3:18:20	3:46:40	3:59:06
0:05:45	0:09:15	0:28:45	0:57:30	1:26:15	1:55:00	2:01:19	2:23:45	2:52:30	3:21:15	3:50:00	4:02:37
0:05:50	0:09:23	0:29:10	0:58:20	1:27:30	1:56:40	2:03:04	2:25:50	2:55:00	3:24:10	3:53:20	4:06:08

Pace Chart (Miles)

Mile Pace	5 Miles	10 Miles	Halfway (13.1M)	15 Miles	20 Miles	Full Marathon
4:45	23:45	47:30	1:02:16	1:11:15	1:35:00	2:04:33
4:50	24:10	48:20	-	1:12:30	1:36:40	2:07:44
5:00	25:00	50:00	1:05:33	1:15:00	1:40:00	2:11:06
5:10	25:50	51:40	-	1:17:30	1:43:20	2:15:28
5:15	26:15	52:30	1:08:50	1:18:45	1:45:00	2:17:40
5:20	26:40	53:20	-	1:20:00	1:46:50	2:19:50
5:30	27:30	55:00	1:12:08	1:22:30	1:50:00	2:24:12
5:40	28:20	56:40	-	1:25:00	1:53:20	2:28:20
5:45	28:45	57:30	1:15:23	1:26:15	1:55:00	2:30:46
5:50	29:10	58:20	-	1:27:30	1:56:40	2:32:56
6:00	30:00	1:00:00	1:18:39	1:30:00	2:00:00	2:37:19
6:10	30:50	1:01:40	-	1:32:30	2:03:20	2:41:41
6:15	31:15	1:02:30	1:21:56	1:33:45	2:05:00	2:43:53
6:20	31:40	1:03:20	-	1:35:00	2:06:40	2:46:03
6:30	32:30	1:05:00	1:25:13	1:37:30	2:10:00	2:50:25
6:40	33:20	1:06:40	-	1:40:00	2:13:20	2:54:47
6:45	33:45	1:07:30	1:28:29	1:41:15	2:15:00	2:56:59
6:50	34:10	1:08:20	-	1:42:30	2:16:40	2:59:09
7:00	35:00	1:10:00	1:31:46	1:45:00	2:20:00	3:03:33
7:10	35:50	1:11:40	-	1:47:30	2:23:20	3:07:55
7:15	36:15	1:12:30	1:35:03	1:48:45	2:25:00	3:10:06
7:20	36:40	1:13:20	-	1:50:00	2:26:40	3:12:17
7:30	37:30	1:15:00	1:38:19	1:52:30	2:30:00	3:16:39
7:40	38:20	1:16:40	-	1:55:00	2:33:20	3:21:01
7:45	38:45	1:17:30	1:41:36	1:56:15	2:35:00	3:23:13
7:50	39:10	1:18:20	-	1:57:30	2:36:40	3:25:23
8:00	40:00	1:20:00	1:44:53	2:00:00	2:40:00	3:29:45
8:10	40:50	1:21:40	-	2:02:30	2:43:20	3:34:07
8:15	41:15	1:22:30	1:48:10	2:03:45	2:45:00	3:36:20
8:20	41:40	1:23:20	-	2:05:00	2:46:40	3:38:29
8:30	42:30	1:25:00	1:51:26	2:07:30	2:50:00	3:42:51
8:40	43:20	1:26:40	-	2:10:00	2:53:20	3:47:13
8:45	43:45	1:27:30	1:54:43	2:11:15	2:55:00	3:49:26
8:50	44:10	1:28:20	-	2:12:30	2:56:40	3:51:35
9:00	45:00	1:30:00	1:57:59	2:15:00	3:00:00	3:56:00
9:10	45:50	1:31:40	-	2:17:30	3:03:20	4:00:22
9:15	46:15	1:32:30	2:01:16	2:18:45	3:05:00	4:02:32
9:20	46:40	1:33:20	-	2:20:00	3:06:40	4:04:44
9:30	47:30	1:35:00	2:04:33	2:22:30	3:10:00	4:09:06
9:40	48:20	1:36:40	-	2:25:00	3:13:20	4:13:28
9:45	48:45	1:37:30	2:07:49	2:26:15	3:15:00	4:15:33
9:50	49:10	1:38:20	-	2:27:30	3:16:40	4:17:50
10:00	50:00	1:40:00	2:11:06	2:30:00	3:20:00	4:22:13

Index